ETHNOMUSICOLOGY
AN INTRODUCTION

To the Memory of John Blacking
(1928–1990)

Ethnomusicologist, Egalitarian

IN THE SAME SERIES

THE NORTON/GROVE
HANDBOOKS IN MUSIC

ETHNOMUSICOLOGY
AN INTRODUCTION

Edited by HELEN MYERS

W. W. NORTON & COMPANY
New York   London

The New Grove and *The New Grove Dictionary of Music and Musicians*
are registered trademarks of Macmillan Publishers Limited, London.

First published in the UK 1992 by
THE MACMILLAN PRESS LTD
London and Houndmills, Basingstoke, Hampshire RG21 2XS
Companies and representatives throughout the world

British Library Cataloguing in Publication Data
Ethnomusicology: Vol. 1
An Introduction – (The New Grove handbooks in musicology).
I. Myers, Helen   II. Series 780'. 89
ISBN 0–333–57631–4 (Vol. 1)
ISBN 0–333–44444–2 (2-volume set)

First American edition 1992

All rights reserved.

W. W. Norton & Company, Inc.,
500 Fifth Avenue, New York, NY 10110
W. W. Norton & Company, Ltd,
10 Coptic Street, London WC1A 1PU

ISBN 0–393–03377–5

Typeset at The Spartan Press Ltd,
Lymington, Hants, Great Britain
Printed in the United States of America

1 2 3 4 5 6 7 8 9 0

Contents

General Abbreviations

AD	anno Domini
add, addl	additional
add(s), addn(s)	addition(s)
ad lib	ad libitum
AK	Alaska (USA)
AL	Alabama (USA)
Alta.	Alberta (Canada)
anon.	anonymous(ly)
appx	appendix
AR	Arkansas (USA)
attrib.	attribution, attributed to
AZ	Arizona
BBC	British Broadcasting Corporation
BC	British Columbia (Canada)
BC	before Christ
bk	book
BL	British Library
BM	British Museum
Bros.	Brothers
c	circa (about)
CA	California (USA)
CBC	Canadian Broadcasting Corporation
cf	confer (compare)
chap.	chapter
Chin.	Chinese
Cie	Compagnie
cm	centimetre(s)
CO	Colorado (USA)
Co.	Company; County
col.	column
coll.	collection, collected by
collab.	collaborator, in collaboration with
comp(s).	compiler(s), compiled by
contribs.	contributors, contributions
CT	Connecticut (USA)
DC	District of Columbia (USA)
DE	Delaware (USA)

Dept	Department
dir.	director, directed by
diss.	dissertation
ed., eds.	editor(s), edited by
edn(s)	edition(s)
e.g.	exempli gratia [for example]
Eng.	English
enl.	enlarged
esp.	especially
etc	et cetera [and so on]
ex., exx.	example, examples
f., ff.	folio, folios
facs.	facsimile
fasc.	fascicle
ff	following pages
fig.	figure [illustration]
FL	Florida (USA)
Fr.	French
frag., frags.	fragment(s)
GA	Georgia (USA)
Ger.	German
Gk.	Greek
Heb.	Hebrew
HI	Hawaii (USA)
Hon.	Honorary; Honourable
HRH	His/Her Royal Highness
Hung.	Hungarian
Hz	Hertz (cycles per second)
IA	Iowa (USA)
ibid	ibidem [in the same place]
ID	Idaho (USA)
i.e.	id est [that is]
IL	Illinois (USA)
IN	Indiana (USA)
inc.	incomplete
incl.	includes, including
It.	Italian

Jap.	Japanese
Jb	*Jahrbuch* [yearbook]
Jg.	*Jahrgang* [year of publication, volume]
jr	junior
kHz	kilohertz [1000 cycles per second]
km	kilometre(s)
KS	Kansas (USA)
KY	Kentucky (USA)
LA	Louisiana (USA)
LP	long-playing record
Ltd	Limited
m	metre(s)
MA	Massachusetts (USA)
MD	Maryland (USA)
ME	Maine (USA)
MI	Michigan (USA)
mm	millimetre(s)
MN	Minnesota (USA)
MO	Missouri (USA)
MS(S)	manuscript(s)
MS	Mississippi (USA)
MT	Montana (USA)
NC	North Carolina (USA)
ND	North Dakota (USA)
n.d.	no date of publication
NE	Nebraska (USA)
NH	New Hampshire (USA)
NJ	New Jersey (USA)
NM	New Mexico (USA)
no., nos.	number(s)
n.p.	no place of publication
nr	near
NV	Nevada (USA)
NY	New York State (USA)
OH	Ohio (USA)
OK	Oklahoma (USA)
Ont.	Ontario (Canada)
op., opp.	opus, opera
opt.	optional
op. cit.	opere citato [in the work cited]
OR	Oregon (USA)
orig.	original(ly)
p., pp.	page, pages
PA	Pennsylvania (USA)

p.a.	per annum
Pol.	Polish
pseud.	pseudonym
pt(s)	part(s)
pubd	published
pubn	publication
R	photographic reprint
repr.	reprinted
rev.	revision, revised (by/for)
RI	Rhode Island (USA)
Rom.	Romanian
rpm	revolutions per minute
Russ.	Russian
S	San, Santa, Santo, Sao [saint]
Sask.	Saskatchewan (Canada)
SC	South Carolina (USA)
SD	South Dakota (USA)
ser.	series
St	Saint, Sint, Szent
suppl.	supplement, supplementary
TN	Tennessee (USA)
trans.	translation, translated by
transcr.	transcription
TV	television
TX	Texas (USA)
U.	University
UCLA	University of California at Los Angeles (USA)
UK	United Kingdom of Great Britain and Northern Ireland
unattrib.	unattributed
unpubd	unpublished
US	United States [adjective]
USA	United States of America
USSR	Union of Soviet Socialist Republics
UT	Utah (USA)
VA	Virginia (USA)
VHF	very high frequency
viz	videlicet [namely]
vol., vols.	volume(s)
WA	Washington State (USA)
WI	Wisconsin (USA)
WV	West Virginia (USA)
WY	Wyoming (USA)

Bibliographical Abbreviations

AcM	*Acta musicologica*	*JMT*	*Journal of Music Theory*
AmF	*Archiv für Musikforschung*	*Mf*	*Die Musikforschung*
AMw	*Archiv für Musikwissenschaft*	*MGG*	*Die Musik in Geschichte und Gegen-*
AMZ	*Allgemeine musikalische Zeitung*		*wart*
AMz	*Allgemeine Musik-Zeitung*	*ML*	*Music and Letters*
AnM	*Anuario musical*	*MM*	*Modern Music*
AnMc	*Analecta musicologica*	*MQ*	*Musical Quarterly*
		MT	*The Musical Times*
BAMS	*Bulletin of the American Musico-*		
	logical Society	*NOHM*	*The New Oxford History of Music*,
BMw	*Beiträge zur Musikwissenschaft*		ed. E. Wellesz, J. Westrup and
			G. Abraham (London, 1954–)
CMc	*Current Musicology*		
		PAMS	*Papers of the American Musicolo-*
DJbM	*Deutsches Jahrbuch der Musik-*		*gical Society*
	wissenschaft	*PMA*	*Proceedings of the Musical Associa-*
			tion
EM	*Ethnomusicology*	*PRMA*	*Proceedings of the Royal Musical*
EMDC	*Encylopédie de la musique et diction-*		*Association*
	naire du Conservatoire		
		RdM	*Revue de musicologie*
FAM	*Fontes artis musicae*	*ReM*	*La revue musicale*
		RISM	*Répertoire international des sources*
Grove1	G. Grove, ed.: *A Dictionary of*		*musicales*
(–5)	*Music and Musicians*, 2nd–5th	*RMI*	*Rivista musicale italiana*
	edns. as *Grove's Dictionary of*		
	Music and Musicians	*SIMG*	*Sammelbände der Internationalen*
Grove6	*The New Grove Dictionary of Music*		*Musik-Gesellschaft*
	and Musicians	*SM*	*Studia musicologica Academiae sci-*
GSJ	*The Galpin Society Journal*		*entarum hungaricae*
		SMz	*Schweizerische Musikzeitung/Revue*
IIM	*Izvestiya na Instituta za muzika*		*musicale suisse*
IMSCR	*International Musicological Society*	*STMf*	*Svensk tidskrift for musikforskning*
	Congress Report		
IRASM	*International Review of the Aesthe-*	*VMw*	*Vierteljahrschrift für Musikwissen-*
	tics and Sociology of Music		*schaft*
JAMIS	*Journal of the American Musical*	*YIFMC*	*Yearbook of the International Folk*
	Instrument Society		*Music Council*
JAMS	*Journal of the American Music-*	*YTM*	*Yearbook for Traditional Music*
	ological Society	*ZIMG*	*Zeitschrift der Internationalen*
JbMP	*Jahrbuch der Musikbibliothek Peters*		*Musik-Gesellschaft*
JEFDSS	*Journal of the English Folk Dance*	*ZL*	*Zenei lexikon*
	and Song Society	*ZMw*	*Zeitschrit für Musikwissenschaft*
JFSS	*Journal of the Folk-song Society*		
JIFMC	*Journal of the International Folk*		
	Music Council		

Contributors

The late JOHN BLACKING (1928–1990), to whose memory the present volume is dedicated, was Professor of Anthropology at the Queen's University of Belfast, Northern Ireland.

Of himself he wrote, 'Born in England on 22 October 1928, he was educated at Salisbury Cathedral and Sherborne schools, where he received his early musical training. During a period of compulsory military service, he was commissioned in HM Coldstream Guards and spent the year 1948–9 in Malaya. He learned the Malay language and, while on military operations in the jungle, visited settlements of the Sakai and Senoi tribesmen who lived there. These experiences, together with many encounters with Malay, Chinese, and Indian people and their cultures, changed the direction of his career and forced a gradual reassessment of his own culture and its values.

'In 1953, Dr Blacking graduated from King's College, Cambridge, with a bachelor's degree in social anthropology. He studied ethnomusicology at the Musée de l'Homme with André Schaeffner. An appointment as Government Adviser on Aborigines in Malaya lasted six days, until he was dismissed after a disagreement with General Sir Gerald Templer in November 1953. Thereafter, he did some anthropological research, taught at a secondary school in Singapore, broadcast on Radio Malaya, accompanied Maurice Clare on a concert tour, returned to Paris for piano lessons in June 1954 and went to South Africa as musicologist of the International Library of African Music.

'He worked with Dr Hugh Tracey on recording tours in Zululand and Mozambique. During 1956–8 he undertook fieldwork among the Venda of the Northern Transvaal, and in 1959 was appointed lecturer in social anthropology and African government at the University of Witwatersrand, Johannesburg. He was awarded his doctorate by the university in 1965, and at the end of the year appointed professor and head of the department. He was also visiting professor of African music at Makerere University, Kampala. In 1969 he left South Africa.'

Dr Blacking carried out ethnomusicological fieldwork among the Gwembe Tonga and Nsenga of Zambia, and in parts of Uganda and South Africa, as well as anthropological research in and around Johannesburg. He is the author of many publications on Venda initiation rites and music and on the relationship between music and culture. Among his publications are two long-playing records of Nsenga music, also *Black Background: the Childhood of a South African Girl* (1964), *Venda Children's Songs: a Study in Ethnomusicological Analysis* (1967), *Process and Product in Human Society* (1969), 'The Value of Music in Human Experience' (1971), *Man and Fellowman* (1972), *How Musical is Man?* (1973), 'A Special Kind of Knowledge' (1982), 'Ethnomusicology and Human Development' (1983), '*A Commonsense View of All Music*': *Reflec-*

tions on Percy Grainger's Contribution to Ethnomusicology and Music Education (1987), 'Coda: Making Musical Sense of the World' (1987) and 'Transcultural Communication and the Biological Foundations of Music' (1990).

HELEN MYERS, editor and contributor, is Professor of Music at Trinity College in Hartford, Conn., where she teaches a wide range of courses from ethnomusicology to music appreciation. She holds degrees in performance, music education, music theory and historical musicology from Ithaca College, Syracuse University and the Ohio State University, and a PhD in ethnomusicology from the University of Edinburgh, Scotland. She has done extensive fieldwork in the Bhojpuri villages of Uttar Pradesh and Bihar, India, and with the Bhojpuri Indian immigrant community in Trinidad, West Indies. The author of innumerable articles, in *The New Oxford Companion to Music*, *The New Grove Dictionaries of Music*, *of Musical Instruments* and *of American Music*, and of *Felicity Trinidad: the Musical Portrait of a Hindu Village* (1984), she is co-author of an introduction to folk music in the United States and editorial consultant in ethnomusicology for all the New Grove titles.

ANTHONY SEEGER, a specialist in Brazilian Indian music, has taught at the National Museum in Rio de Janeiro (1975–82) and at Indiana University (1982–88). He is currently curator of the Folkways Collection and Director of Smithsonian/Folkways Recordings at the Smithsonian Institution in Washington, DC. He has written numerous articles on Brazilian Indians, ethnomusicology, archiving, ethnomusicology audio recordings and the book, *Why Suyá Sing: a Musical Anthropology of an Amazonian People* (1987).

TER ELLINGSON teaches at the University of Washington, Seattle. He has conducted fieldwork in the Himalayan region, particularly Nepal. His writings include numerous articles on Tibetan music ('Musical Flight in Tibet', 1974, 'The Mathematics of Tibetan *Rol mo*', 1979, and his doctoral thesis, *The Mandala of Sound: Concepts and Sound Structures in Tibetan Ritual Music*, 1979). His book on transcription and the search for ethnomusicological paradigms is in preparation.

STEPHEN BLUM teaches at the City University of New York Graduate School. His principal fieldwork was in northeastern Iran. In addition to several papers on Iran and western Central Asia, he has published studies of the music of Charles Ives, North American hymnody, and the history of ethnomusicology in relation to European musical thought. He is co-editor of *Ethnomusicology and Modern Music History* (1990), a collection honouring his principal teacher Bruno Nettl, and Associate Editor of *The Universe of Music: a History* (in preparation).

RICHARD WIDDESS teaches Indian Music at the School of Oriental and African Studies of the University of London. He has conducted fieldwork in India. His writings include 'The Kudumiyamali Inscription: A Source of Early Indian Music in Notation' (1979) and 'Aspects of Form in North Indian Alap and Dhrupad' (1981).

TILMAN SEEBASS teaches historical musicology at Duke University, Durham, North Carolina. His research interests include musical iconography and organology; he has conducted fieldwork in Indonesia, particularly Bali and Lombok. His writings include *Musikdarstellung und Psalterillustration im früheren Mittelalter* (1973), *Die Allgemeine Musikgesellschaft Basel 1876–1976* (1976) and *The Music of Lombok: a First Survey* (1977). He is editor of *Imago Musicae: International Yearbook of Musical Iconography* (1984–).

GENEVIÈVE DOURNON is Head of the Department of Ethnomusicology at the Musée National d'Histoire Naturelle and curator of musical instruments at the Musée de l'Homme, Paris. She has conducted fieldwork in the Central African Republic and in Rajasthan and Madhya Pradesh, India, and has taught organology at the universities of Paris, Montreal and Basle. Her writings include *Les guimbardes du Musée de l'Homme* (1978), *Pour une description méthodique des instruments de musique* (1990), *Guide for the Collection of Traditional Musical Instruments* (1981) and contributions to the *New Grove Dictionary of Musical Instruments* (1984). She has also compiled a number of CDs on various instruments.

JUDITH LYNNE HANNA is Senior Research Scholar at the University of Maryland, College Park. She received her PhD at Columbia University under Margaret Mead. Interested in communication, education and public policy, she has conducted research in villages and cities abroad in addition to theatre stages and school playgrounds and classrooms in the USA. Her publications include *To Dance is Human: a Theory of Nonverbal Communication* (1979), *The Performer–Audience Connection: Emotion to Metaphor* (1983), *Dance, Sex, and Gender* (1988) and *Dance and Stress* (1988).

MARGARET SARKISSIAN is a doctoral candidate in ethnomusicology at the University of Illinois, Urbana-Champaign. She has conducted fieldwork in the Armenian community of Toronto and the Portuguese community of Melaka, Malaysia. Her writings include *Armenian Musical Culture in Toronto: Political and Social Divisions in an Immigrant Community* (1987) and *Cultural Music and the Construction of Identity in the Portuguese Community of Melaka, Malaysia* (1991).

KRISTER MALM is director of Musikmuseet, the Swedish National Collections of Music, Stockholm, and Associate Professor of Musicology at Gothenburg University. He has conducted fieldwork in Chile, Jamaica, Kenya, Nigeria, Sri Lanka, Tanzania, Trinidad, Tunisia and 15 islands of the Lesser Antilles. His publications include *Fyra musikkulturer: tradition och forandring i Tanzania, Tunieien, Sverige och Trinidad* ['Four Music Cultures: Tradition and Change in Tanzania, Tunisia, Sweden, and Trinidad'] (1981), *Folk Music from Venezuela* (1983) and *Big Sounds from Small Peoples: The Music Industry in Small Countries* (1984).

MARK SLOBIN teaches ethnomusicology at Wesleyan University, Middletown, Conn. His early field research was in Afghanistan; he later turned to the study of Jewish music in various settings, historical and contemporary. He has written and edited numerous volumes including *Music in the Culture of Northern Afghanistan* (1976), *Tenement Songs: The Popular Music of the Jewish Immigrants* (1982), and *Chosen Voices: The Story of the American Cantorate* (1990).

SHUBHA CHAUDHURI is Associate Director of the Archives and Research Center for Ethnomusicology in New Delhi, India. She is Editor of *Samvadi: The ARCE Newsletter*, a publication designed to coordinate the collecting and research endeavours of local and foreign scholars of South Asian Music.

BRUNO NETTL teaches ethnomusicology and anthropology at the University of Illinois at Urbana-Champaign. He has done fieldwork in Iran and India and with the Blackfoot people of Montana. His many publications include *The Study of Ethnomusicology: 29 Issues and Concepts* (1983), *Blackfoot Musical Thought* (1989), *The Western Impact on World Music* (1985) and *Comparative Musicology and Anthropology of Music: Essays on the History of Ethnomusicology* (1991).

JENNIFER POST is Curator of the Helen Hartness Flanders Ballad Collection at Middlebury College, Vermont. She is compiler of the 'Current Bibliography' and 'Dissertations and Theses' for the journal Ethnomusicology. Her fieldwork includes research in Maharasthra, India, and northern New England. Among her writings are Marathi- and Konkari-Speaking Women in Hindustani Music, 1880–1940 (1982), 'Recycling Fieldwork: The Challenges of Reusing Fieldwork for Current Research in Ethnomusicology' (1990) and 'Local Song Traditions in Northern New England' (1991).

LAURENCE LIBIN is the Frederick P. Rose Curator of Musical Instruments at the Metropolitan Museum of Art, New York, where he has directed the Department of Musical Instruments since 1973.

KATHRYN VAUGHN is a post-doctoral fellow and visiting lecturer at the Massachusetts Institute of Technology. Her research includes computer applications for ethnomusicology and music cognition and perception. Her writings include 'Exploring Emotion Sub-Structural Aspects of Karelian Lament: Application of Time Series Analysis Digitized Melody' (1990) and *Cognitive and Perceptual Implications of the Tambura Drone: Figure-Ground Interaction with Ten North Indian Scale Types* (1991).

List of Illustrations

List of Examples

Exx. VIII.1 and VIII.2a are reproduced by permission of Cambridge University Press, England.

Illustration Acknowledgments

We are grateful to the following for permission to reproduce illustrative material (every effort has been made to contact copyright holders; we apologize to anyone who may have been omitted): National Anthropological Archive, Smithsonian Institution, Washington, DC: p.5; Archives of Traditional Music, Indiana University: p.10; photo Simha Arom, Paris: p.13, p.56, p.264 (fig.5a), p.274 (fig.22), p.280 (fig.31); Alice Moyle/photo Mr and Mrs B. Chantrill, CMS: p.21; The Laura Boulton Collection, Archives of Traditional Music, Indiana University: p.24; photo K. Kothari: p.35; American Folklife Center, Archive of Folk Culture, Library of Congress, Washington, DC: p.51 (figs.1 and 2), p.366; William P. Malm: p.74; University of California Press, Berkeley, © 1977 The Regents of the University of California: pp.92–3; McGraw-Hill Book Company, New York: p.134, p.196; Society for Ethnomusicology, Indiana University: p.136; Ter Ellingson: p.140 (fig.11a); Macmillan Publishing Company, New York: p.140 (fig.11b); Indiana University Press, Bloomington: p.140 (fig.11c); Centre Nationale de la Recherche Scientifique, Etudes d'Ethnomusicologie, Musée de l'Homme, Paris: p.140 (fig.11d); © 1978 State University of New York Press, Albany: p.143; Charlotte Heth: p.172; University of California, Berkeley: p.181; Gilbert Rouget, Paris: pp.182–3, p.263 (fig.3), p.264 (fig.5b), p.265 (fig.9); Elisabeth Stiglmayr, Wien-Föhrenau: p.185; Dr J. Sundberg: p.186; © 1971 Northwestern University Press, Evanston, IL: p.198; International Council for Traditional Music: p.207; Francesco Giannattasio: p.211; the editors of *The Oral and the Literate in Music*: p.212; Collection Musée de l'Homme, Paris: p.261. p.264 (fig.6), p.275 (fig.29), p.283 (figs.38 and 39); Collection Musée de l'Homme, Paris/photo Daniel Ponsard: p.262 (fig.2b), p.263 (fig.7), p.266 (figs.12 and 13), p.270 (fig.18a), p.271 (fig.20), p.274 (fig.24), p.275 (figs.27 and 28); Collection Musée de l'Homme, Paris/photo Dorine Destable: p.262 (fig. 2c and d), p.266 (fig.11), p.270 (fig.18b); Institute of Anthropology, Coimbra, Portugal, from J. Redinha, *Instrumentos musicais de Angola: sua contruçao e descriçao* (1984): p.265 (fig.8); Collection Musée de l'Homme, Paris/photo José Oster: p.266 (fig.10). p.267 (fig.14), p.271 (figs.19 and 21), p.274 (figs.23 and 25); photo Marcel Griaule, Paris: p.263 (fig.4); photo Geneviève Dournon: p.264 (fig.5c), p.267 (figs.15 and 16c), p.270 (fig.17), p.281 (figs.33 and 34), p.282 (fig.37); photo Monique Gessain, Paris: p.275 (fig.26). p.282 (fig.36); photo Marie-Claire Bataille, Paris: p.280 (fig.30); photo Hugo Zemp, Paris: p.280 (fig.32); photo Jean-Michel Beaudet, Paris: p.281 (fig.35); Wenner-Gren Foundation for Anthropological Research, Inc., New York, reprinted from Samuel Martí and Gertrude Prokosch Kurath, *Dances of Anahuac: The Choreography and Music of Precortesian Dances*, Viking Fund Publications in Anthropology, No. 38, 1965: p.321; Statens Musiksamlingar, Stockholm/photo Roger Wallis: p.358, p.363.

The drawings on pp.55, 58 and 63 are by Bob Woolford. The drawings on pp.255, 257, 259, 267, 287 and 288 are by Jean Laurent. Figs.16a and b are reproduced from G. Dournon and D. Wright, *Les guimbardes du Musée de l'Homme* (1976) by pemission of the publishers, Etudes d'Ethnomusicologie, Musée de l'Homme, Paris.

Acknowledgments

Many individuals have helped in the preparation of this volume. In particular I would like to thank my editorial assistant and Malaysian music specialist, Margaret Sarkissian, who generously checked hundreds of bibliographic entries to source and was untiring in her efforts to ensure factual accuracy. The publishers of this work owe much to my mother, Elsie Myers Stainton, who has used her professional editing skills in full measure on this project. Several editors deserve special thanks for their painstaking work, including Māra M. Vilčinskas of Macmillan, London, Joanne Hinman and Susan Pohl of Cornell University, and Suzanne La Plante of W. W. Norton and Company. For translation work thanks are due to Anthea Bell. Helen Ottaway, illustrations editor for this Handbook series, pursued a picture search around the world to bring this lively subject – ethnomusicology – to life on the printed page.

For my chapter on fieldwork I would like to thank Charlotte Frisbie and Steven Blum for their most helpful suggestions and corrections. For my chapter on field technology I would like to acknowledge the help of my husband, recording engineer Bob Woolford, for assistance with all matters technical. For the chapter on dance by Hanna, thanks go to Robert Dunn, Joan Frosh-Schroder and Carol Robertson, who commented on early drafts. For the chapter on gender and music by Sarkissian we wish to acknowledge the help of Beverley Cavanagh, Ellen Koskoff, James Robbins and Rob Ollikkala for reading an earlier version and making suggestions.

I would like to thank my colleagues at Trinity College, particularly Professor Gerald Moshell and Dean Jan Cohn, for their encouragement, and also the College administration for financial support during the final stages of this project.

This project could never have come to fruition without the unfailing sponsorship of Claire Brook, Vice-President and Music Editor of W. W. Norton and Company; her professional wisdom and her innovative thinking enlighten this volume.

Finally, warmest thanks go to Stanley Sadie, editor of *The New Grove Dictionary of Music and Musicians*, 6th ed., and series editor for these handbooks, who has supported this volume since its inception and guided it steadily to publication. Stanley Sadie early honoured ethnomusicology and has contributed immeasurably to its flourishing around the world. Through the years, I have observed his zeal for perfection, his dedication to detail and his scholarly daring in contemplating the whole musical world – all the places, all the peoples and all the things of that musical universe. It takes greatness of spirit, strong intellectual capacities, organizational skills and even physical stamina to present the music of the world to the world. This he has done.

H.M.

Preface

A famous classic work was the first to claim the title 'Ethno-musicology'; Jaap Kunst's compendium of 1958 introduced the nature, problems, methods, representative personalities and bibliography of a fledgling discipline. Now we use this title a second time for two volumes, *Ethnomusicology: an Introduction* and *Ethnomusicology: Regional and Historical Studies*, appearing in the series of New Grove Handbooks in Music. The growing discipline deserves and has needed this new effort to show the various directions that scholarship in this field has taken and to present the tremendously detailed information that has been discovered in the last half-century. Today, when Eurocentricity is being challenged throughout the world, both philosophically and politically, these glimpses into a discipline that focuses on ethnic diversity will inform everyone confronting the issue.

Although these companion volumes do not remotely resemble a 'World Music Survey', they do make available the tools by which the music of other cultures may be examined, systematically and scientifically, historically and geographically. A second timely factor relates to the teaching of ethnomusicology; there has been up to now no adequate introduction to the subject to serve as a textbook for music majors, be they historians, theorists, composers, performers or educators.

The two volumes consist entirely of contributions written especially for this project. They are intended to serve as a general and wide-ranging guide to the entire field of ethnomusicology. Each volume is self-sustaining and separate but complementary; the first, systematic, discusses theories and methods, and the second, geographical, outlines the early history of ethnomusicology and explores the later manifestations of this study in the continents of the world. Older heads of the field were invited to write on innovative topics and the future of ethnomusicology, while younger scholars of particular promise were commissioned to reassess the much-discussed routine tasks such as ethnography, fieldwork, transcription and analysis. The search for contributors reached beyond Britain and Europe to the USA, Russia, the Near East, India and the Antipodes.

Our aim is to present a comprehensive discussion of ethnomusicology, including definitions, anthropological and musicological approaches, historical ethnomusicology, organology, iconography, biology, technology, dance, gender, preservation and ethics. Appended is a set of fundamental reference aids for the music scholar, at home and in the field, including reference resources (bibliography, discography), lists of the major sound archives, professional societies and their publications, instrument collections around the world, the Hornbostel-Sachs instrument classification, pitch analysis in the light of modern theories of perception and computation, and a table of international mains voltage, frequency and television standards.

In Chapter I, 'Ethnomusicology', I present an introduction to the history of the field and review the burgeoning and often conflicting definitions of the subject, including the anthropology of music, the study of music in culture, the comparative study of musical cultures, the study of non-Western and folk music, of traditional music, of music in oral tradition, and of contemporary music.

In Chapter II, 'Fieldwork', I discuss the general character and purpose of ethnomusicological fieldwork, ethnomusicology as an interpretive and inter-active field, philosophical and epistemological issues including folk versus analytic viewpoints, 'objectivity' and the fallacy of inductive methods, ethics in the field, preparation for fieldwork, entry into the field, participant observation, informants, rapport, interviews, surveys, questionnaires, studies of individual musicians, and basic fieldwork drills for the novice. In Chapter III, 'Field Technology', I offer detailed instructions for recording data (field notes, tape recording, still photography, film and video recording).

Chapter IV, 'The Ethnography of Music' by Anthony Seeger, treats the analysis of music in its cultural setting, including the application of anthropological theories in ethnomusicology, cultural values as reflected in music, and the basic components of musical ethnography: concepts of music and musicianship, attitudes towards music, composition and improvisation; the transmission of music, the learning process, the uses and functions of music, the social role and status of musicians, composers and audience, the ranking of musicians, musical patronage, musical stratification, folk taxonomies of music, aesthetics and a guide for students to prepare a basic ethnography of a musical performance.

Chapter V, 'Transcription' by Ter Ellingson, outlines the purposes of transcription, the relationship between transcription and analysis, prescrip-tive and descriptive transcription, phonetic versus phonemic transcription, the use of Western notation in ethnomusicology, and the problems of ethnocentrism, cultural bias and objectivity in transcription, modern mechan-ical notators and transcription aids including the oscilloscope, sonagraph, stroboscope and the Seeger melograph, mechanical versus aural transcription, and elementary procedures for transcription in ethnomusicology. Chapter VI, 'Notation', also by Ellingson, describes and classifies indigenous systems of visual representations of music throughout the world.

Chapter VII, 'The Analysis of Musical Style' by Stephen Blum, identifies the purposes of analysis in ethnomusicology, cross-cultural comparative approaches, recent approaches based on generative and transformational grammar, analyses of repertories and of individual works, pitch measurement, scales, modes and rhythm, and comparison (both within a culture and cross-culturally) as, for example, Cantometrics, the study of versions, variants and tune families, and universals in music. Chapter VIII, 'Historical Ethnomusicology' by Richard Widdess, describes the study of documents relating to the history of non-Western music, in particular, the critical study of Oriental manuscripts. Chapter IX, 'Iconography' by Tilman Seebass, examines the role of pictorial and sculptural sources for music research.

Chapter X, 'Organology' by Geneviève Dournon, includes definitions of musical instruments, their function as objects of material culture, tools and an extension of the human body; the history of organology including Western and non-Western systems for the classification of instruments, the construction of musical instruments, symbolic and decorative features; and guides for the fieldworker – collecting musical instruments, their transportation and preservation, classification in the field and in the laboratory. Chapter XI, 'The Biology of Music-Making' by the late John Blacking, investigates the biological aspects of music-making – music and the brain, hearing and perception, music and trance, kinesics and performance. Dance, 'the stepchild of ethnomusicology', is discussed in Chapter XII by Judith Lynne Hanna. Chapter XIII, 'Gender and Music' by Margaret Sarkissian, draws together the new scholarship on this topic of the 1970s and 1980s.

Chapter XIV, 'The Music Industry' by Krister Malm, examines the effect of technology on the creation, collection and dissemination of folk and traditional music, including commercial recording in Third World countries, national and transnational phonogram companies, technology and the global music village, and the influence of the music industry on music cultures.

Chapter XV, 'Ethics' by Mark Slobin, asks who owns the music of a culture? Through the discussion of seven case studies, it outlines the central ethical concerns in ethnomusicology: appropriate procedures for obtaining consent for research, payment of informants, protecting the privacy and anonymity of informants, respect for indigenous as well as international systems of copyright, and the conflict between scientific accuracy versus the feelings of human subjects.

Chapter XVI, 'The Preservation of the World's Music' by Shubha Chaudhuri, discusses preservation and collecting as goals in ethnomusicology, the role of archives and museums, the aims and criteria of preservation, cataloguing and documentation, the technical aspects of archiving including multiple copies, and proper storage conditions for magnetic audio and video tape and film.

Chapter XVII, 'New Directions in Ethnomusicology' by Bruno Nettl, looks towards the future of the field – changing perspectives on the world of music, and new concerns in ethnomusicological theory and method: urban and popular music, the music of immigrant and refugee groups, and ethnomusicological studies of Western art music. Nettl reviews fundamental issues of stability and change, marginal survival, acculturation and syncretism, roots and revitalization. As ethnomusicology enters its second century can we aim towards rapprochement with historical musicology, towards a unitary field?

Hartford, Connecticut, 1992   HELEN MYERS

John Blacking: photo by Veronica Doubleday, taken at a picnic on the Antrim coast during the Anthropology of the Body Conference, 1975.

xxiv

PART ONE

Introduction

CHAPTER I

Ethnomusicology

HELEN MYERS

Ethnomusicology, our topic, a broad and challenging topic, is the division of musicology in which special emphasis is given to the study of music in its cultural context – the anthropology of music. The term was coined in 1950 by the Dutch scholar, Jaap Kunst, to replace the label 'comparative musicology' (Ger. *vergleichende Musikwissenschaft*), on the grounds that comparison is not the principal distinguishing feature of this work.

Ethnomusicology includes the study of folk music, Eastern art music and contemporary music in oral tradition as well as conceptual issues such as the origins of music, musical change, music as symbol, universals in music, the function of music in society, the comparison of musical systems and the biological basis of music and dance. Western art traditions are not ruled out, although few studies in this area have been conducted by ethnomusicologists. In general, music in oral tradition and living musical systems are the realms that have most appealed to ethnomusicologists. Often they have studied cultures other than their own, a situation that distinguishes this field from most historical musicology. As a consequence of its broad scope, definitions of ethnomusicology abound, ranging from 'the study of music as culture' and the 'comparative study of musical cultures' to 'the hermeneutic science of human musical behavior' (Alan Merriam, Bruno Nettl, Elizabeth Helser; in Merriam, 1977). Charles Seeger (1970) suggested that the term 'musicology' is more suitable for ethnomusicology, whose purview includes the music of all peoples of all times, than for historical musicology, which is limited generally to Western art music.

Although formal study is relatively recent, amateur interest in non-Western music dates back to the voyages of discovery, and the philosophical rationale for study of foreign cultures derives from the Age of Enlightenment. The *Dictionnaire de musique* of Jean-Jacques Rousseau (1768) reflects the spirit of the age by including samples of European folk, North American Indian and Chinese music. During the 18th and 19th centuries, missionaries, civil servants and world travellers took an interest in 'exotic music', resulting in studies of Chinese music by Jean-Baptiste du Halde (1735) and Joseph Amiot (1779), of Arab music by Guillaume-André Villoteau (1809) and Raphael Kiesewetter (1842), of Indian music by William Jones (1792) and Charles Russell Day (1891) and of Japanese music by Francis Taylor Piggott (1893).

3

As an academic pursuit, comparative musicology, like historical musicology, has a history of just over 100 years, dating from the landmark publication of the Viennese scholar Guido Adler, 'Umfang, Methode und Ziel der Musikwissenschaft' (1885). Adler lists the comparative study of non-Western music as a division of systematic musicology together with music theory, aesthetics and the psychology of music:

> ... die vergleichende Musikwissenschaft, die sich zur Aufgabe macht, die Tonproducte, insbesondere die Volksgesänge verschiedner Völker, Länder, und Territorien behufs ethnographischer Zwedke zu vergleichen und nach der Verschiedenheit ihrer Beschaffenheit zu gruppiren und sondern.

> Comparative musicology has as its task the comparison of the musical works – especially the folksongs – of the various peoples of the earth for ethnographical purposes, and the classification of them according to their various forms (p.14; trans. Merriam, 1977, p.199).

Scientific investigation of non-Western music was first made possible by two technical innovations of the late 19th century: the invention of the phonograph in 1877 by the American scientist Thomas Edison, and the development of the cents system of pitch measurement in 1885 by the English physicist and phonetician Alexander J. Ellis. The phonograph facilitated fieldwork, offering pioneering comparative musicologists the possibility of playback from which to transcribe and analyse. The cents system, by which the octave is divided into 1200 equal units, made possible objective measurement of non-Western scales. In 'On the Musical Scales of Various Nations' (1885), Ellis concludes that 'the Musical Scale is not one, not "natural", nor even founded necessarily on the laws of the constitution of musical sound, so beautifully worked out by Helmholtz, but very diverse, very artificial, and very capricious' (p.526). This finding brought into question the superiority of Western tempered tuning and led the way to open-minded cross-cultural comparison of tonal systems.

Musicologists of the 19th century quickly took advantage of these technological advances, recording small samples on wax cylinders which they added to their collection of musical artefacts – instruments, song notations and photographs. Many early cylinders were collected during general ethnological fieldwork. Psychologists and acousticians of the Berlin Phonogramm-Archiv, including Carl Stumpf (1848–1936) and Erich M. von Hornbostel (1877–1935), studied hundreds of cylinders recorded by German ethnologists in distant colonial territories. From analysis of this limited diverse material they posited ambitious theories about the distribution of musical styles, instruments and tunings – including evolutionary schemes and later *Kulturkreislehre* ('school of culture circles'). Scholars of the Berlin school rarely conducted fieldwork and thereby gave little import in their writings to music as a cultural manifestation (Stumpf studied the Siamese in 1900 during their Berlin tour; Hornbostel did visit the Pawnee in 1906).

Elsewhere in Europe during the 19th century, nationalism motivated a revival of interest in local folk song. In Hungary, Béla Vikár (1859–1945) began recording in the field in 1896. Béla Bartók (1881–1945) notated his first Hungarian folk song in 1904 and in 1905 began collaboration with Zoltán Kodály (1882–1967); from 1906, Bartók used the Edison phonograph in

4

Hungary, Romania and Transylvania. In England, Cecil Sharp (1859–1924) began the study of traditional English folk song during the same decade. In his search for old authentic material he visited the USA (1916–18) where he and his assistant Maud Karpeles (1885–1976) discovered some 1600 English tunes and variants. Harmonizing the material they had collected, Sharp fought for the introduction of folk song in English public schools. The Australian composer, Percy Grainger (1882–1961), emigrated to England where he began recording Lincolnshire folk song on wax cylinders in 1906 and issued in 1908 the first commercial recording of folk song, with the Gramophone Company, London. Nationalist composers throughout Europe turned to peasant song to enrich the classical musical idiom of their country. Composers and amateur collectors made arrangements of folk songs for piano or orchestra; from their love of indigenous folk music, composers also drew inspiration for new compositions based on folk idioms.

American studies during the late 19th and early 20th centuries were practical, descriptive and based on fieldwork, particularly among the indigenous peoples at their doorstep, the American Indians. Early writings on Native American musical life were rich in data and lean in the speculative theories cultivated by contemporary German thinkers. Fearful that native cultures were vanishing, American scholars used the phonograph to preserve Indian music. The ethnologist Jesse Walter Fewkes (1850–1930) was the first

1. *Frances Densmore with the Blackfoot Indian Mountain Chief at the Smithsonian Institution, March 1916, when he used sign language to interpret recordings of Indian songs played on an Edison phonograph*

5

to use the Edison cylinder machine in the field during his research with the Passamaquoddy Indians of the northeastern USA (March, 1890) and later with the Zuni and Hopi Pueblos of Arizona (1890–91).

Especially sensitive American fieldworkers of this generation were women: Alice Cunningham Fletcher (1838–1923), noteworthy for her lifelong collaboration with the Omaha Indian Francis La Flesche (1857–1932), who is now recognized as the first Native American ethnomusicologist (Mark, 1982); and Frances Densmore (1867–1957; see fig.1), the most prolific collector of the period, for 50 years collaborator in the Bureau of American Ethnology at the Smithsonian Institution and author of over a dozen monographs on the Chippewa (1910–13), Teton Sioux (1918), Papago (1929), Choctaw (1943), Seminole (1956) and others. The anthropologist Franz Boas (1858–1942) taught the holistic study of musical cultures through contemporary anthropological fieldwork methods to a new generation of students at Columbia University, including Helen Heffron Roberts (1888–1985) and George Herzog (1901–84; see fig.2). Roberts defined comparative musicology as studies that 'deal with exotic musics as compared with one another and with that classical European system under which most of us were brought up' (1936, p.233), a kind of definition later rejected by ethnomusicologists. Herzog, a German-Jewish émigré and assistant to Hornbostel, was the first to combine in his fieldwork the Boasian anthropological approach with the speculative theories of the Berlin school, a synthesis exemplified in 'The Yuman Musical Style' (1928), an early application in ethnomusicology of the culture-area concept. He saw comparative musicology as a field analogous to comparative linguistics:

> There are many other musical languages, employed by Oriental and primitive-preliterate peoples. The study of these bodies of music is Comparative Musicology, which aims to discover all the variety of musical expression and construction that is to be found within the wide array of types of cultural development all over the world (1946, p.11).

Historical musicologists acknowledged the contributions of these early studies, finding in them evidence for the superiority of Western classical music – a judgement that ethnomusicologists would now avoid. In the first edition of the *Harvard Dictionary of Music* (1944), Willi Apel defined comparative musicology as 'the study of exotic music', and exotic music as 'the musical cultures outside the European tradition' (pp.167, 250). Glen Haydon's standard guide, *Introduction to Musicology* (1941), includes a chapter on comparative musicology and was one of several works during the 1940s that made a point of distinguishing folk music from primitive music and the music of high cultures:

> Of the many ways of studying our art music systematically, one of the most enlightening is to compare it with folk music and non-European musical systems that have grown up more or less independently . . . Although a sharp delimitation of the various fields of comparative musicology is difficult to make, the main subdivisions of the subject are fairly clear. Non-European musical systems and folk music constitute the chief subjects of study; the songs of birds and phylogenetic-ontogenetic parallels are subordinate topics. The extra-European systems are further distinguished in terms of cultural

level and geographical distribution. As applied to musical systems, the term *primitive* is used in two senses; it may refer either to ancient or prehistoric music, or to music of a low cultural level. It is in the latter sense that primitive music is chiefly studied in comparative musicology. The music of the American Indians and the African Negroes, and many native peoples throughout the world may be classed as primitive if it is representative of a low degree of culture. Other musical systems studied are those of highly civilized peoples such as the Chinese, Japanese, and Indians. Folk music is usually studied in terms of national or racial distinctions and in terms of style-species or type (pp.216, 218–19).

But as scholars were pressing on with their new researches, the term 'comparative musicology' was found wanting. After World War II, two professional societies were founded: the International Folk Music Council in 1947 (after 1982, the International Council for Traditional Music) and the Society for Ethnomusicology in 1955. At the organizational meeting in Boston, SEM founding father David McAllester reported that the new field was to be defined not by the music under scrutiny but by a new methodology:

The proper subject matter for the society was discussed at length. The general consensus favored the view that 'ethno-musicology' is by no means limited to so-called 'primitive music', and is defined more by the orientation of the student than by any rigid boundaries of discourse . . . the term 'ethno-musicology' is more accurate and descriptive of this discipline and its field of investigation than the older term, 'comparative musicology' (1956, p.5).

The term 'ethnomusicology' gained currency in the mid-1950s (the hyphen was officially dropped by the Society in 1957), replacing 'comparative musicology'. Over and again the view was expressed, by George Herzog, Jaap Kunst, Willard Rhodes, George List and Curt Sachs that this study was no more comparative than all other fields of knowledge:

But today 'comparative musicology' has lost its usefulness. For at the bottom every branch of knowledge is comparative; all our descriptions, in the humanities no less than in the sciences, state similarities and divergences. Even in the history of music we cannot discuss Palestrina's Masses without comparing them with Lasso's or Victoria's or with his own motets. Indeed, all our thinking is a form of comparison: to speak of a blue sky is comparing it with a grey or a purple one. Walter Wiora is certainly right when he emphasizes that comparison can denote only a method, not a branch of learning (Sachs, 1961, p.15).

Many early definitions of ethnomusicology were scarcely different from those of comparative musicology, identifying the field as the study of primitive, non-Western, folk and Oriental musics.

The study-object of ethnomusicology, or, as it originally was called: comparative musicology, is the *traditional* music and musical instruments of all cultural strata of mankind, from the so-called primitive peoples to the civilized nations. Our science, therefore, investigates all tribal and folk music and every kind of non-Western art music. Besides, it studies as well the sociological aspects of music, as the phenomena of musical acculturation, i.e. the hybridizing influence of alien musical elements. Western art- and popular (entertainment-) music do not belong to its field (Kunst, enl.3/1959, p.1).

Other definitions of the new field stressed the importance of oral tradition:

> Ethnomusicology is to a great extent concerned with music transmitted by unwritten tradition (List, 1962, p.24).

Another view was ethnomusicology as the study of music outside one's own culture:

> Ethnomusicology is concerned with the music of other peoples . . . The prefix 'ethno' draws attention to the fact that this musicology operates essentially across cultural boundaries of one sort or another, and that, generally, the observer does not share directly the musical tradition that he studies . . . Thus it cannot surprise us that in the early stages the emphasis was on comparison, and the field was known as comparative musicology, until, in the 1960's, it was renamed (Wachsmann, 1969, p.165).

By the late 1950s American ethnomusicologists had divided into two camps: those with anthropological training, led by Alan Merriam (1923–80), and those with musicological backgrounds, led by Mantle Hood (*b*1918) (Merriam, 1969, 'Ethnomusicology Revisited'). In 1960 Merriam spoke as anthropologist when he defined ethnomusicology not in terms of subject matter but as 'the study of music in culture' (p.109). In 1973 he modified his definition to 'the study of music *as* culture' and in 1975 gave even greater emphasis to the cultural and social factors stating 'music *is* culture and what musicians do *is* society' (1977, p.204; 1975, p.57; see also Herndon and McLeod, 1979). He criticized the laboratory-based comparative research of the Berlin school in which 'cultural facts were applied more or less indiscriminately to "prove" the already deduced theory' (1964, p.52). Merriam regarded personal fieldwork as an essential part of any ethnomusicological study and proposed a model for the study of musical cultures – the investigation of concepts about music, musical behaviour and musical sound (pp.32–3).

In his dissatisfaction with deductive research, Merriam spoke for most American ethnomusicologists, who considered their current grasp of world music too sketchy to warrant theoretical generalization. Merriam's positivist and particularist approach was nurtured by an increase in fieldwork by scholars, made possible by the advances in commercial aviation following World War II. Studies written during the 1950s and 1960s reflect caution; most are self-contained ethnographic reports based on fieldwork in a particular tradition, an individual ethnic group or a geographic region, aimed at filling the gaps on a map of world musical styles.

Hood, like Merriam, objected to the comparisons of musical cultures undertaken by the earlier generation of musicologists on the basis of insufficient data:

> An early concern with comparative method, before the subjects under comparison could be understood, led to some imaginative theories but provided very little accurate information. Nonmusical standards relating to economic status, technology, and relative social isolation were responsible for the general use of such terms as 'primitive music' and 'exotic music' . . . A vast number of musical cultures of the non-Western world are yet to be

studied systematically and the music of the European art tradition re-examined in the light of newly emerging concepts before comparative methods can 'give musicology a truly world-wide perspective' (1969, p.299).

The American musicological approach stressed mastery of a foreign musical language, 'bi-musicality' (an analogue to bi-linguality), through extended stays in the field of a year or more (Hood, 1960, 1971). This method had its rationale in the teachings of Charles Seeger (1886–1979), the Connecticut Yankee philosopher of musicology, who held that speech and music are incompatible modes of communication. This dilemma, which Seeger called 'the musicological juncture', left the scholar, who must use words to describe music, in a curious position.

> Now, if we are to talk about music we must talk about it in terms of speech. Thus, these polarities, opposites, dichotomies and whatever tend to become regarded as properties or characteristics of the music compositional process. But if you will try to remember what the making of music was when you were making it at your best, most concentrated and probably, most free of extraneous mental activity or feeling, I wonder if you find analogs of the polarities, opposites, dichotomies and other paraphernalia of speech; or, if you do, that they were weak or perhaps obstructive intrusions of extraneous mental activity or feeling. I do. I run afoul of people who talk about meaning in music. If I understand rightly, the meaning of something is what it stands for, unless, by rare exception, it stands for itself, which is next to meaningless. I find that the imputed meaning of music is precisely that. Otherwise, meanings ascribed to the function of music in social contexts are speech meanings in speech contexts (1977, p.183).

One solution Seeger proposed was the study of non-Western performance at home and in the field. Hood gathered at the UCLA Institute of Ethnomusicology a distinguished circle of foreign musician-teachers including José Maceda (Philippines), Kwabena Nketia (Ghana) and Hardja Susilo (Java). Beginning in 1960, Hood's programme offered instruction in Javanese, Persian, Japanese, Mexican, Indian, Balinese, Greek and African musics. The critical mission of ethnomusicology was explicit in his pronouncement of 1961, that 'in the latter half of the twentieth century it may well be that the very existence of man depends on the accuracy of his communications'. These words fired the imagination of American music students and university administrators alike, and ethnomusicology graduates from UCLA found jobs in major American universities. In the series of short articles in the inaugural issues of the *SEM Newsletter*, Hood was one of the first to proclaim ethnomusicology to be the study of any and all musics, paraphrasing the 'Report of the Committee on Graduate Studies', *JAMS*, 1955:

> [Ethno]musicology is a field of knowledge, having as its object the investigation of the art of music as a physical, psychological, aesthetic, and cultural phenomenon. The [ethno]musicologist is a research scholar, and he aims primarily at knowledge about music (1957, p.2).

During the 1960s scholars continued to reject comparison as a feature of ethnomusicology. John Blacking (1928–90) argued against superficial comparisons based on statistical analyses of scales, intervals and rhythms:

> If we accept the view that patterns of music sound in any culture are the
> product of concepts and behaviours peculiar to that culture, we cannot
> compare them with similar patterns in another culture unless we know that
> the latter are derived from similar concepts and behaviour. Conversely,
> statistical analyses may show that the music of two cultures is very different,
> but an analysis of the cultural 'origins' of the sound patterns may reveal that
> they have essentially the same meaning, which has been translated into the
> different 'languages' of the two cultures (1966, p.218).

A curious theme in the short history of ethnomusicology, explained perhaps
by the insecurity of this fledgling discipline within the established academy, is
the persistent preoccupation with definitions. Since Adler, various alternatives
were proposed by the founders of the field: Jaap Kunst, Helen Heffron Roberts,
Curt Sachs and Charles Seeger; and their students: Mantle Hood, George List,
David McAllester, Alan Merriam, Bruno Nettl (see fig.2) and Klaus
Wachsmann. After a century, it is still commonplace to read new publications
laden with new definitions. These range from the grand to the petty: definitions
of ethnomusicology alongside pedantic disputes over the status of the study
(field or discipline, humanity or social science?), to exegeses of commonplace
words (time, space and music), concepts for which the sometimes naïve
ethnomusicologist claims a unique perspective. This dependence on definitions
is not to be wondered at; a developing discipline that sets the entire world of
music – past, present and future – as its province advisedly might seek an
anchor. Fear of drowning in the ocean of world music, of the slippery subjective
nature of cross-cultural research, of the elusive middle ground between the
social sciences and the humanities has motivated ethnomusicologists to impose
definitional limits in their work.

2. *The ethnomusicologist George*
Herzog (left) with his student,
Bruno Nettl, at Indiana University,
1950

The first assignment for a new student in ethnomusicology is customarily a
rehearsal of the old definitions, from Adler to Seeger and beyond. The danger
is that, like the craftsman who never advances beyond sharpening his tools,
the initiate will never emerge from the sea of terminology: such a fate has

befallen some, who have modified definition with redefinition, sacrificing in this exercise the substance of inquiry. Against this risk must be weighed the benefit: that familiarity with the many definitions, greater and lesser, will reveal ethnomusicology to be a multi-faceted lens with abundant powers for diversity and idiosyncrasy, for imagination, intuition, insight and compassion. Definitions can tempt the wise student towards uncharted waters.

First on the agenda in the definitional debate was the search for that single word which identifies this diverse field. Not many scholars use the term ethnomusicology during their fieldwork. The dispute begins back at home in the university setting. There, ethnomusicologists have, since the 1950s, taken custodianship over those aspects of music study that have been long ignored or abandoned by the performers, historians and theorists of Western classical music – hence the hotchpotch of topics that make up our field and defy definition. How is it that the student of new Chinese folk songs is in the same fraternity as the student of old Chinese manuscripts? Yet, in the academy of the 1990s, they share a roof in the ethnomusicology division. Reason itself was on the side of Charles Seeger when he claimed that historians of European art music had 'hijacked' the comprehensive label, musicology, for their parochial pursuits. But other founding fathers of the field have a certain affection for the term ethnomusicology which recalls the pioneering spirit that led in the post-war years to the foundation of the Society for Ethno-musicology. Younger European and American scholars have taken up the identity of ethnomusicologist as the only tag they ever knew, and associate it with the convivial and stimulating environment of the annual meetings of the Society. It is easy to understand, however, the objection of scholars from non-Western continents, such as Africa and Asia (whose music by American consensus is thought to be the subject matter of ethnomusicology), to being identified as the ethno of our musicology.

In the 1990s, the conscientious ethnomusicologist is often at a loss for descriptive words to explain his enterprise, having been stripped during the last several decades of his working vocabulary of vivid, colourful terms. In the kingdom of exiled words live the labels condemned as pejorative: the old-timers, 'savage', 'primitive', 'exotic', 'Oriental', 'Far Eastern'; some newcomers, 'folk', 'non-Western', 'non-literate', 'pre-literate'; and recently 'world'. 'Traditional' survived the trial of the 1970s, leaving ethnomusicologists with an impotent concept that refers, in the world of music, to everything and therefore nothing.

The nature of ethnomusicological studies has been transformed during the last 100 years, although the field has not yet 'come of age' (as was claimed at the 25th meeting of the Society for Ethnomusicology, 1980). Not only musicologists and anthropologists, but also music educators, music therapists, performers of non-Western music and composers who draw on non-Western and folk idioms are using the title 'ethnomusicologist'. The armchair has been abandoned; scholars now conduct their own fieldwork, and experience first-hand the cultures whose music they analyse. Inevitably, this development has improved the standard of work and led to new understanding of the role of music in human life. But have the fundamental issues really changed? Hornbostel understood the insider–outsider debate; Robert Lachmann (1892–1940) saw that the concept of modality was uniform throughout West, South

11

and Southeast Asia; Sachs, in his later writings, argued that non-Western cultures were not 'progressing' towards a Western ideal. 'The grand old men really had the answers' (Nettl, 1975, p.70; personal communication, 1990).

> We are filling gaps in the field, but there are times when the field of ethnomusicology seems to give us substantially no new ideas of what the world of music is like. Have we discovered all musics? I do receive many new ideas of how to work, ideas on methodology and theory, but the substantive descriptions of musical style and musical culture seem to me to have changed relatively little. After carrying out some studies in Persian and Arabic improvisation, I again looked into Robert Lachmann's little book, *Musik des Orients*, and realized that either explicitly or by implication he already, almost 40 years ago, had stated in a few sentences what I had stated in a series of articles (Nettl, 1975, 'The State of Research in Ethnomusicology', pp.70–71).

The 1970s and 1980s saw unification in ethnomusicological theory and method despite a diversification of topics. Anthropological and musicological concerns fused, interest shifted from pieces of music to processes of musical creation and performance – composition and improvisation – and the focus shifted from collection of repertory to examination of these processes.

New approaches to the analysis of music and of its cultural setting were used; these include aspects of cybernetics (the study of control systems), information theory (how information is generated, transmitted and stored), semiotics (the interpretation of phenomena in terms of signs and symbols) and structuralism (the identification of the structural rules governing cultural phenomena). Increased emphasis was placed on decoding the meaning of the musical message. New methods have also stimulated more rigorous musical ethnography, for example, the ethnography of musical performance (McLeod and Herndon, 1980) and the microethnographic analysis of the musical event (Stone, 1982).

Historical studies returned, making new demands on fieldworkers; for example, studies of modernization and Westernization (Nettl, 1985). New subjects came under investigation: ethnopoetics and aesthetic anthropology (Feld, 1982), gender and music (Keeling, 1989), urban music (Nettl, 1978), the music of refugee populations, film music of India and Japan (Arnold, 1985; Skillman, 1986), the impact of tourism on music in rural and urban settings, street music and busking, and the new traditional musics – popular Westernized forms in burgeoning non-Western cities, including Latin salsa, African 'highlife', Congolese *jùjú*, *kwela* and *tarabu* (Blum, 1978; Waterman, 1985, 1990). Local cassette industries sprang up overnight in Africa and Asia (Wallis and Malm, 1984).

The international music industry brought a mixing and matching of musical styles that would have astonished early fieldworkers of the 20th century who searched in their travels only for idealized authentic folk music. Fieldwork took on a new dimension, as the field now comes to the scholar through media broadcasts and locally produced records; artists from Africa and Asia began to visit Western capitals on concert tours. As a consequence of international exchange and renewed ethical awareness, indigenous performers and informants were given recognition for their contribution to music scholarship (Nettl, 1984). In some cases the role of the ethnomusicologist has been to encourage the performer to write his or her own study: the

12

Navajo Blessingway singer Frank Mitchell produced an autobiography (1978) in collaboration with American scholar David McAllester and his student Charlotte Frisbie, and the book by the Scottish traveller Betsy Whyte (1979) was largely inspired by ethnomusicologist Peter Cooke of the University of Edinburgh. Ethics in fieldwork and research are receiving more attention, and attempts have been made to deposit copies of recordings and scholarly publications in archives and libraries of the countries under study.

New methods of field investigation were born of new technology; for example, Ruth Stone's video recording and playback in analysis of musical events among the Kpelle of Liberia (1982). To facilitate transcription of complex polyphonic, polyrhythmic compositions from the Central African Republic, Simha Arom (see fig.3) used stereo recording and audio playback techniques in the field, a method involving the musicians as 'true scientific collaborators' who 'assume totally the determination of the successive stages of the experimental work' (1976, p.495).

3. *The technique of 're-recording' as practised by Simha Arom: the individual parts of two musicians from a horn orchestra of 18 instruments are recorded under the direction of the conductor (Banda-Linda, Central African Republic, 1974)*

The interdisciplinary nature of ethnomusicology and the increasing diversity of methods and theories led George List, in the late 1970s, to state it was no longer possible to draft a single sensible definition of the field:

> That field of study known as ethnomusicology has expanded so rapidly that it now encompasses almost any type of human activity that conceivably can be related in some manner to what may be termed music. The data and methods

used are derived from many disciplines found in the arts, the humanities, the social sciences, and the physical sciences. The variety of philosophies, approaches, and methods utilized is enormous. It is impossible to encompass them all within one definition (1979, p.1).

With innovative studies of modern musical life, the 1970s and 1980s also saw fieldwork resumed in societies largely untouched by Western life, for example Anthony Seeger's research among the Suyá, a remote community of the Amazon (1987), and Marina Roseman's study of the Temiar of the Malaysian rain forest (1984). Steven Feld had to master the local ornithology of the Kaluli people of highland Papua New Guinea, and Monique Brandily that of the Teda of Chad before either could understand these complex musical systems (Feld, 1982, 1988; Brandily, 1982). In isolated settings scholars adapted field techniques to suit the situation. Hugo Zemp elicited the rich detailed musical vocabulary of the 'Are'are people of the Solomon Islands during informal music and language lessons, rather than in formal interviews (1978, 1979, 1981). In these novel approaches, Wachsmann found a solution to the irreconcilability of speech and music, to Charles Seeger's 'thesis of the lingocentric predicament':

> With the discovery of systematic, verbal references to music among the 'Are'are and Kaluli, Hugo Zemp and Steven Feld have provided us with remarkable, promising material of a kind and comprehensiveness that never before was available . . . Zemp and Feld present us with an entirely new game in which the significance of metaphor and synesthesia and the intimate link between music, speech, and the entire experience of ourselves play a central role (Wachsmann, 1982, pp.210–11).

Ironically, new approaches have led back to old issues; for example, comparison, which has returned, but in a new light. Can we compare the music of cultures that share similar social systems or environmental settings, such as music in small-scale egalitarian societies, or music of rain-forest dwellers, of urbanites, peasants and so on? In the mid-1970s, Nettl noted the rediscovery of comparative methods:

> If we are discovering or rediscovering our own past, perhaps we are going back to earlier precepts . . . The reprinting of the work of such scholars as Hornbostel and Brăiloiu is a stimulus for those who feel that it is possible for someone to comprehend a number of musical systems sufficiently well to compare them . . . We are again returning to the idea that musics can be compared, that they lend themselves, at some level of study, to quantified comparison and that one is perhaps unable to absorb information about a new musical culture except by making implicit comparisons to something already known (1975, 'The State of Research in Ethnomusicology', p.71).

Beginning in the late 1970s, renewed enthusiasm was voiced for ethnomusicological studies of Western classical music, but little work was actually published in this area (however, see Wachsmann, 1981 and 1982; Herndon, 1988). Conversely, musicologists (perhaps with a glance over their shoulders at ethnomusicological methods) began taking greater cognizance of extra-musical factors, particularly social milieu, in their analyses of standard repertories.

14

Beginning in the 1980s, the biology of music-making united ethnomusicologists with musicologists, performers and music educators, as well as psychologists and neurologists (Wilson and Rochman, 1988, 1990). Through team-work, fresh approaches were tested to understand the music-specific aspects of brain and motor functions. Ethnomusicologists contributed by comparing findings from different cultures, hearkening back, in spirit if not in method, to the cross-cultural psycho-acoustic studies of the Berlin school in the late 19th century. Are the basic biological functions of human musicality universal, or are they determined by culture? The old nature/nurture question was raised once again.

After a century of work, certain fundamental issues still occupy centre stage in ethnomusicology. Ethnomusicologists generally study non-Western and folk music, and are particularly interested in the match of cultural context to musical style. With the whole world as their oyster, and the essential links between music and the rest of life their abiding concern, ethnomusicologists have resorted to methods and theories from various allied disciplines. Many a recent article describes Mongolian or Bolivian or Samoan music in the terminology of linguistics, interactionism, phenomenological sociology, information theory, structuralism and so on and so on; this makes life hard for experts and amateurs alike, to say nothing of the musicians whose music is under discussion. Delving into the pages of the major periodicals of the field, *Ethnomusicology* and *Yearbook for Traditional Music*, is not light reading for anyone. After wading through pages devoted to definitions of familiar terms like 'performance', 'event' and 'assumption', you may unexpectedly find yourself drowning in a sea of undefined matrices and paradigms, pondering the nature of 'sonic ideation', 'cantometric profiles', 'thick description', or 'semiotico-cybernetic theory'.

In defence of my colleagues, one man's music (say, to the ethnomusicologist) may be another man's Call to Prayer (music is forbidden in Islam); in fact, the seemingly tedious review of first principles is perhaps the major contribution of ethnomusicology to music studies. But tedious it is, nonetheless, and particularly troublesome for editors of reference works such as *The New Grove Dictionary of Music and Musicians* (6th edn.), who seek out (not always in vain) contributors who can tell about another man's music in straightforward English without violating concepts peculiar to that culture.

Conflicts continue: between scholars searching for universally applicable systems of analysis and those attempting to use the cognitive framework of a particular culture as the basis for analysis of its music; between those who believe that detailed analysis of music leads to understanding and those who believe that music can be understood only on its own terms through performance. Although approaches vary and orientations differ, some tenets of ethnomusicology are held in common. Fieldwork remains the focal point of research, and each scholar is expected to collect his own material for analysis. Ethnomusicologists continue to acknowledge the value of written notation; some use mechanical music writers, including computers and the melograph, but a surprising number, armed with various special symbols, still rely on conventional Western notation.

At the very heart of ethnomusicology, the astute reader may discern the fundamental irony of the subject. On the one hand, each scholar is eager to defend the music of his or her own people as special and unique; on the other, no

15

ethnomusicologist will rank the music of his culture over that of his colleague's. Value judgements are not the fashion in today's ethnomusicology – a small price to pay for an even-handed treatment of the world's music. So ethnomusicologists, with their bewildering array of new topics, their barrage of jargon and their pedantic definitions find their place of pride as the great egalitarians of musicology.

Bibliography

J. B. du Halde: *Description de l'Empire de la Chine* (Paris, 1735)

J.-J. Rousseau: *Dictionnaire de musique* (Paris, 1768/*R*1969; many edns. to 1825; Eng. trans. by W. Waring, London, 1771, 2/1779/*R*1975)

J. M. Amiot: *Mémoire sur la musique des chinois tant anciens que modernes* (Paris, 1779/*R*1973)

W. Jones: 'On the Musical Modes of the Hindoos', *Asiatick Researches*, iii (1792), 55–87; repr. in S. M. Tagore: *Hindu Music from Various Authors* (Calcutta, 1875, 2/1882 in 2 pts., 3/1965)

G.-A. Villoteau: 'De l'état actuel de l'art musical en Egypte' and 'Description historique, technique et littéraire des instrumens de musique des orientaux', *Description de l'Egypte: état moderne*, i, ed. E. P. Jomard (Paris, 1809), 607–845, 846–1016

R. G. Kiesewetter: *Die Musik der Araber* (Leipzig, 1842)

G. Adler: 'Umfang, Methode und Ziel der Musikwissenschaft', *VMw*, i (1885), 5; Eng. trans. in Mugglestone (1981)

A. J. Ellis: 'On the Musical Scales of Various Nations', *Journal of the Society of Arts*, xxxiii (27 March 1885), 485–527, (30 October 1885), 1102–11

J. W. Fewkes: 'A Contribution to Passamaquoddy Folk-Lore', *Journal of American Folklore*, iii (1890), 257

C. R. Day: *The Music and Musical Instruments of Southern India and the Deccan* (London and New York, 1891/*R*1974)

A. C. Fletcher with F. La Flesche and J. C. Fillmore: *A Study of Omaha Indian Music* (Cambridge, MA, 1893) [pp.35ff repr. as 'The Wa-wan, or Pipe Dance of the Omahas', *Music*, iv (1893), 468]

F. T. Piggott: *The Music and Musical Instruments of Japan* (London, 1893)

F. Densmore: *Chippewa Music* (Washington, DC, 1910–13/*R*1972)

——: *Teton Sioux Music* (Washington, DC, 1918/*R*1972)

G. Herzog: 'The Yuman Musical Style', *Journal of American Folklore*, xli (1928), 183–231

F. Densmore: *Papago Music* (Washington, DC, 1929/*R*1972)

C. Seeger: 'Music and Musicology', *Encyclopedia of the Social Sciences*, ed. E. R. A. Seligman, xi (New York, 1933), 143

H. H. Roberts: 'The Viewpoint of Comparative Musicology', *Volume of Proceedings of the Music Teachers National Association, Thirty-First Series. Annual Meeting of the Sixtieth Year. Chicago, Illinois. December 28–31, 1936*, ed. K. W. Gehrkens (Oberlin, OH, 1936), 233

G. Haydon: *Introduction to Musicology: a Survey of the Fields, Systematic and Historical, of Musical Knowledge and Research* (Chapel Hill, NC, 1941)

F. Densmore: *Choctaw Music* (Washington, DC, 1943/*R*1972)

C. Sachs: *The Rise of Music in the Ancient World, East and West* (New York, 1943)

W. Apel: 'Comparative Musicology', 'Exotic Music', *Harvard Dictionary of Music*, ed. W. Apel (Cambridge, MA, 1944), 167, 250

G. Herzog: 'Comparative Musicology', *Music Journal*, iv/6 (1946), 11

J. Kunst: *Musicologica* (Amsterdam, 1950, enl. 3/1959/*R*1975 as *Ethnomusicology*)

C. Seeger: 'Systematic Musicology: Viewpoints, Orientations, and Methods', *JAMS*, iv (1951), 240

M. F. Bukofzer: 'Observations on the Study of Non-Western Music', *Les Colloques de Wégimont*, ed. P. Collaer (Brussels, 1956), 33

F. Densmore: *Seminole Music* (Washington, DC, 1956/*R*1972)

D. P. McAllester: 'The Organizational Meeting in Boston', *EM*, i/6 (1956), 3

B. Nettl: *Music in Primitive Culture* (Cambridge, MA, 1956)

W. Rhodes: 'Toward a Definition of Ethnomusicology', *American Anthropologist*, lviii (1956), 457

M. Hood: 'Training and Research Methods in Ethnomusicology', *EM*, i/11 (1957), 2

M. Kolinski: 'Ethnomusicology, its Problems and Methods', *EM*, i/10 (1957) 1

M. Schneider: 'Primitive Music', *New Oxford History of Music*, i, *Ancient and Oriental Music*, ed. E. Wellesz (London, 1957), 1–82

G. Chase: 'A Dialectical Approach to Music History', *EM*, ii (1958), 1

'Whither Ethnomusicology?' *EM*, iii (1959), 99 [essays by Hood, Kolinski, Nettl, Chilkovsky, List, Seeger, Miller, McAllester, Meyer]

M. Hood: 'The Challenge of "Bi-musicality"', *EM*, iv (1960), 55

A. P. Merriam: 'Ethnomusicology – Discussion and Definition of the Field', *EM*, iv (1960), 107

M. Hood: *Institute of Ethnomusicology* (Los Angeles, 1961)

N. Schiørring: 'The Contribution of Ethnomusicology to Historical Musicology', *Report of the Eighth Congress of the International Musicological Society, New York, 1961, Papers*, ed. J. La Rue (Kassel, 1961), 380

C. Seeger: 'Semantic, Logical and Political Considerations Bearing Upon Research in Ethnomusicology', *EM*, v (1961), 77

C. Sachs: *The Wellsprings of Music* (The Hague, 1961)

G. List: 'Ethnomusicology in Higher Education', *Music Journal*, xx/8 (1962), 20

M. Hood: 'Music, the Unknown', *Musicology*, ed. F. Ll. Harrison, M. Hood and C. V. Palisca (Englewood Cliffs, NJ, 1963), 217–326

O. Kinkeldey: 'Musicology', *The International Cyclopedia of Music and Musicians*, ed. O. Thompson (New York, 9/1964), 1428

A. P. Merriam: *The Anthropology of Music* (Evanston, IL, 1964)

B. Nettl: *Theory and Method in Ethnomusicology* (Glencoe, IL, 1964)

C. Marcel-Dubois: 'L'ethnomusicologie, sa vocation et sa situation', *Revue de l'enseignement supérieur*, iii (1965), 38

J. Blacking: 'Review of *The Anthropology of Music*', *Current Anthropology*, vii (1966), 217

M. Kolinski: 'Recent Trends in Ethnomusicology', *EM*, xi (1967), 1

A. Merriam: 'The Use of Music as a Technique of Reconstructing Culture History in Africa', *Reconstructing African Culture History*, ed. C. Gabel and N. R. Bennett (Boston, 1967), 83–114

C. Seeger: 'Factorial Analysis of the Song as an Approach to the Formation of a Unitary Field Theory', *JIFMC*, xx (1968), 33

M. Hood: 'Ethnomusicology', *Harvard Dictionary of Music*, ed. W. Apel (Cambridge, MA, 2/1969), 298

A. P. Merriam: 'Ethnomusicology Revisited', *EM*, xiii (1969), 213

K. P. Wachsmann: 'Music', *Journal of the Folklore Institute*, vi (1969), 164

C. Seeger: 'Toward a Unitary Field Theory for Musicology', *Selected Reports in Ethnomusicology*, i/3 (1970), 171–210

A. Czekanowska: *Etnografia muzyczna: metodologia i metodyka* (Warsaw, 1971)

M. Hood: *The Ethnomusicologist* (New York, 1971/R1982)

C. Seeger: 'Reflections Upon a Given Topic: Music in Universal Perspective', *EM*, xv (1971), 385

G. Chase: 'American Musicology and the Social Sciences', *Perspectives in Musicology*, ed. B. S. Brook, E. O. D. Downes and S. Van Solkema (New York, 1972), 202

V. Duckles: 'Musicology at the Mirror: a Prospectus for the History of Musical Scholarship', *Perspectives in Musicology*, ed. B. S. Brook, E. O. D. Downes and S. Van Solkema (New York, 1972), 32

F. Ll. Harrison: 'Music and Cult: the Functions of Music in Social and Religious Systems', *Perspectives in Musicology*, ed. B. S. Brook, E. O. D. Downes and S. Van Solkema (New York, 1972), 307

J. Blacking: *How Musical Is Man?* (Seattle, 1973)

——: 'Ethnomusicology as a Key Subject in the Social Sciences', *In Memoriam António Jorge Dias*, iii (Lisbon, 1974), 71

S. Blum: 'Towards a Social History of Musicological Technique', *EM*, xix (1975), 207

A. P. Merriam: 'Ethnomusicology Today', *CMc*, xx (1975), 50

B. Nettl: 'Ethnomusicology Today', *World of Music*, xvii/4 (1975), 11

——: 'The State of Research in Ethnomusicology, and Recent Developments', *CMc*, xx (1975), 67

S. Arom: 'The Use of Play-Back Techniques in the Study of Oral Polyphonies', *EM*, xx (1976), 483–519

A. Lomax: *Cantometrics: an Approach to the Anthropology of Music* (Berkeley, 1976)

A. P. Merriam: 'Definitions of "Comparative Musicology" and "Ethnomusicology": an Historical-Theoretical Perspective', *EM*, xxi (1977), 189

Ethnomusicology: an Introduction

C. Seeger: 'The Musicological Juncture: 1976', *EM*, xxi (1977), 179
J. Blum: 'Problems of *Salsa* Research', *EM*, xxii (1978), 137
C. J. Frisbie and D. P. McAllester, eds.: *Navajo Blessingway Singer: the Autobiography of Frank Mitchell 1881–1967* (Tucson, 1978)
K. A. Gourlay: 'Towards a Reassessment of the Ethnomusicologist's Role in Research', *EM*, xxii (1978), 1–35
B. Nettl, ed.: *Eight Urban Musical Cultures: Tradition and Change* (Urbana, 1978)
H. Zemp: ''Are'are Classification of Musical Types and Instruments', *EM*, xxii (1978), 37–67
M. Herndon and N. McLeod: *Music as Culture* (Norwood, PA, 1979 *R*/1982)
G. List: 'Ethnomusicology: a Discipline Defined', *EM*, xxiii (1979), 1
D. P. McAllester: 'The Astonished Ethno-Muse', *EM*, xxiii (1979), 179
B. Whyte: *The Yellow on the Broom: the Early Days of a Traveller Woman* (Edinburgh, 1979)
H. Zemp: 'Aspects of 'Are'are Musical Theory', *EM*, xxiii (1979), 6–48
N. McLeod and M. Herndon: *The Ethnography of Musical Performance* (Norwood, PA, 1980)
K. K. Shelemay: '"Historical Ethnomusicology": Reconstructing Falasha Liturgical History', *EM*, xxiv (1980), 233
E. Mugglestone: 'Guido Adler's "The Scope, Method, and Aim of Musicology" (1885): an English Translation with an Historico-Analytical Commentary', *YTM*, xiii (1981), 1
H. P. Myers: '"Normal" Ethnomusicology and "Extraordinary" Ethnomusicology', *Journal of the Indian Musicological Society*, xii/3–4 (1981), 38
K. P. Wachsmann: 'Applying Ethnomusicological Methods to Western Art Music', *World of Music*, xxiii/2 (1981), 74
H. Zemp: 'Melanesian Solo Polyphonic Panpipe Music', *EM*, xxv (1981), 383–418
M. Brandily: 'Songs to Birds among the Teda of Chad', *EM*, xxvi (1982), 371
S. Feld: *Sound and Sentiment: Birds, Weeping, Poetics, and Song in Kaluli Expression* (Philadelphia, 1982, rev. edn., 1990)
J. Mark: 'Francis La Flesche: the American Indian as Anthropologist', *Isis*, lxxiii (1982), 497
R. M. Stone: *Let the Inside Be Sweet: the Interpretation of Music Event Among the Kpelle of Liberia* (Bloomington, IN, 1982)
K. P. Wachsmann: 'The Changeability of Musical Experience', *EM*, xxvi (1982), 197
H. P. Myers: 'Ethnomusicology', *The New Oxford Companion to Music*, ed. D. Arnold (Oxford, 11/1983), 645
B. Nettl: *The Study of Ethnomusicology: Twenty-nine Issues and Concepts* (Urbana, 1983)
H. P. Myers: 'Ethnomusicology', *The New Grove Dictionary of American Music*, ed. H. W. Hitchcock and S. Sadie (London, 1984)
B. Nettl: 'In Honor of Our Principal Teachers', *EM*, xxviii (1984), 173
M. Roseman: 'The Social Structuring of Sound: the Temiar of Peninsular Malaysia', *EM*, xxviii (1984), 411–45
R. Wallis and K. Malm: *Big Sounds from Small Peoples: the Music Industry in Small Countries* (New York, 1984)
A. Arnold: 'Aspects of Asian Indian Musical Life in Chicago', *Selected Reports in Ethnomusicology*, vi (1985), 25
B. Nettl: *The Western Impact on World Music: Change, Adaptation, and Survival* (New York, 1985)
C. Waterman: 'Juju', in B. Nettl: *The Western Impact on World Music: Change, Adaptation, and Survival* (New York, 1985), 87
T. Skillman: 'The Bombay Hindi Film Song Genre: a Historical Survey', *YTM*, xviii (1986), 133
A. Seeger: *Why Suyá Sing: a Musical Anthropology of an Amazonian People* (Cambridge, England, 1987)
S. Feld: 'Aesthetics as Iconicity of Style, or "Lift-up-over Sounding": Getting into the Kaluli Groove', *YTM*, xx (1988), 74–113
M. Herndon: 'Cultural Engagement: the Case of the Oakland Symphony Orchestra', *YTM*, xx (1988), 134
F. R. Wilson and R. L. Roehmann, eds.: *The Biology of Music Making: Proceedings of the 1984 Denver Conference* (St Louis, 1988)
R. Keeling, ed.: *Women in North American Indian Music: Six Essays* (Bloomington, IN, 1989)
C. Waterman: *Jùjú: a Social History and Ethnography of an African Popular Music* (Chicago, IL, 1990)
F. R. Wilson and R. L. Roehmann, eds.: *Music and Child Development: Proceedings of the 1987 Denver Conference* (St Louis, 1990)

18

PART TWO

Theory and Method

CHAPTER II

Fieldwork

Helen Myers

Introduction

In fieldwork we unveil the human face of ethnomusicology. Whether we select a remote Indian village, European peasant community, Nigerian town or ethnic neighbourhood in a large city such as Tokyo or Paris, whether we study our family or a foreign tribe, our native country or an exotic land, fieldwork is the most personal task required of the ethnomusicologist. Fieldwork is also the most critical stage of ethnomusicological research – the eyewitness report, the foundation upon which all results rest. This great hurdle of the ethnomusicological endeavour is also its great fascination, and more than a few scholars

1. *The Australian ethnomusicologist, Alice Moyle, recording a didjeridu player at Oenpelli, Northwest region, Arnhem Land, Australia, in 1962*

were first attracted to the discipline through the lure and mystique of fieldwork. Its challenges are many, foreseen and unforeseen, mundane and artistic. The strength and weaknesses of our personalities are tested as we adapt to a foreign way of life and document an unfamiliar musical culture. By its very nature fieldwork provides a setting in which we feel awkward and disorientated, a disconcerting reality because fruitful work results from natural, honest, heartfelt and often spontaneous behaviour. Scholars who successfully resolve these dilemmas prove artful fieldworkers, enjoy their research and make lifelong friends.

Fieldwork is a hallmark of many social sciences, including anthropology and ethnomusicology. Gone is acceptance of studies from the 'armchair', in which the musicologist transcribed and analysed material recorded by ethnologists. Today's student is expected to immerse himself or herself in the totality of a foreign culture, usually for a year or more, and experience music first-hand in its diverse settings. During fieldwork the ethnomusicologist assembles primary sources: observations in field notes, recordings of music and interviews, photographs, film and video materials. Unlike the historical musicologist who gleans data from archives and libraries, the ethnomusicologist must collect and document material from living informants. Ethnomusicologists who work in cultures lacking written records must rely on methods designed to investigate oral history. For cultures with written traditions of music theory, the fieldworker must study historical sources, elicit statements about musical practices from informants, and then compare these texts and spoken words with the musical behaviour observed from day to day.

In past decades fieldwork was treated like a rite of passage through which the student had to pass but about which little could be taught. While invoking the name of objectivity, emphasis in fact was placed on insight, intuition, personal charm, happenstance and luck. Because the topic is individual and personal, scholars were reluctant to write candidly about their own experiences in the field. Field notes and diaries, transcriptions of interviews and accounts of day-to-day activities were rarely published (exceptions are Slotkin, 1952; the posthumously published diary of Bronislaw Malinowski, 1967; and Merriam, 1969, 'The Ethnographic Experience'; and an early anthology of personal portraits of informants in Casagrande, 1960). Beginning in the 1960s and 1970s, a body of writings on personal fieldwork experiences was published (Powdermaker, 1966; Henry and Saberwal, 1969; Freilich, 1970; Golde, 1970; Spindler, 1970; Anderson, 1971; Wax, 1971 and 1977; Mead, 1972; Blacking, 1973; Jones, 1973; Pelto and Pelto, 1973; Foster and Kemper, 1974; Béteille and Madan, 1975; Clarke, 1975; Geertz, 1976; Honigmann, 1976; Freilich, 1977; and Dumont, 1978). This movement gained momentum through the 1980s as the pendulum swung to the opposite extreme, and enthusiasts of subjectivity began to argue for psychoanalysis before fieldwork and full confession of the scholar's autobiography (in anthropology, Barley, 1983; Turner and Bruner, 1986; Whitehead and Conaway, 1986; in ethnomusicology, Berliner, 1978; Keil, 1979; and Gourlay, 1978, who appraises the ethnomusicologist's role in the field).

The ethnographic text came to be examined as a piece of literature in its own right, and its form and style, long taken for granted, reconsidered in the light of this new humanism (Bruner, 1986; Clifford and Marcus, 1986). The debate led to an epistemological puzzle labelled 'reflexivity', whereby anthropologists struggled to evaluate and measure their impact on the very topic they sought to study. The act of anthropological observation is obtrusive, inevitably altering the behaviour of the observed; this 'anthropological lens' became for some the very object of investigation (Mills, 1973; Peacock, 1986). Ironically, scholars working in the physical sciences have long accepted these anomalies, especially the subjective element inherent in scientific method (many discoveries are made by accident or luck) and the element of personal interaction with the data, including the much feared self-fulfilling prophecy, for example, the geologist who loudly shouts 'avalanche' on a snowy mountain (Kuhn, 1962; Popper, 1959, 1963, 1972; Ryan, 1973; Myers, 1981).

Definitions: fieldwork, field, informant, performance and recording

Fieldwork may be defined as 'observation of people *in situ*; finding them where they are, staying with them in some role which, while acceptable to them, will allow both intimate observation of certain parts of their behaviour, and reporting it in ways useful to social science but not harmful to those observed' (Hughes, 1960, p.v).

Where is the field? The scope of ethnomusicological inquiry is as broad and varied as the world of music itself. Early studies focused on national folk forms in oral tradition, the music of foreign peasant societies, and music of peoples then called 'exotic' or 'primitive', that is, who had little contact with Western man. The classical musical systems of the Orient, objects of fascination for centuries, have remained popular subjects in modern ethnomusicology. For the 1990s the field abounds with topics, from studies of remote ethnic groups in interior regions of South America, Africa, South and Southeast Asia to modernization, Westernization, urban musical life, popular music and the music industry. For the ethnomusicologist the field can be a geographical or linguistic area; an ethnic group (possibly scattered over a wide area); a village, town, suburb or city; desert or jungle; tropical rain forest or arctic tundra.

Each field situation is unique, but all projects have features in common. First is the informant – the person who supplies the information. This word has troublesome connotations, and many scholars prefer to speak of colleagues, friends, respondents, participants, interviewees, sources or teachers. For better or worse, informant is the term used most widely in the social sciences for those people in the field who talk to us about their lives and their music.

Secondly, all fieldwork includes performances, both musical performances and cultural performances (rituals and ceremonies of traditional life), as well as performances staged especially for the scholar (informal conversations, interviews and recording sessions).

Third is recording, in the form of written field notes, music recordings, cassettes of interviews, still photographs, 16mm film and video recordings. Items acquired in the field – books, records, musical instruments – also form a part of this collection. A major burden in ethnomusicology is the preservation and documentation of recordings, their transportation in the field, and then from field to home to archive (and often back to the field again for checking and further documentation). During fieldwork, travelling by train or local bus,

2. Laura Boulton recording Haitian singers c1938

overflowing with villagers and their livestock, pedlars and their wares, mothers feeding tiny babies, toddlers sucking fruits, old men squatting in the aisles and passenger luggage of various descriptions strapped haphazardly to the roof, guarding the ethnomusicological kit becomes quite a nuisance. At airport check-in counters, with ever more stringent rules about hand luggage and stiff excess baggage charges, these fragile items become a very real handicap; once safely home they are our treasures and our joys as well as the source of all our analyses. The professional ethnomusicologist soon becomes an expert at transporting all manner of things from village A to town B to city C to archive D (for copying before departure from the host country) to airport E to airport F (home) to archive G (for copying or deposit in the home country) – hundreds of open-reel tapes and cassettes, unexposed (outbound flight) and exposed (inbound) film, musical instruments, tape recorders, microphones, batteries and battery chargers, and so on. This inescapable part of the job requires presence of mind and masterful organizational skills.

The earliest guides for field method came from anthropology. In *Argonauts of the Western Pacific* (1922), the Anglo-Polish anthropologist Bronislaw Malinowski (1884–1942) sets out the fundamental issues: the relationship of theory and method; inductive versus deductive research strategies; participant observation; the importance of open-mindedness and self-criticism; the linking of apparently unrelated data; the difference between observation and insight; the distinction between the scholar's observations and ideas expressed by the native informant ('emic' and 'etic' data); the isolation of the anthropological adventure, and the frustration, anxiety and despair of culture shock: 'Imagine yourself suddenly set down surrounded by all your gear, alone on a tropical beach close to a native village', Malinowski writes, 'while the launch or dinghy which has brought you sails away out of sight' (p.4).

But this very isolation, he argues, is the only proper condition for fieldwork:

> cutting oneself off from the company of other white men, and remaining in as close contact with the natives as possible, which really can only be achieved by camping right in their villages . . . to wake up every morning to a day presenting itself . . . more or less as it does to the native (pp.6–7).

As is the custom in the physical sciences, Malinowski recommends a deductive approach to fieldwork, whereby the student's training in theory and method are used to guide but not dominate observation and the systematic collection of data:

> The Ethnographer has not only to spread his nets in the right place, and wait for what will fall into them. He must be an active huntsman, and drive his quarry into them and follow it up to its most inaccessible lairs . . . Good training in theory, and acquaintance with its latest results, is not identical with being burdened with 'preconceived ideas'. If a man sets out on an expedition, determined to prove certain hypotheses, if he is incapable of changing his views constantly and casting them off ungrudgingly under the pressure of evidence, needless to say his work will be worthless. But the more problems he brings with him into the field, the more he is in the habit of moulding his theories according to facts, and of seeing facts in their bearing upon theory, the better he is equipped for the work. Preconceived ideas are pernicious in any scientific work, but foreshadowed problems are the main endowment of a scientific thinker, and these problems are first revealed to the observer by his theoretical studies (pp.8–9).

Planning

SELECTING A TOPIC With the whole world as our oyster and our science only in its infancy, with most of the world's music as yet unstudied, selection of a research problem in ethnomusicology should not be difficult. Ironically the staggering variety of topics and global range of research sites may leave the novice bewildered. Here follow several considerations to help in this selection.

First, personal interest: select a topic you like and that will hold your interest and imagination for the duration of the research and beyond. Open-ended topics that lead on to new research are best. I chose my doctoral project on music of Indian immigrants in Trinidad for this potential; inevitably my investigation led to new problems and projects (Myers, 1984). My post-PhD research led me to northeastern India, the ancestral home of my West Indian informants; this research in turn led me to study similar Indian groups in Fiji and Mauritius, where Indians were also taken by the British during the system of indentured labour, 1835–1919. A carefully chosen PhD topic – well defined, sharply focused and nested within a larger theoretical domain – can be the first phase of a life's work. Continuity of a project capitalizes on the researcher's training in language, musical repertory, bibliography; is attractive to funding agencies; and can readily be recast as a team project involving local scholars.

Most ethnomusicology projects treat a single repertory, either of a village, neighbourhood, urban ethnic group, individual musician or genre. Ethnomusicologists with anthropological inclinations have selected musical cultures that illustrate theoretical issues: the culture area in North American Indian music (Nettl, 1954), structuralism in the society and music of Brazilian Indians (Seeger, 1987), aesthetics among the Navajo (McAllester, 1954) and linguistic models of deep and surface structure in Venda music (Blacking, 1971). Scholars more influenced by musicology have focused on musical structures (Hood's investigation of *paṭet* [mode] in Javanese music, 1954), genres (Wade's survey of North Indian vocal *khyāl*, 1984), instrumental repertories (Berliner's research on the Shona *mbira* [lamellaphone], 1978) or the total repertory of an ethnic group (Capwell's ethnography of the Baul people of Bengal, 1986). Since the 1950s, most studies have been limited to a single culture; cross-cultural studies, the focus of 19th-century German research, are unusual, although senior scholars have written reflective pieces as Nettl's 'Two Cities' (1985), a comparison of musical life in Madras and Teheran. Out of favour is urgent 'survival' ethnomusicology whereby the fieldworker aims to preserve a dying tradition.

Restudies (one scholar retraces the footsteps of another) have borne rich fruit in anthropology, as with the Robert Redfield–Oscar Lewis debate on the village of Tepoztlán in Mexico, Reo Fortune's re-examination of Margaret Mead's data on social roles among the Arapesh of New Guinea, and the Ward Goodenough–John Fisher debate over postmarital residence patterns on a Pacific atoll (Agar, 1980). In ethnomusicology, restudies have the special potential of adding historical depth to understanding oral tradition; they also offer a fresh viewpoint on areas that have come to be associated with the interpretation of a particular scholar (no two observers ever have the same perspective). The role of multiple interpretations is especially critical in the study of expressive culture, but in the small, closely knit society of academic ethnomusicology, the restudy has yet to find its proper place.

FEASIBILITY In selecting a topic, the student must consider all aspects of feasibility.

Scholarly: Is the topic relevant to current theoretical issues in ethnomusicology? Can its intrinsic importance as a contribution to knowledge be justified? Does your training as researcher in ethnomusicology, anthropology, history and musical repertory qualify you to undertake this work? Do you have access to the relevant literary and musical sources (libraries and archives)? Do you know the local language or have a means of learning it in the field?

Political: Can the required visas and research permits be obtained to conduct this work? Steps must be taken to get official permission for the project and enough time allowed for government agencies to clear the proposal. Have you selected a politically sensitive topic or geographical region? Perhaps this project should be postponed for a more suitable moment.

Physical: Does the value of the study warrant the incumbent risks to life and limb, expenditure of time and of money involved? Can funds be raised to do the job properly? Have you allowed enough time to complete the project? Are the required personnel available (particularly assistance in the field)?

ETHICS New methods, theories, and topics have introduced new ethical problems. Should the study of a music be conducted by the 'insiders' – experts with native knowledge of language, culture and music – or by 'outsiders' – who claim objectivity and open-mindedness? The avant garde in ethnomusicology is fostering teamwork between insiders and outsiders, and is helping native artists tell their own life stories (e.g., Frisbie and McAllester, eds., *Navajo Blessingway Singer: the Autobiography of Frank Mitchell*, 1978). The accusation of cultural imperialism, often levelled at outside researchers, is being met by such projects as the Archives and Research Center for Ethnomusicology, Delhi, an organization that assists visiting scholars in depositing copies of their field recordings before leaving India (*Samvādī*, 1984–). Another positive step is dissemination of cultural field materials – recordings and documentation – back to the community of origin, exemplified by the Library of Congress Federal Cylinder Project, through which copies of traditional songs (some collected decades ago and long forgotten) have been returned to Native Americans (Brady and others, 1984 –).

Unless you are studying musical life of wealthy people, prepare for the shock of being rich in a poor country. Every scholar must work out individual justification for spending thousands of dollars to study music when the same money could feed the hungry or heal the sick. Knowledge for knowledge's sake has little meaning when you see a dying child; this issue demands reflection before you meet sick and hungry people in the field. I spent valuable weeks in India struggling with the ethics of music study in a poor country, wondering why no teacher or colleague had alerted me to the conflicting emotions I would experience. You may indeed be able to use part of your grant money for humane purposes, and as a newcomer to the culture, you will be tempted to rush in and help. But think carefully and have respect for the complexity of human deprivation. An obvious panacea to conscience is allocating funds for medicine. Only after handing out many aspirin tablets to feverish Indian villagers did I wonder where blame might fall if a patient worsened or died after taking my over-the-counter medicine.

Whether or not you can help the people you plan to study, you must not harm them. The 'Statement on Professional Ethical Responsibilities' (1983) of the Society for Applied Anthropology outlines the major issues, each of which should be considered before drafting a research proposal:

> 1. To the people we study we owe disclosure of our research goals, methods, and sponsorship. The participation of people in our research activities shall only be on a voluntary and informed basis. We shall provide a means . . . to maintain the confidentiality of those we study . . . [but they] must not be promised a greater degree of confidentiality than can be realistically expected . . .
> 2. To the communities ultimately affected by our actions we owe respect for their dignity, integrity, and worth . . . We will avoid taking or recommending action on behalf of a sponsor which is harmful to the interests of a community.
> 3. To our social science colleagues we have the responsibility to not engage in actions that impede their reasonable professional activities. . . not impede the flow of information about research outcomes and professional practice techniques . . . [and] not prejudice communities or agencies against a colleague for reasons of personal gain.
> 4. To our students, interns, or trainees we owe nondiscriminatory access to our training services . . . Student contributions to our professional activi-

ties, including both research and publication, should be adequately recognized.
5. To our employers and other sponsors we owe accurate reporting . . . We have the obligation to attempt to prevent distortion or suppression of research results or policy-recommendations by concerned agencies.
6. To society as a whole we owe the benefit of our special knowledge and skills in interpreting sociocultural systems . . .

The issue of confidentiality discussed in paragraph 1 is ambiguous in ethnomusicological research, since the artists we study may seek recognition for their work. Stephen Slawek could hardly have falsified the name of the world-renowned artist, Ravi Shankar, in his study of the Hindustani sitar repertory, or Neil Sorrell that of the great *sāraṅgī* virtuoso, Ram Narayan (Sorrell and Ram Narayan, 1980; Slawek, 1987). Ethnomusicologists are generally free to give the names of the musicians they study. Often they sponsor these artists to visit the West on concert tours. Village musicians are also happy to have their names cited in ethnomusicological writings. However, anonymity is sometimes important; Edward Henry withheld the names of his North Indian village informants, since publication of the evocative wedding *gālī* texts he transcribed might embarrass them (1988). If in doubt, ask. Do the musicians wish to be named? How do they wish to be portrayed? Would they like their photograph to appear in your publication? Will they check direct quotations of their words or transcriptions of their music; will they give their imprimatur for these quotations under their name?
A special problem arises when the ethnomusicologist restudies a village already known in the anthropological literature under a pseudonym. Musicians from that village may be keen to have their real names appear, together with transcriptions of their repertories and photographs of performances, a wish in conflict with the confidentiality of the earlier study. Even more perplexing problems arise as informants from much studied villages visit the West; this issue is one from which we cannot escape. A case in point is 'Karimpur', pseudonym for a North Indian village under investigation since 1925, initially by Charlotte and William Wiser and subsequently by several American anthropologists (Wiser and Wiser, 1930). The Wisers disguised the name of the village and of their informants. In recent years as villagers have travelled to large cities in India and the West, they are puzzled to discover on library visits their photographs displayed in anthropological texts without their names. One informant, who served as assistant to several generations of anthropologists, has lectured in British and American universities about the impact of anthropology on his community; he is writing his autobiography, emphasizing the plight of the villager as a subject of anthropological inquiry. By what name should this writer refer to his village? Should anthropologists with whom he worked be identified? Should he give his own name as author of the book? The issue of confidentiality has no single simple solution.

BACKGROUND Senior ethnomusicologists remember days when PhD candidates were required to read the entire ethnomusicological corpus for their doctoral qualifying exams. This is no longer a reasonable requirement, but the prospective fieldworker must master the literature in his or her area –

both geographical region and pertinent theoretical studies. This task requires an interdisciplinary search during which the student can compile a full bibliography – from ethnomusicology, anthropology, history, religion, politics and other fields including fiction (novels of V. S. Naipaul are an important source for Trinidad). Precious days in the field should not be wasted reading or annotating bibliography cards. From a systematic search, students will soon identify scholars who have worked before them in the area. Correspondence with these experts, an essential courtesy, may yield advice as well as names of helpful contacts in the field; pleasant professional relationships based on shared research interests begin in this simple way.

THE RESEARCH PROPOSAL Whether or not the candidate plans to apply for funding, preparing a formal research proposal is helpful in launching a project. This exercise forces discipline on the programme, particularly in budgeting time, money and energy. Committing idealized plans to paper will focus the topic, delineate salient goals, outline their relevance to ethnomusicology and potential contribution to knowledge. You will be forced to calculate a budget and devise the realistic day-to-day schedule that will bring your project to fruition and realize your ultimate intellectual goals.

Preparation of a research proposal can take many months. Familiarize yourself with agencies that offer funding in your area of interest. Many universities have research offices with computerized systems to assist in locating appropriate funding. Basic reference guides such as *The Grants Register* (1991) are helpful and easy to use. Be prepared to tailor the proposal to requirements of specific agencies. This is usually less of an infringement on academic purity than it might seem, and more likely than not may help the candidate focus and improve the proposal.

Write the proposal in simple clear English. Avoid jargon. Make points directly and in a manner that will easily be understood by professionals from other fields. Take care formulating the title and summary description of the project, for it is through the key words in these that proposals are assigned to review committees and adjudicators. Winning grants is a special skill for which advice is available in standard anthropological texts (Pelto, 1970; Agar, 1980; Jackson, 1987).

Participant observation

The main strategy used in ethnomusicological fieldwork is participant observation; the researcher lives in the community, participates in daily life, especially musical activities, records observations and asks community members to comment on them. The participant observer is a privileged stranger, a 'marginal native', and has access to rich data (Freilich, 1970, 1977). Participant observation enhances validity of the data, strengthens interpretation, lends insight into the culture, and helps the researcher to formulate meaningful questions. Anthropological texts have traditionally identified four gradations of the participant observation method: (1) complete participant (observer activities completely concealed); (2) participant as observer (observer activities 'kept under wraps'); (3) observer as participant (observer activities publicly known); and (4) complete observer (in the extreme, observer behind a one-way mirror) (Junker, 1960, pp.35–7). Be careful here as the US Department of Health, Education, and Welfare regulations on human subjects' and informants' consent requires disclosure of the details of the project, the intent of the researcher and consent of the informants. Written records of this information are kept on file. Options 1, 2 and 4 are unethical according to DHEW standards. The balance between participation and observation depends on the personality of the researcher, field situation, host culture and nature of the research. For most ethnomusicological research, option 3 is the only choice.

TRUST Sensitive participant observers gain access to private domains of daily life as community members come to trust and confide in them, especially during long-term field research. (Raoul Naroll's survey of ethnographies shows that researchers who stayed in the field over a year obtained more data on sensitive issues – politics, sex and witchcraft [1962].) Ethical questions soon arise: the scholar may witness crime, overhear plans to smuggle drugs, learn of illegal immigration. Trust when broken hurts researcher and informant and prejudices the viability of the project; but in maintaining trust, the researcher must not break the law. Broken confidence or legal misdemeanour will damage the reputation of ethnomusicology in the community and the country, place future studies in jeopardy and prevent the scholar's future access to that site. Conscience must guide the use of intimate facts. The thoughtful scholar learns that many poignant moments never find their way to the printed page.

ROLE Participant observation is generally credited with reducing 'reactivity' – the degree people alter their behaviour because they are being studied. Ethnomusicologists should not take false comfort in this notion. Disruption is inevitable when one person studies the private life of another. However artful, the fieldworker can never blend without trace into the local scene. Ethics argues against invisible intrusion: through covert recording (the microphone hidden in your bag), or going native. Never let your village friends forget you are studying their music. It is only fair that our equipment – microphones, tape and video recorders, cameras, flashguns – are constant reminders that we have come to study, that we do not belong. Don't people under study deserve the chance to put on their Sunday best? Or do they?

Whatever role the researcher devises, native scrutiny is razor sharp:

> In 1967, a group of white, bearded men came out of the north again . . . They walked about with restless eyes, trying to take it all in . . . This was a group to fatten the ranks of the anthropology clan, and they tried out their remarkable and superficial theories on the lives of the people of my country (Salinas, 1975, pp.71–2).

However closely your appearance and behaviour match norms of the community, the social scientist is always an outsider. The ethnomusicologist who believes he or she has gone native never fools the natives. The Sioux author, Vine Deloria Jr, had no difficulty spotting anthropologists in the Dakotas:

30

Anthropologists can readily be identified on the reservations. Go into any crowd of people. Pick out a tall gaunt white man wearing Bermuda shorts, a World War II Army Air Force flying jacket, an Australian bush hat, tennis shoes, and packing a large knapsack incorrectly strapped on his back. He will invariably have a thin sexy wife with stringy hair, an IQ of 191, and a vocabulary in which even the prepositions have eleven syllables . . . This creature is an anthropologist (1969, p.79).

Ethnomusicologists are more fortunate than anthropologists and sociologists because the private feelings we study are publicly expressed in musical performance. Cultural barriers evaporate when musicologist meets musician. There is no substitute in ethnomusicological fieldwork for intimacy born of shared musical experiences. Learning to sing, dance, play in the field is good fun and good method. Being an appreciative audience is an especially important form of musical exchange. Savour the joy of being a student again; establishing a close relationship with a master musician is a common and successful approach in ethnomusicology (Zonis, 1973; Berliner, 1978; Koning, 1980; Sorrell and Ram Narayan, 1980; Slawek, 1987). By the 1960s students discovered in the literate cultures of India, Japan, Iran and Indonesia, formal systems for music training (not unlike our Western system) in which they could easily enrol. Bimusicality emphasized participation at the expense of observation, and music lessons from a guru captivated many students. However, the ethnomusicologist who remains detached – the outsider looking in – will never plumb the depth of his subject, music, which by its essential nature is personal, expressive, artistic, emotional, even ecstatic. The successful fieldworker achieves a balance between participation and observation, aiming always for scientific, systematic and sympathetic investigation of the art of music.

HOME PRACTICE Participant observation can only be learned in the field, but many component skills can be practised at home. Language competence is the most important. Make every effort to learn the language needed. University courses and self-study kits are available for even the most obscure languages; intensive summer courses can be particularly valuable. Understanding of the culture will increase in tandem with language fluency; as the level of comprehension and expression improves, informants raise their level of discourse, and insight into the culture unfolds spontaneously. (The same is true for fluency in the local musical language.)

Skills of observation, memory and expository writing can also be rehearsed at home. Practise 'explicit awareness', the ability to note and remember details of ordinary life – not as simple as it sounds (Spradley, 1980). An exercise: ask a person who has just checked his watch, 'What time is it?' He will check his watch again because he was not explicitly aware of the absolute time. Anthropological texts offer exercises to improve observation, memory and writing (Agar, 1980; Spradley, 1980; Bernard, 1988). These skills contribute to successful participant observation.

For ethnomusicologists the most essential skills are recording and photography. Be completely familiar with your equipment before you arrive in the field; do not purchase items en route to the village. The cheap camera you pick up in New York may not work (you will miss important pictures waiting to have a test roll developed). The bargain cassette recorder you buy in Singapore on the way to wherever may not use available batteries, may not have leads supplied and may not be compatible with your microphones.

Practise with all your equipment at home. Nothing should be taken into the field which has not been tested in a realistic setting inside and then outside your living room. Record a conversation at your supper table. Then take your recording gear for a test run at a stationary event – for example buskers at an underground station or services in a local church. Next, stretch yourself by recording a moving event with the tape recorder slung over your shoulder and hand-held microphones, preferably outdoors on a windy day: a civic parade, marching band or street market (in which case the recordist will be moving, not the sound source). Finally, record in a setting with loud amplified sound – perhaps a local disco. The more problems that you anticipate and solve at home (wind noise, headphone isolation, setting levels etc), the fewer problems you will have in the field.

ENTERING THE FIELD Before entering the field pause to assess the personal and cultural biases you bring to the project. There is no purely objective research in ethnomusicology (or any subject). Cultural assumptions and personal idiosyncracies guide our observations and colour our findings. The scholar who accepts these biases, deals with them as a part of methodology and acknowledges their influence produces fine research.

Fieldwork can be divided into predictable stages: entry, culture shock and life shock, data collection, holiday periods alternating with more data collection with exhaustion, and leaving the field. Entering the field is a time of excitement, even euphoria, tempered by frustrations, setbacks and hassles. A few simple rules will help during these early days.

First, choose a receptive community. Fieldwork is fraught with problems; if you are not welcome, select another site.

Secondly, take documentation about yourself and your project, purpose of study, and length of stay from your university or funding body. Documentation should make your affiliation clear and be signed by an academic official. Have copies of your documentation drawn up in the local language. Include with your papers pictures of yourself at home with your family; present your human as well as official self, especially to new friends in the village.

Thirdly, in entering a new community, it may be advisable to work through a chain of introductions, courtesy visits to government officials (even the head of state), through the bureaucratic hierarchy to the ministry of culture. From there you may be taken in a number of directions: state schools of music, Westernized professional musicians, radio and TV broadcasting agencies – all interesting (even if none bear on your research). If your destination is the countryside, you will need further introductions. I was lucky during my first weeks in India to meet Shri Ram Sagar Singh of Banaras Hindu University, who lives in a nearby village where he is a leading singer. Within 24 hours of learning I was interested in *dehātī* ('village') music, he had organized village women to sing for me. If you are not that fortunate, you might select a local person to accompany you on your first visit to the village or community – perhaps a government worker from a nearby town. Weigh the advantages and disadvantages: government officials may intimidate villagers and mark you as a government agent; however, an official introduction may lend respect to your work and even serve to protect life and limb.

On arrival it may be wise to start at the top. When entering an Indian village, for example, it is proper to go to the *pradhān* ('head') and ask him to introduce you to musical specialists. I followed this method during my fieldwork in Gorakhpur District, India. In Felicity village, Trinidad, I arrived alone and went directly to the Hindu elementary school; this relaxed informal start, well-suited to the Caribbean venue, set a casual and pleasant style for that field trip. In Southall, London, I simply presented myself at a Hindu temple. Introduction to the community depends on local attitudes; take advice from scholars who have worked in the area and experts on the scene.

Finally, prepare for the inevitable questions: Who are you? What are you doing here? Who pays you? (Are you a spy?) What do you do with the money you earn from selling recordings? Why do people do work like this?

Decide how you will present yourself and abandon any notion of assuming a false role. A pose will quickly wear you out (Jones, 1973). The host society will probably assign a role for you, often a kinship affiliation. Amongst the Mbuti of Ituri forest in Zaire, Colin Turnbull was categorized as a child (despite his actual age) and assigned to a childless couple. His progress through Mbuti childhood was rapid; on a later visit, he was classed as an unmarried adult male – the resident clown (1986). In Karimpur, North India, Charlotte Wiser, who first visited in 1925, was called *dādī* ('father's mother'); Susan Wadley, who came in 1968, was called *buā* ('father's sister'); when I arrived in 1986, the girls called me *dīdī* ('father's daughter').

Spend early days in the field mapping out the geographical setting; walk around, explore and sketch a map. In urban environments, map the social network. Take care that maps and census do not mark you as a spy or tax collector. (Clip boards and pencils on a string make people uneasy.) Be patient. Relax and enjoy your start on a new venture. Note down all first impressions, bad and good. Ethnomusicologists are more fortunate in every way than anthropologists. Problems of entering the field resolve once the music starts.

CULTURE SHOCK AND LIFE SHOCK During the first month, while the fieldworker is establishing a daily routine, 'culture shock' and 'life shock' take their toll. Culture shock is the clash between norms of the native culture and the culture of the researcher. Common sense in the culture of orientation may be nonsense in the native culture. The scholar who tries to integrate his cultural norms with those of the host community is rarely successful, finding himself adrift, without familiar landmarks to guide daily life. Inconveniences of the field – negotiating every hour of every day in a foreign language, adjusting to reduced standards of hygiene, coping with extremes of cold, heat or humidity, and avoiding scorpions, red ants, mosquitos, cobras and other greater or lesser menaces – these liabilities start to irritate. Daily habits of the local people suddenly seem 'backward' and unnecessarily harsh. In India I found myself wincing at the apparently rough treatment of children, the daily tearful scenes of hair combing and beatings for sloppy schoolwork; I felt disheartened with purdah and other 'primitive' methods of suppressing women.

For the novice, 'life shock' is even more distressing. The student may encounter for the first time birth and death, malnutrition and serious illness left untreated (while the family quarrel over who should pay for medicine). The newcomer may be repelled by inescapable features of poverty – deprivation in every area of life including food, housing, clothing, hygiene and sanitation. The notion of scholarly objectivity becomes repulsive and the prospect of an extended stay in the field stressful and depressing. Entry problems, culture shock and life shock are well documented in anthropological texts, for example Napoleon Chagnon's first sight of the Yąnomamö Indians of Venezuela:

> The excitement of meeting my first Indians was almost unbearable as I duck-waddled through the low passage into the village clearing.
> I looked up and gasped when I saw a dozen burly, naked, filthy, hideous men staring at us down the shafts of their drawn arrows! Immense wads of green tobacco were stuck between their lower teeth and lips making them look even more hideous, and strands of dark-green slime dripped or hung from their noses . . . My next discovery was that there were a dozen or so vicious, underfed dogs snapping at my legs, circling me as if I were going to be their next meal. I just stood there holding my notebook, helpless and pathetic. Then the stench of the decaying vegetation and filth struck me and I almost got sick. I was horrified (1968, p.5).

This situation was dramatic, but no fieldworker escapes shock. Honigmann describes a 'dreadful seven weeks' among the Slave and Cree Indians with 'loneliness occasioned by separation from my family, claustrophobic fear of isolation brought on by the flooded rivers and . . . interpreter and informant problems' (Freilich, 1970, p.21). Hortense Powdermaker confesses to being 'totally fed up with native life' (1967, p.100). Researchers working in their own culture face equal difficulties, including lack of privacy – an apparently universal fieldwork problem. M. N. Srinivas describes 'social claustrophobia' during fieldwork in rural India:

> I was never left alone. I had to fight hard even to get two or three hours absolutely to myself in a week or two. My favourite recreation was walking to the nearby village of Kere where I had some old friends, or to Hogur which had a weekly market. But my friends in Ramapura wanted to accompany me on my walks. They were puzzled by my liking for solitary walks. Why should one walk when one could catch a bus, or ride on bicycles, with friends? I had to plan and plot to give them the slip to go out by myself. On my return home, however, I was certain to be asked why I had not taken them with me. They would have put off their other work and joined me. (They meant it.) I suffered from social claustrophobia as long as I was in the village and sometimes the feeling became so intense that I just had to get out (Srinivas, Shah and Ramaswamy, 1979, p.23).

Luckily these crises often coincide with the first opportunity to record music. During culture shock and life shock, the ethnomusicologist can lean on his professional tools: setting the tape recorder running, labelling the first reel, watching Swiss-watch perfection in motion as the second reel follows the first, soothes physical and psychological distress. Working for a long musical evening under the headphones, monitoring off tape (hearing the split-second delay) introduces a timeless suspension from home and field alike, and thoughts turn more to posterity than the here and now. Study of a transcendental medium is our saving grace. When you feel you cannot bear the harshness of native life for another moment, let the music take over; professional equipment (which until then has just been a headache) comes into its own. Nagra or Stellavox, Schoeps or AKG or Sennheiser microphones, Agfa or Ampex or Maxell open-reel tape, all invoke the intellectual goals and professional standards that gave birth to the project.

The sweetness of ethnomusicological fieldwork comes after many days and hundreds of hours of tape recordings, when you and your informants find you are still fascinated with the topic of music. Your village friends will grow accustomed to the intrusion of a live microphone in their homes, temples, schools. In Trinidad and India, I was always more aware than they that a recording was being made, and I soon came to feel that I was living on two planes: the real-now world of people and places and that little-forever world of recorded sound. Before long, culture shock fades and you conduct interviews, construct taxonomies, build theories, tear them down and build them up again. Friendships grow and talk continues late into the night. But in the midst of the many conversations about music, you may find yourself thinking ahead to the playback, the listening-after-the-event, the hours of transcription and analysis to come, the repeated review of those fleeting moments in the field.

3. Geneviève Dournon recording folk musicians in the desert of Rajasthan, 1972

LENGTH OF STAY How long you spend in the field depends on the nature of your research. Major projects by beginners, especially PhD research, require a year (or the equivalent in shorter visits spread over several years). Follow-up studies in the same area can be done on shorter visits. A particularly fruitful fieldwork programme is the 6- to 12-week 'sprint' – convenient for academic holidays; an acceptable absence for mothers or fathers; short enough to work continuously, early morning to late night; and long enough to collect more data than can be transcribed, analysed and written up in a year. Seasoned fieldworkers can start work in a new area with a series of sprints, spread over several years and rotated to cover different seasons. Purists who argue that the one-year stay is the only valid fieldwork style may spend fewer days in the field, measured over their entire career, than more flexible colleagues, who are ready to dash off for a month or two whenever the opportunity presents. Follow-up studies in the same community are particularly rewarding. The ethnomusicologist indicates his sincerity of purpose by returning, and is greeted as an old friend. As the years pass, the original synchronic study acquires historical depth as with Alan Merriam's research among the Basongye of Zaire and Bruno Nettl's with the Montana Blackfoot (Merriam, 1977; Nettl, 1989).

INFORMANTS Selection of teachers and informants involves decisions for which it is difficult to offer guidance. In sociology, random samples of informants are chosen for questionnaire surveys according to complex equations that determine the sample size required for a given population; other equations determine stratified sampling from heterogeneous populations, and probability in proportion to sample size. These statistical operations are rare in ethnomusicology, which usually involves a highly select group of informants, chosen for musical and cultural competence rather than representativeness. Because samples are seldom representative, the statistical validity of our studies may be less precise than in sociology or anthropology.

Ethnomusicologists rely on a few key informants, individuals with special musical knowledge who are willing to share their time. The scholar must decide if their opinions are personal or typical.

Musicians may test the researcher's sincerity before revealing musical secrets. In Zimbabwe, Paul Berliner's reticent Shona *mbira* teacher refused to divulge the secrets of instrumental technique for six years (1978, pp.1–7). Nettl's Blackfoot informant, 'Joe', made him wait: 'Come back and see me next Tuesday, and bring your machine [tape recorder]', he told the naive fieldworker. After several weeks serving as a chauffeur, Nettl was granted an interview and allowed to record a few songs (1983, pp.248–9).

Every ethnomusicologist will need to find ways of thanking and paying informants. Money is not always the best answer (you may be unable to pay), but in some cultures it is appropriate or necessary. Simple gifts, especially from your country, are appreciated, as are copies of field photographs and cassettes. An essential courtesy is returning publications, academic theses, and commercial records or cassettes to the community. Encourage your informants to read your work and comment on it; you will need to supply several copies – one for a local library or archive and others for people in the community who helped with your research. Be prepared to supply more copies as the originals are loaned out, worn out or lost; the next generation will want their own copies.

INTERVIEWS There are as many interview styles as there are interviewers, interviewees, topics, and cultures. Much depends on your personality, ability

36

to relax and to concentrate, listen and respond with quiet enthusiasm, as well as your genuine interest in the topic and the data you are hoping to collect. Interview types vary according to the control the researcher exercises, from the guided conversation (informal interview) to semi-structured open-ended interviews (informant is encouraged to expand topics) to highly structured formats (interviewer follows a written guide and controls the pace and direction of the conversation). Informal interviewing is especially helpful during early phases of fieldwork. Relaxed conversations build rapport and help the researcher to learn basic facts about community life. They reveal fruitful lines of inquiry and provide a working vocabulary. Informal interviews should be written up in field notes on the same day (not the same as a word-for-word transcription, which takes six to eight hours per hour of recorded material). The researcher can draw up interview guides for structured sessions from the data collected in informal and semi-structured sessions.

The first formal interview questionnaire published in ethnomusicology was David McAllester's in *Enemy Way Music* (1954, pp.91–2; repr. in Nettl, 1964, pp.78–81). McAllester had difficulty phrasing questions because the Navajo have no word for 'music'. He revised original questions such as 'What kinds of musical instruments do you have?' to: 'Some people beat a drum when they sing; what other things are used like that?' I experimented with McAllester's questionnaire with East Indian musicians in Trinidad, inquiring, 'Some people beat a drum when they sing. What other things . . . ?' My Hindu informants (for whom 'music' means 'musical instruments') looked puzzled and asked, 'What do you mean? Do you mean instrument? How do you mean "what other thing"? What other music?' A meaningful question for Navajos was foolish for Trinidadians. Interviews must be phrased in culturally expressive terms, taking into account the concepts held in that society using the appropriate words and ways of talking. Highly structured interviews as test instruments cannot be used during the early phases of fieldwork. You will need to record many informal conversations about music and extract from these transcriptions the musical vocabulary, concepts and categories from which to formulate valid interview questions.

A formal interview, however unstructured, is never the same as a simple chat, but artful interviewers aim to make the difference as unobtrusive as possible. The interviewer should act naturally, not contrive a role or a pose; natural behaviour is essential whether you are working with new informants or people who have known you for many years.

Interview technique is best learned through practice; do not wait until you arrive in the field to test your wings. The best way to improve technique is to transcribe your own interviews. Discipline yourself to write down every word you say as well as every word spoken by the subject. Through this tedious process you will discover flaws in your approach – talking too much, interrupting, leading the conversation away from the topics important to the informant. Most novice interviewers feel shy during pauses and jump in quickly, introducing a new topic. Interviews lose depth at these critical junctures; the informant, who perhaps was about to give his or her innermost thoughts, is silenced by your lack of patience and composure. The silent probe encourages your subject to reflect, and offer deeper detailed explanations.

When silences seem too awkward, repeat the subject's last remark (the neutral probe: 'You were explaining that Holī songs are only performed in spring-time . . .'). Let your informant lead the conversation (you will learn something new). Avoid leading questions; as a substitute Lofland suggests 'What do you think about . . . ?' (rather than 'Don't you think that'; Lofland, 1976). Avoid giving emphasis to a point that you (but perhaps not the interviewee) consider important ('Let me note that point down'). Longer questions usually produce longer responses; depending on the informant, you must decide if longer is better. The phrased assertion or 'baiting' (pretending you know more than you actually do) is a journalistic technique that may produce sensitive information; the ethics of this ploy are dubious (Agar, 1980, p.94; Kirk and Miller, 1986; Bernard, 1988, pp.215–16). Relatives and close friends are usually more difficult to interview than strangers; ironically, people are willing to give information to 'the collector who comes from afar and will disappear again' (Goldstein, 1964, p.64; 'stranger-value' is also discussed in Ives, 1980). Friends in the field may hate to tell us what we may not want to hear, so do not spend all your time with people with whom you have good rapport (Wax, 1960, p.91).

Any interviewee will need encouragement – some indication that he or she is supplying the information you want. Offer this support in a transparent effortless manner. Let your face express understanding of the conversation; if you are following intently, this feedback will flow naturally, and you will glimpse the world through your informant's eyes – the ultimate purpose of an interview.

The best way to preserve an interview is to record it. Cassette recorder and electret microphone are ideal. Always ask permission to record, and explain how the recording will be used. Ask the interviewee if he or she wishes to be credited by name for direct quotations (or prefers to remain anonymous). Cassette recorders are a commonplace all over the world, and there is no reason to feel nervous about asking to record an interview. If you feel embarrassed or shy about taping a session, your subject will sense this uneasiness and start to feel uncomfortable, even suspicious.

The good interviewer must be absolutely confident of his technical skills and sure of his recording equipment. After you have set up recorder and microphones, start the tape, check with headphones that all is well (then put them aside for the interview); explain that the equipment is under control, the tape is running, and the interview can begin. Once you give your informant a reassuring go-ahead, do not distract him by fussing with your recording equipment. Pay full attention to the conversation; even glancing down to check the meter levels or to see if the tape is running can spoil the flow. For reel changes, let the click of your cassette recorder snap you out of your utter concentration on his or her words; do not spend the last five minutes of each tape staring anxiously at the cassette.

Field records

Ethnomusicological fieldwork requires orderly record-keeping, accomplished with an imposing list of mechanical aids – audio and video recorders, microphones, typewriters, even lap-top computers. Open-reel and cassette tapes provide the audio record; photographs, both still and moving, the visual. The most reliable technical field aids are pencil and paper with which the ethnomusicologist prepares field notes, diary and log. Many hours in the field are spent preparing records, more hours in their ordering, labelling, numbering, logging, coding, and cross-referencing for personal use, for archives and for other scholars. After months in the field, when with bad luck all the professional equipment has broken down, when the backup and the backup to the backup have failed, take comfort that you can fall back on pencil and paper to record your observations in notes. Their importance has always been recognized in anthropology, but in ethnomusicology, where technology occupies so much attention, they are underrated.

Anthropologists suggest dividing field writing into four categories: (i) jottings; (ii) notes; (iii) diary; and (iv) log. Ethnomusicologists may wish to consider whether this system, which purportedly separates observed fact (notes) from feelings about facts (diary), is suitable for the documentation of expressive culture.

JOTTINGS AND NOTES During the day make jottings in a small notebook that is always with you (ask permission to write during conversations). Note down as much as possible: proper names, ages, kinship relationships, technical terms, song types, lines of texts, ideas about music, instrument names, tunings and so on. Cultivate the habit of noting information on the spot.

Learn one of the many useful systems for recording, coding, and main-taining anthropological and sociological field notes, and train yourself to write notes daily (you will probably need one or two hours). Anthropologists usually set aside evening time for writing; this programme will not work for ethnomusicologists since musical activities often take place after dark. This may put the ethnomusicologist in the position of writing up yesterday's notes – never a good plan since the human memory is a poor storage medium. Select an open time of day for writing; in many tropical countries, the hot midday hours when the locals are resting may be best. Last thing at night after an exhilarating exhausting recording session is never good for me.

Notes are based on rough field jottings; they will cue your memory and supply technical terms needed to fill out your account. You may write as many as 10,000 words of field notes every week (Bernard, 1988, pp.180–202). With this much material to organize, a system is essential. Select a uniform paper size for all notes (the American 8½" x 11" or the European A4 are practical choices). Plan to use plenty of paper, but short notes are easier to order than long ones. Start each new topic or idea on a fresh page. Do not compose long narrative notes covering many subjects; simple expository descriptions of individual topics are easier to compose and index. Some scholars code each page (along the top edge or right-hand margin) according to the 888 topics listed in the *Outline of Cultural Materials* (Murdock, 1945). For music, Murdock gives: '53: Fine Arts (533 – music, 534 – musical instruments, 535 – dancing, 536 – drama, 537 – oratory); 54: Entertainment (545 – musical and theatrical productions, 547 – night clubs and cabarets, 549 – art and recreational supplies industries'). The ethnomusicologist will need to devise a more detailed system suited to musicological research.

Hiding notes from the people about whom they are written always creates suspicion. In Trinidad and India my informants enjoyed hearing me read from my field notes; naturally enough they wanted to know what I was writing in my room. Their comments from these reading sessions proved especially helpful.

DIARY Anthropologists often keep a diary, a personal document in which are recorded feelings, anxieties, frustrations, and hopes; these comments are kept in a volume separate from field notes. The scholar integrates the subjective data from the diary and the purportedly objective facts from the notes at a later stage, evaluating attitudes and moods during the collection of data and their influence on the research. This method may be helpful for some, but I am dubious about trying to make a formal distinction between objective and subjective, and I dislike writing anything in the field that I cannot read back to my informants, indeed anything I would not want published, as for example the posthumously published field diaries of such an eminent scholar as Bronislaw Malinowski:

> Tuesday, 4.24 . . . Last night and this morning looked in vain for fellows for my boat. This drives me to a state of white rage and hatred for bronze-coloured skin, combined with depression, a desire to 'sit down and cry', and a furious longing '*to get out of this*'. For all that, I decide to resist and work today – '*business as usual*', despite everything (1967, p.261).

LOG The key to systematic fieldwork is a log, a running account of plans for spending time (and money). A fairly large bound book with lined pages is suitable for this. Number and date all the pages in advance, allotting one opening for each day in the field. On the left, list your plans for the day, on the right what you actually did. This simple system encourages you to plan ahead: make appointments for specific activities and enter them under the date. Make appointments to interview a singer, photograph the preparing of drum heads, record a particular wedding song, finish a genealogy and enter them in the log. By comparing the real with the ideal on a daily basis, you will learn to budget time and improve your schedule. At least for the beginning of your trip, you might use the log to note down your daily routine, eating and sleeping times and your menus.

NUMBERING In addition to general logs and diaries, the ethnomusicologist will need to keep separate detailed logs for open-reel tapes, cassettes, video tapes and rolls of photographic film. Label all these items as soon as they have been recorded with a number, date and brief identification of contents. Two small self-adhesive labels affixed to the recording spool, one or two on a film canister and the standard self-adhesive compact cassette labels suffice for this purpose. Number each set of materials separately – tapes, cassettes, photo rolls – beginning with '1', in strict chronological sequence (ordering by topic, genre, musician etc should be done through cross-referencing). A simple system for composite identification numbers is useful, for example, *India 6/89/F/131*: the name of the trip (India 6), the year (1989), the format (F – open-reel *F*ield tape), and the number (131st tape); *MAU1/92/CS/39* (Mauritius, trip 1, 1992,

*Ca*S*s*ette number 39); and so on – PH for photographic roll, VC for video cassette, DAT for digital audio tapes.

Health in the field

Give serious consideration to the preservation of personal health in the field, particularly if your field site is away from home, in the tropics or another climatic extreme – arctic, arid, whatever. Make sure your immunizations are current for the area (especially typhoid, cholera, tetanus, yellow fever, polio, hepatitis A; don't forget measles, mumps, rubella [MMR] if you were not immunized in childhood). Many essential immunizations require a course of two or three injections, given over several months. Visit your dentist before departure; take a copy of your eye glasses prescription and a spare pair of glasses (especially important for contact lens wearers).

Be particularly vigilant about malaria, a serious tropical protozoan parasite infection on the increase worldwide (estimated 150 million cases per year with 1 million deaths; Hatt, 1982). If working in a malaria zone (including Africa, Central and South America, the Indian subcontinent, Southeast Asia, the Middle East, and the Pacific Islands), get current advice before your departure from a specialist tropical health centre regarding prophylactic tablets including Chloroquine, Fansidar, Doxycycline, and newer medications such as Mefloquine (Lariam). You *must* take one or a combination of these during your stay. Recommendations about type and dose vary from area to area and from year to year (as resistant strains develop), so check before each trip, even to areas you know well. Many malaria prophylactics must be begun a week before departure and continued for six weeks after your return. If your field site is days away from medical facilities seek advice before departing. In any case carry extra Chloroquine tablets and learn to recognize malaria symptoms: vivax malaria is typified by a cold-shivering-hot-sweating cycle (typically 24 hour cycles repeated every 48 hours, but patterns vary); the potentially fatal falcipurum malaria starts with deceptively mild flu-like symptoms – fever, headache, possibly vomiting and diarrhoea that persist for two days, changing with treacherous swiftness into an overwhelming disease, with liver, kidney or respiratory failure or coma (cerebral malaria). If you experience such mild symptoms and know you could have falcipurum malaria, take four Chloroquine tablets immediately, then two every eight hours for a week. This treatment can save your life, enabling you to reach medical help. Mild symptoms must never be ignored (in the 1980s, one promising young Dutch ethnomusicologist died suddenly in Indonesia from falcipurum malaria). Any disease contracted in a malarial zone must be assumed to be malaria until proven otherwise and treated immediately with Chloroquine by mouth, while seeking urgent and skilful medical attention.

The first line of defence against malaria (and some 80 other dread diseases) is to avoid mosquitoes. Repellents with diethyl toluamide are effective, applied to the skin, clothing and bedding. Keep arms and legs covered, especially in the evenings when the anopheline mosquito bites. Wear socks. Avoid hotels near swamps. Local sprays and mosquito coils are successful deterrents for night-time (set up your coil safely so your room does not catch fire if it breaks). Old-fashioned mosquito nets are very helpful. Beware also of red ants, scorpions (check your shoes), snakes, and rabies-carrying mammals, especially dogs. If bitten seek immediate medical help. Treat even minor cuts and grazes with sterilized water and antiseptic cream.

Ignore the advice that you can slowly build immunity by drinking small amounts of local contaminated water. Water-borne diseases include polio, guinea-worm, leptospirosis, typhoid, paratyphoid, cholera, bacillary dysentery, amoebic dysentery, infective hepatitis, worms and giardiasis. Drink bottled water or develop a system for water purification using boiling, chlorine purification tablets, and perhaps filters. Boiling is the safest method to sterilize water; a brisk five-minute boil is enough, ten minutes very safe. Remember to sterilize water containers. Chlorine tablets are not as effective as boiling (but much better than no protection); however, try to avoid their use for extended periods. They should be added to water at least ten minutes before drinking, preferably longer. If using tablets in boiled water, wait until the water cools. Water filters can be useful to remove sludge and large particles of grit, but need to be cleaned regularly, or they can harbour organisms. Even very hot water kills many germs, so it is always safer to drink tea and coffee than unboiled water. Bottled fizzy drinks are usually safe as the acidity kills bacteria.

In tropical settings and also at high altitudes force yourself to drink more than you feel you need, especially until your natural thirst mechanism adjusts to the setting. Stay out of the noon-day sun and remember that unquenchable thirst is usually helped fastest by hot tea.

Peel all raw foods. Use chlorinated water to wash any raw vegetables or fruits. Avoid raw greens such as lettuce altogether. Prepared milk and milk products also may not be safe. Small roadside restaurants where you can see food cooked over an open fire may be safer than expensive hotels that warm up yesterday's saucy meat dish. In tropical countries, a diet of well-cooked fresh vegetables is best.

Carry standard over-the-counter remedies for pain, diarrhoea, rash, eye infection and dehydration. Your medical kit should include antiseptic cream, tablets for motion sickness (also helpful for nausea), antihistamines (for rash), bandages, electrolyte powder, a course of broad-spectrum antibiotics (Ciproflaxin is particularly effective for severe intestinal disorders), oil of clove (toothache) and any other medications you regularly use. Label all medicines with name, use and dose.

DEPARTURE As there is an art to entering a community, there is an art to leaving. Don't vanish suddenly. Say goodbye in a manner that is appropriate to the culture – with words and actions. Give fair warning of your departure. Stay in correspondence with friends made in the field; they may be relying on a continued relationship, however simple. You may represent an important and unforgettable episode in their life (Alan Merriam discovered when he returned to the Basongye of Zaire in 1974, after an absence of 14 years, that his earlier visit was considered the most important event in recent musical life; Merriam, 1977).

Umesh Pandey from Karimpur, the village in Western Uttar Pradesh studied by American anthropologists since 1925, explained the feelings of the anthropological subject:

'We want friendship, they want information; we want life-long relations, they want information; we want to think of them as part of our family, they want information. Anthropologists come and go like a dream. It is difficult to know what to like or to hate. Still, we love them' (1991, p.1).

Bibliography

GENERAL

B. Malinowski: *Argonauts of the Western Pacific* (New York, 1922)

W. H. Wiser and C. V. Wiser: *Behind Mud Walls 1930–1960* (Berkeley, 1930, rev. 1963, 1971, 1989)

M. Mead: 'More Comprehensive Field Methods', *American Anthropologist*, xxxv (1933), 1

Z. N. Hurston: *Mules and Men* (Philadelphia, 1935/R1969)

B. A. Botkin: *Supplementary Instruction to the American Guide Manual: Manual for Folklore Studies* (Washington, DC, 1938)

A. Lesser: 'Problems Versus Subject Matter as Directives of Research', *American Anthropologist*, xli (1939), 574

A. I. Richards: 'The Development of Field Work Methods in Social Anthropology', *The Study of Society: Methods and Problems*, ed. F. C. Bartlett and others (London, 1939), 272–316

G. P. Murdock and others: *Outline of Cultural Materials* (New Haven, CT, 1945, rev. 5/1982)

M. J. Herskovits: 'The Ethnographer's Laboratory', *Man and His Works: the Science of Cultural Anthropology* (New York, 1948), 79

B. Malinowski: *Magic, Science and Religion and Other Essays* (New York, 1948/R1954)

C. Du Bois: 'Culture Shock', *To Strengthen World Freedom*, Institute of International Education, Special Publication Series, i (1951), 22

J. S. Slotkin: *Menomini Peyotism: a Study of Individual Variation in a Primary Group with a Homogeneous Culture* (Philadelphia, 1952)

R. H. Wax: 'Reciprocity as a Field Technique', *Human Organization*, xi/3 (1952), 34

O. Lewis: 'Controls and Experiments in Field Work', *Anthropology Today: an Encyclopedic Inventory*, ed. A. L. Kroeber (Chicago, 1953), 452

J. H. Bell: 'Field Techniques in Anthropology', *Mankind*, v (1954), 3

——: 'Observation in Anthropology', *Mankind*, v (1955), 55

W. F. Whyte: *Street Corner Society: the Social Structure of an Italian Slum* (Chicago, 1943, rev. 3/1981)

C. M. Arensberg: 'The Community-Study Method', *American Journal of Sociology*, lx (1954), 109

J. P. Dean and W. F. Whyte: 'How Do You Know if the Informant is Telling the Truth?', *Human Organization*, xvii/2 (1958), 34

R. L. Gold: 'Roles in Sociological Field Observations', *Social Forces*, xxxvi (1958), 217

E. Goffman: *The Presentation of Self in Everyday Life* (New York, 1959/R1973)

E. T. Hall: *The Silent Language* (New York, 1959/R1980)

K. R. Popper: *The Logic of Scientific Discovery* (London, 1959, rev. 10/1980)

R. N. Adams and J. J. Preiss, eds.: *Human Organization Research: Field Relations and Techniques* (Homewood, IL, 1960)

J. B. Casagrande: *In the Company of Man: Twenty Portraits by Anthropologists* (New York, 1960)

E. C. Hughes: 'Introduction: the Place of Field Work in Social Science', *Field Work: an Introduction to the Social Sciences*, B. H. Junker (Chicago, 1960)

B. H. Junker: *Field Work: an Introduction to the Social Sciences* (Chicago, 1960)

R. H. Wax: 'Reciprocity in Field Work', *Human Organization Research: Field Relations and Techniques* ed. R. N. Adams and J. J. Preiss (Homewood, IL, 1960), 90 [orig. pubd as 'Reciprocity as a Field Technique', *Human Organization*, xi/3 (1952), 34]

——: 'Twelve Years Later: an Analysis of Field Experience', *Human Organization Research: Field Relations and Techniques*, ed. R. N. Adams and J. J. Preiss (Homewood, IL, 1960), 166

G. D. Berreman: *Behind Many Masks: Ethnography and Impression Management in a Himalayan Village* (Ithaca, NY, 1962)

T. S. Kuhn: *The Structure of Scientific Revolutions* (Chicago, 1962, rev. 2/1970)

R. Naroll: *Data Quality Control – a New Research Technique: Prolegomena to a Cross-Cultural Study of Culture Stress* (New York, 1962)

M. Zelditch Jr: 'Some Methodological Problems of Field Studies', *American Journal of Sociology*, lxvii (1962), 566

D. Nash: 'The Ethnologist as Stranger: an Essay in the Sociology of Knowledge', *Southwest Journal of Anthropology*, xix (1963), 149

K. R. Popper: *Conjectures and Refutations: the Growth of Scientific Knowledge* (London, 1963, rev. 4/1972)

W. A. Smalley: 'Culture Shock, Language Shock, and the Shock of Self-Discovery', *Practical Anthropology*, x (1963), 49

K. S. Goldstein: *A Guide for Field Workers in Folklore* (Hatboro, PA, 1964)

P. E. Hammond, ed.: *Sociologists at Work: Essays on the Craft of Social Research* (New York, 1964)

W. B. Schwab: 'Looking Backward: an Appraisal of Two Field Trips', *Human Organization*, xxiv (1965), 373

E. T. Hall: *The Hidden Dimension* (Garden City, NY, 1966)

F. Henry: 'The Role of the Fieldworker in an Explosive Political Situation', *Current Anthropology*, vii (1966), 552

J. W. Bennett and G. Thaiss: 'Sociocultural Anthropology and Survey Research', *Survey Research in the Social Sciences*, ed. C. Y. Glock (New York, 1967), 269–313

E. Goffman: *Interaction Ritual: Essays on Face-to-Face Behavior* (Garden City, NY, 1967/R1982)

J. Heiss and D. Nash: 'The Stranger in Laboratory Culture Revisited', *Human Organization*, xxvi (1967), 47

E. Liebow: *Tally's Corner: a Study of Negro Streetcorner Men* (Boston, 1967)

B. Malinowski: *A Diary in the Strict Sense of the Term* (New York, 1967)

H. Powdermaker: *Stranger and Friend: the Way of an Anthropologist* (New York, 1967)

W. J. Samarin: *Field Linguistics: a Guide to Linguistic Field Work* (New York, 1967)

T. R. Williams: *Field Methods in the Study of Culture* (New York, 1967)

N. A. Chagnon: *Yąnomamö: the Fierce People* (New York, 1968, 2/1977)

C. C. Lundberg: 'A Transactional Conception of Fieldwork', *Human Organization*, xxvii (1968), 45

V. Deloria Jr: *Custer Died for Your Sins: an Indian Manifesto* (New York, 1969)

F. Henry and S. Saberwal, eds.: *Stress and Response in Fieldwork* (New York, 1969)

R. P. Rohner: *The Ethnography of Franz Boas: Letters and Diaries of Franz Boas Written on the Northwest Coast from 1886 to 1931* (Chicago, 1969)

S. A. Tyler, ed.: *Cognitive Anthropology* (New York, 1969)

R. M. Wintrob: 'An Inward Focus: a Consideration of Psychological Stress in Fieldwork', *Stress and Response in Fieldwork*, ed. F. Henry and S. Saberwal (New York, 1969), 63

N. K. Denzin: *The Research Act: a Theoretical Introduction to Sociological Methods* (Chicago, 1970, 2/1978)

M. Freilich, ed.: *Marginal Natives: Anthropologists at Work* (New York, 1970)

R. Naroll and R. Cohen, eds.: *A Handbook of Method in Cultural Anthropology* (Garden City, NY, 1970/R1973)

P. J. Pelto: *Anthropological Research: the Structure of Inquiry* (New York, 1970, rev. 2/1978)

G. D. Spindler, ed.: *Being an Anthropologist: Fieldwork in Eleven Cultures* (New York, 1970)

B. G. Anderson: 'Adaptive Aspects of Culture Shock', *American Anthropologist*, lxxiii (1971), 1121

J. H. Brunvand: *A Guide for Collectors of Folklore in Utah* (Salt Lake City, 1971)

J. Lofland: *Analyzing Social Settings: a Guide to Qualitative Observation and Analysis* (Belmont, CA, 1971, 2/1984)

M. L. Stein: *Reporting Today: the Newswriter's Handbook* (New York, 1971)

R. H. Wax: *Doing Fieldwork: Warnings and Advice* (Chicago, 1971/R1985)

M. Mead: *Blackberry Winter: My Earlier Years* (New York, 1972)

K. R. Popper: *Objective Knowledge: an Evolutionary Approach* (Oxford, 1972, rev. 6/1981)

J. P. Spradley and D. W. McCurdy, eds.: *The Cultural Experience: Ethnography in Complex Society* (Chicago, 1972)

D. J. Jones: 'Culture Fatigue: the Results of Role-Playing in Anthropological Research', *Anthropological Quarterly*, xlvi (1973), 30

G. Mills: 'Art and the Anthropological Lens', *The Traditional Artist in African Societies*, ed. W. L. d'Azevedo (Bloomington, IN, 1973), 379–416

P. J. Pelto and G. H. Pelto: 'Ethnography: the Fieldwork Enterprise', *Handbook of Social and Cultural Anthropology*, ed. J. J. Honigmann (Chicago, 1973), 241–88

R. Rohner and others: 'Ethnographer Bias in Cross-Cultural Research', *Behavior Science Notes*, viii (1973), 275–317

A. Ryan, ed.: *The Philosophy of Social Explanation* (London, 1973)

L. Schatzman and A. L. Strauss: *Field Research: Strategies for a Natural Sociology* (Englewood Cliffs, NJ, 1973)

M. Speier: *How to Observe Face-to-Face Communication: a Sociological Introduction* (Pacific Palisades, CA, 1973)

R. B. Edgerton and L. L. Langness: *Methods and Styles in the Study of Culture* (San Francisco, 1974)

G. M. Foster and R. V. Kemper, eds.: *Anthropologists in Cities* (Boston, 1974)

M. Harris: 'Why a Perfect Knowledge of All the Rules One Must Know to Act Like a Native Cannot Lead to the Knowledge of How Natives Act', *Journal of Anthropological Research*, xxx (1974), 242

A. Béteille and T. N. Madan: *Encounter and Experience: Personal Accounts of Fieldwork* (Delhi, 1975)

M. Clarke: 'Survival in the Field: Implications of Personal Experience in Field Work', *Theory and Society*, ii (1975), 95

R. J. Grele, ed.: *Envelopes of Sound: Six Practitioners Discuss the Method, Theory and Practice of Oral History and Oral Testimony* (Chicago, 1975)

J. M. Johnson: *Doing Field Research* (New York, 1975)

J. Salinas: 'On the Clan of Anthropologists', *The Human Way: Readings in Anthropology*, ed. H. R. Bernard (New York, 1975), 71

J. H. Brunvand: *Folklore: a Study and Research Guide* (New York, 1976)

C. Geertz: '"From the Native's Point of View": On the Nature of Anthropological Understanding', *Meaning in Anthropology*, ed. K. H. Basso and H. A. Selby (Albuquerque, 1976)

J. J. Honigmann: 'The Personal Approach in Cultural Anthropological Research', *Current Anthropology*, xvii (1976), 243

D. Nachmias and C. Nachmias: *Research Methods in the Social Sciences* (New York, 1976, 3/1987)

K. Blanchard: 'The Expanded Responsibilities of Long Term Informant Relationships', *Human Organization*, xxxvi (1977), 66

M. Freilich, ed.: *Marginal Natives at Work: Anthropologists in the Field* (Cambridge, MA, 1977)

P. Rabinow: *Reflections on Fieldwork in Morocco* (Berkeley, 1977)

M. L. Wax: 'On Fieldworkers and Those Exposed to Fieldwork: Federal Regulations and Moral Issues', *Human Organization*, xxxvi (1977), 321

I. G. Carpenter, ed.: *Folklorists in the City: the Urban Field Experience* (Bloomington, IN, 1978) [*Folklore Forum* special no.]

J.-P. Dumont: *The Headman and I: Ambiguity and Ambivalence in the Fieldworking Experience* (Austin, 1978)

A. W. Johnson: *Quantification in Cultural Anthropology: an Introduction to Research Design* (Stanford, CA, 1978)

R. Sanjek: 'A Network Method and its Uses in Urban Ethnography', *Human Organization*, xxxvii (1978), 257

P. Bartis: *Folklife and Fieldwork: a Layman's Introduction to Field Techniques* (Washington, DC, 1979)

T. D. Cook and D. T. Campbell: *Quasi-Experimentation: Design and Analysis Issues for Field Settings* (Chicago, 1979)

G. M. Foster and others: *Long-Term Field Research in Social Anthropology* (New York, 1979)

L. Sechrest, ed.: *Unobtrusive Measures Today* (San Francisco, 1979) [*New Directions for Methodology of Behavioral Science* special no.]

M. N. Srinivas, A. M. Shah and E. A. Ramaswamy, eds.: *The Fieldworker and the Field: Problems and Challenges in Sociological Investigation* (Delhi, 1979)

M. H. Agar: *The Professional Stranger: an Informal Introduction to Ethnography* (New York, 1980)

B. A. Babcock: 'Reflexivity: Definitions and Discriminations', *Semiotica*, xxx (1980), 1

S. Bochner: 'Unobtrusive Methods in Cross-Cultural Experimentation', *Handbook of Cross-Cultural Psychology*, ii: *Methodology*, ed. H. C. Triandis and J. W. Berry (Boston, 1980), 319–87

R. A. Georges and M. O. Jones: *People Studying People: the Human Element in Fieldwork* (Berkeley, CA, 1980)

G. Fassnacht: *Theory and Practice of Observing Behaviour* (London, 1982)

C. Fischer: *To Dwell Among Friends: Personal Networks in Town and City* (Chicago, 1982)

J. Mark: 'Francis La Flesche: the American Indian as Anthropologist', *ISIS*, lxxiii (1982), 497

J. Ruby, ed.: *A Crack in the Mirror: Reflexive Perspectives in Anthropology* (Philadelphia, 1982)

N. Barley: *The Innocent Anthropologist: Notes from a Mud Hut* (London, 1983)

M. Bulmer and D. P. Warwick, eds.: *Social Research in Developing Countries: Surveys and Censuses in the Third World* (Chichester and New York, 1983)

R. M. Dorson, ed.: *Handbook of American Folklore* (Bloomington, IN, 1983)

Ethnomusicology: an Introduction

R. Lawless, V. H. Sutlive and M. D. Zamora, eds.: *Fieldwork: the Human Experience* (New York, 1983)

H. R. Bernard and others: 'The Problem of Informant Accuracy: the Validity of Retrospective Data', *Annual Review of Anthropology*, xiii (1984), 495

J. P. Goetz and M. D. Le Compte: *Ethnography and Qualitative Design in Educational Research* (Orlando, FL, 1984)

D. R. Gross: 'Time Allocation: a Tool for the Study of Cultural Behaviour', *Annual Review of Anthropology*, xiii (1984), 519–58

S. R. Nachman: 'Lies My Informants Told Me', *Journal of Anthropological Research*, xl (1984), 536

W. F. Whyte: *Learning from the Field: a Guide from Experience* (Beverly Hills, CA, 1984)

M. Borgerhoff Mulder and T. M. Caro: 'The Use of Quantitative Observational Techniques in Anthropology', *Current Anthropology*, xxvi (1985), 323

J. S. Boster: ' "Requiem for the Omniscient Informant": There's Life in the Old Girl, Yet', *Directions in Cognitive Anthropology*, ed. J. W. D. Dougherty (Urbana, 1985)

G. Stocking: *Observers Observed: Essays on Ethnographic Fieldwork* (Madison, WI, 1985)

M. Biesele and S. A. Tyler, eds.: *The Dialectic of Oral and Literary Hermeneutics* (Washington, 1986) [*Cultural Anthropology* special no.7]

E. M. Bruner: 'Ethnography as Narrative', *The Anthropology of Experience*, ed. V. W. Turner and E. M. Bruner (Urbana, 1986), 139

J. Clifford and G. E. Marcus, eds.: *Writing Culture: the Poetics and Politics of Ethnography* (Berkeley, CA, 1986)

J. L. Peacock: *The Anthropological Lens: Harsh Light, Soft Focus* (Cambridge, 1986)

A. K. Romney, S. C. Weller and W. H. Batchelder: 'Culture as Consensus: a Theory of Culture and Informant Accuracy', *American Anthropologist*, lxxxviii (1986), 313

V. W. Turner and E. M. Bruner, eds.: *The Anthropology of Experience* (Urbana, 1986)

L. C. Freeman, A. K. Romney and S. C. Freeman: 'Cognitive Structure and Informant Accuracy', *American Anthropologist*, lxxxix (1987), 310

B. Jackson: *Fieldwork* (Urbana, 1987)

O. Werner and G. M. Schoepfle: *Systematic Fieldwork* (Newbury Park, CA, 1987)

H. R. Bernard: *Research Methods in Cultural Anthropology* (Newbury Park, CA, 1988)

S. C. Weller and A. K. Romney: *Systematic Data Collection* (Newbury Park, CA, 1988)

C. A. Lerner, ed.: *The Grants Register, 1989–1991* (London, 1991)

U. Pandey: 'Anthropologists in Karimpur, 1925–1990' (unpubd MS, 1991)

PARTICIPANT OBSERVATION

F. R. Kluckhohn: 'The Participant-Observer Technique in Small Communities', *American Journal of Sociology*, xlvi (1940), 331

S. M. Miller: 'The Participant Observer and "Over-Rapport" ', *American Sociological Review*, xvii (1952), 97

M. S. Schwartz and C. G. Schwartz: 'Problems in Participant Observation', *American Journal of Sociology*, lx (1955), 343

A. J. Vidich: 'Participant Observation and the Collection and Interpretation of Data', *American Journal of Sociology*, lx (1955), 354

H. S. Becker: 'Problems of Inference and Proof in Participant Observation,' *American Sociological Review*, xxiii (1958), 652

V. L. Olesen and E. W. Whittaker: 'Role-Making in Participant Observation: Processes in the Researcher-Actor Relationship', *Human Organization*, xxvi (1967), 273

G. J. McCall and J. L. Simmons, eds.: *Issues in Participant Observation: a Text and Reader* (Reading, MA, 1969)

B. Jules-Rosette: *Rethinking Field Research: the Role of the Observing Participant* (Washington, DC, 1980)

J. P. Spradley: *Participant Observation* (New York, 1980)

INTERVIEWS

S. F. Nadel: 'The Interview Technique in Social Anthropology', *The Study of Society: Methods and Problems*, ed. F. C. Bartlett and others (London, 1939), 317

S. L. Payne: *The Art of Asking Questions* (Princeton, NJ, 1951)

B. D. Paul: 'Interviewing Techniques and Field Relationships', *Anthropology Today: an Encyclopedic Inventory*, ed. A. L. Kroeber (Chicago, 1953), 430

W. F. Whyte: 'Interviewing for Organizational Research', *Human Organization*, xii/2 (1953), 15

J. P. Dean: 'Participant Observation and Interviewing', *An Introduction to Social Research*, ed. J. T. Doby (Harrisburg, PA, 1954, 2/1967), 225

A. R. Holmberg: 'Participant Intervention in the Field', *Human Organization*, xiv/1 (1955), 23

R. K. Merton, M. Fiske and P. L. Kendall: *The Focused Interview: a Manual of Problems and Procedures* (Glencoe, IL, 1956)

H. S. Becker and B. Geer: 'Participant Observation and Interviewing: a Comparison', *Human Organization*, xvi/3 (1957), 28

W. F. Whyte: 'On Asking Indirect Questions', *Human Organization*, xv/4 (1957), 21

——: 'Interviewing in Field Research', *Human Organization Research: Field Relations and Techniques*, ed. R. N. Adams and J. J. Preiss (Homewood, IL, 1960), 352

R. L. Gorden: *Interviewing: Strategy, Techniques, and Tactics* (Homewood, IL, 1969, rev. 2/1975)

L. A. Dexter: *Elite and Specialized Interviewing* (Evanston, IL, 1970)

J. K. Skipper Jr and C. H. McCaghy: 'Respondents' Intrusion Upon the Situation: the Problem of Interviewing Subjects with Special Qualities', *Sociological Quarterly*, xiii (1972), 237

J. Lofland: *Doing Social Life: the Qualitative Study of Human Interaction in Natural Settings* (New York, 1976)

D. H. Zimmerman and D. L. Wieder: 'The Diary: Diary-Interview Method', *Urban Life*, v (1977), 479

N. M. Bradburn and others: *Improving Interview Method and Questionnaire Design: Response Effects to Threatening Questions in Survey Research* (San Francisco, 1979)

J. P. Spradley: *The Ethnographic Interview* (New York, 1979)

E. D. Ives: *The Tape-Recorded Interview: a Manual for Field Workers in Folklore and Oral History* (Knoxville, TN, 1980)

H. Simons: 'Conversation Piece: the Practice of Interviewing in Case Study Research', *Uttering, Muttering: Collecting, Using and Reporting Talk for Social and Educational Research*, ed. C. Adelman (London, 1981), 27

S. Sudman and N. M. Bradburn: *Asking Questions: a Practical Guide to Questionnaire Design* (San Francisco, 1982)

J. Goyder: 'Face-to-Face Interviews and Mailed Questionnaires: the Net Difference in Response Rate', *Public Opinion Quarterly*, xlix (1985), 234

J. Kirk and M. L. Miller: *Reliability and Validity in Qualitative Research* (Beverly Hills, CA, 1986)

ETHICS AND GENDER ISSUES

H. Barry, III, M. K. Bacon and I. I. Child: 'A Cross Cultural Survey of Some Sex Differences in Socialization', *Journal of Abnormal Social Psychology*, lv (1957), 327

H. Papanek: 'The Woman Fieldworker in a Purdah Society', *Human Organization*, xxiii (1964), 160

R. G. D'Andrade: 'Sex Differences and Cultural Institutions', *The Development of Sex Differences*, ed. E. E. Maccoby, (Stanford, CA, 1966), 174–204

A. Fischer and P. Golde: 'The Position of Women in Anthropology', *American Anthropologist*, lxx (1968), 337

C. Geertz: 'Thinking as a Moral Act: Ethical Dimensions of Anthropological Fieldwork in the New States', *Antioch Review*, xxviii (1968), 139

J. A. Barnes: 'Some Ethical Problems in Modern Field Work', *Anthropologists in the Field*, ed. D. G. Jongmans and P. C. W. Gutkind (Assen, 1967), 193

P. Golde, ed.: *Women in the Field: Anthropological Experiences* (Chicago, 1970, rev. 2/1986)

C. J. Frisbie: 'Field Work as a "Single Parent": To Be or Not to Be Accompanied by a Child', *Collected Papers in Honor of Florence Hawley Ellis*, ed. T. R. Frisbie (Albuquerque, 1975), 98

T. N. Pandey: '"India Man" among American Indians', *Encounter and Experience: Personal Accounts of Fieldwork*, ed. A. Béteille and T. N. Madan (Delhi, 1975), 194

M. A. Rynkiewich and J. P. Spradley, eds.: *Ethics and Anthropology: Dilemmas in Fieldwork* (New York, 1976)

C. A. B. Warren and P. K. Rasmussen: 'Sex and Gender in Field Research', *Urban Life*, vi (1977), 349

M. F. Weeks and R. P. Moore: 'Ethnicity-of-Interviewer Effects on Ethnic Respondents', *Public Opinion Quarterly*, xlv (1981), 245

M. Cesara: *Reflections of a Woman Anthropologist: No Hiding Place* (London, 1982)

E. Brady and others, eds.: *The Federal Cylinder Project: a Guide to Cylinder Recordings in Federal Agencies* (Washington, DC, 1984–)

D. P. McAllester: 'A Problem in Ethics', *Problems and Solutions: Occasional Essays in Musicology Presented to Alice M. Moyle*, ed. J. C. Kassler and J. Stubington (Sydney, 1984), 279

Saṃvādī: Newsletter of the Archives & Research Center for Ethnomusicology (New Delhi, 1981–) from 1988 *ARCE Newsletter*

C. M. Turnbull: 'Sex and Gender: the Role of Subjectivity in Field Research', *Self, Sex and Gender in Cross-Cultural Fieldwork*, ed. T. L. Whitehead and M. E. Conaway (Urbana, 1986), 17

T. L. Whitehead and M. E. Conaway, eds.: *Self, Sex and Gender in Cross-Cultural Fieldwork* (Urbana, 1986)

FIELDWORK IN ETHNOMUSICOLOGY

H. H. Roberts: 'Suggestions to Field-Workers in Collecting Folk Music and Data About Instruments', *Journal of the Polynesian Society*, xl (1931), 103

M. Hood: 'Training and Research Methods in Ethnomusicology', *EM*, i/11 (1957), 2

M. Karpeles, ed.: *The Collecting of Folk Music and Other Ethnomusicological Material: a Manual for Field Workers* (London, 1958)

M. Hood: 'The Challenge of "Bi-musicality" ', *EM*, iv (1960), 55

———: *Institute of Ethnomusicology* (Los Angeles, 1961)

A. P. Merriam: *The Anthropology of Music* (Evanston, IL, 1964)

B. Nettl: *Theory and Method of Ethnomusicology* (New York, 1964)

A. P. Merriam: 'Ethnomusicology Revisited', *EM*, xiii (1969), 213

M. Hood: *The Ethnomusicologist* (New York, 1971, rev. 2/1982)

J. Blacking: 'Fieldwork in African Music', *Review of Ethnology*, iii (1973), 177

K. A. Gourlay: 'Towards a Reassessment of the Ethnomusicologist's Role in Research', *EM*, xxii (1978), 1–35

M. Herndon and N. McLeod: *Music as Culture* (Norwood, PA, 1979, rev. 2/1982)

G. Kubik: 'Field Problems in the Collection of Oral Literature', *Review of Ethnology*, vii (1979), 73

J. Koning: 'The Fieldworker as Performer: Fieldwork Objectives and Social Roles in County Clare, Ireland', *EM*, xxiv (1980), 417

H. P. Myers: ' "Normal" Ethnomusicology and "Extraordinary" Ethnomusicology', *Journal of the Indian Musicological Society*, xii/3–4 (1981), 38

M. Herndon and N. McLeod: *Field Manual for Ethnomusicology* (Norwood, PA, 1983)

H. P. Myers: 'Ethnomusicology', *The New Oxford Companion to Music*, ed. D. Arnold (Oxford, 1983), 645

B. Nettl: *The Study of Ethnomusicology: Twenty-nine Issues and Concepts* (Urbana, 1983)

H. P. Myers: 'Ethnomusicology', *The New Grove Dictionary of American Music*, ed. H. W. Hitchcock and S. Sadie (London, 1984)

B. Nettl: 'In Honor of Our Principal Teachers', *EM*, xxviii (1984), 173

H. P. Myers: 'Return Visit: Thoughts on Fieldwork Method from Felicity, Trinidad', *Bulletin of the International Council for Traditional Music, U.K. Chapter*, xv (1986), 15

REPRESENTATIVE ETHNOMUSICOLOGICAL STUDIES

J. W. Fewkes: 'On the Use of the Phonograph among the Zuni Indians', *American Naturalist*, xxiv (1890), 687

B. I. Gilman: 'Hopi Songs', *Journal of American Archaeology and Ethnology*, v (1908/R1977) [whole issue]

K. Kvitka: *Professional'ni narodni spivtsy y muzykanty na Ukraini: prohrama dlya doslidu yikh diyal'nosti ta pobutu* [Professional Folk Singers and Instrumentalists in the Ukraine: Programme of Study of their Activity and Everyday Life] (Kiev, 1924; Russ. trans. in K. Kvitka: *Izbrannye trudy v dvukh tomakh*, ii [Moscow, 1973], p.xxx)

F. Densmore: *Papago Music* (Washington, DC, 1929/R1972)

J. A. Lomax: *Adventures of a Ballad Hunter* (New York, 1947)

M. Hood: *The Nuclear Theme as a Determinant of Paṭet in Javanese Music* (Groningen, 1954)

B. Nettl: *North American Indian Musical Styles* (Philadelphia, 1954)

D. P. McAllester: *Enemy Way Music: a Study of Social and Esthetic Values as Seen in Navaho Music* (Cambridge, MA, 1954)

C. Brăiloiu: *Vie musicale d'un village: recherches sur le répertoire de Drăguş, (Roumanie) 1929–1932* (Paris, 1960)

A. P. Merriam: 'The Ethnographic Experience: Drum-Making Among the Bala (Basongye)', *EM*, xiii (1969), 74

J. Blacking: 'Deep and Surface Structure in Venda Music', *YIFMC*, iii (1971), 91

E. Zonis: *Classical Persian Music: an Introduction* (Cambridge, MA, 1973)

A. P. Merriam: 'Music Change in a Basongye Village (Zaïre)', *Anthropos*, lxxii (1977), 806–46

P. F. Berliner: *The Soul of Mbira: Music and Traditions of the Shona People of Zimbabwe* (Berkeley, CA, 1978)

C. J. Frisbie and D. P. McAllester, eds.: *Navajo Blessingway Singer: the Autobiography of Frank Mitchell, 1881–1967* (Tucson, 1978)

B. Nettl, ed.: *Eight Urban Musical Cultures: Tradition and Change* (Urbana, 1978)

C. Keil: *Tiv Song: the Sociology of Art in a Classless Society* (Chicago, 1979)

N. McLeod and M. Herndon: *The Ethnography of Musical Performance* (Norwood, PA, 1980)

N. Sorrell and Ram Narayan: *Indian Music in Performance: a Practical Introduction* (Manchester, 1980)

H. P. Myers: *Felicity, Trinidad: the Musical Portrait of a Hindu Village* (diss., U. of Edinburgh, 1984)

B. C. Wade: *Khyāl: Creativity Within North India's Classical Music Tradition* (Cambridge, 1984)

R. Wallis and K. Malm: *Big Sounds from Small Peoples: the Music Industry in Small Countries* (New York, 1984)

B. Nettl: 'Two Cities', in *The Western Impact on World Music: Change, Adaptation, and Survival* (New York, 1985), 40

——: *The Western Impact on World Music: Change, Adaptation, and Survival* (New York, 1985)

C. Capwell: *The Music of the Bauls of Bengal* (Kent, OH, 1986)

R. B. Qureshi: *Sufi Music of India and Pakistan: Sound, Context and Meaning in Qawwali* (Cambridge, England, 1986)

A. Seeger: *Why Suyá Sing: a Musical Anthropology of an Amazonian People* (Cambridge, England, 1987)

S. M. Slawek: *Sitār Technique in Nibaddh Forms* (Delhi, 1987)

E. O. Henry: *Chant the Names of God: Music and Culture in Bhojpuri-Speaking India* (San Diego, CA, 1988)

B. Nettl: *Blackfoot Musical Thought: Comparative Perspectives* (Kent, OH, 1989)

C. Waterman: *Jùjú: a Social History and Ethnography of an African Popular Music* (Chicago, IL, 1990)

HEALTH IN THE FIELD

Ross Institute of Tropical Hygiene: *The Preservation of Personal Health in Warm Climates* (London, 1951, rev. 8/1980)

D. Werner: *Where There Is No Doctor: a Village Health Care Handbook* (Palo Alto, CA, 1977)

J. Hatt: *The Tropical Traveller* (London, 1982)

M. Shales: *The Traveller's Handbook* (London, 1985)

N. Howell: *Surviving Fieldwork: a Report of the Advisory Panel on Health and Safety in Fieldwork* (Washington, DC, 1990)

CHAPTER III

Field Technology

HELEN MYERS

Since ethnomusicology is the study of music – usually unfamiliar music – the professional researcher aims for clean high fidelity professional recordings. The fieldworker should select audio equipment according to these recording needs. The goal is not to produce commercial records, but to ensure the best presentation of material for colleagues and students, facilitate transcription and analysis and preserve the most faithful version of the music for posterity. In the late 1960s, when Swiss portable open-reel recorders first became available in stereo, it seemed inevitable that the quality of field recordings would improve dramatically. In fact the opposite happened: around the same period the market was flooded with medium-quality Japanese domestic cassette recorders, and most professional ethnomusicologists opted for this relatively inexpensive easy-to-use, easy-to-pack, amateur equipment. Just as the transportable equipment of Alan Lomax and the Library of Congress (of the 1930s and 1940s) now appears outmoded (see figs.1 and 2), so our particular miniature machines will soon seem out of date. But the concept and rationale of location recording remains constant.

Open-reel versus cassette

From the 1970s to the 1990s media manufacturers have introduced packaged cassette-like products – the hardcased 3½-inch computer floppy disc versus the paper sleeved 5¼-inch floppy, the helical scan video cassette versus transverse scan open-reel video tape, compact cassettes and digital audio cassettes versus ¼-inch open-reel tape. But the nature of packaged media may place restrictions on its performance and versatility. The latest up-to-date convenience packaging may not meet the exacting standards of ethnomusicological work. For sound recording the cassette medium has restricted signal-to-noise ratio and limited frequency response (particularly at high signal levels), both resulting from the narrow track width (0.024 inches) and slow tape speed (1⅞ i.p.s.), and these result in a noisy recording with background hiss. The undesirable effects have been mitigated with recent improvements in magnetic tape formulation, especially the introduction of chrome and metal oxides. Even with the Dolby B or C noise-reduction (n-r) systems, the mechanical constraints of the cassette shell combined with the slow speed of the system produce results audibly inferior to those of

1. *Sound recording truck purchased by the Library of Congress for field recording folk music*

2. *Recording equipment used by John and Alan Lomax transported in the trunk of their car*

open-reel recording. The defects of the original cassette are exacerbated in copies and become intolerable in copies of copies.

The cassette medium pushes analogue tape technology to its limits: the slightest mechanical or electrical deviation has greater potential for disaster. For example, the cassette shell may crease the tape giving unacceptable random variations in frequency response and output level. Cleanliness of the pinch roller and capstan is critical because of the slow speed; dirt may cause speed variations or errors of azimuth (verticality of the head with reference to the tape) causing loss of high frequencies. Even with Dolby B noise reduction the perceived dynamic range of the cassette is not as good as that of ¼-inch tape running at 7.5 i.p.s. The principle behind these issues is similar to that in photography, whereby the larger the negative, the more information can be registered, and the easier it becomes to produce a faithful print. With tape, the wider the track and the faster the speed, the more magnetic signal is available for sound recording and reproduction. Any technological advance in the cassette-tape medium can equally be applied to the open-reel medium, so that

51

this differential in performance will always exist. For example, although the Dolby n-r systems are commonly associated with the cassette medium, in professional formats they are a standard feature in open-reel recording in broadcast, film and music studios throughout the world. The Dolby S n-r system sets specific standards for the tape transport mechanism and will result in improved stability and reliability when available in battery-powered cassette recorders. Ironically the main criticism levelled at the cassette medium (including DAT [Digital Audio Tape] cassettes) by professional studio users, the virtual impossibility of splice-editing, has no relevance in ethnomusicology, as original field tapes should always be retained intact.

In fieldwork, the results of cassette recordings of music are disappointing at best, but in some 20 years I have never heard anyone comment about the quality of an audio recording at a meeting of the Society for Ethnomusicology or the International Council for Traditional Music. This insensitivity to recorded sound in our profession is difficult to explain.

Monophonic versus stereophonic

However sophisticated the equipment, whether audio or video, monophonic or stereophonic, any recording is only a simulation of reality, an extension of our own selective observation. There are many different methods to record sound and each presents a different view of the original performance: there is no such thing as the definitive recording. Ethnomusicologists need to consider which techniques will produce recordings that will be most useful for their needs.

A monophonic recording is made using only a single recording channel, although it may be made with one or several microphones (using a mixer to attempt a balance between instruments or performers); it may be reproduced through headphones or through one or more loudspeakers. As only one information channel is used, a mono recording contains no information about global placement of sound sources, only their distance, judged by loudness and room sound. If more than one microphone is used even these distance clues are lost. These deficiencies render mono a poor choice for ethnomusicological research (but it is inexpensive).

A stereophonic recording is made using two recording channels, normally carrying left and right information, and requires at least two microphones; it may be reproduced through headphones or two loudspeakers. If the microphones are spaced more than 1½ inches or so apart, then the relative loudness at each will roughly equate with the position of a sound source, with five- to ten-foot spacing arrival time of sounds gives a notion of direction, but phase information is confused. If the microphones are closely spaced (to approximate a single point), then the improved phase (degree of co-incidence of similar frequencies) as well as loudness will give accurate positional information. Stereo is useful to the ethnomusicologist since it tells more about the original sound than mono; for example, with an ensemble the position of performers left to right can be determined in addition to distance. Stereo recording does not compound problems of field recording; in fact, documenting spatial relationships it is more likely to reduce them. 'Quasi-stereo' electronic reprocessing of mono recordings is produced for dubious commercial reasons and is not valid for scholarly or analytic purposes.

Even seasoned fieldworkers believe it is sufficient to record a single performer in mono, forgetting that the lone singer or instrument produces a sound that is characterized by the acoustic setting in which the performance takes place. A stereo recording, by providing a two-dimensional reproduction of this whole ambience, offers the researcher clearer and more useful information than is available with mono.

Mixing and recording the outputs of several microphones spaced throughout an ensemble was originally a ploy to alleviate the shortcomings of mono recording; this product of Western recorded music culture is now used in conjunction with multitrack recorders in studios. Insomuch as it destroys the actual relationships between performers and their environment, it has no value to the ethnomusicologist. Should an analytic recording, highlighting individual performers, be required, the ethnomusicologist can move within the ensemble with the microphones, pausing momentarily by each player. Single-point stereo microphones are ideal for this, being more convenient to hold than a pair. Stereo recording will allow the listener to appreciate spatial relationships of the performers as the microphones are moved through the ensemble. Such recordings present the viewpoint of the performer (as opposed to that of the audience), and are useful in analysis and in teaching the complexities of a foreign musical culture (for example the interlocking parts of East African xylophone ensembles). The roving microphone technique is also ideal for musicians to demonstrate instrumental tunings – bowing or plucking the open strings of fiddles and lutes, plucking the tongues of lamellaphones, or striking in sequence sets of gongs and other metallophones or the individual keys of a xylophone. Other analytic recordings might demonstrate methods of tuning each instrument, from the Trinidadian Indian tuning the goatskin head of a *tassa* drum at an open fire, to sophisticated tuning of the sitar to a different raga as part of a concert performance.

The ethnomusicologist's concern for context should extend even to recording techniques. In fieldwork, it is essential to remember one is recording not only a sound source but also its context, the sound field. The ethnomusicologist's dream of placing all the performers in a professional recording studio (often done by national cultural institutes at great expense) robs the performance of its natural ambience: audience, traffic, animals, conversation, discussion, cooking, eating, drinking – life. Location recording also reminds the ethnomusicologist to observe often neglected musical parameters – timbre, amplification, distortion, dryness, depth, sibilance, boxiness, rapport between musicians and choice of performance venue.

Some cultures express their sound aesthetic through locally produced commercial studio recordings (Wallis and Malm, 1984). For example, recordings made by Creole calypsonians of Trinidad usually have artificial anechoic non-reverberant sound fields, achieved by direct injection of the electronic instruments into the mixing console, very close miking of the acoustic instruments and loudspeakers, and reducing the dynamic range through electronic limiting and compressing. As a contrast, Indian film music is usually recorded with a highly echoic sound field created by reverb, double tracking of the vocal line with a right-left bounce, and wide dynamic range, with the limiter and compressor used only to avoid distortion.

Open-reel recorders

Every ethnomusicologist will need a tape recorder in the field. If the scholar wishes to make recordings of professional quality, for which no apologies need be made, as we approach the year 2000 a professional ¼-inch open-reel stereo machine remains the best choice. At the time of writing the best available were the Swiss-made Stellavox SP9 and Nagra IV-S. These lightweight, easily portable recorders offer full broadcast-quality performance in the field, are exceptionally reliable under the most punishing and adverse conditions (vibration, extremes of heat, cold and humidity) and are remarkably durable (perform within their specifications for 20 years or more). Both can be run at 3¾, 7½ and 15 i.p.s.

The Stellavox SP9 takes 15 AA (Mn 1500) batteries, giving a running time of five to eight hours on NiCad rechargeable cells and 10 to 16 hours on alkaline-manganese cells depending on such factors as current drawn for capacitor microphone powering and use of the internal monitor speakers. It takes 5-inch spools which will hold 900 feet of long-play (1 mil) tape and give 22½ minutes of continuous recording time at 7½ i.p.s. With a simple low-cost adaptor the Stellavox can be used with 10½-inch or even 12-inch spools and gives up to one hour and 42 minutes (10½-inch spool with 3600 feet of long-play tape) or a maximum continuous recording time of two hours and 16 minutes (12-inch spool with 4800 feet of long-play tape).

The Nagra IV-S takes 12 D cells (Mn 1300) giving a running time of four to five hours on NiCad rechargeable cells and 8½ hours on alkaline-manganese cells. The Nagra takes 5-inch and 7-inch spools, and 10½-inch spools with the addition of a costly battery-powered adaptor. The technical specifications of the two machines are equally impressive. The Stellavox is considerably lighter – 5 kilograms (including batteries, tape and carrying case) as compared with 8 kilograms for the Nagra. The Nagra has the advantage of accepting 7-inch reels without adding the adaptor (although this option requires the removal of the lid).

The German-made semi-professional Uher 4200 Report Monitor Stereo is an acceptable choice for those who cannot afford the Nagra or Stellavox. The Uher is a lightweight, simple-to-operate machine with four speeds (7½ i.p.s. is the highest) and a maximum spool capacity of 5 inches. The Uher lacks many professional refinements of the Stellavox and Nagra: predistortion circuitry to compensate for tape distortion at high signal levels, peak-reading level meters (preferable to VU meters because they indicate true rather than average signal level), absolute speed stability from beginning to end of the reel, and speed stability when recording on the move (machine slung over the shoulder). Unlike Nagra and Stellavox, the Uher is unable to provide powering for capacitor microphones (an external power pack is needed). The Uher takes five D NiCad cells or a dedicated rechargeable battery, either giving a running time of three hours; using five D (Mn 1300) alkaline-manganese cells the running time is increased to 4½ hours.

Nagra, Stellavox and Uher all have three magnetic heads (fig.3). Following the path of the tape, the first is the erase head which, when the machine is set in the record mode, removes all previously recorded material. The middle is the record head, which lays signals on the freshly erased tape.

54

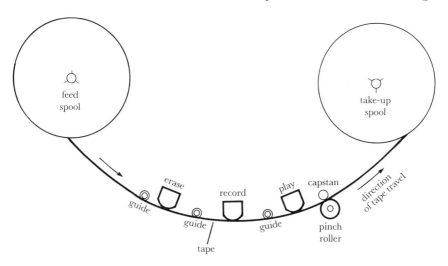

3. Simplified typical audio tape path

Third is the replay head, which produces an electrical signal analogous to the magnetic signal on the tape and relays it to the playback electronics, where it is amplified to feed headphones or loudspeakers. Most domestic cassette recorders have only two heads, an erase head and a combination record/replay head. On three-head machines, the separation of record and replay functions permits reproduction of the recorded signal during the actual recording process, a worthwhile feature given the once-in-a-lifetime nature of ethnomusicological field recording. Through headphones, the recordist can listen to the freshly recorded signal a split second after it has been placed on the tape (for example, on the Stellavox running at 7½ i.p.s. after a 0.236-second delay). This check is critical because any problems with the recording can be immediately spotted, for example, tape drop-out (momentary loss of signal due to irregularities of the tape coating), dirt on the record head, wow (cyclical slow variation of tape speed) or flutter (random rapid high variations of the tape speed). Using a three-head machine, the recordist can also perform an instant 'A-B' check between the incoming signal (monitoring 'input' or 'direct') and the recorded signal (monitoring 'tape' or 'off-tape'); these two signals should match. Any variation can be noted and hopefully corrected on the spot. Cassette machines with combination record/replay heads require the tape to be rewound before the recorded quality can be checked by playback.

A special skill that needs practice is monitoring off tape – listening to the sound that has just been recorded a split-second earlier while watching the musicians perform in real time. Most headphones suitable for fieldwork only offer limited acoustic isolation making it sometimes difficult to differentiate between live and recorded sound. This is especially problematic during loud performances where the performers' acoustic signal is louder than the signal level available within the headphones – an occurrence more frequent than one might expect, in the Third World with the prevalence of over-amplified music, loud group singing in confined spaces and powerful instrumental sounds,

55

especially drumming. Under such conditions, you might try to situate yourself and the tape recorder as far from the performers and microphones as is practicable – difficult if the performers invite you to sit with them.

Digital recording

Open-reel recorders use ¼-inch magnetic tape drawn past the record/replay heads at a fairly high speed (7½ i.p.s./19.05 cms, 15 i.p.s./38.1 cms) to achieve wide frequency response with good signal-to-noise ratio and low flutter. The Digital Audio Tape (DAT) system, by contrast, uses 0.15-inch magnetic tape (in a cassette size 2.875 inches × 2.12 inches × 0.41 inches; mechanically similar to video cassettes), travelling at only 8.15mm/s. A helical (slanting) head assembly rotating at 2000 r.p.m. produces the head-to-tape speed needed to record digital audio signals. The record-playback performance of DAT is exceptional (equivalent to the Compact Disc). The low tape speed enables up to 2 hours of continuous recording; recorders have automatic indexing of the start of each take together with rapid search facilities on playback (200 × play speed).

At the time of writing, portable domestic models were available from Casio and Sony, professional models from Sony and Technics. These machines are about 9 inches × 5½ inches × 1¾ inches in size, and weigh 3 to 4 lbs with batteries and tape. The professional units were originally specified as domestic, but the fidelity of the system is so high that with the addition of microphone input transformers, XLR connectors and minor circuit improvements, these portable recorders now meet or exceed all professional technical specifications. The system is characterized by zero wow and flutter, flat

4. An interactive experiment carried out by Simha Arom using a Yamaha DX7 IIFD synthesizer and a Macintosh SE/30 computer (Gbaya, Central African Republic, 1990)

frequency response ($\pm\frac{1}{2}$dB 10Hz — 22kHz), low distortion, wide dynamic range and excellent signal-to-noise ratio. Running time per battery charge is limited. For ethnomusicological purposes, a drawback of DAT is its sensitivity to humidity; since condensation on the head drum would cause the tape to stick, a sensor shuts down the recorder to prevent damage. The liquid crystal displays (LCDs) used for level metering and other status indications may black out in hot bright sunlight, making operation difficult. The cassette is not splice editable, but digital copying involves virtually no loss of fidelity. Even on domestic models, the outstanding performance justifies use of the best microphones available. Beware the electronic copying restrictions on domestic machines with Serial Copy Management System: it is not readily possible to make digital copies of copies.

Digital techniques offer rich possibilities for the ethnomusicologist working in the field. Computerized and synthesized digital recordings may be used for interactive research. Simha Arom has conducted interactive experiments to further the understanding of the musical scales of central Africa (see fig.4). He adapted a Yamaha DX7 synthesizer to simulate a traditional xylophone, recording the results on a Macintosh SE/30 computer. Using the computer, the musicians were able to correct the tunings to reflect authentic African scales.

Headphones

Every fieldworker will need a comfortable but robust set of circumaural (covering the whole ear), closed-back headphones. This type provides good isolation from ambient sounds and reduces leakage from the headphone monitor signal to the microphones or performers. This isolation is particularly important when you are sitting close to the musicians (and your microphones). Good headphones have a minimum impedance of 200 ohms (Ω) per earpiece and high sensitivity (expressed in dB/mW of input power) to achieve an adequate sound level from the restricted output power available from battery portable recorders. These types of headphones tend to be heavy, bulky and difficult to wear for extended periods. Shop around for a comfortable pair. Closed monitor headphones can also be plugged (via suitable adaptors) into any cassette recorder. In the field, you will also need several pairs of lightweight headphones (as supplied with Walkman recorders) together with split leads to use several pairs at the same time. These are useful as emergency backups, and also give musicians (or audience) a chance to monitor during recording and to listen to playback after the performance.

Cassette recorders

The ethnomusicologist will also need a high-quality cassette recorder. It has many uses in fieldwork: as a backup for the open-reel machine, to record interviews, and to run simultaneously with open-reel machines during important musical sessions (to cover the gaps during open-reel changes, essential for transcription). Cassette recorders are also useful to play back

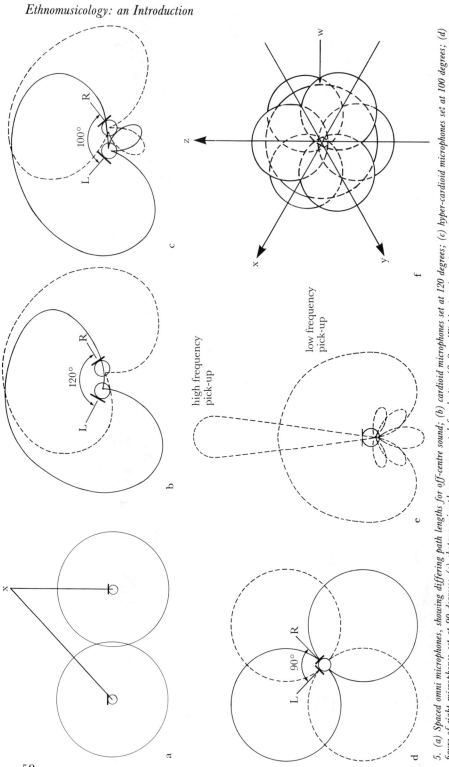

5. *(a) Spaced omni microphones, showing differing path lengths for off-centre sound; (b) cardioid microphones set at 120 degrees; (c) hyper-cardioid microphones set at 100 degrees; (d) figure-of-eight microphones set at 90 degrees; (e) shotgun microphone, exaggerated for clarity; (f) SoundField microphone showing four-channel recording output: X = front-to-back figure-of-eight output; Y = side-to-side figure-of-eight output; Z = up-to-down figure-of-eight output; W = omni, pressure output*

material for informants (to elicit information during interviews) and to make cassette copies of open-reel recordings to give away.

Because the cassette market changes from year to year, it is impossible to recommend any particular brand. The scholar should look for important features such as Dolby B, C or S, fast forward and fast rewind, socket for external microphones (in addition to any in-built microphone), availability of mains adaptor, separate metering for left and right channels, sensible control lay-out (some recorders turn off when laid upside-down), robust construction (metal is better than plastic), ease of access to heads and capstan for cleaning and window on the cassette compartment (to check movement of the tape, running speed and remaining recording time). Since the cassette industry is aimed at the youth culture and changes with annual fashions, you probably will not find all these semi-professional features on one machine. At the time of writing machines worth considering were the Sony WM D6C (Walkman Pro), the Sony TCD5 Pro and the Marantz CP230 and CP430. Of these the Walkman Pro is smallest and lightest while still being easy to use and capable of making recordings of reasonably high quality. The very high battery consumption of the Sony TCD5 is a serious drawback for ethnomusicological fieldwork (two alkaline-manganese D cells last less than two hours). The Marantz has the advantage of right- and left-channel metering (Model CP230) and off-tape monitoring (Model CP430) but tends to record and reproduce hum when used with its mains unit.

Microphones

The choice of microphones is more difficult and more personal (and may even be more costly) than that of tape recorders. The fieldworker who wants maximum flexibility needs a professional-quality single-point stereo microphone for the open-reel recorder, and as backup, a pair of robust dynamic directional microphones; and for the cassette recorder a compact electret microphone (to maintain convenience and portability of the package).

Design of microphones is a specialized mathematical science. The ethnomusicologist needs a good knowledge of the various types to get the best from each in the rapidly changing circumstances of fieldwork, using alternatives as appropriate. Microphones have five basic pickup patterns. (i) Omnidirectional (nondirectional), equally sensitive to sounds from all directions (360-degree pickup), not recommended for stereo recording since a pair needs to be 10 feet or more apart to produce usable left–right information (see fig.5*a*). (ii) Cardioid or unidirectional, a broad pickup pattern, sensitive mainly to sounds from the front and sides, roughly ten times less sensitive to sounds coming from the rear (as compared with the front). For stereo use, a crossed pair of cardioid microphones will give good left–right separation if spaced with their capsules less than 4 inches apart and the bodies of the microphones at 120 degrees (thus emphasizing the combined forward pickup) (see fig.5*b*). (iii) Hypercardioid, which has a narrower front and side pickup than cardioid, and slight rearward pickup (rejects sounds at +/−120 degrees). With this narrower pickup, for stereo a crossed pair should be at 100 degrees. The slight rear pickup collects more indirect room sound than with cardioids (see fig.5*c*). (iv) Bidirectional (figure-of-eight) responds equally to front and rear with zero pickup at the sides (rejects sounds at +/−90 degrees), the ideal choice for stereo use in ethnomusicology, especially indoors. Two figure-of-eight microphones set at 90 degrees provide directional information over a full 360 degrees (see fig.5*d*). (v) Shotgun (club, line, or rifle), with narrow forward pickup and very high side rejection at high frequencies (reverting to cardioid or hyper-cardioid at medium to low frequencies), not recommended for stereo work as the pickup pattern and side colouration varies too much with frequency. This microphone is useful in fieldwork for interviews and documentary filming, as it rejects unwanted sounds without needing to be close to the subject (see fig.5*e*).

Microphones are also categorized by their generating elements, trans-ducers, which convert sound waves into electrical signals. The most com-mon generating elements are: (i) moving coil dynamic, which are robust, can be excellent quality, cover a wide price range, available in all pickup patterns except bidirectional; (ii) ribbon dynamic, which are excellent qual-ity though delicate and generally have very low output level, available in a medium-to-high price range for cardioid, hypercardioid and bidirectional pickup patterns; (iii) electret permanently charged capacitor, of poor-to-high quality (usually related to price), and unlike the foregoing types re-quires a low voltage supply to operate (from an incorporated dry cell), available in omnidirectional and cardioid pickup patterns and can be very small while still of high quality; and (iv) capacitor (condenser), very expen-sive studio-grade units requiring high voltage (48V) to charge the capacitor diaphragm (may be electronically generated within the microphone from a lower voltage supplied from the tape recorder), available in any pickup pattern (some switchable between patterns, either remotely while in use or at the microphone).

Recent developments in mathematics and electronics have led to the development of the SoundField microphone by Calrec Audio (now AMS), UK, the first truly omnidirectional microphone (see fig.5*f*). (The traditional omnidirectional microphone is in fact nondirectional, providing no direc-tional information.) The four outputs available from the SoundField microphone provide precise directional information over the complete sound sphere. If recorded on four channels, complete sound fields – side-to-side, front-to-back, up-to-down and pressure – may be reproduced. If coded on two or three channels, side-to-side and front-to-back horizontal ('quad') may be reproduced. The sound field may be manipulated after the event. Rotating, tilting and apparent raising or lowering of the microphone may be achieved during or even after recording.

The ethnomusicologist will need to select from this variety of microphones to suit his or her peculiar needs. Moving coil (dynamic) microphones from AKG, Beyer, Sennheiser and Shure are excellent for most purposes, especially where they may be subjected to rough handling – vibration, dust, wind or monsoon conditions. A pair is needed for stereo recording. Ribbon dynamic microphones are generally too fragile and sensitive to handling noise for fieldwork. In the electret format, small inconspicuous stereo microphones are available, but these may suffer from hiss and overload distortion. A plethora of electret models are available, ranging from tiny mono tie-tack (as seen on TV), miniature T-shaped stereo, single-point stereo, mono or stereo stick, shotgun and models with screw-on interchangeable heads (for example, cardioid-to-omnidirectional-to-shotgun).

Many Walkman-style cassette recorders have built-in stereo electret microphones, which, though convenient, pick up the electronic and mechanical noises of the recorder. Except in emergencies they should not be used. Recordings will be improved simply by plugging a T-shaped stereo electret directly into the external microphone socket of the recorder (providing isolation from electronic hash and motor servo noise); by using the T-shaped microphone on a short lead you will also gain isolation from mechanical noises of the recorder. This microphone can be clipped to your person and may be useful in conjunction with a cassette machine when recording crowded festivals, wedding processions and street music. However, back in the comfort of home, listening to these recordings on professional monitor speakers, you may regret having opted for convenience and low profile with this inferior microphone and cassette machine to record the hustle and bustle of real musical life – the very stuff of ethnomusicology.

When conditions are less than the most severe, professional capacitor microphones give the very best quality, featuring the widest frequency response with lowest noise. Once you have grown accustomed to the truly high-fidelity recordings these wonderful instruments produce, nothing else will satisfy your ear. Stereo and mono models are available from AKG, Beyer, Sanken, Shure and Schoeps.

Now on the market are the 4011 and 4000 range from B & K of Denmark; these, although electret and mono (requiring a pair for stereo), outperform (and outprice) virtually all other microphones. Since they are reasonably robust, they are worth consideration by the location-recording perfectionist.

To get the most use from professional capacitor microphones, the ethnomusicologist may wish to take into the field a custom-built battery power pack in order to operate these with the cassette recorder. This unlikely combination, sacrificing the benefits of open-reel, may be the only feasible choice for high-quality results in untoward conditions, for example, recording a village springtime Holī festival in North India, where one has in the dark to follow (for several kilometres) a procession of male singers along a narrow slippery dyke separating irrigated fields. (I did do this with a Stellavox, but found reel-changes awkward.)

Microphone stands

The simplest microphone stand – one's hand – is used for recording on the move, but creates noise and is inconvenient and tiring for long periods. Table-top tripods can be used as a handgrip when folded, and double as a camera stand. Clamps are available to clip microphones practically anywhere – chair-back, table-leg, branch of a tree, bicycle handlebars, car dashboard. A light telescopic stand is essential fieldwork equipment; it can position the microphones close to performers, while giving the height necessary for an 'unobstructed view' of an ensemble. A boom arm on the stand can aid in placing the microphones without causing obstruction to the performers, and may be used vertically to provide greater height when necessary. The microphone stand should be as light as practicable but heavy and solid enough to safely support the microphone. Beware of heavy microphones on too light a stand. Stability, particularly when using boom arms, may be improved by suspending a full water bottle at the base of the stand, especially important in crowded settings where the stand may be assaulted.

If using a pair of microphones for stereo, then a stereo rail (bar) with two microphone clips is needed to space the microphones correctly and permit their use on a single stand. A microphone shock mount (elastic suspension that decouples the microphone from mechanical vibrations travelling along the microphone stand – caused by heavy drumming, footsteps, or even knocking against the stand) is basic equipment for the ethnomusicologist who, unlike a studio recordist, has very little control over recording conditions.

Windshields

All microphones are sensitive to wind; unfortunately the microphone of choice for indoor recording (figure-of-eight stereo capacitor) is the most sensitive. For windswept outdoor recordings, the ethnomusicologist needs to use a crossed pair of cardioid dynamic microphones. If a windshield on the capacitor microphone does not reduce noise sufficiently, low-frequency roll-off may also help (labelled *S*peech on Stellavox, Lf1, Lf2 on Nagra).

When recording out of doors, windshields are essential. Windshields of open-cell foam (which permit the passage of sound pressure waves) are most practical for fieldwork; they reduce the effect of wind noise on the microphone diaphragm. Large windshields are effective but inconvenient. Nylon mesh-covered wire or plastic windshields are easily crushed. The film-maker's Zeppelin-style windshield, though extremely effective, probably draws too much attention for ethnomusicological purposes.

Bring windscreens even for indoor recording sessions, to protect against cross draughts, electric fans (especially oscillating fans). If a windshield has to be unexpectedly improvised (draught in the room, performers move outdoors, even air movement caused by candles), a cotton handkerchief or similar light material can be wrapped around the microphone head (for illustration *see* 'Fieldwork', fig.3). For small microphones take spare windshields; these are easily lost. (Many an Indian village boy has received a reward for helping me find electret windshields.)

Leads

The leads connecting microphones to recorder, although outwardly simple, may cause more problems than any other item of field equipment. The electret ranges are usually supplied with connecting leads (often permanently attached). Other microphones (especially higher-priced ones) are not sup-plied with leads, but generally incorporate a three-pin XLR (Cannon) connector (Pin 1 = 'ground', Pin 2 = 'in phase' or 'signal', Pin 3 = 'out of phase' or 'return'). Five pins are needed for stereo. The researcher must have leads with appropriate connectors custom-made (see fig.6). To achieve greatest flexibility with fewest leads, use a Y-lead from the left and right three-pin microphone connectors of the recorder to a five-pin line socket, so the connection from recorder to microphone is a single lead (using another Y-lead to the microphones if separate left and right microphones are used). Both Y-leads should be made with two colours of cable so left and right channels are fully identified (fig.7).

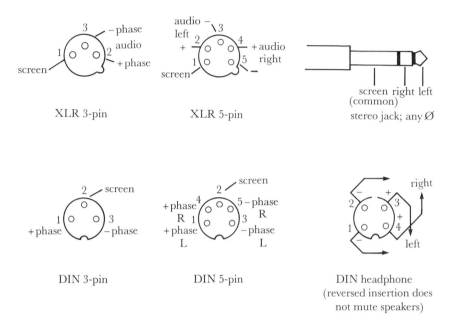

XLR 3-pin   XLR 5-pin   stereo jack; any Ø

DIN 3-pin   DIN 5-pin   DIN headphone
(reversed insertion does
not mute speakers)

6. *Standard connector configurations: Pin 1 of an XLR type connector is always connected to screen (ground); pin 2 of a DIN audio connector is always connected to screen (ground); the lower numbered pin of any audio pair is always + phase (hot)*

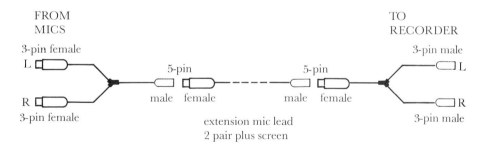

FROM MICS   TO RECORDER

3-pin female   3-pin male

L   L

5-pin   5-pin

R   R

male   female   male   female

3-pin female   3-pin male

extension mic lead
2 pair plus screen

7. *Microphone, Y-lead and five-pin extension lead*

Select the cable with care, choosing a type that lays flat in use, but also has the necessary flexibility to coil neatly for packing. The chosen cable must also have an efficient screen (grounded metal foil or braid around the signal conductors) to reduce pickup of radio interference and hum.

Leads of different lengths are needed in fieldwork. Shortest is a 3- to 4-foot Y-lead from the recorder for use with the machine over the shoulder and hand-held microphone. A second Y-lead of from 10 to 12 feet is practical for recording solo performers or small groups (also as backup for the shorter Y). Medium (10 feet) and long (20 feet) five-pin to five-pin extension leads may be used with either Y-lead to cope with most recording situations. By combining leads the ethnomusicologist and tape recorder may be positioned up to 40 feet from the microphones.

Power supplies

The biggest technical problem in fieldwork is provision of electrical power for recording equipment. Power sources in the field are mains electricity, petrol generator and batteries. The local mains supply should be used with care, preferably only for charging batteries. A petrol generator may be useful where long periods away from mains are envisaged and porterage is no problem (again only for charging batteries because of the noise produced by the generator's motor).

Batteries may be non-rechargeable or rechargeable cells. (i) Non-rechargeable zinc-carbon cells may be the only type available in the field. These inexpensive batteries have low capacity and limited shelf-life. Some leak corrosive acids when discharged, so the ethnomusicologist should always remove them from equipment when a session ends. (ii) Non-rechargeable alkaline-manganese cells are more reliable, leakproof in most conditions, with high capacity and long shelf-life; they are an excellent backup. (iii) Nickel-cadmium rechargeable cells (NiCads) are most useful in fieldwork because they can be charged and discharged some 500 to 1000 times. Their capacity is better than zinc-carbon cells. If C size (Mn1400) or D size (Mn1300) NiCad cells are needed, the ethnomusicologist should search out those of 2-amphour (Ah) and 4-amphour capacity (most types are only 1.2 Ah for each size, compared with 4 Ah and 8 Ah, respectively, for C and D size alkaline-manganese cells). AA (Mn1500) cells have recently become available with 0.8 Ah capacity, but are generally about 0.45 Ah.

Before departure, the ethnomusicologist should inquire about the local electricity supply (availability, voltage, frequency, local plug configurations and light-bulb fittings). The most difficult situation imaginable (and easiest for which to prescribe a solution) is the field site with no electricity. The ethnomusicologist should calculate how many alkaline-manganese cells to take to the field, allowing a reasonable surplus. A fieldworker who has use of mains electricity for part of the day (or week) can use NiCad rechargeable cells; this researcher needs to solve a complicated equation to calculate the number of battery chargers needed, and charging hours required per hour of field recording. He should also carry alkaline-manganese cells so the rhythm of fieldwork is not totally dictated by a battery-charging regime. Under these circumstances solar chargers provide a useful backup.

For field sites where mains electricity is reliably available, the ethnomusicologist can easily establish a daily routine of three to four hours of interview recording on cassette and three to four hours of open-reel music recording using NiCad cells which are recharged at night, thus posing problems when a late night session is followed by a sunrise ceremony. A second set of NiCads is one solution, but these need to have their charge topped up regularly (NiCads quickly self-discharge). It is worth having one or two external NiCad packs custom-made for the open-reel recorder; when the internal batteries are discharged these can be plugged directly into the machine without inter-rupting recording. NiCads require monitoring towards the end of the nominal running time, as they drop off suddenly. Some recorders (such as Stellavox) are designed so the monitor circuits distort the signal on low batteries before the record or motor circuitry give problems, providing early warning of need to change batteries. Alkaline-manganese cells behave differently, with a gradual loss of power. The ethnomusicologist needs to be familiar with discharge characteristics of each type (i.e. with NiCads, make haste!). Virtually discharged alkaline-manganese cells can still power a flashlight (they have a degree of recovery).

Even if mains electricity is available at the recording site it is inadvisable to run your equipment from it. Unrestricted voltage spikes can damage equipment; moreover, the local equipment – cookers, lights, etc. – may put clicks and plops on your recording. (The old notion that speed stability of recorders would be upset by voltage or frequency variations is no longer true, since modern machines use internal reference circuitry to stabilize speed.) Other than for charging batteries, regard local mains only as a backup if the charger or the battery compartment of your recorder fails.

The enterprising ethnomusicologist aims for having all equipment using one battery size. Stellavox users can manage everything on AA (Mn1500) size pencells; Nagra and Uher users will need D cells (Mn1300) in addition to AA. If you do not carry a battery tester, battery condition can be judged by putting the AA cells into a camera flashgun and checking the recycle time.

In most field settings, even when electricity is readily available, the ethnomusicologist may find that the room provided as his base has only one wall outlet, or worse, nothing but a bare bulb hanging from the ceiling. The ethnomusicologist will need to connect many electrical items to the local mains supply at the same time (chargers, open-reel and cassette recorder mains units, light, typewriter, travel kettle). The most practical approach is with a fused IEC (International Electrotechnical Commission) mains distribution board with multiple outlets. By fitting all electrical equipment with standard 6-amp IEC connectors, any combination can be plugged into the distribution board. Only the input leads for the board will require a local connector. Two leads are necessary, one to connect with a wall outlet, the other (in the event your accommodation has no wall socket) to a two-way switched light-bulb connector (Edison screw or bayonet). A five-way distribution board can supply up to 1200 Watts (if the local supply is capable), but the likely loading is around 300 Watts (even with the kettle).

Battery chargers

The ethnomusicologist will need both dedicated and universal battery chargers. Dedicated chargers recharge NiCad batteries inside a specific piece of equipment, and generally also adapt the equipment to operate from mains electricity. The fieldworker may want to have custom battery packs made so cells can be recharging out of the equipment.

Universal chargers will recharge one or more NiCad cells, often of several types (in pairs) at once (but they cannot adapt equipment for mains use). They enable the researcher to charge cells for many items of equipment (e.g. cassette recorders, flashguns, torches and radios). Make sure you have enough chargers to accommodate several complete sets of cells at a time. Solar chargers are available which will trickle (slow) charge one to four AA NiCads, a useful standby where the mains electricity is particularly unreliable or nonexistent. Even a small shadow reduces their efficiency so they cannot normally be considered the primary charging source.

Most NiCad chargers are designed to charge a flat battery fully in 10 to 14 hours (NiCads can be left on these chargers indefinitely), but some are available with a five-hour charge rate. Although useful, they require vigilance, as NiCads can have their capacity reduced if left too long at such higher charges. A partially discharged cell should only be charged at the lower 10- to 14-hour rate. A battery discharger circuit should be used to ensure full discharge of a battery if five-hour charging is used regularly.

Tape

For fieldwork the ethnomusicologist should select ¼-inch open-reel tape with low noise, low print and long playing time. Noise from tape is of two basic forms: noise unrelated to recorded signal including hiss and other low-level noise; and modulation noise, which surrounds and veils the recorded sound – in its own way the most disturbing distortion of analogue tape. High-output tapes accept higher magnetism than normal tapes, but some do not accept high frequencies as well as they do medium and low. Select a tape with good balance between these (expressed in nW/m at 1 kHz and 10 kHz); otherwise the high-output advantage is lost when recording bright sounds. Print-through is transfer of magnetic signals from layer to layer of spooled tape, measured in dB below a standard magnetic reference level (185 nW/m in the USA or 320 nW/m in Europe). The effect is dependent on the recorded wave length, so the audio frequencies at which this is troublesome vary with tape speed. The tape chosen should have a print-through specified better than −58 dB at 7½ i.p.s.

Playing time for given spool size is determined by tape speed and tape thickness. The most useful speed for fieldwork, giving a sensible balance between performance and running time, is 7½ i.p.s. (19.05 cm/s). (If you foresee running out of tape at an unexpectedly lengthy session, switch to 3¾ i.p.s. when changing spools.) The main thicknesses available are 1 mm (.001 inch; in Europe, Long Play) and 1.5mm (.0015 inch; in Europe, Standard Play). Standard-play tape is preferred for studio use, as it has marginally less print-through, and its thicker base is easier to handle for cut and splice editing. Long-play tape is preferable for fieldwork because more footage can be transported to the field; during recording sessions it causes less disturbance from spool changes. Some long-play tapes have less print-through at 7½ i.p.s. than the equivalent standard play; check the specifications carefully. An ideal specification for ¼-inch tape might be:

66

Print: −58 dB
Modulation noise: −58 dB
Maximum signal level @ 1 kHz: +8 dB
Dtot (total distortion) @ reference level 1 khz: 0.5%
Dtot @ maximum level 1 khz: 3% third harmonic distortion

The tape box is unlikely to give any useful information about its contents except length and maybe running time. Specification sheets are available from the manufacturer, or his representative, for their full range of tapes.

Having selected a tape, it is important to align the electronics of the recorder properly to accommodate its particular characteristics. The basic settings are: level (to give equality of input and output); high-frequency level (to give flat [even] overall response); predistortion (to give minimum distortion at peak level; Stellavox and Nagra only); and bias (high-frequency signal [60 kHz or higher] on which the audio signal is superimposed. Bias serves to linearize the transfer characteristic of tape [input to output]; the same frequency is fed at high level to the erase head to saturate the tape coating and erase previous recordings). The bias should be set for minimum noise and distortion. Alignment can take up to an hour, and is best done as part of final servicing by a laboratory technician prior to departure. Scholars who neglect these tasks risk frequency-response errors and high distortion and noise in their recordings, particularly if the tape recorder had previously been aligned for a tape requiring a different bias level.

For audio cassettes the same principles apply, but because of the single slow speed (1⅞ i.p.s. [4.78 cms]) and narrow track width, the requirements are more critical. Unfortunately, the information supplied with cassettes does not help with choice (all cassette tapes have 'lower noise and higher output' than all other cassette tapes – if labels are to be believed). Cassette magnetic formulations are 'improved' (changed) every six months or so; even your favourite brand may suddenly perform differently. Standard lengths for cassettes are C43/45 (21.5–22.5 minutes per side; 43–45 minutes per tape), C60, C90 and C120. For fieldwork the C90 (45 minutes per side) is a good compromise between playing time and reliability. At around .25mm (.00025 inch) cassette tape is too delicate for splice editing, and can easily tangle and be damaged.

Cassette formulations are divided into classes:

I – Ferric	(120 μSpb, low bias)
II – Ferrochrome	(120 μSpb, low bias)
III – Chrome, Pseudochrome	(70 μSpb, high bias)
IV – Metal	(70 μSpb, high bias)

Tapes within these classes are theoretically interchangeable; in practice, although the bias requirements are similar, sensitivity (level) and high-frequency response varies considerably.

The cassette recorder should be aligned by a technician for a given tape before departure, especially as the Dolby B noise reduction circuits are level and frequency dependent (Dolby C even more so). The ethnomusicologist should avoid bottom ranges of tape from any maker, normally specified simply as 'low noise' (although such tapes may have to be purchased in the field if supplies run out). 'New improved' tape will probably have excess top (high frequencies) compared to its predecessor.

For Digital Audio Tape and video cassette recording the choice of tape is, oddly, less critical. Tape that meets minimum requirements for dropout and mechanical stability can produce good recordings. Some DAT and video cassettes stand up better to repeated playback than others, and for archival purposes it is sensible to choose a high-grade tape.

The ethnomusicologist will need to prepare tapes for field use. If tape has been purchased on pancakes (NAB large-centre hubs, without flanges) spool it off onto 5-inch or 7-inch spools (these can be bulk purchased with plain white boxes), leader and box it. This should be done on a mains machine with a tight even wind (not on a portable field recorder). Make leaders around 18 inches long to permit quick lacing of the field recorder during spool changes; use white or green for the start of each spool. Make tails (end leader) the same length but red to indicate recorded reels. Every spool should have blank labels affixed before leaving for the field, so identification numbers can be noted during a music session, to ensure at least a minimum of documentation under pressure.

The recording session

The ethnomusicologist needs to be musicologist, anthropologist, linguist, historian, theoretician and diplomat, and also a one-man recording engineer, photographer, film crew (and all the while a gracious guest). In many communities, he or she must wait patiently for weeks, building friendship and trust, before getting out the tape recorder. With other groups, musicians are puzzled if you do not begin to record straight away. Cassette recorders have found their way to every corner of the globe; if you do not begin to record an important musical function yourself, you may find your informants doing the job for you.

Taking account of attitude towards tape recorders, there are two types of cultures: type 'A', in which members do not mind being recorded by a relative stranger but grow shy as that stranger becomes a friend and confidant (especially for formal interviews); and 'B', in which members test the fieldworker before permitting him to record. It would be a mistake in a type 'A' community to keep your tape recorder packed away too long. There begin work by jumping in at the deep end. Explain you would like to record a representative sample of music, a useful approach – concrete, understandable and feasible. Musicians I have worked with were pleased to think that I got what I came for – a proper sample of the various genres from their community. This is an extremely helpful attitude if you can find it (although in some settings I have had difficulty explaining the need to collect variants). While recording a sample repertory may not represent the fullness of your research goals, it is not a bad start.

The ethnomusicologist as recording engineer must act with grace under pressure, and an act it will surely be with many eyes on every move. Set up as much as possible before leaving the privacy of your room. Lace the open-reel machine with a blank reel of tape; write date, event and next available identification number on the empty take-up spool. Load the cassette machine with a fresh tape and label with date and next identification number. Check that machines have freshly charged (NiCad) or new (alkaline-manganese) cells. Set level controls at minimum (∞), ready for fade-in to ambient sound (if you arrive early) or to the performance (if late). Ensure that cameras have film and that flashgun batteries are fresh.

Before leaving your room check that you have all your recording and photographic equipment, tape and film supplies, backup equipment, notepad and pen packed in carrying bags. If the main recording machine is open-reel, with a single-point capacitor microphone, take along as backup a Dolby cassette recorder, batteries, leads and power supply for the capacitor microphone. Always carry extra tape, film and alkaline-manganese cells. Remember to pack playback equipment, lightweight speakers (or several pairs of lightweight headphones, ¼-inch to mini-jack adaptors and split leads).

For recording stationary performances at a predetermined venue, plan to arrive at least 30 minutes before the music starts. This may be difficult, especially if you are being escorted; try to convince your guide you must be early (often fails).

While setting up, you will usually have a curious audience – an important reason to practise this drill at home. First try to find out where you should sit (are women/men allowed to sit in such and such a place?). Remember rules about taking off shoes or covering the head in certain religious and domestic settings. For Hindu cultures, be prepared to abandon leather objects at the door. Ask where the performers will be. If no one can supply this information, find a quiet corner and start setting up. Often you will not know until the last moment where the performers will sit and where you will be put. Three events may disrupt your progress down this check-list: (i) you may be asked to move; (ii) the performance may start; or (iii) both.

For an open-reel recording, set up as follows:

1. Erect telescopic microphone stand and position by performance site.
2. Screw on stereo bar assembly or shock mount for single-point capacitor microphone.
3. Insert microphone(s) into shock mount(s).
4. Put on microphone windshield (outdoors or for indoor fan or cross-draught).
5. Plug lead(s) into microphone(s).
6. Secure microphone cable to shock mount, with dedicated clip or to microphone stand with cable clips, leaving a slack loop (to isolate microphone(s) from knocks cable may receive).
7. Lay out cable along safe path to recorder. Use rugs or other floor mats to cover (to avoid tripping people up). If necessary, add extension leads.
8. Plug Y-lead into microphone input sockets on recorder.
[*If the performance has started, put machine immediately into record, fade up to a sensible level, set monitor switch to 'tape'; check level meters; go to item 9]
9. Plug in headphones [*if performance has started go to item 11].
10. Set monitor switch to 'direct' setting.
11. Check room sound through headphones, confirm that right and left channels are functioning and microphone perspective is realistic.

12. Unzip or unclip carrying case of recorder [*to 14].

13. Unscrew both spool nuts. Store in pocket.

14. Confirm that tape is securely laced [*running; to 18, 19, then, after first reel change, to 16].

15. If performers have arrived, and are setting up, go and chat with them, adjust your microphone position so as not to inconvenience them (or the audience), aiming always for good height.

16. Unpack camera(s), remove lens cap, attach flashgun (night or indoors).

17. Take your place, headphones on, monitor switch to 'tape' [silence in headphones], main function switch to 'record', fade up to desired levels. Begin recording well before the performance starts to collect a sample of the ambient 'silence'.

18. Set monitor switch to 'direct', then to 'tape' and compare signals (A–B check). Confirm fidelity of recording. Listen especially for drop-out (bad reel of tape?), wow (dirt on pinch roller?), poor frequency response (dirty heads?). If all is well, to 19 (if problems, to emergency repairs).

19. Settle back and relax to cue anyone who may be watching (including performers) that all is well and you are from that moment interested only in the music.

After the bustle of setting up, it requires mental discipline to calm down and allow attention (including yours) to turn to the performance. Your appreciation of the performance will be particularly critical if the session has been arranged especially for you. Try to listen analytically. Some ethnomusicologists take copious notes during the music; I prefer to keep writing to a minimum – quick labelling of tape spools and film canisters. If you are recording on 5-inch spools, be still at least until after the first reel change. People who have never watched you record will be very curious to see what happens when the reel finishes, so be prepared for an audience while changing reels. Do not rush; you will only mislace the machine. Leave the recorded tape wound tail out (red leader showing), and lace up a blank spool. Designate one of your carrying bags (now empty) as a repository only for recorded material – tape, cassettes and film. At the end of the session, remember not to pack headphones, which have magnets, in this bag (or ever to lay headphones down on your recorder).

If photography is permitted and agreed to by the performers, sponsors and others involved, refrain from taking photographs until at least a couple of reels have been recorded. Do not make musicians uneasy during a long musical evening by creeping around the room with a camera. When taking photographs, think 'snapshot'. Estimate settings before pointing the camera at a musician; raise the camera, quickly double check and snap. Your camera is now set for several more quick snaps of that scene without further adjustments. In India, performers appreciate being photographed; in such cultures, remember to photograph all members of the group. If your photography disturbs the performance, stop.

If equipment fails, attempt simple checks without fuss. Always be prepared calmly to resort to your backup cassette recorder (or for photography, your snapshot camera) without displaying frustration, anxiety or disappointment during the crisis (musicians will read these as commentary on their performance).

Do not start and stop the recorder before and after musical items (especially as you may not know what constitutes an 'item' in that culture). Aim for continuous recording of the performance, breaking only for reel changes. Continuous recordings are useful for analysis because they capture more of the event including commentary between musical items (perhaps the musicians talking to you or about you), cueing of playing or singing, ambient sounds and silences, and real-time dimension of the event and spacing of musical items within the time frame. The start and stop method obscures these features, represents a regression to the music-as-artifact age in ethnomusicology, often results in missing the first few seconds of every item and usually does not save much tape.

If you wish to run a simultaneous cassette recording of the performance (as a backup, gift for the performers or to cover gaps in reel changes), you may have to forgo photography. Do not take on too much or you will steal the show. The best way around this problem is to train a local assistant to run your cassette recorder or take snapshots; this approach builds rapport and provides, with the extra pair of hands, an insider's view of what is important. After the performance, musicians (and audience) may want to hear playback of your recordings; a simultaneously run cassette is ideal for this. For cassettes, remember to remove record lock-out tabs as soon as the tape is recorded (punch out with ballpoint pen).

Record up to the end of the performance and beyond. You can begin breaking down equipment while the machine is still running, capturing thus the ambient sound of the emptying room, conversation of the performers as they pack up and audience commentary. Breaking down equipment is harder (but more predictable) than setting up. People will always be impatient to leave, and you will be the last one ready to go. Everyone will want to 'help'. While the machine is still running you can:

1. Pack away cameras and flashguns.
2. Pack away headphones.
3. Tidy recorded tape reels, cassettes and film in designated bag.
4. Screw on spool nuts.
5. Zip or clip open-reel recorder case shut.

The recording is over when you finally:

6. Fade levels to minimum (∞).
7. Stop recorder.
8. Rescue microphone(s): unclip cable letting it fall loose; remove windshields; remove microphone(s) carefully from shock mount(s); place microphone(s) in cases (never rush with these expensive instruments in your hands) and pack away.
9. Unplug cable from microphone input sockets, coil for storage and pack away.
10. Collapse telescopic microphone stand and pack away.
11. Pack away blank tapes, pens, notepads, etc.
12. Close up carrying bags.
13. Move from the site, collecting shoes, coat, etc.
14. When leaving, glance over your shoulder to check if you left anything behind.

Back in your room:

15. Remove last open-reel on the take-up spool from machine, number and label (indicate if tail is blank).

16. Put machine(s) on charge.

17. Collect all discharged NiCad cells from open-reel recorder, cassette recorder, flashgun and charge.

18. Check labelling of tape boxes, spools, cassette shells and boxes, and film canisters.

19. Make sure all microphones and flashguns are switched off.

Stationary events – church or temple services, formal concerts, rehearsals, jam sessions, domestic rituals – are relatively easy to record. More challenging and more common are moving events – processions, wedding celebrations, outdoor festivals and street music. If you have a field assistant, open-reel recording, though difficult, is possible and rewarding. Prepare your machine as for a stationary recording (leaving spool nuts on), using a handgrip for the microphone assembly and your shortest microphone lead. You will always need windshields. Sling the recorder over your head with the strap across your chest. As you must hand-carry microphones, you will not be able to take photographs. You will need a friend to carry blank tape reels and to hold the microphone(s) while you change reels.

If no assistance is available, use a cassette recorder slung over the shoulder or on a belt. Fasten a single-point stereo electret microphone to your person or the recorder strap – wherever it is least likely to get knocked. As you still have both hands free, you can easily operate an SLR camera slung around your neck. Clothes with pockets are really essential for this kind of mobile work, as is a backpack for carrying fresh tape, film and replacement batteries (have spare battery slides loaded and ready to go, cassettes unwrapped, film out of boxes; put recorded material in a separate compartment of the backpack after scribbling a simple ID number '1,2,3,' on it). You will need to practise in this get-up or you will find yourself tangled up in your own straps. As soon as you get back to your room, date and number (in your chronological series) all recorded tapes and films and write up the event in your field notes.

Maintenance of equipment and emergency repairs

No field trip, however brief, will pass without some technical hitch or hiccup; fortunately at least 50 per cent of problems can be resolved on the spot. Whatever happens to your equipment, do not panic, especially during a recording session when insecurity on your part will immediately be relayed to the musicians and spoil their ensemble.

If the open-reel machine stops, most likely the batteries are dead, or making poor contact. If roughing up the contact surfaces of the batteries and recorder does not set the machine going again (fine emery paper is best but even scraping with a knife will do), try a fresh set of batteries. If the machine still does not operate, a drive belt may have snapped or an internal fuse blown; practise changing these at home and carry spares. If the drive belt snaps in mid-spool, it is generally possible to rotate the take-up spool manually; at the end of that spool you will have to decide whether to disrupt the session by fitting a new belt or whether to fall back to your cassette recorder.

If one channel goes out, try by comparing direct and off-tape monitoring to establish if the fault is a record or playback one: if the fault is on the playback side, the signal will be correct when monitored direct, and one should complete the session before investigating further; if the fault is heard both on direct and off-tape, then it is a microphone or record circuit fault. In this case, if it is possible to reach your microphones in a matter-of-fact manner, realign the working microphone for a mono pick-up and continue the session. If there is a break in the performance, try swapping the microphone connections over to establish whether the fault is with microphones, leads or recorder. The first check is to swap connections at the recorder; if the same channel remains faulty, the problem is in the recorder. If the opposite channel now shows the fault, the second check is to replug the recorder correctly and swap connections at the microphones (if separate left and right microphones are used); if the original channel still shows the fault then the cable for that channel is faulty. If the opposite channel shows the fault then the problem lies with the microphone. If a single-point stereo microphone is being used, the first check (swapping connections at the recorder) is possible, but another cable will need to be used to check further. Any ethnomusicologist can learn to re-solder dry or broken joints of cables or recorders, using one of the excellent butane gas soldering irons now available. If the fault is within the microphone or the recorder seek expert advice. By phone or telegram, whatever, it is often possible to receive instructions about quite complex repairs in the field.

Certain tape brands are prone to depositing oxide or other elements onto tape heads or pinch roller, sometimes causing apparent loss of a channel. The ethnomusicologist should regularly clean the tape path; make sure you can find all components of the path (guides, erase, record and replay heads, pinch roller and capstan). The favoured cleaner, 1:1:1 trichloroethylene, is an ozone unfriendly CFC and iso-propylalcohol is now preferred, applied with cotton buds. If no suitable low-residue cleaner is to hand, a spit-moistened tissue is a good (ozone friendly) substitute.

A simple daily routine will help to keep equipment in running order. Clean the tape path as described, and dust off the recorder with the camera brush, paying particular attention to switches and controls. Regularly check the straps of your open-reel recorder and their fixings for security. Dust the camera body, check lens for dust and grime, and blow off any loose dust. Finger marks or persistent greasy deposits may be removed from the protective skylight filter by breathing on it (to moisten it) and wiping it gently with a soft tissue. If necessary replace the filter with another (taken from a spare lens). Do not touch the mirror of your SLR as this is a delicate front-silvered precision surface. The rear element of a lens should always be protected by a back cap when the lens is off the camera, so should never need cleaning.

Video and cine photography

As a direct consequence of sub-professional standards in audio recording in ethnomusicology, more and more scholars – in a blind search for the depth and sweetness missing in typical field documentation – are opting for video recording. Video recordings have an important place in ethnomusicological research, particularly in transcription of dance into Labanotation, making staff notations of xylophone or drumming (to differentiate right- and left-hand movements and separate interlocking parts), and in transcribing tightly knit vocal ensemble genres (Hudson Bay Inuit throat games or Yugoslavian *ganga*). Analytical video recordings such as those of William Malm were first made in the late 1960s (see fig.8). Video recordings are useful in contextual analysis, for example, Regula Qureshi's study of social interaction of Sufi Muslims of North India (1986). It is also a particularly attractive medium for feedback analysis with its instant playback facility without need for laboratory processing as with film (Stone, 1982).

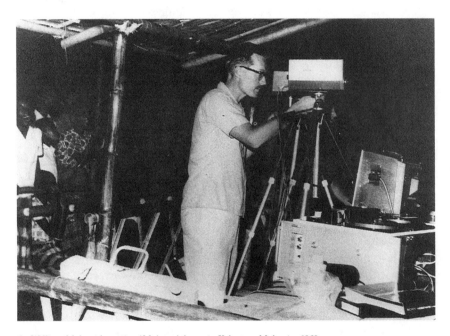

8. William Malm video taping 'Ma'yong' drama in Kelantan, Malaysia, 1969

To make even the simplest video recordings in the field the researcher needs a camera, microphone, headphones, VCR (video cassette recorder), tapes, batteries and chargers and connecting leads; for work of even moderate sophistication, tripods, quartz video lights with battery packs and chargers, a playback VCR and picture monitor, second camera and VCR, additional microphones and a mixer are needed. For convenience in the field, camera and VCR may be combined as a 'camcorder', with a built-in (low-quality) microphone. Camcorders are available from a number of manufacturers (Sony, Canon, Minolta, Panasonic, Fuji, Olympus) for practically every video cassette format (Betamax, Video-8, VHS, and VHS-C [compact VHS, used with an adapter for playback on standard VHS VCRs]). These are lightweight units of varying degrees of sophistication. They may be hand-held, supported on the shoulder for mobile use, or mounted on a tripod for static work. Recording time of the different formats varies greatly, from 20 minutes of VHS-C to 60 minutes of Video 8 to 240 minutes of VHS, but is determined more by the capacity of batteries (from around 20 minutes to 2 hours) than the length of the cassette. All VCRs and camcorders have dedicated NiCad battery packs, needing recharging for 10 to 14 hours. The ethnomusicologist may wish to have external packs made up to ensure adequate recording time; these are available from specialist manufacturers in the form of a belt furnished with appropriate connecting leads. Some camcorders include a caption generator for titling or time and date recording; this can be very useful, but on playback the incrementing numbers in the corner of the frame are a distraction.

For ethnomusicological purposes, the most problematic area of video work is provision of a professional-quality sound track. The easiest solution, use of the built-in microphone, provides the poorest fidelity. The mono sound recorded on the standard analogue audio track of a VCR is poor, with restricted frequency response and dynamic range, and high flutter – all functions of the narrow track (less than 0.5mm), slow linear tape speed, and interference from the video signal ('hash' – high-frequency buzzing and noise due to overlap from the rotating heads). Some models of VHS Hi Fi and Video-8 incorporate stereo audio tracks encoded onto the video signal; this offers dramatically improved performance, particularly if used with high-quality external microphones. For video, at the time of writing, only the Sony Pro Super 8 Camcorder offers stereo sound (using a PCM [pulse code modulation] digital technique); if stereo is a requirement, a separate open-reel recorder is needed with any other model of camcorder.

The advantages of video must be weighed against the quality loss as compared with 16mm film. Although the light weight and simplicity of much video equipment make it attractive to the ethnomusicologist, 16mm film is standard throughout the world, and is readily mass duplicated, whereas there are two incompatible television standards (NTSC 525 lines, 60 Hz; PAL 625 lines, 50 Hz), and many incompatible video formats (Video-8, Betamax, VHS, VHS Super, VHi8). Film or video with its flat, non-stereoscopic picture distorts reality in music documentation in much the same way as do monophonic sound recordings. Stereo sound enhances film or video, but the different viewpoints of camera and microphones may make it impossible to correlate sound and pictures. For movement analysis the individual frame definition of 16mm film is much to be preferred over video. Some video camcorders are fitted with high speed shutters, giving improved definition, but these are only usable with high light levels (and still have poorer definition than 16mm film). Any form of picture recording will need more or less bright lights for night-time work, rendering the ethnomusicologist rather intrusive. For 16mm film a separate sound recorder is necessary, with a pilot synchronizing track (Stellavox and Nagra stereo or mono models are available).

During video work the ethnomusicologist must bear in mind several fundamental problems. First, the autofocus system of the camcorder, which focuses on a central image, may need to be overridden to ensure the main subject is in focus, whatever its position in the viewfinder. Secondly, the cable needed for external microphones restricts mobility. Radio microphones are available, but these may be of low fidelity and unreliable (and in many countries illegal). Thirdly, camcorders are fitted with zoom lenses; change of focal length on a lens alters the pickup angle of the lens, hence the magnification of the image and its apparent distance from the camera. However, it does not alter the perspective of the image; this is only changed by moving the camera with respect to the subject. A close-up of an artist's hands will be of better quality with a close camera wide-angle shot than with a distant camera telephoto shot, even if the picture size remains constant, since the extra depth of field with the wide lens improves sharpness whilst the narrow angle of the telephoto lens exaggerates camera movement, making framing difficult. Finally, in other than rehearsed situations the ethnomusicologist may well miss important data while viewing the scene through the video camera. The camera should as far as is practicable be used locked-off on a tripod, unless a second operator is available. An auto-tracking panning head for camera tripods could be employed, enabling the camera to follow a selected individual. The lone ethnomusicologist will probably have to choose between recording high-fidelity sound or recording the moving image.

The documentary film

The ethnomusicologist who contemplates producing a documentary film must be thoroughly familiar with the field site, have available local assistants and be well-versed in current methods of documentary film-making. Most filming requires a basic crew (film or video) of ethnomusicologist/director, two or three camera operators and sound recordist. Results will need to be assembled, edited, sub-titled and much footage rejected. One camera only severely limits the possibility to portray music in its cultural context. Zemp suggests a crew of two for this, preferably with the ethnomusicologist as camera operator and a local speaker as recordist, and suggests various approaches to single camera work. The National Film School in Beaconsfield, England, and the Centre National de la Recherche Scientifique Audiovisuel, Paris, France, and others offer instruction in the current techniques of documentary filming.

Film-making has a mystique and fascination which should be resisted by the fieldworker seeking an easy route to objectivity (Hood, 1971; Feld and Williams, 1975; Feld, 1976; Zemp, 1988). Many ethnomusicologists turned to film originally in their search for scientific accuracy, selecting the one-camera Cyclops view – a strategy incompatible with human eye-brain function:

> The camera lens system cannot replicate the search pattern of the eye or reproduce *in extenso* the exact signal-to-noise ratio the eyes triggered on. And the camera lens cannot search at the rate the eye searches, shifting soft to sharp focus ratios instantly. This is why it is possible to sit in a chair and observe an action from one place, but impossible to shoot a film of the same observation from the same single sitting position. The camera must move flexibly in order to maintain the framing that includes the information that the eye is triggering on (Feld and Williams, 1975, p.29).

Prospective film-makers should begin by studying ethnographic films, bearing in mind the four simple guidelines suggested by Zemp:

– to film a music piece, and to edit it, in its entirety.
– to keep music performance free from voice-over narration, and to translate song texts with subtitles.
– to film the musician as a human being and not like a thing or an insect, and to show the relationship between filmmaker and musician in the film, rather than hiding it.
– to allow expression of the musician's point of view, respecting his voice and his language through translations in subtitles (1988, pp.393–4).

For still or moving documentation, it is not the camera but the operator that takes pictures. Ethnomusicologists are not making art or commercial movies, have limited time and insufficient budgets to allow for multiple camera work and filming repeated performances (artificialities themselves). The locked-off single camera approach with some panning and zooming (as an adjunct to a high-quality audio stereo recording of the same performance) may be the most appropriate way to preserve ethnomusicological material for notation and analysis.

Still photography

The still camera as used by the ethnomusicologist is called upon to perform many tasks: the wide-angle scenic overview of a locale, portrait of an ethnomusicological subject, group portrait, close-up detail of a portion of a musical instrument, wide-angle picture of an ensemble performance, and time and date recording with databack. For these requirements, the ethnomusicologist needs several different cameras, or a single-lens reflex camera (SLR) with a selection of lenses. Ironically stills often convey more motion than film or video. Movies are a series of fleeting images; stills are time frozen for study, and as such provide one of the finest resources for the ethnomusicologist.

Any fieldworker who has worked in more than one culture will have noticed that people vary in their attitudes towards being photographed. Villagers in North India are photophiles, for example, with an insatiable appetite (not yet satisfied after I have given away over 2000 photographs); many other peoples are photophobic. Because of these sensitivities, always ask if you may take photographs and never fail a promise to give a print. Pictures can be the most satisfying way of thanking people for their time, knowledge and hospitality.

For music studies, the most significant photographic consideration is noise. Musicians will be distracted and recorded tapes ruined by the buzzing, grinding and whirring of motor-driven functions – automatic loading, automatic pop-up flash, automatic film advance, automatic focus, automatic electronic zoom, motor drive, in-focus bleeps, out-of-range bleeps, self-timer bleeps and, finally, the automatic rewind. What may seem a convenience in the camera shop becomes an embarrassment in the stillness of the temple or the tranquillity of a village lane. Even the essentials – click of shutter, flash, manual wind-on – need to be handled with sensitivity.

In the search for a silent instrument the fieldworker may, alas, have to eliminate most of the current generation of cameras, including some of the finest equipment. A further mark against electronically dependent cameras is their total inability to function when the batteries fail – a fatal flaw in remote field settings. The only worthwhile automation is of metering, allowing for aperture priority (automatic speed setting), shutter priority (automatic aperture setting), program (combination setting) or manual operation.

Since most modern SLRs use electronic control of the shutter speed, a sensible choice in an SLR is one with at least one mechanical speed for use either with a flash or if the batteries are dead. Such models are perhaps more readily available on the used-camera market, with Zenith, Nikon FM2, Canon F1 and Leica M6 being the only fully mechanical SLR cameras still manufactured at the time of writing. Nikon's FE, FE2 and FA provide a mechanical 1/125 or 1/250 of a second shutter setting. Models from Pentax, Canon and Olympus are also good. For special purposes a databack (printing time, date or picture number in a corner of the frame or between frames) may be fitted. Most electronic cameras can control the output of a flashgun with metering through-the-lens (TTL flash), but unless long focus lenses are used, the so-called computer or automatic flashgun (which includes its own control circuitry) is satisfactory.

The ethnomusicology student should invest in a basic manual SLR camera early in his or her studies and master the principles of focus, lens aperture and shutter speed setting, depth of field, lens exchange, film speeds and the pros and cons of slide, print, colour and black and white film. As with recording, these photographic skills require trial and error; many user-friendly texts are available for the budding semi-professional photographer (Hood, 1971, offers useful advice).

The main advantage of the SLR over viewfinder (compact) cameras is not the interchangeable lens, but rather that viewing is through the picture-taking lens, so that parallax (framing) problems do not exist and focusing, using split image, micro-prism or ground glass screen is fast and accurate, indeed it soon becomes instinctive. If the ethnomusicologist wishes to purchase additional lenses over and above the standard 50mm, then the first choices are a wide-angle 'landscape' lens or a 100mm short telephoto 'portrait' lens. Since it is worthwhile having a manual compact camera with built-in good-quality 35mm lens (and preferably databack) to serve as your photographic 'notepad' and reserve camera, the choice is between a 100mm and a 28mm wide-angle, for interior shots where space is restricted. The 28mm lens is not satisfactory for portraits since it introduces perspective distortion when used close enough to produce a full frame image of a face; the 100mm is a flattering portrait lens, giving a full frame image at twice the distance from the subject than will a 50mm lens. The opportunity for true portrait work may be limited, but the 100mm lens is very handy for taking detailed photos of parts of an instrument, or of playing techniques, without having to be so close to the subject as to become a nuisance. The standard 50mm or 100mm lenses may also be used with extension rings or close-up lenses for photographing small objects, the 100mm again allowing twice the working distance of the 50mm.

Zoom lenses of high quality are available covering wide focal ranges, but these let in less light than lenses of single focal length, so will be less easy to focus, particularly in dim interior light. Zoom lenses force yet another picture-taking decision at a time when concentration is needed elsewhere and are therefore not suitable for ethnomusicological work. Some all-auto cameras will select the focal length to give portrait images, so reducing this problem. Aim for pinsharp negatives; at home in the lab these can be selectively enlarged at leisure.

For low-light situations an electronic flash may be used. Modern flashguns are very simple to use, requiring none of the complicated equations involving guide numbers, distance scales and aperture settings that turned many a good photographer away from the use of flash in years gone by. Computerized (automatic) flashguns have solved most of the problems (except the nuisance factor of the flash), automatically setting the flash sync speed and appropriate lens aperture for the film in use on electronic cameras, and requiring only the selection of lens aperture (usually with a choice of two or more) and perhaps sync speed on mechanical cameras. If a camera with TTL flash metering is used, then any lens aperture can be used, from wide open (for minimum depth of focus) to the smallest setting that allows enough exposure. In all cases the flashgun will, after the exposure, indicate correct operation by means of Light Emitting Diodes (LEDs) on the back of the gun, often duplicating this indication in the camera's viewfinder. Because the illumination from flash-guns is rather hard and direct, the fieldworker should experiment with diffusers of tissues or handkerchief over the flashtube to soften the light, taking care not to cover the photocell that governs flash output.

The ethnomusicologist will be faced with situations where flash photography is inappropriate, and it will be necessary either to use exposures of 1/15 of a second or longer (using a tripod or other support for the camera) or change to a high-speed film.

For most situations 200 ASA or 400 ASA film is satisfactory, with these slower films having finer grain, allowing greater degrees of enlargement before the image becomes too grainy (fuzzy). For night or interior photography without flash, higher speed films are useful, such as 1000, 1600, or even 3200 ASA.

For critical applications, colour-print film with speeds as slow as 15 ASA offer exceptionally fine grain, permitting 35mm film to rival the picture quality of the traditional 2¼ inch square roll film (used in Hasseblad, Bronica, Rolleiflex reflex cameras). For colour slides the available speeds include 64 ASA, 200 ASA or 400 ASA, with 1000 ASA for low light. For black and white prints the ethnomusicologist will have a favourite film stock, Agfa, Kodak and Ilford all providing excellent ranges. Ilford XP2 is especially useful as this nominal 400 ASA film can be variously exposed from 25 ASA to 800 or 1600 ASA on the same roll, and can be processed by any colour minilab, complete with sepia prints, in the usual one hour. (Although the quality of prints from these minilabs varies around the world, the negative development is normally very tightly controlled by microprocessor; put a test roll through first if having developing and printing done in the field.)

Lists

The efficient fieldworker works from lists. Begin early listing items you plan to take to the field. Everything, however trivial, should be included. Lists are helpful in assembling your equipment, during the final check of your luggage, when buying additional insurance in the field, and when clearing customs and passing security checks at immigration points. Annotate your list during fieldwork so that it will reflect your real needs more accurately on subsequent visits; mark items that you are not using, and note those you wish you had brought. Also note simple items that are available locally so in future you will not pay excess baggage charges unnecessarily for such things as flashlights, umbrellas, water bottles and thermoses, soap, toothpaste and tissues. Collect names and addresses of reliable local suppliers, especially for hard-to-obtain items like open-reel tape, good-quality cassettes and alkaline-manganese cells.

Before each field trip the ethnomusicologist needs to relate his or her technical requirements to his theoretical framework and overall research design; this equation will vary from one tour to the next. The technological requirements for any field project will fall into one of the following categories: 'Minimalist', the most frequently used; 'Professional Standard', the most desirable for ethnomusicology.

1. Minimalist (equipment used only as an extension of a note pad): stereo Dolby cassette recorder, back-up cassette recorder, single-point stereo electret microphone, lightweight headphones, SLR camera, 35mm compact camera).
2. Professional standard (for which no apologies need be made): stereo open-reel tape recorder, stereo Dolby cassette recorder, back-up cassette recorder, single-point stereo capacitor microphone, monitor headphones, SLR camera, 35mm compact camera.
3. Coming professional (state-of-the-art studio performance equipment in the field): DAT battery portable digital audio recorder (with 2-hour record time; Sony, Technics; in place of open-reel recorder), single-point stereo capacitor microphone of highest quality.
4. Video (for movement, context, and event analysis): video camera(s), video cassette recorder (or camcorder), video monitor, open-reel stereo recorder with synchronizing pulse, microphones, headphones, lights (in addition to the equipment listed in 1, 2 and 3).
5. Documentary film-maker (for broadcast or teaching): 16mm cine camera, open-reel recorder with synchronizing pulse, microphones, microphone boom (fish-pole), headphones, lights, pre-planned story-board (shooting list).

Equipment list for 'professional standard' fieldwork

OPEN-REEL RECORDINGS

Professional ¼-inch open-reel stereo tape recorder no.1 with ¼-inch blank reel and take-up spool; leather carrying case and strap; spare spool nuts bolted to strap; record/playback electronics aligned for tape of choice and to NAB or IEC (Europe, broadcast and film only) equalizations

Recorder no.2 prepared as above

NAB 10½-inch spool adaptor (Nagra and Stellavox only) and accessories (for example, 2 spool carriers, 2 NAB centres [4 pieces], 2 drive belts [plus 2 spares], 4 pulleys [large and small])

2 mains power supplies set to local voltage with IEC plugs

2 leads (power supply to recorder)

Monitor grade closed-back 600-ohm headphones

Stereo ¼-inch jack to mini-jack adaptor (to use Walkman headphones as backup)

Single-point stereo variable pattern capacitor microphone

Capacitor microphone shock mount

Capacitor microphone windshield

2 dynamic cardioid microphones (for backup)

2 dynamic microphone windshields

Stereo bar with spacers and microphone clamps to mount dynamic microphones as stereo pair at 120 degrees; fitted with Y-lead from microphone connectors to stereo microphone cable

Adaptor to connect stereo microphone inputs on tape recorder (Y-lead)

Stereo extension lead from adaptor to stereo microphone (medium length)

Stereo extension lead from adaptor to stereo microphone (long length)

Telescopic microphone stand in carrying case

Table microphone stand (double as mini tripod for camera or camera handgrip, thread adaptors as necessary [¼-inch to ⅜-inch])

2 10½-inch metal take-up spools

Professional quality ¼-inch long-play (1mil) tape on 5-inch (or 7-inch) plastic spools (with blank labels)

Professional quality ¼-inch long-play tape as 3600′ NAB pancakes (for use with 10½-inch spool adaptor)

Tool kit (3 spare fuses for mains adaptors, 3 spare fuses for tape recorder, 2 spare drive belts for tape recorder, various thread adaptors, set of allen keys, screwdriver, pair of cutters, tweezers, solder, butane-powered soldering iron, spare electronic modules [Stellavox], spare motor brushes [not for Uher])

Splicing kit (single-edged razor blades, splicing block, splicing tape, coloured leader tape, red-tail tape)

Spare white and coloured labels for tape spools

CASSETTE RECORDINGS

Sony Walkman Pro WM D6C cassette recorder (or equivalent make with Dolby B)

High-grade Walkman headphones

Mains unit/charger set for cassette recorder (set to local voltage)

2 dedicated NiCad rechargeable battery units (for cassette recorder)

Spare carrying strap (cassette recorder)

Stereo recording Walkman (for backup)

4 spare battery slides (for cassette recorders)

Pair of lightweight amplified speakers (for cassette playback)

Miniature electret stereo microphone (with battery, tie-clip lead)

Windshield for miniature electret stereo microphone

One-point stereo electret microphone (with battery)

Table stand for one-point stereo electret microphone (with shock mount and thread adaptors)

Windshield for one-point stereo electret microphone

Blank C90 cassettes

Ballpoint pen for removing cassette record lock-out tabs

PHOTOGRAPHS

SLR camera in case with strap, 50mm lens, fitted with a skylight 1B protective

filter and lens cap; loaded with roll of 400ASA 36-exposure colour-print film
35mm lens for SLR camera (with front and back caps), fitted with a skylight
  1B protective filter
100mm lens for SLR camera (with front and back caps), fitted with a skylight
  1B protective filter
Flashgun (for SLR camera)
Focus-free non-electronic 35mm snapshot camera with databack; loaded with
  roll of 200ASA 36-exposure colour-print film
Colour-print film in a selection of film speeds (200ASA, 400ASA, 1600ASA)
Colour-slide film (64ASA or 100ASA)
Black and white film
X-ray safe shielded film carrying bags
Camera bag (with silica gel)
2 spare lens caps
2 spare back caps
Cable release
Camera cleaning blower brush

TYPEWRITER/LAP-TOP COMPUTER
Portable battery-powered electronic typewriter or lap-top computer with
  portable mini-printer
Typewriter or computer mains adaptor (set to local voltage)
Floppy disks (computer only)
2 small Post-it pads
Typing paper
Typewriter or computer printer ribbons

POWER SUPPLY
3 sets of 15 AA (Mn1500) NiCad batteries (for Stellavox) or 3 sets of 12 D
  (Mn1300) NiCad batteries (for Nagra) or 3 NiCad monobloc packs (for
  Uher)
Alkaline-manganese batteries (AA [Mn1500] for Stellavox, camera flashgun,
  flashlight, amplified speakers, cassette recorders; D [Mn1300] for Nagra or
  Uher)
6 camera batteries (for SLR)
6 camera batteries (for snapshot camera)
6 batteries for miniature electret microphone
6 batteries for one-point electret microphone
2 universal battery chargers (mains powered, with IEC plugs)
4 battery chargers (solar powered)
5-way IEC distribution board with plug-in input lead, fitted with local mains
  plug
Adaptors and extension cords from local mains: (i) for room with light socket
  only: bayonet or Edison screw connector to switched/unswitched
  Y-adaptor (switched half to lightbulb; unswitched via extension cord to
  distribution board); (ii) for room with wall plug: extension cord from local
  plug to IEC socket for distribution board (IEC plugs fitted to all mains
  equipment including open-reel mains units, cassette mains unit, battery
  chargers, typewriter or computer mains units)

MISCELLANEOUS
Swiss penknife
Pen light
Flashlight
Shovel for car (sand, mud)
Car jack and appropriate lug wrenches
Bailing wire (under the seat), useful for fixing many things
Tow rope or chain

DOCUMENTATION, TICKETS, MONEY, PAPERWORK
Passport with local visa
Travel ticket
Traveller's cheques
Cash
Credit cards
International health certificate (with dates of recent vaccinations)
Local government research approvals
Documentation from funding agencies
Address, phone and fax or cable number for closest service headquarters
Letters of introduction from university, archives etc.
Paperwork for equipment (sales receipts, customs receipts, operating and
    service instructions, circuit diagrams)
Copy of travel insurance policy
Address book, stamps (working in own country)
Family photographs
Paper supply for field notes, diary etc.
Music manuscript paper
Pens, pencils
Country, city and area maps
Passport photos
Tourist guide book
Local language to English dictionary (bought locally?)
Light reading
This list

HEALTH AND WATER PURIFICATION
Canteen and cover
Large water bottle (can be bought in field)
Water filter (depending on purification system of choice)
Water purification tablets
Malaria tablets (seek current advice for your area before departure)
First-aid kit with painkillers, antiseptic cream, tablets for motion sickness,
    antihistamines, bandages, electrolyte powder, course of broad-spectrum
    antibiotics, oil of clove, and other medications used regularly

Supplies

Well before departure for the field, the ethnomusicologist will need to calculate
amounts and assemble his or her supplies: open-reel tape, audio cassettes,

video cassettes (if these are being used), alkaline-manganese cells and various types of photographic film. Open-reel tape poses the biggest problem – it is heavy to carry to the field, problematic to mail (often stolen, otherwise dutiable upon receipt) and usually unobtainable in the field. For a two-month stay, the ethnomusicologist can easily go through 150 5-inch spools of long-play tape (56 hours total, 7 hours per week); 50 to 75 C90 audio cassettes (9 to 14 hours per week); 50 to 75 rolls of film; and dozens of packets (sets of 4) of alkaline-manganese cells. Generally, ethnomusicologists who remain in the field a year or more can record and photograph more selectively, but nevertheless they will need at least three times these figures. Many American and European archives, such as the National Sound Archive, London, supply blank tapes in exchange for copies of the original field recordings (or deposit the original recording in the archive, supplying the contributor with a copy).

Professionalism

Faithful field recordings have been part of the ethnomusicological devoir since the birth of the discipline. Any aspiring professional who feels this short list is already too long should give serious thought to choosing another vocation. In the 1990s we face the danger that professional ethnomusicologists, by opting for convenience, are preserving the sights and sounds of music of our time on domestic equipment designed originally as dictation machines or for amateur enthusiasts to make home movies. The rationale is that all will come right on the printed page; any reader who has waded through the pages of our learned journals, *Ethnomusicology* and *Yearbook for Traditional Music*, may have noted equally pedestrian standards of writing. The much-maligned literature of the 19th century was literature indeed; as you read Alice Cunningham Fletcher's elegant work, *A Study of Omaha Indian Music* (1893), consider that the recordings on which it was based were made on the finest equipment available. Modern scholars must bow their heads before the technological standards set by the 19th-century scholars, exemplified by such work as Benjamin Ives Gilman's *Hopi Songs* (1908):

> August 5, 9.45 A.M. I adjusted the instrument to 167 revolutions, and a few minutes later on another count found the rate the same. During the notation of Shiashtasha, Singer No.1, the rate rose in perhaps half an hour to 169. I then set it at 168, and taking the rate at the end of each staff of notation thereafter, no change whatever from this figure revealed itself.
> I concluded thenceforth to adopt this latter method of keeping track of the variations of the phonograph; viz., to examine and record its rate at the end of each staff of the notation. This amounted to taking note of it about every twelve or fifteen minutes, a period during which the experiments with the tuning-fork had indicated that under normal conditions the variation would not be apt to amount to more than about one twenty-fifth of a tone. I carried out this plan for all the rest of the songs, and have written the rates found in the notations at the points where they were taken (p.49).

New ideals of precision and high fidelity in ethnomusicology were contributions of the generation that followed World War II, brought up on the spacious sounds of big band and broad cinema images (from Academy to the widescreen formats – Vistavision, Todd-AO, Cinemascope and Panavision).

This generation had seen the evolution of recorded sound: born in the era of cylinders and shellac discs, raised in the era of wire, paper tape and PVC, and matured in the era of polyester tape, ageing in the digital era. In the late 1960s, this generation saw the introduction of stereo location recording with the portable Nagra and Stellavox machines, and believed that excellence in ethnomusicological recording had arrived. In 1957 Mantle Hood (unable to buy a Nagra) lugged to Indonesia an Ampex 601 mains recorder together 'with a matching playback unit Ampex 620, powered by a 32-volt set of truck batteries [to provide 110 v 60 Hz] through a rotary converter which had a set of vibrating reeds that had to be monitored to be sure the power supply operated constantly at 60 c.p.s.' (1971, p.260). The UCLA Wednesday seminars under Hood's direction were brainstorming sessions for technology in field and lab alike.

The backlash came from the anthropology clan, centred around Alan Merriam. The ethnomusicological literature had grown and its mastery left anthropology students little time for technical training; the intellectual complexity of new theory – linguistics, phenomenology, information theory, cybernetics and semiotics – undermined interest in recording techniques, now taken for granted. Within a decade, excellence in technology became linked with bi-musicality through the charismatic and idiosyncratic figures of Hood and philosopher-musicologist, Charles Seeger; for scholars of anthropological persuasion, their work was theoretically weak. The first generation of American students trained by Hood and Seeger had Hasselblads and Nagras and became university deans; when the second generation came through, the cassette was in and the Hasselblads were locked away in the Dean's office next to the Nagra.

There was no need to sell the bi-musicality philosophy to the TV and Walkman generation, who arrived on American campuses in the 1960s and 1970s – rebellious but serious youth, politically left-wing Vietnam protesters from comfortable middle-class American homes, to whom entering a third-world musical culture with $20,000 in equipment could only be thought of as cultural imperialism. These students were emotionally inclined to invest money in hand-made oriental musical instruments (sitars, gamelan), not hand-finished Swiss recording instruments.

By the 1970s and 1980s, with digital portable recorders coming onto the market, most ethnomusicologists were still using cassette recorders. In the late 1970s the tumultuous cry of tens of thousands of Shi'a Muslims chanting in Firdowsï Square, Teheran – the cry marking the dissolution of international co-operation built over centuries and destroyed in a decade – that cry was recorded on a piano keyboard-style cassette recorder worth less than $50, and reproduced for members of the Society for Ethnomusicology assembled in Montreal on the internal speakers of said cheap recorder held up to a public address microphone. When Mantle Hood himself was drafted in 1985 in the Plaza Ballroom East of the Hyatt Regency in Vancouver to serve as chairman at the combined meetings of the American Musicological Society, the College Music Society, the Society for Ethnomusicology and the Society for Music Theory, it seemed as if the end had come, as cassettes of North Indian *thumrī* were reproduced as if from a leather suitcase on one end of the table in the session entitled 'Improvisation and the Performer-Composer in Courts,

Temples, and Brothels'. It is an embarrassment to our field that on the 100th anniversary of Fewkes's first use of the Edison cylinder machine in fieldwork, modern scholars were found content to rely on amateur domestic equipment, that ethnomusicology had lost the ideals of high-fidelity sound recording and photography that characterized its early years.

Bibliography

AUDIO AND VIDEO RECORDING
A. C. Fletcher with F. La Flesche and J. C. Fillmore: *A Study of Omaha Indian Music* (Cambridge, MA, 1893) [pp.35ff repr. as 'The Wa-wan or Pipe Dance of the Omahas', *Music*, iv (1893), 468
B. I. Gilman: 'Hopi Songs', *Journal of American Archaeology and Ethnology*, v (1908/R1977) [whole issue]
A. P. Merriam: 'The Selection of Recording Equipment for Field Use', *Kroeber Anthropological Society Papers*, x (Berkeley, CA, 1954), 5
G. List: 'Documenting Recordings', *Folklore and Folk Music Archivist*, iii/3 (1960), 2
I. Polunin: 'Stereophonic Magnetic Tape Recorders and the Collection of Ethnographic Field Data', *Current Anthropology*, vi (1965), 227
M. Hood: *The Ethnomusicologist* (New York, 1971, 2/1982)
S. Arom: 'The Use of Play-Back Techniques in the Study of Oral Polyphonies', *EM*, xx (1976), 483–519
M. Clifford: *Microphones – How They Work & How to Use Them* (Blue Ridge Summit, PA, 1977, 2/1982)
C. Card: 'Some Problems of Field Recording for Research Purposes', *Discourse in Ethnomusicology: Essays in Honor of George List*, ed. C. Card and others (Bloomington, IN, 1978), 53
R. M. Stone: 'Motion Film as an Aid in Transcription and Analysis of Music', *Discourse in Ethnomusicology: Essays in Honor of George List*, ed. C. Card and others (Bloomington, IN, 1978), 65
P. M. Honere: *A Handbook of Sound Recording: a Text for Motion Picture and General Sound Recording* (New York, 1980)
E. D. Ives: *The Tape-Recorded Interview: a Manual for Field Workers in Folklore and Oral History* (Knoxville, TN, 1980)
R. M. Stone: *Let the Inside Be Sweet: the Interpretation of Music Event Among the Kpelle of Liberia* (Bloomington, IN, 1982)
C. Fleischhauer: 'Sound Recording and Still Photography in the Field', *Handbook of American Folklore*, ed. R. M. Dorson (Bloomington, IN, 1983), 384
R. Wallis and K. Malm: *Big Sounds from Small Peoples: the Music Industry in Small Countries* (New York, 1984)
R. B. Qureshi: *Sufi Music of India and Pakistan: Sound, Context and Meaning in Qawwali* (Cambridge, England, 1986)
STILL AND MOTION PHOTOGRAPHY
O. Gurvin: 'Photography as an Aid in Folk Music Research', *Norveg*, iii (1955), 181
A. R. Michaelis: *Research Films in Biology, Anthropology, Psychology, and Medicine* (New York, 1955)
J. Collier Jr: 'Photography in Anthropology: a Report on Two Experiments', *American Anthropologist*, lix (1957), 843
K. Reisz and G. Miller: *The Technique of Film Editing* (New York, 1958, rev. 2/1968)
G. Wolf, ed.: 'Rules for Documentation in Ethnology and Folklore Through the Film', *Research Film/Le Film de recherche/Forschungsfilm*, iii (1959), 238
L. de Heusch: *The Cinema and Social Science: a Survey of Ethnographic and Sociological Films* (Paris, 1962)
W. H. Baddeley: *The Technique of Documentary Film Production* (New York, 1963, rev. 3/1973)
G. P. Kurath: 'Photography for Dance Recording', *Folklore and Folkmusic Archivist*, v/4 (1963), 1, 4
G. Kubik: 'Transcription of Mangwilo Xylophone Music from Film Strips', *African Music*, iii/4 (1965), 35
J. V. Mascelli: *The Five C's of Cinematography: Motion Picture Filming Techniques Simplified* (Hollywood, CA, 1965)
J. Collier Jr and M. Collier: *Visual Anthropology: Photography as a Research Method* (New York, 1967, rev. 2/1986)

Institut für den Wissenschaftlichen Film, Göttingen: 'A List of Documentary Films on Ethnomusicological Subjects', *EM*, xii (1968), 397

A. M. Dauer: 'Research Films in Ethnomusicology: Aims and Achievements', *YIFMC*, i (1969), 226

A. Lomax, I. Bartenieff and F. Paulay: '*Choreometrics*: a Method for the Study of Cross-Cultural Patterns in Film', *Research Film/Le Film de recherche/Forschungsfilm*, vi (1969), 505

E. Pincus: *Guide to Filmmaking* (New York, 1969)

H. B. Churchill: *Film Editing Handbook: Technique of 16mm Film Cutting* (Belmont, CA, 1972)

G. Kubik: 'Transcription of African Music from Silent Film: Theory and Methods', *African Music*, v/2 (1972), 28

J. Rouch: 'The Camera and Man', *Studies in the Anthropology of Visual Communication*, i/1 (1974), 37

E. R. Sorenson: 'Anthropological Film: a Scientific and Humanistic Resource', *Science*, clxxxvi (1974), 1079

S. Feld and C. Williams: 'Toward a Researchable Film Language', *Studies in the Anthropology of Visual Communication*, ii/1 (1975), 25

P. Hockings, ed.: *Principles of Visual Anthropology* (The Hague, 1975)

M. Mead: 'Visual Anthropology in a Discipline of Words', *Principles of Visual Anthropology*, ed. P. Hockings (The Hague, 1975), 3

J. Rouch: 'The Situation and Tendencies of the Cinema in Africa (Part I)', *Studies in the Anthropology of Visual Communication*, ii/1 (1975), 52

J. C. Scherer: 'You Can't Believe Your Eyes: Inaccuracies in Photographs of North American Indians', *Studies in the Anthropology of Visual Communication*, ii/2 (1975), 67

A. Sekula: 'On the Invention of Photographic Meaning', *Art Forum*, xiii/5 (1975), 37

E. R. Sorenson: 'To Further Phenomenological Inquiry: the National Anthropological Film Center', *Current Anthropology*, xvi (1975), 267

S. Feld: 'Ethnomusicology and Visual Communication', *EM*, xx (1976), 293–325

K. G. Heider: *Ethnographic Film* (Austin, 1976)

A. J. Ritsko: *Lighting for Location Motion Pictures* (New York, 1979)

D. Bickley: 'The Ethnographic Film as Inquiry: an Interview with David MacDougall', *Newsletter of the University of California Extension Media Center*, i (1981), 2

E. Pincus and S. Ascher: *The Filmmaker's Handbook* (New York, 1984)

H. Zemp: 'Filming Music and Looking at Music Films', *EM*, xxxii (1988), 393–427

CHAPTER IV

Ethnography of Music

ANTHONY SEEGER

Imagine a musical performance. Any performance will do – a rock concert in an American city, an opera in a European capital, classical music in India, popular music in a West African nightclub, a night-long ritual in the Amazon. All these involve musicians, a context in which they perform, and an audience. In spite of their differences, they share certain characteristics.

Before the musicians begin their performance they have usually undergone long training in a musical tradition; the music they will perform will be significant enough to them and to the audience to justify the time, money, food or energy they devote to the event. The musicians have certain expectations of the situation they will be in, of their role in it and of the actions of the audience. The audience, too, attends with certain expectations about the kinds of things that will happen, based on past experiences, concepts about the event, and perhaps knowledge of these particular performers. The time of day and the place of the performance may be significant, as well as the gender, age and status of the performers and the audience. Both may make preparations for the performance including special diet, clothes or activities. When the performers begin, they move their bodies in certain ways, produce certain sounds and impressions. They communicate among themselves through cues to co-ordinate their performance. Their performance has a certain physical and psychological effect on the audience, and some kind of interaction takes place. As the performance progresses, the involvement of the performers and the audience continues, communication takes place, and various levels of satisfaction, pleasure, even ecstasy, usually result. When the event concludes, the performers and audiences have a new experience, by whatever means, through which to evaluate their earlier conceptions about what would occur, and about what will happen next time. These may be formalized in published reviews, internal memoranda, or conversation. That there is often a next time, leads to what we might call a tradition. That the next time is often not the same as the time before, produces what we might call change. The description of these events forms the basis of the ethnography of music.

Musical transcription is the representation (writing) of sounds. Ethnography is writing about people (from the Greek *ethnos*: 'folk', 'people' and *graphein*: 'write') (Hultkrantz, 1960). Ethnography should be distinguished from anthropology, an academic discipline with theoretical perspectives on human societies. The ethnography of music does not have to correspond to an anthropology of music, since ethnography is not defined by disciplinary lines or theoretical perspectives, but rather by a descriptive approach to music going beyond the writing down of sounds to the writing down of how sounds are conceived, made, appreciated and influence other individuals, groups, and social and musical processes. The ethnography of music is writing about the ways people make music. It might be likened to the analytical transcription of events, rather than simply of sounds. It usually includes both detailed descriptions and general statements about a people's music based on personal experience or fieldwork. While ethnographies are sometimes only descriptive and neither interpret nor compare, not all are so.

But what is music? Is it sound? Radios and stereo systems apparently spin out sounds without human agency, but that is an auditory illusion of the medium, not a feature of music. If we, in the 20th century, confuse music with sound, it is partly because most of our recording media capture or reproduce only the sounds of music. Records, tapes and radios do not make music, people do. And other people listen to them. Is it a byproduct of nature? Plato and European theologians of the early Middle Ages wrote that the perfection of creation produced a 'music of the spheres' (Rowell, 1983, pp.43–5) but that was apparently a philosophical illusion – space probes have not recorded it. Is music a species-wide language? Music has been called a 'universal language', but that is probably a romantic illusion – music is as rooted in the culture of specific societies as food and dress, if not language. Confounded by what music probably is not, what might it be?

A general definition of music must include both sounds and human beings. Music is a system of communication involving structured sounds produced by members of a community that communicate with other members. John Blacking has called music 'humanly organized sound' (1973). Alan Merriam, who devoted considerable attention to definitions (1964, p.2f; 1977), maintained that music involved human conceptualization and behaviour, sounds and the evaluation of sounds. Music is a form of communication, along with language, dance and other media. Yet music operates differently from any of these. Different communities will have different ideas of how to distinguish among different kinds of humanly organized sounds – speech from song, music from noise, and so forth. As most of us know from personal experience, one person's music can be another person's noise.

The definition of music as a system of communication emphasizes its human origins and destinations, and suggests that ethnography (writing about music) not only is possible, but is a privileged approach to the study of music. The illusion that music can exist separately from its performers and audiences has led to confusion, long debate and a tendency to treat ethnomusicology as a divided field in which writers either analyse sounds or analyse social and cultural features of music making (Merriam, 1964, p.vii). Although Alan Merriam and Bruno Nettl (1983, p.5) maintain that both groups of writers agree that an ultimate fusion of the anthropological and the musicological would be ideal, the various ideas about what music is have generated very different results. Studies of musical products – sounds – often have not seriously investigated the interaction of the sounds with the performers and audiences. Studies of performers, audiences, and action have sometimes completely ignored the sounds produced and appreciated.

To anyone outside the field, the arguments about what ethnomusicology really is must often appear obscure and uninspiring. The protagonists sometimes may appear to claim and defend conceptual territory rather than to advance understanding. The arguments are often phrased in terms of distant traditions or unheard (only transcribed) musical examples, and people seem to be speaking past one another.

To remedy this appearance of divisiveness and arcane argument, another approach to music might be useful – one that stresses common questions and shared experiences with music, rather than specific answers and studies.

Destinations and 'road maps'

Instead of pursuing the definition of what ethnomusicology ought to be, let us look at the general questions about music that have been shared by Europeans and many other peoples around the world.

1. What is going on when people make music? What are the principles that organize the combinations of sounds and their arrangement in time?

2. Why does a particular individual or social group perform or listen to the sounds in the place and time and context that he/she/it does?

3. What is the relation of music to other processes in societies or groups?

4. What effects do musical performances have on the musicians, the audience and the other groups involved?

5. Where does musical creativity come from? What is the role of the individual in the tradition, and of the tradition in forming the individual?

6. What is the relation of music to other art forms?

These broad questions are general enough to address most kinds of music in most places. They are also fundamental: they ask what happens when people make music. Not every society or every researcher will be interested in them all, and some will be phrased more specifically for investigation. Steven Feld, for example, has proposed a longer and more specific list of questions under six rubrics, many of which can be subsumed under the list above (1984, pp.386–8). Which questions one focuses on and how one tries to answer them depends on a combination of personal interest and professional or cultural orientation.

Within the American academic tradition, those interested in physiology might study the physiological changes in performers and audience; those interested in child rearing might study child socialization through music; those interested in economics might study the economics of performance; those interested in religion might study the relationship of the event to ideas about the cosmos and the experience of the transcendent. Finally, those interested in the sounds might study the sounds and ask quite a few questions about them – about their structure and timbre, about their relationship to previous performances, to instrument design, and many others. Members of ethnic groups may see the character and defence of their group identity in a musical form, while nation-builders may see a pan-ethnic national character emerging in the same forms. Instead of considering these groups to be warring factions, we should see them as different perspectives on the same thing. They are all probably partly right. Each approach can contribute to our understanding of musical events, and each can contribute to discipline (psychology, sociology, economics, anthropology, folklore, musicology, political science) through the study of musical activity.

Of all writers, Charles Seeger most clearly argues for a multiplicity of approaches to music and musicology. Merriam divided the field into two approaches; Seeger demonstrates that there could be many more. In a series of articles he describes different portions of what he calls a 'conspectus of the resources of the musicological process', part of which is reproduced in fig.1. The conspectus is a complex diagram indicating as many of the influences on music as he could imagine, from the physical aspects of the sounds themselves to the historical influences of tradition and the ultimate values and concepts that they express and influence (C. Seeger, 1977, p.125ff). He lists 20 fields involved in the analysis of musical events, from mathematics and logic to myth, mysticism and ecstatics. Fig.1 shows how Seeger divided musicology itself into a systematic and an historical orientation, each of which is further subdivided. The systematic side includes the physical features of music and the semantic features of talking about music; the historical orientation includes both music and speech as human activities and the general needs of human societies for shelter, food and culture.

Frustrated by the inflexibilities of academic language and the mechanical operation of the Hegelian dialectic, Seeger resorts to diagrams to present the field. Of his conspectus he writes:

> By its nature such a schema is static and makes the field it represents – a dynamic, functional thing – appear static . . . In limiting myself to the two dimensions of the conspectus, the best I can do is ask you to begin at the top and as you read down to remember that you are tracing your own progress over the terrain. *When you come to a fork you must decide which path to follow first, but not to stay on it so long that you forget to go back and follow the other fork; for it is the drawing of the two together that is essential to the reading of the table* (1977, p.125, emphasis mine).

Seeger compares his conspectus to a road map, a static representation of many possible 'roads' or lines of investigation. The conspectus is a map of the field as a whole rather than the view of any particular investigator. 'It is a kind of map of the field. How you behave in it is another matter, not structural but functional' (p.126). The map presents large areas for investigation, and there are certainly some missing continents to be discovered (where, for example, are power and hegemony?). Seeger's conspectus reveals the vastness of our subject, and the variety of approaches that have been used in the past, or that each of us may take to it.

Of course the roads on such maps are created by the people who have occupied places on them. One could place much of the history of ethnomusicology into fig.1, with Hermann Helmholtz (1863) and Mieczyslaw Kolinsky (1973) among others, located in the area of aesthetic density, Merriam (1964), Ruth Stone (1982), and much of the ethnography of music in the region of music labelled 'semantic density'. Richard Wallaschek (1893) occupies the middle of the biocultural region of music, while Steven Feld (1982) is found in the study of the left-hand side of that continuum. Some of my own writing is found in the structuralizing of culture on the right-hand side (A. Seeger, 1979, 1980, 1987). Studies of extrinsic determinants include Willard Rhodes (1958) and Merriam (1967), while George Herzog (1930), Helen Roberts (1936), Mervyn McLean (1979), and Nettl (1954) have discussed geographical relations among musical traditions.

IV. MUSICOLOGY

A cross-communicatory, cross-disciplinary, cross-cultural speech study in whose terms the student competent in both arts aims to produce results as valid for the one as for the other.
One phenomenology, one axiology and one evolutional-historical theory may serve both.

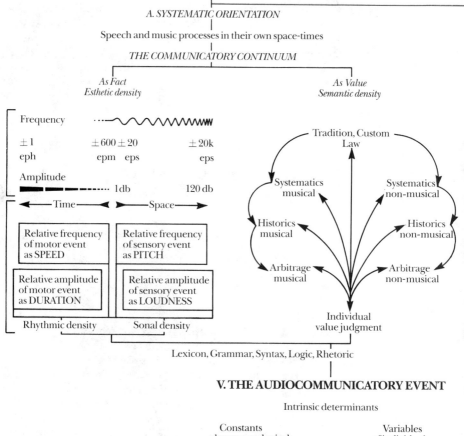

A. SYSTEMATIC ORIENTATION

Speech and music processes in their own space-times

THE COMMUNICATORY CONTINUUM

As Fact
Esthetic density

As Value
Semantic density

Frequency

±1   ±600 ±20   ±20k
eph   epm   eps   eps

Amplitude

1db   120 db

←—Time—◄ ►—Space—→

| Relative frequency of motor event as SPEED | Relative frequency of sensory event as PITCH |
| Relative amplitude of motor event as DURATION | Relative amplitude of sensory event as LOUDNESS |

Rhythmic density   Sonal density

Tradition, Custom
Law

Systematics musical

Systematics non-musical

Historics musical

Historics non-musical

Arbitrage musical

Arbitrage non-musical

Individual value judgment

Lexicon, Grammar, Syntax, Logic, Rhetoric

V. THE AUDIOCOMMUNICATORY EVENT

Intrinsic determinants

Constants
phenomenological
and axiological

Variables
of individual
initiative

Tradition

Form   Style   Genre

The speech event   The music event

1. Excerpt from Charles Seeger's 'Conspectus of the Resources of the Musicological Process' (a fold-out figure in C. Seeger, 1977, pp.114–15)

92

B. HISTORICAL ORIENTATION

Speech and music processes in general space-time

THE BIOCULTURAL CONTINUUM

Music and Speech		Human Beings
	depend, for continuity, upon	

for audible signals   availability of raw materials   for livelihood
which must, for the most part, first be

selected and processed (manipulated)
in accord with particular culturally and socially developed
traditions for rendering them (the raw materials) suitable
for use

as communication,   as food, shelter
discipline and play   and security
by

individuals who cultivate skill in forming the manipulated materials
in concrete products, many of which outlast their producers and serve

to functionalize,   to structuralize
for the members of a society,   the culture,
the values of continuity and variance   giving the members of a society
of the culture and of its potentialities   material evidence of the values
for elaboration and extension   of continuity and variance of the culture

to the extent of their ability to make use of these evidences and potentialities
in the service of whatever may be the aspirations and the destiny of man.

C. IMPLEMENTATION   **VI. THE BIOCULTURAL EVENT (CONTEXT)**

Written Records	Organology	Extrinsic Determinants		
Audiovisual Rec.	Iconography	Geographic	Institutional	Stratigraphic
Archive	Paleography	Families	Dialects of	Idioms
Publication	Archaeology	Languages		Musics
Library	Museum	Ages	Eras	Periods

VII. THE MUSICOLOGICAL EVENT

Science   *Criticism*

This conspectus assembles materials from the present paper and five others, namely;
'On the Formational Apparatus of the Music Compositional Process'; 'Systematic
Musicology: Viewpoints, Orientations and Methods'; 'Factorial Analysis of the Music
Event'; 'Preface to the Critique of Music'; 'The Music Process as a Function in a Nest
of Functions and as in itself a Nest of Functions'.

Seeger's diagrams grew from an appreciation of where research had been done, as well as where it might profitably be attempted. The focus, however, was always on the necessary diversity of questions we must ask in order to understand music and to create an adequate ethnomusicology, or musicology. He often argued that the term ethnomusicology was unfortunate, as true musicology would be ethnomusicological – in the sense that it would include all music and approach it in many different ways (1977, pp.51–2).

During the past 100 years the questions musicologists have asked about music have waxed and waned only to reappear again in different forms. One could say that some parts of the map have been better explored than others. The reasons for the growth of one kind of question and the diminution of another involves social and intellectual history beyond the ethnography of music, but while approaches to some questions have changed over the decades, some of the questions have remained the same. Seeger's figure can serve as an organizing principle for the discussion, although other schemes would do almost as well.

Approaches to the ethnography of music

It is impossible to understand why the ethnography of music developed the way it has without examining some of its roots, at least briefly, here. Other chapters in this volume present fuller treatment, and some excellent book-length histories of ethnomusicology have already appeared (among them, Kunst, 1959; Nettl, 1964, 1983); as well as some synthetic articles (for example Krader, 1980). This section presents a selective discussion of some of the important sources and approaches to writing about music related to general questions about what music is and does in human societies.

THE AUDIO-COMMUNICATORY EVENT: FROM A THOUSAND CIRCUMSTANCES Discussions of historical writings about music must distinguish brief descriptions of song and dance common in the reports of explorers, merchants, travellers and missionaries from longer, intensive, comparative descriptions. Travellers' reports can be useful to later researchers, but they usually are not attempts to establish generalizations about music. More often they are short observations of the type 'when I arrived near the house of the chief I heard a loud noise of singing'. Although sometimes the authors are sympathetic to the sounds – Jean de Léry, who published the first transcriptions of Brazilian Indian songs (made in 1557–8) wrote that they danced in a manner so harmonious 'that no one could say they did not know music' (cited in Camêu, 1977, p.27) – the explorers tended to describe dances and instruments with considerably more care than they gave to musical style.

It was Jean-Jacques Rousseau who laid out some of the basic features of the ethnography of music. In his *Complete Dictionary of Music* (1771/R1975), Rousseau gathered into one place both classical and contemporary information, arranged by entry in alphabetical order. The entry on music is often cited as an early systematic use of non-Western music to make generalizations about music as a whole. Rousseau's initial definition of music was performative: it is 'the art of combining tones in a manner pleasing to the ear'. But later, 'to put the reader in a way to judge the different musical accents of different people' he presented transcriptions of a Chinese air, a Persian air, a song of savages in Canada and the Swiss *ranz des vaches.*

Rousseau drew two important conclusions from the transcriptions. The first concerned the possible universality of musical rules, of physical laws of music: 'We shall find in these pieces a conformity of modulation with our music, which must make one admire the excellence and universality of our rules' (1975, p.266). The second was that the effects songs have on people are not limited to the physical effects of the sounds. To make this point he described how a certain song was outlawed among Swiss troops because of its effect on the listeners:

> The above celebrated Air, called Ranz des Vaches, was so generally beloved among the Swiss, that it was forbidden to be play'd in their troops under pain of death, because it made them burst into tears, desert, or die, whoever heard it; so great a desire did it excite in them of returning to their country. *We shall seek in vain to find in this air any energetic accents capable of producing such astonishing effects. These effects, which are void in regard to strangers, come alone from custom, reflections, and a thousand circumstances,* which retrac'd by those who hear them, and recalling the idea of their country, their former pleasures, their youth, and all their joys of life, excite in them a bitter sorrow for the loss of them. *The music does not in this case act precisely as music, but as a memorative sign* . . . So true it is, that it is not in their physical action, we should seek for the great effects of sounds on the human heart (1975, pp.266–7, italics mine).

In other words, to understand the effects of music on an audience, it is necessary to understand the ways musical performances affect both performers and audience. Music is indeed more than physics. This quotation could be considered one of the earliest justifications for the ethnographic study of music in culture. If we are to understand the 'effects of sounds on the human heart' we must be prepared to retrace with the listeners the 'custom, reflections, and a thousand circumstances' that endow music with its effect.

BIOCULTURAL EVENT: THE ORGANIZATION OF DIVERSITY The centuries of mercantile expansion brought Europeans into contact with a vast variety of human musical and cultural diversity. As the reports of musical life multiplied from all parts of the world, scientists felt it necessary to organize it. In order to do so, they emphasized two basic questions of 19th-century science. The first was an investigation of the origin and development of music (C. Seeger's 'Stratigraphic'), the other was to classify the different styles into groups (C. Seeger's 'Geographic Families'). The answers to both questions were attempts to organize the diversity of musical traditions into patterns – either historical or spatial.

STRATIGRAPHIC PERIODS: ORIGIN AND DEVELOPMENT Some of the best 19th-century studies of music continued to investigate the effects of music on human beings, in the Rousseau tradition. The organization of knowledge, however, was often fitted into an evolutionary framework. Non-Western societies were ascribed a 'primitive' affinity to emotion, and therefore to music and dance, which was believed to have been lost with the acquisition of 'civilization' (one wonders what the authors would have made of 20th-century popular music).

Yet the writers had a great deal to say that cannot easily be dismissed and still requires discussion.

An example of a book-length treatment of music from many parts of the world is Richard Wallaschek's *Primitive Music: an Inquiry into the Origin and Development of Music, Songs, Instruments, Dances and Pantomimes of the Savage Races* (1893). Wallaschek presents a vast quantity of descriptions of musical performances culled from many different sources, a *Golden Bough* compendium of knowledge about music. It has a general theoretical perspective, however. Wallaschek argues that music arose from a general human desire for rhythmic exercise, and developed through the ages to the present.

Although the work has been labelled as mainly of historical interest (Nettl, 1964, p.28), Wallaschek made a number of points that continue to characterize ethnomusicological writing today. One of these is that studying non-European music can be useful because we are able to perceive in the music of other communities aspects of music less obvious to ourselves in music of our own traditions (1893, p.163).

Wallaschek also anticipates much subsequent writing when he notes that ('primitive') music is not an abstract art, but one deeply entrenched in life. He argues that dancing and making music increase group solidarity, organize collective activities, and facilitate association in action (p.294). He describes music as an organizing power for the masses, enabling the tribe to act as one body. This, he wrote, gives musical groups an advantage in the 'struggle for life' over less musical ones, and 'thus the law of natural selection holds good in explaining the origin and development of music' (pp.294–5). Non-musical groups simply could not survive. We can see both the Darwinian influence and a convergence with arguments in favour of 'jazzercise' (an American form of musical exercise in the 1980s). Wallaschek anticipated a great deal of the work that took its inspiration from the French sociologist Emile Durkheim's *The Elementary Forms of the Religious Life*, published some 21 years later (1915).

In spite of some of his prophetic emphases, Wallaschek's work is dated – as much of the anthropology of that day is – by a tendency to view the late 19th century as the height of development. Thus Wallaschek placed the 12-tone scale at the peak of musical development: 'the chromatic intervals in our equal temperament are indeed the smallest possible intervals, not for the ear or the voice or the laws of sounds but for a practical instrument' (p.158). He may have been a keyboard player; had he greater familiarity with Indian music he would probably not have made that argument. He also considered harmony to be a major evolutionary development. And he wrote about the music of different societies by taking their music out of context and comparing the forms according to one or another aspect. None of these things would be done in a contemporary comparative study of music.

Despite Franz Boas's convincing criticisms of evolutionary methodology (1896), the collection of the world's music in order to present a natural history of the development of musical structures and forms continued for another half century. It appeared in Carl Stumpf's *Die Anfänge der Musik* (1911), and continued in various modified forms in Curt Sachs's books on music, musical instruments and dance. For Sachs, in 'primitive' music 'imitation and the involuntary expression of emotion precede all conscious sound formation . . . Ecstasy in the broadest meaning of the word dominates the throat as well as the limbs' (1937, p.175). But the massive accumulation of music from around the world also caused Sachs to caution:

> ... the early history of music can no longer be regarded, as it so often has been, as a direct development from the primitive to the mature, from the simple to the complex and elaborate. This interpretation is outmoded in any case since for scientific method it substitutes 'plausibility', the unfortunate habit of judging by ourselves completely different mentalities many epochs removed from us. 'Primitive' and 'simple', these are indeed concepts which we apply much too casually (1937, p.200).

In the 1960s, Alan Lomax proposed a far more sophisticated and complex correlation between types of society and types of song (1968). He amassed song samples from 233 societies, as well as ethnographic information from the Human Relations Area Files. He developed a coding sheet with 37 different variables, from type of vocal group to articulation of consonants. The subsequent statistical analysis showed that song styles shift according to differences in productive range, political level, level of class stratification, severity of sexual mores, balance of domination between male and female, and level of social cohesiveness (1968, p.6). In its simplest formulation, the song styles could be divided into two groups, model A and model B (1968, p.16).

MODEL A	MODEL B
Individualized	*Integrated, Group-orientated*
Solo	Choral, multi-levelled and cohesive
Metrically complex	Metrically simple
Melodically complex	Melodically simple
Ornamented	No ornamentation
Usually noisy voice	Usually clear voice
Precise enunciation	Slurred enunciation

He wrote of these two groups:

> Model A is the style of exclusive solo dominance and is found all along the highroads of civilization from the Far East all the way west into Europe, or wherever political authority is highly centralized. Model B is the integrated style and has its center among the acephalous and tightly integrated bands of African Pygmies and Bushmen, but turns up in one form or another among very simple people in many parts of the world. Actually, all the singing styles of mankind can be described in terms of their positions on the grid defined by these maximal cases of individualization and integration (p.16).

While the approach was a highly ambitious and comparative one, the Cantometrics ('measure of song') project was heavily criticized on a number of grounds. The most serious of these was sampling, since only ten songs were taken from each of the 233 culture groups. While in some groups song style may be homogeneous, other groups may practise a wider variety of styles that makes categorizing them as either model A or model B quite difficult. Feld, in an examination of his Kaluli data in the light of Lomax's criteria, found that the Kaluli could belong to several different types, depending on which of their songs were taken to characterize them (Feld, 1984, pp.391–2). Although very little work has been done to follow up Lomax's research, he has made Cantometrics training tapes and his original source materials available for further scholarship, and his project was the most serious attempt to reach a global comparative analysis of musical styles ever attempted.

If the history of music could not easily be discerned using an evolutionary model, there were two alternative proposals for organizing the musical diversity of the globe. They both stressed history. One was the study of the diffusion of musical traits over space, which organized the diversity into historical patterns; the other was the definition of culture areas, which organized diversity into geographic areas larger than individual communities.

GEOGRAPHIC FAMILIES: THE ESTABLISHMENT OF CULTURE AREAS Although the definition of musical styles as a means of defining larger musical areas was used in Europe as well as in the USA, it can be particularly identified with some of the students of Boas, especially Clark Wissler (1917), Alfred Kroeber (1947), and in ethnomusicology with Roberts (1936), Boas's student Herzog (1930), and Herzog's student Nettl (1954). Nettl provides a very good discussion of the subject, from the perspective of a person who has done such work (1983, pp.216–33).

The objective of establishing musical areas is to permit generalizations over a larger area geographic or cultural than the individually described 'tribe' or community. The hundreds of native communities in the Americas could be reduced to a varying number of groups by a number of different criteria – language, material culture, ecological zone or musical styles. Often defining an area involved establishing the degree of occurrence of certain traits widely spread throughout a region, which led to problems of sampling. Recent attempts tend to produce areas according to several different criteria. M. McLean's preliminary analysis of musical areas in Oceania according to music structure and instruments produced a map that generally identified contiguous geographical areas as being musically related areas. He was not interested in causal arguments (as was Lomax, 1968) or in verifying existing culture areas (Merriam, 1967), but in 'identifying coherent areal patterns through the correlation of the covariation of a variety of traits' (1979, p.718). McLean's conclusions, however, read much like those of earlier decades. Closely related musical styles of contiguous groups were related to borrowing among them; similarities among distant groups were attributed to similar origins rather than borrowing.

There are advantages and disadvantages to area distribution studies. One of the advantages is that they allow a researcher to speak more generally of styles than is possible by field research alone, and they provide one means to discuss historical relationships among groups and styles. Disadvantages include problems of data (often collected from travellers), of vocabulary (McLean points out that neither travellers nor ethnomusicologists consistently use words such as 'recitative'), of overlooking differences in favour of similarities, of sampling (what kind of selection would provide an adequate sample) and of different degrees of analysis in the sources. Analysts define different areas according to the traits they choose to emphasize and the fineness of their analyses. Thus Erich M. von Hornbostel thought he distinguished an American Indian style, which Herzog rebutted in his influential article comparing Pima and Pueblo musical styles (1936), and Nettl divides native North America into six styles (1954). The world has variously been divided into three (Nettl), five (Lomax), or many different style areas, depending on the objective of the researcher. At the most general level certain musical features are widely shared both within and across geographical areas. As descriptions become more precise, less and less will be found outside of a small geographic or cultural group. Nor, in a general way, has the search for musical areas led to any further understanding of the meaning of music to societies.

Another approach to music emphasizes diversity and understanding in music instead of similarity and historical relations. Each musical tradition is taken as a unit, and the conceptions about music as well as performance traits are treated as an integral whole. This approach addresses more questions, questions that have proved more relevant to the ethnography of music.

Since understanding a musical system requires intensive knowledge of it, the ethnography of music is related to in-depth, first-hand knowledge of the musical tradition and the society of which it is a part. Although this is a characteristic of contemporary field research, it certainly occurred before Bronislaw Malinowski's famous opening chapter of the *Argonauts of the Western Pacific* exhorted anthropologists to live in tents in the native villages (1922). A book resulting from a profound immersion in another society is A. H. Fox Strangways's *The Music of Hindostan* (1914), striking for the clarity of its focus, its admiration of Indian music, its constant comparison between Western music (including that of the author's contemporaries) and Indian music. Fox Strangways argues that Indian music is worthy of study because it lacks the influence of European concepts of harmony, and therefore is similar to song in medieval Europe or ancient Greece. So a study of Indian music should permit a better understanding of European musical history. He argues that an understanding of a musical tradition is necessary to its aesthetic appreciation, but that understanding can be difficult to achieve because we do not know what to make of what we hear (1914, p.2). In descriptions of music he writes 'we do not know what to make of music which is dilatory without being sentimental and utters passion without vehemence' (p.2) and we think of grace notes as added. 'Indian "grace" is different in kind. There is never the least suggestion of anything having been "added" to the note which is graced' (p.182). Strangways undertook his analysis with careful attention to the categories of Indian musicology, which he explained in considerable detail. He opens the book with a chapter on Indian philosophy. His approach is at once specific to a single tradition and comparative with others.

The central focus of Strangways's book is musical structure and form – fairly complex features of Indian music. He does not attempt either a reinterpretation of Indian culture or an interpretation of the meaning of Hindustani music. He does, however, provide some of the social context of the music. In later works this would be developed to a much greater extent.

Context: the relationship of music to social life

What effect does music have on the rest of social life? This question has a long history, and can be related to a number of theories about society itself, as well as about music. Karl Marx held that music was part of the superstructure of a society, and therefore a musical style would be determined by the organization of the means of production.

> Marxist sociology of music follows the principles laid down in Marx's *A Contribution to the Critique of Political Economy*, according to which every movement and change in the social superstructure (the political, legal, religious, philosophical and artistic domains) is determined by changes in the material (economic) basis of society (Boehmer, 1980, p.436).

This general position continues to be a strong force in the study of music, especially in complex, industrialized societies. A degree of independence of music from the economic processes may be posited, but those processes are given considerable weight – especially the economic processes related to music itself. The sociology of music has been defined as a field that 'takes as the basis of its investigation the material circumstances of the production and reception of music, and begins therefore by determining the general social conditions under which music is produced' (Boehmer, 1980, p.432). Yet material forces are themselves created by minds influenced by earlier thought processes, and music may be part of the 'ethos' or general thought patterns of a society. These provide some of the motivation to economic activity and in a sense 'drive' the system, as Max Weber suggested in his study of Protestantism (Weber, 1930).

British and American anthropologists were not as interested in these debates. Influenced far more by Durkheim than by Marx or Weber, they tended to phrase their questions in terms of musical functions. Assuming that music and the rest of social life were interrelated, investigators tried to discover how music functioned to support or destabilize the rest of the social and cultural system.

Merriam was an exponent of this approach, and distinguished between uses and functions:

> When we speak of the uses of music, we are referring to the ways in which music is used in human society, to the habitual practice or customary exercise of music either as a thing in itself or in conjunction with other activities . . . Music is *used* in certain activities, and becomes part of them, but it may or may not have a deeper *function* (1964, p.210).

If music is used to effect a cure, for example, its 'deeper' function might be an unconscious one, discoverable by observers, of 'emotional relief'. Merriam listed a number of likely functions, including emotional expression, aesthetic enjoyment, entertainment, communication, symbolic representation, physical response, conformity to social norms, validation of social institutions and contribution to the continuity and stability of culture (1964, pp.221–5). Merriam's chapter suggests that only the investigator has the clarity of vision to determine functions, while the users appear to be able only to use music, whose functions are unconscious. Yet as investigation has proceeded, it has become clear that many people around the world have theories of music and society that, although phrased differently, are quite as sophisticated as our own. As anthropologists have come to appreciate the cogency of native

100

theories of their society, the distinction between use and function did not hold up.

Nettl took up the issue of functions and uses 17 years later, in another introduction to ethnomusicology (1983, p.159). He suggested that both natives and anthropologists could discuss uses and functions. All these can be arranged in a pyramid, with the base containing 'overt' uses of music, the middle 'abstracted uses' or generalizations about music and finally the most abstract analytic level, which for him is a function:

> The function of music in human society, what music ultimately does, is to control humanity's relationship to the supernatural, mediating between people and other beings, and to support the integrity of individual social groups. It does this by expressing the relevant central values of culture in abstracted form . . . In each culture music will function to express a particular set of values in a particular way (1983, p.159).

From the perspective of this approach, music thus has uses – apparent to native and observer alike – and functions.

No one can deny that people use music consciously. One need only observe the widespread censorship of music around the world and the extensive use of music in advertising to see two very contradictory uses to which it can be put. Yet the search for functions has not usually addressed the particularities of the music itself. If a function of music is to control a group's relations to the supernatural, we need to know why members of a group use music to exercise such control, and why a particular kind of music as distinct from all the other kinds they may employ to other ends. The more general assertions about functions have been too general and have ignored the structure and performance of sounds almost entirely. The split between anthropological and musicological lines of inquiry can partly be traced to the divorce between a search for functions, which requires very little attention to the music, and the search for the structures of the sounds. Drawing them together requires attention to the meaning of the sounds themselves and their various combinations.

The different approaches to the sociology of music share a common goal: to discover the way music is used and the meanings it is given by members of the community that performs it. This goes beyond the interest of Fox Strangways, and appears in a number of contemporary ethnographic descriptions of particular societies.

MUSIC AS VALUE: RECENT ETHNOGRAPHIES OF MUSIC Approaches to musical ethnography over the past 20 years have involved attempts to address more specific questions than are possible through discussions of use or function. Authors have approached music from the native's point of view, using native categories of expression. Although Merriam proclaimed that 'there must be a body of theory connected with any music system – not necessarily a theory of the structure of music sound, although that may be present as well, but rather a theory of what music is, what it does, and how it is co-ordinated with the total environment, both natural and cultural, in which it moves', he was unable to locate it clearly among the Flathead Indians (Merriam, 1967). Other researchers have found it difficult – but possible – to locate (Marshall, 1982).

More recent investigators have searched harder for native ideas about music which may be expressed differently from that of European design. Virtually all contemporary authors focus on sets of native terms, and attempt to analyse music from within the semantic fields employed by members of the society. Some of the earlier works include David Ames and Anthony King's *Glossary of Hausa Music and its Social Contexts* (1971) and Hugo Zemp's *Musique Dan* (1971). Charles Keil's *Tiv Song* begins with a discussion of semantic domains, and investigates the verbs associated with music in particular detail (1979, p.30ff). Stone's *Let the Inside Be Sweet* (1982) addresses Kpelle aesthetics through an elucidation of their phrase 'Let the inside be sweet' and Feld's *Sound and Sentiment* (1982) investigates Kaluli aesthetics through their metaphors and emotions. These books are among the most important ethnomusicological ethnographies of the 1970s and 1980s, and each has made interesting proposals for the ethnography of music.

All the authors note that definitions of what we call 'music' vary widely, and that an inclusive term is often lacking. This means that if we confine ourselves to asking only about what we call music we may be making a partial inquiry into what other people think they are doing. There are several ways to overcome this problem. One is to define carefully a limited object of study, such as the performance event, and to focus on everything that happens in it, whether it is musical or not. The other is to take sets of concepts and actions with respect to music that appear to be related and investigate their inter-relatedness. Stone and Feld have each chosen one of these options.

Stone systematically describes the interaction of performers and audiences in Kpelle music events. She maintains that these events are bounded spheres of interaction, separable for detailed analysis. She studied the interaction of individuals producing music and those who listen to it. Other authors who have focused on the music event or occasion – often inspired by pioneering work by R. Bauman and J. Sherzer (1974) – include M. Herndon and R. Brunyate (1976), N. McLeod and Herndon (1980) and G. Béhague (1984). Feld, on the other hand, embraced a larger gamut of attitudes and beliefs about all forms of sound communication, including weeping and bird cries, to show how analysis of the codes of sound communication could lead to understanding the ethos and the quality of life in Kaluli society.

Feld described Kaluli sound expressions as 'embodiments of deeply felt sentiments' (1982, p.3), and their performances as striving to elicit those sentiments in both audience and performers. Other authors have analysed music as one medium within a set of forms. One of these is Richard Moyle's analysis of Pintupi songs, in which he begins by distinguishing Pintupi singing from other categories of human sound, including recitations, text rehearsals, speaking, crying and dance calls (1979). Another is my own study of Suyá song, which establishes a set of interrelationships among Suyá categories of verbal forms, and then focuses on a group of those forms which define Suyá music (1987). Stone's work is important for the detail with which it approaches what she defines as the music event; Feld's work is important for his approach to music as one among a number of interrelated modes of communication that have profound effects on emotion. If Stone's book focuses on an approach to studying music, Feld's addresses central questions about why people perform music.

Another group of authors began their research with an enthusiasm for a particular instrument or a type of music. We might say they began with an interest in a tradition as aesthetic density (see fig.1) but moved on to study semantic density. The authors were often also performers, and the ethnographies were both engaging descriptions of encounters with musicians in other societies and descriptions of musical life there from the perspective of an apprentice and performer. One of the most successful of these is Paul Berliner's *The Soul of Mbira*, a description of his search for musical and intellectual understanding of the *mbira* (also known as *sanza* and 'African thumb piano'). Berliner described how he learned to play and to understand the aesthetic concepts of the Shona *mbira* players of Zimbabwe: 'The purpose of this book is to draw attention to the *mbira*' (1978, p.xiii) – a very different aim from Feld and Stone. Berliner presents the concepts about and the sounds performed on the instrument – a mode of investigation that leads to many of the same issues treated in the other books. Poetically written, illustrated with transcriptions and supplementary recordings on Folkways records, and providing instructions for constructing a Shona *karimba*, *The Soul of Mbira* is an excellent example of the success with which an enthusiast's approach to another tradition may be transmitted to the reader. Other books whose authors' involvement in the musical performance plays an important role include Hood's description of learning to play in Indonesia (1971) and J. M. Chernoff's description of drumming in West Africa (1979). Hood championed the approach to ethnomusicology known as 'bi-musicality', in which the student learns to perform an instrument as an approach to understanding the music just as he learns a language to speak with the people. Certainly much of the ethnomusicologists' sensitivity to details of other traditions is partly the result of the research being an encounter between musicians.

Regula Qureshi proposed a synthetic approach to music that addressed both the contextual features and the specifically acoustic features of musical performances (1987). The two kinds of analysis she proposed to combine are (i) the system of rules of the musical sound system, which can be obtained especially from the musicians, and (ii) analysis of the context, in terms of concepts and behaviour, structure and process, using anthropological theory and methods of elicitation and observation. Qureshi suggests that analysis should proceed in three steps. First, the musical idiom should be analysed as a structure of musical units and rules for their combination, in the sense of a formal grammar. This can be obtained from the performers. In the Pakistani musical genre she studied there were musicological concepts 'literally for the asking', something not found everywhere. Second is an examination of the performance context as a structure, consisting of units and rules of behaviour. 'This also needs to include a consideration of the larger cultural and social structure behind the specific performance occasion which gives sense to it' (p.65). Third is the analysis of the actual performance process.

In her article, she accomplishes this through an analysis of videotapes and discussions with performers. This stage includes the perspective of the performer, the actions of the audience and the visible interaction between them. Qureshi insists that the focus be on the musician, since the focus is on the music, which is known best to the music maker 'who alone knows the medium of performance' (p.71). Where the focus should be, however, must depend on the questions being asked rather than on the presumed knowledge of a part of the social group. If one wishes to focus on the effect of music in mobilizing audiences, then the focus would appropriately be on the audience.

The sophistication of Qureshi's analysis appeared in the conclusions, where she argued that music is capable of carrying, and does carry meaning in several ways that may be combined or separated to convey a range of intensity. In musical events 'both the performer and listener may choose from among, or combine, several meanings, each of which is itself quite specific' (p.80).

If Qureshi's model is explicit about the performance context, and therefore centrally focused on the music, it is not the only way to approach the ethnography of performance. It suggests areas of emphasis rather than sequential steps of investigation. In the next section I make a suggestion of my own about undertaking such ethnography. I do this in spite of the considerable literature on the difficulty of ethnographic fieldwork and writing (for example, Boon, 1982; Fabian, 1983). While it is important to refine our understanding of ethnography, it is also important to begin doing it as early as possible, and to discover its advantages and shortcomings by undertaking it and reflecting upon it.

A do-it-yourself ethnography of performance

Performances can be analysed by systematically examining the participants, their interaction and the resulting sound, and by asking questions about the event. At the start the questions are those of any journalist: *who* is involved, *where* and *when* is it happening, *what* is being performed, *how* is it being performed, *why* is it being performed and *what* is its effect on the performers and the audience? Although the questions can be applied anywhere in the world, the answers will have to employ significant cultural categories. These questions cover some of the gamut of Charles Seeger's conspectus. The answers to *what* and *how* can describe the sounds (aesthetic density) as well as the categories used to talk about them (semantic density). The answers to *where* and *when* are important parts of the context. The answer to *why* addresses both the historical and the systematic orientation, since it depends both on the historical and on the immediate contexts of the event. Different researchers may choose to concentrate on one more than another, for reasons of their own historical and theoretical development.

Over the years, I have had students prepare a series of ethnographic accounts of musical performances in a small American midwestern college town. Imagine that you are attending a reggae concert in (*where*) the only important nightclub in town. Sitting at a table and watching the audience, the observer can see that its members (*who*) are in groups of both sexes, largely college-age, Caucasian, dressed in apparent informality that in some cases belies considerable expense and care, seated at tables, drinking and talking. A local band (*what*) 'warms up the audience' by providing music to pass the time, to create suspense about the main event and to showcase its own talents before an audience that otherwise might not hear them. When the reggae musicians (more *who*) arrive, they are African-Americans, with dreadlocks, and perform music (more *what*) that developed in Jamaica, a different sound, which is enthusiastically received by the audience. A relationship is established between musicians and audience that enables the creation of an emotional atmosphere, and results in dancing and enthusiastic applause. After a certain period the show ends, the musicians talk with some members of the audience, most of whom leave and return to their homes or dormitories.

That is what one can see by just sitting quietly at a table (earning some dubious looks by sitting too quietly). One can, however, speak to people at other tables and ask questions about the performers, the audience, and the setting. One might learn that the performers are 'the best ever to come to this town', that the audience is 'mostly straight college types with a mixture of regulars', as well as 'friends of the warm-up band' and that there is an undercover police officer in the corner, that 'this place has lousy acoustics but it is the only place in town that books outside shows' and that 'Thursday night is a terrible night to draw a crowd, it should have been scheduled for Saturday'. This part of the investigation yields 'native categories' or the words and phrases people use to define their world and insert themselves into it. These local categories of person, place and time do not make much sense in themselves, but they do form systems with other categories of person, place and time. Taken as a whole, and related to one another, the systems will yield important clues to the significance of the event that is occurring.

Structural analysis argues that things derive their sense from their relationship with other things (Lévi-Strauss, 1963), and native categories are no exception. Further investigation (again by talking with people in the community) might reveal a set of local categories of people (types of *who*): 'college crowd' might contrast with 'local youths', 'Yuppies', and 'old folks'. One might find that different performance spaces in town (types of *where*) are largely reserved for different kinds of music – the 'opera house' does not book reggae, nor do the public library, the churches or the fraternal organizations. Instead, each of those has categories of music that it regularly books and a clientele that regularly attends the events. Other kinds of music may be played at the other locations on different nights of the week (types of *when*). Musicians may overlap by playing different kinds of music in different bands. Audiences may overlap as well since a person may enjoy more than one kind of music. But the audiences are often quite different. Few college students may attend events at the fraternal organizations such as the Rotary Club; many children attend events at the library (directed at children); at the country music bars outside of town there may be fewer students the farther one goes from the university campus; and musical events at churches are often attended according to denomination.

The performance, audiences and performance times can be used to construct a set of expectations about music in the community. Some kinds of music, however, will be appropriate to several locations, times and audiences. It may be that jazz will be performed in the university concert hall, the nightclub, the fraternal organizations and the distant bars to audiences that display a mixture of ages, sexes and backgrounds. If the researcher persists, he or she will find that jazz began in one setting and has moved steadily into others over time. Other types of music, however, will be fairly rigidly differentiated in terms of audience, location and musical style. There are, the analyst usually finds, systems of categories of person, of place and of musical types that are related to one another, if not mutually exclusive and entirely consistent. These can be used to begin an ethnography of a community's performances.

To construct an ethnography of music, however, one needs to do more than sit and talk with one's neighbour in the audience. Musicians, too, have perceptions of what is happening in the performance, although they are not always delighted to talk about it. The college town may be only one stop on a tour, and they may be more concerned with a concert in a big city the next day than with the concert at hand. As professionals, however, they quickly find the level of the audience and play to it. They may, for example, find that Robert Marley songs receive an enthusiastic response, and put more of those into their second set, while soft-pedalling some of their own compositions. They may appreciate the warm reception and compare it with other places they have played. They may have classifications of time, space and audience types that are quite different – but complementary to – those of the audience.

Nor are the musicians and the audience the only people involved in the performance. There are business managers, road managers, nightclub owners, electrical engineers, fire marshals, police, waitresses and bouncers. All of them have perspectives on the event that can be quite instructive. A localized musical event is also part of large economic, political, and social processes that it may protest even as it reproduces them. These processes might be significant, especially for questions relating to the sociology of music. Music is also often part of political processes and censorship, state promotion or political evaluations of performances are frequently important to acknowledge and study.

Interviews can take one a long way toward an analysis, but some very important questions must be answered through interpretation of the answers. These are answers to *why* people participate in music events, *what* are their motivations and what significance the event has to them. These questions are more difficult than those that can be discovered through direct observation, because significance is often the product of past experiences and the relationship of musical events to other processes and events in the community. In spite of their difficulty, these are usually the most interesting questions for anthropologists. Significance can be approached through the relationship of the origin, structure and sounds of music to other aspects of society.

Feld is one of few authors who have investigated the significance of song in this way. In *Sound and Sentiment* he traces the significance of a genre of songs by demonstrating the relationship of human song to birdsong and by analysing the relationship of singing songs that recall areas of the forest and earlier events that evoke intensely felt sentiments on the part of the listeners. He analyses Kaluli myths, their ideas about nature and specific examples of musical performance, and demonstrates that the relationship of human and birdsong are a specific expression of a more general parallel between humans and birds drawn by the Kaluli. The *gisalo* songs are designed to move people to tears, and the audience expresses the success of the singer in eliciting desperate sorrow by burning him with a hot torch.

> These bird sounds and bird sound words reorganize experience onto an emotional plane resonating with deeply felt Kaluli sentiments. When

textual, musical, and performative features properly coalesce, someone will be moved to tears (1982, p.216).

Through investigating both cognitive and emotive aspects of song, Feld provides one of the most careful studies of the significance of song that has so far appeared.

Musical performance has physiological, emotional, aesthetic and cosmological aspects. All these are involved in why people perform and enjoy certain musical traditions. An ethnography of music must be prepared to deal with them – yet so far few writers have done so. Some analyses concentrate on the physiological influence, others on the emotional tension and release obtained through music, and others deal with the social correlates and others with the effects on the cosmic beliefs within the tradition. All are probably involved in any tradition. A combination of field research, investigation of native categories and careful descriptive writing are hallmarks of the ethnography of music.

An anecdote, probably from India, tells about a group of blind men who were taken to visit an elephant. At last, after hearing so much about it, the blind men were led inside the elephant cage and surrounded one of the huge beasts. One man felt the trunk, and concluded that an elephant was long and flexible, like a large snake. Another felt a leg, and concluded that it was circular and stout, like a tree trunk. The one feeling the tail decided it was quite small, while the one standing under its belly felt its oppressive weight, and decided it was huge and heavy. When they left the elephant's cage, they began to compare their impressions of the animal and fell into loud disagreement about the nature of elephants. Each was convinced, by his personal experience, that he was correct.

In many ways music is like the elephant and we are blind men. Deprived of a vision of all its parts, different disciplines and scholars have fixed on certain aspects and declared 'this is what music is all about'. The strength and bitterness of the differences of opinion is evident in journals and books. Instead of defending our own points of view, however, perhaps we should move around more, approach music from different sides, and listen to those who describe it differently. Instead of limiting the kinds of questions we consider acceptable, I believe we should define our research in terms of broad questions, and recognize the power of the diversity of research and writing being done in the 1990s. No one person or discipline has a monopoly on questions we can ask about music. If our answers differ, it is because perspectives on the events are different. If we work apart, like the blind men in the fable, we will never discover what an elephant is. If we work together, we can begin to see the unseen whole, and understand the phenomenon we can only partially perceive by ourselves.

Bibliography

J.-J. Rousseau: *Dictionnaire de musique* (Paris, 1768/*R* 1969; many edns to 1825; Eng. trans. by W. Waring, London, 1771, 2/1779/*R*1975 as *A Complete Dictionary of Music*)

H. L. F. von Helmholtz: *Die Lehre von der Tonempfindungen* (Brunswick, 1863, 4/1877; Eng. trans., 1875/*R*1954 as *On the Sensations of Tone*)

107

Ethnomusicology: an Introduction

R. Wallaschek: *Primitive Music: an Inquiry into the Origin and Development of Music, Songs, Instruments, Dances and Pantomimes of Savage Races* (London, 1893/R1970)

F. Boas: 'The Limitations of the Comparative Method', *Science*, iv (1896), 901

C. Stumpf: *Die Anfänge der Musik* (Leipzig, 1911)

A. H. Fox Strangways: *The Music of Hindostan* (Oxford, 1914/R1966)

E. Durkheim: *The Elementary Forms of the Religious Life: a Study in Religious Sociology* (London, 1915)

C. Wissler: *The American Indian* (New York, 1917, 2/1922)

B. Malinowski: *Argonauts of the Western Pacific* (New York, 1922)

G. Herzog: 'Musical Styles in North America', *Proceedings of the 23rd International Congress of Americanists, New York 1928* (Lancaster, PA, 1930), 455

M. Weber: *The Protestant Ethic and the Spirit of Capitalism* (London, 1930)

G. Herzog: 'A Comparison of Pueblo and Pima Musical Styles', *Journal of American Folk-Lore*, xlix (1936), 283–417

H. H. Roberts: *Musical Areas in Aboriginal North America* (New Haven, 1936)

C. Sachs: *World History of Dance* (New York, 1937/R1963; Eng. trans. of *Eine Weltgeschichte des Tanzes*, Berlin, 1933)

—— : *The History of Musical Instruments* (New York, 1940)

A. L. Kroeber: *Cultural and Natural Areas of Native North America* (Berkeley, 1947)

B. Nettl: *North American Indian Musical Styles* (Philadelphia, 1954)

W. Rhodes: 'A Study of Musical Diffusion Based on the Wandering of the Opening Peyote Song', *JIFMC*, x (1958), 42

J. Kunst: *Ethnomusicology* (The Hague, 3/1959)

A. Hultkrantz, ed.: *International Dictionary of Regional European Ethnology and Folklore* (Copenhagen, 1960)

C. Lévi-Strauss: *Structural Anthropology* (New York, 1963)

A. P. Merriam: *The Anthropology of Music* (Evanston, IL, 1964)

B. Nettl: *Theory and Method in Ethnomusicology* (Glencoe, IL, and London, 1964)

A. P. Merriam: *Ethnomusicology of the Flathead Indians* (New York, 1967)

A. Lomax: *Folksong Style and Culture* (Washington, DC, 1968)

D. Ames and A. King: *Glossary of Hausa Music and Its Social Contexts* (Evanston, IL, 1971)

M. Hood: *The Ethnomusicologist* (New York, 1971, new edn 1982)

H. Zemp: *Musique Dan: La musique dans la pensée et la sociale d'une société africaine* (Paris, 1971)

J. Blacking: *How Musical is Man?* (Seattle, 1973)

M. Kolinski: 'A Cross-Cultural Approach to Metro-Rhythmic Patterns', *EM*, xvii (1973), 494

R. Bauman and J. Sherzer, eds.: *Explorations in the Ethnography of Speaking* (New York, 1974)

T. W. Adorno: *Introduction to the Sociology of Music* (New York, 1976; Eng. trans. of *Einleitung in die Musiksoziolgie: Zwölf theoretische Vorlesungen*, Frankfurt, 1962, 2/1968)

M. Herndon and R. Brunyate, eds.: *Form in Performance: Proceedings of a Symposium on Form in Performance, Hard-Core Ethnography* (Austin, 1976)

H. Camêu: *Introdução ao Estudo da Música Indígena Brasileira* (Rio de Janeiro, 1977)

A. P. Merriam: 'Definitions of "Comparative Musicology" and "Ethnomusicology": an Historical–Theoretical Perspective', *EM*, xxi (1977), 189

C. L. Seeger: *Studies in Musicology 1935–1975* (Berkeley, 1977)

P. F. Berliner: *The Soul of Mbira* (Berkeley, 1978)

J. M. Chernoff: *African Rhythm and African Sensibility: Aesthetics and Social Action in African Musical Idioms* (Chicago, 1979)

C. Keil: *Tiv Song* (Chicago, 1979)

M. McLean: 'Towards the Differentiation of Music Areas in Oceania', *Anthropos*, lxxiv (1979), 717

R. M. Moyle: *Songs of the Pintupi: Musical Life in a Central Australian Society* (Canberra, 1979)

A. Seeger: 'What Can We Learn When They Sing? Vocal Genres of the Suyá Indians of Central Brazil', *EM*, xxiii (1979), 373

K. Boehmer: 'Sociology of Music', *Grove 6*

B. Krader: 'Ethnomusicology', *Grove 6*

N. McLeod and M. Herndon, eds.: *The Ethnography of Musical Performance* (Norwood, PA, 1980)

A. Seeger: 'Sing for Your Sister: the Structure and Performance of Suyá akia', *The Ethnography of Musical Performance*, ed. M. Herndon and N. McLeod (Norwood, 1980), 373

J. A. Boon: *Other Tribes and Other Scribes* (Cambridge, 1982)

R. Falck and T. Rice, eds.: *Cross-Cultural Perspectives on Music* (Toronto, 1982)

108

S. Feld: *Sound and Sentiment: Birds, Weeping, Poetics, and Song in Kaluli Expression* (Philadelphia, 1982, rev. ed., 1990)

C. Marshall: 'Towards a Comparative Aesthetics of Music', *Cross-Cultural Perspectives on Music*, ed. R. Falck and T. Rice (Toronto, 1982), 162

R. M. Stone: *Let the Inside Be Sweet: the Interpretation of Music Event Among the Kpelle of Liberia* (Bloomington, IN, 1982)

J. Fabian: *Time and the Other: How Anthropology Makes its Object* (New York, 1983)

B. Nettl: *The Study of Ethnomusicology: Twenty-nine Issues and Concepts* (Urbana, 1983)

L. Rowell: *Thinking about Music: an Introduction to the Philosophy of Music* (Amherst, 1983)

G. Béhague: *Performance Practice: Ethnomusicological Perspectives* (Westport, 1984)

S. Feld: 'Sound Structure as Social Structure', *EM*, xxviii (1984), 383

R. B. Qureshi: 'Music Sound and Contextual Input: a Performance Model for Musical Analysis', *EM*, xxxi (1987), 56–87

A. Seeger: *Why Suyá Sing: a Musical Anthropology of an Amazonian People* (Cambridge, England, 1987)

CHAPTER V

Transcription

Ter Ellingson

Transcription, which has to do with the writing of musical sounds, has long been considered universally applicable and universally requisite to ethno-musicological methodology. This method provided objectively quantifiable and analysable data that furnished a solid base for ethnomusicology's claim to validity as a scientific discipline. Erich M. von Hornbostel and Otto Abraham declared in 1909 that 'writing down melodies in notation, after all, is essential' for the scientific study that would realize the profits of the 'investment' of field-work and recordings (1909, p.1); and 70 years later, George List made tran-scription the cornerstone of his definition of ethnomusicology: 'For a study to be ethnomusicological the scholar must transcribe the music. . . .' (1979, p.2).

Nevertheless, the view that 'notation is not the ultimate limit of our science' has existed in Western traditions of music study at least since the 4th-century BC Greek theorist Aristoxenus (1902, p.194); and by the late 20th century, changing emphases in ethnomusicological theory and method make it possible to ask whether transcription has not at least declined in importance, or even become a peripheral or anachronistic remnant of outmoded ideas and methods. Thus expressed, the case may seem overstated, but even the possibility of the breakdown and restructuring of a century-old paradigm is an important concern.

Cross-cultural transcription began as a tool of colonial acquisitiveness, a means of appropriating and exhibiting exotic sensory experiences, but was gradually transformed from the 17th century onwards into a form of docu-mentation for supporting scientific theories. From an essentially illustrative device to demonstrate preconceived universalist theories, transcription gradu-ally evolved into a tool for the discovery of cultural diversities. A standardized transcriptional format advanced by Hornbostel and Abraham at the beginning of the 20th century became a kind of musical International Phonetic Alphabet into which nearly every kind of music was transcribed for much of the century. The theoretical understanding of transcription advanced with the formulation by Benjamin Ives Gilman (1852–1933) and Charles Seeger (1886–1979) of a distinction between, in Seeger's terms, prescriptive and descriptive music writing. In the late 20th century, the trend seems to be towards a third type, neither strictly prescriptive nor descriptive, but rather cognitive or conceptual, as it seeks to portray musical sound as an embodiment of musical concepts held by members of a culture. This change reflects a general trend in ethnomusicology away from objectivist intercultural discovery procedures towards problems of conceptualization seen from within a culture and then translation into a broader cross-cultural dialogue.

Notation and transcription both employ written representations of music. Transcription is a subcategory of notation, and logically and historically requires the pre-existence of notation. Since transcriptions and non-transcriptive notations may be closely similar or identical in graphic form, they must be distinguished from one another on other than formal grounds. The clearest difference between them is in their intended functions.

Seeger (1958), in a classic rephrasing of a distinction first identified by Gilman (1908, pp.8–9) at the beginning of the 20th century, draws a basic functional contrast between 'prescriptive' and 'descriptive' notations. The prescriptive corresponds to what ethnomusicological writers usually refer to as 'notations', and descriptive to ethnomusicological 'transcriptions'. Although recognizing possible ambiguities in his description, Seeger introduced the distinction as that 'between a blueprint of how a specific piece of music shall be made to sound and a report of how a specific performance of any music actually did sound' (1958, p.168).

The term 'transcription' in ethnomusicology differs from the usage of related disciplines. In Euro-American classical music studies, 'transcription' usually refers to rewriting music from one kind of notation into another, based on note-for-note substitution without listening to actual sounds during the writing process, while 'dictation' refers to writing notations of sounds actually played or sung in the formalized context of teaching exercises. Linguists use 'transcription' to refer to writing down representations of spoken sounds, but distinguish levels such as 'phonetic' (representation of sounds actually occurring in a language), and 'phonemic' (representations of sound classes that are significantly contrasted with one another). Language scholars also use 'transcription' to refer to rewriting from one system into another; more precise terms are 'transliteration' for letter-by-letter substitution between alphabetic scripts, or 'orthographic transcription' to encompass both alphabetic and non-alphabetic scripts, as in the romanization of Chinese texts.

Similar uses in ethnomusicology, as in the attempts by 19th-century Orientalists or the present-day neo-philological school of historical ethnomusicology (*see* 'Historical Ethnomusicology') to substitute notation symbols between systems without reference to actually performed sounds, could perhaps be considered cases of musical transliteration, transorthography, or transnotation.

The growth of transcription

The tradition of ethnomusicological transcription can be traced to a single line of methodological and intellectual development deriving from key figures such as Alexander J. Ellis (1814–90), Carl Stumpf (1848–1936), and Erich M. von Hornbostel (1877–1935) around the turn of the 20th century. Beyond this period, the roots of transcription can be traced to earlier times, ideas, and practices.

ACQUISITION, UNIVERSALISM, CULTURAL HUMANISM, AND ORIENTALISM Historical writings and oral traditions of various cultures tell of travellers who journeyed abroad and wrote down the music they heard for audiences at home: Kukai of Japan went to China, and Rin chen Bzang po of Tibet journeyed to India. The traditions concerning them are uncertain; but, if they actually transcribed music in their travels, they did so for the prescriptive purpose of fostering change and acculturation in their own countries. Nevertheless, their efforts began with descriptive notations, and are important as early applications of written notations to the problems of cross-cultural musical communication.

European transcription grew out of other motivations, chiefly the acquisitiveness of the early European explorers. The discoverers and conquistadors of Europe carried back not only gold and jewels, but also musical instruments, notations, music theory writings and sometimes even musicians. Some also practised a form of symbolic appropriation. Just as later tourists would 'take' pictures of foreign scenes, European explorers would sketch and paint the cities and ceremonies they could not carry off on their ships; and a few began to sketch the music they heard in the graphic imagery of musical notation. Early examples are shown in Frank Harrison's *Time, Place, and Music* (1973).

Transcriptions thus began as a medium for capturing and preserving exotic sensory experiences. They were written in European notation because this was the only technology available, not for any 'scientific' reasons. However, like the golden religious images and cultural artefacts that later found their way from private hoards into museums, musical artefacts including transcriptions soon were to find scientific applications.

European scholars of the Renaissance and Enlightenment had begun the search for 'laws of nature' to replace or supplement earlier concepts of a divine law, and music played a part in the search because of its perceived relation to mathematics, physics and cultural evolution. Marin Mersenne (1588–1648), a philosopher and mathematician, developed an analysis of the mathematical relationships of musical intervals in an attempt to prove by mathematical

(a)

(b)

1. Transcriptions of songs of (a) Canadian and (b) Brazilian (Tupinambo) Indians: from Mersenne, 'Harmonie Universelle' (1636–7). Neither transcription includes a time signature or barlines although the Brazilian example (b) uses barlines to separate the three songs

ratios that the intervals of the Greek diatonic scale were 'more natural' than other scales (1636–7). To support this proof, he introduced comparative transcriptions of the songs of Canadian and Brazilian Indians (1636–7, vol.ii, p.148; see fig.1).

Mersenne thus produced, by adapting transcriptions from two travellers, apparently the first example of a standardized comparative transcription system. He also introduced what may be the first example of a logical-analogical chain of reasoning that linked the sounds of nature, inanimate objects, animals, children and women with non-European people and their music; the implicit opposition to the sounds of culture, intelligent minds, humans, adults, males and European music would become all too typical of European scholarships as others tried to develop and extend Mersenne's physical-universalist approach to the 'laws' of culture and music. Physical universalism would develop into harmonic universalism as European music theorists gradually discovered the 'laws' of harmony.

Mersenne's paradigm formed the dominant basis for European cross-cultural musical thought for the next two centuries. An alternative viewpoint and transcriptional paradigm emerged in the work of the philosopher Jean-Jacques Rousseau (1712–78). Rousseau maintained that music was not natural, but cultural, and that its effects were due not to sounds but to 'music . . . as a commemorative sign' (1768, p.315). Arguing that members of various cultures would react differently to 'the diverse musical accents of [diverse] peoples', he included transcriptions of Chinese, Persian, American Indian, and Swiss songs (fig.2).

To facilitate comparison, he devised a standard system into which he transnotated all his examples, as Mersenne had done. While Mersenne's system was designed to highlight similarities in support of a theory of physical universalism, Rousseau's had the opposite intent of displaying musical diversities in support of a theory of cultural humanism. For Rousseau, the basic facts of music arose from cultural diversity, and its essence lay not in the physics of sound, but in 'the greatest effects of sounds on the human heart' (p.315).

Harmonic universalism stimulated considerable interest in Chinese music, with its perceived resemblances to 'Pythagorean' theory in Greek music. This interest gave impetus to the translation of Asian music theory texts by Orientalist scholars, often language scholars who had never heard the music in question, and usually of texts dating from ancient music no living person had heard. Nevertheless, Orientalist scholarship encouraged the study of non-European musical concepts and viewpoints in non-derogatory, and often positive, terms; and in some cases was linked with field investigations of musical practice.

Thus, Joseph Amiot (1718–93) introduced descriptions and illustrations of Chinese instruments and performances observed during his 27 years in China, along with an apparent transcription of a Confucian hymn (1779, pp.27f., 176–85). William Jones (1746–94) may have anticipated his own discovery of the Indo-European language family, laying the foundations of comparative linguistics, by his comparison of the features of Indian, Greek, and Persian music (1792, p.135f). Jones was apparently first to suggest that Europeans might learn to perform the music they studied abroad, and showed the importance of field observations of musical practice by pointing out that intervals actually played by Indian musicians seemed closer to a scale of 12

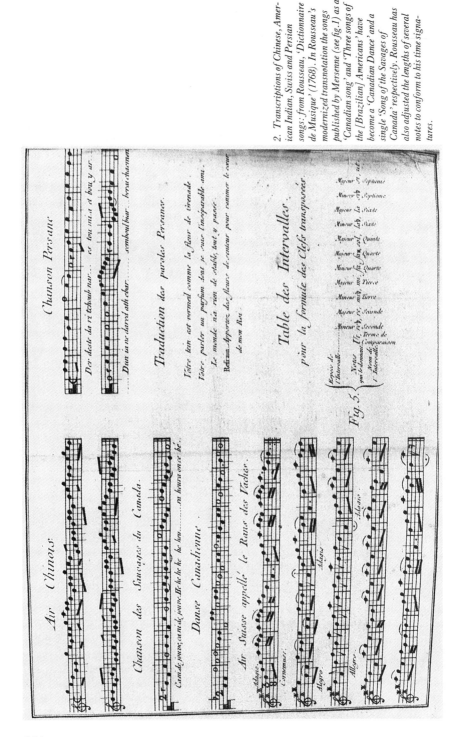

2. Transcriptions of Chinese, American Indian, Swiss and Persian songs: from Rousseau, 'Dictionnaire de Musique' (1768). In Rousseau's modernized transnotation the songs published by Mersenne (see fig.1) as a 'Canadian song' and 'Three songs of the [Brazilian] Americans' have become a 'Canadian Dance' and a single 'Song of the Savages of Canada' respectively. Rousseau has also adjusted the lengths of several notes to conform to his time signatures.

semitones than to the ancient theoretical 22-*śruti* (microtone) system (pp.141–2). Even though some Orientalists emphasized texts to the virtual exclusion of practice, their work as a whole set a precedent of control against Eurocentric speculative views, and later objectivist scholars like Ellis and Hornbostel took the precedent into account in their work on scales and transcription.

TONOMETRY, MUSICIANSHIP AND ETHNOCENTRISM Rousseau had remarked on his comparative transcriptions: 'One will find in all these pieces a conformity of style with our music, which might give rise to admiration in some for the goodness and universality of our rules, and perhaps render suspect to others the intelligence or the accuracy of those who have transmitted these melodies to us' (1768, p.314). The point of accuracy was immediately addressed by Francis Fowke in his study on the Indian *vīṇā* (chordophone): 'You may absolutely depend upon the accuracy of all that I have said . . . It has been done by measurement: and with regard to the intervals, I would not depend upon my ear, but had the *been* [*vīṇā*] tuned to the harpsichord, and compared the instruments carefully, note-by-note, more than once' (1788, pp.193–4). Others quickly followed suit; a friend of Jones reported that Indian and European scales were the same 'when the voice of a native singer was in tune with his harpsichord'; and Dr William Crotch reported that the keys of the Javanese gamelan were in accurate, even 'perfect', intonation compared with the black keys of the piano (Crawfurd, 1820, pp.302, 300). Piano tonometry had the appeal of a hardware-based technological solution to the scale question, and it dominated 19th-century research even after the post-Helmholtz (1863) development of more specialized and accurate tonometric devices (listed in Ellis, 1880, p.16f; Hornbostel and Abraham, 1909, p.18).

Piano tonometry led equally to such important discoveries as the pentatonic scale (Engel, 1864, pp.12–15), and to such misconceptions as the 'latent harmony' theory of Alice Cunningham Fletcher (1838–1923) and John Comfort Fillmore (1843–98). While scientific measurement depends on the use of arbitrary but consistent scales, a standard technically met by the European 12-semitone keyboard, its use was linked to standards of musicianship that imposed a European conceptual system on the music it was used to measure. And European musicians of the period seemed able to assert either identity or difference among scales with the same degree of confidence, and with an equal chance of being right or wrong.

Doubts quickly arose concerning the reliability of exclusively European musical concepts and tools. At the start of the 19th century, Hinrich Lichtenstein warned readers that his transcription of a Khoikhoi ('Hottentot') song was 'approximate' because its intervals 'do not lie in our diatonic scale, but form entirely foreign intervals' which seem to hover between major and minor (1811, vol.ii, pp.378–80, 550–51).

Guillaume-André Villoteau (1759–1839) may have been first to devise special symbols to overcome the 'defects' of Western notation for rendering intervals (1826, pp.41–2). Through the complaints of his Egyptian teacher Villoteau discovered in the course of his pioneering experiment in musical performance study that he had transcribed and performed incorrectly using his European preconceptions (pp.133–5; see fig.3).

Villoteau determined the interval divisions he needed to represent in transcription by studying the frets of Egyptian chordophones and arrived at a figure of about 1/3 tone, a figure that brought him into conflict with Orientalist scholars and led to partial discrediting of his work (Ellis, 1885, p.495). His method of performance study would later be rediscovered by Theodore Baker (1854–1928) and Alice Fletcher, and used to support questionable theories.

Other writers questioned the usefulness of European standards of measurement, notation and universalist assumptions (Lay, 1841, p.81; Kiesewetter, 1842, p.78; Nell, 1856–8, p.201; Day, 1891, p.40). The German musicologist Carl Engel (1818–82) suggested that European transcribers 'considered anything which appeared defective to the unaccustomed European ear as accidental mistakes . . . [and may] have taken the liberty of making alterations which they deemed improvements' (1864, p.134). He complained that the frequent practice of adding piano accompaniments to transcriptions 'obscures its characteristics' and gave 'a ludicrous impression' (1879, p.6). James Davies went so far as to devise a graduated monochord for tonometric studies which convinced him that Maori scales were non-diatonic, and he devised special signs to show quarter-tone differences from European notes in his transcriptions (1854, pp.239–40; see fig.4).

Behind this seemingly esoteric fixation on minute details lies a revolutionary development: Europeans were beginning to discover music as it existed in the

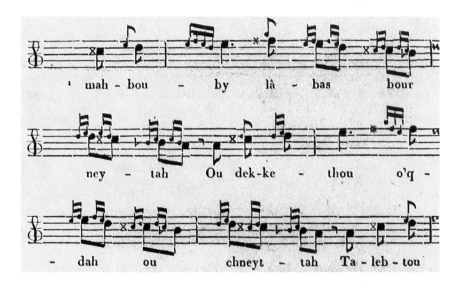

3. *Transcription of an Egyptian song: from Villoteau, 'De l'état actuel de l'art musical en Egypte' (1826). Villoteau may have been the first to devise special symbols to overcome the 'defects' of Western notation: the triangular flat sign used with the note B throughout this example indicates flattening by 1/3-tone; the rounded 'normal' flat sign (♭, not used in this example) indicates 2/3-tone flattening. The signs X (on C throughout the example and F, first line) and ✕ (on F, second line) indicate sharpening by 1/3- and 2/3-tones respectively.*

4. *Transcription of a Maori song: from Davies, 'Appendix: On Native Songs of New Zealand' (1854) in which he uses special signs to show quarter-tone differences from European notes (e.g. the flat signs with displaced ledger lines used everywhere except in the 'normal' flats in the middle of the last two lines)*

real world of cultural diversity, rather than as imagined and misperceived through the constrictions of their own localized practices and theories. A solid scholarly tradition was forming that, towards the end of the 19th century, was developing a consensus that European concepts and methods, including transcription in European notation, gave an inadequate and misleading base for musical understanding. Writers such as Richard Wallaschek (1893, p.25) and Thomas Wilson (1898, p.515) discussed the problems of European notation, and Charles Wead (1902, pp.423, 438) gave a particularly clear analysis of how European notation gave rise to misperceptions of non-European music for 'a musically educated ear'. But the most sophisticated analysis of the problems of European notation was provided by the Indian scholar Sir Sourindro Mohun Tagore (1840–1914) (1874), a major intellectual figure in cross-cultural music studies, who influenced Ellis (1885, p.501; 1891, p.169f), Hornbostel and Abraham (1904, 'Phonographierte indische Melodien' p.119f), and others. Shuji Osawa in Japan was equally influential; and the growing importance of non-European viewpoints is seen by Ellis's reliance on musicians and informants from India, Java, China, Japan and Thailand, who contributed fundamental insights that helped Ellis interpret his tonometric data (1885).

The rapid advance in transcriptional methods and results in the late 19th century is sometimes attributed to increasing tonometric accuracy, but this was a minor factor. Tonometric advances alone could not have advanced transcription and the study of music, because tonometrically significant data were not necessarily regarded as musically significant. European musicians were able to misperceive and misevaluate the sounds they heard, even with pianos and monochords to provide an objective standard of measurement, until their basic musical assumptions and concepts were called into question, and a new level of cross-cultural musical awareness developed. This was achieved in two ways: by de-Europeanization, through the growing entry of non-European scholarship and viewpoints into the cross-cultural musical dialogue; and by de-musicalization, achieved by the participation of scholars other than professional musicians bound to the perspectives of European music. Anthropology and psychology contributed essential elements to the new musical consciousness, as did the intellectually powerful discipline of philology.

BOAS, STUMPF AND ELLIS Philological influence played a formative role in the development of a new perspective on cross-cultural music studies through the work of scholars such as Franz Boas, Carl Stumpf, and Alexander J. Ellis. At the end of the 19th century, philology was a prestigious discipline composed of the two branches of linguistic philology later to become linguistics and literary philology, or historical–comparative literary studies and criticism. Because of achievements such as the discovery of the Indo-European language family, the deciphering of unknown languages and texts, the reinterpretation of familiar texts such as the Bible, and the formulation of laws of linguistic relationship and change, it provided a compelling model for other disciplines; and it had a particular influence on the growth of intercultural studies in music and transcription.

Franz Boas (1858–1942), a professionally trained physicist, is well-known as the main force behind the development of American academic training in anthropology and as the leader of an anti-speculative, anti-reductionist approach that stressed ethnographic description over armchair theorizing. He is less well-known for his work in music, yet he was an enthusiastic musical performer, whose piano and organ playing was so much in demand that it sometimes conflicted with his fieldwork (Boas, 1969, pp.67f, pp.141–2), as well as a promoter of musical research, who encouraged anthropologists to record and study music, and who published over a hundred of his own transcriptions. Among his contributions to music are the discovery of complex rhythmic structures in Northwest Coast songs (1888, 'On Certain Songs and Dances', pp.51–2), an early study specifically devoted to music and culture change among urbanizing tribal peoples (1888, 'Chinook Songs'), and the first intentionally comparative publication of transcriptions of the same songs by different transcribers (1896, 1897). His theoretical interests in music included its role in discovering the processes and principles of culture change (1927, pp.299f, 1938, pp.589f), and its contribution to non-racist understanding of 'primitive' peoples (1889, p.626).

Boas began his philological studies in Berlin in the 1880s after returning from his first Inuit (Eskimo) fieldwork, and quickly recognized that linguistic transcriptions were strongly influenced by sounds expected and misperceived by fieldworkers on the basis of their European cultural conditioning (1889).

His studies brought him into contact with the ideas of the 'neogrammarians' (Robins, 2/1979, p.206), the dominant school of philology at the time, whose emphases included the study of living languages through empirical data and a disdain for speculative theorizing. Osthoff and Brugmann, two leaders of the school, wrote: 'Only that comparative linguist who forsakes the hypothesis-laden atmosphere of the workshop . . . and comes out into the clear light of tangible present-day actuality in order to obtain from this source information which vague theory cannot ever afford him, can arrive at a correct presentation' (quoted in Robins, 1979, pp.184–5). Carl Stumpf, after he and Boas had done collaborative, cross-cultural research in music, wrote: 'Every psychologist, every aesthetician, too, who works his way out of the sphere of influence of the scholar's study and self-observation in order to broaden his horizons through objective investigation of human thought and feelings in other times and places, sees rich tasks for himself here' (1901, p.133).

Stumpf had expressed the same basic idea in 1886: 'What . . . are most needed, are monographs independent of every theory, but with so much the greater conscientiousness of factual description' (p.405), written during collaborative research on a group of Northwest Coast Indians in Germany, with Boas working on philological–linguistic problems, and both Boas and Stumpf on music (Stumpf, 1886, p.408). Stumpf's published musical study included not only linguistic information but also transcriptions furnished by Boas; it was the first publication of transcriptions by both authors. The working relationship continued after Boas's move to North America by co-operation with Stumpf's students Hornbostel and Abraham (1906), and by the move of Hornbostel's student, George Herzog (1901–84), to work with Boas. The early collaboration and continuing relationship established what was in effect a single 'classical' tradition of intercultural music research with a common theoretical and methodological base.

Stumpf, working in Halle with the same visiting Indians Boas had worked with in Berlin, was the first to describe in detail the problems of transcription, beginning with his efforts to transcribe a performance:

> I could only put fragments down on paper, on the one hand because I am not a mighty musical stenographer, on the other hand because the communal dances, in which most steps are performed with both feet at the same time, the uninterrupted drum accompaniment and other circumstances (such as . . . the clapping of the jaws of the monstrous wooden masks . . . the constantly swung rattle of the medicine man) interfered . . . During these proceedings one had, above all, the impression of a heathen uproar, a true devil's music, in the midst of which only here and there distinct tones were drifting by (1886, p.406).

Stumpf's solution was that of a laboratory psychologist – to control complex variables by decontextualizing part of the music for isolated, dissected analytic study. This methodology, despite its potential for musical and cultural distortion, was followed by many later researchers, and Stumpf provides a description of its application that will seem largely familiar even to transcribers working with recordings a century later:

> Nuskilusta now sang for me, softly and . . . unfortunately however not very clearly . . . during four days for 1–2 hours each. I listened first to each melody

119

without writing anything down, in order to receive a certain impression of the melodic and rhythmic construction, but especially to recognize how the notation should be started, whether to write the whole in c major or a minor. For if one begins arbitrarily or with the absolute pitch of the initial tone, then one risks having to continuously insert more sharp and flat signs. Then I wrote, from the second until about the fourth attempt, only the note heads without any durational and rhythmic signs. With an ordinary melody of new music it would create no difficulties for me . . . Here, though, it required repeated new beginnings until the notehead-scaffolding of the collective succession of tones stood in the desired tonality. Then I had the beginning of the melody sung and wrote it, this time from memory, with all its associated duration and rhythm signs. In order to produce the continuation, Nuskilusta had to start over and over again from the beginning; [he] did this, however, with inexhaustible goodwill. And so was accomplished the notation of a song after singing ten times and more, which then on the following day, when something new had come up, would still be subjected to even more controls . . .

Now these experiences awaken in me some mistrust towards the so clear-standing notations of the travellers, who make no mention whatever of the difficulties of transcription . . . Very unclear intervals emerged, according to our conceptions. These were, however, not all simply accidental deviations; one would appear again and again in the same place, and would also be intoned in the same way by Nuskilusta's substitute. The difficulties of notation would be so significantly heightened by such occurrences that one is always tempted at first to perceive a mere accidental alteration and to hear one or another of our intervals in it (1886, pp.406–8).

Stumpf, prevented by language barriers from satisfactory communication with Nuskilusta, resorted to the philological discovery procedure of comparison of parallels and variants to establish musical intention. The procedure would become a basic element of Hornbostel's paradigm; and for Stumpf, it led to the identification of intervals clearly different from those of European scales, and thus not clearly expressible in European notation. Stumpf notated these by diacritical modifying signs (+ for microtonal pitch raising, O for lowering) as had Villoteau for Arabic pitches; but their precise value was unclear until a new advance was made by a professional philologist.

This breakthrough was achieved by Alexander J. Ellis, who effectively demolished harmonic universalism by a study of non-European scales. Ellis produced mathematically precise descriptions of such obviously non-diatonic, non-harmonic scales as the near-equidistant 5-tone Javanese *slendro* and the equidistant 7-tone Thai scales, along with others from Europe, Africa, Oceania, and parts of Asia (1885). He achieved his success through precise measuring tools – his own 'software' – the invention of the cents system, which divided the semitone into 100 equal cents for precise quantification. His conclusion is well-known to ethnomusicologists: 'the Musical Scale is not one, not "natural", nor even founded necessarily on the laws of the constitution of musical sound . . . but very diverse, very artificial, and very capricious' (1885, p.526). Ellis followed this conclusion with the prediction that further progress would depend on 'physicists who have some notion of music, rather than of musicians whose ears are trained to particular systems' (1885, pp.526–7).

Indeed, within 15 years, Charles Wead (1902) completed a study of instrument scales that Hornbostel (1905, p.258) took as proof that some aspects of music are organized by 'extramusical' (*aussermusikalische*) principles, a concept that proved highly influential later.

120

Philological influences underlie Ellis's work with scales. His philological speciality was the transcription of linguistic sounds, practically directed towards efforts at spelling reform, and motivated by political convictions that traditional spelling formed a tool for the oppression of lower classes by creating barriers to achieving literacy and socio-economic advancement (Albright, 1958, p.18f). These motives led to compromises that sacrificed scientific phonetic accuracy to political expediency, and resulted in rejection of his transcription system by other linguists, leaving him somewhat disillusioned (p.20f). His work, which led to the discovery of the phoneme and creation of the International Phonetic Alphabet, was centred on the 'broad' transcription of significant classes of sounds by slight modifications to conventional alphabets, rather than on 'narrow' transcriptions of every detail of sound occurring in a language. His invention of the cents system reflects a 'broad' approach that created diacritical modifiers (cents figures) which permitted retention of a conventional European musical 'alphabet' of pitch and interval designations (G♯, 3rd) – and, by implication, of transcription in cents-modified conventional European notation, rather than 'narrowly' precise and musically meaningless physical representation by vibration frequencies and ratios. He seems to have intended further 'broadening' of his system by giving many of his scales in a 'tempered form in quartertones' rounded off to the nearest 50 cents, a standard of accuracy effectively adopted by Hornbostel and other later transcribers who used signs such as + and − to indicate one level of pitch difference between the European semitones. However, the attempt to round scales off to 50-cent levels failed when confronted with scales such as the Thai 7-tone equidistant with its 171.4-cent intervals. The failure seems to have been taken more as encouragement than disillusionment; and if Ellis's self-assessment of his work in philology has the sense of a 'pathetic confession' (Albright, 1958, p.20), the final sentence of his scale study is more positive: 'At my time of life I must feel satisfied with having shown that such an investigation is possible' (1885, p.527).

20th-century transcription: the Hornbostel paradigm

The new century arrived with a controversy that opposed old and new approaches in a classic struggle of thesis against antithesis, out of which Erich M. von Hornbostel, assisted by Otto Abraham, would create a new synthesis for the transcription and study of music.

The thesis that established the context and terms of discussion, deriving from Mersenne's physical universalism, held that music was the product of natural laws leading to the evolution of Western harmonies. It had not only stimulated harmonic-evolutionist studies of non-European music, but had given rise to the harmonized transcriptions that Engel found misleading and 'ludicrous'. The work of Helmholtz (1863) had seemed to lend new objective scientific support to harmonic universalism, which was given a new injection of vitality through fieldwork experiences and theories derived from them by Alice Fletcher and John Comfort Fillmore.

Fletcher, who used participation in musical performance as part of her research methodology with the Omaha Indians, was aware of the problems of Euro-American cultural conditioning. She described (1893, p.237f) how performance experience had helped her to 'listen below the noise' of first impressions, and noted that her transcriptions of Omaha music in a single melodic line did not reproduce the richness of harmonic overtones of choral performances, nor did piano playback of such transcriptions produce results the Indians recognized or accepted as musical. She found the Indians more willing to accept harmonized piano playback, and might have produced an interesting early example of applied ethnomusicology and acculturation had she simply treated the case as an experiment. However, she chose to regard it as an interdisciplinary problem requiring professional expertise in European music, and sent a transcription to Fillmore for his advice.

Fillmore (1893, 'Report on the Structural Peculiarities') harmonized the transcription and returned it to Fletcher for further experiments with the Indians; the results were so successful that Fletcher published nearly all the transcriptions in her *Study of Omaha Indian Music* (1893) with harmonizations by Fillmore, together with his essay on his discovery of the 'latent sense of harmony' revealed by the transcriptions. By the time of publication, Fillmore had done fieldwork and recordings of his own and in co-operation with Boas, producing a series of publications in which he expanded on the theory of latent harmony and the 'natural and universal law . . . that all folk music runs on chord-lines' (1899, p.311). His descriptions of his transcription methods (1893, 'A Woman's Song', 1895) show an imitation of Fletcher's piano-feedback technique and a patronizing attitude towards the 'dim perceptions' of 'the primitive mind' (1895, pp.287–8). He took the radical position that what the Indians actually sang 'is a matter of comparatively little importance. The really important question is what tone they *meant* to sing' (1895, p.288).

5. Transcription of an American Indian song: from Fillmore, 'The Harmonic Structure of Indian Music' (1899). The transcription includes a melodic line with intervals adjusted to the piano, and piano accompaniments that add pitches required for the 'implied harmony' (e.g. the D-sharps in the middle line)

His transcriptions (fig.5) include a melodic line rendered more or less as the Indians sang it, but with intervals adjusted to the piano, and piano accompaniments that add pitches missing from pentatonic melodic lines, but which were required for the 'implied' harmony (for instance the D♯s in the middle line of fig.5); and sometimes piano imitations of drumbeat patterns were added as well. The harmonic manipulations required for some melodies employed such complex modulations of key that Fillmore concluded the harmonic sense of the Indians was equal only to the latest phase of European Romantic music (1893, 'A Woman's Song', p.62).

Fillmore's theories were initially accepted by Boas (1894) and Frances Densmore (1906), but quickly rejected by both. Boas (1969, pp.178–9) developed doubts about the accuracy of Fillmore's transcriptions and later specifically rejected Fillmore's approach (1927, p.342). Densmore, finding by cumulative statistical studies (1910, 1913, 1918) that relatively few Indian songs could even conjecturally be considered harmonic, and influenced by Wead's opposition (Densmore, 1942, pp.113–14), moved towards less Eurocentric views, and likewise repudiated Fillmore's theory (1927, pp.82–4). Even Fletcher, who supported Fillmore until his death (Fillmore, 1899), abandoned the use of harmonization in her remarkable structural-symbolic study of the Pawnee Hako ritual (1904), devoting her transcriptional energies to 'diagrams of time' which correlated rhythmic structures to cosmological concepts and ritual choreography.

The strongest form of the antithesis to Fillmore's approach was argued by Benjamin Ives Gilman, a Harvard music psychologist, who said that a supposition such as Fillmore's theory of harmonic modulation 'involves an intricacy of musical thought hitherto unknown even in modern European music, and not easily credible of any' (1908, p.11). Gilman sought to eliminate the apperceptive illusion of tones 'continually sounding in the fancy of the European observer' (1908, p.8) from his transcriptions of Zuñi (1891) and Hopi (1908) songs, by distinguishing between transcription as a 'theory of observations' reconstructed from repeated performances and as 'facts of observation' in a recording of a single performance (1908, pp.26–7). In so doing, he discovered the distinction that Charles Seeger would later call the difference between prescriptive and descriptive music-writing:

> The step taken is no other than that separating the indicative from the imperative mood, the real from the ideal. Written music as otherwise known is not a record of occurrence but of purpose . . . [My] Zuñi notations . . . gave memoranda of observation . . . The present notations record similar facts . . . Compared with the customary writing of music, these again are as annals [of a country's history] to laws, as a ship's log to its sailing directions (Gilman, 1908, pp.8–9).

Gilman also anticipated Seeger in suggesting that automatic mechanical–graphic transcriptions might provide more objective and accurate 'indicative' notations. He juxtaposed conventional European-notation transcriptions, of songs 'as noted' according to European-conditioned first impressions, with transcriptions of the same songs 'as observed' by tonometric measurement, notated on a complex equidistant quarter-tone 'staff' expanded up to 45 lines, and accompanied by line graphs comparing melodic motion patterns in the 'noted' and 'observed' transcriptions (fig.6).

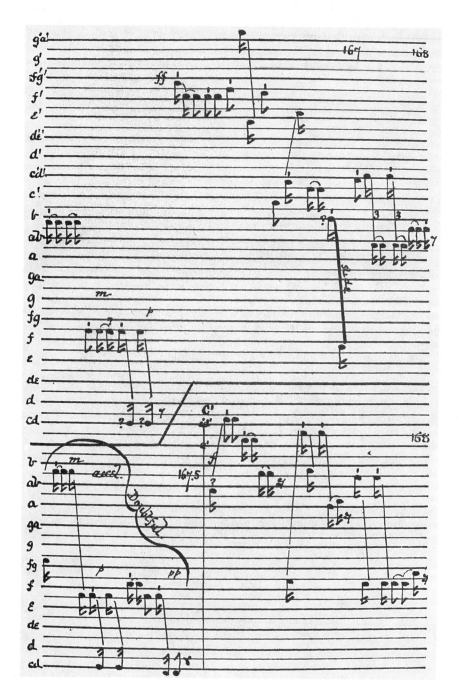

6. Graphic transcription of a Hopi song: from Gilman, 'Hopi Songs' (1908)

He concluded that Pueblo songs 'had no scale' of fixed, precisely determined intervals, but rather embodied a cultural emphasis on freedom (1908, p.14), a conclusion later adopted or substantially paralleled by researchers such as Hornbostel (1928, pp.32–3), Densmore (1929, p.276), Herzog (1936, pp.286–7), and List (1987) in regard to American Indian and other tribal vocal musics. To drive the point home, Gilman took the audacious step of juxtaposing one of his transcriptions with an astronomical star chart superimposed on a diatonic scale to show how well it approximated the diatonic intervals the Indians supposedly 'meant to sing'. Hornbostel and Abraham did not respond to this; but they immediately responded to other aspects of Gilman's approach with their *Proposals for the Transcription of Exotic Melodies* (1909).

THE HORNBOSTEL PARADIGM Hornbostel and Abraham faced the apparent paradox that Fillmore's transcriptions were musically clear and comprehensible but distorted musical truth, while Gilman's were precise and objective, but obscured musicality by their complexity. Their solution was 'a compromise between fluent legibility and objective precision' (1909, p.2) that incorporated aspects of both approaches into a redefined synthesis. Their approach was objectivist in that it proceeded from observation of recorded performances, but it departed from objectivism in two ways: by stressing the importance of musical intent, and by giving a special value to the musical 'impressions' of the transcriber, which in some cases might even override considerations of objective measurement (1909, p.5).

The key to the synthesis was to treat transcription as a tool for discovery of musical intent, assumed to be unknown to the transcriber (as it often was, due to the prevalence of 'armchair' transcriptions of music recorded in the field by others), to be discovered not by speculative theorizing, but by judicious objectivity and a 'music-philological' discovery procedure (1909, p.5f). This procedure, already suggested and put into limited use by Stumpf (1901) and Gilman (1908), was the standard literary-philological method of comparing textual parallels and variants to eliminate unclarities and mistakes, and thus to establish the intent of the author(s)/compiler(s). Applied to music, it required the sounds of a recording to be treated as a 'text' to which similar procedures might be applied.

Philology provided a positive model for development of a comparative method in musical studies (Hornbostel and Abraham, 1904, 'Über die Bedeutung', p.185), pointing the way to a science of 'comparative musicology'. However, it also provided a negative model in its profusion of unstandardized and confusing linguistic transcription systems (1909, p.1). Both models are partly misleading. On the one hand, the apparent unity of the positive model was soon to dissolve into separate disciplinary approaches to language and literature, while Hornbostel's paradigm remained dependent on, and partially confused by, features of both approaches. On the other hand, a standard transcription system had been devised 20 years earlier, and this International Phonetic Alphabet (IPA) became a *de facto* standard followed more or less closely by the majority of 20th-century linguists. Rather than trying to compile another recipe list of transcription techniques, as some later writers tried to do, Hornbostel and Abraham's goal was nothing less than the creation of a musical IPA, an International Phonetic Alphabet for the standardized representation of musical sounds in comparative musicology.

In fact Hornbostel and Abraham were hardly less successful than the linguists in achieving their goal. Like the IPA, their system was accepted in its main outlines and used by a majority of 20th-century transcribers. Nevertheless, the parallel and the success are somewhat misleading. Hornbostel and Abraham chose a modified standard European symbol system as the basis of their approach, thus adopting the 'script' of a single musical language, in contrast to the IPA's Roman alphabet, which had long served as the script of distinct and mutually unintelligible languages. Multicultural perspectives and controls were built into the foundation of the IPA, but were excluded from Hornbostel–Abraham transcriptions. Sounds foreign to their system had to be adjusted to its representational logic. Hornbostel and Abraham's choice meant that their comparative standard would not itself be subjected to comparison and testing, and that musics of other cultures would be measured against European standards less obviously prejudicial, but just as pervasively reductionist, as Fillmore's harmonic analyses.

And yet, the system worked quite well in the hands of culturally sensitive users – due in part to the skill of those who used it, and in part to the fact that many musically derived principles of representation used in European notation (e.g. contrasting discrete pitch and interval relationships, proportional rhythmic organization) are widely applicable to many musics. The partial success of the system can be seen in Hornbostel and Abraham's treatment of Indian rhythms (1904, 'Phonographierte indische Melodien', pp.169–79), where objectivist European-notation transcription and philological discovery procedures led them to the 'conjecture, that the Indians put larger periods together into a unit' (p.178). The 'conjecture' was confirmed by Charles Russell Day's fieldwork-derived explanation of tala, which provided a clearer and more fundamental musical insight than any objectivist discovery procedure attained. It is no wonder that Hornbostel and Abraham, having outlined their transcription system, opened their concluding discussion on techniques by recommending that the best technique would be to learn how to perform the music by lessons from a master musician of the culture concerned (1909, pp.15–16). Although no one transcription could illustrate all their points, fig.7 shows the application of Hornbostel and Abraham's 'Proposals for the Transcription of Exotic Melodies' (1909).

OUTLINE OF HORNBOSTEL AND ABRAHAM'S 'PROPOSALS' Transcription is needed to realize profits from the growing stock of recordings, to provide guidelines for field collectors, for study and communicating music to others. Unified methodology is needed for comparisons and for universal theories. European notation must be modified and supplemented.

(*a*) Choice of tone-script

1. *General aspects*: Notation changes must reproduce music faithfully and not distort usual notation. To avoid expense, limit changes and use simple forms which are easily produced and do not distract attention of reader. New forms should be meaningful and derived from usual ones, so they are easy to learn and retain in memory. Use signs to enable readers to imagine an overall melodic impression. Do not overburden with diacritical signs at the cost of clarity; constant features can be described in accompanying text.

126

7. *Transcriptions of American Indian songs from British Columbia: from Hornbostel and Abraham, 'Phonographierte Indianermelodien aus Britisch-Columbia' (1906) illustrating many of the standard transcription techniques proposed in their 'Proposals for the Transcription of Exotic Melodies' (1909).*

2. *Pitch*: (i) LINE SYSTEM [STAFF]. Retain usual five-line system. Do not use extra lines inserted between staff lines (intensive modification) or added outside staff (extensive modification); Gilman's use of these is impossible to read. Bringing note heads closer to upper or lower lines (Gilman) only works in equidistant staff, and is time-consuming and expensive. For one-tone rhythmic accompaniment, write beats

127

without ledger lines below system; with two-three pitches/sound colours, use one line below system with notes on, above, or below. In graphs, pitch should always be the vertical axis and time the horizontal. Since right angles suggest jerky movement and vertical lines have no time value, better to lay out pitches in spacing corresponding to time value, connected by diagonal lines. Graphs should only represent overall picture, not reproduce every moment. Transcription in staff notation also is needed to establish psychologically significant melodic impression of author. (ii) CLEFS: Restrict number; in most cases, get along with treble clef and show higher or deeper octaves by 8ᵃ, etc. Tenor clefs superfluous; use bass clef only for polyphony and antiphonal song; combinations of several treble clefs for different octaves confuse readers accustomed to piano keyboard. (iii) ACCIDENTALS: Should know absolute pitches, but not always show in notation. To simplify, transpose into key with few accidentals. Not necessary to use same principal tone for all melodies, nor always transpose to key with fewest accidentals. Principal tone c often grounded in scale written with many accidentals. Best to choose neighbouring 'key' (e.g. G instead of A♭, F instead of F♯). Original pitches can be given in text. Primary purpose of the notated image, evoking an acoustic image, requires legibility and recognizability of significant intervals such as 5th and 4th. Hence, close connection with European use of accidentals recommended. Avoid signs for double raising and lowering. For regularly recurring accidentals, use key signature. Never write accidental signs for tones which do not actually occur in melody. For tones which can appear in two octave positions (e and f in treble clef), set accidentals where they correspond to tones that actually occur. For tones which fall between half-tones, write nearest note with + or − above staff. Decision to write next lower or higher tone not exclusively by pitch measurement, but more importantly, music–philological comparisons of parallelisms, subjective impressions, etc, must be considered. If needed, give numbers of vibration cycles. If pitch raisings (lowerings) occasional, notate at appropriate places. For constant occurrence, +(−) can be placed with accidentals in key signature. If accidental exists in signature, place +(−) above the accidental; otherwise put corresponding note in signature as stemless (black) note head with +(−) above, before other accidental signs. (iv) INDETERMINATE PITCHES: If faulty phonogram (scratches, distortions, etc), set ? over note. For very short, weak, or rough tones, set note head in (). If entirely unclear, give rhythm in headless notes [stems and flags]. Wherever possible, philologically reconstruct by comparing parallel usages; show such conjectures by square-bracketing of note head.

3. *Performance practice*: Includes phrasing and tone colour. Both so important for non-European peoples that they deserve special attention and accurate notation. European notation especially poor for this; special signs needed. (i) PHRASING: [Special signs shown in table for text phrasing, staccato/legato/glissando, movement between pitches, pulsation, tremolo, parlando, and audible inhalation.] Other verbal descriptions ('excitedly') abbreviated in words over system or described in accompanying text. (ii) TONE COLOUR: Although very important, almost all descriptions either based on tone source ('trumpetlike') or borrowed from other sense realms ('sharp'). Recommendations: ° for falsetto, natural wind instrument tones, gong strokes, etc. For more special tone colours, put ˣ or other letters over note. Drum rim strokes and strokes in middle of skin distinguished by upward and downward stems. Strokes with flat of hand and fingers shown by ° and ˆ over note, strokes with fingertips unmarked.

4. *Melisma*: Exact writing out is monstrously tedious; usually enough to notate in small notes of indeterminate value, so main melody emerges better. But danger of incomplete tone material if tones appear only in ornaments. Besides usual trill, mordent, etc, special signs given in chart.

5. *Dynamics*: Constant loudness levels given in text, not in notation. Loudness changes shown by *ppp, pp, p, mf, f, ff, fff,* close to where they belong, and under

system. Loudness level continues until new sign introduced. Increase and decrease shown by < and >, never by 'cresc., dim.'. Accents shown by ›: weak (›), medium ›, strong », always over the note. Rhythm (clapping, drumming) given as special voice below system. Sudden piano shown by p‹. [‹] shows accents derived from subjective rhythmic ordering that is objectively unclear.

6. *Rhythm*: Difficult because most complicated, and few clues to intention of musicians. Can follow these points: (i) dynamic accent (clapping, drum); (ii) similar melodic-rhythmic groups, not necessarily same length; (iii) similar numbers of time units. Division by equal 'beats' used only when agrees with first two points. Never follow pedantically: motives often appear augmented or diminished, and strict adherence to equal beat divisions can destroy picture of melodic groups. Decision primarily derived from philological comparison of repetitions and variants. Single groups divided by bar lines. Different possibilities can be shown by double notation or by short lines above system. Dotted bar lines for larger divisions. If no reasonable grouping, use bar lines only at section endings.

Use metric signature at beginning for constant rhythm pattern or constant alternation (3/4 + 2/4). Use 4/4 and 2/4 instead of ¢ or ¢. Bracketed signatures for uncertainty due to rhythmic freedom or exceptions. [Notation chart shows signs for changes, irregularities, and uncertainties.] Time values written in easiest understandable way. For two beats against prevailing three, duplets instead of triplets. Drum rhythms use only one note value; quarters or eighths, but not quarters plus eighths. Rests notated according to rhythmic units (e.g. no half rests for quarter-note beat pattern). For inference of subjective rhythm important to count out long rests to see if fit beat pattern or timeless. Rests philologically reconstructed are square bracketed; inadmissible if not so established. Short pauses without time value (break pauses) shown by ᵛ over system.

7. *Tempo*: Significant for characteristic expression and for instrument/singing techniques. Determine with metronome and give changes with metronome figures. Measure rhythmic places in free rhythm passages, and parenthesize metronome figure. Avoid 'allegro', etc because of vagueness. May use 'slower', 'faster' in free rhythm. Descriptions like 'March', etc, justified only if given by musicians or describe actual use. Special signs for small changes shown in chart. Anticipation or delay of one part against another shown by) and (above note.

8. *Structure*: Grouping of motives in greater periods. Use modified double bars (double dotted, dotted/solid, double solid) corresponding to importance of division. Setting melodic verse lines under one another is clear but expensive. Single sections and periods shown by letters above beginning of section: A, B, C, etc for major divisions, a, b, c, for minor. Variants shown by indices: A₁, A₂, etc, not A', A'', A''', and very first section as A₁, not A. If drum or accompaniment has different structure show by cursive or Greek letters. Repetitions shown by ‖, with number given. Reprises not written out, but indicated by letters. Use double bar only if real end of piece rather than of recording; otherwise end with 'etc', and begin with . . .

9. *Variants*: Minor variants can be given as small notes or in auxiliary system above main system. Very striking, extensive, frequent variants best noted in synoptic score with corresponding beats under each other (no carrying through of bar lines between staves). Short, isolated, but still striking variants notated as footnotes below. Usually suffices to give a frequently occurring variant as main melody; but also theoretically interesting to carefully show all variants. Comparisons show what is essential or how melody can change without losing characteristic form for performer. Avoid constructing melody-types out of parts of different variants. If recitation on one or two tones without interesting details, sketch with stemless notes, whole note for the most significant, stemless quarter for others.

10. *Polyphonic pieces*: For strong variation or isolated simultaneous tones, show both voices in one system with stems in different directions. Use score for continuous or

self-evident polyphony. Voices in unison or parallel octaves notated as one line. If impossible to follow all voices, show clear notes of uncertain voice by special notes (e.g. mensural notes). Double stops and chords shown by note heads on the same stem. For complicated polyphony, may notate composite melodic impression resulting from interplay of voices separately from main score.

11. *Song texts*: Melody affects text, and text alters melody. For tone languages, language–music tone relationships are special problem; melodic motives in many ways determined by text. Musical ethos doubtful other than through text. Give text transcription if possible. Ideal is phonetic transcription with philological commentary, word-by-word translation, and translation according to meaning or rhythmic translation. Not possible from recordings alone; phones altered in singing. Dictation of text by so-called primitives difficult because text never recited alone and can hardly be given without melody. Syllables unclear in recording parenthesized; those heard in recording but missing from text dictation set in square brackets. Long held-out vowels or sonants shown by ——— or – – –; word divisions according to phonetic [characteristics of recorded song]: La– – –mpe, lam– – –pe, lamp– – –e, etc.

12. *Title*: Use non-subjective designations: names given by musicians, functional categories ('Dance song'), indication of content, or beginning of text in original language or translation. Designation from presumed musical or literary ethos ('Melancholie') is unjustified. If none of these possible, give musical category (Chorus, Song, Flute solo), and also as subtitle. Translate and explain all indigenous names.

13. *Ordering of the notated materials*: Not easy even for European folk music. More difficult for exotic music since 'Major and minor', 'Tonic', etc not applicable. Recommended extramusical principles which allow musical–typological to emerge: (i) ethnologically according to people; cultural relationships more important than geographic, political, or somatic (racial); (ii) according to use or function: religion, war, etc; (iii) according to tone source: choral song, instrumental solo, etc; (iv) according to increasing musical complexity when first three impossible or meaningless, when a certain musical factor deserves special interest, or when further division is necessary with much material. Which musical factor is chosen (tone system, melody, rhythm, etc) decided by case.

(*b*) Techniques for transcribing: Phonograph generally used; if impossible, transcribe by ear, which also has advantages. Best to learn music to sing or play to satisfaction of natives. Critics must be musically gifted according to compatriots; make sure approval is not only politeness or disinterest. Safest way to know what is essential to them; their standpoint often varies from European. Demands great patience by teacher and student, unusual musical gifts, good melodic memory, much time and money.

Transcribing from recordings: (i) First listen without writing to gain overall impression. (ii) Adjust speed so not too fast to analyse or so slow that unity disappears. (iii) Try for definitive version from beginning, but beats and divisions only from finished transcription. If some passages unclear, begin with clear ones. Skip difficult passages; initial difficulties disappear with repetition. (iv) Interrupt unclear sounds to isolate them. (v) Listen to fast, complex parts at slower speed. (vi) Study complex rhythms at slow speed with help of a metronome, then control by listening again at normal speed. Rhythmic accompaniments and polyphonic parts should correlate to melody. May add voices progressively to those transcribed first, or transcribe all separately and then combine. (vii) If song text available, use as control for transcription. (viii) Control by repetition, preferably by a second observer, without seeing the first transcription. Not good to stop too long at a difficulty, which could create overall misconception; better to return after long break, and passage will seem completely different.

(*c*) [Tonometric] measurements: Description of apparatus and procedures. Graph ideal for precision. Copy recording to avoid damage to original.

(*d*) Calculations: Procedures for calculating (i) cents, (ii) mean values, and (iii) scales.

(*e*) Scale tables: *Clearest representation of scales is in notation*. All tone steps (including those extending beyond an octave) notated in ascending motion. Use decreasing time values to show relative importance of tones, beginning with whole note for main melodic tone and proceeding through half, quarter, etc, for decreasing importance.

Developments in Theory and Method

QUANTITY AND QUANTIFICATION. New developments quickly changed the situation that had given rise to the Hornbostel paradigm. As recordings accumulated in archives to the point where it became questionable whether they could or should all be transcribed, recordings also began to circulate commercially to the point where it was questionable whether transcription was preferable to the recorded sounds themselves as a way of communicating musical information. Nevertheless, transcriptions increased in quantity, in both Europe and America. In America, Frances Densmore's (1867–1957) development of a statistical-analytic approach to transcription (1910, 1913, 1918) provided a stimulus for producing large quantities of transcriptions which could then be subjected to quantitative analysis. This approach, rationalized as a search for 'adequate statistical samples', was further developed by American anthropologists such as George Herzog (1901–84), and culminated in the mid-century statistical-behaviourist approaches of Alan Merriam (1923–80) (Freeman and Merriam, 1956) and Alan Lomax (*b* 1915) (1968). In Europe, the quantitative stimulus came from compilation of folk songs into collections, sometimes called 'monuments' (*Denkmal*), which were appropriately monumental in scope, and developed into investigations of the 'genetic' relationships of songs. Like all genealogical projects, this required immense databases, in this case transcriptions.

The independent status maintained for music by both the Berlin and American anthropological branches of the tradition encouraged the growth and integrity of a separate discipline of cross-cultural music studies; but it maintained an artificial separation between acoustical and cultural aspects of music that would break down only with the emergence of a new paradigm. This paradigm, which emphasized field research that related musical sounds to elements of culture such as history, ideology and the conceptual and theoretical systems of the culture being studied, is strongly associated with the tradition of research in Indonesian gamelan music deriving from the work of the Dutch ethnomusicologist Jaap Kunst (1891– 1960). Its theoretical formulation emerged slowly over the later part of the century.

TECHNOLOGY AND TONOMETRY. Recording technology transformed transcription. Early experiments, such as James Mooney and John Philip Sousa's use of a disc recorder for American Indian transcriptions in the 1890s, and Stumpf's work with a magnetic band recorder in 1900, did not lead to replacement of the wax cylinder for most field recordings for several decades. However, recording and playback technology gradually advanced from cylinders to discs to wire to tape; and tape recorders developed refinements such as repeating loops, automatic repeat and memory functions, multiple-speed playback and tape log and linear time counters. Transcribers began to use audiovisual technology, first film and then video, to provide multisensory aids to transcription.

Gilman, the first transcriber to work with recordings, had predicted revolutionary implications for transcription and musical research (1908). Recordings of course have aided the accuracy of transcription, but they have also led to distortions. Some writers transcribed recording hum as instrument drones or songs recorded at the wrong speed as falsetto. Other distortions were deliberate. Densmore trained her singers to sing clearly for the phonograph. Many fieldworkers forced performers to shorten pieces, rearrange or drastically reduce the size of ensembles, and make other compromises to adjust to the limitations of recording technology at the time. Even when the initial limitations of microphoneless cylinder recordings were eliminated by improved technology, a 'studio' aesthetic had become so firmly established that a great deal of music continued to be recorded in forms considerably different from actual performances. The technology and aesthetics of 'ethnographic' film added a further temptation to rearrange musical reality to fit the technology and Euro-American theatrical tastes. To the extent that Hornbostel's paradigm is correct in treating music as a 'text' for philological analysis, it must be admitted that a certain amount of transcription and analysis has been done on works of ethnomusicological fiction.

Technological aids to tonometry and the measurement of rhythm (metronometry) have also developed in new directions. Linear time counters on tape recorders have provided relatively accurate automatic indexing, and video control tracks allow automatic timing to an accuracy of .033 of a second in American, and .04 of a second in European video systems. Gerhard Kubik (1965, 1972) and List (Stone, 1978) developed a 'silent transcription' method, using film frames to transcribe and analyse both time and pitch features of xylophone playing; and the transcriptional capabilities of computerized sampling were only beginning to be explored in the 1980s (e.g. Vaughn, 1988).

The monochord, a metal string stretched over a board or box with calibrated pitch scale, was still advocated by Kunst (1959); but, besides the many devices used by Ellis, Hornbostel, and others of the period (tuning forks, Appun's Tonometer, Reisetonometer), new technologies brought a trend towards electronic measurement. Stroboscopic tuners (Hood, 1966; Jones, 1970) were widely used for some time, but their accuracy was compromised by the time required for manual adjustments, limiting their transcriptional applications. By the mid-1970s, some transcribers were using automatic electronic tuners (Ellingson, '"*Don Rta Ddyangs Gsum*"', 1979) with a faster read-out time, which was further accelerated by a change from analogue to digital displays in the 1980s, but at the cost of legibility in fast melodic movement. Both stroboscopic and electronic tuners feature read-out in cents. Tonometric measurements in Hertz, despite a musical opacity that has been recognized since the work of Ellis and Hornbostel, were emphasized as late as some of Kunst's and Hood's publications in the 1950s and 1960s.

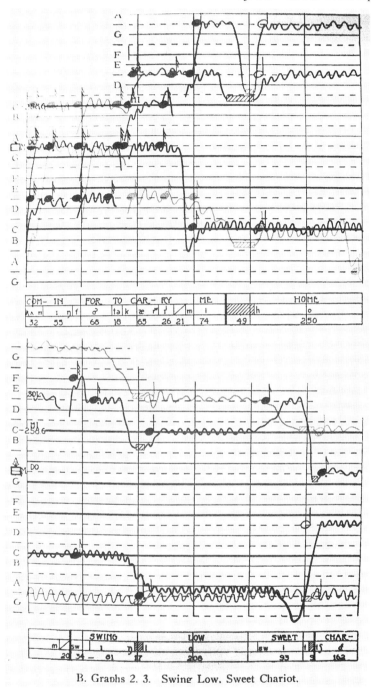

B. Graphs 2. 3.   Swing Low, Sweet Chariot.

*8. Part of a graphic transcription of the African-American song, 'Swing Low, Sweet Chariot',
produced by means of an autotranscription device: from Metfessel, 'Phonophotography in Folk
Music: American Negro Songs in New Notation' (1928).*

AUTOTRANSCRIPTION. Autotranscription machines, invented in the 1870s, had been applied to the study of singing and sound-producing instruments by the 1890s, and both Stumpf and Gilman had suggested their potential usefulness for cross-cultural music study. Pliny Earle Goddard (1906) was one of the first to try such an application. Densmore (1918) made another early experiment in autotranscription; and Milton Metfessel (1928) later used a more complex device for a study of African-American songs (fig.8). Other devices and applications were developed by the Norwegian Folk Music Institute (Gurvin, 1953; Dahlback, 1958) and by Cohen and Katz (1960). However, the most widely used of such devices was the melograph, developed by Charles Seeger (1951, 1958), which produced a simultaneous graph of pitch, amplitude, and overtone spectrum on 16mm film. The machine and its applications were explored in a special issue of *Selected Reports in Ethnomusicology* (1974). As the subjects of study and their accompanying transcriptions show, the melograph lends itself well to

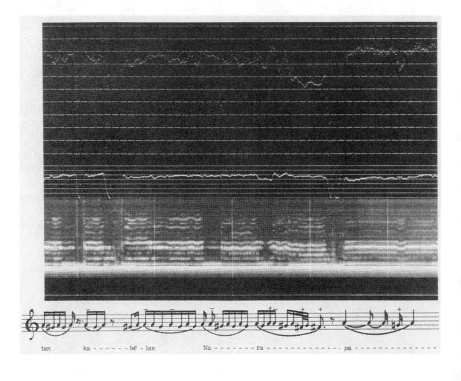

9. A melograph of a Javan 'macapat' song: from Hood, The Ethnomusicologist *(1971). The melograph shows pitch (upper portion: the dotted lines represent the chromatic intervals of Western tuning); amplitude (middle portion: the solid lines represent degrees of loudness in decibels) and overtone spectrum (bottom portion: indicating the spectrum of partials up to 5500 Hz and including at the bottom a reference grey scale as a standard for determining the intensity of each partial represented: the widely spaced vertical lines indicate lapsed time in one-second segments) on 16mm film. The complexity of trying to render these details in Western notation is shown below the melograph*

microanalysis of musical elements not easily explored in manual transcription (fig.9).

Despite their obvious microanalytic value, autotranscriptions produce a curious result of musicality submerged in a sea of acoustic detail, where essential musical illusions vanish into objective complexity and ambiguity. The informational inefficiency of complex detail, and such down-to-earth factors as the high cost and limited accessibility of autotranscription machines, may explain why the technology has not lived up to the dreams of its developers and advocates. Computerized transcription programs (e.g. Vaughn, 1988) hold a promise of further advances in autotranscription.

THEORETICAL ISSUES: PRESCRIPTIVE AND DESCRIPTIVE, 'PHONETIC' AND 'PHONEMIC'. Seeger initially characterized the difference between prescriptive and descriptive notations as the difference 'between a blueprint of how a specific piece of music shall be made to sound and a report of how a specific performance of any music actually did sound' (1958, p.168). He criticized transcriptions in Western notation for selective emphasis of features found in Western music, and for the expectation that readers who did not know the musical tradition should nevertheless be able to read them:

> The result can only be a conglomeration of structures part European, part non-European, connected by a movement 100 percent European. To such a riot of subjectivity it is presumptuous indeed to ascribe the designation 'scientific' (1958, p.170).

This challenge to the notational basis of Hornbostel's paradigm has evoked many theoretical responses, including an acceptance of the evaluation and a proposal of 'three solutions' advanced by Mantle Hood (*b* 1918). Hood suggests the 'Hipkins solution' (named after Ellis's collaborator Hipkins) of adapting the traditional notations of various cultures to their own musics; the 'Seeger solution' of the melograph; and the 'Laban solution' of developing a musical equivalent of Labanotation, a complex pictographic system of dance notation (1971, p.90f). Labanotation-derived systems have been applied to African rhythms by Pantaleoni and others (Serwadda and Pantaleoni, 1968). The linguistically derived contrast between 'phonetic' and 'phonemic' transcriptions has been widely used since the 1950s (e.g. Nettl, 1956, p.43), referring to the difference between more and less detailed transcriptions, and, also following an interpretation of Kenneth Pike's distinction of 'etic' and 'emic' approaches to culture, as the difference between outsider and insider perspectives (1954). Ellis's distinction between 'narrow' and 'broad' transcription is a more accurate label for the differences in detail that many ethnomusicologists take as 'phonetic' and 'phonemic'.

INDIVIDUAL DIFFERENCES AND SUBJECTIVITY. Boas's pioneering experiment in comparing transcriptions of the same music by different transcribers was repeated on a larger scale almost 70 years later by participants in the SEM 'Symposium on Transcription and Analysis' (1964). Collaborative transcription projects were also published by groups working in Japan (Koizumi and others, 1969) and France (Rouget, ed., 1981). Although these projects had different goals and used different methods, their collective result was to highlight factors of individual difference and subjectivity.

The SEM Symposium concentrated the efforts of four transcribers on a San (Bushman) song accompanied by the player on a musical bow, which produced plucked fundamentals and selectively reinforced overtones (fig.10).

The four transcriptions show not only the effects of individual differences, but also of theoretical considerations and analysis. The most obvious difference between the four is Robert Garfias's (G) use of a line graph for the voice. For the bow, Garfias shows only fundamentals, List (L) only overtones, and Rhodes (R) and Kolinski (K) show both. Differences in analytic viewpoints are even more interesting than differences in transcriptional form. Garfias adopted a culture-specific approach, while George List and Mieczyslaw Kolinski both proceed from universalist acoustically based

10. *Transcriptions by four ethnomusicologists of a San (Bushman) song with musical bow accompaniment (SEM 'Symposium on Transcription and Analysis', 1964)*

theories. Willard Rhodes, the most cautious, characterizes his transcription as 'broad'. List remarks, 'In transcribing a musical fabric as complex as [this], I should probably change my opinion concerning certain details on almost every hearing' (1987, p.253).

The Japanese group, regarding individual variation as detrimental to scientific objectivity, devised a complex methodology in which four recordings of the same song by the same performer were transcribed separately by three transcribers, and a composite transcription was synthesized from the resulting twelve transcriptions (Koizumi and others, 1969, pp.30–39, 49–57). An opposite approach was used by the French group (Rouget, ed., 1981), who demonstrated the range of possibilities that might appropriately be selected by different transcribers working with different musics; their results range from autotranscriptions (Mireille Helffer), to colour-coded pitch/tone contrasts (Pierre Salée), to complex structural displays, to simultaneous use of three transcription systems for the same music by the same transcriber (Hugo Zemp). All these projects, whatever their attitude towards the question of subjectivity, tended to emphasize it and to illustrate the debatable status of objectivist theories of transcription.

However, the limitations of subjectivity and difference, whether individual, cultural, or musical, were emphasized by a new controversy. James Reid (1977), influenced by Hood, attacked the use of Western notation, formulated a set of criteria for a more adequately cross-cultural transcription system, and devised a line graph system in which he transcribed a Japanese *hichiriki* (oboe) melody. This approach was criticized by Andreas Gutzwiller, who expressed 'fear that any transcriptional method that tries to deal with any conceivable analytical question in any conceivable musical style would turn out not to be a most desirable tool but a clumsy and deadly weapon . . . A transcription that tries to represent all audible facts ("the truth and nothing but the truth") is bound to fail from the outset' (1979, pp.104–6).

BREAKDOWN OF THE HORNBOSTEL PARADIGM. These developments suggest that the Hornbostel paradigm had begun to break down. Hornbostel himself in later years produced graphic representations of music based on theoretical rather than discovery models, some of which were so complex and obscure that a greater departure from the 'customary notation' standpoint of the *Proposals* is hard to imagine (1920, pp.322–33). Other challenges also developed with the shift of ethnomusicological interests from preoccupation with acoustic–technical features to music as a human and cultural phenomenon, from music considered as a product towards the investigation of process, and from almost exclusive emphasis on 'primitive music' and Oriental classical theory towards the study of a wide range of traditional and popular musics.

Transcription itself began to seem less relevant than other methodologies for investigating important ethnomusicological questions such as social, political, economic and symbolic factors in musical systems.

This weakening showed up in even such a basic element of Hornbostel's paradigm as the concept of scales. Despite the criticisms of Gilman in the *Proposals*, Hornbostel quickly came to accept Gilman's theory of 'no scale' in American Indian music (Hornbostel, 1913, p.23), and to generalize it as a theory of the scalelessness of vocal music in other parts of the world (1928, pp.34–5). He criticized music theorists for being ready 'to take scale instead of melodic structure for the primary element in music' (1928, p.37), and came to some interesting conclusions on notation (1913, pp.13–14):

> The unpsychological view that music assembles itself out of tones is reinforced by notation. It cuts off the work of art from its creators and performers and makes it into a thing, that one gives and takes like any other thing. It abstracts from the living momentary nuance that it can- not at all reproduce, or at least only from afar by strained circumscrip- tions . . . The script keeps the theory, of which it is the fallout, alive.

Herzog (1936, pp.286–7) also regarded intervals as transcriptional artefacts, and List, accepting Gilman's theory, transcribed Hopi songs in a 'pitch band notation' in which the staff positions 'represent a pitch band a whole tone in width rather than specific, discrete pitches' (1987, p.23).

The greatest upheaval in the conceptualization of scales came from another case – Southeast Asian scales. These had formed a vital part of Ellis's tonometric breakthrough, because the discovery and tonometric proof of intentional equidistant interval relationships in 5-tone Javanese *slendro* and 7-tone Thai scales had established not only the structural independence of non-European musical systems, but also their rationality. Stumpf (Stumpf and Hornbostel, 1911, p.105), Hornbostel (1911, pp.6, 14–16), and others, including some scholars of European music, recognized the importance of this discovery.

Later research confirmed the equidistant structure of Thai scales (Morton, 1976, pp.22–9), but not of *slendro* scales. Kunst established that gamelan ensembles were tuned differently, that there is no standard scale; that Javanese musicians recognize many varieties of *slendro*, distinguished by their different interval sizes; and, from measurement of 46 *slendro* gamelan that no two scales were identical, and none was equidistant (Kunst, 1972). Hood (1954, pp.138–42) advanced a logical argument against *slendro* equidistance, and in a tonometric study of two gamelan (1966), showed that their two *slendro* scales were neither alike nor equidistant, and that their interval structures even varied from one octave to another.

Thus, doubt was cast on the concept of scale as a series of 'fixed discrete tone steps'. Equidistant scales were posited for parts of Africa (Kubik, 1969; H. Tracey, 1948) and Melanesia (Zemp, 1979). Nevertheless, Javanese music retained its status as a paradigmatic case not by a restoration of its original place in the tonometric paradigm, but by becoming associated with new paradigms. Kunst's emphasis on explaining Javanese music in terms of Javanese musical concepts, together with Hood's methodology of performance study, created both a new interest in non-European viewpoints and the opportunity for access to them in the professional training of ethnomusicologists. The result was a quiet revolution in transcription, in which Western-notation transcriptions of gamelan music gradually lost place to transcriptions in Javanese number notation (e.g. by Becker, 1981; Vetter, 1981; Sutton, 1985, and many others). The new standard had the advantage for Java specialists of not suggesting fixed, rigid pitch and interval rela- tionships, so that readers could 'hear' the transcriptions in terms of whatever unique gamelan tunings they knew.

African music also began to generate new transcriptional alternatives. Number notations for pitch were used by Kubik (1969), Peter Cooke (1970), Roderic Knight (1972), Pie-Claude Ngumu (1975–6), Lois Anderson (1977) and others. The study of African rhythms gave rise to a wide range of innovative transcriptions; examples include James Koetting (1970), Hewitt Pantaleoni working independently (1972, 'Three Principles of Timing'; 1972, 'Toward Understanding') and together with Moses Serwadda (1968) and S. Kobla Ladzekpo (1970), by Carol A. Campbell and Carol M. Eastman (1984) and many others. Innovation became the norm in African transcription.

Some scholars are disturbed by such developments. Stockmann (1979, p.205) repeated Hornbostel and Abraham's call for standardization and an end to 'arbitrary' experimentation where it was not 'compellingly' necessary. But such experimentation would not be so widely accepted if scholars had not felt its necessity and sought results that European notation could not deliver. The defects of European notation have been known for a hundred years or more; and yet the majority of ethnomusicologists up to the last few decades of the 20th century have considered Hornbostel and Abraham's 'compromise' an acceptable tradeoff for the difficulties of non-traditional notations. Thus, a crucial question becomes whether the compromise can fail in application to a given musical case and lead to misconceptions, violations of musical logic and distortions of objective and acoustic fact.

As an example, we can compare three transcriptions of Tibetan *dbyangs* melody (fig.11).

The traditional notation (fig.11*a*) shows the nature of *dbyangs*: a melody composed of gradually fluctuating tone contours comprised of patterned changes in pitch (rising and falling curves), loudness (thickness of lines) and tone colour (vowels of the text, with prescribed vowel modifications). The pitch-time graph transcription (fig.11*b*, adapted from Ellingson, 1987) illustrates the acoustic result in one performance, and shows, for example, that neither the absolute height of pitches nor the relative 'intervallic' range of the ascending–descending curves is fixed, but varies from one curve (and one performance) to the next. The Western-notation transcription (fig.11*c*, from Kaufmann, 1975, p.45), on the other hand, seems to indicate up-and-down jumps between pitches a distinct chromatic half-step apart, arranged in long–short rhythmic values in strict metric proportion but irregular sequence, giving a syncopated effect. None of these features actually exist; they are artefacts produced in transcription according to the demands of the logic of European notation. The 'G_1' and 'A_1 flat' probably represent peaks and low points in the continuously fluctuating tone contour, but are abstracted and isolated as 'notes' simply because European notation requires it. What the notes represent are moments of a continuous process variable in pitch and range at the wish of the performer; isolating them as separate 'notes' is as reasonable as transcribing a quarter-note drumbeat as a tied string of dotted and double-dotted 8ths, 16ths, and 32nd notes. Because the logic of European notation is in direct contradiction to the logic of the musical system, the transcription ends up distorting objective acoustical facts; and there is no way of making it either 'phonetically' or 'phonemically' accurate.

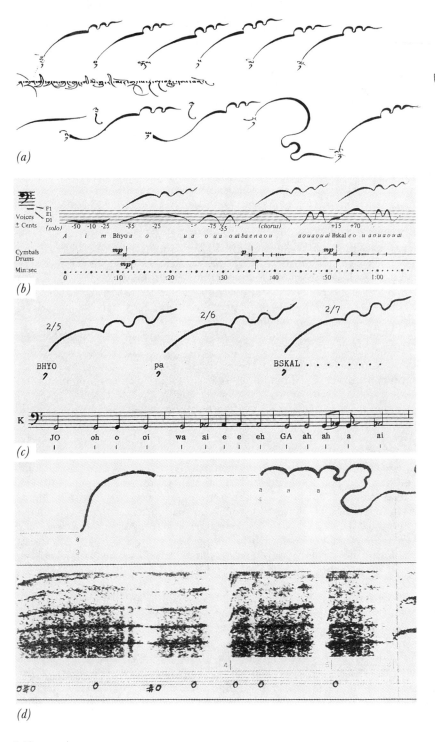

(a)

(b)

(c)

(d)

Autotranscription (fig.11*d*, part of a similar melody from Helffer, 1981, p.13) also does not automatically clarify the phonemic logic of the musical system, although it offers a phonetic advantage. The notation of a similar curve-complex (*top*) is segmented and spaced to coincide with the Sonagram transcription (*middle*), which shows, especially in the higher overtones, a continuously curving fluctuation of pitch corresponding to the notation curves. However, a transcriber working from an objectivist discovery paradigm is likely to overlook this correspondence, since the pitch range is so small and the time duration so great that both musical and transcription-line fluctuations can escape the attention of even cross-culturally experienced observers. Thus, it is possible even with the level of phonetic accuracy provided by the autotranscription, to abstract arbitrary pitch 'levels' from the tone contour fluctuations (*bottom*), and so to distort the musical logic and acoustical facts of the performance.

CONCEPTUAL TRANSCRIPTION. The last example (fig.11) illustrates one of the fundamental paradoxes of ethnomusicology and cross-cultural research: that the very knowledge and concepts which open the door to our being able to understand music also open onto pathways towards misunderstanding it. Nevertheless, some conceptual tools such as the Hornbostel paradigm with its objectivist-discovery orientation and European-notation transcriptional methodology, have worked quite well in solving many ethnomusicological problems. It is only in application to special cases and wider perspectives that they fail; and the broadening and deepening of ethnomusicological research has tended increasingly to show the failure of discovery-model transcriptions despite their apparent continuing success in 'everyday' cross-cultural music studies.

The development of transcription in the late 20th century seems to be away from classical objective-discovery transcriptions towards conceptual transcriptions that seek to furnish a graphic–acoustic definition of the essential concepts and logical principles of a musical system. In classical Hornbostelian transcription, musical features are presumed to be unknown and awaiting discovery in the objective representation of musical sound; and the transcriber is responsible for precisely and exhaustively notating all objective features of musical sound that might lead to any significant discovery whatsoever. In a conceptual transcription, essential features are presumed to be already known through fieldwork, performance lessons, study of traditional written and aural notations and learning and leadership

11. Traditional notation of Tibetan 'dbyangs' (a) compared with a pitch–time graph transcription; (b) of the first three curve complexes; a Western-notation transcription (c) of the same passage and an autotranscription (d) of part of a similar melody. The autotranscription (d) made by Mireille Helffer and Jean Schwarz using a sonogram resembles the pitch–time graph transcription (b) made from measurements with a Korg tuner and a stopwatch in that they both represent melodic movement as smoothly flowing curves, though in (d) the vertical pitch dimension is compressed to about a quarter, and the horizontal time dimension extended to about two times the values in (b). In the lower line of (d) pitch and rhythmic points are extracted from the peaks and valleys of the curves of the sonogram to yield a transcription which resembles that shown in (c). (a) Unpublished manuscript; (b) from Ellingson, Transcription Example 14 for J. Spector, 'Chanting' in 'Encyclopedia of Religion' 3 (1987); (c) from Kaufmann, 'Tibetan Buddhist Chant' (1975); (d) Helffer and Schwarz, 'De la notation tibétaine au sonogramme' in Rouget, ed. (1981)

processes. The transcription then becomes a means not of discovering, but of defining and exemplifying the acoustical embodiment of musical concepts essential to the culture and music.

This is accomplished not by the application of a predetermined universal methodology, but by strategic choices appropriate to the music, performance and culture. In the graph transcription in fig.11*b*, the use of a standard European staff covering more than an octave was rejected because, although such a staff might be relevant to the discovery of significant features of many musics, in the case at hand most of it would be empty informational 'noise' illustrating hypothetical possibilities in music other than the one being transcribed. Graph notation was one of many possibilities, along with European notation, numbers, and so on; for the form of the transcription is secondary to, and is determined by, the musical logic of the melody.

After many such strategic considerations, the transcription is rendered in the form which most clearly and efficiently illustrates the relation between concept and sound in the musical system and performance. It should then be possible to apply discovery procedures at a secondary level (e.g. in fig.11*b*, to determine actual pitch ranges and duration of the tone contour patterns); for the transcription must define the concepts and logic of the musical system in terms of their acoustic manifestations.

Conceptual transcriptions are different from both prescriptive 'blueprints of how a specific piece of music shall be made to sound' and descriptive 'reports of how a specific performance of any music actually did sound' (Seeger, 1958, p.168), by being designed representations of how a performance did and must sound in order to recognize the type of music and the piece. Stockmann (1979, p.214) defines the goal of transcription as 'to represent, precisely and in visually comprehensible form, musical factors essential to a piece and to the carriers of a music culture'. This serves well as a statement of the immediate goal of conceptual transcriptions, and further implications are suggested in Jones's conclusions drawn from the experiment in transcription prompted by his African teacher's criticism of his earlier transcriptions and performances (1959, p.114):

> The graph shows that at point B we were 1/16 sec. off time [in the first transcription] and at point A, only 1/32 wrong. In short, our first version is almost exactly right, and yet when we find out what the African is really doing we discover that it is totally wrong, for it is based essentially on the wrong underlying conception . . . It shows how fatally easy it is for us to think we have found out an African rhythm, when all the time we are wrong, and it shows how necessary it is to . . . find out how he himself regards the pattern. In the last resort that is the thing which really matters.

TRANSCRIPTIONAL ALTERNATIVES. Some transcribers have attempted to extend the usefulness of European notation through complex modifications. The most famous examples are Bartók's transcriptions of Eastern European folk songs (e.g. 1978, i, p.129), which at times grew so complex in minute elaborations that the transcriber added a kind of translation into 'broad' transcription to clarify the melodic line (fig.12).

142

12. *Bartók's transcription of an Eastern European folk song with a 'broad' transcription added to clarify the complex melodic line: from Béla Bartók (ed. B. Suchoff), 'Yugoslav Folk Music' (1978)*

Ethnomusicologists have generally disliked such complexity, but it could be argued that complex transcriptions are the truest representations of musical complexity, and that in some cases a simple form creates illusions and distortions of the music. Villoteau was able to respond to Egyptians' criticisms of his simplified transcriptions by declaring, 'for us the simple melody is the very self of the music'. Gilman's transcriptions (fig.6) are one of the most complex modifications of European notation; but even Gilman's 45-line staff was outdone by Ballantine's transcription of an African ensemble's 21-pitch music with each pitch on its own 5-line staff, creating melodies spaced out over a total of 105 lines (1965). More restrained modifications of European treatment of staves have been used by Andrew Tracey (1970, 1971), Paul Berliner (1978, pp.70ff) and others. Many other kinds of modifications of European notation could be cited; but perhaps the most logical modifications, equidistant-time horizontal spacing and equidistant-pitch lines spaced according to actual intervals, have been proposed (Reid, 1977) but not generally adopted.

Alternatives to European notation are only beginning to be explored. Some are as simple as solfège notation (Kara, 1970) or the use of high-mid-low vocal tone accents derived from Vedic chant notation (Ellingson, 1979, *The Mandala of Sound*, pp.426–9). More complex adaptations of traditional non-European notations include Bonnie Wade's (1984, p.15ff.) use of equidistantly spaced Indian *sargam* solfège syllables and melodic contour lines along with Western notation, producing a multidimensional composite. Graph notations include line graphs (Jones, 1959; List, 1961), bar graphs (Zemp, 1981) and box graphs (Koetting, 1970). Sue De Vale (1984) developed an innovative graphic-iconic system for notating sound texture, an important feature virtually impossible to show in European notation. The most comprehensive use of non-European alternatives has been David Reck's use of graphs in *Music of the Whole Earth* (1977).

Complex displays have been used in forms such as Judith and Alton Becker's (1981) circular depictions of rhythmic cycles and Bernard Lortat-Jacob's (1981) spiral notation of structural development. The most commonly used special display form has been the 'synoptic' alignment of corresponding beats, verses, and sections under one another (Hornbostel, 1920); and the most unique may be Catherine Ellis's 4-colour 3-dimensional topographic map of an Australian Aborigine song (1985, fig.A9).

New dimensions have been admitted to musical research and transcription. Gerhard Kubik (1962) suggested an 'inherent rhythm' in East African music that resulted in different transcriptions of 'the played image' and 'the heard image' of each piece. John Blacking (1973, p.29) gave transcriptions showing how an apparently simple acoustic 'surface structure' could result from more complex deep-structural interactions of a group of players. Sumarsam (1975) posited an 'inner melody' in Javanese gamelan music that, even though not played on any instrument, nevertheless formed the basic conception of the piece for its players. Such concepts demonstrate that 'the music itself' is more than the sound we hear.

Some transcribers have attempted to include extra-acoustical elements of music in transcriptions. An early attempt was Fletcher's rhythmic-cosmo-logical 'diagrams of time'. The Beckers (1981 and other works) have likewise designed transcriptions to show relationships between musical structure and cosmology, and Ter Ellingson (in press) uses transcriptions designed to show effects of architecture and ritual geography on musical forms. On a less symbolic level, Regula Qureshi (1987) uses 'videographs' to show the effects of audience interaction on performances. These are cultural transcriptions, including representation of non-acoustic elements to give a fuller understanding of music than is possible by transcription of sound alone. All such efforts require strategic planning, and in order to explore their possibilities, we must know something of the nature and logic of musical notation systems. All such efforts too will be open to modification, refinement and improvement through use.

Techniques of Transcription

Stumpf attempted the first detailed description of transcription techniques in 1886; and since his time, many transcribers have published accounts of their own work, incorporating various mixtures of descriptive reporting of problems and procedures, and prescriptive suggestions of principles (Stumpf, 1901, pp.132–8; Gilman, 1908, chap.1–2; Densmore, 1942, pp.109–11; Bartók, 1951, pt.1; Jones, 1958; Estreicher, 1957; McColester, 1960; Kubik, 1965 and 1972; Serwadda and Pantaleoni, 1968; Koetting, 1970; Reid, 1977; Gutzwiller, 1979; Beaudry, 1978; Charron, 1978). Some descriptive publications have presented the comparative views and methods of different individual transcribers – in relation to the same piece or pieces (Boas, 1896, 1897; SEM Symposium, 1964), to different pieces and musical styles (Rouget, ed., 1981), or specifically to the methodological strategy of using multiple viewpoints as a control against personal arbitrariness (Koizumi and others, 1969, pp.xiv–xxv, 32–57). Such descriptions can suggest techniques applicable to wider contexts; and a comparative reading of them will reveal some of the effects on transcription of cultural and musical differences between musics, personal viewpoints and purposes of transcribers, and the extent to which transcription techniques not

144

only lead to particular forms of analysis and descriptive communication, but also presuppose and predetermine them.

Hornbostel and Abraham gave prescriptive suggestions on techniques as a minor section of their 'Proposals' in 1909. Since then, a number of authors have tried to construct implicit or explicit, scattered or concentrated prescriptive 'do-it-yourself' recipes in the context of general works on ethnomusicology and discussions of larger issues in transcription; notable efforts include those by Jaap Kunst (1959, pp.37–44, 3–12), the 'Committee of Experts' (*Notation*, 1952), Bruno Nettl (1956, pp.41–4; 1964, chap. 4), Mantle Hood (1971, chap. 2), and Doris Stockmann (1979, p.222ff).

A basic difficulty is that it is not possible to write a manual of transcription in terms of prescriptions for universally valid procedures and techniques for putting notes on paper. The theoretical revolution in late 20th-century ethnomusicology has necessitated the re-evaluation of transcription, as all other aspects of the field. Such a change shows in the work of a writer such as Nettl from decreasing emphasis on a procedural 'recipe' approach (1956, 1964) to an issue-oriented analytic reduction in terms of binary conceptual-methodological alternatives (1983, chap. 6), only one of a range of possibilities for a new theory-conscious treatment of transcription. Stockmann proposes a theoretical-methodological ordering of the transcription process into four 'complexes' – tone height, tone length, structural divisions, and manner of performance – which may be useful as a way of conceptualizing techniques and applications (1979, p.224)

Certain principles of technique can and should be discussed in general texts of ethnomusicology. The first is Hornbostel's insistence that the best technique in transcription would be to learn how to perform the music from a qualified teacher in the tradition, and to obtain feedback and evaluation from discerning listeners in that culture (1909, pp.15–16). Another principle is Ellis's reminder that 'Instruments [or musics] without a native performer seldom record themselves', for by 'record' he meant to write down their sounds in a way that is both descriptively correct and musically meaningful (1885, p.490). It is not always possible to follow either Hornbostel's or Ellis's advice, nor is it desirable to outlaw all transcriptions made without fulfilling their recommendations.

Literacy in Western notation is necessary to understand transcription in ethnomusicology, the bulk of published transcriptions and ethnomusico-logical work based on them. Alternatives to Western notation either are learned through study of non-Western traditions that have their own notations and through reading ethnomusicological studies of them (e.g. Kaufmann, 1967; Tokumaru and Yamaguti, eds., 1986) and studies that use specially invented non-traditional notation systems; or they are invented through a synthesis of imagination, sympathetic musical understanding, logic, con-sistency and awareness of existing theoretical issues and attempted solutions to transcriptional problems.

How do we know that we can 'read' a transcription, or how do we learn to do so? We might try to silently imagine the sounds, but such attempts can lead to the most remarkable forms of vagueness, distortion and self-deception; they concern an imaginary world without sonic reality. A Western music scholar might 'read' a notation by attempting to play it on the piano; but for an ethnomusicological transcription, even the attempt to do so would suggest a failure to grasp the most basic principles of literacy.

Thus, even taking account of Nettl's humorous remarks about semiliterate ethnomusicologists humming under their breath when they read transcriptions (1983, p.72), a sensible option for beginners to acquire transcriptional literacy (and perhaps for experienced transcribers to check and strengthen their fluency) is to treat transcriptions as prescriptive notations and attempt to regenerate the sounds symbolized in them. Even if the specific transcribed instruments are available and one knows how to play them correctly, sight-singing and time-beating are helpful – part by part and with transpositions where necessary, with many repetitions until one is assured that the performance reflects the notation as well as one is capable; and then, for the sake of accuracy and honesty in the next steps, to record the result. As a learning technique, the next step is to compare one's own recording to a recording of the original performance from which the transcription was made. Thus, the concluding step is to go back to the transcription and study it while listening to the original performance with the enriched awareness of experience, and figure out by careful analysis what before had been intuitively assumed to be present in its symbolism. After such an experience one can be prepared for realistic consideration of what sounds one's own transcriptions might suggest to a reader.

When writing transcriptions work with dubbed recordings rather than irreplaceable originals, and work with pencil and eraser rather than pen and ink. Listen to the music again and again; repeat attempts at transcription – come back to them later with a fresh perspective. It may help to begin with simple easy material: solo voices or instruments, music that is not fast or slow, melodies with clear and consistent discrete pitches and cyclic rhythms without complex polyrhythm or syncopation. With more experience one will often return to 'simple' projects and find them more complex than they appeared at first. Give attention to factors such as fatigue, changing perceptions (which can lead in false as well as true directions), the effects of one's own cultural–musical preconditioning, and realization that any transcription entails perceptions and judgments that must be regarded as tentative and hypothetical.

Learning to transcribe in an academic class is valuable since it allows several people to work on the same transcription separately and then discuss problems and solutions together. Or working at least occasionally with another person is helpful. Test your transcriptions with someone else, by having them sing or at least discuss the musical impression the transcription conveys. If there seems to be a problem in musical communication, it may not be the fault of the transcription, but rather a reflection of a special musical feature that, no matter how well transcribed, is difficult to convey. The best transcription, which conveys the essential features of the music, may be the most difficult to read. Alternative solutions should be tried.

The problems of transcription are the problems of ethnomusicology itself. Perhaps the best transcriptional technique is not to regard transcription as a technical procedure, but as a complexly specialized reflection of ethnomusicology. No matter what procedures seem to work best, change them often enough to learn something new. Shift transcribing from familiar to new and unknown music often enough to allow for flexibility and growth in thought and practice.

Transcription is an art that can be learned only through practice, with the aid of formal or informal instruction from experienced transcribers. One goal of transcription is the experience of transcription itself. Thus, Hood speaks of 'exercising the dictation muscles' in the context of developing one's ethnomusicological strengths (1971, p.54), and Nettl suggests that one value of transcription may lie in the concentrated and disciplined attention to music that it brings (1964, pp.126–7).

Further problems arise from the interface between technique and technology. Technological change has removed some of the constraints that hindered earlier transcribers. The availability of offset printing has reduced the expense of transcriptions, and thus has reduced the importance of what Hornbostel believed to be the overriding reason for keeping transcriptions as close to conventional Western notation as possible. A new economic freedom for innovation has arisen that, paradoxically, may be more available in low-budget journals and publications. The appearance of many forms of computerized printing and desk-top publishing may lead to oversimplified transcriptions and eventually to even more freedom for innovation as ethnomusicologists explore the transcriptional possibilities of graphics programs. Some ethnomusicologists are experimenting with non-print forms of transcriptions, as in Hugo Zemp's use of computerized animation to create graph transcriptions, transferred to film, whose lines develop in synchronization with the musical soundtrack.

At the close of the 20th century, ethnomusicology has not dealt with many genres and aspects of traditional music, to say nothing of the new musics that are appearing. The need for innovative procedures remains. Hornbostel's paradigm and staff transcriptions may be like the Buddhist raft that is and should be left behind when we have crossed the river. Implicit in Hornbostel's thought is the notion that increasing knowledge will lead to unitary understanding, a kind of enlightenment that will reveal the concealed pattern behind all music. Do disciplines naturally tend towards enrichment and diversification or towards unitary global enlightenment? At least for ethnomusicology, the 20th century has left this question unresolved.

Bibliography

M. Mersenne: *Harmonie universelle* (Paris, 1636–7/*R*1963; Eng. trans. of the book on instruments, 1957)

J.-J. Rousseau: *Dictionnaire de Musique* (Paris, 1768/*R*1969; many edns. to 1825; Eng. trans. by W. Waring, London, 1771, 2/1779/*R*1975)

J.-M. Amiot: *Mémoire sur la musique des Chinois tant anciens que modernes* (Paris, 1779/*R*1973)

W. Jones: 'On the Musical Modes of the Hindoos', *Asiatick Researches*, iii (1792), 55–87; repr. in *Hindu Music from Various Authors*, ed. S. M. Tagore (Calcutta, 1875, 2/1882 in 2 pts., 3/1965), 125–60

F. Fowke: 'On the Vīnā or Indian Lyre', *Asiatick Researches* (1788), 295; repr. in *Hindu Music from Various Authors*, ed. S. M. Tagore (Calcutta, 1875, 2/1882 in 2 pts., 3/1965), 193

H. Lichtenstein: *Reisen im südlichen Afrika in den Jahren 1803, 1804, 1805, und 1806* (Stuttgart, 1811/*R*1967)

J. Crawfurd: *History of the Indian Archipelago* (Edinburgh, 1820); 'Music and Dancing' repr. in *Hindu Music from Various Authors*, ed. S. M. Tagore (Calcutta, 1875, 2/1882 in 2 pts., 3/1965), 295

G.-A. Villoteau: *De l'état actuel de l'art musical en Egypte* (Paris, 1826)

G. T. Lay: *The Chinese as They Are: Their Moral, Social, and Literary Character* (London, 1841)

R. Kiesewetter: *Die Musik der Araber* (Leipzig, 1842)

J. A. Davies: 'Appendix: On the Native Songs of New Zealand', *Polynesian Mythology and Ancient Traditional History of the New Zealanders*, ed. G. Grey (London, 1854; repr. 1906), 227

L. Nell: 'Introductory Paper on the Investigation of Singhalese Music', *Journal of the Royal Asiatic Society, Ceylon Branch* (1856–58), 200

H. Helmholtz: *Die Lehre von den Tonempfindungen als psysiologische Grundlage für die Theorie der Musik* (Brunswick, 1863; Eng. trans. by A. J. Ellis, as *On the Sensations of Tone as a Physiological Base for the Theory of Music*, 1875/R1954)

C. Engel: *Music of the Most Ancient Nations* (London, 1864/R1929)

S. M. Tagore: 'Hindu Music', *Hindoo Patriot*, September 7 (1874); repr. in Tagore, ed. (1875), 339

——, ed. : *Hindu Music from Various Authors* (Calcutta, 1875, 2/1882 in 2 pts., 3/1965)

C. Engel: *The Literature of National Music* (London, 1879)

A. J. Ellis: 'On the History of Musical Pitch', *Journal of the Royal Society of Arts* (5 March, 1880), 293–336; (2 April, 1880), 400–403; (7 January, 1881), 109–13; repr. in *Studies in the History of Musical Pitch: Monographs by Alexander J. Ellis and Arthur Mendel*, ed. A. Mendel (Amsterdam, 1968), 8–62

T. Baker: *Über die Musik der nordamerikanischen Wilden* (Leipzig, 1882), repr. and Eng. trans. A. Buckley as *On the Music of the North American Indians* (Buren, 1882)

A. J. Ellis: 'On the Musical Scales of Various Nations', *Journal of the Royal Society of Arts* (27 March 1885), 485–527 (30 October 1885), 1102–11

C. Stumpf: Lieder der Bellakula Indianer, *VMw*, ii (1886), 405

F. Boas: *The Central Eskimo* (Washington, DC, 1888/ *R*1964)

—— : 'On Certain Songs and Dances of the Kwakiutl of British Columbia', *Journal of American Folklore*, i/1 (1888) 49

—— : 'Chinook Songs', *Journal of American Folklore*, i/3 (1888) 220

—— : *The Aims of Ethnology* (New York, 1889); repr. in Boas (1940), 626

—— : 'On Alternating Sounds', *American Anthropologist*, ii/1 (1889)

C. R. Day: *Music and Musical Instruments of Southern India and the Deccan* (London, 1891/*R* Delhi, 1974)

A. J. Ellis: 'Appendix: Description of Rajah Sir S. M. Tagore's Śruti Vīṇā' in Day (1891), 169

B. I. Gilman: 'Zuñi Melodies', *Journal of American Ethnology and Archaeology*, 2 (1891) 65

C. Stumpf: 'Phonographierte Indianermelodien', *VMw*, viii (1892), 127

J. C. Filmore: 'Report on the Structural Peculiarities of the Music' in Fletcher (1893), 59

—— : 'A Woman's Song of the Kwakiutl Indians', *Journal of American Folklore*, vi/23 (1893), 285

A. C. Fletcher: *A Study of Omaha Indian Music. Archaeological and Ethnological Papers of the Peabody Museum*, i/5 (Cambridge, MA, 1893)

R. Wallaschek: *Primitive Music* (London, 1893)

F. Boas: 'Review of Alice Fletcher, *A Study of Omaha Indian Music*', *Journal of American Folklore*, vii/25 (1894), 169

J. C. Fillmore: 'What Do Indians Mean to Do When They Sing, and How Far Do They Succeed?', *Journal of American Folklore*, viii/29 (1895), 138

J. Mooney: *The Ghost-Dance Religion and the Sioux Outbreak of 1890* (Washington, DC, 1896, 2/1965)

F. Boas: 'Songs of the Kwakiutl Indians', *Internationales Archiv für Ethnographie*, ix, *Ethnographische Beiträge* (1896), 1

——: *The Social Organization and the Secret Societies of the Kwakiutl Indians. Report of the U.S. National Museum for 1895* (Washington, DC, 1897), 311–737

T. Wilson: *Prehistoric Art: the Origin of Art as Manifested in the Works of Prehistoric Man. Report of the U.S. National Museum 1896* (Washington, DC, 1898), 325–664

J. C. Fillmore: 'The Harmonic Structure of Indian Music', *American Anthropologist*, new ser., i/1 (1899), 297

C. Stumpf: 'Tonsystem und Musik der Siamesen', *Beiträge zur Akustik und Musikwissenschaft*, iii, (1901), 69–138

Aristoxenus: *The Harmonics of Aristoxenus* (Eng. trans. by H. S. Macran, Oxford, 1902)

C. K. Wead: 'Contributions to the History of Musical Scales', *Report of the U.S. National Museum 1900* (Washington, DC, 1902), 421–62

A. C. Fletcher: *The Hako: a Pawnee Ceremony. Twenty-Second Annual Report of the Bureau of American Ethnology*, ii (Washington, DC, 1904)

M. von Hornbostel and O. Abraham: 'Über die Bedeutung des Phonographen für die vergleichende Musikwissenschaft', *Zeitschrift für Ethnologie*, xxxvi (1904), 222; repr. with Eng. trans. as 'On the Significance of the Phonograph for Comparative Musicology', *Hornbostel Opera Omnia*, i: 183–202

—— : 'Phonographierte indische Melodien', *SIMG*, v (1904), 348–401; repr. with Eng. trans. as 'Indian Melodies Recorded on the Phonograph', *Hornbostel Opera Omnia* i: 115–82.

E. M. von Hornbostel: 'Die Probleme der vergleichenden Musikwissenschaft', *ZIMG*, vii/3 (1905–6), 138; repr. with Eng. trans. as 'The Problems of Comparative Musicology', *Hornbostel Opera Omnia* i: 247

F. Densmore: 'A Plea for the Indian Harmonization of All Indian Songs', *Indian School Journal*, vi/4 (1906), 14

P. E. Goddard: 'A Graphic Method of Recording Songs', *Anthropological Papers Written in Honor of Franz Boas* (New York, 1906), 137

E. M. von Hornbostel and O. Abraham: 'Phonographierte Indianermelodien aus Britisch-Columbia', *Anthropological Papers Written in Honor of Franz Boas* (New York, 1906), repr. with Eng. trans. as 'Indian Melodies from British Columbia Recorded on the Phonograph', *Hornbostel Opera Omnia* i: 299

B. I. Gilman: 'Hopi Songs', *Journal of American Ethnology and Archaeology*, 5 (1908)

E. M. von Hornbostel and O. Abraham: 'Vorschläge für die Transkription exotischer Melodien', *SIMG*, xi (1909), 1

F. Densmore: *Chippewa Music* (Washington, DC, 1910/R1972)

E. M. von Hornbostel: 'Über ein akustisches Kriterium für Kulturzusammenhänge', *Zeitschrift für Ethnologie*, xliii (1911), 601; repr. in *Beiträge zur Akustik und Musikwissenschaft*, vii (1913), 1

C. Stumpf and E. M. von Hornbostel: 'Über die Bedeutung ethnologischer Untersuchungen für die Psychologie und Ästhetik der Tonkunst', *Beiträge zur Akustik und Musikwissenschaft*, vi (1911), 102

F. Densmore: *Chippewa Music II* (Washington, DC, 1913/R1972)

E. M. von Hornbostel: 'Melodie und Skala', *JbMP*, xix (1913), 11

F. Densmore: *Teton Sioux Music* (Washington, DC, 1918/R1972)

E. M. von Hornbostel: 'Formanalysen an siamesischen Orchesterstücken', *AMw*, ii (1920), 306

F. Densmore: *Northern Ute Music* (Washington, DC, 1922/R1972)

F. Boas: *Primitive Art* (Oslo, 1927; 2/1955)

F. Densmore: 'The Study of Indian Music in the Nineteenth Century', *American Anthropologist*, xxix/1 (1927), 77

E. M. von Hornbostel: 'African Negro Music', *Africa*, i/1 (1928), 30–62

M. Metfessel: *Phonophotography in Folk Music: American Negro Songs in New Notation* (Chapel Hill, 1928)

F. Densmore: 'What Intervals Do Indians Sing?', *American Anthropologist*, xxxi/2 (1929), 271

G. Herzog: 'A Comparison of Pueblo and Pima Musical Styles', *Journal of American Folklore*, il/194 (1936), 284–424

F. Boas: *General Anthropology* (Boston, 1938)

—— : *Race, Language, and Culture* (New York, 1940)

R. H. van Gulik: *The Lore of the Chinese Lute* (Tokyo, 1940/R1969)

F. Densmore: 'The Study of Indian Music', *Annual Report of the Smithsonian Institution for 1941* (1942), 527; repr. in Hofmann (1968), 101

H. Tracey: *Chopi Musicians: Their Music, Poetry, and Instruments* (1948/R1970)

J. F. Carrington: *Talking Drums of Africa* (London, 1949)

B. Bartók and A. B. Lord: *Serbo-Croatian Folk Songs* (New York, 1951, 2/1978)

C. Seeger: 'An Instantaneous Music Notator', *JIFMC*, iii (1951), 103

Notation of Folk Music: Recommendations of the Committee of Experts (Geneva, 1952)

O. Gurvin: 'Photography as an Aid to Folk Music Research', *Norveg*, iii (1953), 181

P. Crossley-Holland: 'Tibetan Music', *Grove 5*

M. Hood: *The Nuclear Theme as a Determinant of Patet in Javanese Music* (Groningen, 1954)

K. Pike: *Language in Relation to a Unified Theory of the Structure of Human Behaviour*, i (Glendale, 1954)

L. C. Freeman and A. P. Merriam: 'Statistical Classification in Anthropology: an Application to Ethnomusicology', *American Anthropologist*, lviii (1956), 464

B. Nettl: *Music in Primitive Culture* (Cambridge, MA, 1956)

Z. Estreicher: *Une technique de transcription de la musique exotique, experiences pratiques* (Neuchâtel, 1957)

L. Picken: 'Music of Far Eastern Asia 2: Other Countries: Tibet', *New Oxford History of Music*, i (London, 1957)

R. W. Albright: 'The International Phonetic Alphabet: Its Backgrounds and Development', *International Journal of American Linguistics*, xxiv/1 (1958)

K. Dahlback: *New Methods in Vocal Folk Music Research* (Oslo, 1958)

A. M. Jones: 'On Transcribing African Music', *African Music*, ii/1 (1958), 11

C. Seeger: 'Prescriptive and Descriptive Music Writing', *MQ*, xxxxiv/2 (1958), 184; repr. in Seeger (1977), 168

A. M. Jones: *Studies in African Music* (London, 1959)

J. Kunst: *Ethnomusicology* (The Hague, 3/1959)

W. Malm: *Japanese Music and Musical Instruments* (Rutland, vt, 1959)

T. V. Wylie: 'A Standard System of Tibetan Transcription', *Harvard Journal of Asiatic Studies*, xxii (1959), 261

D. Cohen and R. T. Katz: 'Explorations in the Music of the Samaritans: an Illustration of the Utility of Graphic Notation', *EM*, iv (1960), 67

R. McCollester: 'A Transcription Technique used by Zygmunt Estreicher', *EM*, iv (1960), 129

W. Apel: *Harvard Dictionary of Music* (Cambridge, MA, 1961)

G. List: 'Speech Melody and Song Melody in Central Thailand', *EM*, v/1 (1961), 16

G. Kubik: 'The Phenomenon of Inherent Rhythms in East and Central African Instrumental Music', *African Music*, iii/1 (1962), 33

T. Liu: *Liu T'ien-hau's Nan-hu and P'i-p'a Compositions* (Taipei, 1964)

B. Nettl: *Theory and Method in Ethnomusicology* (New York, 1964)

'Symposium on Transcription and Analysis: a Hukwe Song with Musical Bow', *EM*, viii/3 (1964), 223–77

C. Ballantine: 'The Polyrhythmic Foundation of Tswana Pipe Melody', *African Music*, iii/4 (1965), 52

G. Kubik: 'Transcription of Mangwilo Xylophone Music from Film Strips', *African Music*, iii/4 (1965), 35

M. Hood: 'Sléndro and Pélog Redefined', *Selected Reports*, i/1 (1966), 28; repr. in *Readings in Ethnomusicology*, ed. D. P. McAllester (New York, 1971), 35

C. McPhee: *Music in Bali* (New Haven, 1966/R1976)

W. Kaufmann: *Musical Notations of the Orient* (Bloomington, 1967)

C. Hofmann, ed.: *Frances Densmore and American Indian Music* (New York, 1968)

A. Lomax: *Folk Song Style and Culture* (Washington, DC, 1968)

M. Serwadda and H. Pantaleoni: 'A Possible Notation for African Dance Drumming', *African Music*, iv/2 (1968), 47

F. Boas: *The Ethnography of Franz Boas: Letters and Diaries of Franz Boas Written on the Northwest Coast from 1886 to 1931*, ed. R. P. Rohner (Chicago, 1969)

F. Koizumi and others: *Shingi-Shingon Shomyo Shusei/Buddhist Chant of Shingi-Shingon* (Tokyo, 1969)

G. Kubik: 'Composition Techniques in Kiganda Xylophone Music', *African Music*, iv/3 (1969), 22–72

C. Lévi-Strauss: *The Raw and the Cooked: Introduction to a Science of Mythology* (New York, 1969)

P. Cooke: 'Ganda Xylophone Music: Another Approach', *African Music*, iv/4 (1970), 62

A. M. Jones: 'On Using the Stroboconn', *African Music*, iv/4 (1970), 122

G. Kara: *Chants d'un barde mongol* (Budapest, 1970)

J. Koetting: 'Analysis and Notation of West African Drum Ensemble Music', *Selected Reports*, i/3 (1970), 116–46

Ladzekpo, S. Kobla and H. Pantaleoni: 'Takada Drumming', *African Music*, iv/4 (1970), 6

H. P. Reinecke: *Cents Frequenz Periode: Umrechnungstabellen für musikalische Akustik und Musikethnologie* (Berlin, 1970)

A. Tracey: 'The Matepe Mbira Music of Rhodesia', *African Music*, iv/4 (1970), 37

M. Hood: *The Ethnomusicologist* (New York, 1971/R1982)

G. List: 'Ethnomusicology: a Discipline Defined', *EM*, xxiii/1 (1971), 1

A. Tracey: 'The Nyanga Panpipe Dance', *African Music*, iv/4 (1971), 73

R. Knight: 'Towards a Notation and Tablature for the Kora and Its Application to Other Instruments', *African Music*, v (1972), 23

G. Kubik: 'Transcription of African Music from Silent Film: Theory and Methods', *African Music*, v/2 (1972), 28

H. Pantaleoni: 'Three Principles of Timing in Anlo Dance Drumming', *African Music*, v/2 (1972), 50

—— : 'Toward Understanding the Play of Atsimevu in Atsia', *African Music*, v/2 (1972), 64

J. Blacking: *How Musical is Man?* (Seattle, 1973)

150

F. Harrison, ed.: *Time, Place and Music: an Anthology of Ethnomusicological Observation c. 1550 to c. 1800* (Amsterdam, 1973)

J. Kunst: *Music in Java* (The Hague, 1973)

Melograph Issue, Selected Reports, ii/1 (1974)

W. Kaufmann: *Tibetan Buddhist Chant*, (Bloomington, IN., 1975)

P. C. Ngumu: 'Les Mendzanj des Ewondo du Cameroun', *African Music*, v (1975–6), 6

Sumarsum: *Inner Melody in Javanese Gamelan* (diss., Wesleyan U., Middletown, 1975)

E. Leach: *Culture and Communication: the Logic by Which Symbols are Connected* (Cambridge, MA, 1976)

D. Morton: *The Traditional Music of Thailand* (Berkeley, 1976)

T. A. Sebeok and D. J. Umiker-Sebeok, eds.: *Speech Surrogates: Drum and Whistle Systems* (The Hague, 1976)

L. Anderson: 'The Entenga Tuned-Drum Ensemble', *Essays for a Humanist: an Offering to Klaus Wachsmann* (New York, 1977), 1–57

A. Chandola: *Folk Drumming in the Himalayas: a Linguistic Approach to Music* (New York, 1977)

N. Jairazbhoy and H. Balyoz: 'Electronic Aids to Aural Transcription', *EM*, xxi/2 (1977), 275

D. Reck: *Music of the Whole Earth* (New York, 1977)

J. Reid: 'Transcription in a New Mode', *EM*, xxi/3 (1977), 415

C. Seeger: *Studies in Musicology, 1935–1975* (Berkeley, 1977)

N. Beaudry: 'Toward Transcription and Analysis of Inuit Throat-Games: MacroStructure', *EM*, xxii/2 (1978), 261

P. Berliner: *The Soul of Mbira: Music and Traditions of the Shona People of Zimbabwe* (Berkeley, 1978)

C. Card and others, eds.: *Discourse in Ethnomusicology: Essays in Honor of George List* (Bloomington, IN, 1978)

C. Charron: 'Toward Transcription and Analysis of Inuit Throat-Games: MicroStructure', *EM*, xxii/2 (1978), 245

T. Ellingson: Revised transcription Ex. 14 for Johanna Spector, 'Chanting', *Encyclopaedia of Religion*, iii, ed. M. Eliad and others (New York, 1978), 204

R. M. Stone: 'Motion Film as an Aid in Transcription and Analysis of Music', *Discourse in Ethnomusicology: Essays in Honor of George List*, ed.: C. Card and others (Bloomington, IN, 1978), 65

H. Zemp: ''Are'are Classification of Musical Types and Instruments', *EM*, xxii/2 (1978), 37–67

T. Ellingson: '*Don Rta Dbyangs Gsum*: Tibetan Chant and Melodic Categories', *Asian Music*, x/2 (1979), 112–56

—— : 'The Mathematics of Tibetan *Rol mo*', *EM*, xxxiii/2 (1979), 225

—— : *The Mandala of Sound: Concepts and Sound Structures in Tibetan Ritual Music* (diss., U. of Wisconsin, 1979)

A. Gutzwiller: 'Stone Age and Promised Land: an Answer to James Reid', *EM*, xxiii/1 (1979), 103

I. D. Bent: 'Notation', *Grove 6*

G. List: 'Ethnomusicology: a Discipline Defined', *EM*, xxiii/1 (1979), 1

G. Read: *Music Notation: a Manual of Modern Practice* (New York, 2/1979)

R. G. Robins: *A Short History of Linguistics* (London, 2/1979)

D. Stockmann: 'Die Transkription in der Musikethnologie: Geschichte, Probleme, Methoden', *AcM*, lii/2 (1979), 204–45

H. Zemp: 'Aspect of 'Are'are Musical Theory', *EM*, xxii/1 (1979), 5–48

T. Ellingson: 'Ancient Indian Drum Syllables and Buston's *Sham pa ta Ritual*', *EM*, xxiv/3 (1980), 431

J. and A. Becker: 'A Musical Icon: Power and Meaning in Javanese Gamelan Music', *The Sign in Music and Literature*, ed. W. Steiner (Austin, 1981)

M. Helffer and J. Schwarz: 'De la notation tibétaine au sonagramme', in G. Rouget, ed. (1981), 12

R. M. Kessing: *Cultural Anthropology: a Contemporary Perspective* (New York, 2/1981)

B. Lortat-Jacob: 'Danse de Sardaigne: Composition renouvellement', in G. Rouget, ed. (1981), 6

G. Rouget, ed.: *Ethnomusicologie et représentations de la musique* (Paris, 1981)

—— and T. Q. Hai: 'Structure d'un Chant initiatique du Bénin', in G. Rouget, ed. (1981), 10

P. Sallée: 'Jodel et procédés contrapunctiques des Pygmées', in G. Rouget, ed., (1981), 9

R. Vetter: 'Flexibility in the Performance Practice of Central Javanese Music', *EM*, xxv (1981), 199

H. Zemp: 'Le jeu d'une flûte de Pan polyphonique', in G. Rouget, ed. (1981), 8

B. Nettl: *The Study of Ethnomusicology: Twenty-Nine Issues and Concepts* (Urbana, IL, 1983)

C. A. Campbell and C. M. Eastman: '*Ngoma*: Swahili Adult Song Performance in Context', *EM*, xxviii/3 (1984), 467

151

S. C. De Vale: 'Prolegomena to a Study of Harp and Voice Sounds in Uganda: a Graphic System for the Notation of Texture', *Selected Reports in Ethnomusicology*, v (1984), 285–315

B. C. Wade: *Khyāl: Creativity within North India's Classical Music Tradition* (Cambridge, England, 1984)

C. J. Ellis: *Aboriginal Music: Education for Living* (St Lucia, 1985)

R. A. Sutton: 'Musical Pluralism in Java: Three Local Traditions', *EM*, xxix/1 (1985), 56

T. Ellingson: 'Buddhist Musical Notations', *The Oral and the Literate in Music*, ed. Y. Tokumaru and O. Yamaguti (Tokyo, 1986), 302–41

J. Kawada: 'Verbal and Non-Verbal Sounds: Some Considerations of the Basis of Oral Transmission of Music', *The Oral and the Literate in Music*, ed. Y. Tokumaru and O. Yamaguti (Tokyo, 1986), 158

Y. Tokumaru and O. Yamaguti, eds.: *The Oral and the Literate in Music* (Tokyo, 1986)

G. M. Wegner: *The Dhimaybaja of Bhaktapur: Studies in Newar Drumming*, i (Wiesbaden, 1986)

J. Goody: *The Interface between the Written and the Oral* (Cambridge, 1987)

G. Heussenstamm: *The Norton Manual of Music Notation* (New York, 1987)

G. List: 'Stability and Variation in a Hopi Lullaby', *EM*, xxxi/1 (1987), 18

R. B. Qureshi: 'Musical Sound and Contextual Input: a Performance Model for Musical Analysis', *EM*, xxxi/1 (1987), 56–86

H. Zemp: *Head Voice, Chest Voice* (Geneva, 1987) [16mm film]

K. V. Vaughn: *The Music Mapper: a Computer Application for Performance Based Interpretation of Cultural Variance in Digitized Patterns of Melody and Rhythm* (diss., U. of California, 1988)

T. Ellingson: 'The Mathematics of Newar Buddhist Music', *Change and Continuity: Studies in Nepalese Culture of the Kathmandu Valley* (Turin, in preparation)

CHAPTER VI

Notation

Musical notation, the representation of music through means other than the sound of music, is central to two major areas of ethnomusicology: for transcription and for study, in a wider context, of musical cultural symbolic and communication systems. Transcriptions are always artificial – either modified by scholars from pre-existing notation systems, or newly invented without reference to pre-existing models. This chapter focuses on the notation systems that have developed in various cultures to represent music.

The term 'notation' is often used by ethnomusicologists following theoretical distinctions drawn by Benjamin Ives Gilman and Charles Seeger as shorthand for 'prescriptive' notation – that prescribes the sounds that musicians are to perform. The term 'transcription' is often used as shorthand for 'descriptive notation'. Such usages oversimplify and obscure the theoretical issues raised by the study of notation systems. In common parlance, 'notation' connotes a written graphic system of representing pitch, rhythm and other features of music, usually for a prescriptive purpose. Although notation systems that fit such a definition are found in European and Asian cultures, the definition, based on European musical experience, fails to reveal the breadth of musical representation and communication systems in the world, of the depth of the issues they raise for ethnomusicological study.

The study of notation systems, in the broad sense of systems of musical representation and communication, is one of the least-developed areas of ethnomusicological research. We can still hear echoes of 19th-century Eurocentrism in the late 20th-century studies of writers who comment negatively on supposed deficiencies of non-European notations, taking the features of European notation as an implicit standard of what a notation system should represent. Studies of notation have tended to focus on the written notations of the Asian classical traditions. Some work has gone into the construction of descriptive taxonomies of notations based on their external graphic forms, but relatively little theoretical attention has been devoted to clarifying the systems of internal logic that structure and animate all notations, and forge their linkages between sound, concept and culture. Perhaps nowhere in the field of notation studies does the need for theoretical development reveal itself more strongly than in the study of non-graphic, or unwritten systems of musical communication and representation.

153

Non-graphic notations

Various types of non-graphic systems of musical communication exist in different cultures. These include: (i) aural systems representing musical sound by other stylized sounds (e.g. handclap patterns to represent drumbeats), also the important sub-category of verbal systems (e.g. spoken or sung syllables representing instrument sounds used in parts of Africa and Asia); (ii) visual systems (Javanese hand gestures representing gong pitches, or the *mudra* hand gestures indicating scalar and melodic figures in Indian Vedic chant); (iii) kinesic or choreographic systems, in which sequences of body movement play an important role (ancient Egyptian, Gregorian or Tibetan cheironomy), Newar hand movements to direct the performance of rhythmic cycles; (iv) tactile systems (African drummers beating out drum rhythms on the shoulders of student drummers), and others. In cases such as the Sinhalese and Newar music for circumambulation of a *stupa* or other religious structure, the architecture provides a set of prescriptions that determine essential characteristics of the music (Ellingson, in press). Non-graphic notations may include architectural, geographic and cosmological systems making prescriptive impact on the musical performances.

A related subject is the use in various cultures of 'instrument languages' (e.g. as described in Carrington, 1949; Seboek, 1976). These would appear to present a mirror image of notations, in that notations make use of symbols drawn from other media to represent the musical sounds of voices or instruments, while instrument languages make use of sounds produced by instruments as symbols to represent language sounds. However, Kawada, analysing the apparently close parallel between African instrument languages and Japanese syllabic musical instrument notations, posits a fundamental dichotomy between the two kinds of systems (1986, p.170). Rather than thinking in terms of dichotomies, it may be more useful to conceive of oral and written media on a continuum (Goody, 1987). Evidence which contradicts Kawada's hypothesis is the Indo-Newar *mantra-boli*, a system of drum-language in which ritual linguistic messages are 'voiced' by drums and other instruments in structured compositions conceived and evaluated in musical as well as linguistic terms (Ellingson, 1980, 1986).

Theoretical explorations of notation systems by ethnomusicologists have been largely confined to questions of historical continuities. In such treatments, musical communication often seems to be a relatively straightforward, hierarchical process. Such hierarchical conceptions of musical communication have attracted the interest of anthropologists (e.g. Lévi-Strauss, 1969, pp.1–32; Leach, 1976, pp.43–5; Keesing, 1976, p.141), who have proposed general models of symbolic communication based on the relationships between composers, performers, conductors and the orchestral score. However, processes of musical communication may be less hierarchical and less prescriptive than such models suggest. If jazz, for example, is taken as an improvisatory dialogue between equals, then the performer-composers would seem to conduct one another by creative inspiration towards ever-new heights of individual inventiveness: hierarchically precise, comprehensively prescriptive communications would defeat the musical purpose.

154

In contrast to both orchestral and jazz performances, a Balinese *legong* dance embodies a complex web of communication in which the 'notes' of the music are among the least crucial elements in the communication process, and the most significant messages are sent and received at other musical levels. Whether we ask: does the dancer provide a prescriptive 'score' for the drummer in her movements, or the drummer for the other performers, or the set patterns of the gamelan piece for the dancer, or the 'tradition' for everyone, we find ourselves enmeshed in a more complex situation than a 'score' model would suggest, whether taken as a model of musical notations or of symbolism and culture in general. The *legong* and jazz models present a more widely applicable model of both culture and music than the peculiarly rigid, hierarchical nature of the Western orchestral score, although jazz and the *legong* also do not represent universally valid models of music or culture. The score, after all, does have its own place in the world of music, as do still other models of musical communication.

Non-graphic modes of musical communication raise issues basic to the understanding of all notation and transcription. First, the model of the orchestral score and the term 'notation' itself may lead us to narrowly localized expectations of musical communication. 'Prescriptive' seems to be too strongly normative and hierarchical a term to characterize some significant communications to performers about musical sound, communications that might better be conceived as 'suggestive', 'advisory', 'interactive', and even 'inspirational', rather than prescriptions dictated to the performers. Even in cases where performers receive an obligatory message (e.g. the gamelan tempo must be quickened to keep up with a change in the dancer's movement), the prescriptive quality may be that of necessity due to contingent circumstances rather than of fixedly preconceived intent.

Prescriptive content may consist of a skeletal formula (e.g. the *theka* syllables of a North Indian *tāla* cycle) that only provides an audible or conceptual base for performance elaborations; what is prescribed is not the 'music' – 'what we hear' (and perhaps transcribe) – but rather an abstraction out of which music can be created. Important prescriptive communications may focus on message contents other than the 'notes'. Thus, the issue arises of how notations, whether graphic or non-graphic, prescriptive or descriptive, can convey significant musical information, and what criteria determine significance if the primacy of pitch and rhythmic quantification cannot automatically be assumed to be supreme in every case. Should we not include in our definition of 'notation' all significant prescriptive (and in the case of transcriptive notations, descriptive) communications about music, whether or not their main content is 'notes'; and should our transcriptions automatically assume the primacy of pitch and rhythm quantification, or in some cases accord primary emphasis to other significant factors?

Notation systems: logic and strategies

Our knowledge of the number and variety of written notation systems is constantly expanding (see Tokumaru and Yamaguṭi, eds., 1986, for descriptions of several notation systems largely uninvestigated in ethnomusicological literature before the second half of the 1980s). An introductory survey of notations, Western and non-Western, is given by Ian Bent in his article 'Notation' in *The New Grove Dictionary of Music and Musicians* (1980). Readers should also consult more specialized intercultural studies such as Kaufmann's *Musical Notations of the Orient* (1967); Tokumaru and Yamaguti, eds., *The Oral and the Literate in Music*, as well as single-culture studies such as Kunst (1972, pp.346ff for Java), McPhee (1966, Ch.8 for Bali), Malm (1959, appx.2 for Japan). Insight into the comparative logic of notation systems may be gained from a study of Hood's example of transcriptions and transnotations of a single song into 11, mainly Western, notation systems (1971, pp.71–82).

Where scholarship has gone beyond the limits of ethnography, it has dealt primarily with the history of notation systems. Much study of non-Western notations (as well as of older forms of Western notations) has been in terms as much of what they do not do as of they do, that is in terms of their attributes perceived as defects (with a model of perfection provided by Western staff notation). If similar judgements were made about musical sound or social and cultural contrasts with the West, the procedure would strike us as hopelessly old-fashioned and ethnocentric.

The search for an understanding of notations requires a consideration of the musical practices to which they refer and to the concepts and intentions of their users; otherwise we risk the danger, already noted by Sir William Jones two centuries ago, that the study of documentary artefacts without reference to musical practice and musicians can lead to 'mere phrases without clear ideas' and results that are 'insufferably tedious and scarcely intelligible' (1784, pp.132, 151).

Theoretical and conceptual approaches to notation generally work within the bounds of a taxonomical framework inherited from the history of Western music, which arranges notation systems into categories such as 'staff notation', 'neumes', 'tablatures', and other types based on graphic form. Such formalist conceptions are systematically inadequate in that they omit the functional, intentional, communicative and musical dimensions of notation systems, and are also logically deficient. Part of this deficiency lies in apparent inconsistencies: for example, 'tablatures' include guitar fingering charts and Chinese *qin* ideographic notations (Van Gulik, 2/1969, pp.123ff), the first of which depicts and the second of which describes the actions of a player to produce a desired sound pattern; but on the other hand, they also include 16th-century Spanish keyboard pitch number grids (Apel, 1961, p.729) and contemporary Javanese number notations, both of which prescribe acoustic features (pitch expressed as scale degree, duration) of the sounds themselves rather than of the actions that produce them. 'Number notations' include those that use numbers not only to express scale degrees, but also to represent absolute pitch (Hertz measurements), the keys of xylophones (Kubik, 1969), and the ordering of beat groups (Ellingson, 1979, 'Don Rta'). Thus, formalist conceptualizations of notation systems not only fail to reveal the underlying logic of the systems, but actually produce distortion by forcing us to discuss and evaluate notational issues in terms of superficial graphic similarities and differences.

To consider the underlying principles of notation systems, both as subjects for study and in terms of how we adapt them for use in transcription, it is necessary to consider a range of parameters, each of which might be expressed

156

as contrasts. Some of the more important parameters and contrasts, together with representative examples, are shown in Table 1.

TABLE 1
CONCEPTUAL CONTRASTS IN NOTATION SYSTEMS

Contrasts (except Function)	Examples (Function)	
	Prescriptive (Notation) (W = Western staff notation)	Descriptive (Transcription)
Articulatory	W fingering/bowing signs	Labanotation-based diagrams and TUBS diagrams for Africa drumstrokes/tone qualities
	Qin ideographic string/stop numbers and plucking indications	'Are'are panpipe fingerings
REFERENCE		
Acoustic	W pitch/duration signs	Newar drum syllables
	Chinese *nan hu* pitch number notation	'Are'are panpipe pitch bar graphs
Iconic	W high/low staff = pitch	Equidistant modified staff
	Japanese tone-contour curves	All time/pitch graphs
SYMBOLIC MODE		
Abstract	W sharp and flat	Hertz/Cents values, A–B–A
	Japanese radial pitch lines	All number transcriptions
Analog	W ornament signs, time signatures	Animal sound textures patterns
	Tibetan tone-contour curves	*Khyāl* melodic contour curves
ENCODING FORM		
Digital	W written-out ornaments and time-value flags	Animal sound pitches/rhythms written as separate notes
	Tibetan cymbal notations	*Khyāl sargam* pitch syllables
Culture-specific	W harmony	Javanese colotomy letters
	Tibetan *'phar* energy signs	West African bell patterns
MUSICAL CONTENT		
Intercultural	W proportional rhythm	Melodic contour graphs
	Tibetan beat group counts	Rhythmic structure notations

Five main parameters of notation systems are shown: function, reference, symbolic mode, encoding form, musical content. These include some of the primary factors that need to be considered both in the study of notation systems and the design of transcription systems, and they all entail contrasts of emphasis in both kinds of systems. However, in practice few notation systems

157

fall unambiguously into one side or another of the various contrasts. Such parameters and contrasts are useful as tools for the analysis and design of notation systems, rather than as terminological pigeonholes.

1. FUNCTION: PRESCRIPTIVE/DESCRIPTIVE   Following Gilman and Charles Seeger, the function of notation systems is primary: it forms the vertical grid of the chart, and is equivalent to the notation/transcription contrast for purposes of selecting examples. This serves three purposes: (i) to show that virtually any notational logic can function as either prescription or description, as notation or transcription; (ii) to show that functional similarities and differences can occur within any parameter or across any line of contrast; and (iii) to facilitate the inclusion of Western staff notation examples, examples of non-staff notation alternatives, and examples of the most common graphic forms in every division, in order to illustrate how notation systems and graphic forms can embody different and even opposing logical principles. In fact, many of the notation systems cited as examples could be located at different points on the grid by emphasizing features they contain other than those cited in the chart.

2. REFERENCE: ARTICULATORY/ACOUSTIC   Notation systems and symbols may refer either to the articulation of sounds or to the acoustic result. Articulatory notations are subjective in their reference to the actions of a player on an instrument, while acoustic notations are objective in their reference to the sound as an object describable by a perceiver. Articulatory notations refer to actions as the cause of sounds; acoustic notations, to sounds as the effects of actions.

Examples of articulatory notations include the fingering and bowing signs that can be added to piano and violin parts in Western staff notation, and the Chinese ideograph-character notations for *qin* containing numbers of strings to be plucked and positions for stopping the strings, along with abbreviated names of plucking techniques. Among the relatively few transcriptional (descriptive) uses of articulatory notations are the Labanotation-influenced diagrams of Ladzekpo and Hewitt Pantaleoni (1970) and James Koetting's (1970) TUBS system for notating the various handstrokes that produce different qualities of sound in African drumming, both somewhat comparable to the Chinese *qin* ideographs in their level of abstraction from pictographically derived principles, and Hugo Zemp's (1981) more pictorially iconic fingering-diagram notations of 'Are'are panpipe parts.

Acoustic notations include many examples, such as the treatment of pitch and duration in Western notation, and the Chinese *nan hu* notation of Liu Tien-hua (1964), which uses some of the same number characters as *qin* notation, but with reference to the pitches of a scale rather than to string and stop numbers. Descriptive acoustic notations comprise the vast majority of ethnomusicological transcriptions; clear contrasts with our examples of articulatory transcriptions include Wegner's (1986) use of modified syllabic notations for the sounds of the various strokes of Newar drums, and Zemp's (1981) use of pitch/time bar graphs (accompanied by staff notation transcriptions as well) for the same 'Are'are panpipe parts represented by his fingering diagrams.

158

3. SYMBOLIC MODE: ICONIC/ABSTRACT   The mode of symbolization used in notation systems may attempt to make music 'look the way it sounds', or may use abstract and purely conventional symbols. Iconic pictorialism is sensual, relying on synaesthetic parallels with the visual (or another) sense to depict sound, while abstract conventionalism relies on arbitrary logical consistency. The most obviously iconic element in Western staff notation is the equation between high or low staff position and 'high' or 'low' pitch; however, this iconicity is compromised by the abstract conventions of half-step modifications by key signatures and accidentals, to the point where, by the logic of the system, a modified note lower on the staff (b sharp) could be higher in pitch than a note higher on the staff (c flat). To point out that this does not occur in actual notational practice is to emphasize the extent to which cultural and musical conventions, rather than principles of logical or iconographic consistency, shape the development and use of prescriptively based 'natural' notation systems. Thus, in the tone-contour curves of Japanese *karibakase* notations for *shōmyō* chant, gradual and often microtonal pitch changes are also depicted iconically; but in this case, movements to higher pitch ranges may be shown by curves towards the top, right, or left of the page, since the pitch axis is shown at right angles to an abstract, radial constantly shifting pitch base and time axis (Ellingson, 1986).

Iconicity, like abstraction, relies on cultural convention; for although both 'high' and 'low' graphic positions and pitches can be perceived by the senses, their conceptualization and relationships are culturally determined. To a player of the *nan hu*, for instance, what Westerners call 'high' pitches are those which are finger-stopped lower on the strings of the vertically held instrument (see Hood, 1971, p.68, for other examples). However, iconicity in aural notations may be less culture-dependent than in graphic notations: the tones of spoken syllables, for example, may echo the tones of drumbeats in ways obvious even to an outsider. Both iconic and abstract symbolization have been used in a large proportion of ethnomusicological transcriptions, since all pitch/time graphs are inherently iconic, and all number, letter, and syllabic notations are abstract.

4. ENCODING FORM: ANALOG/DIGITAL   Musical sounds (and their articulations) are complex patterns which may be represented by complex synthetic analog symbols, or broken down digitally into their individual analytic components. Analog encoding typically produces complex polynomial symbols which display a structural patterning that corresponds to the patterning of the original and are relatively sparse for the amount and complexity of musical information (Hood, 1971, p.76). Digital encoding produces a dense number of relatively simple monomial symbols for a similar amount and complexity of musical information.

Analog notations include the Western signs for ornaments, such as the turn sign and the zigzags used for trills and mordents, which represent complex event-pattern features by signs patterned to correspond with those features without breaking them down into their separate components; the digital alternative to the analog turn sign is to write out the turn with a separate note for each individual pitch. Kunst's choice (cited in Hood, 1971, p.54), in transcribing a Javanese melodic ornament, of a turn sign in preference to

159

writing out the ornament in a string of separate notes, represents a choice of analog over digital notations, rather than a choice of iconic over abstract, or 'phonemic' over 'phonetic', representation; and Bartók's preference for extremely complex strings of separate notes to represent ornamentation likewise represents a preference for digitalized encoding of musical information (1978).

Tibetan vocal notation utilizes complex curves as an analog of correspondingly complex tone-contour melodic movements (Ellingson, 1979, '*Don Rta*', 1986, fig.20a–b), while Tibetan cymbal notations digitize their beats into separate features of attack and prolongation, represented by separate symbols (Ellingson, 1979, 'The Mathematics'). Bonnie Wade (1984) presents contrasting strategies for the transcription of Indian *khyāl* melodies: graphic contour curves as analogs of melodic contour patterns, and *sargam* 'solfège' pitch syllables which represent the separate pitches of the melodies by separate digitalized components. Sue DeVale (1984) transcribes the texture of animal sounds with complex holistic representations of their sound patterns, while Thomas Wilson (1898, pp.516–17) breaks animal sounds down into components of pitch-time values encoded in separate notes.

Some of the contrasting cases in this group could be interchanged with those in group 3 above; and in general there is a strong relationship between the iconic/abstract and analog/digital contrasts. However, they are not identical. For example, Western time signatures use numerical fractions as structural analogs of proportional duration relationships, without any iconic representation of duration by pictorial synaesthesia. The mordent sign (a zigzag bisected by a slash) depicts the regular down-and-up fluctuation of pitches, but not their levels or number, and the bisecting slash does not depict any significant event in the middle of the sound pattern. Wilson's animal-sound transcriptions are digital and iconic, since their graphic height and length mirrors the pitch height and time-length of the sounds they represent.

Theories of the encoding of information should account for transmittal or carrier media (e.g. the staff in staff notation, itself meaningless but calibrated to carry bits of musical-event information and the empty spaces that separate them), and noise, which interferes with the reception of transmitted information. In devising a transcriptional strategy, one factor to be considered is an efficient relationship between carrier and information, since, for example, the single line often used for single-pitch drumbeat transcriptions could not carry heptatonic-scale pitch information, while to use the five-line staff for single-pitch drumbeats makes the extra lines meaningless rather than carriers of information.

5. CONTENT: CULTURE-SPECIFIC/INTERCULTURAL The content of notation systems, the musical information they convey, is specific to the cultures and musics from which they arise. At the same time, notations will include some information that pertains to intercultural aspects of music, in accord with the features shared by their musics and musics of other cultures. Thus, the information in Western staff notation that pertains to 'functional' harmony is specific to Western musical culture, while information on the proportional organization of rhythm (cycle and beat subdivisions and combinations) reflects a principle of musical organization found in varying forms in many

cultures. The signs in Tibetan cymbal notations for the musical treatment of *'phar* energy patterns reflect a particularly Tibetan principle of musical organization (Ellingson, 1979, 'Mathematics'), while the numbering of beats into counted beat groups in the same notations reflects a form of conceptual abstraction not found in other cultures.

In transcription, the concerns of most scholars have led to the emphasis of interculturally relevant over culture-specific content. However, transcribers have also found it necessary to adapt or devise notations for representing culture-specific musical features; these include the letter notations for what Kunst (1972) called the colotomic subdivisions of the Javanese *gongan* cycle by various gongs, and the asymmetrically alternating long-short 'measures' used by Ladzekpo and Pantaleoni (1970) to show the relationship of other parts to the bell pattern in West African drum ensembles. Features of notation devised to solve special descriptive problems in the music of particular cultures may often be used or adapted to solve similar problems elsewhere.

The parameters and contrasts considered here represent a wide range of components. Contrasts of function and reference represent dimensions of time, space, causality, and person: prescriptive notations are made before the music is performed, descriptive afterwards; and articulatory (subjective) notations refer to a player's causative actions at the place where sounds are articulated, while acoustic (objective) notations refer to sounds as results heard by a listener. Mode of symbolization is a matter of communication and semiotics, and the iconic/abstract distinction could be conceived as sensual/logical and related to concepts of mental processes as formulated by psychological schools as primary/secondary, instinctive/learned, right/left brain, unconditioned/conditioned, and so on. Distinguishing forms of encoding as analog/digital has to do with information theory; while the resultant formal contrast of sparseness/density is a practical consideration. Finally, the content of a system is largely culture-specific, with varying admixtures of features that can be distinguished as having intercultural relevance.

This gradation of components – time, space, causality, person, communication, psychology, information, culture – progresses from a high level of abstractness and generality to a high level of particularity and environment-specific determinism. Formalist and content-oriented thought and approaches to notation, such as those expressed in traditional taxonomic labels like 'neumes' and 'tablature', would thus fall at or near the particularistic, culture-determinate end of the scale.

Although it would seem possible to combine each category distinguished in sets 1 through 5 with any other except its opposite in the same set – that is, we could have descriptive-articulatory-abstract, descriptive-acoustic-abstract, descriptive-acoustic-analog, etc, but not articulatory-acoustic – still, in existing notation systems, there is a strong tendency for certain categories to correlate with certain others. Thus, with limited exceptions, articulatory notations tend to be prescriptive, while descriptive notations tend to be acoustic. Articulatory notations are instrument notations; acoustic notations are often of vocal origin.

In designing transcription systems, the high correlation between descriptive and acoustic rather than articulatory notations is hardly accidental: articulatory notations can describe musical sound only by reference to a specific means of articulation, and in cross-cultural studies it is unlikely that most readers will have the corresponding instrument available. Nevertheless, the capacity of acoustic notations for sound description should not be taken for granted; for they can be compromised in various ways, the most obvious and probably most frequent compromise being to read them as articulatory notations for the piano. However, it is also questionable whether or to what extent description and communication have actually occurred if one never takes transcriptions prescriptively and never attempts to articulate their sounds; for anyone who imagines the sound described by a vocal transcription and then tries to sing it may be surprised at the difference, and anyone who then listens to a recording of the original performance will probably be more surprised still.

A general preference for iconic representation seems implicit in Kunst's and Hood's dictum that a transcription 'should look the way it sounds'. It would certainly be absurd to argue that a transcription 'should look different from the way it (the music) sounds', and there is no denying that iconicity can enhance the communicative power of transcriptions. We might well wonder whether a decision to transcribe non-iconically, accepting all the challenges of reducing music to graphic representations while rejecting the aid of the sophisticated symbolic conventions of verbal descriptions and mathematical formulae, and then further rejecting the special graphic advantages of pictorialism, is not an inefficient use of the power of graphic media. That is, if a representation of music is to be visual in the first place, then why not visualistic, that is, pictorial-graphic? And it could be argued that, at least in some cases, iconicity gives more musical truth than abstract representation.

As for form and content, most late-20th-century writers seem to admit flexibility of choice according to the purpose of the transcription and (presumably) the nature of the music being transcribed. Either analog or digital encoding may lend themselves particularly well to certain kinds of problems. Analog representations run the risk of becoming sparse to the point of ambiguity, and digital representations can become overloaded with discrete bits of data to the point where information turns into noise. The obvious solution is to apply the principle of elegance, holding that the simplicity or complexity of the representation (transcription) should mirror the simplicity or complexity of the phenomenon (music), another dimension of the Kunst/Hood 'look the way it sounds' dictum.

However, here we encounter the same issues of differing perceptions, as well as problems specific to encoding strategies: all things being equal, digital representation will always look more complex because it contains more symbolic elements. This would seem acceptable in return for the high degree of descriptive precision that comes with digital complexity; and yet, there may be deliberately imprecise 'analog' features of music that would be seriously misrepresented by such precision. Finally, in cross-cultural studies, an elegant solution to a problem in one culture or music may be too simple or too complex in another, implying a conflict between elegance and efficiency on the one hand and the quest for a cross-cultural transcriptional metalanguage on the other.

There is a widespread ethnomusicological preference for the notation of culture-specific features of music by interculturally applicable features of notation; but some problems do seem to demand culture-specific notational solutions, and these may subsequently be absorbed into the intercultural metalanguage of transcription. The culture-specific dimension of research and transcription is essential for answering the question, 'What is special about this music?' – a problem left blandly opaque by many conventional transcriptions – while the intercultural dimension is, of course, equally essential for understanding what is human and musical about any and all musics.

Finally, we should recognize that the referential content of notations may include other elements besides music in the narrow acoustic sense. Symbols referring to drumbeats or the pitches of a scale may also connote elements of a cosmology, as in Indian and Newar mantra notations (Ellingson, 1980, 1986) or Chinese (Kaufmann, 1967, p.55) and Balinese scales (McPhee, 1966, p.38). The suprasegmental (significant patterning above the level of atomistic components) patterns of notations may be intended to designate affective (emotional) or cognitive results as well as acoustic ones. We may either dogmatically exclude such features as 'extramusical' and hence of no interest, or admit them to the inclusive study of musical systems in all their aspects, acoustic and non-acoustic.

Bibliography

W. Jones: 'On the Musical Modes of the Hindoos', *Asiatick Researches*, iii (1784)

T. Wilson: *Prehistoric Art: The Origin of Art as Manifested in the Works of Prehistoric Man. Report of the U.S. National Museum* (1896), 325 (Washington, DC, 1898)

B. I. Gilman: 'Hopi Songs', *Journal of American Ethnology and Archaeology*, v (1908)

R. H. Van Gulik: *The Lore of the Chinese Lute* (Tokyo, 1940, rev. 2/1969)

J. F. Carrington: *Talking Drums of Africa* (London, 1949)

C. Seeger: 'Prescriptive and Descriptive Music Writing', *MQ*, xliv/2 (1958), 184; repr. in Seeger (1977), 168

W. Malm: *Japanese Music and Musical Instruments* (Rutland, VT, 1959)

W. Apel: *Harvard Dictionary of Music* (Cambridge, MA, 1961)

T.-H. Liu: *Liu T'ien-hua's Nan-hu and P'i-p'a Compositions* (Taipei 1964)

C. McPhee: *Music in Bali* (New Haven, 1966/R1976)

W. Kaufmann: *Musical Notations of the Orient* (Bloomington, 1967)

M. Serwadda and H. Pantaleoni: 'A Possible Notation for African Dance Drumming', *African Music*, iv/2 (1968), 47

G. Kubik: 'Composition Techniques in Kiganda Xylophone Music', *African Music*, iv/3 (1969), 22

C. Lévi-Strauss: *The Raw and the Cooked: Introduction to a Science of Mythology*, i (New York, 1969)

J. Koetting: 'Analysis and Notation of West African Drum Ensemble Music', *Selected Reports*, i/3 (1970), 116

S. K. Ladzekpo and H. Pantaleoni: 'Takada Drumming', *African Music*, iv/4 (1970), 6

M. Hood: *The Ethnomusicologist* (New York, 1971/R1982)

J. Kunst: *Music in Java* (The Hague, 1972)

R. M. Keesing: *Cultural Anthropology: a Contemporary Perspective* (New York, 1976, 2/1981)

E. Leach: *Culture and Communication: the Logic by Which Symbols are Connected* (Cambridge, MA, 1976)

T. A. Sebeok and D. J. Umiker-Sebeok, ed.: *Speech Surrogates: Drum and Whistle Systems* (The Hague, 1976)

A. Chandola: *Folk Drumming in the Himalayas: a Linguistic Approach to Music* (New York, 1977)

C. Seeger: *Studies in Musicology, 1935–1975* (Berkeley, 1977)

B. Bartók and A. B. Lord: *Yugoslav Folk Music*, ed. B. Suchoff (Albany, 1978)

T. Ellingson: '*Don Rta Dbyangs Gsum*: Tibetan Chant and Melodic Categories', *Asian Music*, x/2 (1979), 112

——: 'The Mathematics of Tibetan Rol mo', *EM*, xxiii/2 (1979), 225

——: *The Mandala of Sound: Concepts and Sound Structures in Tibetan Ritual Music* (diss., U. of Wisconsin, 1979)

I. D. Bent: 'Notation', §I, II, *Grove 6*

T. Ellingson: 'Ancient Indian Drum Syllables and Buston's *Sham pa ta* Ritual', *EM*, xxiv/3 (1980), 431

H. Zemp: 'Le jeu d'une flûte de Pan polyphonique', in G. Rouget, ed.: *Ethnomusicologie et représentations de la musique* (Paris, 1981), 8

S. C. De Vale: 'Prolegomena to a Study of Harp and Voice Sounds in Uganda: a Graphic System for the Notation of Texture', *Selected Reports in Ethnomusicology*, v (1984), 285

B. C. Wade: *Khyāl: Creativity within North India's Classical Music Tradition* (Cambridge, England, 1984)

T. Ellingson: 'Buddhist Musical Notations', *The Oral and the Literate in Music*, ed. Y. Tokumaru and O. Yamaguti (1986), 302

J. Goody: *The Logic of Writing and the Organization of Society* (Cambridge, England, 1986)

J. Kawada: 'Verbal and Non-Verbal Sounds: Some Considerations of the Basis of Oral Transmission of Music', *The Oral and the Literate in Music*, ed. Y. Tokumaru and O. Yamaguti (1986), 158

Y. Tokumaru and O. Yamaguti, eds.: *The Oral and the Literate in Music* (Tokyo, 1986)

G.-M. Wegner: *The Dhimaybaja of Bhaktapur: Studies in Newar Drumming*, i, Nepal Research Centre Publications, xii (Wiesbaden, 1986)

T. Ellingson: Transcription Example 14 for J. Spector, 'Chanting', *Encyclopedia of Religion*, iii, ed. M. Eliade and others (New York, 1987), 204

J. Goody: *The Interface Between the Written and the Oral* (Cambridge, England, 1987)

T. Ellingson: 'The Mathematics of Newar Buddhist Music', *Change and Continuity: Studies in the Nepalese Culture of the Kathmandu Valley*, ed. S. Lienhard (Turin, in preparation)

T. Ellingson: 'The Mathematics of Newar Buddhist Music', in S. Lienhard, ed.: *Change and Continuity: Studies in the Nepalese Culture of the Kathmandu Valley* (Torino, in press)

CHAPTER VII

Analysis of Musical Style

STEPHEN BLUM

Ethnomusicological approaches to the description and analysis of style are founded on different assessments of the conditions in which styles are formed, maintained, modified and abandoned. Methods of analysis differ, both in the extent to which questions of poetics (making) and aesthetics (perception and evaluation) are addressed, and in the underlying conceptions of the relations between creation and reception.

The early history of ethnomusicology includes work in several fields of enquiry – among them, comparative musicology, musical folklore, musical ethnography and cultural anthropology. Depending upon the circumstances in which they worked, some scholars have been more concerned with musical systems, types, genres, 'dialects' or idioms than with styles. The meanings of these terms in relation to one another have varied with the assumptions and procedures of research in different regions.

Many, perhaps most, studies of musical style have been comparative, attempting to distinguish two or more styles or 'stylistic strata' within the practice of one region; to compare the styles of two or more peoples; or to show that different styles are associated with specific types of economic activity and/or social organization. It is very much open to question whether one set of terms and procedures can be used in comparative analysis of music from all parts of the world. Recent improvements in the research techniques of ethnomusicologists have allowed for greater attention to the statements and actions of performers, many of whom are not musicians in the Western sense of the term.

Musical systems, styles and types

The comparative musicology of Carl Stumpf (1848–1936), Erich M. von Hornbostel (1877–1935), Jaap Kunst (1891–1960) and Robert Lachmann (1892–1939) was centred on the study of musical systems rather than on style analysis. Hornbostel's method for the analysis of non-European systems may be understood as an extension and adaptation of familiar Aristotelian and Aristoxenian principles and procedures: the analyst attempts to enumerate the components of a system and to identify their typical functions and relations, distinguishing the more permanent (or 'essential') elements and relations from the more changeable (or 'incidental'). In practice, the analysis of musical systems by comparative musicologists and musical folklorists commonly entailed separate treatment of tone systems and of rhythmic or metric systems.

In Hornbostel's conception, transcriptions and analyses are abstractions that mark certain moments or passages in recorded performances as similar, analogous or equivalent to one another (1909, p.1042):

> In many instances the rhythmic relations can only be disclosed through comparisons of melodically equivalent passages. Like [the analyst's] 'scales', the [rhythmic and formal] division one accepts in the end thus amounts to little more than a theoretical construct, designed to make the articulation of the melody more comprehensible; but [this] does not allow us to draw reliable conclusions concerning the singer's own conception.

As Hornbostel repeatedly warned (1913, pp.13–14; 1917, p.398), such theoretical constructs will inevitably exclude features treated as 'essential' by those who perform and best respond to the music. He realized that comparative musicologists would eventually concern themselves with aesthetic judgments expressed in many non-European languages, but few such statements were available to the members of his circle. Among the rare exceptions were some remarks in Swahili, given by Mwakinyo Makinyaga to the Berlin Seminar for Oriental Languages (Hornbostel, 1909, p.1048):

> ... na tena kama wanaimba sauti nnene ao nyembamba, watu wana-pendezwa zayidi kwimba kwao. Lakini tu kama watu watatu wane wanapocheza katikati, watu hawaipendezwa ile ngoma.
> ... and if they then sing with varying degrees of tonal intensity, people take even more pleasure in their song. Should only three or four persons dance in the middle, people will take less pleasure in such a dance (trans. Blum from Hornbostel's German).

Inasmuch as 'any feature that differentiates one tone from another ... can command attention and mark the tone in question with an accent' (Hornbostel, 1905–6, p.94; 1975, p.265), comparative musicologists came to expect that musicians would call their attention to possibilities of accentuation (as in 'varying degrees of tonal intensity') requiring improved techniques of recording, transcription and analysis (see Wachsmann, 1970, pp.136–8). Transcriptions and analyses can never be wholly 'objective', but some of the analyst's biases may be corrected through careful attention to recurrent features, within single recordings as well as within repertories (Hornbostel, 1909, p.793; 1917, p.406).

The articulation (*Gliederung*) of melodic shapes (*Melodiegestalten*) was one of Hornbostel's most important concerns as he developed a general analytic method for comparative musicology. His procedures were based on the assumption that musical shapes are coherent by virtue of boundaries that may be shifted only within definite limits (1913, p.23). In a performance (or a group of related performances), musicians will normally acknowledge certain of these boundaries, either at regular intervals of time or at predictable moments in the series of events.

Analysis thus begins with *Gliederung* or 'scansion' (Hornbostel, 1917, p.411):

> If the descending direction of the melodic motion be taken into account as
> well, scansion of the periods into their natural components, the motifs, allows
> us to recognize which tones and tone-relations are decisive for the structure.

To identify the motifs in his transcriptions, Hornbostel used bar-lines, letter
schemes and, in at least one instance (1919, pp.483–8), a 'comparative score'
in which the several presentations of each motif are vertically aligned and
deviations from the initial presentation are notated. This technique, which
distinguishes the more variable from the more constant passages, was also
used by Constantin Brăiloiu (1931, pp.250–53; 1973, pp.26–9) and many
others.

Hornbostel's scansion of a Nyamwezi women's dance song (ex.1, from 1909,
no.7) maps structural analogies between two sections of equivalent length
(transcribed as ten measures of 6/4): segments B, C and D in I correspond to
B′, E′ and E in II.

In keeping with his premise that 'the real, in other words the psychological
elements of a melody are motifs, not tones' (1909, p.1035), Hornbostel
provided alternative bar-lines above the staff, to identify recurrent rhythmic
motifs (♪♪♩ in bars 36 and 47; ♩.♪♩ in bars 33, 41, 39, 48). The alternative
barring also contrasts a 'European' interpretation of the metre with the
regular groupings of six time units that Hornbostel found to be most common
in Nyamwezi music (1909, pp.797, 1042).

With his scansion of a Hutu women's song (1917, no. 17, and 1928, p.46;
disc FE 4175, D/9), Hornbostel attempted to show the intersection of
'metrically related' rhythmic motifs, each of them equivalent to ten 8th-notes
but beginning at different points in the time-cycle of 20 8th-notes (ex.2a). The
bar-lines above the staff in his transcription (ex.2b) mark analogous 'periods'
in the handclapping, the soloist's line and the group's response. The most
essential melodic steps are taken simultaneously by soloist and group,
descending to the 'dominant' and the 'tonic', respectively, from their upper
neighbours (or 'leading tones'). The boundaries acknowledged with these
melodic moves are the 'primary main tones': the 'starting point' (dominant)
and the 'goal' (tonic) of the melodic motion. The two upper neighbours
function as 'secondary main tones'. Hornbostel outlined a melody's 'tonality'
– the relations of the main tones to one another and to those of lesser
importance (1909, p.1035) – by means of a scale in which the 'melodic weight'
of each tone is indicated by its relative duration, with brackets connecting the
primary and secondary main tones (exx.1b, 2c). The extent to which the
intonation of each scale degree is consistent – as in the consistently 'low' third
above the tonic in the group response of the Hutu song and in one of its
variants (1917, no.3) – may serve as an index of 'melodic weight'.

The scales abstracted by Hornbostel from his transcriptions are arranged in
tables of tonal types, in order to display regularities of tonal structure not
immediately apparent from the transcriptions and analyses of single items.
The conclusions in his monographs on the musics of various peoples address
both the material at hand and the larger questions of 'a theory of pure melody'
(1917, p.398), diametrically opposed to modern European harmonic logic. In
the Rwanda monograph of 1917 and in most of his subsequent work,
Hornbostel notated his abstractions of scales to descend from the highest tone

Ethnomusicology: an Introduction

Ex. 1 Transcription and analysis of a Nyamwezi women's dance song (from Hornbostel, 1909, Nº7)

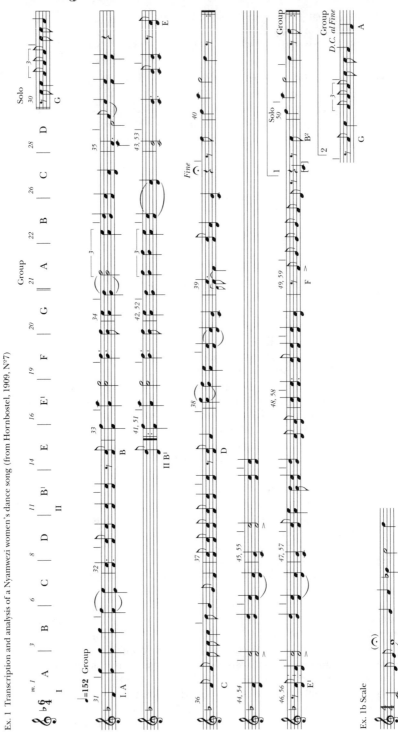

Ex. 1b Scale

168

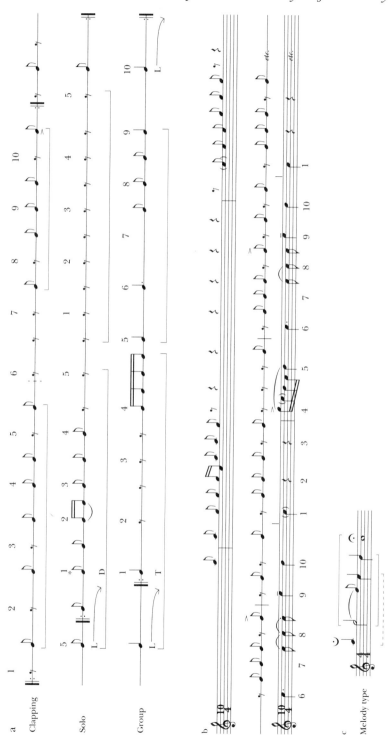

Ex. 2 Transcription and analysis of a Hutu women's song (adapted from Hornbostel, 1917, p. 409)

– following 'the natural motion of melody . . . from tension to rest' (1928, p.34). The analyses of his transcriptions drew upon general conclusions reached in earlier work, such as the judgment that 'in essence only two categories of intervals are to be distinguished' in melodies: steps and leaps (1909, p.1034), with the first class sometimes including major as well as minor 3rds.

Hornbostel's techniques of analysis were developed for use in the reconstruction of music history. He assumed that, given the coexistence of simple and complicated forms within one musical culture, 'the complicated forms may be considered as having sprung from the simple ones' (1928, p.40). His analysis of ex.2 posits the existence of two earlier stages: such devices as the handclapping pattern appear only with the advent of group singing (1928, p.55), and 'purely melodic' responsorial singing between soloist and group leads naturally to overlapping of the periods (1917, pp.403–6). Hutu musical style was characterized by numerous forms of responsorial singing, raising questions about the cultural history of Rwanda. Had the Tutsi overlords deliberately refrained from adopting responsorial practices of their Hutu subjects? Did the example of Twa two-part singing, in which both parts are 'autonomous', stimulate a richer elaboration of responsorial forms among the Hutu (1917, p.412)?

Hornbostel used the term 'style' when speaking of various totalities, notably those involving habitual motor behaviour of musicians: the manner of singing and playing as opposed to *what* is sung and played. Stylistic unity, in Hornbostel's conception, results from the unity of the creator's personality or from the unity of a culture, expressed through techniques of the body (1930, p.14). He was struck by the fact that the distinctive styles of the three peoples living side by side in Rwanda are audible 'the moment they sing' (1921, p.180). As a way of moving to produce sound, 'style' is difficult to analyse without destroying 'just the essential factor contained in an undivided whole' (1948, p.67), and it is more likely to be acquired through inheritance than through cultural exchange. The singing style common to many native peoples of the Americas, from the Polar regions to Tierra del Fuego, seemed to Hornbostel a particularly compelling illustration of the importance of stylistic evidence to the cultural historian (1912, p.180; 1923, pp.414–17; 1936, pp.361–5; 1948, pp.90–95).

Hornbostel's hypotheses, analytic methods, and underlying assumptions were utilized but also challenged by a brilliant group of students and colleagues, including Marius Schneider (1903–82), Mieczyslaw Kolinski (1901–81), George Herzog (1901–83) and Fritz Bose (1906–75). Schneider (1934–5, 2/1969) continued Hornbostel's reconstruction of 'stages' or 'levels' in the evolution of polyphony (understood as 'simultaneous variation'), while Kolinski attempted to refute Hornbostel's theory of pure melody (1957) and devised methods for the comparative analysis of melodic movement (1965, 'The General Direction of Melodic Movements'; 1965, 'The Structure of Melodic Movement'), tonal structures (1961), and metro-rhythmic patterns (1973) in European as well as non-European music. Herzog, on the other hand, reaffirmed the assumptions and procedures of the theory of pure melody. He devoted special attention to degrees of stylistic integration, selecting the highly unified Yuman musical style as the subject of his first monograph (1928).

170

The importance attached by Herzog to questions of style shows his indebtedness to his second mentor, the anthropologist Franz Boas (1858–1942), as well as to Hornbostel. In Boas's view, styles are not necessarily unified wholes:

> There is probably not a single region in existence in which the art style may be understood entirely as an inner growth and an expression of cultural life of a single tribe. Wherever a sufficient amount of material is available, we can trace the influence of neighboring tribes upon one another, often extending over vast distances (1927, p.176).

Herzog described styles as aggregates of 'traits' or 'features' that may or may not constitute 'a harmonious configuration or "Gestalt"' (1935, p.24) and are in either case subject to continual reordering. The type and degree of stylistic integration achieved by a people may be assessed through examination of 'foreign songs' that have or have not been adapted to the prevalent style(s) of that people.

Herzog's most sustained discussion of musical style is found in his dissertation, 'A Comparison of Pueblo and Pima Musical Styles' (1936). He saw the two styles as representative of quite different attitudes:

> . . . Pima style appears to be quite homogenous and closed. Foreign elements are easily detected. Pueblo style, in spite of its great formalization, is exceedingly exuberant and ready to assimilate suggestions from the outside (p.310).

The comparison was designed to cast light on the cultural history of the two peoples and on the maintenance of stylistic boundaries within a region (1936, p.284). Herzog followed Boas (1927, p.146) as well as Hornbostel in assuming that motor habits are most resistant to change, and the Pueblo and Pima manners of singing were thus emphasized in his analysis.

Herzog's account of Pueblo vocal technique supplied details that were missing from Hornbostel's remarks on the 'emphatic' singing manner common to many peoples of the Americas:

> The singing voice is produced with an almost continuous pressure of the vocal organs, notably the epiglottis. On tones initial to a phrase, motif, etc., the attack on a vowel tends to be made with a forceful 'glottal stop' . . . As a rule the pressure is not released entirely during the singing of a unit taken in the same breath, and it is reinforced continually, with almost every tone. The pressure does not affect the vocal organs only, but also some of the facial muscles. This continuous exertion is rather difficult to maintain with a wide-open mouth and the jaws and lips are, in consequence, barely parted (1936, p.288).

The Pima singing style, like the Yuman, was marked by the absence of these features. Although Herzog accepted Hornbostel's suggestion that this 'non-emphatic singing manner' was the more archaic of the two, his method of analysis led to the conclusion that 'the traits which make for these "Indian" or "pre-Indian" types of music are not associated with each other consistently' (1936, p.319). In some cultures but not in others the emphatic vocal techniques seemed to have generated numerous 'secondary tones', allowing

171

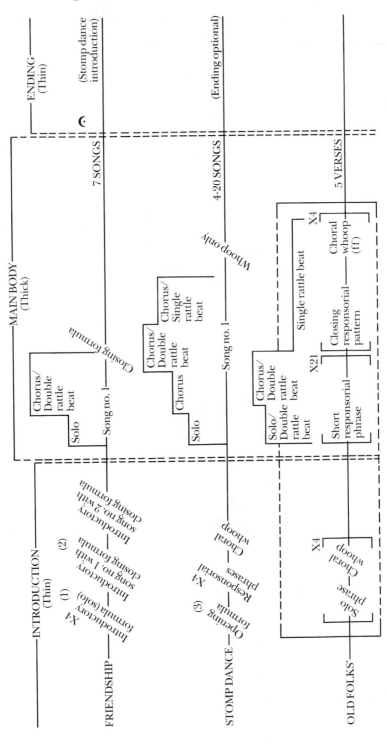

1. *Musical forms of the Stomp Dance (from Heth, 1979, p.133): (1) Introductory formula: a solo phrase (mf) and a choral whoop (f); (2) Closing formula: a responsorial phrase (mf) and a whoop (f); (3) Opening formula: a phrase (mf) begun by soloist and continued by whole group*

for richer melodic growth and greater formal complexity (1936, p.309). Similarly, the non-emphatic manner was only in some instances associated with melodic and structural simplicity.

Herzog abandoned Hornbostel's practice of attaching a short analysis to each transcription. Rather, he formulated generalizations that applied to a limited number of the items transcribed from each culture, in this way using his material to identify 'song-types' or 'sub-styles'. The procedure was feasible only with a larger number of recordings and a richer fund of data obtained through fieldwork: over 400 Pueblo and Pima recordings made by Herzog himself, in comparison to the 43 songs transcribed by Hornbostel from Czekanowski's Rwanda collection. Herzog's meticulous delineation of song types, and his studies of diffusion and mixture of types, are perhaps his most significant contributions to the literature on style analysis.

With modifications, Herzog's approach to the analysis of types proved useful in further studies of American Indian styles. David McAllester's economical description of the style of 84 songs used in the Peyote religion identified 'certain consistencies' in manner of singing, tempo, accompaniment, note values, structure, final tones of phrases and final syllables of texts (1949, pp.80–2). Charlotte Heth's study 'Stylistic Similarities in Cherokee and Iroquois Music' examined one group of formal types, with attention to 'musical reasons for the use of these forms' and 'interrelationships of the performing media' (1979, p.128). Heth's outlines of forms (fig.1) describe whole performance events. Because her analysis is based on observation and documentation of the performers' actions during entire song-cycles, it is a great improvement over Herzog's formal schemes.

Other comparative musicologists active in the 1930s and 1940s also approached difficult questions about the history of musical systems through analysis of musical types. In his study of the smaller of two Jewish communities of the Isle of Jerba, Lachmann found three musical types, each carrying a different social function: women's songs, liturgical cantillation and festival songs. He regarded the three types as products of as many musical systems, differing in the extent to which tonal and rhythmic relations had been rationalized. He interpreted each system as 'a grade in a general course of development' towards greater rationalization, and he believed that systems 'suffer continuous change' (1940, pp.83–5). Lachmann's monograph on Jerba is unique among community studies in viewing a small collection of 22 items as an epitome of several major developments in world music history.

According to Lachmann, the laws governing the women's songs were those of 'a pre-rational or non-rational tone-system' (1940, p.72), inextricably linked to motor impulses. Within a small group of seven women's songs, he distinguished two styles, one of which tempered the expression of psychophysical impulses with greater emphasis on articulation of the melodies (1940, pp.81–2). The most rationalized of the three systems, that of the festival songs, was shared with the several varieties of Tunisian urban music. In the system of liturgical cantillation, rational norms were 'intrusions', assimilated over many centuries without entirely suppressing 'pre-rational' melodic and rhythmic tendencies. An analysis of two readings of one passage by a single cantor (ex.3) shows variants of four 'typical melodic phrases': in Lachmann's

Ex. 3 Transcription and analysis of two readings of Exodus 13:17-18, by one cantor
(from Lachmann, 1940, pp. 87, 98)

a) Transcription:

b) Analysis

Exod. XIII   17: $\frac{b+b}{a^1}$ ¦ d ¦ b+d | d ¦ a^0 ¦ a ‖

18:   c ¦ a^0 ¦ b | a^0 ¦ a ‖

conception, a musical type contains a greater or lesser number of typical shapes, variable within wider or narrower limits. He recommended the use of an 'experimental method' (1940, p.39) to discover these limits gradually by analysing differences between acceptable and unacceptable renderings, as judged by competent performers.

Through the work of Herzog, Lachmann and others, ethnomusicologists began to acquire appropriate techniques with which to examine the coexistence and changing relationships of musical systems, styles and types within specific regions. It did not prove possible to standardize the terminology used in such studies: 'system', 'style', and 'type' have not been given unambiguous, widely accepted definitions.

The full repertory of types cultivated by a group is sometimes said to constitute the 'musical dialect' of that group, and a broad concept of 'regional style' may refer to 'groups of musical dialects with common elements' (Hoshovsky, 1980, p.408). In other writings, however, 'dialect' is the broader term designating 'a special configuration of the known historical styles, whereby individual stylistic elements are integrated into a relatively new formation' (Elschek, 1980, p.134).

'Style' is also used as a synonym for 'type', where the description of a style specifies the techniques of construction that distinguish one type from others. This conception makes it possible to map the geographical distribution of types as accurately as the distribution of musical instruments, without assuming that stylistic boundaries inevitably coincide with national, regional or linguistic boundaries.

Ex. 4 One type of song for the Feast of St John the Baptist (from Kvitka, 1942 and 1967)

a) Notated by M.Czarnowska, 1917, Mogilyev district, Belorussia

b) Notated by K.Kvitka, 1930, Sumy district, Ukraine

Klyment Kvitka (1880–1953), for example, defined one type of eastern Slavic song (for the feast of St John the Baptist) by three features: (i) an octosyllabic line divided into two groups of four syllables; (ii) framed by initial and terminal refrains; (iii) which are identical in words and rhythm but different in melody (ex.4, from Kvitka, 1942, Ger. trans. 1967). Similarly concise descriptions identified other types of harvest and wedding songs, each with a unique distribution in specific districts of Belorussia, the Ukraine and adjacent territories. Whereas Lachmann's analysis of musical types in Jerba referred directly to three 'grades in a general course of development', Kvitka's method produced evidence that might be used by social historians (Kvitka, 1942).

> Calendrical and wedding songs were relatively stable in transmission, and one may assume that the range of distribution of a particular type points to the prevailing social relations of the period in which that type originated and came into use (1967, p.309).

This difference in the underlying assumptions of Lachmann and Kvitka illustrates the characteristic orientations of comparative musicologists and musical folklorists or ethnographers, respectively. The latter were obliged, at an early stage, to classify and analyse large bodies of material. Working with concepts of type, genre, system, style and dialect, many musical folklorists chose not to attach these ideas to general theories of 'rationalization' and 'pure melody'.

An important connection between the concerns of comparative musicology and those of musical folklore was effected, just as the term 'ethnomusicology' began to gain currency, in the late work of the Romanian scholar Constantin Brăiloiu (1893–1958). Brăiloiu's definition of 'system' – 'a coherent set of artistic procedures, governed by intelligible laws' (1948, p.26; 1973, p.153) – is consistent with an Aristoxenian approach to harmonics, rhythmics, and metrics. He argued that certain systems correspond to 'a particular type of civilization, essentially characterized by uniformity of occupations and obedience to an inherited state of things' (1959, p.88; 1973, p.142). Analysis of such a system identifies its permanent elements or resources and the 'natural' principles by which these are exhaustively exploited (1959, p.91; 1973, p.145). Systems, in this sense, predate the styles and dialects that crystallize once a set of resources and principles has been expanded and modified through contact with other sets (1949, pp.329–31; 1973, pp.115–17). By this conception, analysis of a system can enumerate the elements, name the principles and circumscribe the allowable permutations; analysis of a style, however, will show how two or more systems are employed concurrently.

Brăiloiu produced preliminary descriptions of two rhythmic systems: the *syllabic giusto* as used in Romanian peasant song (1948) and the so-called *aksak* rhythms of eastern Europe and western Central Asia (1951). The first of these was extended into an account of a metro–rhythmic system found in children's songs the world over (1956). Brăiloiu also attempted to demonstrate that a system of three tones is one of the oldest and most widespread sets of musical resources (1953).

The system of the *syllabic giusto* was determined by two principles only: (i) exclusive use of two units of duration having the ratio 1:2 or 2:1 and (ii) combination of elementary rhythmic groups comprising two or three such durational units. Brăiloiu listed 256 possible combinations for lines of six or of

176

eight syllables with various patterns of stress. Although his description referred to Romanian peasant song, the intent was to encourage recognition and analysis of the same system in other repertories (see Baud-Bovy, 1956). The system of *aksak* rhythms involves exclusive use of two units having the ratio 2:3 or 3:2; Brăiloiu's inventory of the possible combinations lists 1884 measures with one, two or three elementary rhythmic groups.

Brăiloiu deplored the tendency of comparative musicologists to disregard European peasant music in favour of everything 'non-Western' (1959, p.88; 1973, p.142). He emphasized the study of rhythmic and tonal systems that were 'undomesticated', attempting in this way to link the folklorist's interest in 'authentic' practices with the comparative musicologist's project of reconstructing the earliest stages of music history. Brăiloiu believed that tradition-bound societies were everywhere 'in more or less advanced states of dissolution', and his proposal for a unified approach to the study of natural systems appears to exclude the greater portion of the music investigated by ethnomusicologists in the second half of this century.

Assumptions about the history of musical systems were particularly important in the comparative musicology of the German-speaking world and the musical ethnography of the former USSR. Early stages in the development of musical systems were often described as 'pre-systematic', 'non-rational', or 'incompletely rationalized' (Lachmann, 1935, pp.5, 7). Lachmann's interpretation of liturgical cantillation as 'no longer' controlled by pre-rational tendencies but 'not yet' fully rationalized exemplifies a strategy followed by many of his contemporaries. 'Archaic survivals' were described with reference to idealized practices that 'no longer' retained their full scope and power; modern musical practices were 'not yet' apparent in areas where development remained incomplete.

In the former USSR, studies of 'national musical cultures' attempted to identify the 'vigorous survivals of primitive forms' (Belyayev, 1933, p.422) and the historical stages through which 'higher' forms had evolved. The work of V. M. Belyayev (1888–1968) was particularly influential in outlining three major stages in world music history (summarized, Belyayev, 1965): (i) musical folklore, predominantly vocal; (ii) the professional musical arts that were gradually systematized as 'generalized types of melodic movement' and came to be 'fixed in the scaling of musical instruments' (Belyayev, 1963, 'The Formation of Folk Modal Systems', p.4); and (iii) the 'modern forms of polyphony and harmony', dependent upon musical notation and tempered scales. Belyayev's important textbooks on the history of the music of the peoples of the USSR (vol. i, 1962, trans. Slobin, 1975; vol. ii, 1963, *Ocherki po istorii muziki*) were organized according to this scheme. In his analyses of Turkmen *dutar* compositions, the 'most highly developed repertory of Turkmen music' (trans. Slobin, 1975, p.108), Belyayev described formal structures according to the scales and registers of the sections and according to their functions in the exposition, development and recapitulation of 'themes'.

Close attention to the treatment of musical 'ideas' and 'motifs' is one of the distinguishing features of much Soviet ethnomusicology. Izali Zemtsovsky's monograph on the Russian *protyazhnaya pesnya* (1967), for example, is concerned with development in each song of a 'melodic core' or 'intonational thesis' (following the terminology of Asaf'yev, 1930–47) (ex.5). Zemtsovsky's analyses revealed a correlation between the range of the melodic core (a 5th or a 4th) and the construction of the strophe (1967, pp.193–4).

Ex. 5 Analysis of one *Protyazhnaya Pesnya* (from Zemtsovsky 1967, Ex. 31)

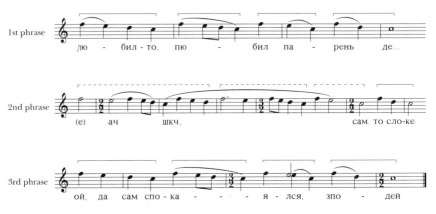

To a far greater extent than comparative musicology, ethnomusicology has been marked by tension between categories of allegedly universal relevance and distinctions of compelling local significance. The latter usually outweigh the former, as scholars seek to analyse the data they have gathered during intensive fieldwork within a community or a region. Most if not all concepts of system, style and type have served to illuminate aspects of certain musical cultures only. Methods of comparative style analysis have been most successful in identifying the stylistic strata in one musical practice or in a group of related practices.

Comparative analysis of styles

In the first half of the 20th century, many concepts shared by comparative musicologists and musical folklorists with art historians, ethnologists and others were used to define styles as ideal types by contrasting certain of their features. The widely admired analysis of Renaissance and Baroque architecture, sculpture, and painting by Heinrich Wölfflin (1915) described two fully developed systems of perception and representation in terms of five polarities. Closely related to less subtle dichotomies between 'naturalistic' and 'geometrical', or 'representative' and 'ornamental' styles of art (see Schapiro, 1953, pp.297–303) were the 'primordial dualisms' of dance styles and singing styles posited by Curt Sachs (1881–1959), a scholar trained in both art history and music history.

The names Sachs gave to 'two different, indeed opposing, singing styles' refer to the processes from which, in his view, they have emerged. Originating in 'passion and motor impulse', the *pathogenic* style traces the gradual slackening of the singer's energy that follows each outburst of strong emotion. Originating in cantillation of sacred texts with one 'high' and one 'low' pitch, the *logogenic* style lends itself to development through extension of the initial nucleus of two notes (Sachs, 1943, *The Rise of Music in the Ancient World*, p.52). Sachs attempted to show that the dualism had been productive, given the 'inevitable' confrontations and combinations of the two styles. His melogenic forms of song do not constitute a third stylistic category but, rather, a large class of melodies born of interaction between the two opposing principles. Similarly, the antithesis between the image dance, 'bound to the body', and the imageless dance, 'free of the body', results in a proliferation of intermediate, hybrid forms (Sachs, 1933, pp.39–42).

These and similar categories have been used in at least three ways to describe attributes of specific recordings or transcriptions. (i) The analyst interprets a given melodic line as a domestication, transformation, or 'rediscovery' of the archaic pathogenic style (Sachs, 1961, pp.52–9; Brandel, 1961, pp.66–7, 70; Sevåg, 1980, p.324); (ii) Tones are labelled (as *affixes* and *infixes*), and melodies are classified, to reveal the successive accretions to the initial nucleus in logogenic melodies (Sachs, 1943, *The Rise of Music in the Ancient World*, pp.37–9; 1961, pp.64–7, 144–5); (iii) The analyst maintains that one melody or genre displays conflicts between two opposing 'urges' and/or structural intervals. According to Sachs, 'an obviously older one-step pattern *g–f* and a double 3rd *f–a–c* are in strong opposition and contention' in a Caribou Eskimo song (ex.6, from Sachs, 1961, p.165).

Ex. 6 Caribou Eskimo Song (from Sachs 1961, 165)

According to A. L. Lloyd (1980), the sung domestic lament in parts of southern and eastern Europe often shifts between emotional outpouring of grief ('lament by tears' in Albania) and more formalized utterance ('lament by voice').

The three techniques were not designed for analytic studies of whole repertories and have seldom been applied in such studies. Sachs generally illustrated his arguments with single examples from disparate cultures, and many of his conclusions concerning the global distribution of tonal structures were premature. In at least one area, however, his interest in conflicting principles of melodic organization shed new light on a large group of related idioms: tracing the hypothetical expansion of a tertial nucleus to chains of two, three, four, five and ultimately six 3rds (Sachs, 1943, 'The Road to Major'; 1943, *The Rise of Music in the Ancient World*, pp.295–305; 1961, pp.145–52) uncovered a melodic predilection shared by many European and Central Asian peoples, which may or may not have conflicted with preferences for quartal and quintal frameworks. Although Sachs assumed such conflicts to be inevitable, more than one idiom allows for frameworks of both types (see e.g., Blum, 1974, pp.108–14).

Methods of comparative analysis currently employed by ethnomusicologists cover a wide spectrum: some are designed to address the broad questions carried over from comparative musicology, while others are deliberately limited to differences that can be shown to matter in the music and musical life of large regions or small communities.

Of the methods at the 'universal' end of the spectrum, the systems of Cantometrics and Choreometrics devised by Alan Lomax (*b* 1915) have received the most attention. Lomax has described the initial observations from which his project developed. These were polarities noted in 1953 and 1955 during field surveys of Spanish and Italian folk singing: vocal tension and solo singing appeared to be correlated with seclusion of women in southern Spain and southern Italy, while choirs of open, well-blended voices seemed to reflect the relaxed sexual mores found north of the Pyrenees and north of the Apennines (Lomax, 1968, pp.vi–viii). Lomax at once proposed that 'vocal stance varies with the strictness of sexual sanctions' in all human societies, and he eventually claimed to have shown that 'song style symbolizes and reinforces certain important aspects of social structure in all cultures' (ibid). Style would function as both symbol and reinforcement if, as Lomax believes, young people learn the behavioural norms of their culture through singing.

As presented in a coding manual and a set of training tapes (Lomax, 1976), the techniques of Cantometrics utilize 37 scales in 'rating' and profiling styles of singing. From left to right on the rating sheet (fig.2), many of the scales extend from minimal to maximal degrees of redundancy or cohesiveness. The profiles of two styles, 'Urban East Asian' and 'African Gatherer', fall mainly at opposite extremes of all 37 measures and exemplify two ideal types of social organization: 'the highly stratified, dominance-oriented empire' and 'the egalitarian, intra-supportive band' (Lomax, 1976, p.19; 1968, p.16). In drawing song performance profiles of over 400 societies, Lomax and his associates rated approximately ten recorded songs from each society. The profiles were arranged in clusters by means of data-processing programs (Lomax, 1968, pp.309–21).

Again and again, the correlations between singing style and social structure generated by the Cantometrics project have associated 'aggressive' singing with social complexity and 'good tonal blend' with social solidarity. Despite the origins of the project in Lomax's journeys through Spain and Italy, analysis by Cantometrics has not shown singing styles to vary with the small-scale differences in subsistence patterns and social stratification that distinguish some communities from their neighbours. However, recent changes in the musical style of some populations have matched certain of Lomax's predictions. Among the Kujamaat Diola of Senegal, for example, changes in community size, subsistence task complexity and hierarchies of political control have affected the mobility and the vocal styles of soloists, with 'a consistent trend toward differentiation and vocal display' (Irvine and Sapir, 1976, p.81).

Lomax insists that the crucial factors in sung communication must also be the most easily identified, when heard with reference to the extremes of his 37 scales. The training tapes juxtapose very short excerpts that illustrate extreme and intermediate degrees along each scale – for example, 'much' glottal shake, 'some' and 'little or none'. Most scales have from 3 to 5 degrees, and none exceeds 13. Although the extreme degrees are usually opposites – 'very precise' enunciation against 'very slurred', for example – this is not true of several measures, including 'Melodic Shape' (classed as arched, terraced, undulating

KEY: URBAN EAST ASIA

AFRICAN GATHERER

Names of the scales   *Precis of the scales*

GROUP ORGANIZATION
1) Social org: Vocal grp — SOLO ONE PART TWO + PARTS
2) Rhy rel'n: Vocal-orch — SOLO ONE PART ..... TWO + PARTS
3) Social org: Orchestra — SOLO ONE PART ..... TWO + PARTS
4) Musical org: Vocal — SOLO ONE PART .... TWO + PARTS

LEVEL OF COHESIVENESS
5) Tonal blend: Vocal grp — INDIVIDUALIZED .... UNIFIED
6) Rhy coord'n: Vocal grp — INDIVIDUALIZED .... UNIFIED
7) Musical org: Orchestra — SOLO ONE PART TWO + PARTS
9) Rhy coord'n: Orch grp — INDIVIDUALIZED .... UNIFIED

10) Repetition of text — FEW REPEATS ..... MANY REPEATS

RHYTHMIC FEATURES
11) Overall rhythm: Vocal — IRREGULAR .... REGULAR
12) Rhy rel'n: Vocal grp — SOLO ONE PART TWO + PARTS
13) Overall rhythm: Orch — IRREGULAR .... REGULAR
14) Rhy rel'n: Orch grp — SOLO ONE PART .... TWO + PARTS

MELODIC FEATURES
15) Melodic shape — ARCHED WAVELIKE DESCENDING
16) Melodic form — COMPLEX .... SIMPLE
17) Phrase length — LONG .... SHORT
18) Number of phrases — MANY .... ONE/TWO
19) Position: Final tone — LOW .... HIGH
20) Melodic range — SMALL .... LARGE
21) Interval size — SMALL .... LARGE
22) Polyphonic type — NONE SIMPLE .... COMPLEX
23) Embellishment — MUCH .... LITTLE

DYNAMIC FEATURES
24) Tempo — SLOW ...... MOD .... FAST
25) Volume — LOUD .... MID ...... SOFT
26) Rubato: Vocal — MUCH .... NONE
27) Rubato: Orchestral — MUCH .... NONE

ORNAMENTATION
28) Glissando — MUCH .... LITTLE
29) Melisma — MUCH .... LITTLE
30) Tremolo — MUCH .... LITTLE
31) Glottal — MUCH .... LITTLE

VOCAL QUALITIES
32) Vocal pitch (Register) — HIGH MID .... LOW
33) Vocal width — NARROW .... WIDE
34) Nasality — MUCH .... LITTLE
35) Rasp — MUCH .... LITTLE
36) Accent — FORCEFUL ..... MID .... LAX
37) Enunciation — PRECISE .... SLURRED

Solo-Dominant   *Integrated-Groupy*

2. Outlines of the Cantometric Scales (from Lomax, 1976)

181

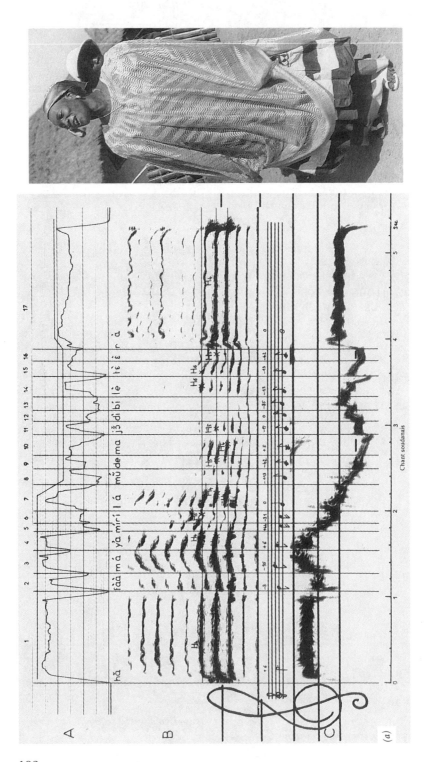

182

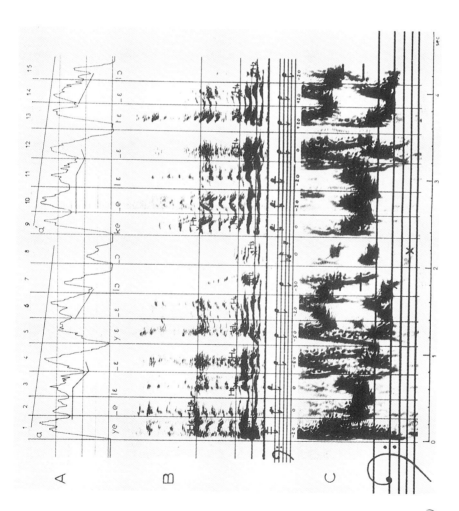

3. Sonagrams of (a) seventeen syllables sung by a Malinké singer and (b) fifteen syllables sung by a Selk'Nam singer (both from Rouget, 1970). The photograph shows Kondé Kouyaté, the Malinké singer whose voice is recorded in (a).

(b)

183

or descending), 'Melodic Form' and 'Overall Vocal Rhythmic Scheme'. Critics have questioned the very possibility of scaling the types of 'Social Organization of the Vocal Group' in such a way that 'the degree of integration among the members of the group increases, roughly, as one proceeds from left to right along the line' (1968, p.38). A related difficulty involves rating the degree of 'simultaneous rhythmic conflict in multi-part music' (1968, pp.52–5; 1976, pp.193–5). Counting the number of phrases in each song is the only technique of scansion included in the Cantometrics rating system, which otherwise emphasizes overall impressions rather than perception of relationships among events in time and of changes during a performance.

Other comparative studies of style depend upon results of acoustical and/or physiological research rather than impressionistic ratings. Use of electroacoustic devices – stroboscope (Metfessel, 1928), melograph (C. Seeger, 1966), Bruel and Kjaer frequency analyser and level recorder (Rouget, 1970), sonograph (Graf, 1967; Rouget, 1970; Födermayr, 1971) – has made it possible to identify distinctive features of vocal and instrumental styles, which stand out particularly well when variable features of one style can be shown to remain constant in a second (Rouget, 1970, p.698; Födermayr, 1971, p.120).

After a careful analysis of two short sequences of sung syllables, by a Malinké and a Selk'Nam singer, Gilbert Rouget concludes that the two systems of vocal production are diametrically opposed to one another in almost every respect. In Rouget's graphs (figs.3*a* and *b*), the profiles of intensity (A) and frequency of the first partial (C) run parallel for the Malinké but not for the Selk'Nam example.

In the latter but not in the former, a descending sequence of pitches is matched by a sequence of vowels (**e ɛ ɔ**) in which the second formants of the vowels are progressively lower (see also Rouget, 1976, p.21). The graphs of the spectra (B in figs.3*a* and *b*) show the extent to which different sung syllables are linked by common upper partials, a type of 'consonance' that is more pervasive in the Selk'Nam than in the Malinké example. The Malinké singer defined each pitch with great precision, approximating, more often than not, one of the pitches of the equiheptatonic tuning of Malinké xylophones (Rouget, 1969). The Selk'Nam singer produced far more diffuse sounds, varying in intensity more than in timbre or 'consonance'. Rouget's analysis of the two styles indicates that Malinké singers are more concerned with the activity of the larynx, Selk'Nam singers with activity of the lungs.

One of the major challenges now facing ethnomusicologists is further development and refinement of methods of stylistic analysis that can identify and utilize pertinent physiological, acoustical and psychoacoustical data. Publications on these subjects necessarily devote considerable space to problems of method, in the hope that the techniques used to obtain and interpret data on one style will prove applicable in studies of many styles. In addition to Rouget's three papers (1969, 1970, 1976), other noteworthy contributions include several studies by Walter Graf (1903–82) and by his student Franz Födermayr.

Graf and Födermayr concentrated their attention on interpretation of sonagrams, produced with the Kay Sonagraph of the Phonogramarchiv, Austrian Academy of Sciences. In contrast to Lomax, they did not assume that

4. Formant frequencies of certain vowels and consonants (from Graf, 1967, repr. 1980)

one style of song expresses the central values of a culture: the 12 sonagrams presented in Graf's survey of Ainu vocal usages, for example, show a remarkable diversity (1967). Whereas Cantometrics excludes 'vocal noises which do not employ discrete pitches and have no rhythmic regularity' (Lomax, 1968, p.36; 1976, p.71), Graf and Födermayr were interested in the full range of sound communication among humans:

> Human societies have at their disposal one or another codification (subject, furthermore, to alterations over time) of prohibited, permitted, and preferred modes of behaviour and expression, which may change from society to society, indeed from situation to situation (Graf, 1967, p.535).

They have published excellent descriptions of several styles that are now or were once cultivated in many societies: ululation and *ololyge* (Födermayr, 1970), yodelling (Graf, 1965, 1980, pp.202–10), epic singing accompanied by a fiddle (Graf, 1967, pp.54–5 and 1980, pp.221–3), singing of the Peyote religion of the North American Plains (Födermayr, 1971, pp.105–19) and artistic singing of the Muslim Near East (Födermayr, 1971, pp.122–39). The last-mentioned study helps to clarify the elaborate Arabic terminology for qualities of voice.

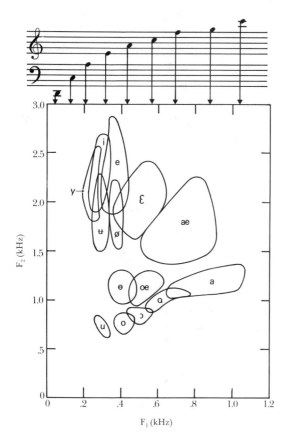

5. *Ranges of the two lowest formant frequencies for different vowels (from Sundberg 1987, p. 61)*

Systematic tabulation of data obtained from sonagrams is extremely useful, not only in identifying the optional and the obligatory features of specific genres of performance, but also in familiarizing the analyst with important variables of sound communication. Graf's analyses make reference to simplified tables of the formant characteristics of vowels and consonants (fig.4, from Graf, 1967; cf. fig.5) and to similar information about various sound-making devices (Graf, 1966, table facing p.84).

By carefully classifying ways of initiating, terminating, and connecting sung syllables, Födermayr's analysis of the genres Salish or 'Flathead' Indian song (1971, pp.35–99) succeeds in separating the features that are idiosyncratic from those that characterize genres.

The sonagraph and the melograph are becoming indispensable tools of ethnomusicological analysis, whether the analyst seeks to identify regularities in personal, local, regional or supra-regional styles. For organologists the utility of sonagrams and melograms increases when instruments are to be classified by 'inspection and faceted or multi-variable grouping' (Kartomi, 1990), taking into account all similarities and differences in, say, the flutes of one region rather than dividing each abstract class by a fixed series of steps, with one variable per step (see Elschek, 1969, 1979). The advantages of 'empirically-based upward grouping' over 'downward classification by logical division' (Kartomi, 1990) are as significant for students of musical style as for organologists.

Attempts at systematic description of two or more styles or musical types may take cognizance of however many similarities and differences. Some but not all methods for classifying songs, tunes, genres and the like either serve to justify or else presuppose a description of 'styles', 'stylistic strata', 'dialects', or 'idioms'. Economy in the number of distinctions registered does not always work to the advantage of ethnomusicological analysis: a complex, multifaceted classification scheme may help scholars to formulate questions and hypotheses about the social and historical processes that have produced and sustained one or another configuration of styles or of musical types. George Herzog's approach to the description of 'song-types' (see above) may be considered an early manifestation of ethnomusicological interest in 'upward grouping', since Herzog noted clusters of similarities and differences that distinguish types without presuming that the latter are necessarily controlled by archetypes or *Ursätze*.

For several decades, scholars of eastern and central European folk music have explored the points at which problems of classification and of style analysis converge and overlap. The rich experience accumulated in this undertaking (see Elschek and Stockmann, 1969; Stockmann and Stęszewski, 1973) holds important lessons for all ethnomusicologists, regardless of specialization. It has gradually become clear that ethnomusicologists need not posit the existence of a sole correct answer to Ilmari Krohn's question 'What is the best method to lexically arrange folk and folk-like songs by their melodic (not textual) constitution?' (Krohn, 1902–3). Much can be learned when one repertory is classified in several different ways (Kerényi, 1956, p.455; Járdányi, 1965, p.289; Elscheková, 1966). Yet the long-standing interest in comparing repertories through use of a single classification scheme (such as Krohn's) has also enhanced our understanding of stylistic differences.

187

No ethnomusicologist has contributed more to the comparative analysis of musical styles than did Béla Bartók (1881–1945). Unity or homogeneity of style was for Bartók the principal attribute of 'peasant music', considered as an ideal type or 'a separate type of melodic creativity which, by reason of its being a part of the peasant environment, reflects a certain uniform emotional pattern and has its own specific style' (1929, p.201; 1976, p.3). The coexistence among most eastern European peasantries of two or more styles – some less unified than others – made it necessary to speak of 'peasant music' in a broad as well as a narrow sense (Bartók, 1931, p.8; 1959, pp.51–2). Together with his contemporary Filaret Kolessa (1871–1946), Bartók realized the importance of contact and 'uninterrupted reciprocal influence' (Bartók, 1941–2, p.155; 1976, p.30) among peoples, not least in the vicinity of linguistic boundaries (Bartók, 1935, p.199). Thus, an appropriate method of style analysis would allow for comparison of the several styles cultivated by speakers of one language and those cultivated by their neighbours.

Classification is the first step, and identification of styles the second, in Bartók's account of the aims of musical folklorists:

(1) To constitute as rich a collection as possible of peasant tunes, scientifically classified, and principally of the tunes of neighbouring peasant classes that are in close contact with one another.
(2) To determine, by careful comparison, every one of the musical styles recognizable in the above materials, and so far as possible to trace them to their origins (1931, p.4).

Following the determination of styles, one may wish to revise earlier procedures of classification. Bartók described an 'old', a 'new' and a 'mixed (heterogeneous)' style of Hungarian peasant music, then made this tripartite division his point of departure for further classification and analysis of the material.

The homogeneity of the new style – a remarkably uniform 'musical dialect' (Bartók, 1933, p.289; 1976, p.102) – was central to Bartók's analysis. He observed the generative capacity of the style at its peak, early in this century, and feared that its popularity would jeopardize the survival of the less uniform (and hence judged more valuable) old style. Common features of the old style included: (i) no association of tunes with special occasions; (ii) pentatonicism; (iii) isometric strophes of four different musical lines; (iv) the main caesura (final note of the second line) a minor 3rd above the final note of the strophe, although two of the four 'dialect-regions' had diverged from this norm; (v) correlation of rhythm with the number of syllables per line: 12-, 8- and 6-syllable lines sung in *parlando–rubato* rhythm; 8-, 6- and 7-syllable lines in invariable *tempo giusto*; 8-, 7- and 11-syllable lines in adjustable *tempo giusto*. The new style was marked by: (i) predominance of the adjustable *tempo giusto* rhythm, used for lines of from 6 to 22 syllables, and (ii) the four 'architecturally rounded structures' AA^5BA, AA^5A^5A, ABBA, and AABA, the main caesura falling in the last case on the final, in the others on the upper 5th degree. Bartók initially found approximately one-half of the repertory to be heterogeneous in style, lacking one or more traits of either the old or the new, but he later incorporated three groups of the 'mixed' tunes within a revised description of the old style. His colleague Zoltán Kodály (1882–1967) preferred to speak of a 'primitive stratum', comprising a yet-to-be-determined number of stylistic types (1960, p.23).

Bartók used his concept of style as an instrument with which to form hypotheses, and he allowed no hypothesis to stand unchallenged. Nor did he assume that every peasant repertory contained one or two homogeneous styles: 'Romanian folk music is not unified but often displays (to a greater or lesser extent, according to region) altogether different, almost opposite characteristics' (1935, p.213). In seeking to identify styles, categories, groups, types or dialects in various eastern European repertories, Bartók asked the same or similar questions – concerning the topics of sung poetry, any association of tunes with special occasions, rhythm and tempo, metric structure of lines and strophes, melodic form, range and scale. Short answers were usually couched in comparative terms:

> In Rumania, suddenly, the text-stanza structure [found in Slovakia and Hungary] disappears (except in songs of urban or semirural origin) though rhymes are still in use; the four-section melody structure is not predominant, since a rather important part of the material has a three-section and a not negligible part a two-section structure; the melodies divide into primary classes according to the different occasions at which they are sung, each of these primary classes having their specific musical characteristics. Going farther south, that is, to Bulgarian and Serbo-Croatian territory, we find again unequivocal changes: no more text-stanza structures and no rhymes (except in songs of urban or semirural origin); two-thirds of the Serbo-Croatian melodies have two-section or three-section structures, much of the remaining third – with four-section structures – is of urban, semirural, or foreign origin. Here, as against the Rumanian material, no primary musical classes would result from a grouping of the melodies according to their function (Bartók and Lord, 1951, p.35).

Longer answers were presented and documented through statistical tables. Bartók devised many ways of tabulating the information that can be read from transcriptions of folk song. To describe a style is to make an inventory of the full range of options. Bartók pursued this goal most exhaustively in tabulating rhythmic schemata (ex.7, from Bartók, 1931, pp.32–3).

Many of the great achievements of eastern European folk-song scholarship are contributions to a comparative musical morphology of the region, with attention to the uses, distribution and history of specific formal types. Transcriptions have been utilized to discover and display the constant as well as the more variable aspects of musical form, for comparative purposes. The comparison may contrast a more unified with a more differentiated 'musical dialect', as in Kolessa's account of the larger but more homogeneous dialect-group of the eastern Ukraine and the smaller but highly differentiated dialect-group of the western Ukraine. Kolessa's description of the latter, like Bartók's of the Hungarian 'old style', emphasized the retention of archaic features, defined in opposition to the more modern features of the eastern group. The diversity of metrorhythmic schemes within one dialect of the western group, that of the Lemki, required an elaborate classification system with ten major divisions (Kolessa, 1929).

In the decades following World War II, eastern European scholars devised increasingly complex schemes of analysis and classification. The earlier

Ex. 7 Rhythmic schemata of Hungarian tunes to eleven-syllable lines, old style (from Bartók, 1931, pp. 32-3)

A. In Isorhythmic Strophes:

1.

2.

3.

B. In Heterorhythmic Strophes:

1.

2.

3.

emphasis on metrorhythmic structures was offset with more detailed consideration of tonal structures. At the Slovak Academy of Sciences, four systems were concurrently employed in the analysis of Slovak folk tunes: structural identification (7 elements to the system), comparative classification or typology (12 data), complex analysis (40 elements) and melodic analysis (5 data). Numerical coding was used for several elements to allow for automatic sorting and tabulating by punch-card machines (Elscheková, 1966). A consensus was reached on the temporal sequence of four stylistic strata: the magico-ritual, old-peasant, shepherd and new (or 'harmonic-melodic') styles (Kresánek, 1951; Elscheková, 1960). The definition of 'style' in this work remained consistent with Bartók's conception: 'the totality of individual melodies with similar structure which – from a national, historical or

190

territorial point of view – constitute a homogeneous unity within a musical culture' (Elscheková, 1960, p.353).

When style is understood as manner of performance rather than as structural framework, the latter may be taken as a constant against which to assess the characteristic ways of realizing one essential idea. Walter Wiora, Walter Salmen and others began to develop a method of 'comparative melodic research' in order to trace adaptations and transformations of common melody types in numerous styles of European song. As defined by Wiora (1969, p.37), melody types either 'determine the course of the melody and hence the sequence of its parts' or are 'aggregates of melodic figures in the framework of one tonality', in which case 'the components remain the same but their order changes'. Bartók's new style of Hungarian peasant music is treated as one melody type by this method, with examples from various times and places arranged in synoptic tables (ex.8, from Salmen, 1954, p.55; see also Wiora, 1952, pp.50–51). One aim is to reveal some of the attributes given to the essential framework by 'stylistically-associated communities' (Salmen, 1954, p.52), defined by region and/or social class. Little has been done as yet to carry out this programme. Salmen argued that the German colonization of eastern Europe in the later Middle Ages marked a point at which 'a great unity embracing all the common forms and styles of popular song, as well as the songs of the upper classes . . . extended from Portugal to the Ukraine' (1960, p.349). It remains to be seen, however, how many 'essential melody types' can be identified through studies that analyse the earliest notated sources of European folk music in relation to field recordings. Wiora's program for 'comparative melodic research' does not take into account the complex stratification of styles revealed by recent studies of eastern Europe (Elschek, 1981, pp.15–17, 29–30), and his method may be most appropriate to research on limited topics, such as the diffusion and adaptation of Protestant church songs in central and northern Europe (Wiora, 1956).

Regional differences among fiddlers in the USA have also been described through comparison of various realizations of common melodic frameworks (Burman-Hall, 1975, 1978). Students of many European and Asian musical practices have concerned themselves with techniques of 'diminution' (under whatever name) that are idiomatic to one instrument within one region. 'Comparative melodic research' is not always designed to illuminate the different habits and preferences of two or more 'stylistically-associated communities' that share a common set of melody types. One regional style is sometimes characterized by a distinctive collection of melodic frameworks as well as by a set of diminution techniques (Thrasher, 1985, pp.240–41). Recent studies of Chinese instrumental repertories (summarized and extended in Thrasher, 1985 and 1988) have attempted to reconstruct some of the techniques by which large portions of a repertory may have been derived from a small number of melodic models.

Interpretation of socio-musical action

The actions of human beings as they perform and respond to music are co-ordinated through 'styles' of acting. 'Styles' in this sense are experienced and analysed by ethnographers as they participate in, observe, document, reflect

Ex. 8 Nine examples of *the Tetonic Quatrain* AA'BA (from Salmen, 1954, p. 55)

upon and compare performances. Style analysis that is 'ethnomusicological' in the strongest sense of the term includes 'interpretive analysis of ethnohistorical and ethnographic data involving the music-making process' (Béhague, 1982, p.12). Such interpretive analysis often aims to describe principles and procedures that are actualized in performance. Working as ethnographers, as historians, or in both capacities, ethnomusicologists have emphasized 'the identification of culturally defined principles that govern the operation of style, including contextual correlates of sound' (Nketia, 1981, 'The Juncture of the Social and the Musical', p.30).

By the late 1950s, as the term 'ethnomusicology' began to gain currency, the principal assumption or axiom guiding ethnomusicological work was the understanding that 'all music carries a social meaning; from society it receives its voices, instruments, timbres, tones, rhythms, melodies, genres and styles, and only within society does its human resonance exist' (Ortiz, 1951, 2/1981, p.37). By what actions is the 'human resonance' of music sustained or reproduced in a given set of circumstances? Many answers to this question are accounts of particular styles or genres, attempting to suggest some of the meanings that have been discovered, created and communicated by musicians familiar with the style or genre.

Through closer attention to the actions of musicians in performance, ethnomusicologists have become more aware of their own styles of action. In an important critique of ethnomusicological research models, K. A. Gourlay charged that performers and scholars had been 'omitted' from several models

A [xx′ aa′ cc′ zz′]

A [xx′ aa′ cc′ zz′]

B [yy bb′ cc′ zz′]

B [yy bb′ cc′ zz′]

A [xx′ aa′ cc′ zz′]

A = k^w *ayinanne,* 'coming out' section, [x & x′] *penan k^wayinan,* 'talk coming out'

[a & a′] k^w*ayinanne,* 'the coming out'

[c & c′] $^{?}i^{?}c^{?}umme,$ 'the strong part'

[z & z′] *waya* or *ya · $^?$ ana,* 'cover' or 'finish'

B = *silnanne,* 'talking about' section, [y y]

[b & b′] *silnanne,* 'the talking about'

[c & c′] $^?i^?c^?umme,$ 'the strong part'

[z & z′] *waya* or *ya · $^?$ ana,* 'cover' or 'finish'

6. Zuni terminology for sections and subsections of the 'Kachina Call' ('sawu'' a·we) genre of song (after Tedlock, 1980, pp.18, 20)

for the same reason: an ill-conceived attempt at 'scientific objectivity' in which 'the chosen terminology acquires a life of its own' (1978, p.9), severed from the choices of human agents. For several decades, unwarranted assumptions and inadequate field techniques hindered the study of musical terminology, instrumental tunings and playing techniques, cueing systems, movement patterns and the like. Needed for investigation of these subjects was the understanding that ' "collection" must be a prolonged interpretative process' (A. Seeger, 1979, p.391) and the development of appropriate strategies linking analysis and interpretation to collection. Replaying and discussing tapes made by Zuni composers and performers, B. Tedlock found that certain Zuñi terms for sections and subsections of songs (fig.6) 'occur in discussions during rehearsals and are used as cues during the performance itself' (1980, p.14).

K. P. Wachsmann (1957, pp.12–15) noted 47 operations carried out by a Ganda specialist to correct the tuning of a newly made xylophone, and he measured the results of several corrections with a Strobosconn. Gourlay (1972) identified six methods of cueing used by Karimojong singers to end songs, begin new songs, change song leaders, introduce a new chorus or vary the length of a solo. What these examples have in common is an interest in signs and interpretations exchanged by the Zuñi, Ganda and Karimojong among themselves.

A concern with what are now termed the multiple channels of musical communication – kinesthetic, tactile and visual as well as aural (Stockmann, 1971; Stone and Stone, 1981) – extends from Hornbostel's programme for comparative musicology to current ethnomusicological practice. This concern has not been as widely shared by analysts of Western classical music, but it is conceivable that future developments in analysis will prove more generally applicable. The desire, and the prospects for realizing it, have been discussed by many ethnomusicologists:

> . . . whether comparative study of style upon a world basis could be initiated in the foreseeable future is a question respecting whose answer we can formulate only a few tentative conclusions (C. Seeger, 1951, p.246; 1977, p.12).

> We need a unitary method of musical analysis which can not only be applied to *all* music, but can explain both the form, the social and emotional content, and the effects of music, as systems of relationships between an infinite number of variables (Blacking, 1971, 'Deep and Surface Structures', p.93).

The major difficulties are the varied, distinctive analytical techniques that have proven to be useful in studies of specific regions.

The development of such regional specializations as 'Indic musicology', 'African musicology' and 'Southeast Asian musicology' has encouraged scholars to define the pertinent levels of style analysis in terms that can be tested and corrected as knowledge of the region increases. Criteria for assessing the function and importance of specific components or levels of style are defined and evaluated most effectively by collaborators who share experiences of the same (or of related) regions. Such collective efforts also provide the best means of opposing the uncritical reproduction of platitudes and stereotypes about one region's musical idioms and stylistic principles. In many regions, musical terminology, pedagogy and analytical techniques have

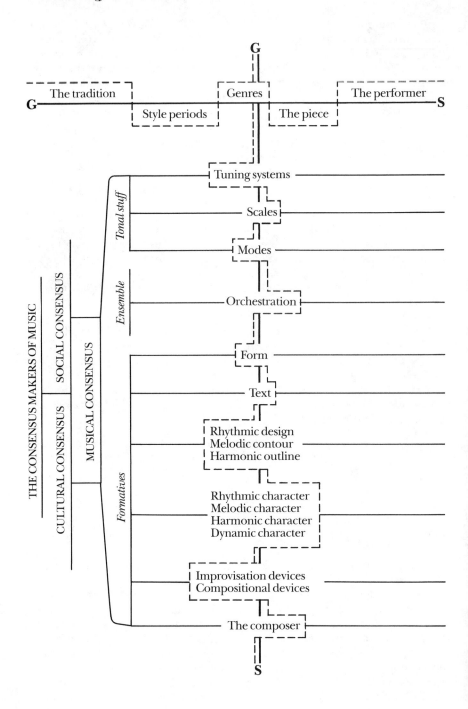

7. *The norms of musical style (from Hood, 1971, p.303)*

been profoundly affected by Western ideas and practices. Ethnomusicologists trained in the West are sometimes slow to acknowledge the concerns of colleagues who do not wish to be labelled 'non-Western'.

Viewed over the long term, the resources and techniques available to the musicians of a given region are often thought to have developed within more or less flexible boundaries. A set of fundamental choices involving the production and reproduction of sounds in appropriate sequences will presumably limit the directions in which the options of musicians are subsequently expanded, reduced, reorganized or otherwise altered. If 'analyses of music are essentially descriptions of sequences of different kinds of creative act' (Blacking, 1971, 'Deep and Surface Structures', p.95), it is desirable to investigate all sets of constraints that may assume varying degrees of importance as musicians act and as others respond to their acts. This task lies beyond the capacities of the individual scholar, and analysis of even a short sequence of musical actions easily becomes a cumulative project, enhanced by attention to constraints that were overlooked at first.

Each of the many analytic strategies adopted by ethnomusicologists offers one or more routes for moving between specific performances and general 'principles' or 'norms' (Hood, 1971, pp.296–312). Mantle Hood illustrates one way of mapping topics that can be investigated from different points of departure (fig.7); the horizontal and vertical lines connecting what is more general and what is more specific may be shifted in any direction, according to the investigator's questions and the available information. A somewhat similar map by Wachsmann (fig.8) treats the results of style analysis as one of four areas of concern, followed through four levels from current practice to the oldest historical and archaeological evidence in order to formulate 'working hypotheses' about the constitution and development of musical practices. Hypotheses of this kind belong to the more 'general' areas of Hood's map, above and to the left of the intersecting (and movable) G-S lines.

Enumeration of a range of alternatives, on the most general as well as the most specific levels, is a fundamental step in many analytic strategies. Surveying the indigenous musical practices of the Philippines, José Maceda has outlined six ways in which musicians' roles have been defined with reference to two principles – repetition and permutation, resulting in 'drone' and 'melody', respectively. Players of drones ensure the 'continuous sounding' or 'periodic reiteration' of one or more tones, whereas players of melodies combine and arrange sounds of indefinite and/or definite pitch. The six possibilities include: (i) one drone only; (ii) two or more drones sounding simultaneously; (iii) sequential rather than simultaneous sounding of drone and melody; (iv) one melody accompanied by one drone; (v) one melody accompanied by several drones; and (vi) several drones that combine to produce one melody (1974). We may expect to encounter additional combinations of drone and melody in instrumental music as well as analogous types in vocal music (1974, p.252); the list of six types is offered as a point of departure for comparative studies of simpler and more complex realizations of the two functions, drone and melody, in various parts of Southeast Asia (1986). Evidence of the antiquity of the former function is provided by the numerous varieties of drone-producing instruments, made of bamboo and many other natural materials as well as of bronze and brass (1974, p.269).

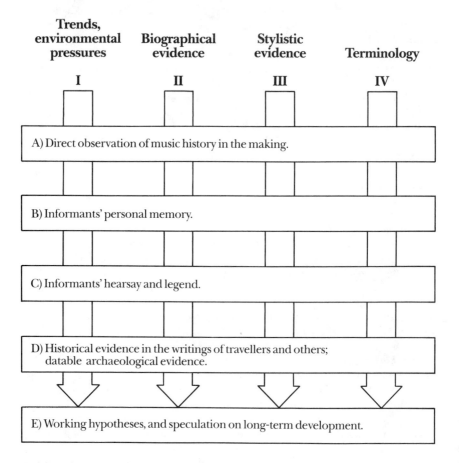

8. Scheme of investigation for ethnomusicology (from Wachsmann, 1971, p.96)

Single instruments that accommodate both functions include bamboo zithers of two or more strings (on which the left thumb-nail produces a drone and the right thumb-nail a melody) and double or triple flutes where only one of the tubes has no stops (1974, pp.266–7).

It is to be expected that ethnographic studies of specific instrumental practices will suggest additions or modifications to Maceda's general account of two complementary functions. In one such study, Manolete Mora analyses a myth of the T'boli people in which the two mallets used to play a wooden percussion beam (*k'lutang*) are transformed into male and female crimson-breasted barbets. The antiphonal singing of two barbets is imitated by the T'boli in one particular *k'lutang* composition, and the principle of complementarity in 'main' and 'subsidiary' parts is elaborated through most of the T'boli instrumental repertory. Since the 'main part' often carries a symbolic meaning, Mora includes this feature in glossing the T'boli terms *tang* ('an underlying tonal/rhythmic support') and *utom* ('melodic and/or rhythmic patterning *plus* the extra-musical symbolic reference of an item of repertoire') (1987, p.202). This pair of terms is related to Maceda's 'drone' and 'melody', but it is not merely a local version of a grand idea. A good overview of major variables in the music history of a large region familiarizes us with musical resources; close ethnographic studies of specific practices show some of the meanings that have been discovered or created by working and playing with the resources.

Quarrels concerning the terms to be used in describing music (on however general or specific a level) are important, since inappropriate terms will convey false or misleading ideas of the musical actions involved. Good examples are the objections raised by Sumarsam to claims that the 'main melody' of a Javanese gamelan composition (*gending*) is played by one instrument, the *saron*, as a 'cantus firmus' or 'nuclear theme'. On the basis of evidence drawn from pedagogy and from performance practice, Sumarsam argues that individual musicians are guided by an 'inner melody', which is 'sung audibly or in their minds'. 'Each musician has to co-ordinate his conception of the inner melody with the range of his instrument and its performing technique when creating melodic patterns for a gending' (1975, pp.7, 12). In this interpretation, 'inner melody' becomes a more accurate translation of Javanese *balungan* (literally 'skeleton' or 'framework').

Similarly, Robert Kauffman (1984) has shown that the social actions by which Shona singers produce multi-part music are more effectively described with Shona terminology than with such European terms as hocket, heterophony, *Stimmtausch* and the like. J. David Sapir's 'grammar' of the *bunansaŋ* genre of funeral songs among the Diola-Fogny is based on four Diola terms for actions that 'serve to define the song's structure' (1969, pp.178–83). By the early 1970s, many ethnomusicologists and folklorists (e.g. Stęszewski, 1972) had familiarized themselves with practices of naming and classification that had escaped the notice of earlier researchers. Looking at the ways in which differences of style are acknowledged within a society, scholars can formulate questions that respect the concerns of that society.

Mwesa Isaiah Mapoma, for example, lists prepositions used in the language ciBemba (northern Zambia) to distinguish styles of dancing, playing and singing according to ethnic group, genre and individual performer. His analysis of the use of this terminology points to a powerful constraint on the performers who are called *ingomba*: each must devise a unique style of composition that refers to existing genres while taking pains not to imitate the style of any other *ingomba*. Guided by this principle, Mapoma's analysis of four individual styles shows four different ways of making reference to one or more genres in new compositions (1980, pp.361–413). He finds a possible explanation for the constraint in the traditional function of the *ingomba* as royal musicians: 'The particular style of an ingomba became the musical insignia of his chief' (1980, p.422).

The extent to which verbal cues are provided to performers (and hence to careful observers) varies greatly within as well as among societies. However, musical performance is quite impossible without 'non-linguistic cues' of various kinds (A. Seeger, 1979, p.374), and ethnomusicological analysis of style necessarily entails investigation of cues and messages. Performers receive messages on how to act from many sources: from the location of a performance in space and time, from the movements of other participants involved in the performance (who may be persons, spirits, winds, animals, birds) and from stories that recount movements through space and time. What do performers know that enables them to respond to cues with appropriate actions? What responses inform performers that their actions are to some degree successful, or unsuccessful? In addressing these and similar questions, several ethnomusicologists have attempted to interpret performance styles with reference to the intentions and desires of participants.

Listing certain traits of two vocal genres of the Suyá Indians (central Brazil), Anthony Seeger describes vocal techniques that move in opposite directions: trying to blend or not to blend, to sing as low or as high as possible, and so on (fig.9).

TRAIT	AKIA	NGERE
Sex of singer	Only men sing *akia*.	Women sometimes sing *ngere* as a group or with the men.
Number of singers	Sung by individuals, each singing his own song, even when several men sing at the same time.	Sung by a group in unison.
Vocal style	Strained, tense, loud. Singers force voices to sing as high and loudly as possible.	Unison, low pitch, moderate volume. Singers try to blend voices.
Pitch	Each singer wants to sing as high in his vocal range as possible. There is no fixed note on which he must begin, however. This varies according to his fatigue, the moment in the ceremony, and his age.	Singers try to sing as low in the vocal range as possible. Songs are often begun lower than some men can sing, then drift up in the first few strophes.
Tempo	Varies with movement of singers and point in the ceremony.	Relatively fixed, varying mostly between classes of *ngere* rather than within a single performance.
Melody contour	'Terraced' or descending contour is typical.	'Flat' contour is typical.
Location of performance	In the center of the village plaza; also outside the village.	Only in the village: in the plaza and in residential houses as well.

9. *Contrast between two vocal genres of the Suyá, 'Akia' and 'Ngere' (from A. Seeger, 1979, p.380)*

The description effectively eliminates the prospect of a cantometric analysis of 'Suyá singing style', since ratings for 'vocal blend', 'register' and the like would vary according to genre. Seeger interprets the list of traits by asking what each genre accomplishes. Having abandoned his mother's household for the men's house and then his wife's household, a man can communicate with his mother and sisters by making his voice heard as he and other men sing their individual *akia* from the centre of the plaza or the outskirts of the village; women comment on the songs and remember those that interest them. As the property of a ceremonial moiety, each *ngere* is performed in unison by persons who have been named to the group; the very existence of the Suyá system of dual moieties depends in large part on performance of *ngere* (1979, pp.379–92). Seeger's analysis focuses on 'the active role music plays in the creation and life of society itself' (1979, p.392). One among several 'necessary tools' of his analysis (1979, p.374) was the Suyá vocabulary for major divisions and subdivisions of songs: terms for the first (*kradi*) and second (*sindaw*) halves of a song in either genre are the same words that distinguish the directions of men's houses associated with 'eastern' and 'western' moieties, where at appropriate times men sing the first and second parts, respectively, of their *akia*. *Sindaw* and *Kradi* also designate the 'upper end' and the 'base' of the throat; for *akia* singers use 'a smaller throat' at the upper end, for *ngere* a 'big throat' at the base (Seeger, 1987, p.180).

Regula Qureshi has developed what she terms 'a performance model for musical analysis', with the aim of identifying 'contextual input into the music . . . through an analysis of the performance process' (1987, p.57). At the centre of the process, in this model, is the performer, whose perceptions of audience responses affect his or her choices from the repertory of available musical options: it is by virtue of the performer's decisions that music conveys specific meanings to listeners. Study of this topic requires analysis of video recordings of audience behaviour during performances. Analysis of the performance process is preceded by two preliminary steps: analysis of the pertinent musical idiom into minimal units and rules of combination, and analysis of 'the performance occasion . . . as a socio-cultural institution with an established setting and procedure, supported by a shared conceptual framework and functioning within a particular socio-economic structure' (1987, pp.68–9). Once the analyst has ascertained the variables and the ranges of variation in both idiom and performance context, analysis of the perform-ance process can show 'how the context of performance affects the music being performed' (1986, p.231).

Qureshi's model served as the basis for her study of *qawwālī*, a genre of sung poetry through which specialist performers minister to the spiritual needs of Sufi devotees in India and Pakistan. The analytic procedures that she recommends proved to be effective in this specific application. The conceptual framework for her analysis of the idiom is that of 'Indic musicology', a product of long-term co-operation between Western and Indian scholars. The distinctive features of one idiom, *qawwālī*, within the larger family of South Asian idioms are to be represented 'in their indigenous form as apprehended by the analyst' (1987, p.66). This task was relatively uncomplicated, since 'participants themselves identify the musical features of *qawwālī* in terms of their association with its function' – spiritual arousal of listeners (1987, p.67).

Only a limited number of these features are subject to variation in response to
'contextual input' (as summarized in fig.10), and most such features offer the
performer only two alternatives.

	Text dimension	Music dimension	Musical presentation
Choice of prelude, introductory verse and song	*language varies:* 1) acc. to *status* *style varies:* 1) acc. to *status* *content varies:* 1) acc. to *identity* 2) acc. to *state* *association varies:* 1) acc. to *identity* 2) acc. to *state*	*tune type varies:* 1) acc. to *status* *rhythm type varies:* 1) acc. to *status*	*performance style varies:* 1) acc. to *status*
Sequencing of song	*type of repetition varies:* 1) acc. to *state* (observed or desired) 2) acc. to *sel. focus* *unit of repetition varies:* 1) acc. to *state* (observed or desired) 2) acc. to *sel. focus* *insert varies:* 1) acc. to *state* (observed or desired) 2) acc. to *status* 3) acc. to *identity* *word call signals vary:* 1) acc. to *status* 2) acc. to *identity*	*type of repetition varies:* 1) acc. to *state* (observed or desired) 2) acc. to *sel. focus* *unit of repetition varies:* 1) acc. to *state* (observed or desired) 2) acc. to *sel. focus* *insert-melodic varies:* 1) acc. to *status* *elaboration varies:* 1) acc. to *status*	*accentuation varies:* 1) acc. to *state* *acceleration varies:* 1) acc. to *state* *actions vary:* 1) acc. to *state* 2) acc. to *status*

10. Summary of contextual input in qawwālī performance model (from Qureshi, 1987, p.78)

To choose wisely, he must assess the status, spiritual identity and state of
arousal of various listeners, and he must decide whether to focus on one or on
several listeners. His choices may convey divergent meanings – a 'low-status'
tune-type rendered in a 'high-status' performance style, for example – or he
may articulate a single message by using all channels to 'say the same thing'
(1986, p.229). Postures, gestures, and actions of the listeners tell the performer
how he is doing.

The guiding principle of several current methods of ethnomusicological analysis, including Qureshi's, has been succinctly enunciated by John Blacking: 'the processes of sharing are as crucial to musical analysis as the sonic product which provides the focus for analysis' (1979, p.12). Different answers to the question 'Who shares what by what means over what period of time?' yield different concepts of style, with varying degrees of emphasis on the production of sounds. It is not always advantageous to separate a 'sonic product' from a 'process of sharing', the 'music' from the 'contextual input'. The latter term is perhaps most appropriate when performers respond to cues from listeners who are not themselves singing, playing, or dancing. Many analyses, such as the studies of Ewe dance-drumming by Hewitt Pantaleoni (1972) and David Locke (1982), concentrate on motions made by one or more members of an ensemble. The cues through which musicians invite others to join in a group performance are also an important subject of inquiry (Chernoff, 1979, p.99; Stone, 1982).

Students of performance must learn to recognize the gestures and words by which performers and listeners indicate that things are going well, less well, or not at all well. This is often accomplished by applications or extensions of the 'experimental method' recommended by Lachmann (see above): while attempting to learn how to play, dance or sing, many scholars have received invaluable criticism of their efforts, conveyed through words and motions. R. F. Thompson, for instance, lists ten objections raised against his dancing by a Yoruba observer (1974, pp.259–60). Replaying videotapes of performances for further comment and response by participants (Tedlock, 1980; Stone and Stone, 1981) also extends the 'experimental method' by soliciting the evaluations and analyses of several interested parties.

Jane Sugarman's study of singing among Prespa Albanian men analyses the dynamics of men's evening gatherings, revealing some of the considerations that determine the order in which men sing, the genres and styles of singing they choose and the responses made by other singers. Sugarman's interpretation of the purpose of the gatherings is developed from the comments of participants and from her observation of many events:

> singing provides . . . a means of engaging all present in the course of a social event, of regulating their participation, and of co-ordinating their progression through an intense and powerful experience that they then apprehend as a collective achievement (1988, pp.30–31).

Her sensitive account of the dangers that must be overcome in the collective creation of a satisfactory evening shows that this 'performance occasion' is, in Qureshi's terms, 'a socio-cultural institution with an established setting and procedure, supported by a shared conceptual framework and functioning within a particular socio-economic structure' (1987, pp.68–9). Indeed as Sugarman indicates (1988, p.34), the performance occasions of *qawwālī* and of the Presparë men's gatherings are two variants of a common 'event structure', widely employed by Sufi brotherhoods and other groups in the Near East and South Asia. However, the fact that Presparë singers are concerned with the responses of other singers rather than with the spiritual arousal of religious leaders (as in *qawwālī*) suggests that 'analysis of the musical idiom into minimal units and rules of combination' should proceed rather differently in the two cases.

The *qawwāl* learns a craft that enables him to identify distinctive features on a relatively small time-scale (e.g. lines that can be repeated) and to choose between several pairs of alternatives. The Presparë men make socio-musical choices that determine the overall quality of single songs in a larger sequence, with details of timbre and timing following naturally from each singer's attitude towards the proceedings and his place in them:

> As their sense of inhibition dissipates, they sing more readily and the intervals between songs become shorter. Their performances become less self-conscious, more spontaneous. Vocal quality is less subdued and more forceful, melodic lines are more intricately ornamented, and exclamatory words and phrases are inserted more often, giving a performance greater expressive weight (Sugarman, 1988, pp.18–19).

Qureshi's ethnography of *qawwālī* justifies an analysis of 'either-or' choices on the performer's part, whereas Sugarman is obliged to deal with several choices that involved 'more' or 'less' of a quality. Analysts have been more successful in constructing 'rules of combination' for choices of either-or than for choices of more-or-less.

Blacking's outline for analysis of 'processes of sharing' emphasizes the study of 'variations between one performance situation and another' (1979, p.11). This programme calls not only for comparative analysis of all styles practised within one culture but also for research aimed at discovering a pan-human 'repertoire of essentially musical values' (1979, p.12). In both respects, styles are to be understood as resources and techniques that acquire specific meanings as they are used and adjusted or transformed, with reference to one another (1967, p.195). As already indicated, there is no consensus among ethnomusicologists with respect to the notions of either 'essentially musical' values or a 'pan-human' repertory. As Blacking suggests, such values would presumably centre on the processes of interaction within ensembles, variously defined.

In an analysis of 56 Venda children's songs, Blacking found that 26 are based on music of the Venda national dance, *tshikona*, and another 21 are related to youths' reed-pipe dances. There is no 'style of Venda children's songs', but most of the songs refer to styles that children experience in attending the national dance and the youths' dances. Children's songs do not refer to the styles of institutions with which children have little contact, such as the possession cult and initiation schools (1967, pp.193–4). The patterns played on the heptatonic set of pipes used for *tshikona* and on the pentatonic set used for youths' dances make available two or three 'harmonically equivalent' pitches at every point in each sequence, so that one has several options in singing 'the same tune' (ex.9).

Each set of pipes has its own history (1971, 'Music and the Historical Process', p.198), as do the possession cult, initiation schools, and other institutions that maintain distinctive styles. Blacking has shown that the reconstruction of Venda music history requires careful analysis of the ways in which stylistic distinctions are meaningful to Venda performers at the present time.

Many of the questions to be addressed through style analysis are posed by the very existence of particular institutions (such as the Bemba royal

Ex. 9 Two versions of One Venda Children's Song (from Blacking, 1967, p. 109) ♩ = 160–176

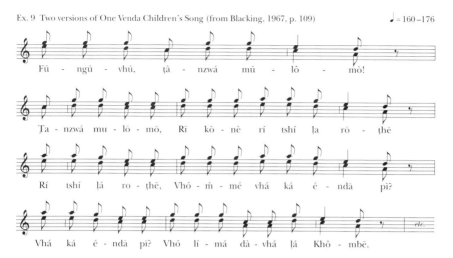

musicians, the Sufi assembly, the Venda possession cult and sets of pipes with different tunings). The *gharānā*s of North India are distinctive lineages of hereditary musicians and their disciples, thought to be recognizable in shared stylistic preferences. In such cases the 'processes of sharing' are complemented by 'processes of refusing to share': groups distance themselves from one another, and individuals compete within as well as outside each group. An analyst may well find it impossible to isolate constant features that mark the styles of groups or individuals – what Blacking (1971, 'Deep and Surface Structures in Venda Music', p.91) terms '*essential* differences'. Variation in the training and interests of both listeners and performers virtually guarantees disputes over what is 'essential' in performances by members of one *gharānā*. Difficulties and areas of uncertainty in the analysis may nonetheless point to alternatives that lie open to performers and listeners.

Bonnie Wade has examined the treatment of one genre, *khyāl*, by members of six *gharānā*s and by singers not identified with one group. Her analysis of recordings is guided by issues raised in statements by musicians and in a large, heterogeneous body of written criticism. These include such topics as cultivation of a wide vocal range or emphasis on one register; typical orderings of the sequence of events in performance; greater or lesser interest in rhythmic play and in specific types of improvisation; and the extent to which repertories incorporate new compositions. The *gharānā* norms appear more as tendencies than as rules, and Wade concludes that 'many musical options are available to *khyāl* singers which do not necessarily characterize either the genre or a group tradition' (1984, p.275). She does not suggest that many of the singer's decisions are predictable but speaks rather of 'the desirability and admissibility of individual creativity', channelled to some extent by the group's preferences.

The much larger repertory of options controlled by competent singers of *khyāl*, in comparison to the restricted number of alternatives in *qawwālī*, illustrates one of the main obstacles facing those who seek to analyse diverse practices by a unified method. In *khyāl*, as in many genres performed for

Ethnomusicology: an Introduction

audiences of connoisseurs, the meaning of a performer's decisions depends, in part, on the attitudes of performers and listeners towards other genres: the ways in which a style of singing *khyāl* can refer to the less public and more prestigious genre *dhrupad* vary over time with changes in the performers' and listeners' experiences and conceptions of the two genres (Wade, 1984, pp.278–9). The issue of reference to other styles and genres cannot be studied entirely by analysis of performer-listener interaction during performance, since the performer's choice of references need not take immediate reactions of listeners into account. The degree to which direct person-to-person contact controls the performer's decisions is in many cases difficult, perhaps even impossible to assess.

Performers' perceptions of the many constraints exerted by changing socio-economic conditions raise similar difficulties, which must nonetheless be faced by ethnomusicologists interested in modern music history. As David Coplan has shown in his study of black South African urban performing arts from the 19th century on, the names given to new styles and the varied uses of the names 'reveal important distinctions in the minds of participants' (1985, p.66). Coplan treats styles as 'complexes of metaphoric symbols, forms and value orientations, labelled and recognized by their participants and used to mark identity' (1985, p.270). Description of styles, in this sense, must roughly outline the range of options that each style makes available to practitioners who pursue specific (and potentially incompatible) goals. In the South African context, such goals are envisioned within a continuing struggle even to reside in urban areas, and participants give different meanings to stylistic metaphors as their needs and aspirations change.

Coplan's method allows for description of several dimensions of the style known as *marabi*, which flourished in the 1920s and 1930s:

> As music it had a distinctive rhythm and a blend of African polyphonic principles, restructured within the framework of the Western 'three-chord' harmonic system. As a dance it placed few limits on variation and interpretation by individuals or couples, though the emphasis was definitely on sexuality. As a social occasion it was a convivial, neighbourhood gathering for drinking, dancing, coupling, friendship and other forms of interaction. Finally, *marabi* also meant a category of people with low social status and a reputation for immorality, identified by their regular attendance at *marabi* parties (1985, p.94).

Very explicit statements of South Africans identify major components of the new style: it was 'a kind of musical *mensetaal*' [a creole language of street gangs]; '*Tickey drai* plus *tula n'divile* [two earlier styles] equals *marabi*'; 'marabi is *ndunduma* Caluzified' [the genre *ndunduma* transformed by applying techniques of the composer Reuben Caluza] (1985, pp.109, 105, 97). Such statements refer to processes of selection and combination, in which meanings of earlier styles and of individual achievements (e.g. those of Caluza) are retained and reinterpreted to create a new set of options.

Coplan dismisses the possibility of circumscribing a 'neat hierarchy of independent and dependent variables' in such circumstances (1985, p.230), and he makes no attempt to enumerate all the metaphors and values that constitute one style. He follows a more realistic strategy, bringing together information from many sources about actions that were taken in particular situations. In interpreting these actions, he attempts to recognize the multiple reference groups with which actors have sought to identify themselves or from which they have kept their distance.

A study of styles as responses to changing socio-economic conditions may also follow the transformations of one genre, as certain of its practitioners find it advantageous to adopt stylistic features from various quarters and as others develop new styles based upon the genre. Peter Manuel, for instance, has shown that specific changes in patronage were responsible for drastic alterations of style in performance of the North Indian genre *ṭhumrī* (1983, 1986). His analytic method is guided by an interpretation of the social meaning of the stylistic options available at various points in the history of *ṭhumrī*.

The approaches to interpretation of socio-musical action as illustrated here through examples drawn from the work of several scholars differ, above all, in

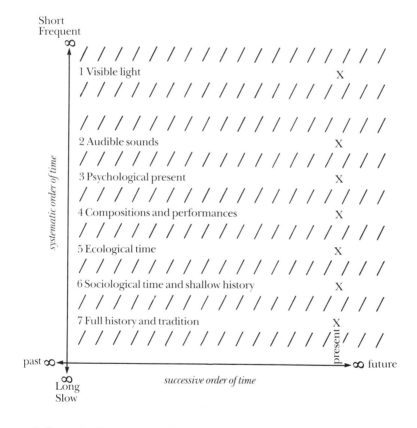

11. *Systematic and successive order of time (from Bielawski, 1985, p.9). 'Seven principa temporal zones characterize human activity and existence. The first two zones are not perceived as time but as light or sound, though from the physical point of view they are temporal frequencies of light waves and acoustic waves. The next four temporal zones are experienced as time. The last zone is conceived only in tradition and history.'*

the time-span covered by the actions with which each scholar is concerned. It is one of the strengths of ethnomusicology that attention is directed to principles exercised during single performances and to principles operating over the longest as well as the shortest periods of history. The achievements of ethnomusicologists in analysis of style include contributions to knowledge of all but the first two of the seven 'time zones' distinguished by Bielawski (fig.11).

Moreover, the growth of regional musicologies makes it increasingly possible to analyse single performances in terms of the long-term variables in a region's music history.

The development of many regional musicologies has cast doubt upon the adequacy of analytical techniques that were designed to be widely or even universally applicable. A case in point is the weakness of the pioneering work on African-derived styles in the Americas, carried out by students and colleagues of Melville J. Herskovits (1895–1963). Many of Herskovits's field recordings from Surinam, Trinidad, and Bahia were transcribed and analysed at length by Kolinski (1936), Waterman (1943) and Merriam (1951, 1963). The analytic method, which Merriam (1951, p.46–7) described as 'instigated by von Hornbostel, and elaborated by Kolinski and Waterman', emphasized computation of 'tonal range', of the number of semitones separating the first and last notes in a transcribed melody, and of the number of occurrences of each interval. On the whole, the results of these computations did not furnish a basis for further research on the music history of the African diaspora. Far more helpful was the list of habits and preferences with which Waterman (1948, 1952) sought 'to characterize [a] rhythmic style' carried by Africans to the Americas: overlapping of call-and-response patterns, emphasis on rhythm-making instruments, responsiveness of dancers to several simultaneous metres and rhythms, predilection of singers and instrumentalists to place melodic accents 'off' or 'between' the 'upbeats' and 'downbeats' of supporting parts and agreement of performers and listeners on a 'theoretical framework of beats spaced regularly in time' so that 'overt or inhibited motor behavior' is coordinated through a 'metronome sense' (1952, p.211).

According to Waterman and Herskovits, these determinants of style were 'carried below the level of consciousness' (Herskovits, 1945, p.22; Waterman, 1948, p.24): analysis of different styles in the Americas and in modern West Africa would show the effects of specific social, musical and religious conditions upon a common inheritance. The approach called for two types of analysis: explanation of the factors responsible for one or another 'reinterpretation', and description of the major components of actual performances. In the latter respect, Waterman's list of habits and preferences (which he termed 'traits') has been refined and extended in subsequent studies of West African performance styles, including those of Thompson (1974, 1983), Chernoff (1979) and Locke (1982). One 'rhythmic style' is no longer the focus of interest; rather, close attention to the actions (including the words) of performers and participants leads to a more concrete understanding of 'selected constituents of structure with set functions' (Nketia, 1981, 'African Roots of Music', p.85).

The cumulative experience of performers and scholars that a 'time line' (Nketia, 1963, p.70) is essential in coordinating ensemble performances across much of coastal West Africa and West-Central Africa (Pantaleoni, 1972, pp.6–9; Locke, 1982, p.243) has been taken as justification for the assumption that 'time-line patterns must have been a rather stable element in African music history', including the history of the diaspora (Kubik, 1979, p.18). Located within this history over the long term, even the most 'essential' functions have not been 'constant' but, at most, 'relatively stable'. The categories needed for reconstruction of the historical process – for example 'modalities of fusion', 'creative models', 'functional substitutes', 'reference systems' (Nketia, 'African Roots of Music', 1981) – do not impose one hierarchy of values, and this point was made clear in the discussion of 'reinterpretation' by Herskovits and Waterman. The point was missed, however, when analysts equated sounds with notes and emphasized numerical formulas. Waterman's list of traits became more meaningful, as scholars learned that 'air beats and other forms of empty beat can be so important in the motor behavior of African musicians that it is impossible to understand the music by writing down its audible aspects only' (Kubik, 1972, p.29).

The comparative musicologists (Hornbostel in particular) initiated a long effort (i) to extend the distinction between 'essential' and 'incidental' elements from analysis of tonal and rhythmic systems (as in the harmonics and rhythmics of Aristoxenus) to the full range of social and musical variables, and (ii) to criticize the limitations of specific analytic procedures (including the 'essential/incidental' dichotomy). Ethnomusicologists have found countless ways in which 'any feature that differentiates one tone from another . . . can command attention and mark the tone in question with an accent' (Hornbostel, 1905, p.94; 1975, p.265). We have described 'processes of sharing' through which human beings are able to define various 'figures' against one another 'ground' (Hornbostel, 1926, pp.702–9), and we have looked for terms that have identified or might come to identify relations of figure and ground with a long history in one region (e.g. Maceda's 'melody' and 'drone'). By resisting the various proposals for 'a unitary method of musical analysis' (Blacking, 'Deep and Surface Structures', p.93), we have learned more than might otherwise have been possible about the multiple meanings of musical activity in many regions.

The analyst's options

We are fortunate that ethnomusicological analysis has not been confined to questions of 'style'. The heritage of our discipline now includes many conceptions of musical systems, genres, types, forms, modes, tastes, languages, dialects and idioms, as well as of styles. Various 'families' of ideas, metaphors, and procedures may be subsumed under each of these headings. Our choices of terms and procedures for musical analysis involve us in the intricate histories of these 'families', as Harold Powers has shown in his study of the 'music-as-language metaphor' (1980).

No single set of metaphors can provide a general foundation for ethnomusicological analysis, given the controversies that flourish within even a single musical practice as well as the fundamental differences that commonly separate one practice from another. Many of the analytic methods surveyed in this chapter have been the subject of vigorous criticism.

Ethnomusicologists are often inclined to say, 'This, too, must be considered.' As a result, we now stand in a better position to resist the appeals of conventional wisdom. We need not agree that 'it is obvious that the basis pattern [of music] resides in [the] two levels' termed 'pitch' and 'duration' (McLeod, 1966, p.182).

The development of regional musicologies has served to quicken scholarly debate concerning the choices that might prove most helpful to students of each region. As Herzog and others realized, it is best not to assume that one 'style', 'stylistic mainstream' or 'musical language' is dominant in the practice of one community or one region. Instances where this is evidently not the case include the Suyá village studied by Anthony Seeger (1979, 1987) and the North Indian village studied by Edward Henry (1976, 1988). As Henry observed, the examination of several genres cultivated in one community calls into question the aims and procedures of the Cantometrics project and similar undertakings (1976).

Concepts of 'musical system' have been extended, so that analysts are now able to consider many aspects of music that may or may not be treated systematically in a given musical practice:

> It would seem that rationalized music systems are in no way dependent upon a written tradition but are inherent in the process of music making, and that what varies is rather the aspect of the music that lends itself to rationalization. Various aspects of gamelan music and Western music, such as tunings, modes, formal structures or styles of improvisation, have been described within the theoretical framework of a rationalized structural analysis. The most successful rationalizations of Western music deal with tunings, but rationalizations of gamelan tunings are the least successful. On the other hand, gamelan *gongan* forms are easily rationalized, but Western formal structures are much more resistant (Becker, 1980, p.144).

The understanding that 'what varies is . . . the aspect of the music that lends itself to rationalization' is an important result of the inquiries initiated by Hornbostel, Lachmann, Max Weber, Brăiloiu and others. We have reason to doubt, however, that 'rationalized music systems' are always 'inherent in the process of music-making'. Perhaps these doubts will be dispelled once we succeed in describing many types and degrees of systematization and rationalization, but this is by no means a foregone conclusion. Our attempts at analysis will continue to meet with sustained resistance, and in each case we must listen closely to the musicians whose work and play does not conform to our expectations. It is conceivable that 'music without system' is not necessarily a contradiction in terms.

An analysis that fails to identify a 'system', 'style' or 'genre' of one or another type may be considered successful, when it helps us to recognize more clearly some of the limitations of particular concepts and methods. Analysts are engaged in honest dialogue with one another and with other musicians only when everything is not proceeding according to a pre-set plan.

The indispensable 'dialogue between informant and investigator' (Sapir, 1969, p.189) is not always advanced by the doctrine that ethnomusicological analysis should never 'remove' music from its 'cultural context'. There are many situations in which musicians interpret music 'by discussing it as though it did have a life of its own' (Powers, 1980, p.8). Such discussions are very much a part of the cultural contexts in which they occur. There is room in the

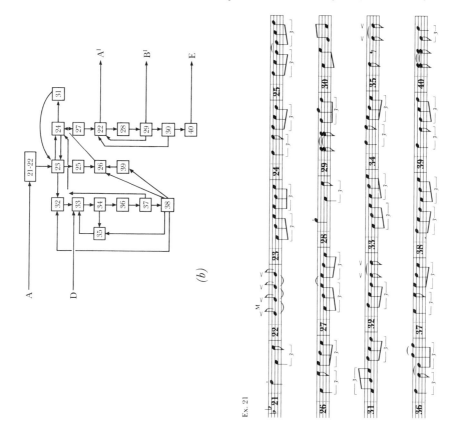

Ex. 21

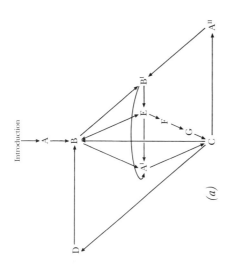

12. *Itinerary of Salvatore Lai in playing the 'Ballu di Villanova' (from Giannattasio, 1982, pp. 29, 19) showing (a) connections of sections, (b) connections of formulae in section B and (c) formulae in section B*

211

vocabulary of musical analysis for metaphors that refer to music's 'autonomous existence outside the memories of men' (Becker, 1980, p.143) – even if, with Becker and Powers, we acknowledge the priority of human actions in the creation and reproduction of musical knowledge.

Actions of many types have been carefully considered in works of ethnomusicological analysis. It has become increasingly common for analysts to include schematic representations of the movements of performers (e.g. Baily, 1977; Moyle, 1984; Staro, 1985). It is possible that studies of movement patterns will encourage more intelligent readings of various conventional notations, which are too often read merely as signs of sounds rather than as signs of relations among movements and sounds.

Very specific answers are required by many of the general questions posed in ethnomusicological analysis, including the 'question of under what circumstances, to what extent, a relationship among sounds may be "detached" in memory and reordered along different "axes"' (Blum, 1975, p.214). Students of some practices have approached this question by reconstructing the 'itineraries' (*percorsi* in Giuriati, 1985) that are available to performers in a given set of circumstances. The numerous terms that denote

13. *An analytical notation of singing and drumming in Nô, showing their rhythmic interrelation (from Fujita, 1986, p.93). X indicates 'the beginning points of patterns, where the drummer prepares himself for a series of drum strokes and his own vocal calls'.*

itineraries created and followed by musicians include Pitjantjatjara *mainkara wanani* ('following the way in the singing'; Ellis, 1984, p.152), Korean *sanjo* ('scattered melodies'), and Persian *radif* ('row'). For some genres, one performer's options may be represented in diagrams that show how sections, and smaller units within sections, have been connected in two or more performances (fig.12), from Giannattasio and Lortat-Jacob (1982).

Among the possibilities suggested by Qureshi's 'performance model for musical analysis' are diagrams that would treat one performer's sequence of moves as 'input' for a second performer. When the choices of two participants in one performance are 'two interdependent variables' (Giannattasio and Lortat-Jacob, 1982, p.33), the itineraries of each performer – an instrumentalist and a dancer, for example – will intersect in specific ways at various points. Ethnomusicologists have begun to develop techniques for discovering and representing points of intersection in the itineraries of two or more performers (fig.13, from Fujita, 1986).

An analyst's choice of terms – 'formula' rather than 'motif' or 'idea', for example – often implies an interpretation of the courses of action followed by a musician in a particular environment. For this reason alone, controversy over the terms and procedures of analysis is certain to continue. In the most fortunate circumstances, controversies among analysts reproduce issues that musicians have addressed and stances that they have adopted, without resolving the disputes. In jazz and in other musical practices, methods for recognizing and dealing with 'formulas', with 'ideas', and with relations between 'formulas' and 'ideas' are a common concern of analysts and performers alike (Gushee, 1970; Kernfeld, 1983).

Musical analysis is a discipline that we learn, above all, from musicians. As analysts, we must continually reshape our tools and our questions as we attempt to interpret some of the actions of musicians and some of the meanings of these actions. Wherever we turn, we can find skilled performers engaged in the exercise of their musical knowledge. It is difficult to avoid the impression that analysts of music often fail to recognize much of the guidance that is readily available to us.

Bibliography

I. Krohn: 'Welche ist die beste Methode, um volks – und volksmässige Lieder nach ihrer melodischen (nicht textlichen) Beschaffenheit lexikalisch zu ordnen?', *SIMG*, iv (1902–03), 643

E. M. von Hornbostel: 'Die Probleme der vergleichenden Musikwissenschaft', *ZIMG*, vii/3 (1905–06), 85; repr. in *Hornbostel Opera Omnia* (1975), 249

—— : 'Wanyamwezi-Gesänge', *Anthropos*, iv (1909), 781, 1033 and musical suppls.

—— : 'Melodie und Skala', *Jahrbuch der Musikbibliothek Peters für 1912*, xix (1913), 11

H. Wölfflin: *Kunstgeschichtliche Grundbegriffe* (Munich, 1915)

E. M. von Hornbostel: 'Gesänge aus Ruanda', in J. Czekanowski: *Forschungen im Nil-Kongo-Zwischengebiet*, i (Leipzig, 1917), 379–412 and musical suppls.

—— : 'Ch'ao-t'ien-tzĕ. Eine chinesische Notation und ihre Ausführungen', *Archiv für Musikwissenschaft*, i/4 (1918–19), 477

—— : 'Musikalischer Exotismus', *Melos*, ii/9 (1921), 175

—— : 'Musik der Makuschi, Taulipáng und Yekuaná, in T. Koch-Grünberg: *Von Roroima zum Orinoco*, iii (Stuttgart, 1923), 397–442; Eng. trans. by M. Herndon, *Inter-American Music Bulletin* (1969), no.71, pp.1–42

Ethnomusicology: an Introduction

—— : 'Psychologie der Gehörserscheinungen', *Handbuch der normalen und pathologischen Physiologie*, ed. A. Bethe and others, xi (Berlin, 1926), 701

F. Boas: *Primitive Art* (Oslo, 1927/*R*1955)

G. Herzog: 'The Yuman Musical Style', *Journal of American Folk-Lore*, xli (1928), 183–231

E. M. von Hornbostel: 'African Negro Music', *Africa*, i (1928), 30–62; repr. in *International Institute of African Languages and Cultures: Memorandum*, iv (London, 1928), 1–35

M. Metfessel: *Phonophotography in Folk Music: American Negro Songs in New Notation* (Chapel Hill, 1928)

B. Bartók: 'Węgierska muzyka ludowa' [Hungarian folk music], *Muzyka*, vi/4 (1929), 201; Eng. trans. in Bartók (1976), 3

F. Kolessa: 'Anordnung und charakteristische Merkmale der lemkischen Volksliedmelodien', *Narodni pisni z halyts'koyi Lemkivshchyny: teksty i melodiyi*, ed. F. Kolessa (Lwów, 1929), lxi–lxxxii

B. Asaf'yev: *Muzikal'naya forma kak protsess* (Moscow, 1930–47). Eng. trans. by J. R. Tull *B. V. Asaf'yev's Musical Form as a Process: Translation and Commentary* (diss., Ohio State U., 1976), 183–564

E. M. von Hornbostel: 'Gestaltpsychologisches zur Stilkritik', *Studien zur Musikgeschichte: Festschrift für Guido Alder zum 75. Geburtstag* (Vienna, 1930/*R*1971), 12

B. Bartók: *Hungarian Folk Music* (London, 1931; Eng. trans. of *A magyar népdal*, Budapest, 1924)

C. Brăiloiu: 'Esquisse d'une méthode de folklore musical', *Revue de musicologie*, xi (1931), 233–67; repr. in Brăiloiu (1973), 5–39

B. Bartók: 'Hungarian Peasant Music', *MQ*, xix (1933), 267; repr. in Bartók (1976), 80

V. Belyayev: 'The Folk Music of Georgia', *MQ*, xix (1933), 417

C. Sachs: *Eine Weltgeschichte des Tanzes* (Berlin, 1933; Eng. trans. 1937/*R*1963 as *World History of Dance*)

M. Schneider: *Geschichte der Mehrstimmigkeit: historische und phänomenologische Studien* i: *Die Naturvölker*; ii: *Die Anfänge in Europa* (Berlin, 1934–35, 2/1968 with iii: *Die Kompositionsprinzipien und ihre Verbreitung*)

B. Bartók: 'Die Volksmusik der Magyaren und der benachbarten Völker', *Ungarische Jahrbücher*, xv/2–3 (1935), 194–258; Ger. trans. of 'Népzenénk és a szomszéd népek népzenéje', *Népszerű Zenefüzetek* (1934), no.3

G. Herzog: 'Special Song Types in North American Indian Music', *Zeitschrift für vergleichende Musikwissenschaft*, iii/1–2 (1935), 23 and musical suppls.

R. Lachmann: 'Musiksysteme und Musikauffassung', *Zeitschrift für vergleichende Musikwissenschaft*, iii (1935), 1

G. Herzog: 'A Comparison of Pueblo and Pima Musical Styles', *Journal of American Folk-Lore*, xlix (1936), 283–417

E. M. von Hornbostel: 'Fuegian Songs', *American Anthropologist*, new ser. xxxviii (1936), 357

M. Kolinski: 'Suriname Music', *Suriname Folk-Lore*, ed. M. J. and F. S. Herskovits (New York, 1936), 489–740

R. Lachmann: *Jewish Cantillation and Song in the Isle of Djerba* (Jerusalem, 1940)

B. Bartók: 'Race Purity in Music', *Modern Music*, xix/3–4 (1941–42), 153; repr. in Bartók (1976), 29

K. Kvitka: 'Ob oblastyakh rasprostraneniya nekotorïkh tipov belorusskikh kalendarnïkh i svadenbnïkh pesen', *Belorusskiye narodniye pesni*, ed. Z. Ewald (Moscow and Leningrad, 1941), 123; Ger. trans. as 'Über die Verbreitung einiger Typen belorussischer Kalender- und Hochzeitslieder', *Sowjetische Volkslied- und Volksmusikforschung: ausgewählte Studien*, ed. E. Stockmann and others (Berlin, 1967), 309

C. Sachs: 'The Road to Major', *MQ*, xix (1943), 381

—— : *The Rise of Music in the Ancient World: East and West* (New York, 1943)

R. A. Waterman: *African Patterns in Trinidad Negro Music* (diss., Northwestern U., 1943)

M. J. Herskovits: 'Problem, Method and Theory in Afroamerican Studies', *Afroamerica*, i (1945), 5; repr. in Herskovits (1966), 43

C. Brăiloiu: 'Le giusto syllabique bichrone. Un système rythmique propre à la musique populaire roumaine', *Polyphonie*, ii (1948), 26–57; rev. as 'Le giusto syllabique. Un système rythmique populaire roumaine', *Anuario Musical*, vii (1952), 117–58; repr. in Brăiloiu (1973), 153–94

E. M. von Hornbostel: 'The Music of the Fuegians', *Ethnos*, xiii (1948), 61–102

R. A. Waterman: '"Hot" Rhythm in Negro Music', *JAMS*, i (1948), 24

C. Brăiloiu: 'Le folklore musical', *Musica aeterna* (Zurich, 1949), 277–332; repr. in Brăiloiu (1973), 63–118

D. McAllester: *Peyote Music* (New York, 1949)

214

B. Bartók and A. B. Lord: *Serbo-Croatian Folk Songs* (New York, 1951/*R*)

C. Brăiloiu: 'Le rythme aksak', *Revue de musicologie*, xxx (1951), 71–108; repr. in Brăiloiu (1973), 303–340

J. Kresánek: *Slovenská l'udová pieseň so stanoviska hudobného* (Bratislava, 1951) [summaries in Ger. and Russ.]

A. P. Merriam: *Songs of the Afro-Bahain Cults: an Ethnomusicological Analysis* (diss., Northwestern U., 1951)

C. Seeger: 'Systematic Musicology: Viewpoints, Orientations, and Methods', *JAMS*, iv (1951), 240

F. Ortiz: *Los bailes y el teatro de los negros en el folklore de Cuba* (Havana, 1951; 2/1981/*R*1985)

R. A. Waterman: 'African Influence on the Music of the Americas', *Acculturation in the Americas: Proceedings and Selected Papers of the 29th International Congress of Americanists*, ed. S. Tax (Chicago, 1952), 207

W. Wiora: *Europäische Volksgesang: Gemeinsame Formen in Charakteristichen Abwandlungen* (Cologne, 1952)

C. Brăiloiu: 'Sur une melodie russe', *Musique russe*, ii (Paris, 1953), 329–91; repr. in Brăiloiu (1973), 342–405

M. Schapiro: 'Style', *Anthropology Today: an Encyclopedic Inventory*, ed. A. L. Kroeber (Chicago, 1953), 287

W. Salmen: 'Towards the Exploration of National Idiosyncrasies in Wandering Song-Tunes', *JIFMC*, vi (1954), 52

S. Baud-Bovy: 'La strophe de distiques rimés dans la chanson grecque', *Studia memoriae Bélae Bartók sacra* (Budapest, 1956), 365–83

C. Brăiloiu: Le rythme enfantin: notions liminaires', *Les Colloques de Wégimont: Ethnomusicologie I* (Paris and Brussels, 1956), 64–96; repr. in Brăiloiu (1973), 267–99

G. Kerényi: 'The System of Publishing the Collection of Hungarian Folksongs Corpus musicae popularis hungaricae', *Studia memoriae Bélae Bartók sacra* (Budapest, 1956), 453

W. Wiora: 'Das produktive Umsingen deutscher Kirchenliedweisen in der Vielfalt europäischer Stile', *Jahrbuch für Liturgik und Hymnologie*, ii (1956), 47

M. Kolinski: 'The Determinants of Tonal Construction in Tribal Music', *MQ*, xliii (1957), 50

K. P. Wachsmann: 'A Study of Norms in the Tribal Music of Uganda', *Ethnomusicology Newsletter*, i/ 11 (1957), 9

B. Bartók: *Slovenské ludové piesne*, i, ed. O. Elschek and A. Elscheková (Bratislava, 1959)

C. Brăiloiu: 'Réflexions sur la création musicale collective', *Diogène*, xxv (1959), 83; repr. in Brăiloiu (1973), 137

A. Elscheková: 'Stilschichten der slowakischen Volksmusik', *Deutsches Jahrbuch für Volkskunde*, vi (1960), 353

Z. Kodály: *Folk Music of Hungary* (London, 1960, rev. enl. 3/1982; Eng. trans. of *A magyar népzene*, Budapest, 1937, rev. enl. 6/1973)

W. Salmen: 'European Song (1300–1530)', *The New Oxford History of Music*, iii *Ars Nova and the Renaissance 1300–1540*, ed. Dom. A. Hughes and G. Abraham (London, 1960/*R*), 349–80

R. Brandel: *The Music of Central Africa: an Ethnomusicological Study* (The Hague, 1961)

M. Kolinski: 'Classification of Tonal Structures, Illustrated by a Comparative Chart of American Indian, African Negro, Afro-American and English-American Structures', *Studies in Ethnomusicology*, i (1961), 38–76

C. Sachs: *The Wellsprings of Music*, ed. J. Kunst (The Hague, 1961)

E. M. von Hornbostel: 'The Demonstration Collection of E. M. von Hornbostel and the Berlin Phonogrammarchiv', FE 4175 [disc notes with commentaries by K. Reinhard and G. List]

V. M. Belyayev: *Ocherki po istorii muziki narodov SSSR*, i [Essays on the history of the music of the Soviet Peoples] (Moscow, 1962); Eng. trans. M. and G. Slobin, *Central Asian Music* (Middletown, CT, 1975)

——: *Ocherki po istorii muziki narodov SSSR*, ii (Moscow, 1963)

——: 'The Formation of Folk Modal Systems', *JIFMC*, xv (1963), 4

A. P. Merriam: 'Songs of the Gege and Jesha Cults of Bahia, Brazil', *Jahrbuch für musikalische Volks–und Völkerkunde*, i (1963), 100–35

J. H. K. Nketia: *African Music in Ghana* (Evanston, 1963/*R*1970)

V. M. Belyayev: 'Folk Music and the History of Music', *Studia Musicologica*, vii (1965), 19

W. Graf: 'Naturwissenschaftliche Gedanken über das Jodeln (Die phonetische Bedeutung der Jodelsilben), *Schriften des Vereins zur Verbreitung naturwissenschaftlicher Kenntnisse in Wien*, cv (1965), 1; repr. in Graf (1980), 202

215

P. Járdányi: 'Experiences and Results in Systematizing Hungarian Folk-Songs', *Studia Musicologica*, vii (1965), 287

M. Kolinski: 'The General Direction of Melodic Movement', *EM*, ix (1965), 240

——: 'The Structure of Melodic Movement: a New Method of Analysis (Revised Version)', *Studies in Ethnomusicology*, ii (1965), 95

A. Elscheková: 'Methods of Classification of Folk-Tunes', *JIFMC*, xviii (1966), 56

W. Graf: 'Zur Verwendung von Geräuschen in der aussereuropäischen Musik', *Jahrbuch für musikalisches Volks– und Völkerkunde*, ii (1966), 59–90

M. J. Herskovits: *The New World Negro: Selected Papers in Afroamerican Studies* (Bloomington, IN, 1966)

N. McLeod: 'Some Techniques of Analysis for Non-Western Music' (diss., Northwestern U., 1966)

C. Seeger: 'Versions and Variants of the Tunes of "Barbara Allen" in the Archive of American Folksong in the Library of Congress', *Selected Reports*, i/1 (1966), 120–67; repr. in Seeger (1977), 273–320

J. Blacking: *Venda Children's Songs: a Study in Ethnomusicological Analysis* (Johannesburg, 1967)

W. Graf: 'Zur sonagraphischen Untersuchung von Sprache und Musik', *Beiträge zur Kenntnis Südosteuropas und des Nahen Orients*, ii (1967), 40; repr. in Graf (1980), 211

I. Zemtsovsky: *Russkaya protyazhnaya pesnya* [The Russian long-drawn-out song] (Leningrad, 1967) [Summary in German]

A. Lomax: *Folk Song Style and Culture* (Washington, DC, 1968)

O. Elschek: 'Typologische Arbeitsverfahren bei Volksmusikinstrumenten', *Studia Instrumentorum Musicae Popularis*, i (1969), 23

O. Elschek and D. Stockmann, eds.: *Methoden der Klassifikation von Volksliedweisen* (Bratislava, 1969)

G. Rouget: 'Sur les xylophones équiheptaphoniques des Malinké, *Revue de musicologie*, lv/1 (1969), 47–77

J. Sapir: 'Diola-Fogny Funeral Songs and the Native Critic', *African Language Review*, viii (1969), 176

W. Wiora: 'Zur Methode der vergleichenden Melodienforschung', *Methoden der Klassifikation von Volksliedweisen*, ed. O. Elschek and D. Stockmann (Bratislava, 1969), 31

F. Födermayr: 'Zur Ololyge in Afrika', *Musik als Gestalt und Erlebnis: Festschrift Walter Graf zum 65. Geburtstag* (Vienna, 1970), 57

L. Gushee: 'Musicology Rhymes with Ideology', *Arts in Society* (Summer, 1970), 230

G. Rouget: 'Transcrire ou décrire? Chant soudanais et chant fuégien', *Échange et communications: Mélanges offerts à Claude Lévi-Strauss*, ed. J. Pouillon and P. Maranda (The Hague, 1970), 677

K. P. Wachsmann: 'Ethnomusicology in Africa', *The African Experience*, ed. J. N. Paden and E. W. Soja, i (Evanston, IL, 1970), 128

J. Blacking: 'Music and the Historical Process in Vendaland', *Essays on Music and History in Africa*, ed. K. P. Wachsmann (Evanston, IL, 1971), 185

——: 'Deep and Surface Structures in Venda Music', *YIFMC*, iii (1971), 91

F. Födermayr: *Zur gesanglichen Stimmgebung in der aussereuropäischen Musik: Ein Beitrag zur Methodik der vergleichenden Musikwissenschaft* (Vienna, 1971)

M. Hood: *The Ethnomusicologist* (New York, 1971; new edn. 1982)

E. Stockmann: 'The Diffusion of Musical Instruments as an Inter-ethnic Process of Communication', *YIFMC*, iii (1971), 128

K. P. Wachsmann: 'Musical Instruments in Kiganda Tradition and Their Place in the East African Scene', *Essays on Music and History in Africa*, ed. K. P. Wachsmann (Evanston, IL, 1971), 93

K. A. Gourlay: 'The Practice of Cueing among the Karimojo of North-East Uganda', *EM* xvi (1972), 240

G. Kubik: 'Transcription of African Music from Silent Film: Theory and Methods', *African Music*, v/2 (1972), 28

H. Pantaleoni: 'Toward Understanding the Play of *Sogo* in *Atsia*', *EM*, xvi (1972), 1–37

J. Stęszewski: 'Sachen, Bewusstsein und Benennungen in ethnomusikologischen Untersuchungen', *Jahrbuch für Volksliedforschung*, xvii (1972), 131–70

C. Brăiloiu: *Problèmes d'ethnomusicologie*, ed. G. Rouget (Geneva, 1973)

M. Kolinski: 'A Cross-Cultural Approach to Metro-Rhythmic Patterns', *EM*, xvii (1973), 494

D. Stockmann and J. Stęszewski, eds.: *Analyse und Klassifikation von Volksmelodien* (Kraków, 1973)

S. Blum: 'Persian Folksong in Meshhed (Iran), 1969', *YIFMC*, vi (1974), 86

J. Maceda: 'Drone and Melody in Philippine Musical Instruments', *Traditional Drama and Music of*

Southeast Asia, ed. M. T. Osman (Kuala Lumpur, 1974), 246

R. F. Thompson: *African Art in Motion: Icon and Act in the Collection of Katherine Coryton White* (Berkeley, 1974)

S. Blum: 'Towards a Social History of Musicological Technique', *EM*, xix (1975), 207

L. Burman-Hall: 'Southern American Folk Fiddle Styles', *EM*, xix, (1975), 47

E. M. von Hornbostel: *Hornbostel Opera Omnia*, ed. K. P. Wachsmann, D. Christensen and H. P. Reinecke (The Hague, 1975)

Sumarsam: 'Inner Melody in Javanese Gamelan Music', *Asian Music*, vii/1 (1975), 3

B. Bartók: *Béla Bartók Essays*, ed. B. Suchoff (New York, 1976)

E. O. Henry: 'The Variety of Music in a North Indian Village: Reassessing Cantometrics', *EM*, xx (1976), 49

J. T. Irvine and J. D. Sapir: 'Musical Style and Social Change among the Kujamaat Diola', *EM*, xx (1976), 67

A. Lomax: *Cantometrics: a Method in Musical Anthropology* (Berkeley, 1976)

G. Rouget: 'Chant fuégien, consonance, mélodie de voyelles', *Revue de musicologie*, lxii/1 (1976), 5

J. Baily: 'Movement Patterns in Playing the Herati *Dutār*', *The Anthropology of the Body*, ed. John Blacking (London, 1977), 275–330

C. Seeger: *Studies in Musicology, 1935–1975* (Berkeley, 1977)

L. Burman-Hall: 'Tune Identity and Performance Style: the Case of "Bonaparte's Retreat"', *Selected Reports in Ethnomusicology*, iii/1 (1978), 77

K. A. Gourlay: 'Towards a Reassessment of the Ethnomusicologist's Role in Research', *EM* xxii (1978), 1–35

H. Zemp: '"Are'are Classification of Musical Types and Instruments', *EM*, xxii (1978), 37–67

J. Blacking: 'The Study of Man as Music-Maker', *The Performing Arts: Music and Dance*, ed. J. Blacking and J. W. Kealiinohomoku (The Hague, 1979), 3

J. M. Chernoff: *African Rhythm and African Sensibility: Aesthetics and Social Action in African Musical Idioms* (Chicago, 1979)

O. Elschek: 'Melographische Interpretationscharakteristika von Flötenmusik', *Studia Instrumentorum Musicae Popularis*, vi (1979), 43

C. Heth: 'Stylistic Similarities in Cherokee and Iroquois Music', *Journal of Cherokee Studies*, iv (1979), 128–62

G. Kubik: *Angolan Traits in Black Music, Games and Dances of Brazil: a Study of African Cultural Extensions Overseas* (Lisbon, 1979)

A. Seeger: 'What Can We Learn When They Sing? Vocal Genres of the Suyá Indians of Central Brazil', *EM*, xxiii (1979), 373

J. Becker: *Traditional Music in Modern Java: Gamelan in a Changing Society* (Honolulu, 1980)

O. Elschek: 'Czechoslovakia', §2, *Grove 6*

W. Graf: *Vergleichende Musikwissenschaft: Ausgewählte Aufsätze* (Vienna, 1980)

V. Hoshovsky: 'Union of Soviet Socialist Republics', §10/2, *Grove 6*

A. L. Lloyd: 'Lament', *Grove 6*

M. I. Mapoma: *The Determinants of Style in the Music of Ingomba* (diss., UCLA, 1980)

H. S. Powers: 'Language Models and Musical Analysis', *EM*, xxiv (1980), 1–60

R. Sevåg: 'Norway', §2, *Grove 6*

B. Tedlock: 'Songs of the Zuni Kachina Society: Composition, Rehearsal, and Performance', *Southwestern Indian Ritual Drama*, ed. C. J. Frisbie (Albuquerque, 1980), 7

O. Elschek: 'Stratigraphische Probleme der Volksmusik in den Karpaten und auf dem Balkan', *Stratigraphische Probleme der Volksmusik in den Karpaten und auf dem Balkan*, ed. A. Elscheková (Bratislava, 1981), 15

J. H. K. Nketia: 'The Juncture of the Social and the Musical: the Methodology of Cultural Analysis', *The World of Music*, xxiii/2 (1981), 22

—— : 'African Roots of Music in the Americas: an African View', *IMSCR*, xii *Berkeley 1977*, ed. D. Heartz and B. C. Wade (Kassel, 1981), 82

R. M. and V. L. Stone: 'Event, Feedback and Analysis: Research Media in the Study of Music Events', *EM*, xxv (1981), 215

G. Béhague: 'Folk and Traditional Music of Latin America: General Prospect and Research Problems', *The World of Music*, xxiv/2 (1982), 3

F. Giannattasio and B. Lortat-Jacob: 'Modalità d'improvvisazione nella musica sarda: due modelli', *Culture musicali*, i/1 (1982), 3–35

D. Locke: 'Principles of Offbeat Timing and Cross-Rhythm in Southern Eve Dance Drumming', *EM*, xxvi (1982), 217

217

R. Stone: *Let the Inside Be Sweet: the Interpretation of Music Event Among the Kpelle of Liberia* (Bloomington, IN, 1982)

B. Kernfeld: 'Two Coltranes', *Annual Review of Jazz Studies*, ii (1983), 7–66

P. L. Manuel: *Thumri in Historical and Stylistic Perspective* (Diss., UCLA, 1983)

R. F. Thompson: *Flash of the Spirit: African and Afro-American Art and Philosophy* (New York, 1983)

C. J. Ellis: 'Time Consciousness of Aboriginal Performers', *Problems and Solutions: Occasional Essays in Musicology Presented to Alice M. Moyle*, ed. J. C. Kassler and J. Stubington (Sydney, 1984) 149–85

R. Kauffman: 'Multipart Relationships in Shona Vocal Music', *Selected Reports in Ethnomusicology*, v (1984), 145

R. Moyle: 'Jumping to Conclusions', *Problems and Solutions: Occasional Essays in Musicology Presented to Alice M. Moyle*, ed. J. C. Kassler and J. Stubington (Sydney, 1984), 51

B. C. Wade: *Khyāl: Creativity within North India's Classical Music Tradition* (Cambridge, England, 1984)

L. Bielawski: 'History in Ethnomusicology', *YTM*, xvii (1985), 8

D. Coplan: *In Township Tonight! South Africa's Black City Music and Theatre* (London and New York, 1985)

G. Giuriati: '"Percorsi" improvvisativi nella musica strumentale dell'Italia centro-meridionale', *Forme e comportamenti della musica folklorica italiana: Etnomusicologia e didattica*, ed. Giovanni Giuriati (Milan, 1985), 15

P. Staro: 'Analisi del repertorio di danza della Val Po', *Culture musicali*, iv/7–8 (1985), 57–90 [with xix pls]

A. Thrasher: 'The Melodic Structure of *Jiangnan Sizhu*', *EM*, xxix (1985), 237

Takanori Fujita: 'Structure and Rhythm in *Nô*: an Introduction', *The Oral and the Literate in Music*, ed. Y. Tokumaru and O. Yamaguti (Tokyo, 1986), 88

J. Maceda: 'A Concept of Time in a Music of Southeast Asia (A Preliminary Account)', *EM* xxx (1986), 11–53

P. Manuel: 'The Evolution of Modern *Thumrī*', *EM*, xxx (1986), 470

R. B. Qureshi: *Sufi Music of India and Pakistan: Sound, Context and Meaning in Qawwali* (Cambridge, England, 1986)

M. Mora: 'The Sounding Pantheon of Nature: T'boli Instrumental Music in the Making of an Ancestral Symbol', *AcM*, lix (1987), 187–212

R. B. Qureshi: 'Musical Sound and Contextual Input: a Performance Model for Musical Analysis', *EM*, xxxi (1987), 56–86

A. Seeger: *Why Suyá Sing: a Musical Anthropology of an Amazonian People* (Cambridge, England, 1987)

J. Sundberg: *The Science of the Singing Voice* (Dekalb, IL, 1987)

E. O. Henry: *Chant the Names of God: Music and Culture in Bhojpuri-Speaking India* (San Diego, 1988)

J. C. Sugarman: 'Making *Muabet*: the Social Basis of Singing among Prespa Albanian Men', *Selected Reports in Ethnomusicology*, vii (1988), 1–42

A. Thrasher: 'Hakka-Chaozhou Instrumental Repertoire: an Analytical Perspective on Traditional Creativity', *Asian Music*, xix/2 (1988), 1–30

M. J. Kartomi: *On Concepts and Classifications of Musical Instruments* (Chicago, 1990)

CHAPTER VIII

Historical Ethnomusicology

RICHARD WIDDESS

Ethnomusicology is often represented as a discipline concerned mainly, or even exclusively, with the present – with the performances of living musicians and the roles of such performances in present-day societies. Yet each music, as each society, is the temporary result of continuing historical processes, processes that may or may not be important to the performer, but are arguably important to the outside observer. These processes can be observed in both the recent and the more remote past, and include both profound changes and significant continuities; the evidence includes early sound recordings, oral history, written documents and organological, iconographical and archaeological data. The methodologies required for studying these materials are often derived from other disciplines, and are of course different from those most closely identified with ethnomusicology: one cannot do fieldwork in the past. But it is clear from the work done in many areas that any picture of the present that is not informed by an appreciation of the historical dimension is sadly incomplete.

There is no consensus on the agenda or methodology of historical ethnomusicology, and a wide variety of historical materials and approaches to their study can be observed. On the one hand, recent changes in musical culture, especially under the impact of Western influences, and early European encounters with the wider musical world (e.g. Harrison, 1973; Hardgrave and Slawek, 1988; Woodfield, 1990) are among the accepted concerns of the ethnomusicologist. On the other hand, it is not only during the period of contact with the West that musical change has occurred, or for which evidence is available. Many cultures have preserved iconographic, archaeological or documentary records, by means of which historical processes in pre-modern times may be traced; these may be regarded as direct historical evidence, artefacts created at the time in question. Oral histories, song texts, or the present-day structure and distribution of musical styles, repertories and instruments, may also offer indirect but significant clues to past events. Among the changes attested by such evidence, 'external' and 'internal' have been distinguished (Merriam, 1964, p.307; Nettl, 1983, pp.183ff), referring to influences imposed from outside a culture and changes generated from within the culture; but these are not always clearly distinct.

Historical enquiry, especially where written documents are lacking, may focus on external change, associated with migration, conquest, colonization, trade, stimulus diffusion and other inter-cultural relations, for which evidence is sought in musical instruments, systems and styles (e.g. Sachs, 1943; Jones, 1964; Lomax, 1968; Blacking, 1971; Picken, 1975, pp.570ff; Blench, 1984). Such studies can contribute to the general history of a region (see for example various contributions to Wachsmann, 1971), though hypothetical relationships adduced over very wide areas, or on the basis of simplistic models of migration or conquest, may be difficult to sustain, especially in the absence of 'direct' evidence (as defined above). A written literature, on the other hand, may shed light on the history of musical ideas, practices and institutions within a culture, and on internal changes both in music itself and in its social, ritual and other functions; such literature is available for the 'high cultures' of the ancient Mediterranean, Europe, and much of Asia, and has been extensively but by no means exhaustively studied (many major Asian sources remain unpublished), with a view to tracing the history of music within the culture concerned as well as contributing to wider perspectives.

Textual scholars tend to give documentary evidence a privileged status in relation to other forms of evidence, such as oral tradition. Oral tradition may also be acceptable as a historical resource, and often records different kinds of information from written documents: in India, for example, musical treatises rarely concern themselves with performers as individuals, about whom there is however a rich oral history. However, oral history seldom has a time depth of more than a few centuries, and may tell us more about the present situation than about the past to which it ostensibly refers (Kippen, 1988, p.84ff). Thus Gilbert Rouget distinguishes the history constructed by historians from 'traditional history', defined as 'the sum total of knowledge the group possesses concerning its past', which 'justifies the position of the group in society and provides it with the basis for its rights' (1971); such histories, 'always *ex parte* statements' (Fage, 1971), need careful interpretation in the light of both the present social environment and the material historical record. Written documents and other 'direct' evidence must of course be viewed equally critically, in relation to the past in which it was created. Nevertheless, artefacts offer a degree of intimacy with the past that is lacking in other types of evidence; in their absence some questions, such as the search for musical origins and pre-historic evolution, may never be definitively resolved (on the value of 'speculative' history, compare John Blacking's assault [1973, pp.56f] and Bruno Nettl's defence [1983, p.167ff]).

Nettl makes an important distinction (1983, pp.172ff) between the *content* of musical change – 'particular events and their relationship' – and the underlying *processes* of change, assigning study of the former to 'historical musicologists', the latter alone to ethnomusicologists. It may be doubted, however, whether the two aspects can be separated; processes, after all, *are* relationships between particular events, and the study of process cannot logically precede that of content. 'Historical ethnomusicology', if it can be defined as a discipline, might well take as its twin objectives the uncovering of historical events, and the study of their relationships in terms of processes of change, taking into account all available evidence, including that of socio-musical continuity and change observable today.

To illustrate the working methods and underlying approach adopted by a number of musical historians, let us consider the historical documentation of music in Asia. The materials in this field include: (i) non-musical literature with incidental references (often detailed) to music (for two striking examples, see Picken and Mitani, 1979; Picken, 1984); (ii) treatises on music theory (see for example, Gimm, 1966; te Nijenhuis, 1970; Lath, 1978; Shringy and Sharma, 1978; Wright, 1978; Provine, 1988); (iii) notations of music, occurring either as examples in theoretical works, or as separate scores, part-books or anthologies (see later).

The study of these documents takes as its models the disciplines of Oriental studies and historical musicology, both of which ultimately derive their outlook from the Western tradition of classical scholarship, with its emphasis on philology and on literary and textual criticism. Of his work and that of his pupils on Japanese court music, Laurence Picken writes:

> Our method in the study and transcription of the earliest scores of the Tōgaku-tradition surviving in Japan has throughout been: to read them with no more information than that given in the manuscripts themselves, deliberately ignoring the living tradition and performance-practice of today . . . Our collective approach, analysing the documents in question in their own terms, is one widely practised by Sinologists in recent times, and is to be seen at work [for example] in the translations of Karlgren and Waley – who laid aside the accumulated interpretations of the commentaries – of the *Book of Songs* . . . It is the attempt to determine what an ancient text meant at the time when it was written (Picken and others, 1981, p.11).

The connection with literary criticism is explicit here, the parallel with historical musicology obvious (the emphasis given here to the evidence of the manuscripts themselves does not preclude the authors from drawing on the evidence of other sources that are contemporary with or earlier than the manuscripts in question). This approach, however, is in some respects different from that of other branches of musicology and ethnomusicology. In Europe, on the one hand, there is no question of an unbroken 'living tradition and performance practice' for the majority of pre-18th-century music (except plainchant), and there has been rapid, extensive and well-documented change in every aspect of repertory and performance. Elsewhere, a far greater degree of continuity from the remote past is often assumed, especially by the bearers of ancient and prestigious traditions. Such assumptions often need to be qualified in the light of documentary evidence (e.g. Marett, 1985; Wright, 1987). The results of a Western historical approach to a living tradition may therefore be at variance with the conception of music history held by the living bearers of that tradition – or may seem so to them. The historical ethnomusicologist may, and should, be able to reconcile the 'outsider's' and 'insider's' viewpoints to his own satisfaction, but he may have difficulty convincing his critics in the culture concerned. This is a problem faced, in some degree, by most ethnomusicologists; but unlike his colleagues the historical ethnomusicologist is by definition unable to accept at face value the concepts and values of the living musician, for they are a product of the very historical processes of change that he is attempting to trace. The assumption that the performance practices of today may be projected into the past is criticized by Jonathan Condit (1976, 'The Evolution of *Yŏmillak*'): 'in cultures relying on aural transmission of music, a piece can undoubtedly be preserved in the performing repertory for a period of several centuries, but the assumption that a piece has remained unchanged for such a period should be viewed with skepticism' (see also Marett, 1985).

For the sake of brevity we shall concentrate here on the third type of documentation, notated music; partly because this is an area of growing interest, partly because its methodologies apply also in some measure to the other types of musical document, and partly because it is arguably the most important of the three types in that it gives direct evidence for music's definitive features – sounds and temporal organization. Even so, the diversity of notation systems and sources makes any generalizations about methodology hazardous. One question is central to the study of any musical score: what is the relationship between the structure of the music as notated, and its realization in sound? The answer to this question, and the extent to which an answer is possible, is likely to be different for each culture, notation system and source.

Study of a source of early musical notation may be divided into four activities: bibliographical research, interpretation of the notation, transcription and analysis. These activities may be concurrent rather than sequential, for the results of each may be relevant to the other.

Bibliographical research

In order to interpret a musical notation it is necessary to know the history of the source and its functions in the musical culture concerned. We wish to know, if possible, the author or authors, date and provenance of the source, the method of textual transmission, the number of copies available, and their relationship to each other and to the original, with a view to establishing a text as close to the original as possible. Processes of compilation, interpolation, abbreviation and other editorial changes may have to be taken into account, as well as straightforward copyists' errors. (See, for example, Allan Marett's [1987] bibliographical study of the manuscripts of a 14th-century *tōgaku* flute score.) Equally important, the functions that the source and its notations were intended to serve will have a bearing on its relationship to performance: for example, a dynastic record including notation of court music, a theoretical treatise on modes and an instrumental instruction book, are likely to give very different perspectives on a music repertory. Unfortunately our knowledge of a repertory is often dependent on a single type of source, and it is necessary to take into account other evidence, such as iconography, to fill out our picture of performance practice. Finally, the relationship of the source to other sources in the same tradition must also be considered: it may for example include materials derived from earlier sources reflecting an earlier period of history, and/or it may have exerted a significant influence over later sources (and even over performance practice). Indian theoretical writings, for example, regularly derive their material (including, in many cases, their notated examples) from earlier sources. Moronaga's 12th-century edition of the *tōgaku* repertory drew both on earlier scores and on current performance practice, and considerably influenced later and modern practice (see ex.1; p.233). As Robert Provine has shown (1988), 15th-century notations of ritual music from Korea are to be seen in the context of a Chinese tradition of ritual

222

and musical theory going back to the 6th century BC; this music is still performed in Korea today.

Interpretation of the notation

It is generally acknowledged that any method of music writing yields an imperfect representation of performance, and few, if any, notation systems even purport to be 'descriptive' (Seeger, 1958). Every notation assumes some familiarity with at least the style of the music represented: the more familiarity is assumed, the less detail is encoded in the notation. Some notations may not permit transcription without reference to modern practice (apparently the case with Tibetan and Vedic chant notations; see Helffer, 1980; Howard, 1977), which is not necessarily reliable as historical evidence. For some ethnomusicologists, the value of early notations is therefore severely limited. But the object in studying notations is not necessarily to recreate musical performances (though it may be valuable to do so as a test of the practical and musical plausibility of one's interpretation [see Condit, 1984]), but rather to draw conclusions of a historical and analytical nature, both from the notation system itself and from whatever musical parameters it represents.

The method of interpretation and the extent to which a definitive interpretation is possible depend on the nature of the notation system itself and its function. The symbols of a notation system may be physical gestures, spoken or sung syllables, or written signs of various kinds: letters, numbers, syllables, lexigraphs, words, graphic signs or pictures. Musical parameters represented include pitch (absolute or relative), pitch sequence (ornament, accent, direction of movement, contour, melodic formula), vocal production, dynamic, instrumental technique or sonority, formal and rhythmic structure, meter, beat and duration. Notation systems are conditioned by, and therefore shed light on, methods of transmission and performance, and by fundamental concepts of musical order, as well as by such extra-musical factors as the availability of writing materials, the cultural status of writing, and the writing system for language in the culture concerned (see, for example, Treitler, 1981 and 1982; Bent, 1980). Interpretation must take all these factors into account.

Beyond the characteristics of the notation system itself one must also take into account the intention of the notator: to what extent was it his purpose to represent the music as he would himself have performed it? Here again it is impossible to generalize, except to point out the frequent conflict between the desire to codify and preserve a repertory by writing it, and an equally strong desire to ensure its secrecy from the uninitiated, which may result in the omission from the notation of important features of performance practice. Thus the 9th-century copyist of the Sino-Japanese lute-manuscript *Fushi-minomiya-bon biwa fu* marked it 'For oral transmission only', and commented: 'according to the Tang notation, one presses only at one fret and plays it: according to the teachings of the Master, one strikes, adding many strings, and plays it. Again, in Tang notations, there are few ornamental notes: in the teachings of the Master, there are many ornamental notes' (Wolpert, 1977, pp.135f, 150). This passage might describe the relationship between notation and performance typical of many notations, but it can also be interpreted, as

Rembrandt Wolpert has suggested, as indicating a historical change in performance practice, the notation preserving its conventional form, hallowed by age and provenance.

In interpreting the symbols of a notation, both intrinsic and extrinsic evidence must be brought to bear. The meaning of the symbols may be partially known from other written or oral sources, but this and other extrinsic evidence must be confirmed by a rigorous examination of the text itself. Intrinsic evidence includes the results of both statistical and structural analysis; thus the rhythmic interpretation of ex.2 (pp.234–5) rests on a statistical analysis of the frequency with which different squares on the notation grid are occupied by pitch symbols (rather than on the extrinsic knowledge that triplet rhythms are characteristic of Korean music today).

The scale structure of ex.3 (p.236), which is not explicit in the syllabic notation, is deduced from a structural analysis of the use of consonant intervals in the melody, as well as from a knowledge of early and later Indian scale theory.

Extrinsic evidence includes parallel notations of the same music from other sources; the known features of a musical language or the known properties of instruments; and such quasi-universals as the preferences for descending contours, small intervals rather than large inversions and consistent ambitus, at least in vocal music. Extrinsic evidence also includes modern performance practice, but here one must exercise caution. Certain performance features of very great antiquity may be preserved; but it is also clear that, even where the same composition remains in the repertory for centuries, its interpretation by performers can change radically (a point to be discussed under 'Analysis' below). Hence it is essential, in the first instance, to interpret a notation in the light of contemporary evidence only, as advocated by Picken, though of course this approach may lead to conclusions rather different from hitherto accepted assumptions.

Transcription

The purposes of transcription (or transnotation) are first to test an interpretation of the original, and second, to make the results of that interpretation accessible to others. Is it then not simply a question of exchanging one set of symbols for another? This approach might seem ideally objective, but as with transcription from recordings or performance, it is doubtful whether such a mechanical process would be desirable, even if it were actually possible. As with translation from another language, some element of interpretation is essential, and the use of a different notation system may force interpretive decisions on the transcriber. The charge of subjectivity can be guarded against by ensuring that the reader is able to reconstruct, in all significant details, the original notation from the transcription: in this way one is not falsifying the evidence, even if some interpretive decisions happen to be mistaken.

It is common for ethnomusicologists to deplore the limitations and ethnocentric implications of staff notation; yet there is no universally accepted substitute. For most transcription purposes, at least in cases where the original notation specifies a sequence of identifiable pitches, staff notation provides the most suitable vehicle. This limits the readership to scholars conversant with the Western system: but it is undoubtedly convenient for comparative purposes to have transcriptions of different repertories and from different sources in a single notation (but *see* 'Transcription').

One of the 'limitations' of staff notation is that it may be, in some respects, more precise than the original notation system. This may force the transcriber to make interpretive decisions in areas that are imprecise, deliberately or through the accidents of transmission, in the original source. If the original notation is not specific about octave register, for example, the use of staff notation may require one to postulate the octave register of each pitch, as in ex.3. The melody is here transcribed by choosing at every point the smallest available interval – 2nds rather than 7ths, 3rds rather than 6ths etc – except where this would lead to a complete change of register for the remainder of the melody (see the interval a'-d' near the end of the melody). This method sometimes allows alternative solutions, and other factors – such as parallel passages in other melodies – must then be taken into consideration.

Similarly the use of Western time values when transcribing from mensural notation carries implications about tempo that may not be explicit in the original: one must choose whether to represent the basic rhythmic unit of one's source by a quarter-note or a whole note (for example), and one's choice may depend on one's overall view of the history of performance practice in the tradition concerned. Thus, if transcribed in accordance with the modern reading of similar modern notations, exx.1 and 2 would be written with much longer note values. Condit argues persuasively against the modern reading of early Korean sources (1979, p.13), as does Picken for *tōgaku* (Picken and others, 1981, pp.5–14, etc).

On the other hand staff notation may not be sufficiently precise in other respects; additional signs or other modifications may have to be improvised for denoting ornaments, indeterminate time values, pitch inflections and the like, as they often are when transcribing from performance. In some cases, it may be helpful to include the original notation in combination with the transcription (see Marett, 1981), although it should normally be possible to reconstruct the original notation from the transcription.

Finally, one further advantage of staff notation may be mentioned; it is well suited to synoptic display, where a number of melodies, or segments of a single melody, are set out in parallel, or otherwise disposed about the page, in such a way that the structure of the music can be more readily perceived by the reader.

Analysis

Analysis is an indispensable part of the study of early notation; some analytical exercises may be necessary, for example, in determining the meaning of the notational symbols, or the functions of the notation in the source. But once a repertory is transcribed in its entirety, it becomes available for more thorough analysis of the musical language, or of the relationship of the repertory to other music. Analysis here need not be seen as necessarily an artificial, 'etic', or ethnocentric exercise, filtering the music through an alien mesh, though it may often appear so. A more positive view would be that the original notation itself involves an act of analysis on the part of members of the musical culture concerned, for notation preserves those aspects of the music which *the notator* considers essential for its transmission or recall. In analysing an early notated repertory, therefore, we are in fact carrying a stage further the analysis already undertaken by members of the culture concerned.

The analysis of early Asiatic music that has so far been undertaken may be broadly characterized as *structural* and *comparative*. Some analyses consider the music in question in its own terms, without reference (in the first instance) to other music. The objective here may be to identify the compositional processes, the grammatical rules of the musical language, its rhythmic, modal or formulaic structure and the like. A classic essay in this genre is Picken's study of Tang ritual melodies: the equidurational, four-square rhythm of the melodies lends itself well to the statistical analysis of melodic movement between the notes of each mode, from which modal dynamics and compositional principles can be deduced (Picken, 1956, p.172). Noël Nickson's analysis of early *tōgaku* melodies, which uses similar methods, is designed to demonstrate not only the methods of the original composers, including 'the technical devices of musical composition of repetition, sequence, transposition and inversion, with or without variation', but also the 'quality' of the music, as shown by 'felicitous touches of craftsmanship', 'skill in avoiding the commonplace and monotonous', 'ingenuity and musicality' (Picken and others, 1985, *Music from the Tang Court*, ii, pp.72–99 and subsequent volumes). Analysis here overlaps with criticism, an activity in which ethnomusicologists perhaps too rarely permit themselves to indulge. The critical approach, which is regarded as valuable in both the 'mother disciplines' of Oriental studies and musicology, is used in this case to support the historical hypothesis that the music in question was composed at the Tang court (since the hypothesis would presumably become untenable if the music could be shown to be crudely constructed). The hypothesis is not, however, dependent on qualitative criteria, the validity of which many ethnomusicologists would be disinclined to accept.

In another direction, structural analysis can also throw light on the relationship between text and music, as Picken has shown in his studies of early Chinese song. In two of his many essays on this subject, Picken uses analysis of the texts speculatively to reconstruct essential characteristics of the music of the Chinese *Shi Jing* and Tang lyric poetry, for which no music survives in contemporary sources (Picken, 1977 and 1981).

For all the insights that can be gained from it, structural analysis is often characterized by starkly statistical computations, requiring a considerable effort of imagination to relate them to musical experience. One of the advantages of staff notation is that it can be used as an analytical tool, either for synoptic display or for reduction of the melody to a simpler outline, the advantage being that the analysis can be read as music, or at least 'proto music' and hence easily related to the original. Elizabeth Markham's analysis of the early Japanese *saibara* (court song) repertory uses synoptic transcriptions to show that the many different song texts were sung to variants of a few 'stock' tunes, themselves of a formulaic structure, and hence easily malleable to fit diverse text structures (1983, ch.5). In my own analyses of early Indian music, the original melody itself is first displayed synoptically in such a way that repeated material is vertically aligned – the melody becomes, as it were, its own analysis. Below this, reductions and analytical formulas of various kinds, usually in staff notation, can be derived from and co-ordinated with the display (see ex.3). This type of analysis makes it possible to compare both the formal and modal structure of different melodies (Widdess, 1989, 1992).

Many studies compare the repertory in question with other music of the same or different periods. In the first case little has been done beyond the comparison of different instrumental partbooks in *tōgaku* (for example, Picken and Wolpert, 1981), but Markham has made a valuable comparison of the *saibara* and *tōgaku* repertories leading to important suggestions about their inter-relationships (1983, ch.4). Diachronic comparative analysis has on the other hand produced spectacular results, particularly in the comparison of early notations with modern performance practice. The demonstration that melodies in current *tōgaku* repertory can be recognized in early (10th–12th centuries) partbooks, and almost certainly derive from pre-9th-century China and Central Asia, although performed now in a radically different style, is the achievement of Laurence Picken (1967; see also Picken and others, 1985, pp.5–14) and his research group, whose collaborative publication *Music from the Tang Court* is undoubtedly the most ambitious project in historical ethnomusicology yet undertaken (ex.1). Picken's observation that the original melodies of *tōgaku* are preserved in the lute and mouth-organ tablatures, and not in the highly decorated wind parts as commonly supposed, illustrates the radically new light that a historical perspective can throw on modern practice; the importance of this perspective for understanding the complex relationships between the different instrumental parts in *tōgaku* has been demonstrated by Marett (1985). Melodies preserved in 15th-century Korean sources have been compared with successively later notations by Condit (1976 'The Evolution of *Yŏmillak*', and 1981); this comparison demonstrates processes of embellishment and expansion by which the 15th-century versions have become transformed (and incidentally confirms Condit's reading of the mensural notation). In some cases, a single original melody has given rise to several versions in the modern Korean repertory: Condit is thus able to relate items of current repertory to each other and to earlier stages in their development. A similar achievement is Markham's comparison of the *saibara* melodies as they survive in 12th-century manuscripts, and as they are performed today (Markham, 1983, ch.6); here a set of transformations, including modal and rhythmic changes and the imposition of ornamental formulae derived from Buddhist chant, have been convincingly adduced (ex.4; p.237). In this case the extent of the changes observed is perhaps less surprising in view of the fact that the performing tradition was reconstructed, after a period of neglect, during the 17th century – an example of the 'revival of tradition' which forms an interesting and topical aspect of historical research.

This type of analysis has so far been carried out mainly with regard to East Asian musics, due to the richness of that area in historical documents. For South Asia the 17th-century notations for *vīnā* of Somanātha have attracted attention (te Nijenhuis, 1976; Ayyangar, 1980), but these (like most historical notations of Indian music) are unmeasured, quasi-improvised *ālāpa* preludes, not fixed compositions that might have survived as such into present practice. It is therefore musical forms and modes that can be compared with present practice, rather than specific melodies. My own work focuses on Indian sources of the 7th to 13th centuries that include notation; these sources show that some of the structures and techniques of improvisation characteristic of modern Indian art music were already current by the 13th century or earlier (see ex.3), but one cannot juxtapose early and modern versions of the same melodies as one can for Korean and Japanese court musics (Widdess, 1981 'Aspects of Form', 'Tala and Melody', 1989, 1992). More immediately comparable with the latter is the case of Turkish instrumental art music. Wright's comparative analysis of compositions preserved in 17th-, 19th- and 20th-century Turkish sources (1987) reveals a remarkable degree of melodic expansion and elaboration, which can be partly explained in terms of 'transformational rules'. The Turkish, Japanese and Korean materials together furnish a remarkable body of evidence for the operation of oral and written transmission over long periods, and for processes of progressive retardation and elaboration to which Picken first drew attention. It may be noted that the relationship of oral and written transmission is also an important aspect of Western musical history (Treitler, 1974, 1981, 1982; Tokumaru and Yamaguti, 1986).

In this preliminary overview of 'historical ethnomusicology' we have emphasized the problems, methods, and results of textual studies. But does a historical approach, whether text-based or not, really belong to the ethnomusicological field, except insofar as it coincides geographically with areas of interest to ethnomusicologists? Many of the musicologists whose work has been discussed above would disclaim the prefix 'ethno-' with its implications of a social-science orientation. But there is no reason to assume that the anthropological perspective is the only valid one in ethnomusicology, and in any case generations of ethnomusicologists have grappled with historical questions as part of their normal activities (Nettl, 1986). The challenge is therefore (since ethnomusicologists like to feel they are working as part of a concerted endeavour) to integrate historical enquiry into the overall scheme of ethnomusicological studies.

A response to this challenge is provided by Timothy Rice's 're-modelling' of ethnomusicology (1987), in which 'historical construction' is seen as one of the 'formative processes' that brings music into being, and as organically related to two other such processes, 'social maintenance' and 'individual creation and experience':

> Historical construction can be explained in terms of both changes in patterns of social maintenance and individual creative decisions. Individual creation and experience can be seen as determined partly by historically constructed forms as learned, performed, and modified in socially maintained and sanctioned contexts. Social maintenance can be seen as an ongoing interaction between historically constructed modes of behaviour, traditions if you will, and individual action that recreates, modifies and interprets that tradition.

This approach does not require all ethnomusicologists to become historians (or anthropologists), but helps us to relate the work of specialists working in different traditions, and encourages us to seek a diachronic as well as a synchronic, a historical as well as a social understanding of musical phenomena.

228

Significantly, although he acknowledges the historical interests of many ethnomusicologists, Rice himself does not refer to any of the text-based research quoted in this chapter; it is Kay Shelemay who, in her response to Rice (1987), observes: 'We need to incorporate what are often for ethnomusicologists neglected manuscript and archival sources whose study requires source-critical and text-critical skills'. Both Rice and Shelemay advocate a rapprochement with the heavily text-oriented scholarship of Western music, leading to 'a unified, rather than a divided, musicology' (Rice). Historical ethnomusicology thus offers to bridge the conventionally accepted but artificial boundary between 'ethnomusicology' and 'musicology', a development desired by many in both camps. For this to happen, however, specialists in historical ethnomusicology must maintain and develop intellectually rigorous source-critical methods that can be taken seriously by Western-music historians, while at the same time addressing questions of 'social maintenance' and 'individual creation and experience', in the light of the anthropology and psychology of music. This is a severe challenge; but if it is met, we may hope to see historical ethnomusicology develop an important role within a re-united, global musicology.

Bibliography

C. Sachs: *The Rise of Music in the Ancient World, East and West* (New York, 1943)

L. E. R. Picken: 'Twelve Ritual Melodies of the T'ang Dynasty', *Studia Memoriae Belae Bartok sacra*, ed. Z. Kodály and others (Budapest, 1956), 147

B. Nettl: 'Historical Aspects of Ethnomusicology', *American Anthropologist*, lx (1958), 518

C. Seeger: 'Prescriptive and Descriptive Music Writing', *MQ*, xliv (1958), 184; repr. in Seeger (1977), 168

A. M. Jones: *Africa and Indonesia: the Evidence of the Xylophone* (Leiden, 1964)

A. P. Merriam: *The Anthropology of Music* (Evanston, 1964)

B. Nettl: *Theory and Method in Ethnomusicology* (New York, 1964)

M. Gimm: *Das Yüeh-fu tsa-lu des Tuan An-chieh: Studien zur Geschichte von Musik, Schauspiel und Tanz in der T'ang Dynastie* (Wiesbaden, 1966)

L. E. R. Picken: 'Secular Chinese Songs of the Twelfth Century', *SM*, viii (1966), 125–72

W. Kaufmann: *Musical Notations of the Orient: Notational Systems of Continental East, South and Central Asia* (Bloomington, IN, 1967)

R. C. Pian: *Song Dynasty Musical Sources and their Interpretation* (Cambridge, MA, 1967)

L. E. R. Picken: 'Central Asian Tunes in the *Gagaku* Tradition', *Festschrift Walter Wiora* (Kassel, 1967), 545

A. Lomax: *Folk Song Style and Culture* (Washington, DC, 1968)

E. te Nijenhuis: *Dattilam: a Compendium of Ancient Indian Music* (Leiden, 1970)

J. Blacking: 'Music and the Historical Process in Vendaland', *Essays on Music and History in Africa*, ed. K. P. Wachsmann (Evanston, 1971), 185–212

J. D. Fage: 'Music and History: a Historian's View of the African Picture', *Essays on Music and History in Africa*, ed. K. P. Wachsmann (Evanston, 1971), 257

G. Rouget: 'Court Song and Traditional History in the Ancient Kingdoms of Porto-Novo and Abomey', *Essays on Music and History in Africa*, ed. K. P. Wachsmann (Evanston, 1971), 27–64

K. P. Wachsmann, ed.: *Essays on Music and History in Africa* (Evanston, 1971)

J. Blacking: *How Musical is Man?* (Seattle, 1973)

E. Harich-Schneider: *A History of Japanese Music* (Oxford, 1973)

F. L. Harrison: *Time, Place and Music: an Anthology of Ethnomusicological Observation c.1550 to c.1880* (Amsterdam, 1973)

R. C. Provine: 'The Treatise on Ceremonial Music (1430) in the Annals of the Korean King Sejong', *EM*, xviii (1974), 1

L. Treitler: 'Homer and Gregory: the Transmission of Epic Poetry and Plainchant', *MQ*, lx (1974), 333–72

L. E. R. Picken: *Folk Musical Instruments of Turkey* (Oxford, 1975)

W. Kaufman: *Tibetan Buddhist Chant* (Bloomington, IN, 1975)

J. Condit: 'Differing Transcriptions from the Twelfth-Century Japanese Koto Manuscript *Jinchi yōroku*', *EM*, xx (1976), 87

G. Chase: 'Musicology, History and Anthropology', in *Current Thoughts in Musicology*, ed. J. W. Grubb (Austin, 1976)

J. Condit: 'The Evolution of *Yōmillak* from the Fifteenth Century to the Present Day', *Articles on Asian Music: Festschrift for Dr Chang Sa-Hun* (Seoul, 1976), 231–64

E. te Nijenhuis: *The Rāgas of Somanātha* (Leiden, 1976)

W. Howard: *Sāmavedic Chant* (New Haven, 1977)

L. E. R. Picken: 'The Shapes of the *Shi Jing* Song-Texts and their Musical Implications', *Musica Asiatica*, i (1977), 85

C. Seeger: *Studies in Musicology, 1935–1975* (Berkeley, 1977)

R. F. Wolpert: 'A Ninth-Century Sino-Japanese Lute-Tutor', *Musica Asiatica*, i (1977), 111–65

M. Lath: *A Study of Dattilam: a Treatise on the Sacred Music of Ancient India* (New Delhi, 1978)

R. K. Shringy and P. L. Sharma: *Saṅgītaratnākara of Śārṅgadeva*, i (Delhi, 1978)

O. Wright: *The Modal System of Arab and Persian Music A.D. 1250–1300* (Oxford, 1978)

J. Condit: 'A Fifteenth-Century Korean Score in Mensural Notation', *Musica Asiatica*, ii (1979), 1–87

L. E. R. Picken and Y. Mitani: 'Finger Techniques for the Zithers Sō-no-koto and Kin in Heian Times', *Musica Asiatica*, ii (1979), 89

D. R. Widdess: 'The Kuḍumiyāmalai Inscription: a Source of Early Indian Music in Notation', *Musica Asiatica*, ii (1979), 115–50

R. V. Ayyangar: *Gamaka and Vādanabheda: a Study of Somanātha's Rāgavibodha in its Historical Context* (diss., U. of Pennsylvania, 1980)

I. Bent: 'Notation', §I–II, *Grove 6*

M. Helffer: 'Neumatic Notations', §VII, *Grove 6*

K. K. Shelemay: '"Historical Ethnomusicology": Reconstructing Falasha Liturgical History', *EM*, xxiv (1980), 233

J. Condit: 'Two Song-Dynasty Chinese Tunes Preserved in Korea', *Music and Tradition: Essays on Asian and Other Musics Presented to Laurence Picken*, ed. D. R. Widdess and R. F. Wolpert (Cambridge, England, 1981), 1–40

A. J. Marett: '"Banshiki Sangun" and "Shōenraku": Metrical Structure and Notation of Two Tang-Music Melodies for Flute', *Music and Tradition: Essays on Asian and Other Musics Presented to Laurence Picken*, ed. D. R. Widdess and R. F. Wolpert (Cambridge, England, 1981), 41

L. E. R. Picken: 'The Musical Implications of Chinese Song-Texts with Unequal Lines, and the Significance of Nonsense-Syllables', *Musica Asiatica*, iii (1981), 53

—— and others: *Music from the Tang Court*, i (Oxford, 1981)

L. E. R. Picken and R. F. Wolpert: 'Mouth-organ and Lute Parts of Tōgaku and Their Interrelationships', *Musica Asiatica*, iii (1981), 79

L. Treitler: 'Oral, Written, and Literate Process in the Transmission of Medieval Music', *Speculum*, lvi (1981), 471

D. R. Widdess: 'Aspects of Form in North Indian *ālāp* and *dhrupad*', *Music and Tradition: Essays on Asian and Other Musics Presented to Laurence Picken*, ed. D. R. Widdess and R. F. Wolpert (Cambridge, England, 1981), 143–83

——: 'Tāla and Melody in Early Indian Music: a Study of Nānyadeva's Pāṇikā Songs with Musical Notation', *Bulletin of the School of Oriental and African Studies*, xliv/3 (1981), 481

R. F. Wolpert: 'Tang-Music (Tōgaku) Manuscripts for Lute and Their Interrelationships', *Music and Tradition: Essays on Asian and Other Musics Presented to Laurence Picken*, ed. D. R. Widdess and R. F. Wolpert (Cambridge, England, 1981), 69–121

——: 'A Ninth-Century Score for Five-Stringed Lute', *Musica Asiatica*, iii (1981), 107

L. Treitler: 'The Early History of Music Writing in the West', *JAMS*, xxxv (1982), 237–79

E. J. Markham: *Saibara: Japanese Court Songs of the Heian Period* (Cambridge, England, 1983)

B. Nettl: *The Study of Ethnomusicology: Twenty-Nine Issues and Concepts* (Urbana, 1983)

R. Blench: 'The Morphology and Distribution of sub-Saharan Musical Instruments of North-African, Middle-Eastern, and Asian, Origin', *Musica Asiatica*, iv (1984)

J. Condit: *Music of the Korean Renaissance: Songs and Dances of the 15th Century* (Cambridge, England, 1984)

L. E. R. Picken: 'Instruments in an Orchestra from Pyū (Upper Burma) in 802', *Musica Asiatica*, iv (1984), 245

A. J. Marett: 'Tōgaku: Where Have the Tang Melodies Gone, and Where Have the New Melodies Come From?', *EM*, xxix (1985), 409

L. E. R. Picken and others: *Music from the Tang Court*, ii and iii (Cambridge, England, 1985)

M. Honegger and C. Meyer, eds.: *La musique et le rite, sacré et profane* (Strasbourg, 1986) [report of the Congress of the International Musicological Society, 1983]

B. Nettl: 'Some Historical Thoughts on the Character of Ethnomusicology', *Exploration on Ethnomusicology*, ed. C. J. Frisbie (Detroit, 1986)

Y. Tokumaru and O. Yamaguti, eds: *The Oral and the Literate in Music* (Tokyo, 1986)

A. J. Marett: 'An Investigation of Sources for *Chū Ōga Ryūteki Yōroku-fu*: a Japanese Flute Score of the Fourteenth Century', *Musica Asiatica*, v (1987), 210–67

T. Rice: 'Towards the Remodelling of Ethnomusicology', *EM*, xxxi (1987), 469

K. K. Shelemay: 'Response to Rice', *EM*, xxxi (1987), 489

O. Wright: 'Aspects of Historical Change in the Turkish Classical Repertoire', *Musica Asiatica*, v (1987), 1–108

R. L. Hardgrave Jr and S. M. Slawek: 'Instruments and Music Culture in 18th-century India: the Solvyns Portraits', *Asian Music*, xx (1988), 1–92

J. R. Kippen: *The Tabla of Lucknow: a Cultural Analysis of a Musical Tradition* (Cambridge, England, 1988)

R. C. Provine: *Essays on Sino-Korean Musicology: Early Sources for Korean Ritual Music* (Seoul, 1988)

D. R. Widdess: 'Sugar, Treacle and Candy: History and the Concept of *rāga* in Indian Music', *Ethnomusicology and the historical dimension*, ed. M. L. Philipp (Ludwigsburg, 1989)

M. L. Philipp, ed.: *Ethnomusicology and the Historical Dimension* (Ludwigsburg, 1989)

I. Woodfield: 'The Keyboard Recital in Oriental Diplomacy, 1520–1620', *JRMA*, cxv (1990), 33–62

D. R. Widdess: *The Rāgas of Early Indian Music: Modes, Melodies and Musical Notations from the Gupta Period to c.1250* (Oxford, 1992)

Notes to Music Examples

Ex.1 (source: Picken *et al.*, *Music from the Tang Court*, iii, pp.34–5, 1985)

Tang-music (*Tōgaku*): court instrumental ensemble music of Japan, believed to have been introduced from the Tang court of China not later than the 9th century AD. Transcribed by Picken and others (1985, p.34f) from part-books for (1) mouth organ (*shō*; 1244); (2) mouth organ (1303); (3) long zither (*sō-no-koto*; *c* 1171); (4) lute (*biwa*; *c* 1171). The incomplete part for flute (3a) is preserved as a series of marginal glosses, in archaic flute tablature, in (3). The parts differ from one another (*a*) in instrumental technique and ornamentation; (*b*) in metrical structure (suggesting divergent performance traditions); and (*c*) in mode (as a result of Fujiwara no Moronaga's revision of the string parts in the 12th century). Nevertheless they are clearly versions of a single original melody, possibly composed in China. Like all unmeasured preludes (*jō*), this piece has been dropped from the repertory and is no longer performed; modal clashes between string and wind parts survive, however, as a general feature of modern performance practice (Picken *et al*, 1981, pp.26–8).

Ex.2 (source: *Musica Asiatica*, iv, pp.37 and 39 [fig.10.1, 10.3])

Korean instrumental notations: a page from An Sang's *Zither Tablature Book (Kŭm hapcha-bo*, 1572). The columns of rectangles are read vertically from top to bottom; the rectangles denote metrical units (not necessarily equal), grouped into larger units by the heavy horizontal lines. The columns contain, from right to left (1) relative-pitch numeric notation for zither (*kŏmun'go*); (2) the same melody in zither tablature; (3) the same melody in mnemonic syllables for zither; (4) a song text (the vocal melody is not given); (5) a part for flute in relative-pitch numeric notation; (6) mnemonic syllables for the flute; (7) and (8) pictographic notation for hourglass drum and barrel drum. The transcription is by Condit (1984, p.39), who interprets the larger metrical divisions as equal, and the smaller units (rectangles) as unequal:

Note the heterophonic independence of the flute and zither parts.

Ex.3 (source: Widdess, 1989)

Early Indian *rāga* melody of *ālāpa* type from a treatise by Yāṣṭika, preserved in the *Bṛhaddeśī* of Mataṅga (late first millennium AD) (Trivandrum Sanskrit Series 94, p.121). (1) Original syllable notation in transliteration; (2) transcription; (3) synoptic display showing division of the melody into three sections, and their relationships; (4) analysis showing material common to all three sections, and variants in parentheses; (5) analysis of melodic structure in terms of consonant relationships (beamed notes), modal function (◊ = Predominant (*aṃśa*)), emphasis (₀ = reiterated note), and prolongation (∪, ∩). Rhythmic values are regarded as imprecise: notes with tails (corresponding to an –ā or –ī in the notation syllable) are probably longer than those without. Note the gradual increase in range in the three sections, a feature reminiscent of modern *ālāp* performance.

Ex.4 (source: Markham, 1983, p.338)

Vocal parts for the Japanese court-song (*saibara*) 'Mushiroda' (1) as performed today, and (2) as reconstructed from 12th-century sources. Strokes on the clapper (*shakubyōshi*) are shown as X and x; other instrumental parts are omitted.

Ex. 1

Ex. 2

Ex. 3

1 pā dhā mā dha ni dhā pā pā pa dha ni dhā mā mā dhā ni sā sā sa ni dha ni sā sa ni dhā ni sā ni sā dhā sā dha ri mā mā dhā ni ni dhā pā pā pa ma ma dha ni sā sā sa ni sā sā sa ni ga ri ma
ma mā ga ri sa sa dha ni pā dhā mā sa ri mā dhā ri ma pā pā

Ābhīrī

Ex. 4

CHAPTER IX

Iconography

TILMAN SEEBASS

'Iconography' and 'iconology', like many other terms of Western scholarship, were compounded from Greek words. Originally applied to the study of emblems and ancient archaeological and numismatic evidence they have since acquired new meanings; musical iconography means the study of artworks with musical subject matter.

Musical iconography is concerned with pictures or more generally visual evidence, as used for research in music – apart from other sources such as recorded music, notated music, transcriptions, musical instruments and archival or literary evidence. In other words, musical iconography involves research in the pictorial documentation of music. No categorical difference is made of the media involved, from paintings to sculptures, photographs, or whatever. But as R. Hammerstein (1984), J. McKinnon (1982), T. Seebass (1987) and others have pointed out, there is a danger in this concept, because it might lead scholars to treat pictures the same as they treat other 'visibles', such as a melographic chart or a musical instrument, without taking into account that an artist has given an interpretation of a scene or activity. Scholars are required to analyse the pictures as products of artists in the visual medium, and to apply in their analysis and interpretation the methods developed by art historians. Musical iconography, then, should be considered as a discipline between two others, art history and musicology (including ethnomusicology). A student of it needs to be familiar with the methods of these two fields.

It is obvious that in trying to understand a picture like that on p.240 we will need to use all our knowledge of musical instruments and insight into performing practice in order to relate what is depicted to the actual music as it may have sounded at the time and place of performance. Yet, as long as we do not know what story the relief illustrates or the purpose for which it was created, we cannot connect the depiction to contemporary reality. To find answers to such questions we must turn to art historians. They look at pictures from a different perspective (best summarized by Panofsky, 1939). They first describe the formal elements of the picture and deal with the factual meaning of each element. In a second step they take into account the cultural convention that influenced the depiction of those elements, and they attempt to describe the origin of the elements in a story or scene, and to discuss the 'transnatural', allegorical or metaphorical meaning intended. This stage of descriptive analysis is called iconography.

A third level of understanding a picture is reached through iconology. Here the scholar tries to establish the intrinsic meaning of the picture when it is seen as a manifestation of an artist's personality, a patron's wish or a public's expectation. Iconology explains the picture as a symptom and representative of a given culture. The analogy of ethnography and ethnology (or of the less common pair organography and organology) is worth mentioning. The meaning of '-graphy' from the Greek 'graphein' ('to write', 'to describe') enforces the conclusion that the field mentioned in the first part of the compound will be explored by a descriptive form of research. Such activity assumes of course knowledge of comparative material, that is informed description with qualitative weighting. The meaning of '-logy' on the other hand, from the Greek 'logos' ('word', 'thought'), suggests intellectual penetration on an interpretative, hermeneutical level. Most musicological or ethnomusicological research in the visual arts happens on the pre-iconographical or iconographical level. The term musical iconology, favoured by E. Winternitz, invites expectations which are rarely met and is therefore avoided by most scholars. Thus 'musical iconography', a less presumptuous term, has become the most commonly accepted label for our field of study.

Sources

In principle, any document that visualizes music either concretely or abstractly is an artist's reflection on music, hence an object for iconographers. The pictorial material may range from photographs to abstract and figurative art. These sources include depictions of music-making, dance and musical instruments as well as portraits of musicians and music patrons, and also representations of musical ideas – where music-making might not be depicted at all. Examples of the last are the transformation of a mandala into a musical form (Ellingson, 1979), laws of decoration that seem to be equally valid for music structures (as advocated by al Faruqi, 1985), a *rāgamālā* miniature that represents a musical concept (see Gangoly, 1935; Powers, 1980), or the drawing of a 'flying dragon clasping the clouds' which shows a specific fingering on the Chinese *qin* (reproduced in van Gulik, 1940, fig.10). We must include also the figurative or non-figurative decoration on musical instruments and the musical instrument as an image, the stage decoration for music drama and the design of places and buildings in which music is performed. A special case are pictures that inspire musicians to new forms of music-making (as analysed by Staiti, 1988, in the instance of 18th-century Sicily).

Every culture provides us with various types of sources, but not each type to the same degree. Their differences depend on the character of the culture, literate, semi-literate or non-literate. Certain types of sources are typical only for a particular social or cultural stratum: book and manuscript illustrations belong to the realm of a court and the class of the *literati* (see Vickers, 1985); figurative reliefs are found on the walls of temples in which people from various classes (but sharing the same religious beliefs) gather for worship, or they are part of the decoration of rooms inside palaces where a few people are lavishly entertained; illustrated single sheets of

Relief from Borobudur, central Java, first half of the 9th century

music or illustrated covers of record jackets appeal to the taste of specific consumer groups (see Slobin, 1988).

Other pictures are created for an individual only, such as the carved horse's head on the pegbox of a fiddle which is an icon of the spirit of the instrument, awakened or conjured down into the instrument by the player (Tsuge, 1976). Another is the painted surface of the Siberian Shaman drum, on which the Shaman has depicted the cosmos through which he travels in search of the spirits while playing the drum (Emsheimer, 1988). Other instances of 'user-related' art are the decorations burnt into the African *mbira* or the carvings on a New Guinean slit-drum (Penney, 1980). Although in most of these examples the image is a product by and for an individual, it is at the same time a symbol typical of its culture as a whole and can be described in comparative stylistic and thematic terms.

Problems of qualification and evaluation

An important goal in iconography is the analysis of the music depicted in relation to actual musical performance. The priorities of artists differ from those of musicians or ethnomusicologists. Aesthetic considerations, pictorial models and artistic traditions may be more important to them than accuracy in depicting an object or situation. A patron with mundane motivation might impose non-musical conditions on the design. The artistic medium may limit the amount of detail or forbid a complete rendering of a scene: concessions will have to be made when sculpting a harp player in clay or fitting a 'complete' and 'accurate' picture of the battle music of a royal army in the margin of a manuscript.

In order to understand a music picture it is crucial first to establish its relation to the story or myth which led to its making, and then to gauge more precisely how it was understood by the original viewers. The task is comparatively easy when dealing with illustrations for a text as in manuscript illumination. Here we can directly compare what is said in the text with what is depicted, and occasionally also with what is written into the picture or supplied as a caption. This provides a basis for deciding whether the illustrator followed the text or a pictorial model or both combined, and how far he used his own knowledge of the music of his time.

A series of wall paintings or reliefs is one step more difficult to decipher than textual illustrations, but often can be identified. In most other instances it is far more difficult to establish the proper context. To find answers to these questions one usually needs the collaboration of colleagues in literature, religion and ethnology. Interviews with artists, priests, patrons and viewers are a rewarding aspect of iconographic analysis for ethnomusicologists in the field; through them we can usually learn more about musical concepts than by directly asking musicians to explain their art.

Even if artists are keen observers and genuinely interested in music, different cultural and social roots can prevent them from depicting things 'correctly'. For instance, in a 17th-century painting of Italian folk musicians by a Dutch artist in Italy, Febo Guizzi discovered that the meticulously depicted bagpipe did not match any type known in Italy at that time or later, but was rather a precise representation of a type then used in the Low

Countries (Guizzi, 1983). An example of social trends influencing art appears in the canvases of a Franco-Swiss artist from the early 19th century. He depicts Italian folk musicians as innocent heroes and by such means satisfies the Romantic interests of his noble clients (Seebass, 1988).

Often the problem is not a contrast between everyday life and the art of a literate society; sometimes the contradictions and inconsistencies are farther reaching. The relief in fig.1 appears on the lower frieze of the main wall of the Borobudur, an immense Buddhistic temple, built in the first half of the 9th century in central Java. The picture is carefully spaced out; symmetries and pairing can be found throughout. In the centre, a Bodhisattva sits with his consort on a canopy, to the right there are priests, trees, horses and elephants, to the left we see a dancer, slightly oversized, and next to her two rows of musicians, the upper row females with cymbals, the lower males with various instruments. Contrasting with the reliefs on the base of the temple, which show scenes from indigenous Java, this relief (as all the others on the upper terraces of the temple) takes us into the realm of Indian culture. It illustrates a story from the '*Gandavynha*' (see N. J. Krom and T. van Erp, 1920–31). In most instances we cannot connect the scenes from the upper terraces of the temple to anthropological evidence from Indonesia. The music shown here is perhaps the only music that existed at Indianized courts. This hypothesis has some credence, because on Bali, an island where the Indianized culture was never challenged by Islam, a distant relative, gamelan *Gambuh*, has survived. Be this as it may, the relief proves that this music existed in Java, if not as a reality at least as a vision entertained by the literate class who designed the monument.

The dichotomy between the cultural background of artists and the musicians they depict reached an extreme in the illustrated travel books of Western colonizers – an invaluable source for the ethnohistory of music, as Frank Harrison was the first to emphasize – and in the sketches and photographs of the ethnologists and ethnomusicologists who followed them a few hundred years later. Iconographic questions merge with questions of ethnomusicological subjectivity and objectivity. The task of artists assessing, sketching, photographing – visualizing – a music which is not theirs, is conceptually not far from the tasks of ethnomusicologists who are trying to describe and understand other musical cultures.

State of scholarship

Aside from archaeological studies on ancient cultures in the Near East and Middle East and publications on the iconography of South Asian sources, research is sparse. A few book-size studies, beginning with Kunst and Goris (1927) and Marcel-Dubois (1941), restrict themselves to a descriptive, organological analysis of pictorial material. Other authors, compiling music histories of a particular music culture, such as the Chinese or Japanese, have used pictorial evidence for historical documentation of instruments and performance practice (*see* 'Historical Ethnomusicology'). The serial publication *Die Musikgeschichte in Bildern*, founded by Heinrich Besseler and Max Schneider in 1961, now edited by Werner Bachmann, has helped significantly to make scholars aware of how useful iconography can be and how untapped

242

the riches of pictorial source material are. If the main scope of this serial was to stimulate iconography as an ancillary discipline, what is now called for is an interpretation of the pictures as images in their own right. In this respect ethnomusicology still lags behind. If scholars insist on a proper conceptual framework for their fieldwork and correct methods for interviewing and evaluating the social, religious and aesthetic context of music, the same standards are needed for analysis of pictures – no matter whether these sources are the product of an 18th-century Japanese woodcutter or a photo taken by Frances Densmore.

Except for Guizzi's essay (1983) methodological studies specifically in ethnomusicological iconography are yet to come. There are some publications in which methods are discussed on the basis of material from Western art. But during the 1980s a number of ethnomusicological articles appeared that demonstrate possibilities in method. For the future it seems preferable not to insist on a universal method for iconography. Some recent studies are convincing and innovative because the authors, while keeping to Panofsky's principles of research in pictures, tailored their methods to the nature of their sources and to the aesthetic tenets of the cultures in which picture and depicted music originated (Gramit, 1985; Emsheimer, 1988; Staiti, 1988; Seebass, 1988).

Bibliography

BIBLIOGRAPHIES AND PERIODICALS

F. Crane: *Bibliography of the Iconography of Music* (New York, 1972)
Imago Musicae: International Yearbook of Musical Iconography, ed. T. Seebass (Kassel, and Durham, NC, 1984–88; Lucca, 1989–) [with annual bibliography]

METHODOLOGY

E. Panofsky: 'Iconography and Iconology: an Introduction to the Study of Renaissance Art', *Studies in Iconology* (New York, 1939), 3; repr. in Panofsky, *Meaning in the Visual Arts* (Woodstock, NY, 1974), 26
E. Winternitz: 'The Visual Arts as a Source for the Historian of Music', *International Musicological Society, Report of the 8th Congress, New York, 1961*, ed. J. LaRue (Kassel, 1961), 109
J. Białostocki: 'Iconography and Iconology', *Encyclopedia of World Art* (New York, 1963), 769
I. Mačak: 'Zur Verifikation ikonographischer Informationen über Musikinstrumente', *Studia Instrumentorum Musicae Popularis*, iv (Stockholm, 1976), 49
H. M. Brown: 'Iconography of Music', *Grove 6*
J. McKinnon: 'Iconography', *Musicology in the 1980s: Methods, Goals, Opportunities*, ed. D. K. Holoman and C. Palisca (New York, 1982), 79
F. Guizzi: 'Considerazioni preliminari sull'iconografia come fonte ausiliaria nella ricerca etnomusicologica', *RIM*, xviii (1983), 87
T. Seebass: 'Prospettive dell'iconografia musicale: considerazioni di un medievalista', *RIM*, xviii (1983), 67
R. Hammerstein: 'Musik und bildende Kunst: Zur Theorie und Geschichte ihrer Beziehungen', *Imago Musicae*, i (1984), 1
T. Seebass: 'Introduzione all'iconographia musicale', *Iconografia Musicale in Umbria nel XV Secolo* (Assisi, 1987), 9

MUSICAL ICONOGRAPHY

N. J. Krom and T. van Erp: *Beschrjiving van Barabudur* (The Hague, 1920–31)
O. C. Gangoly: *Rāgas and Rāgiṇīs* (Bombay, 1935)
R. van Gulik: *The Lore of the Chinese Lute: an Essay in the Ideology of the Ch'in* (Tokyo, 1940, 2/1969)

K. Kos: 'St Kummernis and Her Fiddler: an Approach to Iconology of Pictorial Folk Art', *SM*, xix (1977), 251

T. J. Ellingson: *The Mandala of Sound: Concepts and Sound Structures in Tibetan Ritual Music* (diss., U. of Wisconsin, 1979)

H. S. Powers: 'Illustrated Inventories of Indian Rāgamālā Painting', *Journal of the American Oriental Society*, x (1980), 473

L. I. al Faruqi: 'Structural Segments in the Islamic Arts: the Musical "Translation" of a Characteristic of the Literary and Visual Arts', *Asian Music*, xvi/1 (1985), 59

D. Gramit: 'The Music Paintings of the Capella Palatina in Palermo', *Imago Musicae*, ii (1985), 9–49

E. Emsheimer: 'On the Ergology and Symbolism of a Shaman Drum of the Khakass', *Imago Musicae*, v (1988), 145

M. Slobin: 'Icons of Ethnicity: Pictorial Themes in Commercial Euro-American Music', *Imago Musicae*, v (1988), 129

N. Staiti: 'Identificazione degli strumenti musicali e natura simbolica delle figure nelle "Adorazioni dei pastori" siciliane', *Imago Musicae*, v (1988), 75–108

T. Seebass: 'Léopold Robert and Italian Folk Music', *The World of Music*, xxx/3 (Berlin, 1988), 59

MUSICAL INSTRUMENTS AS IMAGES

C. Sachs: *Geist und Werden der Musikinstrumente* (Berlin, 1929/*R*1975)

G. Tsuge: 'Musical Idols: Beasts in the Form of Instruments', *Festschrift for Dr Chang Sa-hun: Articles on Asian Music* (Seoul, 1976), 407

D. Penney: 'Northern New Guinea Slit-Gong Sculpture', *Baessler Archiv*, xxviii (1980), 347

D. A. Olsen: 'The Flutes of El Dorado: Musical Effigy Figurines of the Tairona', *Imago Musicae*, iii (1986), 79

MUSICAL ICONOGRAPHY FOR THE DOCUMENTATION OF MUSIC

J. Kunst and R. Goris: *Hindoe-Javaansch Muziek-Instrumenten* (Weltevreden, 1927); Eng. trans. as *Hindu-Javanese Musical Instruments* (The Hague, 1968)

C. Marcel-Dubois: *Les Instruments de Musique de l'Inde Ancienne* (Paris, 1941)

F. Hoerburger: 'Das Bilddokument und die Tanzfolklore', *Deutsches Jahrbuch für Volkskunde (Festschrift Wilhelm Fraenger)*, vi (1960), 127

Die Musikgeschichte in Bildern, ed. W. Bachmann (Leipzig, 1961--) [Serial begun by H. Besseler and M. F. Schneider in 1961; 24 volumes written by various authors have appeared so far, half dealing with ethnomusicological subjects]

G. H. Tarlekar and Nalini: *Musical Instruments in Indian Sculpture* (Poona, India, 1972)

F. Ll. Harrison: *Time, Place and Music: an Anthology of Ethnomusicological Observation c.1550 to c.1800* (Amsterdam, 1973)

E. Stockmann and E. Emsheimer, eds.: *Studia Instrumentorum Musicae Popularis*, iv (Stockholm, 1976) [11 short articles devoted to iconography of musical instruments]

F. Willet: 'A Contribution to the History of Musical Instruments Among the Yoruba', *Essays for a Humanist: an Offering to Klaus Wachsmann* (New York, 1977), 350–386

Kunitachi College of Music, Research Institute, Study Group of the Iconography of Music: *Musical Scenes in Japanese Art: a Catalogue of Musical Instruments in Pictures from the Heian Period to the Edo Period* (Tokyo, 1984) [in Japanese]

W. Denny: 'Music and Musicians in Islamic Art', *Asian Music*, xvii/1 (1985), 37–68

R. L. Hardgrave Jr and S. M. Slawek: 'Instruments and Music Culture in Eighteenth-Century India: the Solvyn Portraits', *Asian Music*, xx/1 (1988–9), 1–92

R. Pejovič: 'Folk Musical Instruments in Mediaeval and Renaissance Art of South Slav Peoples', *Studia Instrumentorum Musicae Popularis*, viii (Stockholm, 1985), 126

A. Philipzuk: *Elfenbeinhörner im sakralen Königtum Schwarzafrikas* (Bonn, 1985)

A. Vickers: 'The Realm of Senses: Images of the Court Music of Pre-Colonial Bali', *Imago Musicae*, ii (1985), 143–177

D. Waterhouse: 'Korean Music, Trick Horsemanship and Elephants in Tokugawa Japan', *The Oral and the Literate in Music*, ed. Y. Tokumaru and O. Yamaguti (Tokyo, 1986), 353

J. Bor: *The Voice of the Sarangi: an Illustrated History of Bowing in India* (Bombay, 1987) [as xv/3/4 and xvi/1 of the *Quarterly Journal of the National Centre for Performing Arts*]

H. D. Bodman: *Chinese Musical Iconography: a History of Musical Instruments Depicted in Chinese Art* (Taipei, 1987)

244

CHAPTER X

Organology

GENEVIÈVE DOURNON

The diversity of instruments is born of the actual union of music with life. It seems that this material condition widens our musical sense. Too limited from the viewpoint of its works alone, music gains from being seen in the naturalism of these instruments as well. (André Schaeffner, 1936)

What is organology?

HISTORICAL SURVEY   When Praetorius gave the title *De organographia* to the second volume of his treatise *Syntagma musicum* (1618), he was the first to name the discipline that would become the science of musical instruments – organology.

The term comes from the Greek *organon*, meaning a tool or instrument used in some activity or trade (even an organ of the body). It was used for musical instruments as well as for the organs governing the human voice. When the Latin term *organum* (*organa*) is used to describe certain aspects of instrumental music, it is by analogy with vocal polyphony. A more precise application to instruments, the organ in particular, is found in St Augustine quoted by P. Williams (1984, p.838) in the commentary to Psalm cl. In classical antiquity the musical instrument was denoted by the Latin term *instrumentum*, and in the Middle Ages by the expression *instrumentum organicum*.

The description of medieval instruments is imprecise in the West, perhaps, as André Schaeffner points out (1946, p.16), because of the long pre-eminence of liturgical chant over instrumental music. Only from the 16th and 17th centuries onwards did major Western works on musical instruments appear, including the treatise by Praetorius mentioned above, *Musica getutscht und ausgezogen* by Sebastien Virdung (1511), *Musica instrumentalis deudsch* by Martin Agricola (1529), *Harmonie universelle* by Father Marin Mersenne (1636–7), and Pierre Trichet's *Traité des instruments de musique* (1640). Centuries earlier, however, ancient civilizations had approached the subject of musical instruments methodically. We know about the Oriental instrumentarium from rich and extensive documentation in the chronicles and in the ancient treatises of Chinese, Arab and Indian theoreticians. These works give the names and classifications of instruments, indications of the way in which they were played and their part in rites and ceremonies, and details concerning musicians and their training.

From the 16th century onwards the great discoveries, explorations and the colonial conquests brought objects, specimens and musical instruments of other civilizations – Arab, Chinese, Indian, Native American and African – back to Europe. As early as 1620, Praetorius published plates in the *Theatrum instrumentorum* showing African instruments, including perfectly recognizable depictions of horn, bell, drum, harp and pluriarc; the *Gabinetto armonico*, an organological work by Father Filippo Bonanni (1722), has some remarkable illustrations of African musicians.

The opening of the Western mind to the customs and arts of other civilizations owes much to the observations of travellers, navigators and missionaries, and to the works of those scientists who travelled the world after the 16th century. Such works included *Mémoire sur la musique des Chinois tant anciens que modernes* by Jean-Joseph-Marie Amiot (1779), and the *Description historique, technique et littéraire des instruments de musique des Orientaux* by Guillaume-André Villoteau (1813). Foreign music, musicians and instruments aroused the curiosity of the great travellers. Accounts of African music span the centuries from the *Journal of the Voyage of Vasco da Gama* (1497–8) and O. Dapper's *Description de l'Afrique* (1674), to the works of W. Burchell (1822–4), G. Schweinfurth (1873) and many others, up to André Gide in our own period describing the fanfares blown on great wooden trumpets in his *Voyage au Congo* (1927) (see bibliography of Schaeffner, 1936, and Arom, 1985). Other sources are the observations of the Chevalier Chardin in Persia (1711), the accounts of Captain Cook's voyages in the Pacific (1785), the Abbé J. A. Dubois's work on the customs and ceremonies of India (1825) and the monumental *History of Java* (1817) by Sir Philip Raffles, the first to bring a Javanese gamelan to Europe. All these preceded the first works by anthropologists.

Valuable musical instruments from distant lands found their way into the 'cabinets of curiosities', the pride of princely courts since the Renaissance (such as Louis XIII's 'Cabinet du Roy'), into royal libraries, and into the collections of powerful religious orders and enlightened amateurs.

Subsequently, they became the initial stock of collections in museums of art and ethnography, in conservatories of music and in universities. The late 19th century saw the first publication of methodical catalogues, notably by C. Engel (1869), G. Chouquet (1875) and Victor-Charles Mahillon (1880–1922). The systems of classification then worked out provided organology with its scientific basis, making an important contribution to the development of the new discipline of ethnomusicology.

Organology (Ger.: *Instrumentenkunde*) covers the field of musical instruments in general, from every musical tradition – 'classical' or 'art' music, 'folk' or 'ethnic' music, 'Western' and 'non-Western' music (the terminology in present use). It is hardly surprising that its boundaries are not precise, and that perspectives differ between historical musicology and ethnomusicology. Nevertheless the contribution of ethnomusicology (organology included) has been very important for the study of music.

Some ethnomusicologists, like Mantle Hood, try to distinguish between organography and organology, intending to separate simple description from the information that bears on problems of taxonomy (1971). In 1941 Nicholas Bessaraboff used the term 'organology' in a narrower sense, to distinguish 'the scientific and engineering aspects' of musical instruments from the wider study of music. To André Schaeffner (1946, p.13), the essential subject of organology is 'the enumeration, description, localization and history of even the least of the instruments used in all human civilizations and periods to produce tones or sounds either for purely aesthetic ends or solely for some religious, magical or practical purpose'. Organology should be primarily the study of actual musical instruments (inventory, terminology, classification, description of construction, shapes and technique of playing) but the study cannot disregard musical production (the analysis of acoustic phenomena and musical scales) or data on the use of the instrument, socio-cultural factors and beliefs which determine that use, or the status and training of the players. Even study of the symbolism and aesthetics of the instrument, both as an artistic object and a musical 'tool', are relevant to organology.

The history, origin and relationship of existing and obsolete instruments are also legitimate parts of the discipline. Knowledge of this kind may be acquired from the iconographic sources provided by Sumerian, Hittite, Assyrian, Egyptian, Greek and Roman, Celtic and Etruscan sculptures, vase ornamentation, paintings and carvings. Other evidence is provided by the New World codices and the rare depictions carved in the rocks of prehistoric cave dwellings. Archaeological excavations regularly dig up instruments made of material that has resisted the passage of time. Most of them are related to instruments still played today, in different places but in an almost unchanged form: they include lyres and harps from Ur, Chinese lutes from the treasure of Shosoin of the 8th century AD, bronze bells of the 1st millennium BC, brass horns from Scandinavia, and the reed or clay pipes used as wind instruments by the ancient Egyptians and the Amerindians. Many even older finds have been made in Europe, including a Magdalenian bull-roarer of reindeer horn (discovered in southwest France) and fragments of prehistoric bone aerophones some 15,000 years old, already showing the little 'slot' typical of air duct flutes. The number and variety, as well as the great age of surviving depictions of instruments and players, bear witness to the importance of music in almost all civilizations of the world.

Like a kaleidoscope, organology presents many facets. Two fundamental aspects of the study of musical instruments are dealt with here: the theoretical and the practical playing, and musical context of the instrument.

Musical instruments: definition and classification

WHAT DO WE MEAN BY A MUSICAL INSTRUMENT? Organology considers any apparatus or device made by man in order to produce a sound or sounds as a musical instrument. The definition given by Alexander Büchner (1980, p.14) is both more elaborate and narrower: 'A musical instrument is a source of intentionally produced sound, constructed and employed for musical production, objectively capable, by virtue of its acoustic properties, of participating in a musically artistic effect, since its acoustic properties correspond to the cultural standards of a given people at a specific historical period.' Erich M. von Hornbostel's view (1933, p.129) was that 'for purposes of research everything must count as a musical instrument with which sound can be produced intentionally'. However, he distinguished between musical instruments in the conventional sense and sound-producing instruments. It fell to Schaeffner (1936, p.9) to formulate the question properly: 'If an object can produce a sound, how do we recognize that it is musical? What qualities, of what kind, cause it to be ranged with other musical instruments?' He provided the reply himself in a later work (1946, p.13), in stating that all musical instruments share 'a characteristic timbre, either for producing a sound or sounds of a definite pitch, or at least for providing material for noises produced successively in a time sequence, which may be described as musical rhythm'. This definition, which sets out the parameters of timbre, pitch and rhythm, opens up the organologist's field of investigation to all the 'usual tools of music' – from the tapping of a bamboo to the harpsichord – independently of their construction, however rudimentary or sophisticated it may be, of the way in which they are used, of their geo-cultural origin and their history. The concept of an instrument, like the concept of music itself (when such a notion exists), differs from one culture or period to another depending on the function it is seen to fulfil. Tools, weapons, vessels and other utensils may be used as rhythmical instruments during a festival or a ritual and are then returned to their ordinary use.

Empiricism is the rule in instrument-making, the aim of which is usually to increase sound resources. The aesthetics of every culture appear in the choice or combination of the means employed: the multiplication of sounds by augmenting the size or number of components (as in panpipes) or the improvement of the component (finger-holes), the addition of resonators (xylophones, chordophones), the combination of timbres (small pellet bells on the bows of fiddles in India), and other jingling devices added to some chordophones and membranophones in Africa. The result is an extraordinary quantity of more or less affiliated instrumental types showing the imaginative diversity of which the human mind is capable in the structure of its musical instruments. Only acoustic instruments will be dealt with here. For mechanical (automatophonic) and electrical (electro-acoustic and electronic) instruments, the reader may consult the works of Alexander Büchner (1956, 1980) and the authors he mentions in his bibliography, as well as the relevant articles in *The New Grove Dictionary of Musical Instruments* (also see Reference Aid 3).

Systematics

Classification is preliminary to all studies of general organology or of organology applied to the musical instruments of a region, culture, religion or specific socio-cultural group (ethnic, social, caste etc). To understand and select the most useful of the various systems devised in the West since the end of the 19th century, we must look at their theoretical bases and practical application.

Classification is essential for keepers of collections, organologists, musicologists, ethnomusicologists and anthropologists, who emend or even devise new systems themselves. It is not surprising that classifications tend to arise from the researches of curators of instrumental collections, particularly collections consisting entirely or partially of instruments relevant to ethnomusicology. Johannes de Muris' (14th century) conventional tripartite division into strings (*tensibilia*), wind (*inflatibilia*) and percussion instruments (*percussibilia*) has proved notoriously inadequate in this area. Such curators include V. C. Mahillon (Musée Instrumental du Conservatoire Royal de Musique, Brussels), Curt Sachs (Instrumental Museum of Berlin), G. Montandon (Musée d'Ethnographie, Geneva), A. Schaeffner (Musée de l'Homme, Paris), and N. Bessaraboff (Museum of Fine Arts, Boston).

The objectives of classification and the methods of practitioners differ from those of theoreticians. Practitioners base their theory on the analysis of collections of musical instruments, in order to determine a common concept, so that the whole range of ancient and modern, European and extra-European instruments may be placed in large categories. Once broad categories have been defined, subdivisions and hierarchy must be worked out, so that the multiplicity of specimens may be logically arranged and types and sub-types defined. One of the difficulties, as Hornbostel and Sachs pointed out, is that 'the objects to be classified are alive and dynamic, indifferent to sharp demarcation and set form, while systems are static and depend upon sharply drawn demarcations and categories' (Hornbostel and Sachs, 1914; Eng. trans., 1961, p.4; hereafter all references to this article refer to the English translation. See Reference Aid 3). The classificatory process is a difficult exercise which must compromise between principles and reality; consequently, though some systems are more satisfactory than others, none is perfect.

Theoreticians try to look beyond the material structure of the instrument and take account of acoustics, scales, the musician, performance practice, and to integrate historical and genetic data as well as socio-cultural factors and beliefs which determine the function of the instrument. These two approaches, the first organological, the second holistic, have produced works that are two complementary stages in the study of instruments.

The aim of the first approach is to provide a conceptual tool with a view to practical application. The second aims for an 'ideal organology', developing a body of linked data to produce a schematic model of analysis which requires the assistance of the computer. H. Heyde (1975), O. Elschek and E. Stockmann, (1969, pp.11–41) and W. P. Malm with his 'Musinst' project (1974) represent the second approach; their differences are well summed up by Klaus Wachsmann (1984) in the article 'Classification', in *The New Grove Dictionary of Musical Instruments*, in which he sets out his own principles for 'the study of instruments as objects and as aspects of biological and social musical activity . . .'. Thinking along similar lines Mantle Hood (1971) aims to go 'beyond the usual requirements of a descriptive taxonomy' and establishes a 'symbolic taxonomy' taking into account a complex ensemble of considerations to be codified as 'organograms'.

Heyde (1975) distinguishes between 'natural' and 'artificial' approaches to classification, and suggests that we should 'take into account the historical genesis and development of the instruments; the latter are based on any arbitrary viewpoint that disregards "genetic" factors'. According to him, the Hornbostel and Sachs system belongs to the 'artificial' category. Heyde's 'natural' system uses 11 constituents to establish the analytical profile of an instrument. As Wachsmann remarks, 'The desire, evident in Heyde's book, to place musical instruments in some kind of evolutionary sequence had already found strong expression in Sachs's *Geist und Werden der Musikinstrumente* (1929)' (1984, p.410).

Hans-Heinz Dräger's important study, *Prinzip einer Systematik der Musik-instrumente* (1946) stands by the principles of his masters Hornbostel and Sachs, and extends them into more fields, thus extending the limits of classification towards a global approach to musical instruments.

Although scientifically attractive, the 'global' approach which aims to generate an 'ideal organology . . . would require for its applications a wealth of data . . . not available on a worldwide scale', and the application of such systems to everyday organological analysis is not easy in practice. This kind of analysis involves a more exhaustive and analytical study of instruments than the necessarily reductive process of classification.

Supporters of the organological approach set about satisfying two imperatives: 'a system of classification has theoretical advantages as well as practical use . . . the first requirement of a classificatory system is surely that the principle of demarcation remains the same throughout for the main categories . . . Herein will always be found the leading test of the validity of the criteria upon which the system is based' (Hornbostel and Sachs, 1961, pp.5–6).

Since we are dealing with sound-producing tools, the fundamental principle of classification must be related to the vibrating material itself. This basic concept was developed not in the West but in other civilizations, with or without a written language.

THE CHINESE SYSTEM   The science of musical sounds and notes dates from ancient China. The classification of instruments integrated was the Chinese concept of the world, including cosmic forces and elements. In about the 8th century BC, Chinese theory classed musical instruments into eight groups corresponding to the eight winds and defined by the material destined either to produce the sound (the silk of strings, the skin of drums, the metal of bells, the wood of scrapers and clappers, the stone of lithophones) or to contain the vibrating air (the bamboo of tubular flutes, the clay of globular flutes, the gourd for the air chamber of the mouth organ). This division into eight classes, conceived for a precise instrumentarium (i.e. a finite number of instrumental types), could not be adopted on a universal scale, unlike the Indian system.

THE INDIAN SYSTEM   The ancient Indian classification of musical instruments into four classes is presented in one of the many technical treatises of Sanskrit literature, the *Bhāratiya-nātya-shāstra*, or 'teaching of dramatic art', attributed to Bhārata. This encyclopaedic work, dated around the beginning of our era, deals with the theatre and its associated arts, particularly poetry and music. Musical instruments, *vādhya*, are divided into four classes, determined by the nature of the vibrating component: *tāta* (from *tan*, to stretch) *vādhya* corresponding to strings; *avanaḍha* (attached or covered) *vādhya* to drums covered with a skin; *sushira* (hollow or pierced) *vādhya* for pipes into which the player blows; and *ghana vādhya* (from *han*, to strike a solid material, particularly metal), forming a distinct category. Western organologists undoubtedly drew inspiration from the quadripartite Indian system.

ETHNIC SYSTEMS (BASSARI AND 'ARE'ARE) The Bassari system (Senegal) was drawn to Western attention by two French ethnologists, Marie-Thérèse de Lestrange and Monique Gessain (Paris, 1976, pp.92–4). Bassari class their musical instruments into four groups, depending on the way they produce sounds: 'horned' instruments (flutes, clarinets, trumpets), including what are usually called wind instruments; 'rung' instruments (rattles, bells etc), including instruments that are shaken; 'beaten' instruments, including percussion like the xylophone and drums as well as such chordophones as the zither and harp; and 'cut' instruments including the fiddle (to-and-fro movement of the bow rubbing the strings) and the scraper (the stick rubbing on the indented body).

Hugo Zemp's study (1978) tells us that the 'Are'are of the Solomon Islands distinguish different types of 'bamboo music' and classify their instruments as 'struck bamboos' and 'blown bamboos', each group subdividing according to whether the playing is individual or collective. These two examples suggest that other cultures with an oral tradition may have implicit or explicit classificatory systems or 'folk classifications' based on quite different concepts which have yet to be elucidated (see van Thiel, 1969).

THE MAHILLON AND HORNBOSTEL–SACHS SYSTEMS At the end of the 19th century Victor-Charles Mahillon, Curator of the Musée Instrumental of the Conservatoire Royal de Musique in Brussels, developed his *Catalogue analytique et descriptif du Musée Instrumental*, an 'attempt at methodical classification of all instruments, ancient and modern, based on the different nature of the bodies employed as sources of sound'. Based on the classification devised ten years earlier by his director, F. G. Gevaert, dividing instruments into four classes – string instruments, wind instruments, membrane instruments, and auto-phones – Mahillon adopted a subdivision into branches and sections on the Linnaean model. His work gave organological definitions to the large categories, in particular the new class of autophones 'made of solid bodies, elastic enough in themselves to maintain the vibratory movement set up by one of the three following modes of agitation: percussion, plucking or friction'.

The concept of 'the physical characteristics of sound production as the most important principle of division' was taken up again by Hornbostel and Sachs in 1914, in their 'Systematik der Musikinstrumente' (translated into English by A. Baines and K. P. Wachsmann, 1961). The four categories are: chordophones, in which 'one or more strings are stretched between fixed points'; aerophones, in which 'the air itself is the vibrator in the primary sense'; membranophones, in which 'the sound is excited by tightly stretched membranes'; idiophones, in which the substance itself, 'owing to its solidity and elasticity, yields the sounds, without requiring stretched membranes or strings'. The principles, problems and weaknesses of the system are set out in an introduction which is of great interest to organologists.

By comparison with Mahillon's system, the two German theoreticians modified the principle and number of the subdivisions, determined 'only on those features which can be identified from the visible form of the instrument avoiding subjective preferences and leaving the instrument itself unmeddled with'. The ranking of data follows the Dewey decimal system.

The regrouping of idiophones (the term preferred to autophones) into a class distinct from membranophones (as in ancient Indian theory) splits up the heterogeneous section of 'percussion' instruments, including instruments of any material functioning by various modes of sound production.

One of the contributions made by 'ethno-organology' has been to render obsolete the conventional tripartite division into string, wind and percussion instruments. That classification is still current in the Western orchestra, although it is described by Hornbostel and Sachs as 'not only inadequate but also illogical'; Schaeffner, like most organologists, saw it as 'inapplicable to the exhaustive and scientific study of instruments'. For the complete text of the Hornbostel–Sachs classification, *see* Reference Aid 3.

The works of early organologists uncovered the amazing richness of many 'sounding objects' that are rattled, shaken, rubbed or struck, which often appear primitive but are living or extinct witnesses to the power of the human imagination in sound production; it also gave them a status as real musical instruments.

The Hornbostel–Sachs classification was widely adopted by organologists, musicologists, ethnomusicologists, ethnologists and keepers of collections, to whom it was particularly addressed. They followed the main principles, adding modifications or developments – as in the case of Dräger (1946) – in the light of their objectives or the type of collection concerned. Weaknesses, particularly the lack of consistent criteria for the subdivisions, are discussed by Jaap Kunst (1959, p.5).

The first to adopt and modify the system was G. Montandon (1919), whose catalogue of musical instruments in the Musée Ethnographique of Geneva remains faithful to its model apart from some judicious adjustments, particularly in the chordophone category. N. Bessaraboff (1941), drawing up the catalogue of a collection comprising many classical Western instruments, introduced as the first subdivision the notion of instruments 'controlled directly, by a keyboard, by automatic motion'. More recently the English scholars J. Montagu and J. Burton (1971, pp.49–70) proposed terminology making it possible to define musical instruments without the series of numbers involved in the decimal system. Tetuo Sakurai's *The Classification of Musical Instruments Reconsidered* (1981) questions the Hornbostel–Sachs categories; Sakurai suggests classification on three levels, leading to a division of instruments into 'seven main classes with sub-classes in each. The sub-classes are based on the number of the primary vibrators of each instrument'. This approach, claimed to be 'intermediate between scientific accuracy and practical utility', is not easy to apply.

During the last decade the Comité des Musées et Collections d'Instruments de Musique (CIMCIM) of the ICOM (International Committee of Museums) devised a classification for the use of museum curators and keepers of collections. The principles adhere to the principles of Hornbostel and Sachs, while integrating more subdivisions relating to the material and formal structure of the instrument, so that it is possible to deal more precisely, and conjointly, with instruments of the two kinds of collections known, for want of better terminology, as 'art' or 'historical' and 'folk' or 'ethnic' instruments. The results have been published in various numbers of the *CIMCIM Newsletter* (1983–4; 1985; 1987).

THE SCHAEFFNER SYSTEM   André Schaeffner did not entirely adhere to the system of the two German theoreticians (he published a French translation in 1935), although he freely expressed his esteem for and indebtedness to the work of Hornbostel and Sachs (whose presence, friendship and ideas he was able to appreciate during his years of exile in Paris) (1933–7). From 1930 onwards he worked on another classification, original in being bipartite. The principles of this classification are outlined in 'Projet d'une classification nouvelle des instruments de musique' (1931) and in 'D'une nouvelle classification méthodique des instruments de musique' (1932).

In his contribution to *La musique des origines à nos jours* (1946, p.18), Schaeffner points out that the first bipartite division of musical instruments was made by Arab theoreticians, quoting Al-Fārābī (*d* 950), according to whom 'the striking organ is either the human hand or the respiratory apparatus'. The interest of the Schaeffner system, which Wachsmann describes (1984, p.408) as 'logically perfect and coherent', is that it is based on a uniform principle: the nature and structure of the vibrating material. Schaeffner defines two principal categories: instruments with solid vibrating bodies (subdivided into those 'not susceptible of tension', those that are 'flexible' and those that are 'susceptible of tension') and instruments in which the air itself is the primary vibrator.

The subdivisions are based on 'factors of an immediately appreciable character' (1931, p.21): the material (wood, metal, stone etc), the form or structure of the sound-producing component (stick, lamella, plaque, tube, husk, block) in the case of those 'not susceptible of tension' and those that are 'susceptible of tension' (string, stalk, thong); the membranes are classed by the body of the instrument (vase, tube, frame) on which they are stretched. In the category of instruments with vibrating air, Schaeffner distinguishes those for which the vibrating air is not confined – or 'air-ambient' – as for example the bull-roarer, from wind instruments proper, which are subdivided into single pipe, pipe with natural reeds and reed pipe.

Schaeffner does not introduce the means of setting an instrument in vibration as a criterion of subdivision, but simply as a complementary indication for certain types (concussion sticks, struck boards, scraped bones, plucked lamella, skin set vibrating by direct or indirect percussion etc). He thus makes optional something that was a useful classificatory sub-criterion in Hornbostel–Sachs and Mahillon, at least in three of their four categories.

Schaeffner's has not been widely used, despite its undoubted interest, perhaps because the user must revise and complete the subdivisions himself. Moreover, Schaeffner's work on the origin of musical instruments, which is fundamental to ethnomusicology and organology and includes his classification, has never been translated from its original French into any other language (except a recent Italian version).

Attempt at synthesis

One can say, with Mantle Hood (1971, p.126), that 'tackling the problems of instrumental classification constitutes a worthy exercise for the critical faculties of searchers'. Over 20 years of practical experience, study of the collections of musical instruments in the Musée de l'Homme (some 8000 today), together with fieldwork, teaching and the training of young research-ers, and participation in collective works (including those of the CIMCIM, mentioned above) has led me to reconsider the compatible features of the various systems in order to devise the classification below for practical and didactic purposes. My sole aim is to provide the museum curator, the ethnomusicologist and the student with a guide making it possible to identify any (acoustic) instrument, whether in current use or obsolete. I have tried to clarify and arrange in ranking order the criteria differentiating instrumental types and sub-types; those criteria are based on direct observation of the data (structure, shape and material).

Like the Hornbostel–Sachs system (to which it is faithful in broad outline), this classification adopts the Dewey numerical system rather than a tree-like presentation. This 'open' system allows the development of certain headings and the integration of new data, necessary because 'with increasing knowledge especially of extra-European forms, new difficulties in the way of consistent classification will constantly arise' (Hornbostel and Sachs, p.8). Attempts to improve the system constitute a fascinating challenge.

What vibrates? How does it vibrate? These are the first questions to be asked in classifying any musical instrument. The data will concern the main vibrating material, the way in which it is set in vibration, and the structure of the instrument. These data constitute the organological definition of the instrument and should allow anyone to identify it.

Schaeffner's opposition between solids and air for the main vibrating material which produces the sound has the advantage of allowing a primary, unambiguous distinction, and lends itself to logical combination with the Hornbostel–Sachs quadripartite system. Those instruments for which the vibrating solid material (either rigid or flexible) is not stretchable come into the category of idiophones. When the vibrating material (membrane or string) is stretchable, instruments belong either to the category of membranophones or to that of chordophones. When air is the prime element set in vibration, we are dealing with aerophones.

The distinction of instruments within each of the categories thus defined is based on the relation between the ways in which they are set in vibration and the structure of the instrument.

Although the guiding principle must be scrupulously followed throughout, there are sometimes good reasons to invert the hierarchy of secondary data, in order to adapt them to the logic of the instrument itself and respond better to the purposes of classification: intelligibility and practical application. Like the German systematicians, 'we have purposely not divided the different main groups according to one uniform principle, but have let the principle of division be dictated by the nature of the group concerned, so that ranks of a given position within a group may not always correspond between one group and another' (Hornbostel and Sachs, p.9).

Thus the method of setting the instrument in vibration may not occur at the same level of subdivision in all four categories. Let us see how this combination of characteristics may operate in view of the logic peculiar to instruments belonging to the same category.

CHORDOPHONES   All chordophones consist of one or more strings stretched at

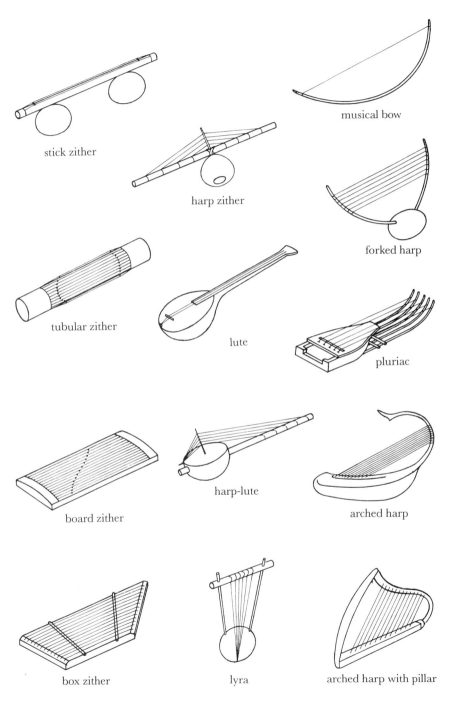

stick zither

musical bow

harp zither

forked harp

tubular zither

lute

pluriac

board zither

harp-lute

arched harp

box zither

lyra

arched harp with pillar

A. Schematic chordophone types

the two extremities on a supporting structure or sound body. A classification of chordophones according to the way they are set in vibration – by plucking, friction, striking, blowing – would have the disadvantage of dispersing instruments belonging to the same type (for instance, zithers) because in some the strings are plucked, in others struck or rubbed, or even agitated by the wind, and at the same time would group together instruments of different types (lute, lyre, harp, musical bow, zither etc) simply because their strings are plucked.

It is more useful to prefer an obvious structural characteristic of the instrument: the relationship between its construction and the disposition of the strings. The body structure of the instrument follows either a straight or a curved line, separating two organological groups: that of the zither and lute, the other of the musical bow, which gave rise to the pluriarc and the harp (fig.A). Another distinctive feature is the existence of a neck, a distinct component connected with the body of the instrument (the soundbox), and to which one end of the string is attached. The presence or absence of a neck will ensure a practical distinction between zithers and other string instruments. The strings of zithers (or at least of their vibrating portion) are arranged parallel to each other and to a soundbox the structure of which determines the sub-type (bar, stick, tube, raft, board, box). (The principle of the box zither is found combined with a mechanism in keyboard instruments such as the clavichord, spinet, harpsichord and piano.)

For instruments with a neck, the first distinction depends on whether it is attached directly to the body (lute, harp) or attached indirectly by the means of two arms (lyre). Another primary characteristic is the plane of the instrument: either the neck and the body are on the same plane (lute, harp-lute) or the neck (straight or arched) and the body, which are on two planes, form an angle, or a curve (harp). The plane of the strings – parallel or not parallel – in relation to the plane of the instrument has a direct effect on the method of playing. In the first case, the vibrating length of the string may be modified by pressing it down on a point on the neck (the fingerboard, with or without frets); in the second case, the strings are played open.

These structural data distinguish the principal types of chordophones, especially those whose construction integrates the characteristics of two different kinds, such as the harp-lute and harp-zither. The structure is that of the lute in the first case, and that of the stick or bar zither in the second, and in both cases there is a disposition of the strings (and thus a way of playing) similar to that of the harp, by means of a vertical bridge. Once the main types of chordophones have been thus defined, the way in which the strings are set in vibration (plucking, friction, striking, blowing) is given for each (in full, by a letter or by a symbol).

IDIOPHONES   If a care for consistency leads us to try applying structural data to the other three instrumental categories as the first level of subdivision, the idiophones will pose a problem of classification. If structure or shape were retained as the primary subdivision (as Schaeffner does retain it), we would find instruments with nothing in common in the same section: for instance, instruments made of slabs, plates and plaques would include clappers, along with xylophones, metallophones and lithophones, the distinction between

256

a) Stretched on soundbox, trunk or vessel (single or double head)

CYLINDRICAL

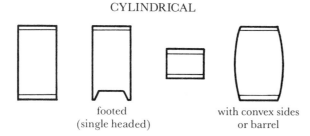

footed
(single headed)

with convex sides
or barrel

TRONCONICAL   DOUBLE TRONCONICAL

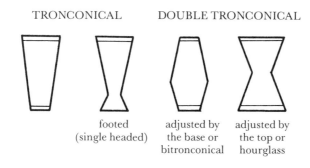

footed
(single headed)

adjusted by
the base or
bitronconical

adjusted by
the top or
hourglass

VESSEL (single head)

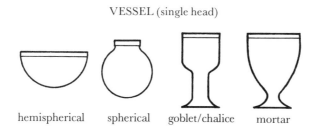

hemispherical   spherical   goblet/chalice   mortar

b) Stretched on frame (one or two membranes)

CIRCULAR   QUADRANGULAR   POLYGONAL

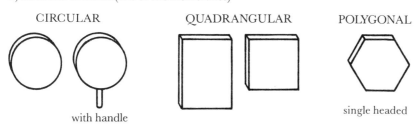

with handle

single headed

B. Some schematic shapes of skin drums

257

which must depend on a heading 'material'. By starting with the way the instrument is set in vibration (as in the Hornbostel–Sachs system), the parameter of structure/construction is used to better effect in imposing order on the extraordinary diversity of this instrumental category.

Idiophones, then, are subdivided into seven modes of playing: concussion, striking, stamping, shaking, scraping, friction and plucking. (This is preferable to the subdivisions of Hornbostel–Sachs, 'struck directly' or 'indirectly', that increases the number of digits in the coding.) However, some instruments require specific adjustments. (For instance, to avoid having different kinds of bells under different headings because of the way they are played, bells with a free or separated clapper and those with an attached clapper have been combined under the heading 'striking', although in the second case it is the action of shaking that causes the clapper to strike the inside of the bell.)

Other oppositions relating to structure (solid body, vessel-shaped or hollowed-out body; single or serial vibrating element), which if necessary will complement the shape and material of the vibrating component, may be useful in creating subdivisions. Thus, among gongs, we find two 'solid-bodied' types: made of a solid plaque (circular or triangular), and those with a raised rim like vessels. (The size of the rim may range from a few centimetres to a height equal to or greater than the diameter of the circular plate, as for example the 'bronze drum'.) For bossed groups, two kinds of data are important: the proportion of the depth of the body to diameter, or their setting: hung (the Javanese *gong agĕng*) or supported on a frame (the set of *pencon* of the *bonang*). Structural criteria alone are not enough to establish the difference between a struck 'vessel idiophone' of the 'bronze drum' type, and another of the bell type, without taking into account complementary data of a morphological and acoustic nature (the vibrations of the former are stronger near the vertex; the contrary is the case with the latter). Hence idiophones form this large and varied instrumental category, particularly resistant to systematic classification, and containing some of those 'calculated lacks' with which any classificatory system must come to terms.

MEMBRANOPHONES   There is little difficulty in identifying the skin drums which constitute the membranophone category. The vibrating material, stretched over an opening or two openings in the soundbox, may be set in vibration by percussion or friction. Indian instruments (the *gopīyantra* and *apang*) regarded by some authors (Hornbostel and Sachs, p.19, and Picken, 1981, p.29) as 'plucked drums' appear to be more at home among the chordophones, because the primary vibrating element is the string which induces resonance of the membrane covering one of the openings in the soundbox. Conversely, but according to the same principle, the small string or 'timbre' underlying the membrane on certain frame drums and vibrating at the same time as the membrane does not make those instruments chordophones.

Once that first distinction has been applied, the diversity of types and subtypes of skin drums is considerable. The organologist must look at the structural elements successively: the number of vibrating membranes (one or two) and the standard or 'schematic' shapes of the soundbox or frame (see fig.B). For a typology of drums, the material of which the body is made is critical (wood, bamboo, metal, earthenware), as is the way in which the membrane or membranes is or are attached: lacing, glueing, nailing, pegging, hooping, and various combinations.

AEROPHONES Aerophones are of two types according to the manner of inducing vibration. For the first (free aerophones or whirling aerophones) the vibrating air is not confined (e.g. with the bull-roarer a sharp-edged spatulate blade provokes an airstream vibration by a spinning motion); for the second type the air is enclosed within a tubular or a globular vessel; its vibration is provoked by action of breath or wind. The way the air is made to vibrate allows us to define the three main types of wind instruments: (i) for flutes, the flow of

(a) edge mouthhole

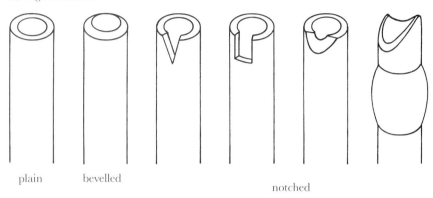

plain   bevelled

notched

(b) air-duct mouthhole

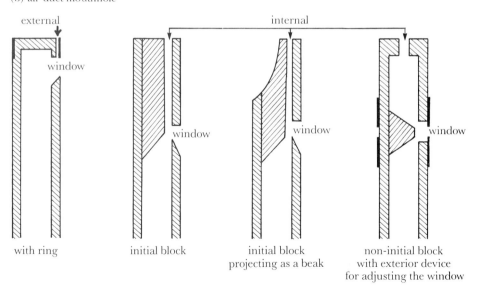

external   internal

window

window   window   window

with ring   initial block   initial block   non-initial block
                            projecting as a beak   with exterior device
                                                for adjusting the window

C. Endblown flutes

259

air is directed against an edge situated on the mouthhole or connected with it by means of an air duct (see fig.C); (ii) for reed instruments, the airstream is acting on a lamella, a free or a beating reed (single or double); and (iii) for horns and trumpets the airstream passes through the player's vibrating lips. The position of the mouthhole (end or side of the pipe) combined with the structure of functional devices (mouthpiece or reed) determine the ranking between sub-types.

Kazoos are half-way between two categories because the breath sets in vibration both the air contained in a pipe and the membrane over one end of it; they can be classified as either membranophones ('singing membrane' as defined by Hornbostel–Sachs) or better as aerophones, because the membrane does not yield a note of its own but modifies the speaking or singing.

Classification

To facilitate the comprehension and use of this classification, examples of the types and sub-types of instruments have been given, often illustrated by a photograph. Most have been chosen from *The New Grove Dictionary of Musical Instruments*, so that the reader can usefully find more information about ethnic origin, geographical origin, history and the use of an instrument by referring to the relevant entries.

1	**Idiophones** solid/non-stretchable material
11	CONCUSSION between 2 (or more) similar elements, independent or linked = clappers
111	solid body
111.1	concussion sticks/blocks: *claves* (Mexico); *tsuke* (Japan)
111.2	plaques (wood, bamboo, bone, ivory, metal, others)
111.21	2 components (wood): *cerek* (Malaysia); *tengere* (Bozo, Niger) (fig.1).
111.211	with jingles (metal discs or rings): *kartāl* (India); *sinh tiên* (Vietnam)
111.22	2 + 2 components: *kartāl* (Rajasthan)
111.23	3 to 6 elements: *p'ai-pan* (Taiwan); *pak* (Korea)
112	body hollow or partially hollow = 'vessel clappers'
112.1	castanets (wood, bone, ivory): *castañuelas* (Spain)
112.11	double: *qarqab* (Ngawua, Morocco)
112.2	spoons (wood or metal): *koutalia* (Greece)
112.3	cymbals (metal): *manjīrā* (India); *chāp* (Thailand)
112.31	crotales or 'finger cymbals'
112.32	on a fork: *zilli maşa* (Turkey)
112.4	spheres (husks or fruit which may or may not contain loose grains): *tekeya* (Gbaya, Central Africa)
112.5	plaques (metal) rolled into a banana-shape with slit: *kěmanak* (Java)
112.6	tubes = 'bamboo clappers'

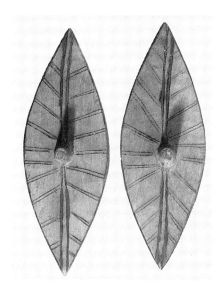

*1. Wooden clappers (*tengere*), Bozo, Niger*

12	STRIKING the vibrating component is struck by a beater (stick, hammer, other)
121	solid body in various forms (plaque, plate, disc, stem, board, stick, bar, beam etc) and made of various materials (stone, wood, gourd, bamboo, metal)
121.1	single component
121.11	stick, bar, beam or plaque (of wood, stone, metal): *amagala* (Uganda); *klepalo* (Yugoslavia); *kyè-zi* (Burma)
121.111	with resonator (also called 'one-key xylophone'): *kĕrtok kĕlapa* (Malaysia); *ilimba* (Zambia)
121.12	disc (metal) = flat gong: *ghanta* (Orissa) (fig.2*a*). (cf flat gong with raised rim with and without boss [122.51–512])
121.2	set of 2 (or more) bars of graduated length
121.21	xylophones (wood)
121.211	free-key xylophone
121.211.1	on legs: *atranatra, kilangay* (Madagascar)
121.211.2	on banana trunks or 'log xylophone': *gbo* (Ivory Coast)
121.211.3	on a pit or 'pit xylophone': *doso* (Benin); *lingassio* (Central Africa) (fig.3).
121.212	fixed-key xylophone
121.212.1	on a box resonator: *gambang* (Java)
121.212.2	with a set of resonators: *bala* (Mali); *kalangba* (Central Africa); *timbila* (Mozambique); *marimba* (Guatemala) (fig.4).
121.22	lithophones (stone)
121.221	hanging plaques (L-shaped, other shapes): *bianqing* (China)
121.222	resting plaques or bars: *picancala* (Kabre, Togo); *goong lu* (Vietnam)

(a)

(b)

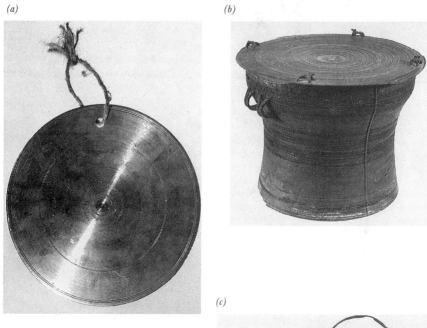

(c)

2. (a) Flat circular gong (ghanta), Nepal; (b) vessel
gong or 'bronze drum' (hpà-si), Burma; (c) Hanging
bossed gong with raised rim (kĕmpul), Java; and (d)
set of resting gongs or gong chime (jengglong), Java.

(d)

*3. Double pit xylophone (*doso*), Benin*

*4. Mounting a Maninka xylophone (*bala*) with a set of resonators, Mali*

(a)

(b)

(c)

5. *Struck inverted gourd vessels (a) on the ground, Banda-Dakpa, Central African Republic, and (b) on water, Maninka, Guinea; (c) struck metal tray containing water (jaltal), Rajasthan (harmonics are produced by manipulation of a pottery lid over the tray containing water)*

6. *Wooden slit drum with several slits, Kissi, Guinea*

264

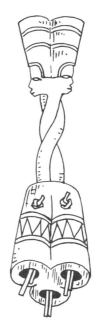

*7. Iron double clapperless bell with superimposed bodies (*agogo*), Yoruba, Nigeria*

*8. Wooden clapperbell with several bodies and clappers (*tsingalagala*), Cabinda, Angola*

9. Gourd 'thigh tapper', Itcha, Benin

265

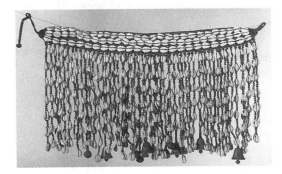

10. *Jingling dance belt, Bambara, Mali*

11. *Jingles: cluster of shells tied on a stick, Thoru, Nepal*

12. *Gourd rattle with external strikers, Burkino Faso*

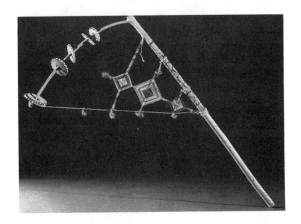

13. *Sistrum made from six gourd discs gliding on a forked stem* (wasamba), *Kissi, Guinea*

266

14. *Hollow notched iron scraper*(nkana), *Senufo, Mali*

15. *Hollow notched scraper with extra clappers* (chara), *Muria, Madhya Pradesh*

(a)   *(b)*

(c)

16. *The two main types of jew's harp: (a) with projecting tip of tongue set in vibration directly by plucking; (b) with enclosed tip of the tongue set in vibration indirectly by pulling a string attached to the opposite end of the frame. The photograph (c) shows a jew's harp of the second type being played* (ghorāliyo *of Rajasthan*)

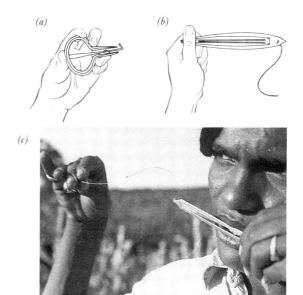

267

121.23	metallophones (sets of slabs or keys of iron, bronze, others)
121.231	on a box resonator: *saron* (Java)
121.232	with a set of resonators: *gĕnder* (Java)
121.232.1	with keyboard: *celesta* (Western)
122	hollow-bodied or partly hollow = vessel (wood, bamboo, vegetable husk or pod, metal)
122.1	'wooden slit drum' = hollowed block of wood or bamboo
122.11	single slit: *lenga* (Central Africa); *mu-yü* (China); *krŏng* (Thailand); woodblock (Western); *lali* (Fiji); *koturka* (Madhya Pradesh)
122.111	with 1 inner central protuberance: *garamut* (New Guinea); or 2 central protuberances: *ikoro* (Igbo, Nigeria)
122.12	2 or more slits = 'xylophone drum': *kende* (Kissi, Guinea) (fig.6).
122.13	2 opposed tongues: *teponatzli* (Mexico); *tunkul* (Yucatan)
122.2	hemispherical percussion vessel (gourd, calabash, bowl, cover lid, pot)
122.21	standing upright: *ghaṭam* (India); *kin* (Japan)
122.211	set of bowls containing water: *jaltarang* (India)
122.22	inverted on the ground: *gaasay* (Songhay) (fig.5a).
122.23	inverted on water = 'water drum': *assakhalebo* (Niger); *jícara de agua* (Mexico); *jaltal* (Rajasthan) (fig.5b and 5c).
122.3	tubular percussion vessel (bamboo): *patang-ug* (Kalinga, Philippines)
122.31	set of tubes = bamboo 'xylophone': *tinglik* (Bali)
122.4	inverted cylindrical vessel = 'bronze drum': *hpà-si* (Burma); *tonggu* (China); steel drum (Trinidad) (fig.2b).
122.41	set of cylindrical vessels: steel band (Trinidad)
122.5	circular plaque with rim = gong: *gangsa* (Philippines); *thall* (India); *luo* (China)
122.51	with central boss
122.511	narrow rim (hanging): *gong agung, kempul* (Java) (fig. 2c).
122.512	high rim or 'kettle gong' (resting on a stand or box resonator)
122.512.1	single element: *kenong* (Java)
122.512.2	as a set: *jengglong, bonang* (Java); *không mön* (Thailand) (fig. 2d).
122.6	bell mouth vessel = bell (with or without handle); various shapes and materials (metal, wood, horn, ivory, vegetable husk)
122.61	with hammer not attached or clapperless bell
122.611	single body: *bonsho* (Japan); *nzoro* (Zandé, Central Africa)
122.611.1	as a set: *blangzhong* (China); *carillon* (France)
122.612	double body (metal)
122.612.1	superimposed: *agogo* (Yoruba, Nigeria) (fig.7).
122.612.2	side by side: *kuge* (Hausa, Nigeria); *gonga* (Zaire)
122.62	with attached clapper(s) or clapperbell
122.621	internal clapper(s)
122.621.1	single body (metal, wood, bamboo, horn, ivory, earthenware)
122.621.11	single clapper: *drll bu* (Tibet); *irna* (Madhya Pradesh); *clochette* (France); *gbwini* (Guinea)

122.621.12	several clappers
122.621.2	double body hourglass-shaped (metal, wood): *uyara* (Igbo, Nigeria)
122.621.3	multiple bodies (wood) with one or more clappers: *tsingalagala* (Angola) (fig. 8).
122.622	external clapper(s) (wood): animal bells (Southeast Asia)
13	STAMPING OR TAPPING the vibrating component taps or stamps another element (the human body, a mortar, the ground, water, mud etc)
131	solid (stick, bar, beam, pestle etc): *jāwan* (Bedouins of Iraq)
132	hollow: stamping tube or stamping vessel (gourd, bamboo, wood, metal): *ˏau ni mako* (Solomon Islands); *ipu hula* (Hawaii); *ganbo* (Haiti); 'thigh-tapper', *bara* (Kissi, Guinea); 'water' or 'mud drum' (Sepik, New Guinea) (fig.9).
132.1	with split end: *ṭokā* (Assam); *duri dana* (Nias); *balingbing* (Philippines)
14	SHAKING
141	pellet bell (small free ball(s) inside a perforated vessel)
141.1	as a set or cluster worn on the body or tied on a stick: *ghuṅgrū* (India); *zang* (Tuva, USSR); *suzu* (Japan); *cascabels* (Spain)
142	vessel rattle with internal strikers (pebbles, sand, seeds, beads etc)
142.1	single body with or without handle (shapes: tubular, spherical, ovoid, circular, conical, others; materials: bamboo, wood, earthenware, wickerwork, metal, gourd, tortoise-shell, others): *chocalho* (Kayapo, Brazil); *maracas* (Mexico); *ichaka* (Nigeria); *hochet* (France)
142.2	double (in the shape of a dumb-bell or with two superimposed bodies) (Central Africa)
142.3	raft (vegetation stalks, porcupine quills, tied side by side): *kayamba* (Digo, Kenya)
143	vessel rattle with external strikers, vibrating components arranged on a net around a vessel (gourd, calabash): *segbureh* (Sierra Leone); *agbe* (Nigeria) (fig.12).
144	jingles = set or cluster of vibrating components (nuts, fruit shells, animal hooves, others)
144.1	attached to various parts of the body: *sonaja* (Mexico); *ekpiri* (Nigeria) (fig.10).
144.2	attached to a stick: *trideksnis* (Latvia) (fig.11).
145	sistra (discs, rings, caps of gourds, sliding on a stem): *wasamba* (Maninka, Guinea); *siak* (Martinique); *sonaja* (Mexico) (fig.13).
146	oscillating tubes (bamboo): *angklung* (Java)
15	SCRAPING notched element scraped with a stick = scrapers
151	solid body
151.1	notched stick (wood or stem): *gwasak* (Birom, Nigeria)

17. *Double-headed drum, hooped and laced on a cylindrical metal body*
(dhol), *Rajasthan*

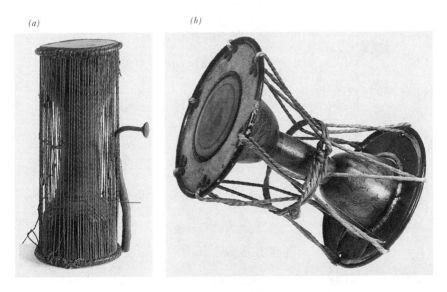

18. *Double-headed hourglass drums: (a) hooped and parallel laced* (tama), *Senegal, and (b) hooped and cross laced* (kotsuzumi), *Japan*

19. Double-headed hourglass drum
*with striking balls (*damaru*), Tibet*

20. Single-headed friction drum
*(*zambomba*), Spain*

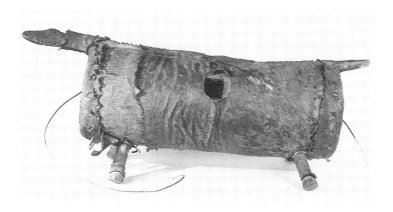

21. Double-headed friction drum, Senufo, West Africa

271

151.11	with extra resonator attached: *hiohkat* (Arizona); *ekola* (Namibia)
151.2	corrugated plaques: washboard (African-American)
151.3	jawbone: *quijida* (Afro-Cuban)
151.4	notched wheel or 'cog rattle': *crécelle* (France); *carraca* (Spain)
152	notched hollow body = vessel scraper
152.1	gourd: *güiro* (Cuba); *reco-reco* (Brazil)
152.2	slit tube (metal): *kirgicha* (Madhya Pradesh); (bamboo): *kargach* (Rajasthan) (fig.14).
152.21	with extra clappers attached: *chara* (India) (fig.15).
152.3	box: *yü* (China); *ŏ* (Korea)
16	FRICTION of a smooth surface or edge
161	solid body or 'rubbing block': *launut* (New Ireland)
161.2	metal band rubbed with bow: musical saw (Western)
162	vessels
162.1	bowls, glasses: musical glasses (Western)
162.2	tortoiseshell: *áyotl* (Maya-Quiche, Mexico)
17	PLUCKING of a flexible tongue or lamella(s)
171	tongue fixed to or cut out of a frame = jew's harp; bamboo/reed (idioglot), metal or mixed (heteroglot); using mouth cavity as resonator
171.1	projecting free tip; directly plucked: *vargan* (USSR); *morcang* (India); *guimbarde* (France) (fig.16*a*).
171.2	non-projecting free tip; set in vibration by plucking/striking of the frame; pulling a string: *röding* (Vietnam); *ghořaliyo* (India); *genggong* (Bali) (fig.16*b*).
172	set of lamellas of graduated length fixed on a board or box = lamellaphone
172.1	vegetable lamellas
172.11	on a board (wood, raffia): *kakolondondo* (Zaire); *kasandji* (Gabon)
172.12	on a soundbox: *sanza* (Cameroon); *mbira* (Venda, South Africa)
172.2	metal lamellas
172.21	on a soundbox: *sanza* (Zaire, Cameroon)
172.211	with extra resonator: *tshisaji* (Zaire); *sanza* (Central Africa)
2	**Membranophones or skin drums** solid stretchable material: skin(s) covering a soundbox or a frame (when the depth of the body is equal to or less than the radius of the membrane); ways of fixing of the skin(s): glued, nailed, pegged, laced (as II, X, V, Y-shapes), hooped and laced, other combinations and different stretching and tuning devices (loops, wedges, or mechanism: pedal, rods)
21	PERCUSSION directly with hands, beaters, hand and stick or indirectly with striking balls
211	1 membrane or single-headed drum
211.1	stretched over a vessel or trunk (wood, metal, earthenware)
211.11	hemispherical = kettledrum: skin laced: *bāyā* (India); *naqqāra* (Tunisia); nailed: *naas* (Chad); other means of tightening: *timbale* (France)
211.111	containing water: *tamamápka* (Creek, Eastern America)
211.12	cylindrical or tubular (the opposite side can be open or closed): *apinti* (Surinam)
211.13	goblet/chalice

211.131	glued: *darbukka, tarija* (Morocco); *dombak* (Iran)
211.132	laced: *thōn* (Thailand)
211.14	mortar: *tindé* (Tuareg, Niger)
211.15	hourglass
211.151	hooped/glued (with handle): *kundu* (New Guinea)
211.152	laced: *kalali* (Kotoko, Chad)
211.16	cask: *atabaque* (Brazil); footed: *atumpan* (Ghana)
211.17	truncated cone, pegged; laced; mixed: *mutumba* (Zimbabwe)
211.18	spherical (gourd): *binderi* (Mossi, Burkina Faso)
211.19	other shapes
211.2	stretched over a frame (circular, quadrangular, polygonal, with skin glued, nailed, laced, hooped)
211.21	circular: *cang* (Rajasthan)
211.211	with extra sounding devices
211.211.1	timbre 'snare drum': *bendīr* (Morocco); *teueikan* (Cree, Ontario)
211.211.2	jingles (rings, tiny cymbals, others): *dāyre* (Kurdistan); *ṭār* (Morocco)
211.212	with handle: *uchiwa-daiko* (Japan); *kilaut* (Inuit, Canada)
211.22	quadrangular
211.23	octagonal: *gherā* (Rajasthan)
212	2 membranes or double-head drum
212.1	stretched over a trunk
212.11	cylindrical: laced: *langorony* (Malagasy); hooped/laced: *t'bol* (Mauritania); *bombo* (Argentina); *dhol* (India) (fig.17).
212.12	truncated cone, laced: *mādar* (India)
212.13	double trunconical laced: *mṛdaṅga, tablā* (India)
212.14	barrel: laced: *ḍholak* (India); *kĕṇḍang* (Java); nailed: *tsuri daiko* (Japan)
212.15	hourglass: laced: *tama* (Senegal); *kotsuzumi* (Japan); variable tension by squeezing the lacing (armpit, hand) (fig.18).
212.151	with striking balls tied to a cord: *damaru* (Tibet, India) (fig.19).
212.2	stretched over both sides of a frame
212.21	circular: *caja* (Argentina)
212.211	with handle: *dhyângro* (Nepal)
211.211.1	with striking balls: *sogo* (Korea)
212.22	quadrangular: *deff* (Morocco); *adufe* (Portugal, Brazil)
22	FRICTION of a thong, stick attached at the centre of the skin
221	1 membrane stretched on a vessel (wood, cork, gourd)
221.1	internal friction stick: *mukuiti* (Congo)
221.2	external friction stick/brush: *buhai* (Romania); *rommelpot* (Flanders); *cuíca* (Brazil) (fig.20).
222	2 membranes stretched on a wooden body with external friction strips (Senufo, Ivory Coast) (fig.21).
3	**Chordophones or string instruments** solid stretchable material: one or more strings attached at both ends on a bearer or soundbox; the combination of criteria like the structure of the instrument and mounting of the strings determines the types and sub-types; means of setting in vibration: striking = S, plucking = P, friction or bowing = F, blowing = B (the

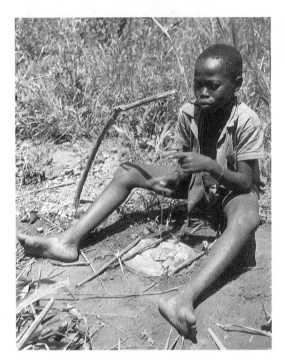

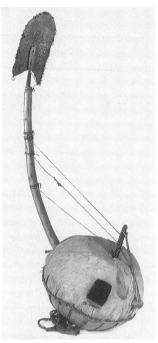

22. *Arched harp on a pit or single-stringed 'ground harp', Central African Republic*

23. *Arched harp with bridge and extra sounding device (*bolon)*, Guinea*

24. *'Forked harp' with attached gourd resonator, Toma, Guinea*

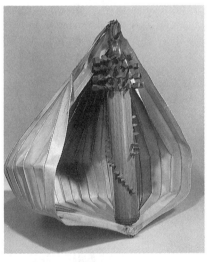

25. *Heterochord tube zither with a palm-leaf resonator (*sasando)*, Timor*

*26. Idiocord stick zither, with mouth as resonator (*etemb*), Bassari, Senegal*

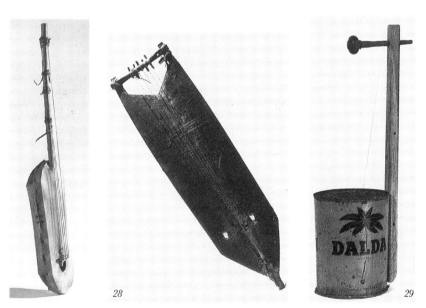

*27. Lute with neck inserted through the cowhide sound-table (nkomi), Bambara, Mali; 28. Lyre with wooden flat soundbox (bridge missing), (*naryukh*), Siberia; 29. Variable tension chordophone (apang), Rajasthan*

275

number and role of strings, the tuning [pegs or other devices], the presence of frets, fingerboard etc should be taken into account in an extensive study)

31	MUSICAL BOW a string stretched between the 2 ends of a curved bearer (branch or stick); vibration: striking, plucking, blowing, friction
311	mouth resonator: *mbela* (Central Africa) = S; *umrubhe* (South Africa) = F
311.1	segmented or braced string: *chipendani* (Shona, Zimbabwe) = S
311.2	with feather vibrator: *gora, lesiba* (South Africa) = B
312	with extra resonator (gourd, wood, metal, pot)
312.1	attached to bow: *berimbau* (Brazil) = S
312.2	resting on the ground: *villu* (Kerala) = S
32	PLURIARC combined musical bows arranged in a soundbox or on a plaque; set in vibration by plucking
32.1	soundbox (wood, gourd): *banga* (Kissi, Guinea)
32.2	plaque: *kondingi* (Susu, Sierra Leone)
33	HARP strings stretched between a soundbox and a straight or curved neck forming an angle between them (or between the ends of an arched or forked component, see 333); strings plane perpendicular to that of the instrument; set in vibration by plucking
331	arched harp (with a curved neck)
331.1	over a pit which acts as a soundbox or 'ground harp' (single-stringed): *tekpede* (Dan, Ivory Coast) (fig.22).
331.2	with soundbox attached to a neck
331.21	ovoid/indented/boat-shaped soundbox (skin sound-table): *kundi, ngombi* (Zaire, Central Africa); *saung gauk* (Burma)
331.22	hemispherical soundbox (skin sound-table): *ardīn* (Mauritania)
331.221	with a bridge: *bolon* (Manding, Guinea) (fig.23).
331.23	prismatic soundbox (wooden sound-table)
331.231	with supporting pillar (1 or 2 rows of strings): Irish harp; *arpa* (Paraguay); various Western concert harps
331.3	curved neck passing through sound-table: *waji* (Afghanistan)
332	angular harp (with straight neck): *changi* (Georgia)
333	'forked harp': strings stretched between the ends of a curved or forked bearer, with resonator attached: *do* (Guere, Ivory Coast); *juru* (Baoule, Ivory Coast) (this instrument could also be regarded as a musical bow with several strings and a resonator attached) (fig.24).
34	ZITHERS strings stretched over a straight bearer, strings parallel to each other and with the plane of the bearer; setting in vibration: striking = S; plucking = P; friction = F; blowing = B
341	on a stick or a bar = stick or bar zither
341.1	idiocord (1 or more string(s) cut from the bark of the stick): *etemb* (Bassari, Senegal) = S (fig.26).

341.2	heterocord (added strings tied on the stick): '*au pasiawa* (Solomon Islands) = P
341.21	with resonator(s) attached: *bīn, jantar* (India) = P; *sāṭiev* (Cambodia) = P; *zeze* (Zaire) = P
342	on a tube (usually bamboo) = tube zither
342.1	idiocord: *valiha* (Madagascar) = P; *gintang* (Assam) = S
342.2	heterocord: modern *valiha* = P
342.21	with resonator attached: *sasando* (Timor) = P (fig.25).
343	parallel arrangement of stalks or raft zither (usually idiocord): *pandaa* (Burkina Faso); *yomkwo* (Birom, Nigeria); *dendung* (Orissa) = P
344	on trough/hollow dish = trough zither: *inanga* (Burundi) = P
345	strings stretched on a convex board = board zither: *koto* (Japan) = P; *ajaeng* (Korea) = F
346	on box = box zither
346.1	trapezoid shape
346.11	isosceles: *santur* (Iran); *Hackbrett* (Switzerland) = S
346.12	rectangular or wing shape: *qānūn* (West Asia) = P
346.121	with mechanism (keyboard, pedals, other): piano = S; harpsichord = P
346.13	other forms: dulcimer (Appalachians) = P; *langspil* (Iceland) = S
347	over a frame: 'Aeolian harp' = B (sounded by natural wind)
35	LUTES AND FIDDLES one or more strings stretched between a soundbox and a straight neck; both strings and instrument are on 2 parallel planes; vibration: plucking (fingers, plectrum) for lutes, friction with a bow or wheel for fiddles; to be taken into account: structures of the 2 components (soundbox, neck); shape of the soundbox and/or sound-table (see fig.E); eventually its material; relation of length between the neck (short/long) and the soundbox; strings and pegs when these features are relevant to differentiate sub-types
351	LUTES
351.1	monoxyle structure (neck, soundbox and peg-box carved from a single piece of wood)
351.11	oval or pear-shaped sound-table
351.111	made of skin: *qanbūs* (Yemen)
351.112	made of wood: *biwa* (Japan); *pipa* (China)
351.12	circular sound-table
315.121	made of skin: *ravaj* (Rajasthan)
351.122	made of wood
351.13	waisted skin sound-table (double-chested soundbox)
351.131	with sympathetic strings: *rabāb* (Iran); *sarod* (India)
351.14	other shapes
351.2	composite structure (neck and soundbox are 2 distinct components tied together in different ways)
351.21	neck (fretted or not) fixed to the soundbox
351.211	soundbox made of a single piece (wood, gourd, metal)

351.211.1   circular soundboard (wood): *tamburā* (India)
351.211.11   with sympathetic strings: *sitar* (India)
351.211.12   waisted/bilobed sound-table (made of skin): *tār* (Iran)
351.211.13   quadrangular skin sound-table: *shamisen* (Japan)
351.211.14   other shapes
351.212   soundbox assembled from several parts (with wooden sound-board)
351.212.1   triangular soundboard (over a prismatic soundbox): *balalaika* (USSR)
351.212.2   oval/circular/triangular soundboard with rounded sides (over a rounded or pear-shaped soundbox)
351.212.21   short neck (equal or smaller than length of the soundboard): *ud* (Middle East, North Africa)
351.212.22   long neck: *saz* (Turkey); *setār* (Iran); *dombra* (Central Asia)
351.213   soundbox with ribs (sidewalls connecting the bottom and soundboard)
351.213.1   circular soundboard: *yueqin* (China)
351.213.2   waisted soundboard: *guitare* (France)
351.22   neck passing through the skin sound-table (soundbox made of a single piece): *khalam* (Senegal); *tidinit* (Mauritania) (fig.27).

352   FIDDLES
352.1   with bow or bowed lutes (similar subdivisions as for lutes)
352.11   monoxyle structure
352.111   oval sound-table (spoon or boat-shaped soundbox)
352.111.1   skin sound-table: *gusle* (Yugoslavia); *rebāb* (Tunisia)
352.111.2   wooden soundboard: *gadulka* (Bulgaria); *lyra* (Crete)
352.112   circular skin sound-table (hemispherical soundbox)
352.112.1   with sympathetic strings: *kamayāicā* (Rajasthan)
352.113   waisted skin sound-table (double chested soundbox): *hārangī* (Rajasthan)
352.113.1   with sympathetic strings: *sārangī*, *sārindā* (India)
352.114   other shapes
352.12   composite structure
352.121   neck fixed to the soundbox
352.121.1   waisted shaped soundboard with ribs or sidewalls = *viole, violon* (France)
352.122   neck inserted through the soundbox
352.122.1   soundbox made of a single piece
352.122.11   circular sound-table
352.122.111   over a cylindrical soundbox (bamboo, wood, metal); with skin sound-table: *nerhu* (China); *indingidi* (Uganda); with wooden sound-table: *haegum* (Korea)
352.122.112   over an hemispherical soundbox (gourd), skin sound-table: *goge* (Hausa, Nigeria)
352.122.12   quadrangular skin sound-table (prismatic soundbox): *bana* (Madhya Pradesh); *masenqo* (Ethiopia)
352.122.2   soundbox as a quadrangular frame: *morin khuur* (Mongolia)
352.122.3   other shapes

278

352.123	neck prolongated with a spike (various shapes of soundbox and sound-table): *rebab* (Java); *kamânche* (Iran); *joze* (Iraq)
352.124	neck inserted through the skin sound-table (hemispherical soundbox): *imzad* (Tuareg, Chad)
352.2	with bow and keyboard: *nyckelharpa* (Norway)
352.3	with wheel: *vielle à roue* (France); hurdy-gurdy (England); *vevlira* (Sweden)
36	HARP LUTE lute structure (body and straight neck on the same plane) but the strings (usually 2 rows) are raised by a vertical bridge in a perpendicular plane (as for harp); set in vibration by plucking: *kora* (Gambia); *soron* (Guinea)
37	HARP ZITHER stick zither structure but the strings (usually idiocord) are raised by a vertical bridge in a perpendicular plane (as for harp); set in vibration by plucking: *mvet* (Gabon)
38	LYRE strings stretched between a soundbox and a neck ('yoke') linked by 2 arms (symmetrical or not); set in vibration by plucking (more rarely by bowing: *strakharpa*; Sweden)
381	bowl-shape soundbox with skin sound-table
381.1	symmetrical arms: *kissar* (Sudan)
381.2	asymmetrical arms: *beganna* (Ethiopia)
382	flat soundbox with wooden soundboard: *naryukh* (Siberia) (fig.28).
39	CHORDOPHONE WITH VARIABLE TENSION (usually single-stringed)
391	with straight neck and peg: *apang* (Rajasthan) (fig.29).
392	with forked neck and peg: *gopīyantra* (Bengal)
393	without neck (manual tension): *bhapang* (Rajasthan); *khamak* (Bengal)
4	**Aerophones or wind instruments** air is the primary vibrating agent, confined or not confined in the instrument
41	air enclosed within a pipe or vessel
411	FLUTES OR EDGE AEROPHONES air stream blown against an edge, situated on the mouthhole (terminal or lateral) or connected with it; at a typological level of study, more data must be taken into account; detailed mouthhole devices, fingerholes (number and position), open/stopped/partially stopped pipe; given the great diversity of flutes only the main sub-types will be mentioned here
411.1	end-blown flutes: air stream directly over the rim of a terminal mouthhole or connected with it by means of an air duct (see fig.C)
411.11	edge on the rim
411.111	plain mouthhole (pipe cut straight)
411.111.1	single pipe: *hindewhu* (Babenzele, Central Africa) (fig.31).
411.111.2	set of pipes of graduated length = panpipes
411.111.21	arranged in a row: *nai* (Romania); *'au paina* (Solomon Islands)

30. Endblown nose flute
(pangupangu), *Tonga Islands*

31. Endblown flute with plain rim mouthhole
(hindewhu), *Babenzele, Central African
Republic*

32. Bundle panpipes ('au waa), *'Are'are, Solomon
Islands*

*33. Endblown airduct double flute (*bandha bā̃sī*), Rawaut, Madhya Pradesh*

*34. Sideblown double airduct flute (*muralī *or* ara bā̃sī*), Rawaut, Madhya Pradesh*

*35. Ensemble of idioglot clarinets with tube resonators (*tule*), Wayãpi, Guiana*

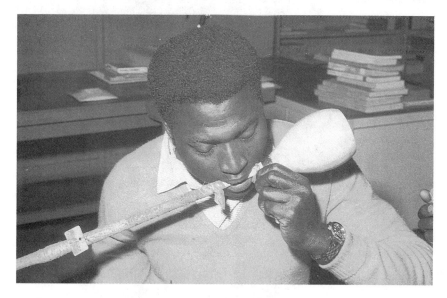

36. *Transverse idioglot clarinet with extra bell* (embekow), *Bassari, Senegal*

37. *Double clarinet* (pūngī) *player mounting the two single beating reeds into the wind chamber, Kalbeliya, Rajasthan*

282

38. Endblown pottery trumpet, Mochita culture, Peru

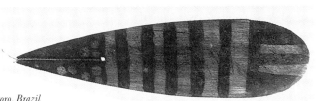

*39. Bullroarer (*aige*), Bororo, Brazil*

411.111.22	two rows: *siku* (Bolivia)
411.111.23	bundle: *'au waa* (Solomon Islands) (fig.32).
411.112	bevelled (to a more or less marked extent): *ney* (Iran); *nar* (Rajasthan); *kaval* (Turkey, Bulgaria), often played in a slanting position
411.113	notched (U-shaped, V-shaped, crescent-shaped or double crescent-shaped): *kena* (Bolivia); *shakuachi* (Japan); *miele* (Kenya); *endere* (Uganda)
411.12	with airduct: the air stream is directed through a narrow duct against the sharp edge of a chamfered orifice open in the wall of the tube ('window')
411.121	internal airduct: the duct is inside the wall of the flute and formed by an inserted block or plug (situated at the upper end = initial or not initial)
411.121.1	initial block
411.121.11	at level with the pipe
411.121.111	single pipe: *caval* (Moldavia); *algōjā* (Madhya Pradesh)
411.121.111.1	with extra blowing tube: *fujara* (Slovakia), played in a vertical position; *mohoceno* (Aymara, Bolivia), played in a transverse position
411.121.122	double pipe: *cyla diaré* (Albania)
411.121.12	projected as a beak
411.121.121	single pipe: recorder (England); *flûte à bec* (France); *masul* (Morocco); *satara* (Rajasthan); *pincullu* (Peru)
411.121.122	double pipe: *dvoinice* (Yugoslavia)
411.121.123	vessel-shaped: *molinukai* (Lithuania); *bulbul* (Georgia)
411.121.2	non-initial block with an external tied-on cover (band, slip

	or piece of wood) to adjust the chamfered orifice open in the wall
411.121.21	adjustable band (vegetable, cloth, others)
411.121.211	single pipe: *bāsī, bāsurī* (Madhya Pradesh)
411.121.212	double pipe: *bānsri* or *bhanda bāsī* (Madhya Pradesh) (fig.33).
411.121.22	adjustable 'groove': *sul* (Apaches, Northeast America)
411.122	external airduct
411.122.1	the duct is outside the wall of the pipe and formed between a chamfered node and an external tied-on ring: *suling* (Java)
411.122.2	attached airduct; a feather quill serves as an airduct and is fastened by means of wax at a suitable angle to the pipe: *gaita* (Colombia)
411.2	side blown: air stream directed over the edge of a lateral mouthhole or through an airduct against a chamfered orifice open in the wall of the pipe and connected with the mouthhole
411.21	edge mouthhole
411.211	tubular pipe: *basuri* (Nepal); *ryūteki* (Japan); *taegum* (Korea); with extra kazoo: *di* (China), with mouthpiece and keys: transverse flute (Western)
411.212	vessel flute: *ocarina* (Italy); *nōkan* (Japan)
411.22	with airduct: pipe segmented in 2 parts, each with a block and external adjustable device: *muralī* or *ara bāsī* (Madhya Pradesh) (fig.34).

412	REED(S) vibrating lamella(s) cut into or tied on the pipe, through which the air stream has intermittent access to the air column causing its vibration
412.1	free reed (lamella narrower than the orifice in which it is cut or on which it is tied), adjusted on a pipe or case
412.11	single pipe or horn: *töki* (Jörai, Vietnam)
412.111	set of pipes (on 1 or 2 rows) with an air chamber = mouth organ
412.111.1	1 circular row: *sheng* (China)
412.111.2	2 parallel rows: *khāen* (Laos)
412.111.3	2 divergent rows: *mbuat* (Vietnam)
412.111.4	2 convergent rows: *raj qeej* (Hmong, Vietnam)
412.12	on small cases: harmonica (Western)
412.121	with bellows and keyboard: *accordéon* (France); *concertina* (former USSR)
412.122	with bellows, keyboard and pedal: *harmonium* (Western)
412.2	single beating reed (clarinets, saxophones, bagpipes) = reed wider than the orifice into which it is cut (idioglot) or onto which it is tied (heteroglot)
412.21	1 pipe (with or without extra bell)
412.211	end-blown clarinet: *zhaleyka* (USSR)
412.211.1	with extra tubular resonator; *tule* (Wayãpi, Guiana) (fig.35).
412.212	side-blown clarinet: *tukpolo* (Gwari, Nigeria) (fig.36).
412.22	two pipes (equal/inequal length) with or without bell: *zummāra* (Iraq); *mijwiz* (Lebanon); *arghūl* (Egypt)
412.23	three pipes (1 chanter, 2 drones): *launeddas* (Sardinia)
412.3	double beating reed or concussion reed: 2 lamellas beating one

against the other under the action of the breath (through them intermittent access of the air stream to the air column) = oboe, bassoon, bagpipes

412.31	oboe with cylindrical bore: *balaman* (Azerbaijan, Armenia)
412.32	oboe with conical bore (most of the oboes with flared end or attached bell): *ghayṭa* (Maghreb); *zūrnā* (West Asia); *śahnāī*, *nāgasvaram* (India); *rgya-gling* (Tibet); *selompret* (Java); *chirimía* (Guatemala)
412.4	beating reed(s) with air chamber
412.41	rigid = double clarinet with air chamber (gourd or wood): *pūngī*, or *muralī* (India) (fig.37).
412.42	flexible = bagpipe
412.421	2 pipes with single reed: *tsambouna* (Greece); *maśhak* (Rajasthan)
412.422	2 pipes or more with single and double reed (various combination of chanters and drones): *biniou* (France); *gaita* (Spain); Scottish Highland bagpipe
412.422.1	with bellows: *musette*, *cabrette* (France)
412.423	3 pipes with double reed: *zampogna* (Italy)
413	LIP-VIBRATED WIND INSTRUMENTS = trumpets and horns: the column of air is intermittently set in motion by lip vibration against a mouthhole situated at the end or at the side of the instrument
413.1	end-blown trumpets (subdivisions according to various features like plain or composite structure/shape of the pipe/bore/and, when relevant, material)
413.11	cylindrical bore (bone, bamboo, wood): *rkangling* (Tibet); *vaccine* (Jamaica); *didjeridu* (Australia)
413.111	with finger-holes: *bāns* (Madhya Pradesh)
413.112	with extra bell: *trutuka* (Mapuche, Chile); *trumbita* (Poland)
413.113	with kazoo (membrane glued to one end): *nyastaranga* (India)
413.12	conical bore
413.121	straight shape with flared end (wood, metal): *bucium* (Romania); *alphorn* (Switzerland); *ragai* (Lithuania); *ongo* (Broto, Central Africa); *didjeridu* (Australia); *nafīr* (Morocco, Northern Nigeria); *kakaki* (Chad, Cameroon, Nigeria)
413.121.11	with telescopic parts: *dung-chen* (Tibet)
413.122	curved shapes: S-shape, various coiled pipes (horn, ivory, wood, earthenware, metal, seashell): *shofar* (Israel); *akum* (Madhya Pradesh); *oliphant* (France); *narsinga* (Nepal); as well as seashell conch trumpet (with or without extra mouthpiece): *sankh* (India); *puutaatara* (Maori, New Zealand) (fig.38).
413.122.1	with playing holes: *cornet*, *serpent* (Western); *sarv* (Finland)
413.122.2	other devices for modifying the pitch (mouthpiece, valve, piston, sliding tube): bugle, french horn, trombone etc (Western)
413.2	side-blown trumpets (same subdivisions as for end-blown trumpets)
413.21	cylindrical bore (wood, bamboo, metal): *inkanka* (Rwanda)
413.211	with added bell: *pututu* (Bolivia)

413.212	with kazoo (membrane covering 1 end of pipe) (Africa)
413.22	conical bore (horn, ivory, wood, metal, earthenware, gourd, seashell)
413.221	straight shape
413.222	curved and various coiled shapes: *aporo* (Uganda); *tori* (Madhya Pradesh); seashell conch: *davui* (Fiji)
42	AMBIENT AIR air not confined by the instrument or free aerophone; set in vibration by the whirling of a sharp-edged device
421	whirling blade attached to a string = bull-roarer (ovoid or fish-shaped, edge smooth or indented, wood, metal, bone): *egburburu* (Zaire); *balum* (New Guinea); *juco* (Nicaragua); *burunga* (Madhya Pradesh) (fig.39).
422	whirling tube of bamboo (India); of plastic (Western sounding gadget)
423	buzzing disc: *fur-fur, uvuru* (Bushmen, Xhosa, South Africa); *diable des bois* (France)

Terminology in question

In providing data relevant to the definition of the main instrumental types, the support of systematics proves to be essential for the establishment of adequate terminology. However, many terminological problems still remain in organology, and only a few are mentioned here. Although the writers of more or less specialized works today hardly ever speak of the 'African guitar' or the 'Chinese violin', descriptions such as 'reed flute' and other equally ambiguous terms may still be found. With string instruments, one of the principal sources of confusion arises from the old word *kithara*, denoting a type of lyre in ancient Greece, which became *cithara* in Latin. Everyone knows that the term *cithare* in French, 'zither' in English and German, and deriving from that word, denotes quite a different instrumental type today. The word *lyra* itself is now found from Crete to the Dodecanese and the Turkish shores of the Black Sea for various bowed lutes, while *lera* and *vevlira* are hurdy-gurdies in the traditional music of the Ukraine and Sweden. The confusion of terms is nothing new. Bragard, De Hen and Ferd (1973, p.234) note that as early as 1511 Virdung was commenting 'that which one calls a harp, another names lyre'; the same authors also quote a Latin poem of the late sixth century concerning a musical instrument that 'the Roman calls "lyre", the barbarian "harp", the Greek "achiliaca" and the Breton "chrotta"', although one and the same instrumental type, the lyre, is concerned. Mediaeval writings call the lyre *cithara teutonica*, while the Irish harp is described as *cithara anglica*.

Confusion of this nature could be considerably reduced if the generic term referring to an organological definition of the instrument were distinguished from the vernacular term peculiar to a particular country or ethnic group. For instance: *guimbarde* in French, jew's harp in English, *Maultrommel* in German, *morchang* in Hindi and *vargan* in Russian may be regarded as so many vernacular names referring to the same type of plucked idiophone.

The extension of a vernacular name to a generic term gives rise to further confusion. Such is the case with the term *balafo* or *balafon*, which has become current usage for any kind of African xylophone, despite the fact that the name

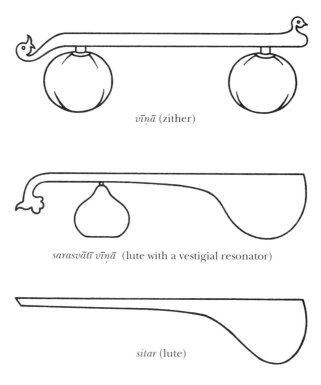

vīṇā (zither)

sarasvātī vīṇā (lute with a vestigial resonator)

sitar (lute)

D. *An example of the organological relationship between the Indian stick zither and lute*

varies from one ethnic group to another; in fact *bala* (*balafo* means to play the *bala*) refers solely to the Maninka instrument. And what are we to make of the use of the term *tamtam* (or tom-tom as in jazz band percussion), originally the name for a Southeast Asian gong, denoting any kind of drums or percussion instruments as well as the music of African dances? The same applies to the originally Spanish term *maracas*, which has become the popular equivalent of a rattle of any species or origin.

The organologist faces another kind of problem in dealing with two Indian instruments: the *sitar* lute and the *vīṇā* zither, the organological relationship between which is obvious (see fig.D). In the north of India the *vīṇā* (or *bīn*) is a fretted stick zither which has two additional hanging gourd resonators. Supposing one of these resonators is turned over and closed, it becomes a soundbox now firmly associated with the stick, which itself acts as a neck, and the *vīṇā* zither becomes the *sitar* lute. The second resonator is found vestigially preserved in the *sarasavatī vīṇā* of South India. Despite its name, this instrument, like the *sitar*, belongs to the lute category, which does not simplify the problem for researchers either Indian or European (the latter being further confronted with the homophony of sitar/ cithare/zither). Such 'fluctuating' terminology can be explained by the fact that the words *vīṇā*, *bīnā* and *bīn*

287

QUADRANGULAR

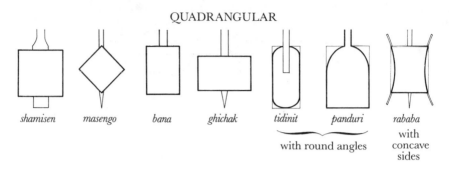

shamisen masengo bana ghichak tidinit panduri rababa

with round angles

with concave sides

TRAPEZOIDAL

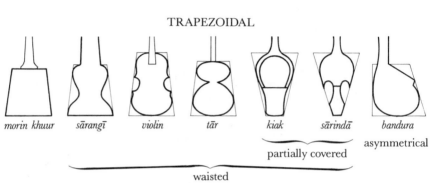

morin khuur sārangī violin tār kiak sārindā bandura

partially covered

asymmetrical

waisted

LOZENGE

TRIANGULAR

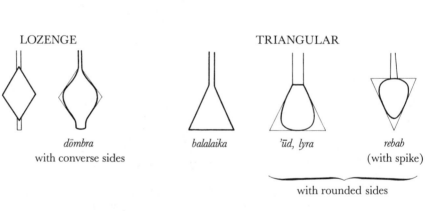

dömbra

with converse sides

balalaika 'ūd, lyra rebab

(with spike)

with rounded sides

POLYGONAL

CIRCULAR

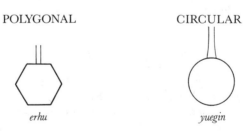

erhu yuegin

E. *Some schematic shapes of lute sound-tables*

288

have been used indiscriminately for thousands of years to designate several kinds of string instruments in India and other South Asian countries.

Some instruments have been given names referring to their function rather than their typology: the 'courting flute', a duct flute of unique construction (see 411.121.22) played by Native Americans; 'shamanic drums' for various Asian and Native American frame drums, and 'talking drums', this last term being applied to both membranophones and idiophones (wooden slit drums) because of their use in the transmission of messages.

It must be admitted that a few organological terms do not always avoid the pitfall of ambiguity. If a terminology aiming to avoid all ambiguity (in other words one term has a single meaning) is to be imposed at every level of analysis it is necessary to draw up glossaries, both general and relating specifically to a particular instrumental type or sub-type. An unequivocal terminology would also allow a clear distinction between certain elements or component parts, for instance between soundbox and resonator: the first is an integral part of the instrument, while the resonator is an added element which can be removed without destroying the structure of the apparatus producing the sound. The same applies to general morphology: most notably shapes of sound-tables and soundboxes in string instruments and drums (see figs. B and E for some standard 'patterns'). Standardization of technical terms would make a considerable contribution to the description of instruments (see Montagu/ Burton, 1971; Rick, 1977).

This ambiguity is most notably the case with the term 'drum', which should be reserved solely for membranophones. However, we use the word 'wooden drums' and 'bronze drums' among struck idiophones for want of a more suitable term (such as 'hollowed block' or 'vessel-gong'). 'Drum', in this case, covers a double reality: percussion exerted on a stretched membrane as well as on a wooden or bronze body. This counters the distinction of membranophones from idiophones. Similarly, the box zither of the south of France, with its struck strings, must certainly owe its misleading name of *tambour de Béarn* or *tambour à cordes* to the way in which it is set in vibration. (Fortunately, although it is often regarded as a percussion instrument, the piano has escaped being nicknamed 'keyboard drum'.) As for the term 'tambour' itself, the French word for drum, should its distant origin be sought in lutes with plucked cords, the *ṭanbūr*, *tandūrā*, *tambūrā* and *tampūrī* of Central Asia? The field of organology verges here upon etymological and semantic research linked to the history and geo-cultural distribution of musical instruments to which Sachs reserved a large part of his *Geist und Werden du Musikinstrumente* (1929).

If taxonomy and terminology are of primary importance in organology and constitute a necessary stage in research, any kind of classification system must become part of a wider perspective. The study of musical instruments is a complex process which must combine two main aspects. The first concerns the identification and description of the characteristics of the 'tool' which produces the sound: the principal vibrating element and the ways of setting it; the structure of the instrument (the arrangement of the functional elements); its construction (shape, dimensions, the material of its constituent part or parts, the additional sound-producing components [e.g. jingles]); and any ornamentation and accessories proper to it. This standard description could be used as a guide allowing apprehension of the structural, formal and technical complexity of the musical instrument.

The second aspect embraces many data of a different order, but essential regarding the geo-cultural origin and use of the instrument, the playing techniques, the musical rendering and the social context.

While properly so-called classification and description call chiefly on acquired knowledge and data observed, the ethnomusicological documentation which must accompany it should be gathered in the course of research and work in the field.

Building up collections of musical instruments

Traditional musical instruments, threatened everywhere sooner or later by their likely disappearance or transformation, are of interest to museums and other scientific institutions throughout the world, particularly where cultural concepts and heritage have acquired a wide and truly anthropological significance. Building up and enlarging musical collections can be a part of ethnomusicological research. Fieldwork is the best way to go about the task, and it is the only way to collect representative sets of instruments directly and methodically, along with adequate documentation furnished by ethnomusicological investigation.

RESEARCH AND COLLECTING IN THE FIELD   Fieldwork is a necessary part of research for the human sciences, ethnomusicology in particular. The field simultaneously represents a laboratory, a university, a training ground and the location of a unique experience. It involves knowledge, abilities and human qualities of great importance. Like all other research, it has its own ethics and methods. Observing the ethics is imperative, while the application of the methods calls for rigour and flexibility at once. Empiricism and improvisation both have their place in an activity where experience is valuable so long as it is open to amendment and will accept being questioned as places, circumstances and the aim of research may demand.

Following the work done by Constantin Brăiloiu and Béla Bartók on methods of collecting and studying musical folklore, some ethnomusicologists, notably Gilbert Rouget (1963), S. Arom (1976) and José Maceda (1981), have suggested methodological bases for investigation and techniques of sound recording in the field derived from past experience. The recommendations made in the *Guide for the collection of traditional musical instruments* (Dournon, 1981) concern the three stages of collecting. First comes the preparatory phase, when basic documentary material is assembled, written works and discographical publications on the region or culture concerned are consulted, information is gathered from ethnomusicologists and anthropologists with experience in the chosen field, and the rudiments of a language for communication are acquired. Next comes the phase of investigation and collecting proper, to be carried out with the aid of investigation protocols and taking into account various ethical principles relating to the research worker's behaviour and respect for the customs of another environment, and to problems of human relations and linguistic communication with the people of the culture whose aid the researcher is seeking: the musician, the instrument maker, those who provide information or act as occasional assistants. The art of offering suitable remuneration in a proper way should not be neglected either. The final phase is the collecting of documentation on and assessment of the material collected.

Although the 'keys to ethnomusicology' are not automatically handed to today's novice researcher before he sets out, he now has at his disposal an increasingly powerful body of technical equipment (tape recorder, photographic and video cameras) to complement the irreplaceable notebook. The purpose of it all is to collect documentation – sound, visual or written – which only fieldwork can provide.

In traditional musical cultures with which we are concerned, instruments are not objects like any other: they are artefacts which both produce sounds and convey meaning. In fact, the musical instrument has an extra dimension determined by its functional and symbolic role in society. Its use is frequently linked to beliefs, to the spiritual or temporal power, the institutions, the cycle of life, and various other circumstances, some codified and some not. Hence the specific ceremonies accompanying the consecration of an instrument, the unwritten rules defining its part in a ritual, the taboos presiding over its making and its use, and the myths (written or orally transmitted) about its origin (natural or supernatural), which are evidence of the importance the social group attributes to it. In traditional societies the musical instrument is seldom neutral, never insignificant.

It follows that methodical research can lead to the collection of a whole complex of information of a musical, technical, aesthetic, symbolic, historical and ethnological nature. We may learn how playing techniques influence the resulting sound (for instance, continuous or discontinuous blowing in various aerophones). The construction of instruments can provide information about the various techniques employed – basket-making, pottery, metal-casting and forging, wood carving – and even at times about the musical concepts which may underlie it. (For instance, research into the making and measurement of the panpipes of the 'Are'are has brought to light a whole folk musical theory [Zemp, 1971–2].) We may also discover whether an instrument is regarded as indigenous or imported from another cultural tendency (e.g. the spread of certain instruments to India, Indonesia and elsewhere by way of Islam, the existence of African instruments in the New World etc). The anthropomorphism or zoomorphism connected with certain instruments may cast light on aspects of cosmogony or social organization.

The basic information, however, concerns the part assigned to the musical instrument in a community or socio-cultural group, and the factors regulating its use (initiation ceremonies, segregation of the sexes, liturgies, magic, rituals, agrarian calendar etc).

Field research is a diverse and complex activity to be approached with as much knowledge as possible, in the right frame of mind, and with the appropriate tools.

The following recommendations for investigation pose the main questions the research worker should ask about the instrument, its maker, the musician, the way it is played, its repertory and socio-cultural function; he will need to modulate and adapt these questions in line with his aims, the environment and the unexpected circumstances in which he is working.

Investigation into the instrument

THE INSTRUMENT   (*i*) Vernacular name: term denoting it in the local language, pointing out what that language is, and its meaning. (*ii*) Locality: geographical and ethnic (places of use and of origin). (*iii*) Description: local names of the functional components, the material of which they are made, and the decorative components (with their underlying meaning). (*iv*) Construction: manufactured or made by a craftsman; identity, age, sex, ethnic group and training of the maker or makers; construction techniques; ritual observances linked to the making of the instrument. (*v*) Use: musical, as signals or messages, imitation of the voice, other. Place, time and circumstances of use. (*vi*) Playing: position of the player and the instrument, playing techniques (fingering, blowing etc); tuning. (*vii*) Modes of performance: solo; accompaniment to singing, poetry, drama or dance; ensemble of one or several similar instruments or different instruments (which instruments?) (*viii*) Property: individual or collective. (*ix*) Origin: indigenous (mythical origin) or borrowed from another cultural group. (*x*) Storage: Where? By whom? How? Is it destroyed after use?

THE PLAYER   (*i*) Identity: name, sex, approximate age, membership (of ethnic group, caste, phratry, clan, brotherhood etc), birthplace and place of residence. (*ii*) Social status: professional musician (*griot*, poet, other); occasional musician (usual occupation: medicine man, shaman, priest, secular or religious leader, farmer, shepherd, blacksmith, instrument maker, other). (*iii*) Social position: high/low/indefinite. (*iv*) Remuneration: in money or kind, other. (*v*) Training and transmission of music: individual (from a master), collective (initiation society, religious community, traditional music school), mode of transmission (oral/written). (*vi*) Repertory: undifferentiated/specific (liturgy, music drama, ceremonial, epic ballads, concert, other).

FUNCTION AND USE   (*i*) Masculine, feminine or children's activities (hunting, war, gathering, pastoral, agricultural or ludic activities). (*ii*) Ceremonies and rituals (birth, marriage, funerals, investiture of a secular or religious leader, initiation, other). (*iii*) Cults (ancestors, twins, tutelary deities); liturgies (Buddhist, Islamic, Hebraic, Shinto, Christian, other). (*iv*) Therapeutic cures (shamanism, possession). (*v*) Festivals and rejoicings (harvest, courting, eulogies, quests). (*vi*) Theatrical performances (dance drama, puppet plays, shadow plays, other). (*vii*) Periodicity: seasonal, regular, undifferentiated.

Investigation into the music

Documentation of instruments includes sound recordings. Whether we are dealing with instrumental music, accompaniment to songs and dances, or essentially vocal music, there should be equal and parallel collection of the documentation relevant to musical pieces which will constitute a body of material for study or for the enrichment of sound archives in museums, universities and conservatories, musical libraries and cultural institutions. As recording techniques have been discussed elsewhere in this volume, only the main items of information to be assembled concerning the musical piece, its interpreters, its text, and its socio-cultural function will be given shortly here (see *Fieldwork, Field Technology*).

THE MUSICAL PIECE   (*i*) Identification: title or incipit (vernacular name and its meaning). (*ii*) Genre or repertory: epics, *chantefables*, liturgy, art music. (*iii*) Place of the piece in the repertory: episode, fragment, integral version. (*iv*) Language of the text: spoken, sung, recited. (*v*) Composer: known or anonymous. (*vi*) Performance: the piece is: (*a*) essentially instrumental, accompanies singing (proceed as for the instrument, above: number, names and methods of playing instruments etc); (*b*) essentially vocal (solo, duet, choral, soloist and chorus (give the number and sex of the performers; the singing styles: responsorial, antiphonal, other); (*c*) in the case of a dance, mention basic choreography, clapping of the hands, stamping of the feet etc, and all sounding devices carried on the body. (*vii*) Circumstances of performance: spontaneous, at request, out of context. (*viii*) Place and time of performance: indoors or out of doors; night or day; prescribed or not.

THE INTERPRETERS   (Compare the player in the preceding protocol.) Name, age, sex, social status, places of birth and residence, training, transmission.

THE TEXT   A literal translation, or failing that, the general significance of the sung or spoken text; translator (if used): name, age, sex, group membership, mother tongue/other languages, training.

FUNCTION OF THE MUSIC   The same kind of investigation as for instruments.

Whatever the order and manner in which the documentation is collected (and it should be adapted depending on the people, places and circumstances involved), this information must be rigorously recorded, so proper use can be made of it subsequently.

Collecting musical instruments

When fieldwork involves the acquisition of musical instruments, various recommendations concerning the ethics and methods of collection must be taken into account. Whether carried out on behalf of a local or a foreign institution, the acquisition of instruments is not an end in itself. It must be an integral part of research, must have the approval of the traditional depositaries and the authorization of the local authorities. The customs and usages of the country and its legislation on the preservation of its heritage must be scrupulously observed. Collecting must be neither a raid nor a shopping expedition.

In some cases the acquisition of musical instruments is not recommended: in particular, when the owner shows any reluctance to let an instrument go, when it has a sacred value, when its use has become rare, and when its acquisition might entail the disappearance of a repertory or ceremony. When the instrument cannot be acquired, its music and social context should be investigated exhaustively. Complete the investigation with a photographic or video record.

From the practical point of view, the acquisition of instruments and the rewarding of any collaboration should take account of local usage, the requirements of the vendor, and the relationship the research worker has with the members of the community who have taken him in and given him the benefit of their hospitality and their knowledge.

If collecting is done without disturbance to the culture, and with regard for ethical, psychological and material imperatives, it may at best be a catalyst, stimulating the memory and creativity of musicians and instrument makers, reviving extinct repertories or ceremonies. It can also contribute to the on-the-spot training of young local research workers.

Conservation and utilization

The instruments collected in the field – along with information and documentation gathered – will be dispatched to whatever national or regional institution (museum, university or research institute) has taken responsibility for their conservation and preservation, study and utilization (particularly by means of publications and exhibitions).

The transport of instruments to their place of storage is an important stage of the work, and should not be underestimated; it would be unfortunate if carelessness meant that instruments of considerable cultural and scientific value, often acquired in difficult circumstances, deteriorated during their risky delicate journey. The protection of acquisitions must be assured, taking into account three factors: the fragility of the instruments, the shortage of packing materials on the spot, and the means and duration of transport, which will vary depending on distance and local conditions.

Musical instruments and all the documentation collected must then go through a process giving them legal and official status. The process may vary from one institution to another, but it always follows the same general principles: (*i*) Registering the instruments in the institution's records. (*ii*) Giving each a chronological registration number. (*iii*) Indelibly marking the registration number on each item. (*iv*) Cleaning, disinfection and protection against parasites or other destructive agents. (*v*) Taking photographs for the documentary files. (*vi*) Drawing up all the documentation relating to the instrument. (*vii*) Classifying, arranging and keeping items in the storage or display areas.

The generation of documentation is an essential phase. Complementary information relating to an instrument or a collection of instruments must be compiled, using various aids: field notes, recorded tapes, photographs and films. The data are of various orders: (*i*) museographical (the registration number, the collector's name, the method of acquisition); (*ii*) organological (identification, description); (*iii*) ethnomusicological (playing, scales, tuning, repertory, use). All this information must be kept in suitable media: card indexes, technical files, computer records.

Several kinds of index cards may be used, depending on the levels of information required. In all cases the minimum information needed is: (*i*) instrument's museum registration number; (*ii*) the organological and vernacular names; (*iii*) the provenance (place of origin and group using the instrument); (*iv*) a brief description (structure, main material, dimensions, condition); (*v*) social and musical function; (*vi*) the name of the collector; (*vii*) the existence of any sound or photographic records; (*viii*) the place or medium where all other information may be consulted (files, field notes, catalogue cards, computer records etc). Models of index card entries for instruments or tape recordings can be found in various specialist publications (see Dournon, 1981). (Sound archives follow a process analogous to that of instrumental collections, and their conservation draws on specific techniques.)

The care of musical instruments should take a number of factors into account:

(*i*) their constituent materials (wood, reed, shell, skin, metal etc); (*ii*) adequate storage facilities; (*iii*) conditions of preservation in the storage or display areas (control of humidity and temperature, protection against shocks, parasites, dust and light). The general principles are to be found in professional periodicals, including the *Technical Bulletin* and the *Canadian Conservation Institute* (iv, 1978), and in articles in *Museum* and the *CIMCIM Newsletter*, as well as in publications dealing with the delicate question of the restoration or reconditioning of instruments (Sachs, 1934; Berner, 1967; Abondance, 1981).

Instrumental collections can provide various publications (e.g. catalogues, monographs, organological and musical works, gramophone records, etc), exhibitions, and supply teaching data. The job of the researcher, organologist and curator is not only building up, keeping, and studying musical instrument collections as representative of human cultures, but also bringing that part of the musical inheritance of mankind to the awareness of specialists, students and the national and international public, including in particular its traditional depositaries.

The aim of this study has been to cast light on two fundamental aspects of the study of musical instruments: theoretical, in the sphere of taxonomy, and practical, in the sphere of fieldwork. Major publications devoted to the subject – in particular the remarkable book by Margaret Kartomi, *On Concepts and Classifications of Musical Instruments* (Chicago, 1990), which was published when this article was in press – and dealing with complementary aspects cited in the bibliography, will allow the interested reader to gauge the full extent of the multi-faceted science of organology.

Bibliography

GENERAL AND REGIONAL ORGANOLOGY

S. Virdung: *Musica getuscht und ausgezogen* (Basle, 1511; repr. 1931/*R*1970)
M. Agricola: *Musica instrumentalis deudsch* (Wittenberg, 1529/*R*1969, enl. 5/1545)
M. Praetorius: *Syntagmatis musici tomus secundus* (Wolfenbuttel, 1618, 2/1619/*R*1968); with *Theatrum instrumentori* (Wolfenbuttel, 1620/*R*1958)
M. Mersenne: *Harmonie universelle* (Paris, 1636–7; Eng. trans. of the book on instruments, 1957)
P. Trichet: *Traité des instruments de musique* (1640), ed. F. Lesure, *AnnM*, iii (1955), 283–387; iv (1956), 175–248; edn. pubd separately (Neuilly-sur-Seine, 1957)
F. Bonanni: *Gabinetto armonico pieno d'instrumenti sonori indicati e spigate* (Rome, 1722, rev. enl. 2/1766)
J. J. M. Amiot: *Mémoire sur la musique des Chinois tant anciens que modernes*, ed. P. J. Roussier (Paris, 1779/*R*1973) and *Mémoires concernant l'histoire des sciences, les arts, les moeurs, les usages des Chinois*, vi, ed. J. J. M. Amiot (Paris, 1780), 1–254
G.-A. Villoteau: 'Description historique technique et littéraire des instruments de la musique de l'antique Egypte', *Descriptions de l'Égypte*, ed. E. F. Jomard (Paris, 1809–22, 2/1821–30)
V.-C. Mahillon: *Catologue descriptif et analytique du Musée instrumental et Conservatoire royal de musique de Bruxelles* (Ghent, 1880–1912; i, 2/1893; ii, 2/1909)
C. R. Day: *The Music and Musical Instruments of Southern India and the Deccan* (London, 1891)
H. Balfour: *The Natural History of the Musical Bow: a Chapter in the Developmental History of Stringed Instruments of Music* (Oxford, 1899/*R*1976)
C. Sachs: *Real-Lexikon der Musikinstrumente, zugleich ein Polyglossar für das gesamte Instrumentengebiet* (Berlin, 1913/*R*1962)
E. M. von Hornbostel and C. Sachs: 'Systematik der Musikinstrumente: ein Versuch', *Zeitschrift für Ethnologie*, xlvi (1914), 553–90; Eng. trans. by A. Baines and K. P. Wachsmann, as 'Classification of Music Instruments', *GSJ*, xiv (1961), 3

C. Sachs: *Die Musikinstrumente Indiens und Indonesiens* (Berlin, 1915, 2/1923)

———: *Die Musikinstrumente Birmas und Assams im K. Ethnographischen Museum zu München* (Munich, 1917)

———: 'Die Maultrommel: eine typologische Vorstudie', *Zeitschrift für Ethnologie*, xlix (1917), 185

G. Montandon: *La généalogie des instruments des musique et les cycles de civilisation: Étude suivie du Catalogue raisonné des instruments de musique du Musée ethnographique de Genève* (Geneva, 1919)

C. Sachs: *Handbuch der Musikinstrumentenkunde* (Leipzig, 1920, 2/1930)

R. d'Harcourt and M. d'Harcourt: *La musique des Incas et ses survivances* (Paris, 1925)

W. Kaudern: 'Musical Instruments in Celebes', *Ethnological Studies in Celebes*, iii (Göteborg, 1925–9)

C. Sachs: *Geist und Werden der Musikinstrumente* (Berlin, 1929/R1985)

H. G. Farmer: *Studies in Oriental Musical Instruments* (London, 1931)

A. Schaeffner: 'Project d'une classification nouvelle des instruments de musique', *Bulletin du Musée d'Ethnographie du Trocadéro*, i (1931), 21

V. Goloubew: 'Sur l'origine et la diffusion des tambours métalliques', *Prehistorica Asiae Orientalis*, ii (Hanoi, 1932), 37–157

A. Schaeffner: 'D'une nouvelle classification méthodique des instruments de musique', *ReM*, xiii/129 (1932), 215

E. M. von Hornbostel: 'The Ethnology of African Sound-instruments [comments on C. Sachs: *Geist und Werden der Musikinstrumente*], *Africa*, vi (1933), 129, 284; vii/1 (1934), 277–311

K. G. Izikowitz: *Musical and Other Sound Instruments of the South American Indians: a Comparative Ethnographical Study* (Göteborg, 1934/R1970)

P. R. Kirby: *The Musical Instruments of Native Races of South Africa* (London, 1934/R1953; 2/1965)

J. Kunst: *De Toonkunst van Java* (The Hague, 1934; Eng. trans. as *Music in Java*, 2/1949, enl. 3/1973)

O. Boone: *Les xylophones du Congo belge* (Tervuren, 1936)

T. Norlind: *Systematik der Saiteninstrumente*, i: *Geschichte der Zither* (Stockholm 1936), ii: *Geschichte des Klaviers* (Stockholm, 1939, 2/1941)

A. Schaeffner: *Origine des instruments de musique: introduction ethnologique à l'histoire de la musique instrumentale* (Paris, 1936/R1968; 1980)

F. E. Williams: *Bull-roarers in the Papuan Gulf* (Port Moresby, 1936)

F. W. Galpin: *A Textbook of European Musical Instruments: their Origin, History and Character* (London, 1937, 4/1956)

C. Sachs: *Les instruments de musique de Madagascar* (Paris, 1938)

A. Chottin: *Tableau de la musique marocaine* (Paris, 1939)

J. Kunst: *Music in Nias* (Leiden, 1942)

N. Bessaraboff: *Ancient European Musical Instruments* (Cambridge, MA, 1941)

C. Marcel-Dubois with J. Auboyer: *Les instruments de musique de l'Inde ancienne* (Paris, 1941)

J. Kunst: *Music in Flores: a Study of the Vocal and Instrumental Music Among the Tribes Living in Flores* (Leiden, 1942)

H.-H. Dräger: *Prinzip einer Systematik der Musikinstrumente* (Habilitationsschrift, U. of Kiel, 1946; Kassel, 1948)

E. Emsheimer: 'Schamanentrommel und Trommelbum', *Ethnos*, xi (1946), 66

A. Schaeffner: 'Les instruments de musique', *La musique des origines à nos jours*, ed. N. Dufourcq (1946), 13

O. Alvarenga: *Musica popular brasileña* (Mexico City, 1947; Port. orig. 1950; It. trans. 1953)

H. Hickmann: *Terminologie arabe des instruments de musique* (Cairo, 1947)

H. Tracey: *Chopi Musicians: Their Music, Poetry, and Instruments* (London, 1948/R1970)

J. F. Carrington: *Talking Drums of Africa* (London, 1949)

H. Hickman: *Catalogue général des antiquités égyptiennes du Musée du Caire: Instruments de musique*, nos. 69201–852 (Cairo, 1949)

C. Vega: *Los instrumentos musicales aborigenes y criollos de la Argentina* (Buenos Aires, 1949)

J. Kunst: *Musicologia: a Study of the Nature of Ethno-musicology, its Problems, Methods and Representative Personalities* (Amsterdam, 1950, enl. 2/1955 as *Ethnomusicology*, 3/1959; suppl. 1960)

O. Boone: *Les tambours du Congo belge et du Ruanda-Urundi* (Tervuren, 1951)

A. Schaeffner: 'Le lithophone de Ndut Lieng Krak' (Vietnam), *RdM*, xxxiii (1951), 1

———: 'Les Kissi: une société noire et ses instruments de musique', *Cahiers d'ethnologie, de géographie et de linguistique*, ii (Paris, 1951/R1990 as *Le sistre et le hochet*)

F. Ortiz: *Los instrumentos de la musica afro-cubana* (Havana, 1952–5)

P. Wirz: *A Description of Musical Instruments from Central North-Eastern New Guinea* (Amsterdam, 1952)

M. Trowell and K. P. Wachsmann: 'The Sound Instruments', *Tribal Crafts of Uganda* (London, 1953), 309–422

J. A. R. Blacking: 'Musical Instruments of the Malaysian Aborigines', *Federation Museums Journal*, new ser., i–ii (1954–5), 35

S. Martí: *Instrumentos musicales precortesianos* (Cordóba, 1955, rev. 2/1968)

T. Alexandru: *Instrumentele muzicale ale poporului romîn* (Bucharest, 1956)

A. Büchner: *Hudebnie nastroje od pravedu k dnesku* (Prague, 1956; Eng. trans. as *Musical Instruments through the Ages*, 1956, 4/1962)

K. M. Klier: *Volkstümliche Musikinstrumente in den Alpen* (Kassel and Basle, 1956)

B. Söderberg: *Les instruments de musique du Bas-Congo et dans les régions avoisinantes: étude ethnographique* (Stockholm, 1956)

D. Yupho: *Khruang dontri Thai* (Bangkok, 1957, 2/1967; Eng. trans. as *Thai Musical Instruments*, 1960, 2/1971/R1987)

H. Fischer: *Schallgeräte in Ozeanien, Bau und Spieltechnik, Verbreitung und Funktion* (Strasbourg, 1958); Engl. trans, as *Sound-Producing Instruments in Oceania* (Boroko, Papua New Guinea, 1983)

W. P. Malm: *Japanese Music and Musical Instruments* (Rutland, vt, 1959)

J. -S. Laurenty: *Les cordophones du Congo belge et du Ruanda Urundi* (Tervuren, 1960)

A. Schaeffner: 'Genèse des instruments de musique', *Histoire de la musique* (Encyclopédie de la Pléiade, Paris, 1960, i, 76–117)

H. Tracey: 'A Case for the Name Mbira', *African Music*, ii/4 (1961), 17

J. -S. Laurenty: *Les sanza du Congo* (Tervuren, 1962)

Chuang Pen Li: *Panpipes of Ancient China* (Taiwan, 1963)

K. Vertkov, G. Blagodatov and E. Yazovistkaya, eds.: *Atlas muzikal'nikh instrumentov narodov SSSR* (Moscow, 1963, 2/1975 with 4 discs)

W. Bachmann: *The Origins of Bowing* (London, 1964)

V. Chenoweth: *The Marimbas of Guatemala* (Lexington, 1964)

F. Harrison and J. Rimmer: *European Musical Instruments* (London, 1964)

A. M. Jones: *Africa and Indonesia: the Evidence of the Xylophone and Other Musical and Cultural Factors* (Leiden, 1964, enl. 2/1971)

B. Dietz and M. Babatunde Olatunji: *Musical Instruments of Africa: Their Nature, Use and Place in the Life of a Deeply Musical People* (New York, 1965)

C. Mcphee: *Music in Bali* (New Haven and London, 1966/R1976)

D. Rycroft: 'Friction Cordophones in South-Eastern Africa', *GSJ*, xix (1966), 84

E. Veiga de Oliviera: *Instrumentos musicais populares portugueses* (Lisbon, 1966)

I. Aretz: *Instrumentos musicales de Venezuela* (Cumaña, 1967)

J. Ling: *Nyckelharpan: studier i ett folklit musikinstrument* (diss., U. of Uppsala, Stockholm, 1967)

B. Sarosi: *Die Volksmusikinstrumente Ungarns: Handbuch des europäischen Volksinstrumente*, ed. E. Emsheimer and E. Stockmann, I/i (Leipzig, 1967)

K. S. Kothari: *Indian Folk Musical Instruments* (New Delhi, 1968)

J. Kunst: *Hindu-Javanese Musical Instruments* (The Hague, 2/1968)

J. -S. Laurenty: *Les tambours à fente de l'Afrique Centrale* (Tervuren, 1968)

F. Bebey: *Musique de l'Afrique* (1969; Eng. trans. 1969 by J. Bennett as *African Music: a People's Art*)

O. Elscheck: 'Typologische Arbeitsverwahren bei Volkmusikinstrumente', *Studia instrumentorum musicae popularis*, i (1969), 23

—— and E. Stockmann: 'Zur Typologie de Volksmusikinstrumente', *Studia instrumentorum musicae popularis*, v (1969), 11

J. Rimmer: *Ancient Musical Instruments of Western Asia in the Department of Western Asian Antiquities, British Museum* (London, 1969)

P. van Thiel: 'An Attempt to the *Kinyankore* Classification of Musical Instruments', *Review of Ethnology* (1969), no. 13, 1

A. F. Weisbebtson: 'The Launeddas: a Sardinian Folk-music Instrument', *Acta ethnomusicologica Danica*, i (Copenhagen, 1969)

A. Baines: *Bagpipes* (Oxford, 1970)

J. Blades: *Percussion Instruments and their History* (London, 1970, 2/1974)

R. Leydi and S. Mantovani: *Dizionario della musica popolare Europea* (Milan, 1970)

M. Hood: *The Ethnomusicologist* (New York, 1971, 2/1982)

J. Montagu and J. Burton: 'A Proposed New Classification System for Musical Instruments', *EM*, xv/1 (1971), 49

G. Tintori: *Gli strumenti musicali* (Turin, 1971)

K. P. Wachsmann: 'Musical Instruments in Kiganda Tradition and their Place in the East African Scene', *Essays on Music and History in Africa*, ed. K. P. Wachsmann (Evanston, il, 1971), 93–134

Ethnomusicology: an Introduction

H. Zemp: *Musique Dan: la musique dans la pensée et la vie sociale d'une société africaine* (Paris, 1971)

———: 'Instruments de musique de Malaita', *Journal de la Société des Océanistes* xxvii/30, (1971), 31; xxviii/34 (1972), 7–48

F. J. de Hen: 'Folk Instruments of Belgium', *GSJ*, xxv (1972), 87–132; xxvi (1973), 86 129

A. Spycket: 'La musique instrumentale mésopotamienne', *Journal des savants* (1972), 153–209

R. Bragard and F. de Hen: *Les instruments de musique dans l'art et l'histoire* (Brussels, 1973)

M. Brandily: *Instruments de musique et musiciens instrumentistes chez les Teda du Tibesti* (Tervuren, 1974)

L. Kunz: *Die Volksmusikinstrumente der Tschechoslowakei* (Leipzig, 1974)

J. -S. Laurenty: *Systématique des aérophones de l'Afrique Centrale* (Tervuren, 1974)

W. P. Malm: 'A Computer Aid in Musical Instruments Research', *Festschrift to Ernst Emsheimer* (Stockholm, 1974), 119

R. Moyle: 'Samoan Musical Instruments', *EM*, xviii (1974), 57

H. Heyde: *Grundlagen der natürlichen Systeme der Musikinstrumente* (Leipzig, 1975)

A. Janata: *Musikinstrumente der Völker* (Vienna, 1975)

L. Picken: *Folk Musical Instruments of Turkey* (London, 1975)

H. Boone: 'De hommel in de Lage Landen', *Brussels Museum of Musical Instruments Bulletin*, iii (1976) [with Eng. summary]

V. Chenoweth: *Musical Instruments of Papua New Guinea* (Ukarumpa, 1976)

J. Jenkins and P. Rovsing-Olsen: *Music and Musical Instruments in the World of Islam* (London, 1976)

M. -T. Lestrange and M. Gessain: *Collections Bassari: Sénégal, Guinée*, xv/4, ser. C (Paris, 1976), 84, 258

I. Vandor: *La musique du Bouddhisme tibétain* (Paris, 1976)

A. Kebede: 'The Bowl-lyre of Northeast Africa, *Krar*: the Devil's Instrument', *EM*, xxi/3 (1977), 379

D. Reck: *Music of the Whole Earth* (New York, 1977)

E. Bassani: *Gli antichi strumenti musicali del'Africa nera: dalle antiche fonti cinquecentesche al Gabinetto Armonico del Padre Fillipo Bonnani* (Padua, 1978)

P. Berliner: *The Soul of Mbira: Music and Traditions of the Shona People of Zimbabwe* (Berkeley, 1978)

B. C. Deva: *Musical Instruments of India: Their History and Development* (Calcutta, 1978)

G. Dournon-Taurelle and J. Wright: *Les guimbardes du Musée de l'Homme* (Paris, 1978)

S. Olędzki: *Polskie instrumenty ludowe* [Polish folk instruments] (Kraków, 1978)

Seong Gyong-Rin: *Traditional Instruments of Korea* (Seoul, 1978) [slides and tape recording]

H. Zemp: ''Are'are Classification of Musical Types and Instruments', *EM*, xxii/1 (1978), 37–67

F. Anoyanakis: *Greek Popular Musical Instruments* (Athens, 1979)

H. Camêu: *Instrumentos musicais dos indigenas brasileiros* (Rio de Janeiro, 1979)

R. Leydi: *La zampogna in Europe* (Como, 1979)

J. Lindsay: *Javanese Gamelan: Traditional Orchestra of Indonesia* (Kuala Lumpur, 1979)

C. Ziegler: *Les instruments de musique égyptiens au Musée de Louvre* (Paris, 1979)

S. Bandhyopadhyaya: *Musical Instruments of India* (Varanasi, 1980)

X. Bellanger: 'Les instruments de musique dans les pays andins (Equateur, Bolivie, Pérou), i: Les instruments dans le contexte historique-géographique', *Boletín des Instituto Frances de estudios Andinos*; ix/3–4 (1980), 107–49; x/1–2 (1981), 23

J. Gansemans: *Les instruments de musique Luba* (Tervuren, 1980)

S. Q. Hassan: *Les instruments de musique en Irak et leur rôle dans la société traditionnelle* (Paris, 1980)

C. Marcel-Dubois with M. Pichonnet-Andral and others: *L'instrument de musique populaire, usages et symboles* (Paris, 1980)

G. Rouget: *La musique et la transe: Esquisse d'une théorie générale des relations de la musique et de la possession* (Paris, 1980); Eng. trans. as *Music and Trance: a Theory of the Relations between Music and Possession* (Chicago and London, 1985)

F. R. Tranchefort: *Les instruments de musique dans le monde* (Paris, 1980)

B. Bachmann-Geiser: *Die Volksinstrumente der Schweiz* (Leipzig, 1981)

F. Flores and L. G. Flores: *Organologia aplicada a instrumentos musicales prehispanicos: Silbatos Mayas* (Mexico City, 1981)

C. Lund: 'The Archeomusicology of Scandinavia', *Archaeology*, xii/3 (1981), 246

L. Picken: 'The "Plucked" Drums: gopî yantra and ânanda lahari', *Musica Asiatica*, iii (1981), 29

R. J. M. van Acht: *Volksmuziek en volksinstrumenten in Europa: een beeldverhaal* (The Hague, 1982)

A. Büchner: *Encyclopédie des instruments de musique* (Prague, 2/1982)

H. Boone: *La cornemuse* (Brussels, 1983)

M. Helffer: 'Observations concernant le tambour *rnga* et son usage', *Selected Reports in Ethnomusicology*, iv (1983), 62–97

C. Marcel-Dubois and others: 'Typologie et classification en organologie musicale', *CIMCIM Newsletter*, xi (1983–4), 36

F. Borel: 'Quelques observations à propos des objets vibrants non identifiés', *Objets prétextes, objets manipulés* (Neuchâtel, 1984), 57

A. Chamorro: *Los instrumentos de percusion en Mexico* (Mexico City, 1984)

J. Redinha: *Instrumentos musicais de Angola: sua contruçao e descriçao* (Coimbra, 1984)

K. P. Wachsmann: 'Classification', *The New Grove Dictionary of Musical Instruments*, i (1984), 407

P. Williams: 'Organ', *The New Grove Dictionary of Musical Instruments*, iii (1984), 838

U. Wegner: *Afrikanische Saiteninstrumente* (Berlin, 1984) [with tapes]

S. Arom: *Polyphonies et polyrythmies instrumentales d'Afrique centrale: structure et méthologodie* (Paris, 1985; Eng. trans. as *African Polyphony and Polyrhythm*, Cambridge, 1991)

E. Bermudez: *Los instrumentos musicales en Colombia* (Bogota, 1985)

H. Boone: *De mondtrom* (Brussels, 1986)

F. Borel: *Les sanza* (Neuchâtel, 1986)

E. Vega de Oliviera: *Instrumentos musicais populares dos Açores* (Lisbon, 1986)

L. Liavas, ed.: *Music in the Aegean* (Athens, 1987)

W. Maioli: *Le origini il suono e la musica* (Milan 1987; French trans. by S. Valici as *Son et musique, leurs origines*, Paris, 1991)

Å. Norborg: *A Handbook of Musical and Other Sound-producing Instruments from Namibia and Botswana* (Stockholm, 1987)

L. Rault-Leyrat: *La cithare chinoise zheng: un vol d'oies sauvages sur les cordes de soie . . .* (Paris, 1987)

S. Cloutier: 'Les instruments musicaux des indiens zoros-pangueyens', *Recherches amérindiennes au Québec*, xviii/4 (1988), 75

S. Ghosh: *String Instruments of North India*, i: *Plucked Instruments* (Delhi, 1988)

S. C. De Vale: 'Musical Instruments and Ritual: a Systematic Approach', *JAMS*, v (1988), 14

M. T. Brincard, ed.: *Sounding Forms: African Musical Instruments* (New York, 1989; Fr. trans., 1990 by L. Albaret as *Afrique: Formes sonores*)

M. Desroches: *Les instruments de musique traditionelle* (Fort de France, 1989)

G. Dournon: 'Une flûte qui trompe: parallèle entre deux aérophones indiens', *Cahiers de Musique traditionnelles*', ii: *Instrumental*, ed. L. Aubert (Geneva, 1989), 13

R. Moyle: *The Sounds of Oceania* (Auckland, 1989)

Å. Norborg: *A Handbook of Musical and Other Sound-producing Instruments from Equatorial Guinea and Gabon* (Stockholm, 1989)

G. Dournon and J. Schwarz: *Instruments de musique du monde/Musical Instruments of the World* (Paris, 1989), LDX 274675 CM251 [discs and notes]

N. Sorel: *A Guide to the Gamelan* (London, 1990)

L. Aubert: *Planète musicale* (Geneva, 1991)

DICTIONARIES, ENCYCLOPEDIAS, SERIES AND COLLECTED WORKS

Dictionaries and Encyclopedias:

A. Lavignac and L. de la Laurencie, eds.: *Encylopédie de la musique et dictionnaire du Conservatoire* (Paris, 1920–31)

E. Wellesz, J. A. Westrup and G. Abraham, eds.: *New Oxford History of Music* (London, 1954)

F. Michel, F. Lesure and V. Féderov, eds.: *Encyclopédie de la musique* (Paris, 1958–61; Sp. edn. by M. Valls Gorna, Barcelona, 1967)

S. Marcuse: *Musical Instruments: a Comprehensive Dictionary* (Garden City, NY, 1964/R1975)

Histoire de la musique, Encyclopédie de la Pléiade (Paris, 1960)

Diagram Group: *Musical Instruments of the World: an Illustrated Encyclopedia* (London, 1976)

S. Sadie, ed.: *The New Grove Dictionary of Musical Instruments* (London, 1984)

S. Sadie, ed.: *The New Grove Dictionary of Music and Musicians* (New York and London, 1980)

Series:

H. Besseler and M. Schneider: *Musikgeschichte in Bildern* (Leipzig, 1961–87)

E. Stockmann, ed.: *Studia instrumentorum musicae popularis* (1961–81)

L. Aubert, ed.: *Cahiers de musiques traditionelles*, ii: *Instrumental* (Geneva, 1989)

ACOUSTICS

A. Bouasse: *Verges et plaques, cloches et carillons* (Paris, 1927)

——: *Tuyaux et resonateurs* (Paris, 1929)

A. Bouasse: *Instruments à vent* (Paris, 1929–30)
E. Leipp: *Acoustique et musique* (Paris, 1971, 4/1984)

ACCOUNTS OF TRAVELS

O. Dapper: *Naukeurige beschrijvinge der Afrikaenishce gewesten* (Amsterdam, 1668, 2/1674; Eng. trans., 1897, 2/1899, 3/1906)
C. Chardin: *Voyages de M. Chevalier Chardin en Perse* (Amsterdam, 1711)
T. Cook: *A Voyage to the Pacific Ocean* (London, 1784)
P. Raffles: *The History of Java* (London, 1817)
W. Burchell: *Travels in the Interior of Southern Africa* (London 1822–4/R1953)
C. Defremery and B. R. Sanguinetti: *Voyages d'Ibn Battuta* (Paris, 1853–8)
A. Morelet: *Journal du voyage de Vasco da Gama en MCCCXCVII* (Lyon, 1864)
G. Schweinfurth: *The Heart of Africa: Three Years' Travel and Adventures in the Unexplored Regions of Central Africa from 1868 to 1871* (London, 1873)
J. -A. Dubois: *Hindu Manners, Customs and Ceremonies* (Oxford, 1897, 2/1899, 3/1906)
A. Gide: *Voyage au Congo: carnets de route* (Paris, 1927)

FIELD RESEARCH; CARE OF MUSICAL INSTRUMENTS

G. Rouget: 'L'enquête ethnomusicologique', *Histoire de la musique*, Encyclopédie de la Pléiade, II (Paris, 1960), 333–48
A. Berner, ed.: *Preservation and Restoration of Musical Instruments* (London, 1967)
C. Brăiloiu: 'Esquisse d'une méthodologie de folklore musical', *Problèmes d'ethnomusicologie* (Geneva, 1973), 5–39
S. Arom: 'The Use of the Play-back Techniques in the Study of Oral Polyphonies', *EM*, xx (1976), 483–519
F. Hellwig: *The Care of Musical Instruments: a Technical Bibliography for Conservators, Restorers and Curators* (Bratislava, 1977)
J. Jenkins, ed.: *International Directory of Musical Instrument Collections* (Buren, 1977)
R. L. Barclay: 'Care of Musical Instruments in Canadian Collections/Le soin des collections canadiennes d'instruments de musique', *Technical Bulletin*, iv (1978), 1
F. Abondance: *Restauration des instruments de musique* (Fribourg, 1981)
G. Dournon: *Guide pour la collecte des instruments de musique traditionelle* (Paris, 1981; Eng. and Spanish trans.)
J. Maceda: *A Manual of Field Music Research with Special References to Southeast Asia* (Quezon, 1981)
G. Dournon: 'L'Heritage muséographique d'André Schaeffner: les collections d'instruments de musique du Musée de l'Homme', *RdM*, lxviii (1982) [Schaeffner festschrift]
F. Hellwig, P. Kurfurst and I. Macak, eds.: *Contributions to the Study of Traditional Musical Instruments in Museums* (Bratislava, 1987)
G. Dournon and others: *Pour une description méthodique des instruments de musique* (Paris, 1990, unpubd)

CHAPTER XI

The Biology of Music-Making

JOHN BLACKING

First the ethnomusicologist needs to address the general problem of assessing the roles of nature and culture in forming the particular cultural activities called 'musical', which are defined variously from one society to another. Second the researcher must examine the suitability and the limitations of the human body for performing available musical tasks: it is assumed here that what one human being has invented, and others have accepted as a conventional mode of musical communication, could in principle be done or understood by any other normal human being. Given the psychic unity of mankind, then, a third consideration is the biological foundation of music-making and the extent to which musical ability springs from a specific human propensity or from the application to music-making of more general capabilities.

Culture, nature and music-making

Ethnomusicological research, it so happens, has raised more problems about the biology of music-making than it has resolved. It has questioned arguments about universal, elementary musical structures, learning processes and emotional reactions, around which a coherent theory of the biological foundations of music-making might be based, chiefly because it has revealed a diversity of human perceptions and definitions of music and of affective responses that cannot be explained in naturalistic terms.

First, Alexander J. Ellis (1814–90), the so-called 'father of ethnomusico-logy', developed a theory of music derived from the psycho-acoustical discoveries of Herman von Helmholtz (1821–94). He argued (Ellis, 1877) that 'all musical scales, and hence all music, has depended, and must depend, from all time to all time' on the mathematically determined, physical facts that relate partial to fundamental tones, and the number and character of overtones to timbre. But when he tested this theory, he found it deficient. By measuring scientifically the scales of certain Asian musics, he showed that at least some musical systems were very diverse, artificial and man-made, and not necessarily derived from natural laws relating the pitch and consonance of sounds to the mathematical proportions of their vibrations and ratios (Ellis, 1885). The importance of mathematically calculated tonality, consonance and dissonance in the tonal music of Europe after 1600 was the result, it appears, of cultural choice, and not an inevitable development in the evolution of a human capacity for making music with parameters biologically determined. Definitions and measurements of people's musical aptitude in relation to their comprehension of the natural laws of sound and their mastery of increasing acoustical complexity – all are culture-specific.

Secondly, young children's musical competence does not proceed in all cultures according to some universal syntax related to acoustical complexity, that is, from two- and three-tone ditties to five-, six- and seven-tone melodies, and from isorhythmic to polyrhythmic and additive rhythmic patterns: it develops in different ways in different musical cultures. It seems that learners of different musical systems lack the common denominators and the common children's syntax that appear to be universal features of language learning.

Thirdly, in spite of claims to the contrary, the meanings of similar musical sounds and 'languages' vary greatly from one culture and one individual to another, depending on the performance, and the status and role of performers and participants. Although bodily resonance is a prerequisite of effective musical communication, there is no convincing evidence that the same musical patterns will have the same meanings for people brought up in the same society, let alone for those reared in different cultural traditions. Nor is there evidence that particular melodies, rhythms or timbres will in themselves precipitate altered states of consciousness such as trance or general feelings of joy, sorrow or nostalgia.

Although ethnomusicological research has provided timely warnings against over-generalization about human musicality, it has also contributed to arguments in favour of a species-specific musical competence. For example, studies of musical practice in Sub-Saharan Africa and Southeast Asia show that in communities with cultural systems that value general musical competence, all normal human beings are proficient in dancing, singing and instrumental performance. These facts can be and have been interpreted in three ways.

1. Musical ability is acquired independently of human biology: music is a social fact, with characteristics defined in many ways throughout the world and the practice of which must be learnt in a variety of social contexts. The ability to understand music and participate in its performance depends largely on the emphasis given to musical activity in a cultural system, and on the opportunities to participate in music-making.

2. Musical ability is genetically inherited in such a way that its incidence will vary from one individual to another. Widespread music-making in some populations rather than others could therefore be explained by an increased expression of genes for music-making (as socially defined) in their society. This would be like the prevalence of thalassemia, sickle cell anaemia, blue eyes, red hair or other genetically transmitted characteristics in certain populations.

3. Musical ability is genetically inherited, but in the same way as the biological potentialities necessary for speech (Lenneberg, 1967, p.28ff). That is, musical ability is specific to all normal humans and is part of their general biogrammar (indeed may be a primary modelling system for thought and communication). If absent in some individuals, this lack is the result either of trauma, such as brain damage, or of social and cultural inhibition which deprives individuals of the interaction necessary to develop the capability.

(This deprivation would be comparable to the atrophy of speech in children who have been isolated from the human intercourse necessary to develop their language potential.) This third possibility would explain how some people can assimilate the rules of musical systems without notation or formal instruction, and can generate novel patterns of sound even during early childhood (Blacking, 1967). It could explain why musical aptitude tests in the European tonal tradition show correspondence with milestones in cognitive and physical growth, and to stabilize round about puberty (Gordon, 1987).

These three interpretations recur in different societies' conceptualizations and practice of the musical art. Because words cannot convey the significance of musical experience, ethnomusicological analyses incorporating insights expressed in the language of myth are no less valid than observations in the language of scientific method. Of particular importance are the definitions and contradictions and consistencies in the arguments held in different musical communities or in one musical community on the ways in which these relationships vary from one social class to another.

For example, biological theories of exceptional musical ability have been widely held in Europe and North America, especially since the development of genetics, and studies of outstanding composers and performers have often drawn attention to the musical activities of their 'blood' relatives.

When, however, the same idea that musicians are born, not made, is expressed in many Asian and African societies, it does not necessarily refer to a belief in biological inheritance. If a person is described as being 'born a musician', the definition is social: she or he is a member of a family or clan of musicians, and hence is expected to perform music well, particularly if they go with their parents and close kin to musical events, sit next to them, hold their instruments and perhaps take minor parts in performance. If people believe in reincarnation, as in the Hindu caste system, the children of musicians clearly cannot inherit their musicianship biologically, since their 'reborn' individual souls could not have been musicians in their immediately previous incarnation.

From earliest recorded history, many societies and individuals have held beliefs relating to the common theme that exceptional musical ability is a divine gift which can be acquired only by grace or by spiritual exercises, in addition to assiduous practice of technique. These are not inherently biological theories, although their phraseology sometimes suggests it. First, a belief in the divine origins of musical ability is frequently invoked to explain the exceptional musical interest and talent of someone who was not born into a family of musicians. Secondly, such beliefs are used as explanations of vocation rather than of any innate ability: it is also believed that other people could make music, as they often do, and that all people should be able to understand and appreciate it, but that only some are expected to devote extra time to music. Thirdly, such beliefs place music-making as one of a number of ways in which people can express the divine essence of all existence: thus the divine nature of the expression is more significant than its particular manifestation in music-making.

The belief that musical ability has divine origins has been held in many sub-Saharan African societies. In the traditional musical system of the Venda people of the Northern Transvaal, outstanding ability in music was generally considered to depend partly on the assistance of the spirit of a deceased ancestor (who may not necessarily have been an outstanding musician), and partly on the commitment and efforts of a person to develop the musical abilities with which all human beings were endowed by virtue of being human. Observation of Venda musical practice suggested that people's special interest in music tended to be influenced by their gender and social status, so that there were more than an average number of musicians who were women of noble families or men who were commoners. If individual musicality were genetic, the Venda evidence would suggest that it was sex-linked in a rather unusual way.

Of the three interpretations of musical ability, the first and third are most common, and they are frequently invoked on different occasions by the same people and for different reasons, or by different people in the same society. In some modern industrial societies, schools and music teachers use variations of the first or the third interpretation to persuade large numbers of young people to devote hours to rehearsal, even if the children may not be interested, on the grounds that everyone has ability and it is a task of teachers to develop it. This cultural tax on children's time and parents' income can contribute to the employment and continuity of the music profession, whose economic role in society is publicly expressed in frequent music competitions. At these events, the uneven performance of different competitors is interpreted as the success or failure of particular teachers or pupils, depending on the values that people attach to efficient education, individual motivation, and general human potential.

Although few people notice it, the musical socio-economic system is regularly threatened when some enthusiastic adjudicator declares that a performer is a 'born' musician – the second interpretation. If the most successful performers really were genetically different from the rest, then parents and pupils should save their money and time, even at the risk of making music teachers redundant. This does not happen, partly because the presence of music in society is supported by its social and political uses, quite apart from the pleasure that music-making gives to less 'successful' individuals, and partly because few people really believe the genetic theory: it conflicts with their sense of their own musicality.

People's sense of their own musicality is a deeper and more visceral experience than anything that is culturally acquired, such as membership in a particular organization or proficiency in some skill. Although the musical conventions with which it can be expressed are part of a cultural system, like the syntax of a language, participation in performance (by listening carefully as well as by actually playing) can involve the body's sensorimotor system in such a way that people's responses to the music are felt as an expression of the very ground of their being and an intrinsic part of their human nature. In literally being moved, both internally and externally, by participation in musical performance, they can become more aware of the human body and its repertory of sensations and emotions.

Thus, however much a musical system and people's responses to performance may be cultural constructs, some relatively unchanging biological processes must be taken into account. None of these processes in themselves may be peculiar to music-making, of course, but at the same time a reductionist approach will not explain the uniqueness of music-making as human experience. Comparisons of isolated features, such as patterns of movement, breath control, emotional response, and so on, in music-making, with similar phenomena in ritual, sports activities, painting, sculpture, poetry or drama, cannot explain particular musical structures and responses. Music-making and a person's sense of musicality are the outcome of interpersonal interaction with at least three sets of variables: symbolically ordered sounds, social institutions, and a selection of the available cognitive and sensorimotor capabilities of the human body.

Whether some or most of the capabilities selected are specifically 'musical' and/or specially suitable for music-making, or whether they are taken from a general store of capabilities that can be selectively applied to music, they are socially constructed as much as they are genetically conditioned. Supposing it emerged that there were links between left-handedness and certain kinds of musicality, as there appear to be between left-handedness, exceptional mathematical and artistic abilities, or a person's susceptibility to dyslexia, immune diseases, epilepsy and migraines, such syndromes would have to be tested cross-culturally, to ensure that they were not consequences of socially constructed attitudes to left/right, male/female, sacred/profane, and so on, and of corresponding values attached to left-handedness and to certain related activities. An informal study of art students showed that an unusual number (45 per cent) were left-handed and that many had developed an interest in art as a result of doodling with the left hand while they wrote, as required, with the right hand.

If 'musical' proclivities are part of the genetic constitution of some or all human beings, to what extent are differences in behaviour due to differences in genetic constitution or to differences in experience and vice versa? And how far are 'musical' proclivities finite? Hearing music is part of the experience necessary for developing musicality and music-making, but is there a limit to what one can learn as music? 'Organisms come into the world with proclivities for learning some things but not others . . . chaffinches might soon get into difficulties if they imitated every sound that they heard, so it is predetermined that they learn only songs with a note-structure resembling that of normal chaffinch song' (Hinde, 1975, p.117). What is most significant of birds, and applies no less to children's learning of speech (and music?), is that the experience of learning their normal song occurs some months before the bird starts to sing, so that the information must be stored in some way (Hinde, 1975, p.114).

Biology of musical performance and response

A. L. Kroeber was one of many anthropologists who argued that culture is entirely learned and superorganic, and that its development is independent of biological evolution. This view tends to reduce the role of the human body, and especially of affect, in the invention of ideas and artefacts. Although composers who work with notation intended for singers and instrumentalists, and some contemporary composers who work with machines, may seem to reduce the human factor in music-making, there is a sense in which their work is no less 'organic' than those who compose without notation, often as they develop pieces of music during performance. The organic element in musical composition has been emphasized by Victor Zuckerkandl (1973, pp.248, 337ff), who described it as a process of 'thinking in motions'.

It is hard to see how making sense of music can be superorganic: for it requires some degree of bodily resonance, as does monitoring speech, and music-making is a physical performance that engages the body in ways which may or may not suit its 'nature'. 'Nature' must be broadly defined because the plasticity of the human body is such that its postures, gestures and performance can be, and are, developed in many ways: what is suitable for one human body may be difficult for another, and an apparent limitation of body use need not restrict musical invention. Many European ethnomusicologists have found it difficult to sit in the culturally appropriate way for playing some Asian instruments, but the dexterity of good sitar players has not been hindered by their 'failure' to use all fingers of the left hand.

Thus, although the responses of composers, performers and audiences can never be entirely objective or detached from associated bodily experiences, neither are the bodily experiences automatically determined responses to certain stimuli. They are mediated by culturally learned habits and attitudes and by the different ways in which people have come to use their bodies. For example a person's perception of consonance and dissonance cannot be determined objectively in terms of less or more complex ratios of intervals: some people hear minor 2nds as dissonant, but others find them harmonious and consonant, especially when they stand close to each other and sing so that they feel the tension of the beats in their bodies (see Messner, 1980). Similarly, some people may be excited by driving drum beats, but the claim of Andrew Neher that a particular speed of drumming will induce trance-like states has been shown to be quite untenable (Rouget, 1985, pp.172–6).

On the other hand, the neurophysiologist and concert pianist Manfred Clynes has presented interesting evidence to support his claim that through the fantasized emotions of music, someone can generate a precise emotional state in others by repeatedly producing its typical expression, or 'essentic form'. He argues that there is a biological basis for sharing emotion through music (Clynes, 1974, 1977, 1982): people are able to resonate with the inner pulse of music through the sense of their own musicality, because biologically determined, expressive movements (essentic forms) are programmed into human bodies, and emotional gestures have precise representations in the brain. Music is 'a language of essentic forms', which can be used 'to communicate emotions and qualities to others who recognise the language. Access to essentic forms is part of what musical talent means: the most gifted musicians are those who are able to achieve the greatest purity of essentic form' (Clynes, 1974, p.53).

Clynes's theory relates in particular to Gustav Becking's (1928) observations that the underlying pulses of the music of Haydn, Mozart, Beethoven and Schubert are quite different, though they often use similar melodic phrases; to Susanne Langer's concept of the logical form of feeling; to Paul Ekman's work on the structures of emotions and moods; and to findings of another neurophysiologist, Karl Pribram, who demonstrated that emotions are neural processes which structure input as an alternative to instrumental action, and so influence patterns of thought and imagination.

The claim that essentic forms are stable and universal across individuals and across cultures need not conflict with anthropological and ethnomusicological data on the variability of cultural forms and musical systems.

306

'Fantasized' emotions are cultural constructs, and the same expressive movements of the body can be given many different meanings, especially in the conventional contexts of dance, music, drama and ritual. Clynes's essentic forms for the specific emotions of anger, grief, hate and the like need not be universally associated with those emotions.

On the other hand, there are problems with this theory, and with several other theories that resemble it. It seems to imply that there must be precise correlations between the feelings of two persons, fantasized or actual, for effective communication to take place; and that the wrong response, or absence of response, is in some respects a measure of a person's musical insensitivity. It leans towards a questionable theory of musical communication that relies on identity of interpretation and strict correlations between sound and meaning that must be shared by co-performers.

In practice, interpretations of 'the same' symphony by different orchestras vary greatly in expression and tempo, and yet concert and record sales and reviews show that each appeals to different, but discerning, listeners. Clynes attributed the stability of Toscanini's performing times of the Brahms 'Haydn' Variations with the NBC Symphony Orchestra in 1935, 1938 and 1948 to a constant conception of the music and great precision of emotion. However, there are many performances of the same work by the same orchestras and soloists whose tempi have varied greatly over the years, each performance bringing new insights into the work. Surely the hallmark of a musical masterpiece is not the singularity of its emotional message, but its polysemy and the fact that many people find satisfaction through it on many occasions; this is certainly the case in the Venda music of spirit possession, which moved different people in different ways on the same occasion, and differently on different occasions, even when the tempo and the general sound of the music varied little from one performance to another (see Blacking, 1985).

Emotion and mood are important in the composition, performance and appreciation of music, but aesthetic and social factors can be equally salient. Also, they are much more difficult to quantify and predict. The growing interest in the biology of music-making, especially by neurologists, psychologists and psychiatrists, has not been prompted by a belief in biological determinism, but rather by a conviction that a clearer understanding of the interactions between human biology and musical cultures can benefit the further development of music-making in human society.

Social and musical conventions can help some people in their music-making but hinder others, largely because of biological inheritance. For example, in some societies congenital blindness was associated with certain classes of semi-professional musicians, and especially court musicians, who were required to play before women whom others were not allowed to see. Thus music provided a promising career for many who were physically handicapped. Deformities of the trunk and legs, such as kyphosis (humpback) and rickets, could affect music-making when it was intimately associated with dancing: in some African societies, humpbacks seemed almost driven to overcome their sense of physical disability by a passion for step-dancing and its associated singing, while persons with rickets tended to express themselves musically through instruments using the top of the body, such as zithers, lyres and bowharps.

307

A most striking feature of many traditional African societies, which incidentally supports arguments in favour of an innate human predisposition to music-making, was that physically disabled persons seemed positively to use music and dance to overcome any stigma of social abnormality. A similar disregard for physical limitations or predispositions is found in the recruitment of musicians within the more circumscribed world of so-called European classical music. For instance many fine pianists have not had 'pianist's' hands; and small pianists like Alicia De Larrocha are able to negotiate the large stretches required in the music of the pianist–composer Isaac Albeniz. The size of cellists can range from Casals's 1.37 metres, with small, thick hands, to Piatigorski's 1.96 metres, with long arms and fingers.

Schumann's unfortunate experiments with his fourth finger serve as a reminder that some physical limitations of the body cannot easily be overcome, and that instrumentalists are as susceptible to injuries as are singers to severe voice strain (see Bunch, 1982). Although performance anxiety is a general condition that can affect musicians and non-musicians alike, and is therefore not peculiar to the biology of music-making, some disorders appear to arise because of the instruments people play, such as dental and lung problems among wind players, left-hand tension in violin and viola players, and neck and shoulder troubles among pianists.

This evidence suggests that a better understanding of all aspects of the biology of music-making could contribute to the practice and theory of music therapy, which has tended to develop by a process of inspired empirical trial-and-observed success, rather than by a systematic theory and testing of hypotheses. Thus there is little doubt that instrumental ensembles such as Balinese and Javanese gamelan may be more practical than European instruments for music therapy: they can involve a large number of people in a corporate activity which both requires awareness of others and saturates individual bodies in a rich oscillation of organized sound; and the variety of instruments and their different contributions to the ensemble allow for participants with a wide range of abilities. But the potential of gamelan and other musics for human growth cannot be fully exploited until the biogrammar of possible relations between social and physical body, music, affect, mind and brain is better understood, and until there is a more general theory of music-making to reconcile the structures of a cultural phenomenon with its biological foundations.

Musical systems and techniques have been invented and developed by people with basically the same bodies, but cultural conventions and individual idiosyncrasies have influenced the ways in which they have used and extended those bodies. Thus what may have come easily to one person may have to be acquired with difficulty by others, not only because of physical barriers or facility, but also because good musicians do not play with their bodies so much as through their bodies.

Pianists, especially in the idiom of jazz, seem to have been able to acquire dexterity with a remarkable variety of 'natural' and 'unnatural' postures of the wrists and fingers. Much of Chopin's, Debussy's and Ravel's piano music seems to flow quite 'naturally' from a certain way of holding the hands, which presumably became habitual for those composers and was not unrelated to the development of the piano in the 19th century as well as to prevailing ideas about musical expression. It is probably unlikely that keyboard players used their hands in those ways during the time of Carl Philip Emmanuel Bach and Mozart. In some musical traditions of sub-Saharan Africa, symmetrical and physically 'easy' movements of the body, combined with culturally appropriate ideas, social situations and musical instruments, have given people the stimulus to create an infinite variety of compositions (Blacking, 1961, 1973, p.12ff). Since music-making often involves patterned movement in relation to the active surface of a musical instrument, the intrinsic modes of operation of the sensorimotor system can influence the shapes of musical structures (Baily, 1985).

As in ballet and many styles of dancing, some uses of the body in music-making can stretch the body to its limits and often go against what might seem 'natural' postures and gestures. Although techniques that were developed with extreme difficulty in one generation have become standard practice in subsequent generations, it cannot be assumed that accompanying bodily tensions have thereby been resolved. What is to be made of the argument that some of Paganini's extraordinary feats of dexterity were first accomplished because he had a disease of the connective tissue which allowed him hypermobility and hyperextensibility of the joints (Smith and Worthington, 1967), and hence made the movements comparatively easy? If a pathological condition of the body gives rise to a new musical technique, does the adoption of that technique by subsequent generations of violinists make them susceptible to abnormal physical or psychological stress? Or are the reported physical and psychological disorders of musicians a consequence of different social attitudes towards music and music-making and to the role of musicians rather than the nature of the musical tasks?

The widespread positive evidence of the ability of musicians to overcome serious disabilities, of physical disability giving rise to musical innovation, and of individuals feeling their way beyond the boundaries of social convention, together with the negative evidence from some societies of musicians with physical ability succumbing to musical stress, confirm the influence of culture in a person's responses to the challenge of music-making. But they also reinforce claims that musical performance can help people to transcend cultural restrictions and physical and psychological disadvantage. This view of the power of music-making is so widely held in pre-industrial societies (see Blacking, 1973, p.51) that one suspects the disorders afflicting professional musicians in modern industrial societies spring not so much from music-making in itself, as from the conditions in which music is made.

Towards a theory of musical intelligence

Social and cultural conditions, and especially the professionalization of music-making, can create problems for musicians and inhibit the full expression of human musicality, but conditions do not altogether determine musicality. Whatever view is taken of the relative influences of cultural and biological factors in musical performance and response, some music-making, it appears, requires that various parts of the brain and body work together in particular ways – an effort that cannot be adequately explained by the individual's use of any uniquely constructed, culturally defined musical system in changing social situations.

In other words, music-making is not entirely a human invention created as part of an ideology of social life: it also resulted from the discovery and use of a set of interrelated capabilities as intrinsic to defining an organism's humanity as its capacity to speak a natural language. The essence of music is non-verbal and hence cannot be conceived as a product of word-based ideological construction. The varieties of musical thought and practice in the world presuppose innate musical intelligence, even though ethnomusicological research has shown that music is a social fact, that musical systems are cultural systems woven into the larger web of the cultures of communities, and that the variety of these symbol systems precludes a universally valid definition of music or universal agreement on what constitutes music as distinct from non-music or noise.

'Musical intelligence' can be usefully distinguished from 'musical thought'. 'Musical thought' refers to the culturally defined processes involved in composing, performing, listening to and talking about what different societies categorize as special ('musical') symbol systems and special kinds of social action. The concept of 'musical intelligence' is proposed as a working hypothesis to define the cognitive and affective equipment with which people can (i) make music and (ii) make musical sense of the world.

The existence of a special musical intelligence has been inferred chiefly from observations of individual successes and failures in monitored music-making and in responses to aural tests (see Critchley and Henson, 1977; Gardner, 1983; Sloboda, 1985). Although there are few studies of performance practice in different social contexts, and although the musical thought observed has been almost entirely within the system of European tonal music and with assumptions about perception that have been questioned (Ellis, 1885), a profile of 'the musical mind' is emerging which can be refined and extended by more systematic cross-cultural research, and which suggests very strongly that biological factors cannot be ignored in the analysis of music- making.

Howard Gardner has revived interest in Franz Joseph Gall's theory of multiple, modular intelligences, arguing that 'the brain can be divided into specific regions, with each emerging as relatively more important for certain tasks, relatively less important for others' (1983, p.54). Gardner identified seven basic human intelligences and defined one of these 'frames of mind' as 'musical'. He drew his evidence from the study of outstanding musicians (also in 'Western' music) and of *idiots savants*, who were able to perform music with great success but in other respects were of subnormal intelligence.

The evidence of ethnomusicological research suggests that 'musical intelligence' cannot be defined in strictly acoustical terms, and that although its most characteristic and effective embodiment is in music-making, it is a basic intelligence prompting many kinds of action. This explanation would not dispose of the possibility that there is a species-specific musical intelligence, but rather would broaden the notion of 'musical'. Instead of arguing that music-making is the result of applying more general capabilities to music, it could be said that musical intelligence can be a modelling system for a variety of non-musical activities, just as it need not be the source of all 'music-like' sounds. Thus, culturally defined musical structures have been derived from patterns of body movement applied to instruments (Baily, 1985), and musical intelligence can be used to organize cultural phenomena that are not usually described as 'musical', such as architecture, mathematics (especially Boolean algebra), rhetoric and poetry.

Musical intelligence seems to be as much a social intelligence as it is cognitive and affective. It can play a crucial role in contemporary social life, drawing people together in close association, coordinating and integrating the different modes of thought characteristic of the left and right hemispheres of the brain, and allowing the imagination to thrive without being bound to any particular conceptual scheme. Because it is the epitome of non-verbal communication, it probably played a major role in the evolution of the two culture-bearing species before modern *homo sapiens*: *homo erectus* and *homo sapiens neanderthalensis*. These species did not have speech as we know it, but they were able to communicate and transmit cultural traditions on which all subsequent human societies were founded (Blacking, 1976).

The evidence for modular intelligence and the occurrence of amusia and of musical *idiots savants* raise the question whether increased knowledge in gene mapping will show that certain genes can be associated with some of the skills and aptitudes that are needed for successful performance in most of the world's musical systems. On the other hand, most genetic predispositions so far confirmed seem to relate to physical functions and states of health and disease, rather than to specific cognitive capacities and affective tendencies. For example research in the 1970s disproved earlier claims that aggressive behaviour and criminality were more likely in men born with an additional male chromosome; and no convincing correlations have been shown between a person's excellence in music and possession of abilities that are claimed to be inherited, such as perfect pitch and exceptional melodic memory. On the contrary, some of the 'musical' abilities considered rare among children in European industrial societies appear to be quite common in for example African rural societies, where they have probably been learned through intensive early interaction in musical situations.

It seems that understanding of music, like comprehension of speech, requires the same cognitive equipment as the production of music and that in many societies everyone is musically competent. Thus, it is most likely that if human beings possess genetically inherited biological predispositions for music-making, those capabilities will be general to the species rather than peculiar to particular individual members – the third of the possible interpretations of the facts about musical ability.

If the biological predispositions are not general capabilities that have been applied to music-making, but a special set of capabilities that can be called 'musical', there should be signs of musical competence of the same kind that Lenneberg (1967) and others have observed for speech. Moreover, if there *are* specific biological propensities for music-making, musical skills and their analogues would have to be acquired differently from a cultural tradition that is learnt and handed down from one generation to another. That is, there ought to be no need for teaching 'musical' activities, just as speech is not taught and as programmed training has no significant effect upon the rate of language acquisition.

If musical communication is biologically based, understanding of its rules should emerge as part of the process of biological maturation. This seems to have been the case in pre-industrial societies, where music is transmitted orally (see Blacking, 1967), and it is probably no less true of literate societies. It seems that children, especially in their pre-school musical activities, in their playground songs, in their creative responses to pop music and in their intuitive solutions to musical problems, acquire some kind of musical 'grammar' without any formal instruction. There is therefore no need to argue that the appropriate genes have a higher frequency in the populations of some pre-industrial societies than they do in the populations of literate societies.

There are several reasons why musical languages could be acquired in much the same way as speech, even though there is far less evidence available, especially in literate, industrial societies. First, even the acquisition of speech is not biologically determined like the eruption of teeth: it depends both on basic physiological processes relating to activating, monitoring and processing speech, and on interaction and meaningful dialogue with others. Widespread absence of musical competence, therefore, does not rule out biological foundations of music any more than aphasia and speech disorders discredit a biological theory of language acquisition. In many societies, speech communication is so heavily emphasized that an innate ability to communicate musically could be inhibited. Secondly, even within sophisticated musical traditions which seem to depend on cultural learning, many people have been able to perform complex music well by ear and without tuition, and Jeanne Bamberger has shown that children develop untutored, but musically effective, strategies for making sense of unfamiliar musical material (1990). Thirdly, there seems to be evidence in the motor and vocal behaviour of infants of elementary music-making capabilities; but, like the cooing and babbling of congenitally deaf infants, it is not developed through interactive use. Finally, it appears that musical ability is not necessarily accompanied by or related to ability in other cultural fields. Similarly, although certain mentally retarded children have difficulties with speech, all normal human beings possess the ability to speak well a natural language, regardless of race, class, and even measured intelligence (Lenneberg, 1967).

Although there are attractive arguments in favour of the biological foundations of certain human behaviours that may be called 'musical', there are serious problems in identifying their forms. This complication is caused partly by the diversity of musical systems ethnomusicologists have found, partly by the difficulty of pinpointing any musical universals and partly because it seems to be necessary to show that special muscles and cognitive capacities have evolved suitable for music. If speaking were simply a matter of using the organs for eating and breathing to enhance communication, there would hardly be a case for the biological foundations of language. Likewise, similar relationships between form and behaviour are necessary for any theory of the biological foundations of music.

It will, perhaps, be easier to approach the problem in terms of the more general categories of 'aesthetic response' and 'aesthetic work'. At least, an evolutionary function has been claimed for aesthetic communication by the biologist J. Z. Young, and the phenomenon of aesthetic transcendence contradicts arguments that artistic creation and response are superorganic and culturally determined. Young writes: 'Creation of new aesthetic forms, including those of worship, has been the most fundamentally productive of all forms of human activity. Whoever creates new artistic conventions has found methods of interchange between people about matters that were incommunicable before. The capacity to do this has been the basis of the whole of human history' (1971, p.519).

Transcultural musical communication can be explained in terms of (i) social, political and commercial pressures on people's taste (which accounts for the widespread appeal of much popular music); (ii) different kinds of aesthetic satisfaction with the same sounds through each person's own, culturally influenced, musical intuition; and (iii) biologically based capabilities that enable people to make culture-free, aesthetic judgments. Only in the third type of situation is there a possibility that two individuals might experience the same musical sounds in the same ways. And because those experiences would inevitably involve the same 'movements' of the body, such as people experience in monitoring speech, any investigation of the biology of music-making will probably need to consider music and dance (or structured movement systems) as a single category, as was, and still is, the case in many African and Asian societies.

It can be hypothesized that 'musical intelligence' is a species-specific capability that is older than speech in human phylogeny, that it is expressed with modes of thought and of non-verbal communication now characteristic of the processing in the right hemisphere of the brain, and that its survival value has not been superseded in human evolution, because it enables people to transcend immediate responses to environment and to create imaginative, secondary strategies. Music-making is, as Alfred Schütz suggested, 'a meaningful context which is not bound to a conceptual scheme', but 'can be communicated' (1951, p.76). It is an aesthetic experience, but it is also an archetype of the communicative process that underlies all social relationships, a '"mutual tuning-in relationship" upon which alone all communication is founded. It is precisely this mutual tuning-in relationship by which the "I" and the "Thou" are experienced by both participants as a "We" in vivid presence' (ibid).

If it is hypothesized that musical intelligence is species-specific, the search for its presence or suppression in the activities of all human beings must be rigorous, as it is for speech. The development of 'musical' behaviour in different cultural contexts, and especially its emergence in infants and children, can then be studied in new and interesting ways. For example, the structures of children's preverbal communication and of their strategies in early music-making, could reveal many of the elementary structures of musical intelligence. If the varying emphases on other forms of communication in different societies help or frustrate infants and children in the development of their 'musical' skills, and if children require mastery of structured non-verbal communication at a very early age but are deprived of opportunities for development, this lack could affect subsequent development.

Although musical intelligence is probably concerned with expressive and 'logical' feeling-responses to situations, it is unlikely that specific feelings will be associated with particular structures, as Clynes (1974) suggested. Musical intelligence is essentially a way of thinking and interacting, a mode of reflection on being rather than an immediate response to basic needs.

Systematic research into the biology of music-making could probably produce significant findings in a very few years if greater use was made of the

313

broad range of contrasting conceptualizations of music, performance practice and contextualized response which ethnomusicological research and methods can reveal.

Bibliography

A. J. Ellis: *On the Basis of Music* (London, 1877)

——: 'On the Musical Scales of Various Nations', *Journal of the Society of Arts*, xxxiii (1885), 485–527

G. Becking: *Der musikalische Rhythmus als Erkenntnisquelle* (Augsburg, 1928/R1958)

S. Langer: *Philosophy in a New Key* (Cambridge, MA, 1942)

A. L. Kroeber: *Anthropology* (New York, 1948)

A. Schütz: 'Making Music Together: a Study in Social Relationship', *Social Research*, xviii/1 (1951), 76

S. Langer: *Feeling and Form* (London, 1953)

J. Blacking: 'Patterns of Nsenga kalimba Music', *African Music*, ii/4 (1961), 26

——: *Venda Children's Songs: a Study in Ethnomusicological Analysis* (Johannesburg, 1967)

E. Lenneberg: *Biological Foundations of Language* (New York, 1967)

R. D. Smith and J. Worthington: 'Paganini: the Riddle and Connective Tissue', *Journal of the American Medical Association*, cxcix/11 (1967), 820

K. H. Pribram: 'The Foundation of Psychoanalytic Theory: Freud's Neuropsychological Model', *Brain and Behaviour*, iv: *Adaptation* (London, 1968), 395–432

J. Z. Young: *An Introduction to the Study of Man* (Oxford, 1971)

J. Blacking: *How Musical is Man?* (Seattle, 1973)

V. Zuckerkandl: *Man the Musician* (Princeton, 1973/R1976)

M. Clynes: 'The Biological Basis for Sharing Emotion: the Pure Pulse of Musical Genius', *Psychology Today*, viii/2 (1974), 51

R. A. Hinde: 'The Comparative Study of Non-Verbal Communication', *The Body as a Medium of Expression*, ed. J. Benthall and T. Polhemus (London, 1975), 107–42

J. Blacking: 'Dance, Conceptual Thought and Production in the Archaeological Record', *Problems in Economic and Social Archaeology*, ed. G. de G. Sieveking, I. H. Longworth and K. E. Wilson (London 1976), 3

K. H. Pribram and M. Hill: *Freud's 'Project' Reassessed* (London, 1976)

M. Clynes: *Sentics: the Touch of Emotions* (London, 1977)

M. Critchley and R. A. Henson: *Music and the Brain: Studies in the Neurology of Music* (London, 1977)

F. Messner: *Die Schwebungsdiaphonie in Bistrica* (Tutzing, 1980)

M. Clynes, ed.: *Music, Mind and Brain* (New York and London, 1982)

M. A. Bunch: *Dynamics of the Singing Voice* (Vienna and New York, 1982)

H. Gardner: *Frames of Mind: the Theory of Multiple Intelligences* (New York, 1983)

J. Baily: 'Music Structure and Human Movement', *Musical Structure and Cognition*, ed. P. Howell, I. Cross and R. West (London and New York, 1985), 237

J. Blacking: 'The Context of Venda Possession Music: Reflections of the Effectiveness of Symbols', *YTM*, xvii (1985), 64

G. Rouget: *Music and Trance: a Theory of the Relations between Music and Possession* (Chicago, 1985); Eng. trans. of *La musique et la transe: Esquisse d'une théorie générale des relations de la musique et de la possession* (Paris, 1980)

J. Sloboda: *The Musical Mind: the Cognitive Psychology of Music* (Oxford, 1985)

E. E. Gordon: *The Nature, Description, Measurement, and Evaluation of Music Aptitudes* (Chicago, 1987)

F. R. Wilson and R. L. Roehmann, eds.: *The Biology of Music Making: Proceedings of the 1984 Denver Conference* (St Louis, 1988)

J. Bamberger: 'The Mind Behind the Musical Ear', *Music and Child Development: Proceedings of the 1987 Denver Conference*, ed. F. R. Wilson and R. L. Roehmann (St Louis, 1990), 291

J. Blacking: 'Music in Children's Cognitive and Affective Development', *Music and Child Development: Proceedings of the 1987 Denver Conference*, ed. F. R. Wilson and R. L. Roehmann (St Louis, 1990), 68

CHAPTER XII

Dance

JUDITH LYNNE HANNA

The discipline and conceptualization

A 'step-child' of ethnomusicology, as well as of the arts and scholarship, dance in non-Western and folk cultures has been researched primarily by anthropologists. At the beginning of the 20th century, some dances were sketchily described, usually in the context of their society, culture, history and ecology. Evans-Pritchard's 1928 article is an early landmark. Since the 1950s, anthropologists have studied different dance forms and movement analysis. This training permits more complete accounts of dance that include not only the context but also the text, that is, description of the body movement itself. Dance scholars come also from the disciplines of music, ethnomusicology, folklore, theatre, performance studies and literature (Vatsyayan, 1968) as well as dance.

Historical and critical assessments of contributions, theories, and methods and bibliographical annotations and anthologies of dances in world cultures appear in Kurath, 1960; Royce, 1977; Kaeppler, 1978, 1986; Hanna, 1979 'Movements Toward Understanding Humans'; 1989 'The Anthropology of Dance'; 1990 'Dance and Semiotics'; Spencer, 1985; Fleshman, 1986; Forbes, 1986; and Cohen, 1991.

Anthropology encompasses four major fields (archaeology, physical anthropology, linguistics and social and cultural anthropology – the last also referred to as ethnology and sometimes as anthropological semiotics), and numerous subfields. Borrowing from anthropology, several university dance and music departments call the exploration of non-Western and folk dance cultures 'dance ethnology'. It remains more often textually descriptive than theoretical and explanatory.

The discipline of anthropology overlaps the arts, humanities and social, behavioural and physical sciences. Anthropologists, as artists, have expressively and representatively translated dance cultures in articles, books, museum exhibits, films and dramatic format as the re-enactment of ritual or secular events to convey a sense of another culture's dance. Staged dances informed by research are a kind of 'applied' or 'practising' anthropology. Katherine Dunham, searching for her African roots, carried out ethnographic fieldwork in the Caribbean, observing and participating in the social life there. Then in the 1940s, she transformed dances from these areas for the stage. In her lifetime, Dunham choreographed an extensive repertory, some of which continues to be performed today by such companies as the Alvin Ailey American Dance Theater. Anthropologists also conduct research and then teach non-Western and folk dances to teachers for use in the classroom (Kealiinohomoku, 1981; Honko, 1984, on issues involved in the appropriation of other peoples' dances).

As part of the humanities, anthropology seeks to understand dance through a holistic perspective that fits parts together, the dance text itself and the context which provides underlying premises. Qualitative and sometimes quantitative description attempts to answer the question, 'What is it?'. The anthropologist looks at intentionality, the aims and purposes of the doer, the meaning of signs created and their importance. Concern is with the historically and culturally unique. Explanation (ethnology) follows.

As a science, anthropology uses methods that impose a categorical scheme from outside the dance content and abstract elements from a range of examples. Selected analytic categories imposed on dance data are a kind of 'deconstruction' that may be ethnocentric, developed from the researcher's own traditions. However, the categories, not fixed entities but the most applicable at the time of study, are open-ended and altered in light of new theoretical formulations and empirical research. The principal concern of a scientific approach to dance is expressed in a question: is a particular hypothesis supported by available valid and reliable evidence that has been gleaned from a representative sample of the universe in question?

A comparative perspective reveals the uniqueness of a culture as well as the similarity of many cultures. From a broad overview arise hypotheses of greater generality and greater interpretive insight than is possible from a single case. The question is posed: what determines the specific ways in which groups look at the world and how do these views shape their dances? Comparison forces intellectual probing for causes of variability.

Because a researcher's theories and methods in some way determine the results of inquiry, a combination of approaches from these different domains of knowledge may provide the fullest understanding of dance.

Within a number of disciplines, dance often appears under headings such as aesthetics, arts, celebrations, communication, courtship, creativity, economics, education/transmission of culture/acculturation/assimilation, ethnicity, expressive behaviour, folklore, funerals, human movement, initiation rites, mythology, music, non-verbal communication, play, politics, psychology, recreation, reflection of social forces, ritual, semiotics, symbolism, urbanism and war. These headings suggest the scope and significance of dance in human affairs.

A conceptualization of dance creates an analytic unit and is therefore of critical importance for a field of study. Moreover, a conceptualization allows comparison. Although there is no consensus among scholars about what constitutes dance, an analysis since the 1950s of informant specifications, empirical observations, and a survey of the literature on behaviour called dance has led to the following conceptualization: dance is human behaviour composed (from the dancer's perspective, which is usually shared by the audience members of the dancer's culture) of purposeful, intentionally rhythmical and culturally patterned sequences of non-verbal body movements other than ordinary motor activities, the motion (in time, space and with effort) having inherent and 'aesthetic' value and symbolic potential (discussed in Hanna, 1979, 'Movements Toward Understanding Humans'; 1979, *To Dance Is Human*).

Dance is a form through which people represent themselves to themselves and to each other. Because a symbol condenses a number of affectively linked associations within a meaning system, it has an affective charge (Hanna, 1983). Perhaps this is why dance has long held pride of place in religion, ethnic and gender identity, and social stratification (Hanna, 1979, *To Dance Is Human*; 1988, *Dance, Sex and Gender*; 1988, 'The Representation and the Reality'; Kapferer, 1983; Chaki-Sircar, 1984). Whereas words express in sequential form what exists simultaneously in reality, images offer a density of information and immediate insight into what is depicted.

From research on cognition, emotion and non-verbal communication, we know that the kinetic imagery of dance is language-like. It requires the same underlying faculty in the brain for conceptualization, creativity and memory as does verbal language in speaking and writing. Both forms have vocabulary (steps and gestures in dance), grammar (rules for putting the vocabulary together) and semantics. Dance, however, usually assembles these elements in a manner that more often resembles poetry, with its multiple, symbolic, emotional and elusive meanings, than it resembles prose. Yet classical Indian dance, with its ancient elaborate system of codification, has gestures and movements with fixed denotation and prose-like renditions. An American choreographer, Merce Cunningham, made abstract dances that paralleled avant-garde 20th-century writers and poets such as Gertrude Stein, James Joyce and T. S. Eliot. Rather than being a universal language, dance is many languages and dialects.

Some anthropologists study Western performance genres along with non-Western dances because the former are often transformations of the latter or of folk, social and religious dance (Kealiinohomoku, 1969–70; Hanna, 1979, *To Dance Is Human*; 1983, 1986, 1988, *Dance, Sex, and Gender*). Often Western elite dance forms serve as a model for non-Western cultures, in content, style or theatrical convention or as material to parody (for example, Mitchell, 1956; Hanna, 1965, 1983; McKean, 1979). Concern with the gamut of dance genres, a comparative perspective, can be a mind-stretcher and a prejudice-dissolver in understanding human thought and action.

The anthropologist's time frame may be synchronic (dance in a limited period) or diachronic (dance as it changes over time). Much research falls under the rubric of culture change. Dance is often considered in discussions of nature and nurture, what is biologically based or socially determined, including sex roles, and public policy and the arts.

To focus only on the dance text (an internalist perspective) is to leave performances without dancers, choreographers, producers and audiences. Structuralist studies (not in the A. R. Radcliffe-Brown or Claude Lévi-Strauss traditions of comprehending social organization) identify physical movements in space, time and effort or 'steps', phrases, rules for combining these and the resulting regularities in dance form. To focus only on the dance context (an externalist perspective) is to deny the meaningful, expressive articulation and communication of the human body. Functionalist studies, in which the

317

meaning of dance lies in its presumed consequences for the individual and society, have tended to slight the text. Consequently, some anthropologists espouse an integrated paradigm of the micro and macro, the objective and subjective, an examination of both the text and the context of dance and their interrelationship and how the rules of social life impinge on the rules of dance-making.

Dance/music relationships

Dance and music are similar. At times separate, they often co-occur, intertwine with equal status, or depend one upon the other. Dance may be an adjunct of music or vice versa. The variation of relationships between dance and music within and among groups worldwide is yet to be fully explored.

The key element of dance – physical movement – is also an element in the performance of music, but music need not be a component of dance. Movement does not occur separately from sound, while in dance, sound may be a byproduct of movement. Both dance and music use time, space, dynamics and the human body. However, dance and song use the human body as an instrument, whereas instrumental music-making usually uses the human body to animate an inanimate object. In dancing, the human moving body is the critical end product; in music-making humanly organized sound is most significant.

Dance and music have intentionality in rhythm and patterned, temporarily unfolding phenomena. They use accent, the significant stress with which energy is released; duration, the relative length of time of actions; metre, the underlying consistent patterns of beats and accents; and tempo, the rate or speed at which actions follow one another. Both musicians and dancers have the ability to alter time and lead individuals into altered states of conscious-ness (Rouget, 1985; Hanna, 1988, *Dance and Stress*). Alan Merriam (1979, p.13) says that 'the powerful nature' of Basongye musicians' skill makes them rather dangerous'. The Dogon of Mali describe the rapid *gona* dance movement 'as a relief, like vomiting' (Griaule, 1965, p.188).

Through its kinetic images, dance permits greater and less abstract symbolic manipulation of time. For example, more concretely and less ambiguously than music, dance can articulate the biological time of heart-beat, ageing, energy expenditure and fatigue.

The use of time merges dance and music. Korean drum-dances range from a performer dancing with a simple hour-glass drum slung in front of the body by a neck strap to elaborately choreographed dances executed inside frames from which nine drums are suspended. In the Japanese *nohgaku*, the *o-tsuzumi*, *ko-tsuzumi* and *taiko* drummers perform with stylized movements contrapuntally designed for maximal visual impact. Their strokes interact with the musical patterns. An American tap dancer has to sound good as well as look good. Indeed, Chuck Green's tap dancing was broadcast on radio.

Musicians may occasionally leave their music-making role during a performance event and take on the role of dancer, as Flamenco singers and guitar players do. A Balinese *kebyar* performer dances, makes stylized movements in playing the *trompong* (a row of gong-kettles) as part of the gamelan ensemble, and then frees himself from the instrument to dance again.

318

Patterns of musician–dancer relationships include mirroring, opposing or interplaying with each other (Blom and Kvifte, 1986). Dancers may accompany themselves with instruments, such as castanets in flamenco. They may sing, hum, stamp or tap their feet; or they may beat out body sounds with claps, slaps or finger snaps. African-Americans in Dallas, Texas, beat out body sounds and dance their songs and sing their dances during free time at school (Hanna, 1986). Among Nigeria's Ubakala Igbo, young girls sound the pellet bells tied about their chests when they shimmy, sometimes adding yet another rhythmic pattern to the instrumental music. The Ubakala word for dance is also the word for drum and play.

The Inupiat dance song *sayuun* has meaningful words that have traditional fixed dance movements. By contrast, the *atuutipiag* does not; dancers freely create dance movements to the vocables depending on how they feel (Pulu and others, 1979, p.1). Whereas the drummers sing the tunes but do not dance, the dancers may choose whether or not to sing (p.4).

Westerners have tended to view dance as the handmaiden of music: generally, the more complete the music, the less suited it is to dance. However, some dances are performed without music, for example, Bosnia's *licko*, *glamoc* and *vrlicko* (Larry Weiner, folk dance leader). Jerome Robbins's ballet 'Moves', created in 1959, is silent. Dancers may forgo music for various reasons, including the search for rhythms inherent in life (such as breathing and muscular dynamics), emotion, dramatic effect or calling attention to the sound of the moving body.

Dancing may guide music-making. When J. Chernoff (1979, p.66) told Ghanaian Dagomba drummers that he wanted to learn to play their music, he was told, 'I hope that you are also trying to learn the dancing . . . you have to mind the dancers . . . the drum beaters should be following the dancers'. In Bali, the gamelan instrumental ensemble follows the dancer's improvisation in telling a story in the 'Baris' and 'Topeng' dances.

Attracting attention and evoking physiological responses in performers and observers, both dance and music are multisensory. There is physical movement, the feeling of kinesthetic action or empathy; the sight of performers, and sometimes the audience; the touch of body to performing areas as in standing or locomotion, to the performer's own body or to another's body in dance, the touch of the body to the instrument in music-making; the sound of physical movement, the impact of the feet or other body supports on the 'stage', and heavy breathing in high energy presentations in dance, the sound of the instrument in music; the smell of physical exertion and perhaps the smell of the ingestion of food and drink that accompanies a performance event. With the exception of conducting, the visual/kinesthetic senses are primary in dance, whereas the auditory/kinesthetic senses predominate in music-making.

Although the primary products of dance and music differ, the structural processes of production and performance, the relationship of text (physical movement for dance and sounds for music) to context, and devices and spheres of encoding and decoding meaning are similar (see Hanna, 1979, *To Dance Is Human*, pp.76–82). Individual, social and/or physical elements catalyse a dance or music performance. The dancer, or musician, performing a social role, perceives a situation, such as a wedding or political conflict. For both there are motivations, incentives and desired rewards. The performer makes movement or sound choices with some intention (to inform, evaluate, prescribe and/or effect) or without specific intention but with the possibility that information transfer may occur. Intent becomes transformed through the communication medium or channel of performance, the body in dance and the body and instrument in music. Messages are sent through the performance. Rules about what is required, preferred or permitted govern the combination of dance or music elements. (In some performances the rule may be to ignore the usual rules.) The performer encodes messages using devices that operate in one or more spheres within the rules governing the combination of these elements through the channel of performance. The performance may include adjunct channels, such as costume.

If there is no interference, the audience decodes messages of intrinsic form and/or extrinsic reference and makes some assessment. The audience reaction may have a recognized or unrecognized effect. However, the performance has implications for the performer, the audience and the context of the performance.

Methods of data collection and analysis

Because dance and music differ in instrument used and senses stimulated, the research methods and analytic categories of analysing their texts differ. Movement data categories (Hanna, 1979, *To Dance Is Human*, pp.245–6) are less relevant to music. Sound categories are often irrelevant to analysing dance.

MOVEMENT Ethnography, developed as a reaction to speculative history, entails a researcher engaging in participant observation, joining in dances where this is acceptable. Seeing and physically moving in culture's dance shapes, time and dynamics aid the researcher in describing dance movement.

Highly trained movement analysts may variously perceive, interpret and notate a dance (van Zile, 1986; Davis, 1987). Among the other problems with dance notation, accurate and speedy notation of a dance, using any of several systems (such as Labanalysis or Benesh) in its field context is nearly impossible. Or some dances may be performed only once during a research visit, and some dancers may be unable or unwilling to replicate a performance, as is necessary for notation. Consequently, anthropologists now preserve dance behaviour on film and video.

These recording processes make what happens more objectively accessible to the researcher and others. Nonetheless, some selectivity in what is filmed and how it is filmed is unavoidable. An ideal situation would involve several camera people shooting from different perspectives. Audiovisual recording permits valid and reliable analysis and reanalysis of units of movement in slow motion, in much the same way a musicologist uses a tape recording to prepare a transcript and describe patterns (Hanna, 1989, 'African Dance Frame by Frame').

Whereas some researchers use the ideographic movement notation of Labanalysis, others describe movement using Rudolf Laban's movement categories (Hutchinson, 1954; Dell, 1970) to make their work accessible to a

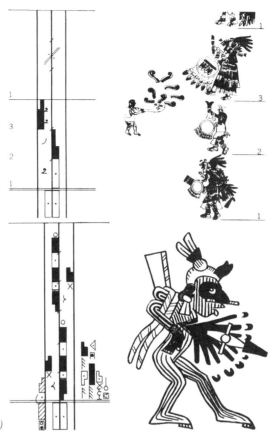

Gods dancing to a drum (Codex Borbonicus; top) with Labanotation (left) reading step forward right; flex right knee, touching left toe; brush left forward and sacrificial victim (Codex Borgia; bottom) with Labanotation (left) reading flexed back leg and withdrawn posture; backward stepping with double bounce on each foot (from Hanna, 1979)

wider audience and to identify reoccurring patterns (Hanna, 1979, *To Dance Is Human*, pp.245–6). Many movement categories are applicable to music-making.

MEANING Although there were tools for describing movement in the 1970s, none existed to probe its meaning. A semantic grid was developed to meet this need (Hanna, 1979, *To Dance Is Human*, pp.40–46; 1979, 'Toward Semantic Analysis'); at least six *devices* for conveying meaning may be utilized in dance.

1. A *concretization* is movement that produces the outward aspect of something as in courtship dances showing potential lovers' advance and retreat tactics. In music, sounds that imitate nature (birds, thunder, crashes) – such as in Beethoven's 'Pastoral Symphony', Vivaldi's 'Primavera', the Ugandan Ankole's imitation of noises made by cattle or the Central African Ba-Benzlele's 'bee-buzzing' in a honey-hunting song – are concretizations.

2. The *icon* represents most properties or formal characteristics of a thing, event, or condition and is responded to as if it were what it represents. For example, a Haitian possessed by Ghede, god of love and death, who manifests his presence through dancing, may be treated with genuine awe by the

321

Haitians and with behaviour appropriate to their gender – as if he were the god (Deren, 1972).

3. A *stylization* encompasses arbitrary and conventional gestures or movements as the *danseur* pointing to his heart as a sign of love for his lady. In music, cultures assign meaning to arbitrary sound as the military bugle call. Detective movies use the wailing sax to evoke the 1940s big city at night.

4. A romantic duet representing a more encompassing relationship, such as a marriage, is a *metonym*. A war dance, or song, as part of a battle, is another example.

5. A *metaphor* is the expression of something in place of another that it resembles to suggest an analogy between the two, such as a fairy tale love story between animals to denote the situation between human lovers. Dancing the role of a leopard, or playing the song of a leopard, may denote the power of death.

6. An *actualization* is a portrayal of one or several of a dancer's usual roles. This occurs, especially in theatrical settings where there is not a rigid boundary between performer and spectator, when dancers express their own sexual preferences through dance (heterosexual or homosexual seduction of a spectator) and the audience member accepts or rejects a dancer. Louis XIV danced the role of king and was treated as such in contrast to how he was treated when dancing other roles. Oscar Levant, the cynical composer, plays himself in the movie 'Ten'.

The devices for encapsulating meaning in dance and music seem to operate within one or more of eight *spheres*: (i) the dance event, as when people go to the ballet or opera to be seen socially or to seek sexual partners or fantasy, dance-viewing or opera-watching being incidental; (ii) the total human body in action, as in girl- or boy-watching; (iii) the whole pattern of the performance which may emphasize form, style, feeling or drama; (iv) the sequence of unfolding movement, including who does what to whom and how in dramatic episodes or sound configurations; (v) specific movements and how they are performed, for example, a male dancer parodying a woman on *pointe*, or specific sounds; (vi) the intermesh of movements or sounds with other communication modes such as speech or costume; (vii) dance or music as a vehicle for another medium, like serving as a backdrop for a performer's poetry recitation; and (viii) presence, the emotional turn-on through projected sensuality or raw animality. Singly, or in combination, the devices and spheres allow us to consider message material.

Anthropologists have demonstrated that we must turn to society and not just to the dancer's experience to understand the meaning of dance. It is a reflection of social forces (Spencer, 1985). At the same time, dance may be more than epiphenomenal and serve as a vehicle through which individuals influence social forces. That is, dance may reflect what is and also influence what might be (Hanna, 1979, *To Dance Is Human*; 1986, 1988, *Dance, Sex, and Gender*; 1988, *Dance and Stress*). Individual choreographies take shape in cultural material that is used to maintain or challenge the status quo.

Among the Ubakala Igbo of Nigeria, dance conveys traditional values about family roles, political processes, economic patterns, and religious precepts. At the same time dance is a vehicle to assert what should be. The 1929 'Women's War' is a notable example of dance catalysing change.

Inattention to women's danced grievances about taxation and abuses of indigenous representatives of the colonial government led to subsequent violence and moved the mighty British to alter their colonial administration of what was then called Eastern Nigeria.

Because the body is the instrument of dance, anthropologists look at attitudes toward the lived-in, ubiquitous, sentient body in a people's cultural system. People's experiences with the first form of power, their bodies, tap potent, dramatic, and easy-to-recall sources of images that influence their responses to dance as participant or observer. Using the signature key of sexuality, essential for survival and desirable for pleasure, dance resonates universal instincts and particular concerns. The medium is part of the dance message.

Precedents of meaning in everyday use of the body and movement are part of a choreographer's and spectator's cultural inheritance. Dance-makers seek signs and symbols people can relate to, as well as sometimes to create new ones. Social relations of who does what when, where, why and how, alone and with or to whom appear in the dance.

Western theatrical dance is compartmentalized in the sense of being largely relegated to the sphere of entertainment or art for its own sake. By contrast, dance in many societies is an integral part of religious, social, economic, or political life. Irrespective of time and place, however, dance is a powerful means of communicating a group's values and beliefs and transmitting them from one generation to the next.

Dances derive from and contribute to evolving culture. In much the same way as animal ritualized displays, the motion of dance attracts attention. As a result, dance 'frames' messages and thereby bestows power upon them. The optical array of dance messages may lead to reinforcing ongoing patterns of social behaviour, acquiring new responses, weakening or strengthening inhibitions over fully elaborated patterns in a person's repertory, and facilitating performance of previously learned behaviour which was unencumbered by restraints (see Bandura's modelling theory [1972], on how we learn through images).

Prior to 1957 anthropologists generally had viewed people as existing in a culture and described their patterns of behaviour. More recently culture is presupposed to be in people's heads; culture is considered a branch of cognitive psychology (see Shweder and LeVine, 1984, on controversies and approaches to the study of culture).

Reliance upon an informant's verbal exegesis alone for indigenous cultural description and analysis, however, may preclude understanding some people's dance. The language of dance is non-verbal and not easily translatable lexically. Indeed, people express themselves non-verbally in part because words are less adequate for some communication (see Barko, 1977). Renowned American dancer Isadora Duncan put it this way: 'If I could *tell* you what I mean, there would be no point in dancing'. In many cultures, instruction and learning occur through dancing and watching, that is, without recourse to words. Yet contemporary theories of socialization have nothing to say about what people convey to each other through dance.

Lexicality is only part of a culture. There are alternative ways of knowing, glossing experience, and different types of competencies, including bodily kinesthetic competence (Gardner, 1983). Some people think, express themselves and learn through images (Gazzaniga, 1985, p.32). People also take cognizance of smoke and act upon olfactory information without being able to put into words the attributes and meanings of smoke itself.

Many features of dance lie beyond the conscious awareness of dancers and viewers. In American culture, most social dancers do not know the names of specific steps in such dances as the waltz, rock and roll or disco (Cottle, 1966). Just as the grammarians and linguists are knowledgeable about vocabulary and syntax, so movement analysts are familiar with the comparable elements in dance.

S. Krebs, in a valuable, innovative approach, used film playback of Thai dance for Thai informants to elicit meaning (1975). However, even when an informant tells the researcher a dance movement name or symbolic meaning, it is necessary to know what actually is being said. Things taken for granted may not be articulated; lies, rationalizations, jokes, and metaphors are possibilities. Like poetry, dance is polysemous, that is, layered with many meanings. Dance is also similar to a Rorschach ink blot test which each person interprets on the basis of individual experience and culturally influenced perception. Of course, some dance cultures (for example, classical Western ballet and classical Indian dance) have codified systems with names of steps and specific meanings. Even so, participants in these cultures may not engage in further reflective dance discourse or analysis.

When a group does not have its own (emic) verbalized aesthetic views about its dance culture, the researcher's intervention in trying to elicit verbalization rather than see the action may in fact be imperialistic and trigger a new way of thought for the native, namely, an outsider (etic) phenomenon.

Some anthropologists follow the tenets of always questioning their own assumptions and apparent facts and observations, attempting to discover the insiders' or 'natives'' points of view, to describe their behaviour, to note the relationship between what is said and what is done and to convey information about a group to other outsiders. Certainly, there is variation within a group based on such factors as age, gender and other elements of social stratification (Pelto, 1975).

HISTORY Researchers sometimes explore movement and meaning through time. Resources to recover behaviour and thought include archaeological artefacts, ancient texts, travel and newspaper reports, key informants, and critics' reviews. As social agents of a culture, the critics fulfil a role assigned to those who convey knowledge. Criticism is often the only record of a performance. Reading the critics can be a form of interviewing and historical content analysis (Hanna, 1988, *Dance, Sex, and Gender*).

'Ethnomusicologists often neutralize dance for fear of lacking interpretive knowledge, but dance is often central to what they study' (Robertson, 1989). In many cultures movement reveals the structure and performance of sound; through embodying a people's dance in one's own physicality, one can gain an understanding of their music. Illustratively, in Nigeria, Tiv music has multiple metres within its percussive whole. When an anthropologist was directly challenged to dance, she arrived at the essential truth of the matter: ' "Teach me then", I retorted. Duly, she and the other senior women began my instruction: my hands and feet were to keep time with the gongs, my hips with

324

the first drum, my back and shoulders with the second . . .' (Bowen, 1954, p.123).

Compared to music and ethnomusicology, the scholarly field of dance is less developed. Only recently has the academic world considered dance a significant element of human culture and behaviour and therefore a legitimate subject of study. Impediments include the disparagement of dance because of prejudices reflecting distrust of the body and emotion and the inferior social status of many theatrical performers. Both the French and Industrial revolutions placed emphasis on the mind; the body was made the vehicle of production. Verbal, not non-verbal, language took pride of place. Besides, scholars had tended to be men, and in Anglo-Saxon culture men's dancing had effeminate, homosexual overtones.

Some scholars early on rationalized the neglect of dance study on the grounds that it was not subject to notation and recording. But verbal descriptions of movement and systems of notation have a long history, and now audiovisual recording is available – although the costs often are prohibitive.

Since the 1960s there has been a greater acceptance of the body, an increase in female scholars, the explosion of all forms of theatrical dance performance, a recognition and appreciation of the intertwining of mind and body, cognition and emotion, the discovery of how we learn from images and the appearance of new nations whose cultures pique curiosity. These changes catalysed the blossoming of dance scholarship in new book and journal publications, university dance programmes, and research centres throughout the world.

Bibliography

E. Evans-Pritchard: 'The Dance', *Africa*, i (1928), 436
C. Sachs: *Eine Weltgeshichte des Tanzes* (Berlin, 1933; Eng. trans., 1937/*R*1963)
E. Bowen [L. Bohannan]: *Return to Laughter* (New York, 1954)
A. Hutchinson: *Labanotation* (New York, 1954, rev. and enl. 2/1970)
J. Mitchell: *The Kalela Dance* (Manchester, 1956)
G. Kurath: 'Panorama of Dance Ethnology', *Current Anthropology*, i/3 (1960), 233
M. Griaule: *Conversations with Ogotemmeli* (London, 1965)
J. Hanna: 'Africa's New Traditional Dance', *EM*, ix/1 (1965), 13
T. Cottle: 'Social Class and Social Dancing', *Sociological Quarterly*, vii (1966), 179
K. Vatsyayan: *Classical Indian Dance in Literature and the Arts* (New Delhi, 1968)
J. Kealiinohomoku: 'An Anthropologist Looks at Ballet as a Form of Ethnic Dance', *Impulse: Extensions of Dance* (1969–70), 24
C. Dell: *A Primer for Movement Description Using Effort-Shape and Supplementary Concepts* (New York, 1970)
A. Bandura: 'Modeling Theory: Some Traditions, Trends, and Disputes', *Recent Trends in Social Learning Theory*, ed. R. D. Park (New York, 1972), 35
M. Deren: *Divine Horsemen: Voodoo Gods of Haiti* (New York, 1972)
S. Krebs: 'The Film Elicitation Technique: Using Film to Elicit Conceptual Categories of Culture', *Principles of Visual Anthropology*, ed. P. Hockings (The Hague, 1975), 283
P. Pelto: 'Intra-cultural Diversity: Some Theoretical Issues', *American Ethnologist*, ii/1 (1975), 1
C. Barko: 'The Dancer and the Becoming of Language', *Yale French Studies*, liv (1977), 173
A. Royce: *The Anthropology of Dance* (Bloomington, IN, 1977)
J. Chernoff: *African Rhythm and African Sensibility: Aesthetics and Social Action in African Musical Idioms* (Chicago, 1979)
A. Kaeppler: 'Dance in Anthropological Perspective', *Annual Review of Anthropology*, vii (1978), 31

J. Hanna: 'Movements Toward Understanding Humans through the Anthropological Study of Dance', *Current Anthropology*, xx/2 (1979), 313

—— : *To Dance Is Human: a Theory of Nonverbal Communication* (Chicago, 1979/*R*1987)

—— : 'Toward Semantic Analysis of Movement Behaviour: Concepts and Problems', *Semiotica*, xxv/1–2 (1979), 77

P. F. McKean: 'From Purity to Pollution? The Balinese Ketjak (Monkey Dance) as Symbolic Form in Transition', *The Imagination of Reality: Essays in Southeast Asian Coherence Systems*, ed. A. Becker and A. Yongoyan (Norwood, PA, 1979), 293

A. Merriam: 'Basongye Musicians and Institutionalized Social Deviance', *YIFMC*, xi (1979), 1

T. Pulu and others: *Inupiat Aggisit Atuutinich Inupiat Dance Songs* (Anchorage, 1979)

J. Kealiinohomoku: 'Ethical Considerations for Choreographers, Ethnologists, and White Nights', *Journal of the Association of Graduate Dance Ethnologists*, v (1981), 10

H. Gardner: *Frames of Mind: a Theory of Multiple Intelligences* (New York, 1983)

J. Hanna: *The Performer-Audience Connection: Emotion to Metaphor in Dance and Society* (Austin, 1983)

B. Kapferer: *A Celebration of Demons: Exorcism and the Aesthetics of Healing in Sri Lanka* (Bloomington, IN, 1983)

M. Chaki-Sircar: *Feminism in a Traditional Society: Women of the Manipur Valley* (New Delhi, 1984)

L. Honko: 'Do We Need an International Treaty for the Protection of Folklore?' *NIF* [Nordic Institute of Folklore] *Newsletter*, xii/3 (1984), 3

R. Shweder and R. LeVine: *Culture Theory: Essays on Mind, Self and Emotion* (Cambridge, 1984)

M. Gazzaniga: 'The Social Brain', *Psychology Today*, xix/11 (1985), 29

G. Rouget: *Music and Trance: a Theory of the Relations between Music and Possession* (Chicago, 1985)

P. Spencer, ed.: *Society and the Dance: the Social Anthropology of Process and Performance* (Cambridge, 1985)

J.-P. Blom and T. Kvifte: 'On the Problem of Inferential Ambivalence in Musical Meter', *EM*, xxx (1986), 491

B. Fleshman, ed.: *Theatrical Movement: a Bibliographical Anthology* (Metuchen, 1986)

F. Forbes: *Dance: an Annotated Bibliography, 1965–1982* (New York, 1986)

J. Hanna: 'Interethnic Communication in Children's Own Dance, Play, and Protest', *International and Intercultural Communication Annual*, ed. Y. Y. Kim, x (Beverly Hills, 1986), 176

A. Kaeppler: 'Cultural Analysis, Linguistic Analogies, and the Study of Dance in Anthropological Perspective', *Explorations in Ethnomusicology: Essays in Honor of David P. McAllester*, ed. C. Frisbie (Stuyvesant, 1986), 25

J. van Zile: 'Do You See What I See? Do You Say What I Say?' [Paper presented at the Conference on Researching Dance Through Video and Film sponsored by the Congress on Research in Dance and the Human Studies Film Archives, Smithsonian Institution] (Washington, DC, 1986)

M. Davis: 'Movement Studies: Observer Agreement', *Journal of the Laban/Bartenieff Institute of Movement Studies*, ii (1987)

J. Hanna: *Dance, Sex, and Gender: Signs of Identity, Dominance, Defiance, and Desire* (Chicago, 1988)

—— : 'The Representation and Reality of Divinity in Dance', *Journal of the American Academy of Religion*, vi/2 (1988), 281

—— : *Dance and Stress: Resistance, Reduction, and Euphoria* (New York, 1988)

—— : 'African Dance Frame by Frame: Revelation of Sex Roles through Distinctive Feature Analysis and Comment on Field Research, Film, and Notation', *Journal of Black Studies*, vi (1989), 422

—— : 'The Anthropology of Dance', *Dance: Current Selected Research I*, ed. L. Overby and J. Humphrey (New York, 1989), 219

C. Robertson, personal communication, 31 May, 1989

J. Hanna: 'Dance and Semiotics', *Semiotics in the Individual Sciences*, ed. W. Koch (Bochum, 1990), 352

S. Cohen, ed.: *International Encyclopedia of Dance* (Berkeley, 1991)

PART THREE

Ethical Concerns and New Directions

CHAPTER XIII

Ethical Issues

MARK SLOBIN

All ethnomusicologists have probably had a moment of ethical awareness at some point in their work, yet few, if any, see fit to publicize such moments, so there appear to have been no self-reflective statements on ethical issues in ethnomusicology until the 1970s. In the USA, the notion of open discussion of ethics came about as a result of the parallel situation in anthropology. Racked by internal dissension over the uses of anthropological research in Asia and Latin America in the late 1960s, members of the American Anthropological Association began a highly vocal, public debate which reached the ears of American ethnomusicologists. The panel on ethics at the Society for Ethnomusicology (SEM) meeting at Toronto in 1972 was the first of such events, held spontaneously every few years since then. Beginning also in the 1970s, scholars began to mention ethical issues and dilemmas in their publications. Barbara Krader's brief comment on ethics in *The New Grove Dictionary of Music and Musicians*, under 'Ethnomusicology' (1980), was the first such discussion in a standard reference work.

A consideration of ethical issues in the discipline can draw on several sources: (i) material generated within the Committee on Ethics (1973–80) of the Society for Ethnomusicology; (ii) statements of the American Anthropological Association (AAA); and (iii) writings of ethnomusicologists and others on ethics. By and large, such discussion as has emerged within ethnomusicology has been based on five assumptions.

1. Ethics is largely an issue for 'Western' scholars working in 'non-Western' societies. Thus, Nahoma Sachs's 'Introduction' to a proposed (but not completed) 'Handbook on Ethics of the Committee on Ethics' states: 'Having not consensually agreed upon higher authority to legitimize our suggestions, we have agreed to orient them to the special needs and problems of the population to whom they are addressed: ethnomusicologists who are members of Western society.'

2. Most ethical concerns arise from interpersonal relations between scholar and 'informant' as a consequence of fieldwork. For example, the 'Preamble' to the AAA's 1971 'Principles of Professional Responsibility' begins: 'Anthropologists work in many parts of the world in close personal association with the people and situations they study.'

3. Further arenas of ethical consideration include such headings as are detailed in the outline for the proposed SEM ethics handbook: relations with

the host government, relations with local institutions (these topics still relate to fieldwork), relations with one's own government, sponsorship of research, relations with other scholars, archival agreements, relations with publishers (including sound recording), relations with the public and relations with students.

4. Ethics is situated within what Ralph Beals has called 'the declared purpose' of the researcher: 'the increase of knowledge in the ultimate service of human welfare' (1969, p.2). Thus, the 1963 'Code of Ethics' of the Society for Applied Anthropology, a group especially concerned with the effects of fieldwork, sees ethics in the light of the scholar's 'responsibilities to his client, to science and to his fellow men', the three apparently having an equal claim on his conscience. The 'Code' also states that 'when these responsibilities are in conflict, he must insist on a redefinition of the terms of his employment,' which puts a great deal of strain on the system in view of the high probability of potential conflict.

5. Discussion of ethical issues proceeds from values of Western culture (of which point 4 above might well be an example).

These assumptions have produced some concomitant results: first a lack of discussion of other potential ethical arenas, for example work in Eastern-bloc countries on local musics, work in 'Third World' countries by local scholars, or work by Western scholars on Western musics. The last-named category has some resonance for American scholars, based on factors such as a sensitivity to the long-term appropriation and profiteering of minority musics by the music industry and to the politics of a large, multi-ethnic democracy. Yet another area not yet discussed is the ethics of non-Westerners studying Western musics. Insofar as it has been foreseen, it has been viewed optimistically, as in Krader's statement in *The New Grove Dictionary of Music and Musicians* (6th edn) or Charles Keil's notion (1979, p.5) that as 'more of "them" may want to study "us", a more interested anthropology will emerge . . . in the sense of intersubjective, intercultural . . . critical, revolutionary'. This stance implies that 'they' are more likely to be better at handling ethical issues than 'we' are, but still defines proper action in terms of Western values only, leading to a second point: the lack of a cross-cultural approach to value systems. This issue touches on a philosophical position pointed out by Antonio Gramsci; he cites what he calls Kant's maxim, 'Act in such a way that your conduct can become a norm for all men in similar conditions' (which could almost be a summary of a standard approach to ethics in ethnomusicology), then criticizes it as presupposing 'a single culture, a single religion, a "world-wide" conformism' (1971). Although one can find commentary on this situation in the social sciences at times – 'Whose ethics shall be favoured?' (Beals, 1969, p.82), it is an issue rarely raised in ethnomusicology.

How does one recognize violations of the appropriate ethical norms? Are not violations in the eye of the beholder, since ethics tends to be situational? It is easier to identify what Beals calls 'obvious causes of misunderstandings and conflicts' which may lead to breaches of ethical codes. His convenient, but partial, list includes 'the researcher's choice of a sensitive research topic, his acceptance of questionable sponsorship, his concealment of information and misrepresentation of facts, his invasion of privacy and inadequate protection of his subjects, his overidentification with his subjects and his failure to be personally perfect from his host's point of view, his host's national pride and expectation that the research will be relevant to local needs as well as abhorrence of any suggestion of neocolonialism or imperialism, special interest group's pressures, and the area's saturation with researchers' (1969, p.25). Added to this for ethnomusicologists are the myriad problems arising from the learning, collection, exporting and dissemination (some class all this as 'appropriation') of a group's expressive culture, specifically its music and perhaps its musical instruments.

Thus the embryonic state of ethical awareness in ethnomusicology is evident. It is due partly to the apparent and overwhelming apathy of professional ethnomusicologists towards public airing of such issues. When the Ethics Committee of the SEM attempted to stimulate such a discussion in the mid-1970s through techniques adopted in the AAA (questionnaires, a regular ethics column in the Newsletter), responses were so negligible as to indicate lack of interest in ethics as an openly broached topic. In the late 1970s, however, scholars began to touch upon the epistemological and implicit ethical issues faced in their work as they presented their research findings in print.

An early and articulate example of this trend is the 'Introduction' in Paul Berliner's 1978 book *The Soul of Mbira* (see also a more radical self-critique in Keil's 1979 *Tiv Song*). In it, the author recounts the difficulties he faced getting the 'real' tuning system for an African instrumental style. Finally, a key musician gave him the necessary data, thanks to the hard-won personal relationship achieved between researcher and informant: ' . . . he decided that I was worthy of being entrusted with the single piece of information that I sought to collect from him only after six years of studying *mbira* music, three trips to Africa, and many rigorous tests' (1978, p.7). What is the implicit ethical stance behind Berliner's description? First, it is understood that ethical issues arise from the *role* of researcher: this is the problem of the prying outsider, frequently discussed in anthropology. Secondly, the *personality* of the ethnomusicologist comes into play: it is possible for individuals to transcend the basic role, thereby overcoming the mistrust often inherent in outsider status. Implied here, and often explicitly stated in fieldwork manuals, is the notion that *tact* will win the day, involving a show of persistence and respect by the researcher which will impress those whom he needs for his work. As always, the work is understood to be the gathering of 'accurate' data for the purpose of 'scholarship', called 'science' by some early ethnomusicologists.

If that were all to Berliner's account, it would be noteworthy only for its honesty about the problems of getting 'reliable' data and would still be grounded in the older positivistic approach to ethnomusicology which saw 'science' as the goal. Here, the only ethical problem is whether the appropriation of insiders' knowledge about music is done in the right spirit. However, there is more to Berliner's agenda. By revealing the fragility and incompleteness of the 'scientific' knowledge about *mbira* he had reached prior to the 'transcendental' fieldwork moment, he implicitly criticizes the propriety of most, if not all, scholarship arrived at by such methods. The alert reader begins to wonder how much of the following chapter's description of *mbira* is based on understandings reached before a 'decisive' interview was achieved, a question the author does not answer. Though rooted in the old ways, Berliner's introduction points to a newer ethical dilemma: how should we do our work if we no longer believe in positivism? After all, we now do our work in an age where philosophers of the social sciences say that 'it is generally agreed that the manner in which objectivity in meaning is achieved, along with a specification of the rules for when it is not, remains unsatisfactorily explicated' (Gergen, 1986, p.138).

The present discussion does not move towards consideration of these issues, since they overstep the notion of ethics as presently understood in the field. Nevertheless, it is worth pointing out for the future that once the 'interpretive turn' (Geertz, 1983, p.23), as defined in the social sciences and anthropology, becomes an important issue in ethnomusicology, new ethical questions will arise in a post-positivist age.

Ethnomusicologists have lagged somewhat behind anthropology on this issue; anthropologist Raymond Firth was already reporting on a well-advanced trend when in 1973 he identified a 'retreat from empirical reality', including 'the recognition of observer-effect' and 'a challenge to positivism' (1973, p.125). By 1986, the anthropologists G. E. Marcus and M. M. J. Fischer could note that 'the most interesting theoretical debates in a number of fields have shifted to the level of method, to problems of epistemology, interpretation and discursive forms of representation themselves, employed by social thinkers; . . . social thought . . . has grown more suspicious of the ability of encompassing paradigms to ask the right questions, let alone provide answers, about the variety of local responses to the operation of global systems' (1986, p.9), all of which suggests that a new approach to professional ethics must eventually accompany this shift in sensibility towards ethnographic work. Current statements from philosophy make it clear we are liable to be at sea for some time, for example Bernard Williams's bald statement that 'the resources of most modern moral philosophy are not well-adjusted to the modern world' (1985, p.197).

For the present, it seems best to remain within the bounds of problems raised by the earlier modes of inquiry, looking at a few sample situations. There have been two modes of public discussion of ethics: hypothetical case studies and personal accounts; for example, the former was adopted at the 1972 SEM panel, the latter at a 1978 discussion. Another approach, the hearing of ethical complaints and censuring of scholars, was raised and rejected by SEM, partly on the advice of veterans of the anthropology battles in the USA, who noted that making moral pronouncements about individuals' activity was bad for the morale of a scholarly society and perhaps itself an unethical practice. Any discussion of particular situations involving ethical dilemmas quickly reveals the situational nature of ethics: no generalized response provides an easy answer in light of the very specific nature of the immediate circumstances surrounding each case. This weakens the usefulness of arguing even hypothetical cases, since context is lacking. This situation may help explain the apathy towards ethics discussions: if everything depends on context, why bother talking about the issues? The answer suggested here is: confronting ethical dilemmas may not yield timeless wisdom, but it certainly sharpens the mind.

Following is a selection of sample cases illustrating standard areas of ethical concern, with brief discussion of implications and alternatives. This is the method still used in the 'Ethical Dilemmas' column of the Newsletter of the

AAA. Some of the cases cited here are based on actual experience, while others are purely hypothetical.

CASE 1: THE RARE MUSICAL INSTRUMENT You are doing fieldwork and encounter an old musician with an unusual instrument, seemingly the only one of its kind. Should you buy it and place it in a museum for preservation?

Against acquisition: leave culture and its artefact where they belong. To remove an instrument is to mutilate local culture, particularly if the object is not immediately replaceable.

For acquisition: it is essential to preserve a record of the world's music in all its diversity in publicly accessible places. Otherwise, musical change, an inevitable part of history, will erase the memory of the instrument and its repertory (which you can tape). If the tradition is a viable one, local musicians will revive it; if not, it is best to save it for the future, even for the group itself.

This case highlights the kinship of ethnomusicology to anthropology and archaeology, which often face dilemmas based on the acquisition of indigenous artefacts. Those disciplines have not developed clear-cut answers to such issues, as the notion of acquisition can be differentially understood by all actors in the process and is variable over time; ethnomusicology has not even formulated any policy in this area.

CASE 2: A DOCUMENTARY FILM Due to your success as a fieldworker, an old practitioner has granted you permission to film sacred ceremonies, with the proviso that you must be present when the film is shown to avoid misinterpretation by the audience. What should the ultimate disposition of the film be after you die?
    1. Give the film to the practitioner's family. This raises problems of their reliability vis-à-vis the understanding you reached with the old man, now gone: can you trust them to keep the faith?
    2. Put the film in an archive with instructions that it is not to be viewed. Then of what use is this 'scientific document' to the future of knowledge, the supposed aim of research?
    3. Train someone you trust to present the film as you presented it. This continues the spirit of the original agreement but builds in a risk of future breaches.
    4. Destroy the film. With your death, the original agreement and hence the film have lapsed. Of course, 'science' loses a document, but there may be ways to fill this slight gap.

This case involves a different sort of artefact than Case 1: the ethnomusicological object is created by the scholar with complicity by the informant. A great deal of dispute in ethnomusicology centres on the production and fate of such artefacts, which 'capture' local musics, usually in the form of film or sound recordings in a variety of media. Case 2 avoids the usual issues of permission and royalties (cited below) and goes directly to the question of the understanding reached between scholar and subject about presentation. There seems no clear solution to the problem of how to 'satisfy' the ethnomusicologist, the musician and 'science', despite the hope of ethical codes that one can do so.

CASE 3: RECORD ROYALTIES On your first field trip, you paid a musician to play for you, explaining that people in your country will be interested in his music. You return to the field and give the musician a copy of the documentary sound recording you made. You can:

1. Assume that the generous fee you gave him originally covers his appearance on the record.

2. Tell him that this record has brought you no income at all, and that if it ever does, you will send him some money.

3. Give him an extra flat fee as a recording royalty.

4. Give him multiple copies of the record for his friends.

5. Try to arrange for a local company to distribute the record.

. . . Or any number of other possible arrangements.

This is an area of extremely grey ethical consideration in which it is hard to presuppose a solution without a great deal of contextual information. Most ethnomusicologists would probably feel that the rapport with the particular musician is the major factor here, rather than a uniform policy on royalties. Two or three solutions might be needed for different musicians from varied locales or local status levels. The question of whether the record was premeditated or evolved as a project after fieldwork makes some difference here. There are roving pseudo- or quasi-ethnomusicologists who have muddied these waters by producing records after the most casual of contact with local musicians without informing them of the intention to market their music; such behaviour would probably be universally condemned in the discipline, and could lead to a situation such as Case 6 below.

CASE 4: PARTIAL PERMISSION IN THE FIELD You have been given access to a hitherto esoteric ceremony by a member of a ritual group and arrive with recording gear. It becomes clear that agreement about your presence is not unanimous.

1. You excuse yourself and leave. In this conflict situation, 'science' loses and rapport with and sensitivity to group feelings wins. However, you've left your friend high and dry. There are many such situations in which divisions within a group, between groups, between groups and local authorities or local and national agencies, place fieldworkers in a variety of conflict situations resulting in self-censorship, external pressure or even exclusion from the group or the country. The possible consequence of the last-named outcome, future denial of access to other researchers, is often cited in the literature as a 'worst-case scenario' resulting from bad fieldwork. It is unclear as to whether this dread of exclusion is due more to the loss to 'science' or to career possibilities.

2. You appeal to your friend's authority and see if it holds; if so, there is no reason not to proceed. This is a situational issue in which conventional ethical practice might suggest you are allowed to leave the decision up to the local factions and hope it is possible for science to benefit from the outcome.

3. Aware of tensions, you nevertheless covertly record the ceremony. This is not a viable choice from the standpoint of conventional ethics, which would

dictate that going against local opinion is not good and that any secret behaviour is an even worse option. Nevertheless, a great deal of covert recording has been done by ethnomusicologists and doubtless continues to be done, usually justified by an appeal to the needs of 'science' though often motivated by the researcher's self-interest.

CASE 5: PROBLEMS ON TOUR You bring a local musician, one of your informants, to the West on tour. He wants to perform pieces you feel inappropriately represent his tradition to Westerners, as the genre reinforces Western stereotypes about the musician's homeland.

This case raises the question: do you have the right to overrule the insider when he is on your territory? Are there situations where you can protect the local tradition better than 'they' can? The more usual dilemma posed by the context of Case 5 is the reverse: you want the musician to perform material inappropriate for presentation to a non-initiated audience; this seems merely to indicate the very real possibility of exporting the fieldwork atmosphere and its problems.

CASE 6: RECORD LINER NOTES You are called by a record producer who is publishing a documentary sound recording of a pseudo-ethnomusicologist who has worked in 'your' region. The collector failed to notify musicians of his intention to make a record, and now the producer wants you to do the liner notes since the collector is incapable of the task.

1. You refuse the assignment and denounce the producer and the collector in every forum open to you. The problem with this solution is that the record will be distributed anyway, with misleading notes, which may go against your code of protecting the musicians, the music and 'science'.

2. You agree to write the notes to save the situation. Here you run the risk of being implicated, which goes against the stricture of not polluting the field, as the country of origin may decide to restrict you and others after this record appears.

There are of course palliatives to this dilemma. In solution 1, you can always provide improved notes along with your denunciations in scholarly journals, and elsewhere, to balance things. In solution 2, you might write the notes anonymously to protect yourself as well as 'science' and the musicians.

Notice that the option of forcing the record company to disown the disc is not included; scholars have in fact little influence on entrepreneurs. In general, this case is but one example of a type of ethical dilemma: how to mitigate the unethical work of others, particularly if they work in the same region you do.

CASE 7: PUBLISHING THE 'FACTS' Included in your data are facts about informants which, if published, might lead the local government authorities to act against them. Solutions may or may not be forthcoming to this dilemma; possible issues include:

1. Disguising the informants' names and locales may not work, since even the barest outlines of the region and activity could lead clever investigators to your data source.

2. Leaving out the relevant information may damage your scholarly work from the 'scientific' point of view, hence injuring yourself (and 'science')

instead of your informants. Similarly, choosing other data to work with may produce a weaker dissertation, article or book. Perhaps this is the altruism expected of proper ethical behaviour.

Indeed, the sort of internal conflict suggested here has led to some anthropologists dropping out of their discipline altogether, an extreme admission that, properly understood, ethics means you either do not work with informants at all or you do not publish your findings. While the existence of ethnomusicology indicates that not everyone has adopted this stance, a great deal of either callous disregard or individual soul-searching must be going on within the discipline constantly. One hopes for more of the latter than the former, and that by maintaining a continuous discussion of thorny issues and anticipating those to come, ethnomusicology will not solve its ethical problems – since in the nature of human activity this is not a possibility – but will shore up damage done and keep building a framework for future, carefully considered action.

Bibliography

R. L. Beals: *Politics of Social Research* (Chicago, 1969)

A. Gramsci: *Selections from the Prison Notebooks* (New York, 1971)

R. Firth: *Symbols: Public and Private* (Ithaca, NY, 1973)

P. F. Berliner: *The Soul of Mbira: Music and Traditions of the Shona People of Zimbabwe* (Berkeley and Los Angeles, 1978)

C. Keil: *Tiv Song: the Sociology of Art in a Classless Society* (Chicago, 1979)

B. Krader: 'Ethnomusicology', *Grove 6*

C. Geertz: *Local Knowledge* (New York, 1983)

B. Williams: *Ethics and the Limits of Philosophy* (Cambridge, MA, 1985)

K. J. Gergen: 'Correspondence versus Autonomy in the Language of Understanding Human Action', in *Metatheory in Social Science: Pluralisms and Subjectivities*, ed. D. W. Fiske and R. A. Shweder (Chicago, 1986), 136–62

G. E. Marcus and M. M. J. Fischer: *Anthropology as Cultural Critique: An Experimental Moment in the Human Sciences* (Chicago, 1986)

CHAPTER XIV

Gender and Music

MARGARET SARKISSIAN

Gender combines a principle of social organization and a set of ideas which, while appearing to be natural, based on common sense and biological difference, is in fact culturally constructed and variable. Despite the arbitrariness of characteristics associated with male and female identity, many scholars feel that 'all contemporary societies are to some extent male-dominated, and although the degree and expression of female subordination vary greatly, sexual asymmetry is presently a universal fact of life' (Rosaldo and Lamphere, 1974, p.3). Others have gone further and suggested that even our most basic 'premises such as universal sexual asymmetry, are ideological constructs that have their history in Western European society and misrepresent the thought and experience of people in other times and places' (Atkinson, 1982, p.238; see also Yanagisako and Collier, 1987, p.18).

Since the 1970s, increased attention given by feminist scholars to the study of gender and the place of women in society has raised a number of basic questions. Can we really conceive of culture as a homogenous whole comprising complementary halves or should we examine separate and autonomous male and female domains? Is the binary male–female division adequate or should we consider it in conjunction with other factors such as age and social status? Has the distinction between public and domestic spheres – the former generally male-dominated and open to outsiders, the latter often female-oriented and closed – determined the kinds of research that scholars (female and male alike) have been able to conduct? Are female researchers bound by an academic discipline controlled by men and constructed from a male-oriented perspective? Is our very notion of 'science' really grounded in an objective reading of data or must it, too, be reconsidered, having emerged from a particular male-dominated set of social conditions (see Farganis, 1989)? Such questions have contributed to a vigorous debate that criticizes and challenges the prevailing androcentric (male-centred) bias, attempts to redefine the position of women within the larger cultural matrix and focuses on gender as a unifying rubric.

There is a danger that the appropriation of gender by scholars concerned with restoring women to view and expressing themselves without domination from men can lead to the creation of an alternate forum, separating gender analysis and women's studies from the main stream of academic discourse (Strathern, 1987, p.278; Wood, 1980, p.287). Conferences, seminars and essay collections devoted to women's studies may contribute towards margin-alization (see, for example, Rosaldo and Lamphere, eds., 1974; MacCormack and Strathern, eds., 1980; Ortner and Whitehead, eds., 1981; Collier and Yanagisako, eds., 1987; and Koskoff, ed., 1987). But while we cannot fully understand women's lives in isolation from those of men, it is only after an adequate body of data focused specifically on such issues has been gathered that new theories concerning gender-related behaviour and ideology can be formulated (Rosaldo, 1980, p.395; Keeling, ed., 1989, p.86).

In ethnomusicology, there has been a gradual awakening of interest in gender-related studies. Although many pioneers of our field were women (see Frisbie, 1989 and 1991), little attention has been addressed to the musical expression of women as distinct from that of men, perhaps because of 'the dominant role of men in determining approaches and methods' (Nettl, 1983, p.334). Passing references to particular songs or genres performed by women abound in the literature, compensatory studies describing women's musical activities address lacunae; but only in the last decade, with momentum generated by developments in the feminist movement and anthropology, has attention been drawn to the examination of links between sex, culturally constructed notions of gender and musical behaviour. Collections dedicated to the study of women's music in various cultures are now beginning to appear (Koskoff, ed., 1987; Keeling, ed., 1989) and to a revision of the historical canon (Bowers and Tick, eds., 1986). While such contributions advance the possibility of a gender-sensitive approach, calls for a feminist criticism of the canon itself are still regarded by many women in musicology as 'invitations to professional suicide' (McClary, 1988, p.ix).

This chapter explores a number of different ways in which scholars have approached the study of music and gender. (For a comprehensive overview of the ethnomusicological literature dealing with women and music, see E. Koskoff's introduction to *Women and Music in Cross-Cultural Perspective*, Koskoff, ed., 1987.) Recurrent themes – for example, the importance of musical performance in the process of socialization (simultaneously expressing and shaping social order), or the segregation of female and male musical worlds as part of a conceptual tendency towards binary opposition – are derived from established anthropological models. Other approaches – including studies of musical behaviour as an indicator of gender-based power relations, feminist approaches to musical analysis and deconstructions of the portrayed image of women (particularly in opera) – reflect more recent academic interests.

Anthropologists have been concerned with the ways in which a society perpetuates itself, and in particular how ritual and ceremonial practices serve to reinforce shared beliefs and values and to maintain group solidarity. These practices, whether or not perceived as such by participants, are at the same time models *of* and models *for* expected social behaviour:

> culture patterns have an intrinsic double aspect: they give meaning, that is, objective conceptual form, to social and psychological reality both by shaping themselves to it and by shaping it to themselves (Geertz, 1973, pp.93–4).

Ethnomusicologists have examined musical performance as a special means of instilling and perpetuating basic gender values. J. C. Sugarman, for

338

example, has suggested that singing styles are so important in the socialization process of Prespa Albanians that they can be considered a metaphor for local conceptualizations of gender (1989, pp.193 and 207). The dialectical nature of the relationship is also stressed: '[in] the case of Prespare, singing is indeed constrained by community notions regarding gender. But singing may also be seen as a means both of acquiring those notions and of suggesting ways in which they might be refined or modified' (ibid, p.206). Similarly, according to S. Auerbach, musical behaviour provides a model of acceptable domestic female experience for Greek women: 'women's prescribed musical roles as singers and lamenters may thus be viewed generally as gender behaviour, that is, models of and for their ideal home-centered gender role' (1987, pp.40–41).

Once appropriate gender behaviour has been assimilated, musical events often provide a context for the progress of inter-gender relations. In Malta and Albania, for example, festivals provide opportunities for singing and dancing, contexts in which courtship may occur under the watchful eyes of village elders (McLeod and Herndon, 1975, p.82; Sugarman, 1989). In the Philippines, Maranao parents traditionally keep an unmarried daughter in a special chamber 'which is off-limits to visitors and suitors . . . The only opportunity for the suitor, and for everybody, to subject her to an eagle-eyed scrutiny is when she participates in the *kulintang* performance' (Cadar, 1973, p.248). U. H. Cadar notes further that 'many couples in Lanao have started their romantic past with an exciting exchange of *kulintang* and drum passages!' (ibid, p.245). Music is also used as a medium of communication between the sexes in informal contexts. The Hmong jew's harp, for example, 'is tradition-ally used almost exclusively by lovers for their secret and intimate courtship dialogues' (Catlin, 1982, p.185). The quiet instrument not only ensures intimacy in a place where absolute privacy is impossible, but it also acts as a *lingua franca*, overcoming the dialectal differences between villages, and by avoiding direct speech, protects a potential lover from acute embarrassment (ibid, p.193).

Anthony Seeger has shown how Suyá men, after reaching the age of puberty, sing to communicate with their mothers and sisters (relatives who are socially and spatially distant and with whom direct communication is no longer socially acceptable). A man may visit his mother/sister's house to sing *ngere*, a communal genre in which the blending of voices and the submersion of individuality are important, but he can only communicate with them directly as an individual through *akia*, a genre performed in the men's central area. In the latter genre, men sing together, but each performs his own distinctive song in an individual style (Seeger, 1979).

Changes in musical behaviour often reflect more widespread changes in society as a whole. J. Vander observes that the growing economic independ-ence of Shoshone women since the 1950s has provided the momentum for them to take on new roles in reservation institutions. This independence has also led to increased musical opportunities, including the assumption of what had previously been exclusively male singing and dancing roles at the powwow (1989, p.9). The growing frequency with which Prespa Albanian immigrants in North America now sing together as married couples also suggests adaptation to new social contexts (Sugarman, 1989, p.208). Changes in gender relations may be inspired by contact with external, particularly colonial, systems (Rapp, 1979, p.505). For example, the number of musical genres performed by Ojibway women was greatly reduced through 'historical forces and culture contact' (Vennum, 1989, p.21). Eastern Algonkian gender relations were fundamentally altered by the 'patriarchal value systems and notions of family' imposed by Jesuit missionaries and resulted in decreasing female musical participation (Cavanagh, 1989, p.56). In India, while the Victorian British colonial morality spawned social reform movements and severely curtailed performance by the *devadasis* and other professional women (Post, 1987, p.104), it also led to the present acceptance of musical ability as a desirable feminine accomplishment.

Taking a different approach, Alan Lomax tried to show that singing style itself can be a measure of gender relations, reflecting the severity of sexual mores and the imbalance in authority between males and females in a particular society. Tense vocal production, narrow range and highly ornate vocal lines, he suggests, are indicative of societies in which women are repressed: more equal power relations, on the other hand, tend to produce music that stresses well-blended ensemble singing and relaxed vocal styles (Lomax, 1968). Lomax's Cantometrics system is based on the androcentric assumption that the only relevant human universals are the division of labour and the means of production in a society. To have considered other universals, such as the primary role that women play in the socialization of children, or male insecurity generated by the exclusive female reproductive capacity, would have necessitated a new series of Cantometric correlations (Riley, 1980, p.78).

The association of female and male spheres with binary pairs of Lévi-Straussian-style structural anthropology – for example, domestic/public, nature/culture and self interest/social good – has been particularly wide-spread in gender studies (see Rosaldo, 1974; Ortner, 1974; and Strathern, 1981). Structuralists have

> sought to establish the universal grammar of culture, the ways in which units of cultural discourse are created (by the principle of binary opposition), and the rules according to which the units (pairs of opposed terms) are arranged and combined to produce the actual cultural productions (Ortner, 1974, p.135).

Consideration of the domestic/public and female/male dichotomies in relation to musical behaviour has produced a number of studies which document the existence of separate or complementary musical domains. There has been a general inclination to regard the public domain as a male sphere of activity. As Bruno Nettl observes, 'in many cultures men are the people who live a more or less public life and are thus responsible for dealing with the outside world – which includes ethnomusicologists' (1983, p.335). Where there is a strong distinction between female and male worlds, independent musical domains develop and these may be viewed as expressions of female or male solidarity, and as contexts in which the restrictions that operate in the common male–female domain may be suspended. For example, V. Doubleday describes Afghan professional all-women bands that perform only in segregated contexts: '[they] play music for women: separate parties for women. There's hardly a man in sight' (1988, p.195). A similar tradition of all-women ensembles that perform 'a special repertoire [at] events where attendance is restricted to women' has developed in Tunisia (Jones, 1987, p.81). Alternate venues for female performance also existed in 19th-century European society; although women were allowed increasing access to musical education as conservatories spread, 'they remained less employable than men. The sense of frustration women felt under these circumstances led them to organize. One response was to form women's orchestras and chamber-music groups' (Bowers and Tick, 1986, p.8). Less formal separation has been documented by K. A. Gourlay, who noticed that Karamojong women organized musical groups that appeared to be a counterpart to men's age-grade societies but seemed to have no clear purpose and did not exclude male singers who wanted to join (1970, p.115).

In cultures where the female/male dichotomy is not clearly articulated, women's roles and activities are often considered complementary to, rather than separate from, those of the men. Among the Shoshone, for example, the Sun Dance has been described as a 'beautiful metaphor' for the co-operation required in a society where labour is divided between men as hunters and women as gatherers:

> The male lead singer begins the Sun Dance song, his opening phrase is repeated by the rest of the male singers who accompany themselves on the drum. After this repetition of the opening phrase, women join the singing. This sequence occurs in every repetition of the song. Midway through the final repetition of Sun Dance songs, the men stop singing [and drumming] and allow the women to finish (Vander, 1989, p.7).

Complementarity may also extend into the realm of the supernatural. Men may be the primary recipients of songs in Eastern Algonkian communities, but they are often received from women in dreams (Cavanagh, 1989, p.63). M. Roseman's work among the Temiar of Malaysia demonstrates that symbolic inversion of roles can cross-cut categories of kinship, pedagogy and gender, concurrently stating and undermining differences (1984, 1987). At a symbolic level, then, gender differences can be reversed, '[t]he free-ranging male of the everyday domain becomes the earth-bound male of the ritual domain, whose consort is the ritually free-ranging female component' (1984, p.433).

The existence of separate male and female musical spheres, whether autonomous or complementary, raises the issue of boundary crossing and sanctions that may be invoked when, for example, a woman performs in the public (hence male) arena. In cultures with strongly marked female and male realms, such women transgress acceptable norms of behaviour, and there is frequently a real or implied association with prostitution. In Malta, for example, there is a clear contrast between women who sing song duels among themselves during the day within the domestic courtyard and those who sing *bormliza* at night in bars often with or accompanied by male musicians. 'Women who sing in public are regarded as "prostitutes"; women who are not prostitutes do not sing in public places' (McLeod and Herndon, 1975, p.91). This association is further magnified in situations where there is also a strong religious antipathy towards music. Such attitudes are especially prominent in traditional Islamic contexts where male and female worlds are strictly segregated (see Jones, 1987, p.73; Sakata, 1987, p.86; Doubleday, 1988).

Although the domestic/public dichotomy has been emphasized in this chapter, other oppositions, including nature/culture, remain equally relevant. Regarding the nature/culture debate, S. B. Ortner suggests that 'the male . . . lacking natural creative functions, must . . . assert his creativity externally, "artificially," through the medium of technology and symbols' (1974, p.75). If one accepts the premise that the voice is the most natural of instruments, then accounts which highlight the fact that in many cultures women sing while men play instruments are pertinent to this discussion (e.g. see Post, 1987, p.100; Jones, 1987, p.77; Shehan, 1987, p.47; and Sutton, 1987, p.111 – all appearing in the same volume – regarding India, Tunisia, the Balkans and Java, respectively).

During the last 20 years, a Marxist-derived theoretical perspective has become increasingly influential in anthropological studies, treating culture as a means of legitimation and replication of an existing exploitative social order largely through the mystification of the sources of inequality (Ortner, 1984, p.140). The 'surface forms of what the British called "social structure" are seen as native *models* of social organization that have been bought by anthropologists as the real thing, but actually mask, or at least only partially correspond to, the hidden asymmetrical relations of power that are driving the system' (ibid, 1984, p.139; emphasis in original; see also R. Rapp, 1979, pp.508–10). The concept of asymmetrical power relations is particularly appropriate for studies of gender. Attention is drawn to an examination of the *practical* ways in which domination is achieved. 'Gender conceptions in any society are to be understood as functioning aspects of a cultural system through which actors manipulate, interpret, legitimize and reproduce the patterns of cooperation and conflict that order their social world' (Collier and Rosaldo, 1981, p.311).

Even in situations in which male and female roles appear to be complementary, there are often restrictions that create inequality. In some North American Indian cultures, for example, the singing of men and women may be valued equally but taboos exist that restrict female participation in ceremonies during menstruation (see Frisbie, 1989, p.31, and Vander, 1989, pp.5–7). While Shoshone women and men may perform together, the men always start the song and it is considered a breach of etiquette for a woman to correct or prompt a male song leader (Vander, 1988; 1989, p.9). Perceptions of equality may also vary depending on the viewpoint of the observer: Transylvanian adolescents may consider their masculine and feminine song and dance movements as 'complementary and of equal value' but 'local spectators (especially women) interpret the differentiated patterns as symbols of a pre-established hierarchy of power' (Giurchescu, 1986, p.47).

The issues of power and the internalization of *status quo* are complex and deceptive. In cultures with courtesan traditions, female performers may appear to have more freedom than ordinary women, but such freedom is often illusory; these women still have 'to fulfill certain male-defined expectations identified with their profession' (Post, 1987, p.102). For Prespa Albanians, 'the internal consistency and logic of the fundamental relationships upon which [the system] is based are so pervasive that concepts regarding gender appear to be utterly natural and unquestionable' (Sugarman, 1989, p.192). Among the Gahuku-Gama of Papua New Guinea, on the other hand, far from being unquestioned, the *status quo* is maintained through complex mutual deception:

> The women know the men's secrets but pretend not to know in order not to damage the men's self esteem. The men not only know that the women know and are pretending but themselves pretend that the women do not know but actually believe the stories which they themselves admit are pretence (Gourlay, 1975, p.117).

Gender-based asymmetry is also manifested in what Ortner and H. Whitehead have described as 'prestige structures' (1981, p.13), in which 'male as opposed to female activities are always recognized as predominantly important, and cultural systems give authority and value to the roles and activities of men' (Rosaldo, 1974, p.19). Combined with the value assigned to men's activities is a corresponding tendency to devalue women's activities. The connection between gender and value is clearly demonstrated by H. L. Sakata, who notes that in Afghanistan musical instruments are generally played by men. The *daira* (tambourine), usually played by women, is not considered a 'real' instrument unless, for some special reason, a man should use it as an accompanying drum in an ensemble (1987, p.88). Similarly, lullabies sung by women are for the express purpose of putting babies to sleep; stylized lullabies sung by men and accompanied by a two-string lute, are for male social entertainment and are valued more highly (ibid, p.89). The different values attached to Afghan male and female musical expression are reiterated by Doubleday, who observes that although there was considerable overlap in repertory, women always learned songs *after* they were established in the male repertory and minstrel women never performed classical or devotional music (1988, p.182).

Not only are women's songs often less valued than men's, but, as Sugarman points out of the few Albanian women who did successfully perform men's songs: '[so] long as they maintained a feminine demeanour and vocal timbre as they sang, their forays into the men's repertoire were viewed as evidence of an unusual degree of intelligence and talent' (1989, p.208). Men, on the other hand, were embarrassed to associate themselves too closely with the women's style or repertory (ibid). Women who sang men's songs – with the proper degree of deference – were praised; men who sang women's songs were denigrated.

In addition to the low status derived from their association with prostitution, women who perform in public are often structural outsiders in other ways. For example, in Tunisia female musicians were generally slaves 'of exotic race or religion' (Jones, 1987, p.71); in Java, *klèdèk* (female dancers hired to perform at *tayuban*, male drinking and dancing parties) were usually hired from outside the village (see Geertz, 1960, p.299; Wolbers, 1986; Hefner, 1987); in Afghanistan and India female musicians often came from hereditary castes (Doubleday, 1988, p.167; Post, 1987, p.99). In each case, it would seem that employment of women who are in some way outsiders gives licence to behaviour that would not otherwise be tolerated. As R. W. Hefner has pointed out of the *klèdèk*, 'with a paid professional from outside the village, men would feel free of moral constraints which might bind them when dancing with local women' (1987, p.90).

The marginal status of female performers is only one aspect of the extraordinary nature of certain public events during which normal behaviour may be suspended. For example, during the Javanese *tayuban*, the usually unacceptable drinking of alcohol and physical contact between dancers are tolerated (Geertz, 1960, p.300; Sutton, 1984, p.121, 1987, p.113). Greek festivals provide an opportunity for 'a change in the permitted movements and activities of women' (Auerbach, 1987, p.31). One should not forget, however, that these structural aberrations pertain to a wider field than inter-gender relations. And in musical contexts, the low status of public performers is not necessarily gender based but can apply equally to male musicians; for example, Maltese male singers have a public image of being troublemakers (McLeod and Herndon, 1975, p.86). The strong correlation between perceived freedom from social norms and low status is not always negative. L. J. Jones (1987) and J. Post (1987) both suggest that female courtesans in Tunisia and India had more access to education than other women and Doubleday observes that although Afghan women generally looked down upon Minstrel women, whose 'image as exotic and daring outsiders' had so attracted her as a researcher (1988, p.158), they were 'secretly envious of the parties and the endless music-making' (ibid, p.195). Not only did Minstrel women bare their faces to strangers, but they also had more freedom to travel and could negotiate and argue with men over payment (ibid, p.163).

New approaches to the study of music and gender have been inspired by work from the fields of cultural studies and literary criticism. Studies considering opera as text, for example, have subjected the presented image of women – as characters and as performers – to close scrutiny, drawing attention not only to 'the gender politics that require the death of the heroine but also [to] the racism and imperialism that opera often so unapologetically celebrates' (McClary, 1988, p.xii). Deconstruction of the meaning underlying such texts emphasizes the androcentric basis of opera as a genre. As L. Treitler suggests of *Lulu*, female characters become an amalgamation of roles projected onto them by men 'out of their own needs, fantasies, and fears about Woman' (1989, p.283). C. Clément extends this line of argument to encompass the performers themselves, proposing that the figure of the *prima donna* is nothing more than a male-constructed fantasy (1979).

Popular music in British and American society has been an especially fruitful area for recent research. S. Frith and A. McRobbie's article, 'Rock and Sexuality' (1978), was a pioneering attempt to examine the sexual messages inherent in rock and pop. They suggest that for Western adolescents, rock is the medium for simultaneous expression and construction of conventional notions of masculinity and femininity, and situates performers and audience alike along clearly established gender lines. Males are identified as active participants and females as passive consumers. Musically the distinction is marked by the contrast between 'cock rock . . . an explicit, crude, and often aggressive expression of male sexuality', and 'teenybop', a romanticized image of 'the young boy next door: sad, thoughtful, pretty and puppylike' (1978/*R*1990, pp.5–7; see also Frith, 1985/*R*1990, p.420).

This musical distinction has been further explored analytically by Shepherd, who describes gender stereotypes according to parameters of timbre, pitch and rhythm, and suggests that these parameters operate in classical as well as popular music spheres and are linked to 'male hegemonic processes of gender typing and of cultural reproduction and resistance' (Shepherd, 1987, p.152). 'Cock rock', characterized by a hard and rasping vocal sound, is contrasted with 'soft rock', an expansion of Frith and McRobbie's 'teenybop', whose triple subdivision distinguishes the sound of the 'woman-as-nurturer' (a warm, resonant, chest-centred vocal sound) from that of 'the boy next door' (where softness and warmth is a result of head, rather than chest, tones) and the 'woman-as-sex-object' (which introduces a certain edge to the sound) (ibid, pp.166–7).

Ambiguity and the blurring of gender boundaries, subjects rarely discussed in mainstream ethnomusicological literature, have received long overdue attention in studies of popular music. During the 1960s and 1970s, conventions of masculine and feminine sexuality gradually converged, particularly in British rock: the Beatles' image was 'neither boys-together aggression nor boy-next-door pathos'; David Bowie and Brian Ferry exuded sexual ambivalence; and Garry Glitter and Suzi Quatro were 'campy' (Frith and McRobbie, 1978/R1990, pp.13–14; Savage, 1988, pp.154–7). In the 1980s, this convergence culminated on one hand in 'gender benders' like Boy George and Marilyn and on the other in a group like Bronski Beat, packaged simultaneously as gay in Britain and straight in the USA (Frith, 1985/R1990, pp.422–3; the crucial influence of gay subculture on every style from the Teds to the 'feminized New Man' of the late 1980s has been thoroughly discussed in Savage, 1988).

Ethnomusicological scholars, while benefiting from the perspectives of their colleagues in anthropology, women's studies and cultural studies, have recognized that female and male identities are culturally variable constructions. This standpoint has allowed us to break away from the classification of music based on a premise of seemingly natural biological differences. Increasingly varied discussions of the ways in which musical performance and behaviour can contribute to maintaining gender distinctions within a social system are now beginning to appear. We must take care, however, not to separate gender from other bases of identity. Age, for example, frequently affects apparently gender-specific behaviour. Loss of child-bearing capacity may lessen a woman's perceived sexuality and can lead not only to changes in dress and demeanour but also to increased social status and freedom of musical expression. Growing consciousness of ethnic identity may lessen gender distinctions as group solidarity is valued above internal divisions. The importance of gender within a society can also vary. While gender may be 'situated at the core' of Prespa Albanian logic, it is neither a polemical issue nor a central organizing principle among the Wana of Sulawesi (Sugarman, 1989, p.192; Atkinson, 1982, p.257).

On a more positive note, the recent increased focus on gender studies in ethnomusicology has begun to redress the imbalance in favour of women, to fill the gaps in our knowledge of women's musical behaviour and activities, and to reinterpret existing historical material. While the study of music and gender is still in its infancy and an extensive retrospective is premature, it is encouraging that such research continues to expand in scope and sophistication.

Bibliography

C. Geertz: *The Religion of Java* (Chicago and London, 1960)

A. Lomax: *Folk Song Style and Culture* (Washington, DC, 1968)

K. A. Gourlay: ' "Trees and Anthills": Songs of Karamojong Women's Groups', *African Music*, iv/4 (1970), 114

U. H. Cadar: 'The Role of Kulintang Music in Maranao Society', *EM*, xvii (1973), 234

C. Geertz: 'Religion as a Cultural System', *The Interpretation of Cultures* (New York, 1973), 87– 125

S. B. Ortner: 'Is Female to Male as Nature Is to Culture?' *Women, Culture, and Society*, ed. M. Z. Rosaldo and L. Lamphere (Stanford, CA, 1974), 67

M. Z. Rosaldo: 'Women, Culture, and Society: a Theoretical Overview', *Women, Culture, and Society*, ed. M. Z. Rosaldo and L. Lamphere (Stanford, CA, 1974), 17

—— and L. Lamphere: 'Introduction', *Women, Culture, and Society*, ed. M. Z. Rosaldo and L. Lamphere (Stanford, CA, 1974), 1

—— and L. Lamphere, eds.: *Women, Culture, and Society* (Stanford, CA, 1974)

K. A. Gourlay: *Sound-Producing Instruments in Traditional Society: a Study of Esoteric Instruments and Their Role in Male-Female Relations* (Port Moresby and Canberra, 1975)

N. McLeod and M. Herndon: 'The *Bormliza*: Maltese Folksong Style and Women', *Women and Folklore*, ed. C. R. Farrer (Austin and London, 1975), 81

S. Frith and A. McRobbie: 'Rock and Sexuality', *Screen Education*, xxix (1978), 1; repr. in S. Frith and A. Goodwin (1990), 370

C. Clément: *L'opéra ou la défaite des femmes* (Paris, 1979); Eng. trans. as *Opera or the Undoing of Women* (Minneapolis, 1988)

R. Rapp: 'Anthropology', *Signs: Journal of Women in Culture and Society*, iv (1979), 497

A. Seeger: 'What Can We Learn When They Sing? Vocal Genres of the Suyá Indians of Central Brazil', *EM*, xxiii (1979), 373

C. P. MacCormack: 'Nature, Culture and Gender: a Critique', *Nature, Culture and Gender*, ed. C. P. MacCormack and M. Strathern (Cambridge, England, 1980), 1

C. P. MacCormack and M. Strathern, eds.: *Nature, Culture and Gender* (Cambridge, England, 1980)

A. McRobbie: 'Settling Accounts with Subcultures: a Feminist Critique', *Screen Education*, xxxiv (1980), 36; repr. in S. Frith and A. Goodwin (1990), 66

J. Riley: 'Women and World Music: Straining Our Ears to the Silence', *Heresies*, x (1980), 74

M. Z. Rosaldo: 'The Use and Abuse of Anthropology: Reflections on Feminism and Cross-cultural Understanding', *Signs: Journal of Women in Culture and Society*, v (1980), 389

E. Wood: 'Women in Music', *Signs: Journal of Women in Culture and Society*, vi (1980), 283

J. F. Collier and M. Z. Rosaldo: 'Politics and Gender in Simple Societies', *Sexual Meanings: the Cultural Construction of Gender and Sexuality*, ed. S. B. Ortner and H. Whitehead (Cambridge, England, 1981), 275–329

S. B. Ortner and H. Whitehead: 'Introduction: Accounting for Sexual Meanings', *Sexual Meanings: the Cultural Construction of Gender and Sexuality*, ed. S. B. Ortner and H. Whitehead (Cambridge, England, 1981), 1

——, eds.: *Sexual Meanings: the Cultural Construction of Gender and Sexuality* (Cambridge, 1981)

M. Strathern: 'Self-interest and the Social Good: Some Implications of Hagen Gender Imagery', *Sexual Meanings: the Cultural Construction of Gender and Sexuality*, ed. S. B. Ortner and H. Whitehead (Cambridge, England, 1981), 166

J. M. Atkinson: 'Anthropology', *Signs: Journal of Women in Culture and Society*, viii (1982), 236

A. R. Catlin: 'Speech Surrogate Systems of the Hmong: From Singing Voices to Talking Reeds', *The Hmong in the West: Observations and Reports*, ed. B. T. Downing and D. P. Olney (Minneapolis, 1982), 170

B. Nettl: *The Study of Ethnomusicology: Twenty-nine Issues and Concepts* (Urbana and Chicago, 1983)

S. B. Ortner: 'Theory in Anthropology since the Sixties', *Comparative Studies in Society and History*, xxvi/1 (1984), 126–66

M. Roseman: 'The Social Structuring of Sound: the Temiar of Peninsular Malaysia', *EM*, xxviii (1984), 411–45

R. A. Sutton: 'Who is the *Pesindhèn*? Notes on the Female Singing Tradition in Java', *Indonesia*, xxxvii (1984), 119

S. Frith: 'Afterthoughts', *New Statesman* (23 Aug 1985); repr. in S. Frith and A. Goodwin (1990), 419

J. Bowers and J. Tick: 'Introduction', *Women Making Music: the Western Art Tradition, 1150–1950*, ed. J. Bowers and J. Tick (Urbana and Chicago, 1986), 3

——, eds.: *Women Making Music: the Western Art Tradition, 1150–1950* (Urbana and Chicago, 1986)

A. Giurchescu: 'Power and Charm. Interaction of Adolescent Men and Women in Traditional Settings of Transylvania', *YTM*, xviii (1986), 37

P. A. Wolbers: 'Gandrung and Angklung from Banyuwangi: Remnants of a Past Shared with Bali', *Asian Music*, xviii/1 (1986), 71

S. Auerbach: 'From Singing to Lamenting: Women's Musical Role in a Greek Village', *Women and Music in Cross-Cultural Perspective*, ed. E. Koskoff (Westport, CT, 1987), 25

J. F. Collier and S. J. Yanagisako, eds.: *Gender and Kinship: Essays Toward a Unified Analysis* (Stanford, CA, 1987)

R. W. Hefner: 'The Politics of Popular Art: *Tayuban* Dance and Culture Change in East Java', *Indonesia*, xliii (1987), 75

L. J. Jones: 'A Sociohistorical Perspective on Tunisian Women as Professional Musicians', *Women and Music in Cross-Cultural Perspective*, ed. E. Koskoff (Westport, CT, 1987), 69

E. Koskoff, ed.: *Women and Music in Cross-Cultural Perspective* (Westport, CT, 1987)

J. Post: 'Professional Women in Indian Music: the Death of the Courtesan Tradition', *Women and Music in Cross-Cultural Perspective*, ed. E. Koskoff (Westport, CT, 1987), 97

M. Roseman: 'Inversion and Conjuncture: Male and Female Performance among the Temiar of Peninsular Malaysia', *Women and Music in Cross-Cultural Perspective*, ed. E. Koskoff (Westport, CT, 1987), 131

H. L. Sakata: 'Hazara Women in Afghanistan: Innovators and Preservers of a Musical Tradition', *Women and Music in Cross-Cultural Perspective*, ed. E. Koskoff (Westport, CT, 1987), 85

P. K. Shehan: 'Balkan Women as Preservers of Traditional Music and Culture', *Women and Music in Cross-Cultural Perspective*, ed. E. Koskoff (Westport, CT, 1987), 45

J. Shepherd: 'Music and Male Hegemony', *Music and Society: the Politics of Composition, Performance, and Reception*, ed. R. Leppert and S. McClary (Cambridge, England, 1987), 151

M. Strathern: 'Producing Difference: Connections and Disconnections in Two New Guinea Highland Kinship Systems', *Gender and Kinship: Essays Toward a Unified Analysis*, ed. J. F. Collier and S. J. Yanagisako (Stanford, CA, 1987), 271

R. A. Sutton: 'Identity and Individuality in an Ensemble Tradition: the Female Vocalist in Java', *Women and Music in Cross-Cultural Perspective*, ed. E. Koskoff (Westport, CT, 1987), 111

S. J. Yanagisako and J. F. Collier: 'Toward a Unified Analysis of Gender and Kinship', *Gender and Kinship: Essays Toward a Unified Analysis*, ed. J. F. Collier and S. J. Yanagisako (Stanford, CA, 1987), 14–50

V. Doubleday: *Three Women of Herat* (London, 1988)

S. McClary: 'Forward. The Undoing of Opera: Toward a Feminist Criticism of Music', *Opera, or the Undoing of Women*, ed. C. Clément (Minneapolis, 1988), ix

J. Savage: 'The Enemy Within: Sex, Rock, and Identity', *Facing the Music: a Pantheon Guide to Popular Culture*, ed. S. Frith (New York, 1988), 131–72

J. Vander: *Songprints: the Musical Experience of Five Shoshone Women* (Urbana and Chicago, 1988)

B. D. Cavanagh: 'Music and Gender in the Sub-Arctic Algonkian Area', *Women in North American Indian Music: Six Essays*, ed. R. Keeling (Bloomington, IN, 1989), 55

S. Farganis: 'Feminism and the Reconstruction of Social Science', *Gender/Body/Knowledge: Feminist Reconstructions of Being and Knowing*, ed. A. M. Jaggar and S. R. Bordo (New Brunswick, NJ, 1989), 207

C. J. Frisbie: 'Gender and Navaho Music: Unanswered Questions', *Women in North American Indian Music: Six Essays*, ed. R. Keeling (Bloomington, IN, 1989), 22

——: 'Helen Heffron Roberts: a Tribute', *EM*, xxxiii (1989), 97

R. Keeling, ed.: *Women in North American Indian Music: Six Essays* (Bloomington, IN, 1989)

J. C. Sugarman: 'The Nightingale and the Partridge: Singing and Gender among Prespa Albanians', *EM*, xxxiii (1989), 191

L. Treitler: 'The Lulu Character and the Character of *Lulu*', *Music and the Historical Imagination* (Cambridge, MA, 1989), 264–303

J. Vander: 'From the Musical Experience of Five Shoshone Women', *Women in North American Indian Music: Six Essays*, ed. R. Keeling (Bloomington, IN, 1989), 5

T. Vennum Jr: 'The Changing Role of Women in Ojibway Music History', *Women in North American Indian Music: Six Essays*, ed. R. Keeling (Bloomington, IN, 1989), 13

S. Frith and A. Goodwin, eds.: *On Record: Rock, Pop, and the Written Word* (New York, 1990)

347

C. J. Frisbie: 'Women and the Society for Ethnomusicology: Roles and Contribution from Formation through Incorporation (1952–1961)', *Comparative Musicology and Anthropology of Music: Essays on the History of Ethnomusicology*, ed. B. Nettl and P. V. Bohlman (Chicago, 1991)

CHAPTER XV

The Music Industry

KRISTER MALM

Music technology

When general technology is applied to music, one speaks of music technology. Making even a simple musical instrument requires a certain technology. In common use, however, the term music technology refers to the specific mechanical, electro-mechanical and electronic technologies that developed in Europe and North America during the 19th and 20th centuries. As these technologies have been applied to music, profound changes have resulted.

These technologies until recently have been part of the expertise mainly of industrialized countries. But the products resulting from the application of the technologies due to better communications, colonization and worldwide transport have been introduced to all continents, starting in the 19th century and with accelerating momentum during the 20th century. The two main categories of products are hardware, usually some kind of 'music machine', and software, that is packaged musical data to be processed and decoded into music with the help of hardware.

Musical instruments form a special category of hardware, being used more as tools than as machines. The construction of conventional musical instruments in almost all cultures has been improved by the use of mechanical technology. During the 19th century the mechanical design of keyboard instruments became more sophisticated, and wind instruments got valves. Mechanical and semi-mechanical instruments were invented, such as music boxes and pianolas. The consequence of these developments has been a subject well-explored by traditional organology.

Another kind of hardware is electronic equipment that, combined with conventional musical instruments, goes to make up electro-mechanical systems such as microphones, amplifiers and loudspeakers. Yet another category of hardware is the media machines: phonographs, gramophones, all kinds of radio, TV, CD players, film and video equipment.

Software includes the many kinds of recordings such as phonograph cylinders, records, audio cassettes and compact discs, as well as film and video-recordings and laser video discs.

Electronic musical instruments such as electric organs and synthesizers combine software and hardware in one unit.

All these products have been linked to industrialization in the field of music;

most modern music technology is actually music-industry technology. The industrialization process has in turn been linked with monetary economy, with profitability 'laws' relevant to mass production and with the establishment of international music and media corporations. Since this is a fairly homogeneous conglomerate of phenomena, usually introduced at the same time into the music culture of different geographical regions and ethnic groups, it is difficult to single out the effects of technological developments from those of economic and organizational developments in the areas. However, it is possible to describe some of this interaction between music industry technology (including related economic and organizational phenomena) and traditional music.

Recording technology

The single technological development that has most influenced the field of music is the invention of sound recording in 1877. For the first time people had the ability to preserve, transport and reproduce at a specific time and place sounds that were originally produced elsewhere. During the period 1877–90 recording was mainly used for speech and only to a limited extent for music. By the mid-1890s two systems were available. First was the Edison phonograph system, which used wax cylinders and could both record and play back on the same machine, representing record/play or two-way recording technology. The other, the Berliner gramophone system, was built on play only or one-way recording technology. It was designed for the mass production of sound recordings through a number of stages, from the recording of the sound onto an original wax disc, through the production of metal stampers, to the pressing of a number of identical gramophone discs to be played back on a special machine, the gramophone. The Edison phonograph became the most important tool in the early documentation of sound for research purposes, while the Berliner gramophone became the main vehicle of the commercial recording industry.

The principles of the gramophone record have, in gradually more sophisticated versions, remained essentially the same until the 1980s, when laser compact-disc technology was launched. In the 1930s, cutting equipment for one-off acetate lacquer discs was developed; by the 1950s, both the cylinder and the lacquer disc were replaced by the record/play system of tape-recording technology.

The commercial recording industry

Although there were some preludes in the 19th century, it was only after the turn of the century that the commercial recording industry started to grow. The growth was based on sales of hardware, that is phonographs and gramophones, with recorded music on cylinders and discs as the main software. The recording industry right from the start was concentrated in a few companies, mainly due to the restricting effect of patents. In the USA the dominant companies were the Victor Talking Machine Company (later RCA), the Columbia Phonograph Company (later CBS), and the Edison Company. In Europe the British Gramophone Company (later EMI), the German Lindström Company (later Polygram) and the French Pathé

Company dominated the industry. Beside these six companies a number of smaller concerns were operating, especially in Europe, but most of the big trans-national music corporations of today are direct descendants of those six early companies.

The expansion of the recording industry was rapid. By 1910 the six big companies had established branches not only throughout Europe and South America but also in Asia and Africa. The gramophone did not require any special operating skills. With its clockwork mechanism and acoustic amplification, it could be used by anybody anywhere. Recording companies soon found that in order to sell gramophones they had to provide records of music that was in demand by potential customers. In Europe and the USA the light music and art music of the upper classes had become fairly homogeneous in the whole area during the 19th century, partly due to the activities of music publishing companies and of international impresarios like P. T. Barnum. Since the upper classes also were the people who could afford a gramophone, the recording industry concentrated on the established international music styles in Europe and the Americas. This strategy would not work in other parts of the world: recordings of local music had to be made in each region and language area.

In 1902 the Gramophone Company sent a young American, Fred Gaisberg, to India and other Asian countries to 'open up new markets, establish agencies, and acquire a catalogue of native records' (Gaisberg, 1942; Gronow, 1981). At about the same time Fred's brother Will Gaisberg and others were sent to Armenia, Georgia, Ukraine and elsewhere in the Russian empire. In 1903 Fritz Hampe of the Gramophone Company started to record in Cairo and in 1907 a regional branch of the Gramophone Company was established in Alexandria. This branch carried out activities in the Near East, Turkey, Greece and Albania, while a French branch was active in Morocco, Algeria and Tunisia.

By 1910 the Gramophone Company, partly owned by Victor, had made over 14,000 recordings throughout Asia and North Africa (Perkins, Kelly and Ward, 1976) excluding the Caucasus and Central Asia. In an agreement of 1907 the two companies divided the world market into two separate spheres of interest. Victor got the Americas, China, Japan and the Philippines, while the Gramophone Company got the rest of the world. Columbia was active in Latin America, Japan, China and Eastern Europe. The Pathé Company had branches in North Africa, Russia and Japan. The Lindström Company and other German companies were recording in North and South Africa, the Near East, Southern Asia and the Far East.

In Europe, the USA and Latin America the recording companies soon tapped the upper-class market and then turned to issue records of local music. In the USA, special record series were made for different ethnic groups (Norwegian, Swedish, Finnish and Ukrainian). In Latin America, recordings were made in the Caribbean Islands and on the mainland. Gradually the recording industry began introducing music from one country to the others. The flow was mainly from the USA and Europe, but there were also cases of local music from Latin America being exported to the USA and Europe (for example, the introduction of the Argentinian tango to Europe in the early 1900s).

By 1914 recording technology had been introduced to local music cultures in almost all parts of the world and the gramophone record was well-established as a mass medium. Although in many places only a few recordings were issued with local music, to help sell the hardware locally, these recordings must have influenced the further development of local music, since they usually were highly regarded and could be replayed over and over.

World War I put an end to the first period of intensive activities of recording companies. After the war the expansion of the recording industry picked up momentum. In the USA many local music styles were affected, especially different kinds of African-American music. By 1930 independent or semi-independent record companies had been started in some countries of the Third World (Japan, India and Egypt), but the dominance of a few big companies continued. Recording activities started in West and East Africa around 1930.

New electric recording technology and the emergence of radio in the 1920s brought new hardware and more sophisticated software on the market. The introduction of sound movies around 1930, the activities of radio corporations and the worldwide depression halted the expansion of the recording industry until the 1960s.

The introduction of tape-recording in the 1950s made it possible to record long sequences of music outside special recording studios. The long-playing disc was the major means of marketing these recordings, but the 78 rpm record still dominated the market in the Third World, since electricity was needed to run open-reel tape recorders and LP playback systems.

In the 1960s locally owned recording companies were established in many of the newly independent countries of the Third World. These companies had their own recording studios but were in most cases still dependent on the big trans-national companies for mass production. The records mainly contained local popular music or representative, nationalistic music sponsored by the new ruling local elites.

The introduction of transistorized amplifiers and cassette tape-recording technology around 1965 meant that relatively inexpensive, easy to use record/play technology was available. The cassette radio-recorders could work on small batteries and be taken anywhere. The cassette recording technology penetrated in a very short time from around 1973 to 1980 into almost every human settlement on the globe. Before roads, running water and mains electricity, cassette recorders and amplifiers reached the most remote villages. And with the recorders came the software, most of it produced by a few trans-national corporations. By the early 1980s for the first time the world had a youth population where almost everybody had heard the music of the Western superstars of the 1970s: the BeeGees, ABBA, Boney M and Michael Jackson.

Low-cost cassette technology also soon gave rise to a booming Third World local recording industry. This industry is partly based on recordings of local music, and partly on the reissuing of hit records originally published by the trans-national companies. Reissuing is extremely profitable since little investment is required and fees are not paid to performers. It is also illegal according to copyright legislation in most countries. As this legislation is seldom enforced, the so-called 'cassette pirates' thrive.

By the mid-1980s the trans-national music industry launched a new high-cost, one-way music medium – the compact disc. Around the corner, however, lurks a low-cost, two-way version of digital sound recording technology; the digital audio tape. Soon personal computers will also be used to distribute music to the masses. Of course these changes will in time also affect the recording industry in the Third World.

Although many new companies have started over the years, they have usually been integrated into the structure of the handful of big companies that were producing both the hardware and the software right from the start. Through mergers and take-overs the link between electronic hardware and software production has been maintained so that by the 1980s, in spite of the local cassette industry boom, more than 50 per cent of all commercial recordings sold worldwide were produced by eight trans-national companies.

The aim of the commercial recording industry is of course to make money. During the first expansion period recordings of local music were made in order to sell the hardware. In the 1920s the selling of records became a profitable business; the more copies sold of a recording, the higher the profit. With the spread of broadcasting – to a great extent based on commercial records – and later film and television, the recording industry acquired very efficient marketing channels.

The strategy became to sell the same music to as many customers as possible. This meant finding the lowest common musical denominator for the largest possible market. Since the biggest single market was, and still is, the English-speaking communities of North America and Europe, it was the target of the bulk of record production. The Spanish-, French- and German-speaking markets and some others were also big enough to make record production aimed at them profitable. As investment costs in studio and mass reproduction equipment rose, it became harder to produce records for small language and music culture areas at a profit. This trend was temporarily halted by cassette technology but has culminated in the very high costs of compact-disc production. As a result, small culture areas have mainly served as marginal markets for the sale of left-overs from the larger mass markets. This situation can lead to the total integration of the smaller music cultures into the larger ones, starting with a change in the musical preferences of youth groups in the smaller cultures.

Soon the recording industry discovered that small cultures could provide music to be sold to a larger audience not belonging to the small culture itself. The big companies have used these small music cultures as sources of new music to market, most of the time in adapted second-hand versions. The blues, jazz, the tango to the bossa nova, Indian film music and reggae are a few of the many examples of this phenomenon. Small local recording companies first put recordings of such minority musics on the market, fulfilling the role of testers and risk takers. In order to keep track of what is catching on, the major companies try to handle the distribution of records from small companies. They often provide the mass-reproduction equipment and sometimes even the recording studios, thus keeping control of production facilities and at the same time easing the burden of investment for small companies. In this way there is both competition and symbiosis between the trans-national and the small local companies.

Technology and ethnomusicology

Record/play versions of recording technology, from the phonograph to the multitrack cassette 'portastudio' and digital recording equipment, have been of great importance to ethnomusicology. The possibility of recording music in the field and instantly playing it back there opened up a whole world of new methods for studying music. Combinations of recorded sound and still or moving pictures (film and video) made the methodological possibilities even greater. The systematic recording of traditional and other musics for scientific purposes had started before the turn of the century. In 1899 the first sound archive was established in Vienna, Der Phonogrammarchiv der Österreich-ischen Akademie der Wissenschaften, which is still active. Later many more archives were established at universities or by government authorities, and radio stations also compiled archives of recordings of traditional music. The aims of these archives were often quite different from those of the commercial recording industry. While ethnomusicologists generally recorded ceremonial and other music belonging to closed contexts and small populations, the music industry recorded more widespread kinds of entertainment music. Today both categories of recordings provide important source material for ethnomusico-logical research.

Some of the music collected as part of ethnomusicological fieldwork has also been published as commercial records. There were a few remarkable series of such recordings of ethnic and folk music issued on 78 rpm records by the Library of Congress in Washington, DC, Hugh Tracey in South Africa and others before 1950. In the 1950s a series of field recordings of traditional music from different parts of the world was issued by Alan Lomax on Columbia and by several collectors on Folkways. These were the first of many such editions to appear: for example the UNESCO Collection (issued on a number of labels), the French Ocora Series and the American Nonesuch series. The best of these LP albums have extensive written commentaries and documentary photo-graphs that form a unique media product.

Documentary recordings have been of great importance in preserving traditional music. In many countries they have been the main source of information when young people start to revive older kinds of music.

Technological hardware like different variants of melographs, sonagraphs and oscillographs have also been used by ethnomusicologists to study the structure of various musical traditions. The possibilities in this respect opened up by the development of computer and synthesizer technology are still to be tapped.

Recording technology has provided musicologists and ethnomusicologists with a means for preserving, duplicating and moving raw data in a way that many other disciplines were not able to do until the advent of computer technology. For many years musicologists made only limited use of the capabilities offered by recording technology. Most early musicological work was confined entirely to the realm of the written word. Since the 1950s ethnomusicologists have started to use sound recordings as an integral part of their scholarly texts. However, this is only a start. There is still much to be done in order to take full advantage of the inherent possibilities for publishing the results of ethnomusicological work as a combination of text, sound recordings and moving pictures. After all, one can never describe the sound of an instrument or a kind of music to somebody who has not heard it before without at least one recording.

An interaction model

Recording technology and the recording industry have been at the centre of contacts between technology and music during the 20th century. The music industry, however, is surrounded by a network that includes many kinds of organizations and institutions. During 1979–83 a survey was carried out by Roger Wallis and myself in 12 small countries in order to chart the effects of technological, organizational and economic developments on musical life (Wallis and Malm, 1984). The project, called 'The Music Industry in Small Countries' (MISC), gave rise to an interaction model as a means of describing the continually more complex network of relationships in the field of music (see fig.1).

The model has three main levels of action: the global or international, national and, finally, the local level.

The international level includes copyright and other international conventions. Included also are associations and organizations like the non-governmental UNESCO-affiliated International Music Council (IMC) with all its independent member organizations (the International Federation of Musicians, the International Society for Music Education, the International Council for Traditional Music, and the International Publishers' Association), and further the World Intellectual Property Organization (WIPO) and the International Federation of Producers of Phonograms and Videograms (IFPI). It also includes the trans-national industry dominated in the mid-1980s by the Big Five: Polygram, Warners, CBS, RCA and EMI, and by the related media and electronics hardware and software industries including transborder satellite broadcasting corporations.

At the national level, sovereign governments can make decisions that affect the field of music. Operative here are the national organizations from copyright societies and musicians' unions to fan clubs, and also the music industry, both the nationally owned companies and the subsidiaries of trans-nationals, national mass media, show business and institutions for formal music education.

The local level comprises all the musical activity in communities and neighbourhoods, including different musical sub-cultures and mini-cultures, and musical societies. This is the level of the 'public at large'.

The interaction within and among the three levels has grown in intensity from the 1960s. So far, the national level has been a mediator between the international and local levels. But with large international marketing campaigns, starting with disco music in the 1970s and on to satellite broadcasting of music videos in the 1980s, the direct interaction between the international and local level is rapidly increasing.

With increasingly sophisticated musical technology, the network of institutions and legislation trying to monitor the use of the technology gets ever more complicated. Still it seems virtually impossible to keep up with the rapid technological developments. For instance, the whole international and

IMPORTANT FACTORS	ORGANISATIONS	AREAS OF ACTIVITY

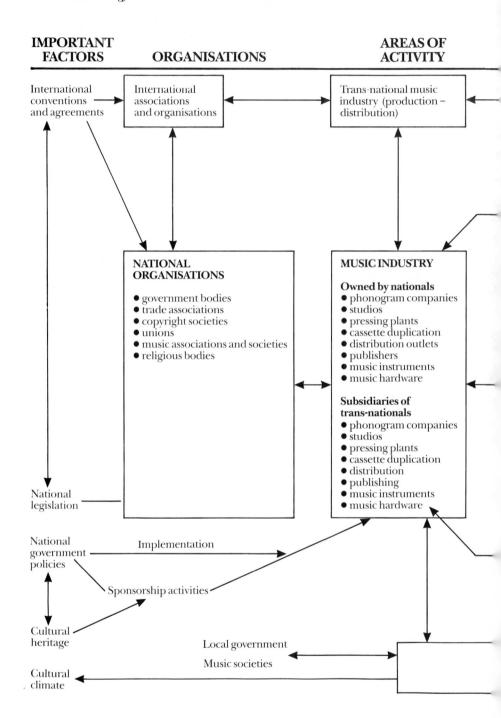

1. *MISC interactive model*

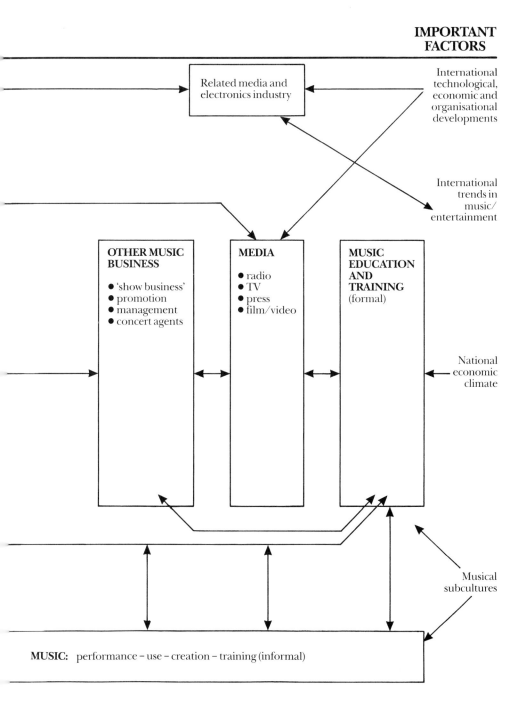

national system of copyright conventions and legislation has, through constant additions promoted by new technology, grown into a patchwork of regulations that is almost impossible to implement. That so much music is played through an ever-increasing number of media channels, on all levels and at all hours of the day and night, is making the problem of identifying usage of music, for the purpose of correctly remunerating creators and performers, an almost insoluble problem. The present copyright system can handle neither the transfer of copyright monies from industrialized countries to the Third World, nor counter transborder satellite broadcasting or home taping and piracy – not to mention the problems that will be caused by the digital audio tape-recording technology. Another challenge to the system is posed by local traditional music becoming part of an international 'packaged music' not protected by international copyright conventions or even, with a few exceptions, by national legislation.

Music industry technology and patterns of change

The products of music industry technology have permeated all kinds of societies regardless of their individual state of development. With each wave of new products this penetration is becoming more rapid. This has resulted in much of the hardware and software of the music industry during the past decades reaching countries in the industrialized world and the Third World almost at the same time. A survey carried out by the MISC team in 1983 in the small village of Pitipana, Sri Lanka, showed that 35 per cent of the households

2. A cassette recorder on sale at the market in the isolated town of Douz, in the Sahara desert, Tunisia

had cassette players (Malm and Wallis, 1985, p.289). A survey carried out in Sweden just a few years earlier showed that 52 per cent of the households had cassette recorders (Malm, 1982, p.67). The difference in general conditions between Sri Lanka and Sweden is enormous, but the percentage of households having cassette recorders is quite similar.

The presence of music industry products profoundly affects music and musical life wherever they penetrate. Although traditional societies and their music in different countries and ethnic groups can be dissimilar, the changes resulting from the introduction of music industry technology seem to follow common basic patterns (Wallis and Malm, 1984, pp.269–311). Many changes are brought about by use of different kinds of hardware to disseminate music and by the adaptation of local music to the constraints of mass media, recording technology and phonogram markets. One can term this the 'mediaization' of music and music life.

Before the advent of music technology all music was performed live and could be heard only within a limited space. The introduction of music technology brings an increasing distance between music makers and audience. Microphones, amplifiers, loudspeakers, recording studios and radio transmitters are inserted between musicians and listeners, separating the music from a specific context. With a Walkman-style cassette machine you can listen to any kind of music anywhere. Music becomes an independent, abstract sound phenomenon. Many languages do not traditionally have a word meaning music. With music technology such a word is usually introduced into these languages.

The shift from live-music to various forms of media-disseminated situations also brings a shift in audience attitudes from active, participating listening to passive hearing. Music is increasingly used as a time-filler and as a background to other activities.

The musicians become specialized professionals, stars and even idols far removed from the public at large, lessening possibility of interaction with their audience. In extreme cases the only feedback from the audience to the artist is in the form of money. 'Media stars' tend to become fewer, concentrating the amount of money invested in technological equipment and 'production'. For example, only a handful of superstar singers perform on the sound tracks of the high-cost Indian film productions.

Mediaization both changes traditional music and gives birth to new music. The open forms of many traditional kinds of music are replaced by closed forms with a distinct beginning and end. The 3-minute 78 rpm record format has moulded many kinds of traditional music into pieces of music of around three minutes duration. Longer forms of music such as epic songs are often excluded from the media. The use and function of traditional music also changes. They become representative and are used in national and other official functions, often performed in stylized and arranged versions on stage by official music groups. Traditional music is also used in advertising and the tourist industry.

At some point in the mediaization process copyright legislation is introduced. In many traditional music cultures neither the concept of individual ownership nor the Western art-music concept of a composer is applicable, both of which are basic concepts of copyright conventions. The problems

Development of National Pop and Rock (N P and R) 1960s–early 1980s in Tanzania, Tunisia, Sweden and Trinidad

	1960s	Early 1970s	Mid 1970s	Late 1970s and early 1980s
TANZANIA	'Jazz' bands playing popular music from Zaire migrate to Tanzania. European string and wind instruments. African percussion. Style influenced by jazz and Caribbean music. Sung in linguala (Zairean patois). Tanzanian groups formed imitating the Zairean 'jazz'.	First groups formed copying Western rock and soul and using electric guitars. Texts in English. Groups imitating Zairean music and start to sing in Swahili and develop 'Tanzanian' style. First recordings made and pressed in Nairobi, Kenya.	Electric instruments gradually replace wind instruments. Almost all texts in Swahili on Tanzanian topics. Melodic and rhythmic elements from traditional *ngoma* mixed with Zairean and Afro-American elements form 'Swahili jazz'. 'Jazz bands' sponsored by co-operatives, trade unions and students' associations. Radio Tanzania starts regular live broadcasts with 'jazz'.	Approximately 120 'jazz' bands active in major towns. N P and R regarded as representing development by ruling elite. Supported by National Music Council. Afro 70 Band represent Tanzania at FESTAC 77 in Nairobi with full set of electric instruments including synthesizer. In early 1980s no electric instruments imported due to lack of foreign currency.
TUNISIA	Strong influence of Libanese and Egyptian film music and French pop music.	Electric organs introduced in wedding party music in urban areas. Youth groups formed to play music patterned on film music and trans-national rock. Much emphasis on solo singers.	Electric organs adapted to Arabic scales. Groups experiment with N P and R. African-American and Arabic stylistic elements mixed, but with limitations. Government counteracts influence of trans-national P and R by extensive youth activities in network of culture houses. Many youth orchestras play Arabic film music.	Imitations of trans-national P and R still common. N P and R not firmly established. In early 1980s a new form 'musique engagée' with political texts in Arabic is developed by young intellectuals. Music style a mixture of traditional Tunisian music and French popular music.

SWEDEN	Numerous groups imitating Beatles, Stones etc. 68/69 groups emerge singing in Swedish. Ignored by established media. New groups in opposition to older forms of Swedish popular music.	'Swedish trend' develops. Groups mix Swedish folk music with trans-national rock into N P and R. Enthusiasts start record companies for N P and R. Many texts carry political commitments. Electric groups appear all over the country.	'Music movement' develops. Associations formed to support live N P and R. New record companies form own association to confront IFPI. Much opposition from establishment, although some grants given to N P and R groups by National Council for Cultural Affairs. Synthesizers introduced but not getting common in N P and R due to association with trans-national ABBA music.	N P and R gets more diversified and sophisticated. Elements from non-European musics introduced. Young punk groups emerge, first singing in English, then in Swedish. Increased support for N P and R from established media and government. N P and R groups find it hard to retain 'angry' identity.
TRINIDAD	An indigenous non-transnationalized folk/popular music firmly established: calypso played by 'brass bands' and steel bands. Indian film music and US hits imitated by some groups.	Electric instruments used in calypso bands. In spite of massive output of soul, Beatles, etc in mass media, little imitation of that music. Trans-national record company operations taken over by local enthusiasts.	Soul and reggae rhythms filter into the calypso music resulting in new N P and R style called 'soca' (soul-calypso). From 1977 adopted by most bands. The heavy soca beat depends totally on electric instruments.	Soca fad continues. Synthesizers adopted by most bands. Some soca tunes banned in mass media due to content of text. Steel bands start to play soca.
ALL FOUR COUNTRIES	PA systems used. Introduction of electric instruments. Imitations of trans-national pop and rock music by local groups.	Electric instruments adopted by many groups. Groups start to compose own music instead of copying. Experiments with singing pop and rock in local languages, mixing trans-national music styles with national music. The emerging N P and R groups try to find venues (new clubs, festivals of Woodstock type etc) and mass media outlets.	Fully developed N P and R styles are accepted by youth audience.	Disco boom causes setback of live music scene and demand for a more heavy beat (i.e. more powerful amplifier systems and sophisticated multitrack studio facilities). Some kinds of N P and R accepted by government authorities and national mass media.

361

caused by this conflict have affected the development of local music in many ways. While local kinds of music are used as raw material by the recording industry, this borrowing often means that certain pieces of traditional music are registered with copyright societies and thus become the 'property' of persons who have had nothing to do with their original creation. Copyright legislation combined with this kind of 'theft' of music has led to instances in which local media have to pay somebody in another part of the world in order to disseminate a piece of local music.

The introduction of amplification has changed the style of musical performance. Many traditional vocal styles have been moulded by the use of microphones and amplification. One obvious example is the rapid 'softening' of the Muslim prayer calls during the past decade. All kinds of traditional instruments are now played with amplification and Western electro-acoustic and electronic instruments, especially electric guitars and synthesizers, can be found in all parts of the world. These instruments are usually imported and expensive; here is a significant factor changing the economics of local music-making.

Amplified and electronic instruments can be used as substitutes for traditional instruments; for example, a synthesizer programmed to give the appropriate sound can be used instead of a bagpipe at a Tunisian wedding. A synthesizer can also be used to imitate music styles marketed by the trans-national music industry. They are often used to create new kinds of local mediaized music, which usually borrows stylistic features both from local traditional music and international hit music. This kind of 'hybrid' media music has developed in most small regions and countries since the 1960s. In the MISC project this music was called 'National pop and rock music'. Table 1 shows the stages in the development of such music in four otherwise very different societies: Tanzania, Tunisia, Sweden and Trinidad. The parallels are striking.

Sometimes the adaptation of local music to the media can go so far that, like Jamaican reggae, it becomes almost entirely a product of the recording studio. It is only in the sophisticated recording studios of Kingston, Jamaica, that the reggae sound the world has come to know is created. Live performances of reggae are rare, since the demands on equipment are so great and the finances of all but a few top reggae artists so limited. Reggae can be heard live in Jamaica only at major events directed towards tourists. On the other hand, giant discothèques, called 'sound systems' in Jamaica, dominate the local music scene, where live performance is by local disc jockeys who often improvise lyrics ('toast') over reggae rhythm tracks ('dubs').

Local, regional and national mass media play as important a role today for music and music life in the Third World as in the industrialized world. In most countries local musicians more or less have access to the broadcasting media or at least to recording technology and legal or illegal distribution of recordings. If the broadcasting media project only certain officially accepted kinds of music or just act as megaphones for the trans-national music industry, local cassette companies tend to take over the mass distribution of other kinds of music. In the village of Pitipana in Sri Lanka, the most popular music in 1983 was *baila*, a Sri Lankan popular music with topical texts seldom played

3. *One of the many record pressing plants in Jamaica*

on the air by the Sri Lanka Broadcasting Corporation, but sold on prerecorded cassettes.

'Transculturation'

Music technology has played many roles in processes of cultural exchange, cultural domination and cultural imperialism. It has also brought about a new kind of process that can be termed the 'transculturation' of music. This process involves the combination of features from several kinds of music in an industrial process, the result being a music without roots in any specific ethnic group. Disco music, constructed by producers in the recording studios of Munich, was probably the first such 'transcultural' music.

An increasing number of national and local music cultures contribute features to transcultural music. For example, a European record producer travels to Africa with a portable 8-track tape recorder and records local drumming. Once back in one of the music capitals of the world, he feeds some of this into his sampling synthesizer, adds synthetic brass sounds, backing vocalists, mixes in some effects from a recording with a Mongolian singer from a sound archive and produces a hit record to which everyone can sing along but which sounds unique.

Today, in the 1990s, as people all over the world sit in front of their small battery-powered Japanese synthesizers and try to relate to the pre-programmed rhythms and sounds produced when they press buttons which say 'Big Band', 'Waltz', 'Cosmic' or 'Koto', 'transcultural' music structures are quickly spread. Will this lead to a 'greyout', a global music style, or even a global music culture? Or will all the possibilities brought about by music and media technology add a wealth of new kinds of music to those already existing in living tradition and on recordings waiting for revival?

Much research remains to be done before the impact of music-industry technology on music cultures is fully understood. One can safely predict that this will be one of the main areas of ethnomusicological research in the immediate future. The results of such research will be an important resource in the formation of national and international cultural and communication policies.

Bibliography

F. Gaisberg: *The Music Goes Round* (New York, 1942/*R*1977)

J. F. Perkins: 'On Gramophone Company Matrix Numbers 1898–1921', *Record Changer*, xxiii/3–4 (1976), 51

P. Gronow: 'The Record Industry Comes to the Orient', *EM*, xxv/2 (1981), 251

K. Malm: 'Phonograms and Cultural Policy in Sweden', *The Phonogram in Cultural Communication*, ed. K. Blaukopf (Vienna and New York, 1982), 43

R. Wallis and K. Malm: *Big Sounds from Small Peoples: the Music Industry in Small Countries* (London, 1984)

—— : 'The Baila of Sri Lanka and the Calypso of Trinidad', *Communication Research*, xxii/3 (1985), 277

CHAPTER XVI

Preservation of the World's Music

SHUBHA CHAUDHURI

Of the many definitions of ethnomusicology, none explicitly or implicitly includes the concept of preservation as a major purpose or component of the field. Yet the preservation of music in various forms has all along been one of the major activities. The early history of our field is particularly characterized by this urge, but it continues with us in the present. (B. Nettl, 1983)

Collection and preservation of sound recordings in ethnomusicology

The systematic collection of sound recordings is closely linked to the development of ethnomusicology. Accounts of the earliest ethnomusicological works, though differing in interpretation, all mention sound recording as integral to the discipline. In 1890 the anthropologist Jesse Walter Fewkes recorded songs of the Passamaquoddy Indians on the phonograph, these being the earliest ethnomusicological recording. Dietrich Schuller states that 'All areas of ethnomusicology, however, share as their common base, and regard as by far and away their most important source, the sound recording . . . Just how essential sound recording was to become, was demonstrated by A. J. Ellis' study of various musical scales which are regarded as the beginning of ethnomusicology' (Schuller, 1983, p.121).

With the importance of the collection of music and folklore recordings came the recognition of the need to preserve them. Music and other oral arts exist in a state of flux, and traditions and performance are constantly changing. Early anthropologists and folklorists were concerned that many musical and performing traditions were becoming 'extinct' and regarded recording collections as the sole manifestations of such material. Thus sound archives came into being to provide repositories for the systematic storage of field recordings.

Sound archives, or centres of recorded collections like the sound archives in Vienna and Berlin in Europe or the Library of Congress in the USA, provided a base for the discipline of ethnomusicology before the institutional structure now provided by university departments (see illustration). Archives provided support for the systematic collection, documentation and collection of sound recordings. Some historic landmarks in the development of sound archives are: (i) 1899, establishment of the Phonogrammarchiv in Vienna; (ii) 1900, Société d'Anthropologie in Paris; (iii) 1900–5, establishment of the

Phonogrammarchiv in Berlin, under the directorship of the ethnomusicologist Erich. M. von Hornbostel; (iv) 1902–3, establishment of sound archives in Leningrad.

Sound archives, even those that focus on musical material, were not

Robert W. Gordon, head of the Archive of American Folk Song at the Library of Congress, with part of the cylinder collection and recording machinery, c1930

established for research. In most cases archives housing music collections and related material have their origins either in the recording industry or in broadcasting. There are government and state archives that are intended to serve national public needs in most countries today: some of these have had their origin in broadcasting or recording archives and most such sound archives house recordings of speech and other sound resource material in addition to music.

All types of sound archives are primarily committed to the physical preservation of their material, which provides a base of similarity in their operation. However, it is the nature of its users that determines the structure and organization of a sound archive. Policies concerning acquisition, administration, cataloguing, and access all differ. Some of these factors are: (i) public access versus research and educational use; (ii) international versus regional or national representation; (iii) commercial versus non-commercial use.

Ethnomusicology archives

Ethnomusicology archives are research-orientated, and have research and educational use as guiding principles. These archives are generally so-known when they are part of ethnomusicology programmes in universities or are seen as being based on fundamental ethnomusicological principles. This is especially apparent in acquisition policies and cataloguing methods. Such archives comprise music collections from all over the world, providing essential support for study and training in ethnomusicology. Popular and contemporary trends in music and related arts, integral in the study of a culture, are included in such archives. This is an antithesis to the belief that sound archives should only house recordings of musical traditions that are threatened with extinction.

Cataloguing systems are constantly being influenced by developments in ethnomusicology and by the needs of ethnomusicologists using such archives.

Access and dissemination

The role of archival preservation is not limited to physical preservation, though that is undoubtedly the most crucial task, as the loss or deterioration of recordings cannot be compensated in any satisfactory way. Such stringent and rigorous measures are involved in this task, that archivists are at times accused of seeing physical preservation as an end in itself, which can lead to questions of whether the high costs of physical preservation in archive maintenance are justified. This is particularly true of archives in developing countries where the meagre funding available must be channelled into physical preservation that appears to require disproportionate sums of money. Such countries also tend to be in parts of the world where climatic control becomes much more crucial as, for example, in most areas of Asia and Africa.

It is for these reasons that archivists must constantly keep before them the question 'Preservation for whom and for what?' Though it may seem self-evident, preservation entails many complex factors beyond those of physical preservation of recordings. If this is not borne in mind, archives will be considered as mere storehouses, where collections of recordings have limited use for a few people.

All archivists face the unenviable task of balancing on a tightrope between the requirements of physical preservation and the provisions of access to users. Since the handling, playing and even movement of recordings damage them by wear and tear, weakening of the magnetic signal, or deterioration due to climatic or physical factors, allowing indiscriminate or free use becomes out of the question. However, if we accept that recordings are preserved for the use of future generations, procedures can be devised by which use of recordings does not damage them. Duplicate copies do not necessarily provide the required protection. Many archives are not able to have duplicates or working copies of all master tapes, either due to material or manpower limitations. Therefore, many situations exist where an archivist must make a decision that will compromise one or the other criteria. In all cases, however, it would be retrograde to follow a course which could damage a unique recording for short-term convenience of either the archive or the patron.

Access to archival material not only entails physical access to tapes and recordings, but also to information. Documentation and any information that would be useful for a greater understanding of the material must be cross-related and made accessible. Insufficient documentation and cataloguing lead to inadequate access, as these are vehicles of communication to the user of the recordings.

Archives must also consider levels of access. In physical terms, this would be the difference of allowing a user to physically handle a tape, versus listening facilities where recordings are played for users from a controlled environment. However, the issue of access is more complex than that. Most archives today have degrees of access stipulated in their contracts. In some form or other this would mean restrictions on the making of further copies, copies being available for purposes of research, or commercial use and broadcast.

Archival collections do exist where material is not made accessible to any user and is stored for posterity alone. An archive grows by the use that is made of its holdings. If criteria of physical preservation become the sole guiding principle, providing better access at a later stage becomes more difficult.

Access to archival material, however free, remains a somewhat passive means for an archive to reach users, as it is restricted to people who can interact with the archive on an individual basis. This is important, and most archives do answer queries by mail and respond to an individual's needs. Publications of catalogues, finding aids, recordings, monographs and reports enable a greater cross-section of users to gain access to archival sources. Exhibitions, sponsoring of seminars and conferences are all vital means by which an archive can reach out to a wider audience. Broadcasting is another avenue through which an archive can legally disseminate its holdings. Archives and institutions also support research ventures that augment the archive's collections, or provide further documentation and updating of the archival resources. Archives can participate more actively in this area by development of programmes that interact with teaching and educational institutions.

Technical considerations of preservation

The core aspect of preservation must be physical preservation. If archival material in the form of recordings or documentation is damaged or lost, it is a permanent loss. This is particularly true of original recordings. Even if the material has a duplicate elsewhere in the world, the costs of making multiple copies and archival environmental control are high. Copies could perhaps be procured again, but at a very high cost. Poor cataloguing, inadequate legal procedures, and lack of dissemination can all be compensated for at a later stage, but nothing can compensate for the loss of the recording.

STORAGE Storage of tapes is the most central aspect of physical preservation. Magnetic tapes should ideally be stored at temperatures between 16 and 18 degrees centigrade, and 40 per cent humidity. It is important to protect them from direct sunlight and ultra-violet rays and this should be a decisive factor when choosing a room for tape storage. Dust and humidity are the other major dangers and closed shelving may be preferred in many situations. In tropical countries this provides a further level of protection against dust, and reduces to some extent the direct impact of temperature and humidity variations in the storage area. The issue of metal versus wooden shelving remains a controversial one. Wooden shelving provides safeguards against magnetic and electrical charges, but may be prone to insects and pests. Certain glues and varnishes also may have acidic properties or secrete oily substances over a period of time that damage tapes. If electrical wiring is safely covered and well maintained, metal shelving, especially with enamel finishing, is a safe option. If painted surfaces are required, polyurethane paint is considered the safest option.

The crucial factor in the maintenance of an archival environment is that temperature and humidity should not fluctuate: it is better not to have humidity control than have wildly varying levels. Air conditioning provides a basic level of humidity control, but archives in humid climates should use dehumidifiers. Temperature and humidity should be regularly monitored to avoid extremes. Excess and varying humidity can cause permanent damage by altering the condition of the emulsion leading to dropouts, peeling, crimping and mould. Phonodiscs also are permanently damaged by mould. Mould and fungus are a major hazard to all recorded material – from cylinder recordings to digital tape.

PRESERVATION OF DOCUMENTATION   The major drawback of archival recordings is that they are preserved without the context in which they are performed. This greatly diminishes the value as the context is not self-evident. Archivists have the disadvantage of being responsible for the preservation of recordings for the use of future users without knowing who they will be and what they may need to know. Hence all details by which such information can be provided, no matter how trivial they may seem at the time, are an integral part of an archive's holdings.

The emphasis required and given to recordings can undermine the care that is necessary to preserve documentation that accompanies the recorded material directly or indirectly. It is not uncommon to hear of tapes in archives and institutions that are unidentified or uncatalogued because of the lack of documentation.

Documentation should be clearly marked so that it identifies the material it accompanies. If this consists of notes and journals, the yellowing and crumbling of paper is likely to be the chief hazard. Documentation can be microfilmed or copied on acid-free paper. Photocopies are less acidic than printing inks. Newspaper cuttings should be photocopied, as their highly acidic nature can harm paper that is stored in the same file or file drawer over a period of time. Archive supplies of acid-free materials are available in most Western countries, and although they are expensive, are worth the cost. Typewritten labels are better than using ball points or spirit-based markers. Documentation in the form of written transcriptions of text and music is an important aid to the preservation of recordings, as is also the music in a wider sense. Good documentation available to users can reduce the need for handling recordings, saving time and contributing to longer tape life in the final analysis.

Tape care and maintenance

Tapes come in varying formats. Archives often must choose between options that suit their needs. Although audio cassettes are increasingly used in the field, open-reel tape is still considered the safest option; 1.5 mil quarter-inch tape is the generally accepted archival format. Cassette tape is not considered a format suitable to long-term preservation. Apart from the frailty of the plastic casings, the formulas of emulsions and backing used are not maintained at professional levels as is the case with open-reel tape. Chrome and metal cassette tapes, however, do enable very high grade recordings, though they deteriorate perceptibly with repeated playing. Tape should not be subjected to rapid changes in temperature even before recording. It is advisable to allow tape to reach the temperature of the space where recording is to be done before actually making the recording.

It is currently thought that print-through does not occur due to contact of magnetic signal on tape surfaces which is caused by poor storage. Print-through is highest in the 24 hours immediately following recording, after which it tends to reduce. To avoid this being a permanent problem, tapes should not be shelved in an archive immediately. After 24 hours of storage, they should be wound back and forth twice before being permanently shelved. Rewinding of tapes every six months is no longer considered necessary. (It may be a wise idea to play and check older recordings for brittleness, dropout, and degeneration of signal or physical condition of tape.) According to the Technical Committee of the International Association of Sound Archives (IASA) print-through on older tape can be practically eradicated by playing it through in the fast mode a couple of times. This must be done with discretion in the case of ageing tape. Use of leader tape is also necessary. Tapes should be stored with the tail (end of the tape) out. It is sometimes advised to rotate the sides of the boxes in which tapes are stored. Master tapes or preservation copies should not be stored with splices. Also, even winding is necessary for archival storage, and tapes that have been played in a faster than normal mode should not be shelved before they are played on normal mode. No tape manufacturer today is in a position to guarantee tape life that archives need. Tapes should therefore be checked every few years and be copied on to new tape if they are found to be degenerating.

To understand the technical aspects of tape care it is necessary to know about the backing and emulsion used. There is an increasing amount of literature on this and the IASA through its publication *Phonographic Bulletin* provides regular updates of information, and is a valuable resource in this area.

Care of recording equipment is crucial in producing recordings that will be preserved over long periods of time. Recording equipment should be clean and dust-free and regularly calibrated to specifications required by the tape manufacturer. The recording heads should be regularly demagnetized and replaced promptly when they show signs of wear.

ANALOG AND DIGITAL RECORDING   Archival storage must be designed for posterity and that sometimes necessitates that conservative choices be made in favour of tried and trusted systems. This is the main reason that digital recordings are not yet being used for archival preservation though most archives use some form of digital recording for making of recordings.

Digital recordings used most frequently are PCM, DAT, and compact discs. PCM recordings have a digital audio signal on videotape. Compact discs are the most stable and likely to be the most permanent format of these.

However, these are only being produced industrially. Videotape is not likely to have a long life, and the life expectancy of DAT tapes is the lowest. These newer, more compact forms of recording where the information is compressed on relatively little area are also more prone to damage of the recorded signal by physical factors such as dust or mould, and malfunctioning of equipment.

The major advantage of digital recordings apart from the generally high standards of recording is that the recorded signal does not wear out over time, and does not degenerate with repeated playing. It is possible to generate copies of equal fidelity as the original. The emergence of an archival standard of digital recording will definitely solve major problems of sound archives today.

Cataloguing

The development of adequate cataloguing systems of unpublished sound recordings is one of the major challenges for ethnomusicology archives. The crux of the problem is that sound recordings consist of serially ordered information that is not easily accessible in any physical terms, placing great demands on the cataloguing system for adequate retrieval of data. As sound archives are a relatively recent phenomenon, cataloguing standards have not reached the levels of standardization that are, for example, available for libraries.

Cataloguing of recordings is an irreplaceable element of preservation. If recordings are to be used by future generations, the information accompanying them must be detailed and complete. Numbering of tapes, shelf lists, and accession records forms the basis of a successful cataloguing system. Accompanying documentation, notes, photographs and any related artefacts must be related to recordings through the cataloguing system. In a sound archive, complete technical information of the tape type, recording equipment and technical standards used should be a part of the cataloguing information.

Standardization of terminology and technical vocabulary are other criteria of professional cataloguing. National and international standards are being developed and will go a long way in the successful sharing of information among archives. Standardization is also vitally necessary in in-house systems. Subject thesaurus and authority lists are also important tools for the standardization of cataloguing standards.

Before the widespread use of computers, most archives provided one primary point of access like a geographical index, and further detailed subject information through cross-referencing. This task has now been made much easier. Cataloguing on computers provides ease of retrieval on an unprecedented scale. Most computer-based retrieval systems provide for easy and multiple cross-referencing. Searches by keyword and access words have reduced the burden of designing a system that will accommodate a host of specialized needs. Sharing of archival resources on networks across continents reduces the onus for an archive to catalogue all its published material in-house, and allow searches of material housed in other archives with relative ease. The limitation of such on-line systems in accommodating specific requirements of institutions is compensated by the possibility of resource sharing. An ideal situation for most archives would be access to national and international networks supplemented by in-house databases which cater to specific research needs.

The basic structure of a cataloguing system would depend on the anticipated nature of the users. However, primary information on the time, place, performers and the nature of performance should be common to all systems. It is, however, a near impossible task to anticipate or predict the user's needs. It is debatable whether cataloguing standards should be limited by an archivist's evaluation of user needs. One hears only too often that 'nobody ever asks us for this'. Users will also base their demands on what they consider reasonable to ask for and demand more from cataloguing systems once they know what is available. The extent of detailed cataloguing is dependent on the level of available information. Recordings generated by researchers in the field are bound to have a qualitatively different standard of documentation available for cataloguing than incidentally collected recordings of an identical event.

Preservation and the role of archives

As agents for preservation, archivists are in a position to make decisions that have very long-term effects: not only are physical preservation criteria involved, but also many ethical issues. It is very tempting for archivists to 'play God' as they often have the sole responsibility in determining how a recording should be used and by whom. The archivist, more often than not, is in a pivotal position between the fieldworker or researcher, the performer or performing community and the patrons or users.

The archivist must ensure that copyright and ethical demands are met by all concerned. Legal opinions must be sought so that these aspects are not violated by an archive. Most archives have legal contracts that stipulate the conditions for use. It is often difficult to decide who has the right to restrict or release recordings. This also varies between countries and communities, and archives must often take a stand. In so far as possible, archivists should not perpetrate a system where they have a discretionary right over the use of the material.

Researchers should be encouraged to leave copies of the recordings they make in a regional or national archive in the field area, and archivists can take an active role in ensuring this. Archives can work with researchers to procure performers' permissions as well as advise on local ethical issues.

Though the aim of archives is preservation, it does not follow that they do not have a role to play in contemporary ethnomusicology. If fieldwork is an established component of research in ethnomusicology, archives should have a supplementary if not parallel place. Collections of sound recordings should enable comparative and analytic studies of field recordings, and archives serve this need by the systematic centralization of such material. Though recordings in archives are handicapped by existing out of context, they are not restricted by factors of time and place. Archival collections enable cross-cultural studies on a range that is not possible for an individual. More significantly, archival recordings alone can provide for research of oral traditions based on historical perspectives. Computerization now facilitates analysis of hitherto impossible amounts of data. This also changes and expands the scope of ethnomusicological research. By providing sufficient documentation and thorough cataloguing, archives can, and do, provide a range of recordings enabling research that cannot be accomplished through fieldwork.

Bibliography

J. Kunst: *Musicologica: a Study of the Nature of Ethno-musicology, its Problems, Methods and Representative Personalities* (Amsterdam, 1950, enl. 2/1955 as *Ethnomusicology*, 3/1959; suppl., 1960)

B. Nettl: *Music in Primitive Culture* (Cambridge, MA, 1956)

A. Breigleib: 'Ethnomusicological Collections in Western Europe: a Selective Study of Seventeen Archives', *Selected Reports in Ethnomusicology*, ii (1968), 77

M. Hood: *The Ethnomusicologist* (New York, 1971, 2/1982)

D. Lotichius: 'Safety First – Essential in the Preservation of Recordings', *Phonographic Bulletin*, v (1972), 8

H. Spivacke: 'Broadcasting Sound Archives and Scholarly Research: Background Paper for Discussion', *Phonographic Bulletin*, vii (1973), 6

R. Edwards, ed.: *The Preservation of Australia's Aboriginal Heritage* (Canberra, 1975)

R. B. Carneal: 'Controlling Magnetic Tape for Archival Storage', *Phonographic Bulletin*, xviii (1977), 11

IASA Technical Committee: 'Standard for Tape Exchange between Sound Archives', *Phonographic Bulletin*, xix (1977), 42

G. A. Knight: 'Factors Relating to Long-term Storage of Magnetic Tape', *Phonographic Bulletin*, xviii (1977), 16

M. M. Agar: *The Professional Stranger: an Informal Introduction to Ethnography* (Orlando, 1980)

A. Moyle and G. Koch: 'Computerised Cataloguing of Field-Recorded Music', *Phonographic Bulletin*, xxviii (1980), 19

H. Harrison: 'Selection of Sound Material for Current and Future Use', *Phonographic Bulletin*, xxxi (1981), 14

R. Schuursma: 'Problems of Selection in Research Sound Archives', *Phonographic Bulletin*, xxxi (1981), 17

W. D. Storm: 'The Establishment of International Re-Recording Standards', *Synergetic Audio Concepts*, viii/4 (1981), 1

P. T. Bartis: *A History of the Archive of Folk Song at the Library of Congress: the First Fifty Years* (diss., U. of Pennsylvania, 1982)

K. Compaan: 'Compact Disc – Digital Audio: the Optical Way of Sound Recording', *Phonographic Bulletin*, xxxiv (1982), 33

Library of Congress: *Ethnic Recordings in America: a Neglected Heritage* (Washington, DC, 1982)

D. Lance, ed.: *Sound Archives: a Guide to their Establishment and Development* (Milton Keynes, 1983)

B. Nettl: *The Study of Ethnomusicology: Twenty-nine Issues and Concepts* (Urbana, 1983)

V. A. Newton: *Mexican Institutions and Archives: Their History and Development* (diss., U. of Texas, Austin, 1983)

D. Schuller: 'Preliminary Recommendations for Fire Precautions and Fire Extinguishing Methods in Sound Archives', *Phonographic Bulletin*, xxxv (1983), 21

——: 'The Technical Basis of Sound Recording', *Sound Archives: a Guide to their Establishment and Development*, ed. D. Lance (Milton Keynes, 1983), 10

J. Blacking: 'Dialectical Ethnomusicology: Individual Development and the Invention of Culture', *Working Papers from the Seminar and Workshop on Documentation and Archiving in Ethnomusicology*; ARCE; AIIS (Pune, 1984)

H. P. Harrison: 'Selection in Sound Archives', *Collected Papers from IASA Conference Sessions Special Publication*, v (1984)

A. Seeger: 'Is it Traditional? Is it Music?', *Resound: a Quarterly of the Archives of Traditional Music*, iii/3 (1984)

A. Seeger: 'The Collection, Preservation and Archiving of Field Materials', *Working Papers from the Seminar and Workshop on Documentation and Archiving in Ethnomusicology*; ARCE; AIIS (Pune, 1984)

W. D. Storm: 'Construction and Rationale of Building the Belfer Audio Laboratory and Archive at Syracuse University', *Phonographic Bulletin*, xxxix (1984), 9

UNESCO: *The Protection of Movable Cultural Property*, i: *Compendium of Legislative Texts* (Paris, 1984)

M. Ames: *Museums, the Public and Anthropology: a Study in the Anthropology of Anthropology* (New Delhi, 1985)

E. J. Dick: 'Access in Sound Archives: Equality for Users – Inequality for Recordings', *Phonographic Bulletin*, xliii (1985), 9

S. Frangos: 'Cataloguing Field Recordings on OCLC', *Resound: A Quarterly of the Archives of Traditional Music*, iv/3 (1985)

D. Hull: 'National Sound Archives: the Case for Creative Access', *Phonographic Bulletin*, xliii (1985), 12

M. A. Kenworth, M. E. Ruwell and T. Van Houten: *Preserving Field Records: Archival Techniques for Archaeologists and Anthropologists* (Los Angeles, 1985)

G. Koch: 'Who are the Guardians? Problems in Retrieval at an Ethnographic Sound Archive', *Phonographic Bulletin*, xliii (1985), 17

N. Yeh: *Cataloguing Sound Recordings on Computer: a Progress Report from the UCLA Ethnomusicology Archives* (Los Angeles, 1985)

E. S. Johnson: 'Exchanging Copyright Sound Materials between Universities, Sound Archives, Students and Researchers', *Phonographic Bulletin*, xliv (1986), 11

A. Seeger: 'The Role of Sound Archives in Ethnomusicology Today', *EM* (1986), 261

A. L. Whitehead and M. E. Conway, eds.: *Self, Sex and Gender in Cross Cultural Fieldwork* (Urbana and Chicago, 1986)

B. Jackson: *Fieldwork* (Urbana and Chicago, 1987)

A. Seeger: 'Contacts with Patrons', *Resound: a Quarterly of the Archives of Traditional Music*, vi/1 (1987)

J. G. Bradsher: *Managing Archives and Archival Institutions* (London, 1988)

D. Holzberlain with D. Jones: *Cataloguing Sound Recordings: a Manual with Examples* (New York, 1988)

W. H. Leary: 'Managing Audio Visual Archives', *Managing Archives and Archival Institutions*, ed. J. G. Bradsher (London, 1988), 104

L. Sercombe: 'Ethical Issues in Sound Archives', Paper read at the annual meetings of the Society of Ethnomusicology (1988).

Papers from the Joint Technical Symposium on Archiving the Audio Visual Heritage: Shifting Deutsche Kinematic (Berlin, 1988)

CHAPTER XVII

Recent Directions in Ethnomusicology

BRUNO NETTL

Since 1960, ethnomusicology has moved in a number of new directions. We have seen both consolidation and fragmentation of the field. Concepts and issues that had hardly been considered earlier have taken up much attention in the 1970s and 1980s, but it is possible also to trace in the 1980s some of the fundamentals of the field as it was established in the decade of the 1880s. This chapter briefly surveys some areas that have been emphasized in the last two decades, and goes on to mention several major issues of concern before assessing some of the ways ethnomusicology has affected the world of music and scholarship.

A look at publications of the 1880s shows the continuing strands of concern. Two publications stand out in the early development of ethnomusicology: Alexander John Ellis's 'On the Musical Scales of Various Nations' (1885) and Guido Adler's 'Umfang, Methode und Ziel der Musikwissenschaft' (1885). Adler's study is ordinarily regarded as the point of origin of musicology as a whole, since it is the first work that lays out the entire discipline, provides subdivisions (beginning with the division into historical and systematic branches) and makes a claim for a discipline of musicology to include all types of learning and research about music. Rather than separating out historical research, it builds a discipline in which ethnomusicological concerns are included at various points. Overall, Adler presented ethnomusicology as definitely part of the musicological discipline, although he also noted its prospective major contributions to anthropology. Ever since, in encyclopedic definitions and in actual academic practice, ethnomusicology has been a part of musicology, and secondarily it has been a sub-discipline of anthropology. All definitions of musicology subsume ethnomusicology.

Ellis's major contribution was the establishment of a comparative, relativistic basis for research in musical systems, maintaining that they are all equally natural and, at least in certain respects, equally good, and that they could best be understood by being compared with one another and measured through a unified analytical device, the cent. The use of comparative perspective, while occasionally subject to criticism, has remained with the field. The emphasis on pitch as the pre-eminent phase of music has also, for better or worse, continued as the touchstone of analytical procedure. And the avoidance of a normative view, the conception of the world of music as a group of systems that are at bottom basically equal, is even more than ever a governing principle of ethnomusicology.

Other publications of the 1880s were seminal. To mention only a few, in order to show their relationship to the most recent history, Carl Stumpf's monograph on the music of the Bella Coola (1886) set the stage for monographs and studies dealing with repertories of individual cultures. The literature of ethnomusicology for its first decades was dominated by works that aimed to provide a proper sampling of the music of a culture, to describe its style in a way that might be applicable to many of the world's musics, and to provide transcriptions in Western notation. The basic assumption was that a single way of dealing with all of the world's musics could be developed, and that one must view the music to some extent in its cultural context. Transcription into Western notation was possible, and, the early scholars insisted, desirable as documentation and as a kind of proof of the existence of the music, and as a technique of showing that this was indeed music in the proper sense of the word (like the Western art music whose existence was regarded as residing primarily in its notated form). One cannot claim that surveys of small cultures any longer dominate the field, but the basic assumptions inherent in Stumpf's monograph are still around: description element by element, transcription, relationship to culture and, most import-ant, conception of the world of music as a group of separable musics, each a system with internal logic and coherence.

Another early seminal publication is Theodore Baker's dissertation on American Indian music (1882), a work that emphasizes music as a part of culture and gives a sophisticated discussion of singing style, divided into parameters. Further, we may look to the work of Franz Magnus Boehme, renowned as folk-song collector and editor, whose history of dance in Germany (1886) exhibits interests of continuing importance: close relationship of dance and music; acculturation between German and other dances; popular social dances of cities; and the reconstruction of history through study of contempor-ary forms. Finally, the attitude towards taxonomy of musics within a society, something frequently emerging from considerations of folk music, turns out (in statements by Gustav Weber, for example) to have been a good deal more sophisticated than one might have expected. Weber (see Pulikowski, 1933) makes it clear that he considers the world of song to consist of a number of overlapping categories (including folk, popular, art, 'volkstümlich', 'choral'). The question of taxonomy, and of developing a general one along with culture-specific ones, is still very much around in the 1990s.

Is it possible to state briefly what ethnomusicologists regard as the fundamental questions of their field in 1991? I have no surveys, and can only make some impressionistic remarks based on the literature and on formal and informal communications at scholarly meetings.

Defining, circumscribing and determining what actually comprises the field of ethnomusicology remains a major area of concern (see e.g. Merriam, 1977; Nettl, 1983, pp.1–14). A substantial literature speaks to this question, extending from rather trivial definitional matters to issues involving the taxonomy of musical activity and fundamental questions of value. For example, the degree to which it is possible to do comparative work at all and to understand properly a musical system outside one's own culture is a major issue of debate. Techniques, methods, technologies – recording, video recording, computer applications – have played a major role. An interest in shifting the focus of the field from the examination of static forms to the understanding of processes characterized ethnomusicology in the 1980s (see the special issue of *World of Music*, xxviii/1, 1986). Also there remains the question of social, intellectual and ethical responsibility, that is, the issue of what rights and obligations a scholar has in dealing with, promulgating, and judging the music of another culture, and the way in which he may discharge his debts to the original owners of that music. For a recent set of approaches to the history of ideas in ethnomusicology, see Nettl and Bohlman (1991).

These are but contemporary forms and current statements of abiding issues; they are evident at least by implication in the literature of the 1880s. And yet, of course ethnomusicology has changed enormously in recent times. An overview of what may be called 'new directions' and areas particularly emphasized in recent times may conveniently be divided into three parts: musics and cultures including new kinds of music being studied, new processes recognized as venues for study and new techniques and methods.

Musics and cultures

The earliest literature of comparative musicology adheres to a taxonomy of musics to be studied: primitive or tribal music, art music of the Orient and folk music. In some ways, these areas are still what most ethnomusicologists study. Scholars are somewhat uncomfortable with the terms, however, and have therefore come to prefer dividing the musical world into other categories. Whereas these sometimes coincide with the earlier classes, and while in any event the same music is often involved (albeit in a pie sliced differently), the newly recognized categories of music provide changes of emphasis. However, the change in attitude about taxonomies has also motivated ethnomusicologists to study musics that had not previously come under the purview of their field.

WESTERN ART MUSIC The most obvious addition, and the one that is perhaps most significant, is Western art music and its culture. The idea that ethnomusicological approaches could be beneficial to the understanding of this music goes back to early studies of popular music (Cantrick, 1965), early Marxist-derived analyses of musical culture (Finkelstein, 1960), and the study of folk and non-Western musics as sources for art music. Alan Merriam (1964) avoided defining ethnomusicology as the study of any particular music or culture, and in his most general book liberally included illustrations from Western society. In the later 1970s and 1980s, a number of papers and publications have tried to break down the barriers, some by suggesting disciplinary (and basically political and social) recombination, and a few by substantive study (see C. Seeger, 1977; Brook and others, 1972).

One may ask, of course, what kind of study of Western music would have to be undertaken to qualify as ethnomusicology. As an answer, one might look at four principal characteristics of the field widely accepted: interest in the study of music in culture, comparative study of the world's musics, field research and the study of all types of music in a society. Thus, the study of music as an aspect of culture, systematically and broadly conceived, might involve the study of the concept of talent as a special feature of Western music education, and as a principal issue in understanding the history of Western art music (see Kingsbury, 1988). Or it could include a study of the concept of W. A. Mozart in 20th-century musical thought, the relationship between fact and legend, and the degree to which the particular way in which Mozart is perceived by historians and musicians has determined understanding and analysis of his music. It might include a study of the relationship between musical excellence and moral superiority, and therefore, the ways in which historians have evaluated the attitudes of musicians in order to make their personas conform. Thus, ethnomusicologists might wish to examine the widespread musicological criticism of works dealing with Beethoven's unconventional treatment of his nephew and other relatives, or Mozart's supposedly uncouth behaviour (as depicted in Peter Shaffer's *Amadeus*), or Wagner's antisemitism.

The definition of ethnomusicology as the comparative study of world musics would require that Western music be studied with the approaches also used to study non-Western systems. This study would have to include some areas that are rarely treated by conventional musicology, such as timbre, singing styles and differences among performances, to give just a few examples from many. The concept of ethnomusicological fieldwork in Western music could lead to the study of musical taste and behaviour in audiences, or the description of musical events such as concerts, church services, recording sessions and rehearsals. Also, the notion that ethnomusicology is interested in all types of music in a society suggests the study of norms in addition to ideals, the relationships among various classes of music (an area which, in the case of the relation of folk and art musics, has actually been widely approached) and matters of folk taxonomy.

VERNACULAR MUSICS While there has been a good deal of discussion of the desirability of including studies of Western music in the purview of ethnomusicology, actually not much has resulted. However, significantly, ethnomusicological conceptualization has had an impact on historical musicology, whose practitioners have shown increased awareness of ethnomusicological methods and concepts. They have become more interested in musics outside the framework of 'art' music, sometimes giving the term 'vernacular music' to popular, light and semi-classical genres along with folk music; they have participated in the growing interest in symbolic and semiotic studies; and they have been fascinated by the role that oral tradition may have played in the development of the European written repertories. They have become more inclusive.

So in fact have ethnomusicologists as well. The fact that both musical taxonomies and cultural categories have changed in Western academic life and culture has tended to focus more attention on kinds of music previously neglected or at least not singled out for specific concern. In other words, while ethnomusicologists have always been interested in all kinds of music, their earlier concern with authenticity, cultural boundaries and oral tradition led them to draw lines among musics and to focus on the musical universe in terms of these boundaries. However, changes in concern brought about changes in the conventional taxonomies, and the new groupings of musics stimulated changes in the emphases of research. Thus, one now finds ethnomusicological interest focused on 'popular', 'urban', 'ethnic' music and on the music of specific groups within the population, such as women.

POPULAR MUSIC The addition of popular music to the conventional arsenal of ethnomusicology, which began around 1970, but had roots in the late 1940s (Waterman, 1948; Cantrick, 1965; *Popular Music*, i, 1981), signified a willingness to abandon some of the concepts dominating ethnomusicology from its beginnings. Ethnomusicological study of popular music began with an interest in African-American musics as a confluence of African and European styles; and with that mixture the idea of ethnomusicology as the study of the unspoiled, unmixed, and thus totally authentic began to give way. Indeed popular music is, throughout the world, the opposite of these early ideals. It frequently exhibits cultural and stylistic combinations, is often ephemeral, maintaining its character over short periods, is not regarded as high art by its society, and does not signify important rituals or cultural performances. It was once the kind of music that all types of musicologists eschewed as not worthy of study and perhaps not worthy of performance. With the growth of cities in the Third World and with increased interest in culture change on the part of model-disciplines of ethnomusicology such as anthropology and folklore, ethnomusicologists came to recognize popular musics the world over as the types of music to which the majority of the world's population gave allegiance. Thus, studies of popular genres of African derivation in the Caribbean and Latin America, the use of music in protest movements in Africa, the combination of Western and non-Western elements in popular genres of the Middle East and Indonesia, the study of film music in India have all played a major role in recent decades. It would be reasonable to expect this role to increase in significance.

URBAN AND 'ETHNIC' MUSIC The growth of urban populations and the willingness of ethnomusicologists in recent times to retreat from the work in the isolated rural 'field' – along with the growth of the sub-discipline of urban anthropology – have stimulated our field to begin strenuous research in urban environments. This new trend has much to do with the acceptance of popular musics as legitimate research, but it is also related to the growing interest in populations and musics that have moved among cultures, nations and social contexts. The lifeways of African music in Bahia, New Orleans and Chicago, or of Polish folk songs in Detroit neighbourhoods, the relations between Hispanic and African-American cultures in New York, but also the fate of country and western music when it moved from Tennessee to Chicago and, on the other hand again, the changes and consistencies in German classical music performed by Jewish musicians in Central Europe after its importation to Israel – all are examples of the kind of studies that have interested ethnomusicologists in moving to explicitly urban venues. (See Reyes Schramm, 1975; Pawlowska, 1961; Erdely, 1979; Béhague, 1984). Of course, earlier research too was carried out in cities; students of Indian and Japanese music studied in Delhi and Madras, in Tokyo and Kyoto. What is new is the attention given to the explicitly urban environment, the confluence of cultures and musics that characterize modern cities, the notion of a city as a single, comprehensive environment for the study of musical culture.

Closely related is the concept of 'ethnic' music, a useful category in the political climate of the period since 1960, and one that has been used to get around the undesirable aspects of older terms such as folk, popular and art music as they apply to particular groups. Problems such as the need to attribute rural origin or at least primacy in folk music, or the basic difference in origin between Chinese opera in San Francisco (an 'art' music) and Czech street bands in Chicago ('popular' or perhaps 'folk' music) could be avoided by use of the term 'ethnic' for both. The difficulty of distinguishing between 'ethnic' and other musics has not really been faced. Some scholars have taken a great interest in the definition or redefinition of folk music, but the widespread use of the term 'ethnic' may just have substituted new problems for old. The concept has nevertheless provided a home for areas of ethnomusicological inquiry that have been around for a long time but have really come into their own since 1960, that is, studies of minority and immigrant repertories. In particular, the fate of musics removed from their original home such as African-American, overseas Indian, European and Asian immigrants in the Americas, European and Middle Eastern repertories in Israel have come to be of special interest (see for examples the several studies in *Asian Music*, xvii/2, 1986; Baumann, 1985; *Selected Reports in Ethnomusicology*, iii/1, and vi). The degree to which isolated musics retain older characteristics, and the ways in which they change when placed into contact with strange musics and into new cultural and social contexts is of course the theoretical touchstone of this interest.

The role of music as cultural emblem is an important aspect of this area of interest. The assumption that each culture group associates itself principally with one music, repertory or style goes back to early ethnomusicological history and accounts for the willingness to draw conclusions from small samples. Its logical successor is the theory that while a society or a person may participate in many musical repertories and styles, there may be one music which is properly *the* music of the culture.

Ethnomusicologists increasingly have recognized that a society may be divided musically along various lines, and scholars have therefore begun to concentrate on the repertories and musical behaviour of segments of a population. Whereas they once looked at small samples of the songs of a tribe with the assumption that these examples signified a homogeneous repertory, they have since come to study linguistic, religious and ethnic minorities. This has led to increased interest in other segments of society largely neglected in the past, in particular women and children (see Ellis, 1970; Blacking, 1967; Frisbie, 1980). A large literature is on the verge of developing, however, as suggested by the special sessions on music and gender at 1987 conferences of the International Council for Traditional Music and the Society for Ethnomusicology (see also Koskoff, 1987). It has long been assumed that there is a children's music with a style of wide geographic distribution, and recent studies have tested and contributed to this supposition. The separate study of women's music in individual societies as well as on a larger scale, and of women's distinct repertories as well as their participation in general repertories and musical life is a new area of exploration.

Processes

If ethnomusicological research of the 1980s is distinct from what went before, it is distinguished chiefly by an increased interest in the study of processes, and of music as process rather than simply as a product. Perhaps one can say that there is now more interest in how things happen than in how things are. A survey of some of these processes (and their grouping) inevitably parallels some of the listing of repertories under musics and cultures, as these are the results of processes.

CHANGE AND ACCULTURATION The paradigm was once thus: historical musicology took a diachronic view, and ethnomusicology a synchronic view. The paradigm was never satisfactory, but in recent years especially, the diachronic view has actually come to dominate ethnomusicology. A survey of studies in the major journals during the 1970s and 1980s shows that more than half of the subjects are in a substantial way concerned with music as a changing phenomenon (Nettl, 1986). Ethnomusicology is still distinct from the characteristic study in historical musicology, which is concerned far more with specific events and changes than with generalizations and patterns. Ethnomusicologists are indeed concerned with seeing how, in general, music changes, by what mechanisms and with what regularities. Attempts have been made to classify types of change, beginning with Merriam's suggestion that one can distinguish between change stimulated from within a culture, and perhaps inherent in the cultural and musical systems, from change that results from contact with other musics and cultures (1964, pp.306–7). Most attention has been given to the latter, as the kinds of events that can be observed typically involve rapid and readily documented contact among cultures. Changes coming from internal stimuli are likely to be slower and to result from a large number of individual actions difficult to document for one from outside the culture, and difficult also to organize in patterns. The kinds of change that make up the bulk of the history of Western music fit readily into the internally stimulated category, and of course they might profitably be analysed with an ethnomusicological perspective.

In any event, the study of musical change is a significant new direction of ethnomusicology (see e.g. the special issue on 'Mechanisms of Change' in *World of Music*, xxviii/1, 1986). Typically, it has been approached by seeing each, and how cultures that have come into close contact have affected each, how new forms have come about from the contacts – the various ingredients of the concept of acculturation.

WESTERN INFLUENCES The most important avenue of acculturation has been the passing of elements of Western music and musical culture to other cultures; and indeed, one might consider the coming of Western music to all cultures to be the most significant event in world music history of the 20th century. Although it is a subdivision of general culture-contact studies, the study of Western influence may be separated from the rest for several reasons, among them the thorough knowledge of Western music and musical culture available to the typical scholar, the existence, on the whole, of a unified system of music in Western society, and the comparative perspective afforded by the possibility of viewing Western impact upon many cultures. The study of these influences requires, indeed, the recognition of certain central features and concepts of Western music – the system of functional harmony, for example, or the importance of the large ensemble, the prevalence of notation, the predominance of certain instruments such as piano, violin and guitar, the importance of composed works known by their composers, the concept of public concerts, and the notion of the general availability of music to anyone and at any time in contrast to social and ritual restriction (for illustrations see Nettl, 1985). This idea has underscored the concept of the world of music as a set of separable musics, each associated with a society and having central traits. As a consequence, confrontation among musics has been the model for study, leading to the identification of responses of the world's societies to the coming of Western musical culture.

Thus, some societies have rejected Western intrusions and maintained their traditional music essentially intact, while others have virtually abandoned the tradition, keeping it only in vestige. More commonly, we find societies that have created new musics from a combination of the traditional and Western, while others have, as it were, divided the society into sectors, each with a principal musical allegiance. In some cultures, Western elements have had an impact on musical style, and in others, principally on musical institutions and behaviour, or on ideas about music. Some societies have 'museumized' their traditions, keeping them alive in isolated pockets of culture; and others have adopted Western music but kept the older traditions for use in special cultural performances. A number of classificatory systems have been suggested. Blacking (1978) distinguishes among different types and degrees of change. I myself suggested eleven responses, two of which encompass others, that is, 'modernization', which involves the adaptation of Western features to enhance but not replace the central musical values of the tradition, and 'Westernization', which is the substitution of central Western musical values for the traditional ones (Nettl, 1978). M. Kartomi (1981) suggests another group that is in part parallel, while A. Shiloah and E. Cohen (1983) provide a continuum of nine types resulting from the interaction of traditional and Western musics, based on musical style and type of audience. M. McLean (1986) goes further in this direction in a study specific to the events in Oceania.

THE MASS MEDIA A process related to and overlapping the spectrum of Western influence is the dispersal of musical sound (and behaviour) through the mass media. Again, early ethnomusicologists might have avoided the study of this phenomenon (had it been an extant issue), preferring instead almost to pretend it did not exist. Ethnomusicology virtually came into existence because of the invention of recording, but the fact that commercial recording companies began very early in the 20th century to record non-Western (mainly Asian) and ethnic (mainly North American) music, including that of American Indians, and that they produced, early in the 20th century, records principally for the consumption of these ethnic groups, was long ignored (Racy, 1976; Gronow, 1982). From this point on, records, radio and eventually films and television have been important sources of transmission in the musical cultures of the world. Only in the early 1960s did ethnomusicologists begin to show much interest in the role of the media in societies; and at first it was largely a matter of using early recordings as sources. The degree to which the existence of the media affected the musical cultures has been studied so far largely with the use of Middle Eastern and also American ethnic material (for recordings), and with music of India (for film; Arnold, 1985). Recent studies of popular music in the Middle East, Africa and Indonesia (see articles in *Popular Music*, 1981–5) have made substantial contributions to the understanding of the record industry. It seems appropriate to suggest, conversely, that the 20th-century history of Western art music could be enhanced by more detailed study of the use of recordings and other media in the transmission of performance practices, and in the moulding of audiences.

Ethnomusicologists have always been interested in the study of oral tradition; but only recently have they begun to look at the variety of sound sources that mediate between the purely oral and the written as ways of transmitting music. Thus, the study of the role of the mass media is important not only because the media play a major role in the world's musical cultures, but because it would as well increase the sophistication with which the matter of musical transmission at large is approached.

URBANIZATION Since a branch of ethnomusicology devoted particularly to urban studies has been established, one of its principal tasks is to understand the process of urbanization as it applies to music. When we speak of 'urban ethnomusicology', however, we really refer to a preoccupation with the study of 'secondary urbanization', the transformation of cities which are the focuses of individual cultures into multicultural centres; and the establishment of urban centres that are multicultural from the start, such as certain African cities that virtually grew in the 20th century. While there are surely European cities that once served and continue to serve a variety of cultural functions and that brought together a number of otherwise separate societies well before the 20th century – Vienna, London and Istanbul come to mind – the rapid growth of cities which united and served as the venue for confrontation among social groups, including groups of recent immigrants from abroad or from the countryside, is essentially a phenomenon of the late 19th and 20th centuries. Most characteristic are cities such as Mexico City, which have grown enormously as a result of influx from rural populations; Lagos, in which the several ethnic groups comprising the nation of Nigeria are combined with labourers from other parts of West Africa and Europeans; Detroit, which in the late 19th and early 20th centuries saw the coming of poor white farmers from the highland South, blacks from the villages and plantations of the former confederacy, and immigrants from many European and particularly Eastern European countries. All of these ethnic groups in part maintained an independent existence and at the same time established relationships of conflict, co-operation and exchange; and each of them tended to divide itself into sectors with varying degrees of allegiance to older customs and values.

The task of ethnomusicology has been to investigate the way these groups used music to accomplish their ends, and the ways musical style and repertory, musical behaviour, as well as ideas about the nature and function of music may change in the course of urbanization. The three kinds of studies that principally have been carried out involve the fate of rural folk music, mainly European, when brought to the city (see Erdely, 1979); the fate of Asian classical music in a modernizing urban environment (see Riddle, 1983); and the establishment of genres of popular music from a combination of other, extant musical styles and genres (see Coplan, 1985). Not much general theoretical material has been developed, but a certain amount on methodology, especially concerning field methods and interpretation, has been published (see Reyes Schramm, 1982). In carrying out these studies, ethnomusicologists have been made particularly aware of the importance of music as a cultural emblem, as something that is used by a population group to express its uniqueness to other groups, bringing about cohesion but also serving as a medium of intercultural communication. These scholars have not yet come to general conclusions about the way music is affected by an urban environment as a whole, but the effects of certain ingredients of this environment have been studied: the development of popular music; the influence of the media, close relationships and confrontations among culture groups; and the development of occupational specialization. The growing interest in urban cultures has intensified issues that have fascinated ethnomusicologists for decades. I have in mind the great diversity of musical cultures, and the possible growth of a single, homogeneous musical culture with worldwide distribution.

SURVIVALS A discussion of the study of processes should include mention of survivals of various sorts, although these are in a sense 'negative' processes; that is to say, they retain culture elements in situations where change is otherwise taking place. Most obvious, and also oldest in the history of ethnomusicology, are the so-called marginal survivals, a retention of older cultural elements at the edges of a culture's geographical distribution. Characteristically this has been studied in New World contexts, with the use of repertories of European folk music, in African-American contexts, and later among other overseas and immigrant populations. The earliest students of the phenomenon, including, for example, Cecil Sharp (studying English folk songs in the USA) or Georg Schünemann (studying German colonists in Russia), were principally interested in the possibility of uncovering early and generally unknown songs, styles, repertories and instruments, and to a smaller extent in discovering principles governing the relationships of culture centres to their surroundings. A second wave of interest involved African-American music and the degree to which it reflected (and contained survivals of) African music. These studies had political overtones, as they concerned the degree to which African-Americans were capable of artistic creativity, were still genuinely African in nature, or might simply be borrowing European materials. These questions were mitigated through the application of more sophisticated and realistic approaches to research (see the bibliography in Westcott, 1977).

The study of marginal survivals in the 1960s to the 1980s has taken new turns, in two directions: towards the study of musical immigration, or survival of musical materials in an environment including an essentially different language, and towards an interest in the survival of institutions and practices aside from musical style and sound, including in particular the analysis of performance as carried out by American folklorists since 1970.

The study of 'survivals' should seek to answer questions about the extent to which the survival of older forms is related to distance from a culture centre, and to what degree it results from the social needs of a culture group surrounded by other cultures – and further, to what extent the stylistic relationships of a music in a new environment affect its retention. While the earlier studies of immigrant music were made mainly with European folk cultures transplanted to the New World, and with African materials (whose similarity to the European was made explicit by the theory of syncretism), new and perhaps different questions arise in the study of the interaction of Asian, that is, Asian-American, musics with mainstream American styles.

Examples of studies of Asian survivals in the Americas include works by Ronald Riddle, Amy Catlin, Isabel Wong and Alison Arnold (all 1985). They show that older Asian forms persist but that they also adapt to new social environments. They largely involve urban genres transplanted to new but also urban environments (in contrast to the European folk music which, of rural origin, came to New World cities and soon exhibited major changes in social function). They also indicate that music may become very quickly an emblem of ethnicity, as in the case of immigrants at the end of the Vietnam War, and that music may retain this function for many decades, as in the case of Chinese opera in San Francisco. While the Americas have provided the principal exemplars of immigrant music, other areas make comparison possible. One culture very widely studied is that of Israel, where the retention of folk musics of Middle Eastern origin has been examined with particular thoroughness, but where the role of Western art music as a mechanism for retaining cohesion of a culture group has also been studied (see the survey by Gerson-Kiwi and Shiloah, 1981). In general, the interest in survivals of the ancient has played less of a role in recent ethnomusicology, having been replaced by an interest in the processes of recent change.

HISTORY Interest in history in the conventional sense has not decreased, however. That ethnomusicologists are principally involved with non-written traditions has moved them to study processes of change as they occur, and to analyse what is presumed to be the result of change. There was in the 1980s far less interest in such historical study as the extrapolation of strata from geographic distribution, or the construction of evolutionist schemes, than there was early in the 20th century. But ethnomusicologists are taking greater account of archaeological evidence, following the greater sophistication in archaeological research at large (see the symposium on archaeo-musicology edited by Ellen Hickmann, 1985). There is also the study of history in the traditional sense, as the use of early documents including theoretical treatises emanating from the cultures studied and early reports of travellers, missionaries, and government emissaries, as illustrated in the compendia of F. Ll. Harrison (1973) and H. Oesch (1984). Also, there is much interest in seeing history from the perspective of the world's societies, as exhibited, for example, in the project, 'Music in the Life of Man', whose purpose was to compile a panorama of world music history written, wherever possible, by scholars native to the societies treated. (See also Blum, Bohlman and Neuman, 1991.)

It is important to note the changed conception of music in these historical studies. While primary focus may still be on the musical artefact and on musical style, ethnomusicological historians have been much more inclined to see music as consisting of sound and context, or indeed, to accept (not always explicitly) Merriam's tripartite model of music. Thus, changed functions or interpretations of music have come to play a role in their work.

REVITALIZATION One of the characteristics of 20th-century social history is the increased interest in ethnic identity and ancestry of individuals and groups – the concept of 'roots'. It has to do with the widespread movement of population groups, changing political borders, creation of new nation states, forced and voluntary emigration. Ethnomusicologists have recognized the importance of music in revitalization movements, the recovery of earlier music as a way of integrating society and fostering ethnic identity, and the importance of music as a marker of cultural boundaries.

ET CETERA The processes thus far mentioned involve change in total musical cultures and repertories. But the issues to which attention has been given in recent years also include processes operating in the life of the individual. Thus, ethnomusicologists have worked in the area of biography, producing general life histories of people concerned with music in non-Western and folk cultures (Ives, 1964; Vander, 1988), as well as explicitly musical biographies (Nettl, 1970). Beyond this, they have paid more attention to the uniqueness of the individual than may have been the case several decades ago, when the concept of cultural homogeneity overshadowed the need to understand the diversity within cultures. Related to this kind of thinking is the interest in learning and teaching, and in the way in which music is transmitted. The study of oral (and related) traditions has played a major role, and has been one of the areas in which ethnomusicologists and historians of European music have come to join forces (Treitler, 1974; 'Transmission and Form', 1982).

Methods and techniques

If ethnomusicology of the last 25 years can be characterized by its interest in types of music that it had previously neglected and in a shift from emphasis on the static to concentration on processes, its present state can be even better represented by its use of new (or revised) methods and techniques. In many ways, these changes in method reflect the changes in materials and processes studied, but they are also related to innovations in the approach to research in general, and to changes in society and in academic life.

IMPACT OF ANTHROPOLOGY AND LINGUISTICS Ethnomusicology began as a kind of offspring of musicology and anthropology, but it has participated in the growth of linguistics as an independent discipline since the 1950s, and in the growing interrelationship of anthropology and linguistics (Feld, 1974). It seems logical for a field that maintains an interest in music as *culture*, that makes a study of *all* of the world's music, all societies and all strata, and that gathers its data in the field, to be closely associated with anthropology. Yet there are scholars who would prefer to avoid the association, citing negative aspects of the emphasis on tribal cultures in anthropological method and the emphasis on the context of music rather than on music as an art. It may also be suggested that the positive aspects of the close association with anthropology had negative results, such as the decreased association, especially in North

America, with other fields such as psychology, sociology and biology, whose methods might well have played a salutary role in the study of world music (Blaukopf, 1983; Simon, 1978). Thus, despite the occasional foray or the isolated psychologist speaking at an ethnomusicological meeting, the absence of data on biological aspects of music-making (but see Blacking, 1977, 1978), or of experimental studies of perception and judgment seen interculturally seems to me to be a result of the predominance of the anthropological perspective.

Of the new methods in anthropology that have played a role in ethnomusicology, three areas stand out: ethnographic method, statistical correlation and semiotics. The sharpening of field methods and of interpretation of field data is of course at the heart of socio-cultural anthropology, and in the period around 1960, the question was attacked from several perspectives. Increased emphasis accrued to the idea that there may be significant differences between the perspectives of the cultural insider and the fieldworking outsider, abbreviated as 'emic' and 'etic', and between the fieldworker's imperative to present the world as seen by the culture. Attention was also drawn to the related conception that the 'inside' view has validity for interpreting the culture whether or not supported by 'objective' facts. The concept of ethno-science, the way the world's societies classify and divide their cultures, began to have a role in ethnomusicology, particularly in establishing the classes of musical types and genres. At the same time, the concepts of cognitive anthropology (Dougherty, 1985), and of the study of culture as a set of symbols (Turner, 1974), or more broadly, cultural anthropology as the study not so much of what humans do and the artefacts they produce as of the way they use and think about them, played a role in the establishment of new approaches to musical ethnography.

If culture is how people think about what they do, the ethnomusicological counterpart of 'culture' should be the concept sector of Merriam's model; and, indeed, the late 1970s and 1980s produced studies that deal principally with the ideas about music in various cultures. Lorraine Sakata's (1983) work on Afghanistan, Steven Feld's (1982) on New Guinea, Charles Keil's (1979) on West Africa, and Anthony Seeger's (1987) on Brazilian Indians all concentrate on 'concept', using musical sound and observed behaviour as a background, rather than – as was often done before – using the articulated theory of a culture to explain why its music had a particular style. Dealing with ideas about music in fieldwork and analysis requires much refinement in technique, especially if the ultimate purpose is to create a framework for the comparative study of musical conceptualizations. Theoretical models for this type of study are discussed by Feld (1984).

Quantification as a way of expressing the nature of musical data goes back to the late 19th century in ethnomusicology, and formal statistics at least to Merriam and L. C. Freeman's pioneering study of 1956 (Freeman and Merriam, 1956). The large-scale use of correlations between components of musical style and elements of culture as a way of explaining the relationship of musical and cultural types may be seen most clearly in the work of Alan Lomax and his associates in the so-called 'Cantometrics' project. Previewed in a study published in 1959, it was carried out largely in the 1960s and 1970s (Lomax, 1959, 1962, 1968). Its purpose was to examine music as a complex of components, mapping them in relationship to each other in order to show their geographic distributions individually and in clusters, thus characterizing each musical style or culture with a 'profile'; then to establish a typology of cultures, mainly on the basis of social structure and the quality of interrelationships among people, along with economic and political considerations; and then to find significant correlations. The project has been inhibited by the difficulties of determining just what constitutes culture types and musical styles, by problems that concern the measurement of musical and cultural similarity and difference. The conclusions reached have been occasionally criticized (Henry, 1976). Nevertheless, it has generally been agreed that the Cantometrics project has dealt with central problems of ethnomusicology – the reason for stylistic difference among musics, and the relationship of musical style to social structure and lifestyle. From the viewpoint of method, the attack on these relationships on a worldwide basis with the use of statistics has been an important contribution, and its continuation and improvement should be a major direction for the future. It is interesting to see that the project has been much more warmly welcomed by anthropologists than by musicologists, and that it has been regarded mainly as an anthropological study.

A third ethnomusicological approach traceable to the intellectual environment of anthropology is frequently referred to as 'semiotics', but it is in fact considerably broader than this term implies, since it encompasses both the general idea that music can be analysed as a symbol or set of symbols as well as analytic methods derived from the general conceptions of structuralism. The 'semiotic' movement in ethnomusicology can be said to encompass analysis using methods derived from linguistics, structural approaches to the analysis of culture and myth developed by Claude Lévi-Strauss, and the study of symbolic systems generally. A considerable number of publications have emanated from this approach, and it has stimulated ethnomusicologists and indeed musicologists of all kinds to become acquainted with the fundamentals of modern linguistics and with some of the literature of anthropology. A number of articles and books providing analyses of specific musical works and repertories have flowed from the approach, and in the early 1970s a general movement in its direction could be identified (Boilès, 1973; Nattiez, 1973; Pelinski, 1981). It did not maintain its momentum, however, in part because its publications, while methodologically sophisticated, rarely told musicians things for which they did not already have the tools. Furthermore, few musicians wish evidently to extend themselves to the degree of analytical rigour necessary for using linguistic techniques. Nevertheless, the semiotics movement continues to have an impact. Concepts from linguistics play a role: the importance of myth as an indicator of cultural values is recognized, and the notion that structural analysis is a way of making objective judgements parallel to the presentation of a culture as it sees itself is an important concept in recent research. In all of this, semiotics and structuralism, while not replacing other methods, have had substantial influence on the field as a whole.

LEARNING AND TEACHING One way ethnomusicology has changed since the 1950s involves the vastly increased importance of learning and teaching. Three facets of this process are important. First, and most general, ethnomusicologists have become increasingly interested in the ways in which societies teach their musical systems, that is, in the way music is transmitted. They wish to discover such general matters as the nature of oral tradition, and to analyse the way music is broken down into units for transmission. They are interested in the acquisition of music by children, and in the way music may be used for enculturation, in early life and throughout the life of an individual.

Second is the explicit study of teaching and learning. This includes diverse components: devising materials specific to teaching, exposition of the way in which general principles of music making, intellectual and technical, can be incorporated into teaching materials and translated into actual music; study of the relationship between student and teacher; examination of the social role of teaching; research on techniques of giving lessons and practising; review of concepts of learning such as discipline and talent; and emphasis on the role of teaching institutions (see the symposium, *Becoming Human Through Music*, 1985). In earlier times, such issues, while recognized, played a small part in ethnomusicological research, but today it is understood that one can hardly comprehend a musical system without knowing how it is taught, learned and transmitted in its own society.

Third among these concerns for learning and teaching is the issue of field research. The question is: how can ethnomusicologists learn the musical systems of the societies with which they work, how internalize them? A major change in ethnomusicology field methods was effected when fieldworkers began, in the middle 1950s, systematically and routinely to study perform-ance of musics. Many scholars and graduate students came to believe that their own minimal competence in performance provided an appropriate background for more serious research, and also gave them credibility in their host communities. This approach was widely adopted, particularly in North America and Australia, and now, a generation later, it is being enhanced through increased sophistication and a critical understanding of the varied roles of performance in the music-making conceptualizations of the world's societies (see Hood, 1971, pp.230–41). For example, while making the 'right' musical sounds may be appropriate, a foreign performer may or may not 'feel' like a native music-maker. The roles of memorization and improvisa-tion may be handled differently by native musician and outsider. Social and ritual roles of performers may or may not be replicable with outsiders. The social relationship between teacher and student may be quite different if an outsider rather than a native is involved. Therefore, while ethno-musicologists continue to try to enter into a foreign musical culture by becoming students within it, they also recognize the degree to which this approach must be fine-tuned to the way in which each culture teaches its music.

Non-Western societies have, on the whole, accepted the notion that foreigners try to study their musics as active participants. This results from long-term exposure to ethnomusicologists and other fieldworkers. However, it may relate to the acceptance of music as an artefact of the modern world, something that all are permitted to hear and witness, that may be combined with other musics and performed by anyone. Temporal, personal and ritual restrictions give way to the musical culture of modern nation states, with its concert life and its mass media. All of this, of course, not only has made ethnomusicologists more welcome as participants but also has separated the teaching systems from their integral roles in the musical culture.

APPROACHES FROM MARXIST SCHOLARSHIP It is difficult to show explicitly all of the approaches in ethnomusicology that may be derived from the cultural climate of Marxism; they extend from a general interest in music of the 'masses', in folk and popular music, to a concern with the debts owed by scholars from colonial and capitalist powers to the poor nations; from the use of particular schemes of cultural evolution based on successions of economic systems to the concept of music as part of a superstructure of culture based on the relationship of classes; from the suggestion that the scholar must take an active role in improving the lot of human society to the interpretation of musics as instruments of protest. However, while various social sciences and humanistic fields have come to participate in Marxist styles of analysis (which may in fact be unrelated to a specific political stance), ethnomusicologists have actually made relatively little use of them. A number of studies in the journal *Popular Music* are clearly Marxist-inspired, as some of the studies in Eastern European, especially eastern German, periodicals (*Beiträge zur Musikwissenschaft*; see also Gourlay, 1978, Keil, 1982). A few publications show awareness of and influence by the Frankfurt school and by the work of Theodore W. Adorno (1949, 1962). However, many publications in the mainstream of ethnomusicology show subtle and general influences of Marxist thought.

They are influences largely traceable in style of thought, perhaps even in mood. These publications tend to accept the musics of a society as being qualitatively equal, and there is a certain scorn of 'elite' traditions. There is an interest in popular music, in repertories as a whole, as these reflect (both specifically and in method) the interest in groups and classes, not individuals. There is acceptance of certain basic principles of Marxism, such as the class struggle and the economic base of culture, and a desire to treat music as their reflection and illustration. But there is not yet an explicitly Marxist ethnomusicology.

RESTUDIES There may have been a time when the ideal model for the society of ethnomusicologists was to identify musical cultures, assigning to each a scholar who would collect its music, analyse, interpret and say the last word about it. One spoke of musics in terms of their having been 'done', or 'not yet done'. When the main task was for the field to get its bearings, as it were, this may have been a reasonable approach, though one not consciously carried out. Two changes in attitude motivated the development of restudy, the return, after elapsed time, to a particular venue in the field. One was the interest in change; the second stemmed from the recognition that music and culture are not simply hard and fast facts, but rather, that the contribution of the ethnomusicologist is in a broad sense interpretive. Both motivations followed the lead of anthropology, which began to take a serious interest in change in the 1940s, and in which the concept of restudy developed from the work of Robert Redfield (1930) and Oscar Lewis (1951).

390

In ethnomusicology, restudy takes at least two forms. First, the continuing return of fieldworkers to the same venue may be interpreted as restudy, as the repeated visits of scholars to one society not only reveal changes in the culture but also exhibit the changed approaches of the researcher. For example, the continuous work of David McAllester among Navajo people through several decades shows changes in his view of the culture. Alan Merriam's return, after 14 years, to the Basongye in Zaire shows him not only interested in quite different things, but also reveals the changes that took place in the interim (Merriam, 1964, 1977).

More characteristic of the 'restudy' concept is the fieldworker who examines a culture investigated by another, perhaps long ago. Nazir Jairazbhoy in the 1980s retraced the field trips in India made by his teacher, Arnold Bake, in the 1930s. Much of the recent research in Javanese gamelan music follows the footsteps of Jaap Kunst, using this pioneer's work as point of departure and as template for critical new approaches. Restudies, observation of change and showing the different approaches of several scholars to one culture have been important in shaping ethnomusicology since around 1960.

A related phenomenon is field research by cultural 'insiders' (or proximate insiders), following the footsteps of Western fieldworkers. Studies by Asian, African and Native American ethnomusicologists seek to re-examine situations once described by Europeans and North Americans, frequently taking on a corrective function, and exhibiting, as well, the difference of views of a musical culture from the perspectives of different cultures.

TECHNOLOGY One might expect that the enormous changes in technology, particularly sound recording, video-taping and computers, would have had a major effect on ethnomusicological techniques. There has surely been a substantial impact, and yet the effects have been surprisingly small. There have been changes in the kinds of data produced, but ordinarily not of the sort that would lead to radically altered conclusions. For example, far better recordings are made now than in 1950, but actually researchers are not using them much differently. Visual recording has played a greater role, but we are only at the beginnings of using video-tapes for analysis to supplement the analysis of sound, and so far, video has been largely a tool for education.

The use of computers in analysis of musical and other data has been advocated by musicologists for over two decades (Lincoln, 1970). A number of experimental studies appeared in the 1960s, but except for indicating how computers might be used for sophisticated processing of musical data, they produced few insights that go beyond those of early attempts such as Bronson's use of punch-cards in the 1940s (Bronson, 1949). Since then, except for the Cantometrics project, computer applications on a large scale have not had major impact, although ongoing projects are progressing. However, it is likely that we are on the verge of major changes and that certain uses of computers will become standard techniques.

Yet the fact that ethnomusicologists did not quickly seize the opportunity of being in the technological vanguard may be significant, as it points up again the essentially individualistic methodology of this field. The mass production of data that can be processed by computers is not compatible with the practice of individual scholars to work intensively with one or a few consultants, or with the emphasis on differences rather than similarities among musics. It is thus surprising but in the end not illogical that ethnomusicology, in most respects a forward-looking area among the fields of music, has not been in the front lines of technological application.

ABANDONMENT OF DOCTRINE It may be hard to distinguish some methods and techniques from the concepts and approaches of an earlier age, but it would be a mistake to exclude from a discussion of contemporary methodology the abandonment of doctrinaire taxonomies. Ethnomusicologists are now willing to look at the totality of a musical culture, to accept the taxonomy of music as it is presented by the society being studied. They no longer separate 'unspoiled' or 'uncontaminated' and therefore 'authentic' material from that which results from stylistic combinations or from intrusions of other cultures. Purity and refinement now play only a small role. This change in attitude is somewhat related to a willingness to look at various forms of music-making in the same terms – composition and improvisation, for example, and the various kinds of interaction between and combinations of the two. The result is a modest but growing literature of studies of improvisatory repertories, the process of improvisation and the relationship between models and points of departure on the one hand and the resulting improvised performances on the other (see Nettl, 1987). The discussion of these issues as well as those of oral and literature traditions is carried on in a series of papers edited by Tokumaru and Yamaguti (1986).

And surely also related is the avoidance of sharp distinctions between Western and non-Western, and between folk and art, that was once part and parcel of the ethnomusicologist's arsenal. The assumption that a different set of methods and attitudes is needed for the study of traditions that are non-Western (as opposed to Western), folk (as opposed to art), one's own (as opposed to foreign), or oral (as opposed to written) has virtually been abandoned as at once unnecessary and oversimplified. One major result, perhaps foremost, in a consideration of new directions is the gradual inclusion of Western and Western-derived music in the ethnomusicological purview. All of this shows ethnomusicology as a whole becoming broader, less doctrinaire, and more inclined to derive its methods from the nature of the material to be studied rather than imposing frameworks for study from the outside. The change has not been dramatic, but is significant.

ATTITUDES There is little consensus about the attitudes of ethnomusicological research in the early 1990s. One trend is a gradual abandonment of the division of the field into 'musical' and 'anthropological'. It is widely accepted that a scholar needs to be at least competent and interested in both. However, there are no official policies; no society has made a statement about the official qualifications needed to be a proper 'ethnomusicologist', and few if any charismatic scholars who stand out as principal leaders. But issues of widespread concern remain.

FACT AND VALUE There is a widespread tendency to move ethnomusicology where many feel it has belonged all along, into the mainstream of musicology (bringing with it, not at all abandoning, the interest in culture). For good reason, this is debated by those whose principal allegiance is anthropology. This argument aside, the debate remains about the basic value structure of musicology at large, and of ethnomusicology in particular. An aspect of this debate is the music historians' attitude of advocacy (of the kinds of music they study) in contrast to the ethnomusicologists' more egalitarian approach. The historian of the 1990s is interested in establishing facts in contrast to the ethnomusicologist's greater interest in extrapolation and generalization (once also widely done by historians; see Brook, 1972; Kerman, 1985; Meyer, 1967). The historians' view of themselves as 'insiders' to Western culture of all periods, contrasts with the ethnomusicologists' emphasis on facts as functions of approach and attitude.

The terms 'fact' and 'value', subjects of a symposium in Vancouver attended by about a thousand music scholars of all types in 1985 ('Fact and Value', 1986), illuminate what ethnomusicologists take to be their ultimate task. The question is whether we are to maintain a strictly objective attitude, trying to learn the nature of music and its cultural context, ascertaining what is happening, what has happened and why; or whether we should be guided by the differential of artistic accomplishment in the various cultures of the world, identifying and studying the world's best music, working to preserve and improve it, and in other ways imposing a well-considered value structure on our work. Along with music historians, theorists, composers and performers, ethnomusicologists are engaging in a kind of debate about the view of the musical world that should be taken by the musicians and music scholars of the world's cultures. However, it is already clear that, if values are a major issue, they must be the values of individual cultures seen from the perspective of each, and that social and ethical values are involved probably more than strictly musical ones; and surely that matters of musical excellence are approached intra- and not inter-culturally.

INSIDERS AND OUTSIDERS Research is supposed to uncover facts, but the 'facts' can be only somebody's interpretation, and if a multiplicity of cultures is involved, the validity of the insider's and outsider's views becomes a major issue. In the 1970s and 1980s ethnomusicologists became particularly concerned with the contrastive roles of the two. In part it is a matter of ethics: what is the right of a society to control entirely its cultural products, and who speaks for such a society? What is one to do about individual internal differences, and indeed, is a 'society' defined by the outside anthropologist's taxonomy or by the citizenship laws of modern nations? The current picture shows again, the abandonment of strict doctrine. At one time, the virtues of the outsider's objectivity were considered essential, and ethnomusicology was sometimes defined as study by the outsider; around 1970, in part as a result of political and social currents in North America and Europe, the vast number of 'outsiders' who populated the field showed an appropriate inclination to defer to the 'insiders', though sometimes mindlessly defining these very broadly – according 'insider' status in all African musical cultures, for example, to any African scholar. By now, the complexities of the issue are better recognized, and the interrelationships of insider and outsider, as both scientifically objective and interpretive, are better understood.

However, the question is not only who should be permitted or encouraged to study a musical culture, but how to help anyone to carry out such study – in particular, the members of a society who wish to do ethnomusicological work in their own backyards. They characteristically want to learn Western-derived approaches and methods, but in doing so, they may simply become part of the army of Western investigators. They may wish to avoid operating in the framework of a comparative discipline, but the approaches they wish to learn are precisely those fashioned for comparative study. They are almost always people who have some background in and respect for the master composers and works of Western classical music, and thus they find themselves hard put to reconcile those musical values with the ones of their own tradition (a dilemma they sometimes solve by recourse to a music-in-culture approach), but they do not wish their music to be of merely ethnographic interest. Resolution of this group of problems is one of the great needs of ethnomusicology. (For detailed discussion, see Nettl, 1983, pp.247–302; Koizumi and others, 1977).

INVOLVEMENT Very broadly speaking, an important issue for scholars in the recent past and the immediate future is the kind and degree of involvement they should seek in the cultures and music they study. Can one work jointly with an Indian or Indonesian colleague, or with a native field consultant? Should the ethnomusicologist get involved in political and social problems? Rational and serious considerations of such questions have begun to replace the characteristic self-flagellation of white scholars for their participation in exploitation of the non-white world. It is an old question, but it remains: can one carry out responsible scholarship and still participate in what is being studied; or can one actually do so without this involvement?

BOUNDARIES In a number of ways that are superficially distinct, ethnomusicology has been concerned with boundaries, and in this aspect it has continued to expand. The decreasing firmness in the attitude regarding the boundaries among musics and between disciplines, and the greater sophistication in the study of musical and cultural boundaries seem nevertheless to be related. With the greater flexibility in disciplinary boundaries and taxonomies came a greater awareness of the degree to which the societies of the world use music to mark boundaries. Thus, political boundaries were shown by Blacking (1965) to be marked by music in the culture of the Venda, age boundaries among Australian peoples (Waterman, 1956), and ethnic boundaries in cultures with significant minorities (Bohlman, 1984). It has become clear that the divisions of the world, be they social, political, national or supernatural, are often marked by music. Indeed, as in some instances among European-derived and American Indian minorities, music and dance may be the most significant markers of ethnic boundaries; when Indians of North America wish to show their ethnic identity to themselves and to others, they do so most typically with the use of dances and songs. A future task for ethnomusicology is the development of methods for systematic and detailed study of this phenomenon.

UNIVERSALS AND THE UNIQUENESS OF CULTURES Since 1970, a number of organized attempts have been made to study and identify universals of music (most recently in a special issue of *World of Music*, xix/1/2, 1977). Before that, ethnomusicologists tended more to revel in the infinite diversity of human cultures and musics, and they answered assertions of universal characteristics by citing exceptions. They wished to show that what was regarded as a worldwide norm by European musicians was not valid, and that not all non-Western musics were governed by the same principles. More recently, partly in concert with anthropology, ethnomusicologists have revived the interest in universals. There are actually few published statements that try specifically to identify universals. A number of authors have tried to establish definitions of the concept, and provide some methodology for the search. Some draw on approaches from other fields, and indeed, the increasing interest of ethnomusicologists in biology and psychology are partly motivated by the interest in universals.

DISCIPLINE OR FIELD This has been an issue for 100 years. All along, many scholars have maintained that what ethnomusicologists do is part and parcel of musicology; yet most musicologists, while paying lip service to their interest in ethnomusicology, have regarded its musical object of study to be inferior, its cultures too distant, and have therefore accepted this field only on the fringes of their discipline. But since about 1900, ethnomusicology has also been classed as a subdivision of socio-cultural anthropology. In the 1950s, born from a feeling of rejection, the idea of a separate discipline became widespread. The notion of 'taking over' musicology as a whole by ethnomusicological concerns and approaches, suggested by Charles Seeger (1977, pp.116–17), was considered less seriously. The issue has been less one of directing the individual scholar's work than one of establishing an academic base and programmes of teaching and training, and of prescribing the role of non-Western music in the general education of the Western musician. Nevertheless, the notion that ethnomusicology asks the most fundamental questions about human music continues as a principal motif in successive attempts to state its nature and character (see Rice, 1987; Qureshi, 1987).

Impact of ethnomusicology

Has ethnomusicology had any effect on the world? Its avowed purpose was never to have a wide impact on musical life and on the general public, as ethnomusicologists have usually been scholars who spoke to and wrote for each other, and whose arguments seemed scarcely to be noticed even by academics in related areas. Nevertheless, after a hundred years of activity, ethnomusicologists can claim that they have contributed importantly to changes in the world's musical experience. To illustrate, one can look at contemporary concert life, at the system of teaching musics and at developments in composition.

Composition may be most germane. Non-Western music has influenced Western composers for centuries, and the impact of gamelan music on Claude Debussy is frequently cited as a landmark leading to a century of close association. However, of course the use of folk music by 18th- and 19th-century composers is a well-recognized part of the Romantic movement. New in the recent past is mainly an increased acceptance not only of the externals of non-Western music – instruments and tunes – but of central principles of tone colour, texture, rhythm and the perception of time. The interest of composers in musics from cultures outside their experience is surely not the result entirely of ethnomusicological awareness. However, at American and European institutions of musical education, composers have come to take a special interest in ethnomusicology, often making it a second area of specialization. Their interest has not been exclusively in the nature of sound but also in the conceptual sector of the musical spectrum as well, and also in the variety of attitudes towards music that may be found in the world's societies. Thus, they have taken a special interest in processes such as composition and improvisation, audience participation and the different ways in which sound may be perceived.

In the 1960s, the sounds of East Asian or Middle Eastern singing, of *mbira* or *didjeridu*, could evoke laughter or disgust from the typical American or European who chanced to hear these sounds; and surely, there would arise questions about the status of these sounds as proper music. Today, concepts such as gamelan, sitar and *tablā*, the master drummer, Peking opera, *kabuki* and *kathakali*, are well-known and widely accepted in educated Western society; and the jazz and popular music communities include aspects of Indian, African and Middle Eastern musics in their purview. Non-Western music is widely accepted as part of the Western musical scene; its sounds are regarded as music, and some of the basic terms (raga, gamelan and koto) have become part of the generally used vocabulary of musicians.

This development owes much to the determination of ethnomusicologists to bring these sounds – usually in the form of concerts, records, broadcasts – to their students and to the general public. The growth of non-Western music in American and European concert life is substantially the result of efforts by ethnomusicological individuals and institutions. Music life in the 1990s in Europe and the Americas now includes a significant proportion of non-Western music, sponsored by the major patrons of classical music, by academic institutions and by organizations of ethnic groups. All of this activity is surely related also to the tendency of ethnic minorities to use music as a way of fostering social integration, as well as to the desire of composers to experience new sounds and concepts; however, ethnomusicological thought was certainly also in good measure supportive of the kind of cultural relativism necessary for accepting the sounds of non-Western music, and provided the kind of intellectual background necessary for intelligent and informed appreciation of this music. It was ethnomusicologists who made the acquaintance of Asian and African musicians in the field and often determined to bring them to their own countries to perform and teach.

We have already touched upon the impact that ethnomusicology has had on other kinds of music scholarship, particularly historical musicology and music theory. The increased influence is shown also in that the College Music Society, the largest and most representative body of music educators in higher education in North America, maintains a regular seat for an ethnomusicologist on its 12-person Board of Directors. However, ethnomusicology has had its most significant impact on the musical education of European and, even much more, North American cultures. Some influence on primary and secondary schooling is evident. In some communities, music teachers are expected to have a modicum of background in musics outside the mainstream of Western art music and some sense of the study of music in culture; and they may avail themselves of the musical materials belonging to those of their students who come from minority or non-Western populations in order to teach general musical principles. Much more important, however, is the impact of ethnomusicology in university music departments, which may teach courses in world music for hundreds of students specializing in music and in other fields, and some of which include some exposure to world music and to ethnomusicological approaches in the standard curricula for training musicians. Although progress has been slow, it has been remarkably steady since the 1950s, and in the 1990s it is widely taken for granted that most musicians confront, even if they do not always accept, certain basic principles promulgated by ethnomusicologists. Significant among these are the importance of an essentially relativistic view in comparing musics and cultures and the conception of music as something best understood as part of the culture from which it comes. Most musicians and music lovers in Europe and North America now seem to have a sense of this; it seems to me that the musicians elsewhere, and their audiences, have characteristically taken it for granted all along.

Bibliography

T. Baker: *Über die Musik der nordamerikanischen Wilden* (Leipzig, 1882)

G. Adler: 'Umfang, Methode und Ziel der Musikwissenschaft', *VMw*, i (1885), 5

A. J. Ellis: 'On the Musical Scales of Various Nations', *Journal of the Society of Arts*, xxxiii (1885), 485

F. M. Boehme: *Geschichte des Tanzes in Deutschland* (Leipzig, 1886)

C. Stumpf: 'Lieder der Belakulla Indianer', *VMw*, ii (1886), 405

R. Redfield: *Tepotzlán: a Mexican Village* (Chicago, 1930)

J. von Pulikowski: *Geschichte des Begriffes Volkslied im musikalischen Schrifttum* (Heidelberg, 1933)

R. A. Waterman: '"Hot" Rhythm in Negro Music', *JAMS*, i (1948), 24

T. W. Adorno: *Philosophie der neuen Musik* (Tübingen, 1949)

B. H. Bronson: 'Mechanical Help in the Study of Folk Song', *Journal of American Folklore*, lxi (1949), 81

O. Lewis: *Life in A Mexican Village: Tepotzlán Restudied* (Urbana, 1951)

E. and R. Sterba: *Beethoven and His Nephew: a Psychoanalytic Study of their Relationship* (New York, 1954)

L. C. Freeman and A. P. Merriam: 'Statistical Classification in Anthropology: an Application to Ethnomusicology', *American Anthropologist*, lviii (1956), 464

A. Lomax: 'Folksong Style', *American Anthropologist*, lxi (1959), 927

S. Finkelstein: *Composer and Nation* (New York, 1960)

H. Pawlowska: *Merrily We Sing: 105 Polish Folksongs* (Detroit, 1961)

T. W. Adorno: *Einleitung in die Musiksoziologie* (Frankfurt, 1962)

A. Lomax: 'Song Structure and Social Structure', *Ethnology*, i (1962), 425

E. D. Ives: *Larry Gorman: the Man Who Made the Songs* (Bloomington, 1964)

A. P. Merriam: *The Anthropology of Music* (Evanston, 1964)

J. Blacking: 'The Role of Music in the Culture of the Venda of the Northern Transvaal', *Studies in Ethnomusicology* (New York), ii (1965), 20

R. B. Cantrick: 'The Blind Men and the Elephant: Scholars on Popular Music', *EM*, ix (1965), 100

J. Blacking: *Venda Children's Songs* (Johannesburg, 1967)

L. Meyer: *Music, the Arts, and Ideas: Patterns and Predictions in Twentieth Century Culture* (Chicago, 1967)

M. Harris: *The Rise of Anthropological Theory* (New York, 1968)

A. Lomax: *Folk Song Style and Culture* (Washington, 1968)

B. Nettl: 'Biography of a Blackfoot Indian Singer', *MQ*, liv (1968), 199

C. J. Ellis: 'The Role of the Ethnomusicologist in the Study of Andagarinja Women's Ceremonies', *Miscellanea Musicologica* (Adelaide), v (1970), 76

H. Lincoln, ed.: *The Computer and Music* (Ithaca, 1970)

M. Hood: *The Ethnomusicologist* (New York, 1971)

B. Brook and others, ed.: *Perspectives in Musicology* (New York, 1972)

C. Boilès: 'Sémiotique de l'ethnomusicologie', *Musique en jeu*, x (1973), 34

F. Ll. Harrison, ed.: *Time, Place, and Music: an Anthology of Ethnomusicological Observation c. 1550 to c. 1800* (Amsterdam, 1973)

J.-J. Nattiez: 'Linguistics: a New Approach for Musical Analysis', *IRASM*, iv (1973), 51

S. Feld: 'Linguistic Models in Ethnomusicology', *EM*, xviii (1974), 197

L. Treitler: 'Homer and Gregory: the Transmission of Epic Poetry and Plainchant', *MQ*, lx (1974), 333

V. Turner: *Dramas, Fields, and Metaphors* (Ithaca, 1974)

A. Reyes Schramm: *The Role of Music in the Interaction of Black Americans and Hispanos in New York City's East Harlem* (diss., Columbia U., 1975)

E. O. Henry: 'The Variety of Music in a North Indian Village: Reassessing Cantometrics', *EM*, xx (1976), 49

A. J. Racy: 'Record Industry and Egyptian Traditional Music, 1904–1932', *EM*, xx (1976), 23

J. Blacking, ed.: *Anthropology of the Body* (London, 1977)

F. Koizumi and others, eds.: *Asian Music in an Asian Perspective* (Tokyo, 1977)

A. P. Merriam: 'Music Change in a Basongye Village (Zaire)', *Anthropos*, lxxii (1977), 806

C. Seeger: *Studies in Musicology, 1935–1975* (Berkeley, 1977)

W. Westcott: 'Ideas of Afro-American Musical Acculturation in the U.S.A.', *Journal of the Steward Anthropological Society* (Urbana) viii, (1977), 107

J. Blacking: 'Some Problems of Theory and Method in the Study of Musical Change', *YIFMC*, ix (1978), 1

K. A. Gourlay: 'Towards a Reassessment of the Ethnomusicologist's Role', *EM*, xxii (1978), 1

C. J. Frisbie and D. P. McAllester, eds.: *Navajo Blessingway Singer: the Autobiography of Frank Mitchell* (Tucson, 1978)

B. Nettl: 'Some Aspects of the History of World Music in the Twentieth Century', *EM*, xxii (1978), 123

——, ed.: *Eight Urban Musical Cultures: Tradition and Change* (Urbana, 1978)

A. Simon: 'Probleme, Methoden und Ziele der Ethnomusikologie', *Jahrbuch für musikalische Volksund Völkerkunde*, ix (1978), 8

S. Erdely: 'Ethnic Music in America: an Overview', *YIFMC*, xi (1979), 114

C. Keil: *Tiv Song* (Chicago, 1979)

H. Zemp: 'Aspects of 'Are'are Musical Theory', *EM*, xxiii (1979), 6

C. Frisbie, ed.: *Southwestern Indian Ritual Drama* (Albuquerque, 1980)

E. Gerson-Kiwi and A. Shiloah: 'Musicology in Israel, 1960–1980', *AcM*, liii, (1981), 200

M. Kartomi: 'The Processes and Results of Musical Culture Contact: a Discussion of Terminology and Concepts', *EM*, xxv (1981), 227

R. Pelinski: *La musique des Inuit du Caribou* (Montreal, 1981)

Popular Music, vols i–v (Cambridge, 1981–6)

S. Feld: *Sound and Sentiment: Birds, Weeping, Poetics, and Song in Kaluli Expression* (Philadelphia, 1982)

P. Gronow: 'Ethnic Recordings: an Introduction', *Ethnic Recordings in America, a Neglected Heritage* (Washington, 1982), 1

C. Keil: 'Applied Ethnomusicology and a Rebirth of Music from the Spirit of Tragedy', *EM*, xxvi (1982), 407

A. Reyes Schramm: 'Explorations in Urban Ethnomusicology: Hard Lessons from the Spectacularly Ordinary', *YTM*, xiv (1982), 1

'Transmission and Form in Oral Tradition', *Report of the Twelfth Congress of the International Musicological Society, Berkeley, 1977*, ed. D. Heartz and B. Wade (Kassel, 1981), 139 [symposium]

K. Blaukopf: *Musik im Wandel der Gesellschaft* (Munich, 1983)

B. Nettl: *The Study of Ethnomusicology: Twenty-nine Issues and Concepts* (Urbana, 1983)

R. Riddle: *Flying Dragons, Flowing Streams: Music in the Life of San Francisco's Chinese* (Westport, CT, 1983)

H. L. Sakata: *Music in the Mind: the Concepts of Music and Musician in Afghanistan* (Kent, OH, 1983)

A. Shiloah and E. Cohen: 'The Dynamics of Change in Jewish Oriental Ethnic Music in Israel', *EM*, xxvii (1983), 227

G. Béhague: 'Patterns of *Candomblé* Music Performance: an Afro-Brazilian Religious Setting', *Performance Practice: Ethnomusicological Perspectives*, ed. G. Béhague (Westport, CT, 1984), 222

H. Oesch: *Aussereuropäische Musik*, i (Laaber, 1984)

A. Arnold: 'Aspects of Asian Indian Musical Life in Chicago', *Selected Reports in Ethnomusicology*, vi (1985), 25

M. P. Baumann, ed.: *Musik der Türken in Deutschland* (Kassel, 1985)

Becoming Human Through Music: the Wesleyan Symposium on the Perspectives of Social Anthropology in the Teaching and Learning of Music (Middletown, CT, 1985)

A. Catlin: 'Harmonizing the Generations in Hmong Musical Performance', *Selected Reports in Ethnomusicology*, vi (1985), 83

D. Coplan: *In Township Tonight* (London, 1985)

J. Dougherty, ed.: *Directions in Cognitive Anthropology* (Urbana, 1985)

E. Hickmann: 'Musikarchäologie als Traditionsforschung', *AcM*, lvii (1985), 1

J. Kerman: *Contemplating Music: Challenges to Musicology* (Cambridge, MA, 1985)

B. Nettl: *The Western Impact on World Music: Change, Adaptation and Survival* (New York, 1985)

R. Riddle: 'Korean Musical Culture in Los Angeles', *Selected Reports in Ethnomusicology*, vi (1985), 189

I. K. F. Wong: 'The Many Roles of Peking Opera in San Francisco in the 1980's', *Selected Reports in Ethnomusicology*, vi (1985), 173

'Fact and Value in Contemporary Musical Scholarship', *CMS Proceedings, the National and Regional Meetings, 1985*, ed. W. E. Melin (Boulder, CO, 1986), 1

O. T. Hatton: 'In the Tradition: Grass Dance Musical Style and Female Pow-wow Singers', *EM*, xxx (1986), 197

M. McLean: 'Towards a Typology of Musical Change: Missionaries and Adjustive Response in Oceania', *World of Music*, xxviii/1 (1986), 29

'Mechanisms of Change', *World of Music*, xxvii/1 (1986), 3 [series of articles]

B. Nettl: 'World Music in the Twentieth Century: a Survey of Research on Western Influence', *AcM*, lviii (1986), 360

Y. Tokumaru and O. Yamaguti, eds.: *The Oral and the Literate in Music* (Tokyo, 1986)

E. Koskoff: *Women and Music in Cross-Cultural Perspective* (Westport, CT, 1987)

B. Nettl: *The Radif of Persian Music: Studies of Structure and Cultural Context* (Champaign, 1987)

R. B. Qureshi: 'Music Sound and Contextual Input: a Performance Model for Musical Analysis', *EM*, xxxi (1987), 56

T. Rice: 'Toward the Remodeling of Ethnomusicology', *EM*, xxxi (1987), 469

A. Seeger: *Why Suyà Sing* (Cambridge, 1987)

H. Kingsbury: *Music, Talent, and Performance* (Philadelphia, 1988)

J. Vander: *Songprints: the Musical Experience of Five Shoshone Women* (Urbana, 1988)

S. Blum, P. V. Bohlman and D. M. Neuman, eds.: *Ethnomusicology and Modern Music History* (Urbana, 1991)

B. Nettl and P. V. Bohlman, eds.: *Comparative Musicology and Anthropology of Music: Essays in the History of Ethnomusicology* (Chicago, 1991)

PART FOUR

Reference Aids

Research Resources in Ethnomusicology

JENNIFER C. POST

Ethnomusicological research

This directory of research resources gathers together references to information useful to students and scholars engaged in ethnomusicological research. It seeks to identify important bibliographic sources, in both printed and online format, sound archives which may house information useful in historical and comparative research, and associations and organizations which may serve as contacts for ethnomusicologists working in specific areas. While it is selective, not exhaustive, it should be especially useful to researchers looking for background materials, scholars and teachers seeking sources for information on a specific topic, and students compiling bibliographic data for papers.

Like all scholarly work, ethnomusicological research can present major bibliographic challenges to a researcher taking anything from a cursory to an exhaustive look at a subject. Research in ethnomusicology is a multi-faceted process which grows in complexity as the discipline matures. The very interdisciplinary nature of the field complicates the literature search at every turn. While research for many ethnomusicologists involves fieldwork, during the preliminary search for information, and at all stages of data compilation and writing, students and scholars work with library collections, are in contact with archival resources and research centres, and sometimes seek information from national and international organizations.

Research in musicology relies heavily on printed media found in musical scores and historical writings, as well as aural media. Social scientists, and anthropologists in particular, on the other hand, rely on book and journal literature in addition to primary data, which may be aural or visual, but also may include manuscripts, newspapers, government documents, or statistical data. Ethnomusicological research traditionally combines aspects of the two, utilizing research resources in a number of formats, housed in various locations. In current practice, it is clear that while scholars frequently cite theoretical constructs drawn from musicology and/or anthropology in their research, they in fact draw from a number of other fields for theoretical and methodological frameworks as well as for general source materials. In fact, the literature used by ethnomusicologists is not always produced specifically by specialists in either musicology or anthropology, but by scholars in other disciplines in the humanities and social sciences such as linguistics, history, literature, religion, and folklife. An informal survey of articles and monographs on ethnomusicological topics published recently cited bibliographic literature in the following fields (in addition to all musicological sub-disciplines and anthropology): art, biography/autobiography, communication, dance/kinesics, economies, ethnography, folklife, geology, history, linguistics, literature, management, mythology, philosophy, political science, popular culture, psychology, religion, sociology.

Many students are at a disadvantage when beginning research in ethnomusicology. While academic programmes concentrate on processes of field collecting, and on research and writing skills, techniques for accessing materials in libraries, archives, and information centres may be neglected. The wide variety of online bibliographic tools are not always introduced, and methods and resources for finding visual, aural, and manuscript data are sometimes left for students to discover on their own. In addition, unlike more traditional disciplines, ethnomusicology has few guides to research; nor is the field served comprehensively in general bibliographic studies. See, for example, W. Webb and others: *Sources of Information in the Social Sciences* (Chicago, 1986), an excellent general source guide for social science research which all but neglects ethnomusicology. In Blazek and Averse, *The Humanities: a Selective Guide to Information* (Englewood, CO, 1988) materials to support ethnomusicological research are not fully recognized. The most comprehensive source is probably the latest edition of *Music Reference and Research Materials* by Duckles and Keller (New York, 1988), although only some of the available bibliographic material is cited.

Types of Research Resources

A wide array of research resources is available to ethnomusicological scholars. In addition to book and journal literature, information may come from: dissertations and theses, dictionaries and encyclopedias, audio and video recordings and their documentation, microform collections or other data archives stored on optical disk, public documents, original manuscripts, or other archival material.

BOOKS AND JOURNALS   Book and journal literature is the most widely used resource material for any scholarly research. It is valued not only for its theoretical, historical, and descriptive content, but also for the bibliographic and discographic citations included which may lead researchers to a related body of literature on the subject.

DISSERTATIONS AND THESES   Like book and journal articles, dissertations and theses can offer important theoretical and descriptive content as well as bibliographic and discographic citations to additional research material.

DICTIONARIES, ENCYCLOPEDIAS AND HANDBOOKS   Encyclopedic summaries of information about a specific topic can provide valuable background data during research. Of particular interest to ethnomusicologists are *The New Grove*

Dictionary of Music and Musicians (ed. S. Sadie, 1980) and *The New Grove Dictionary of American Music* (ed. H. W. Hitchcock and S. Sadie, London: Macmillan, 1986) with their numerous articles on specific geographic regions, instruments, musical styles, forms and theory. More regionally or topically specific sources such as regional encyclopedias of music and glossaries of musical terms, as well as general area studies handbooks, can also provide relevant information.

SOUND RECORDINGS   Commercially produced sound recordings, especially those containing field recordings, are valuable both for their musical content and for background information, descriptions, photographs, and citations provided in accompanying literature.

VIDEOS, FILMS AND PHOTOGRAPHS   Like sound recordings, visual information can be used as both primary and secondary source material in ethnomusicological research. Unfortunately, like sound recordings, videos, films or photographs without any accompanying documentation may be of little or no use to scholarly research.

MICROFORMS AND OPTICAL DISKS   Projects to microfilm large collections of historical newspapers, manuscripts and books have provided scholars with a tremendous amount of material for research during the last three decades. Indexes to microform collections such as *Microform Research Collections: a Guide* by Suzanne Cates Dodson (Westport, CT, 1984) or *Guide to Microforms in Print* (Westport, CT, 1978–) should be consulted. These preservation projects have now moved into electronic media and the optical disk has provided a medium for preservation of materials in a variety of formats.

DATA ARCHIVES   For anthropologists and ethnomusicologists, one of the more important archives are the data archives found in the Human Relations Area Files (HRAF). This ethnographic resource compiles coded materials reproduced from articles and books on cultures from throughout the world. Files for these archives have been distributed on microfiche and are available at a number of academic and larger public libraries.

PUBLIC DOCUMENTS   Government publications, town records, and other public documents have always provided a broad spectrum of information for research in history and the social sciences. National government offices or official publications of a country may provide historical, statistical, or political information directly related to ethnomusicological research. Government documents and town records can be important sources for regional census information and genealogical data.

ARCHIVAL MATERIAL   Many kinds of materials are retained by libraries and archives for their historical as well as intellectual value. Those frequently consulted by ethnomusicologists include field recordings and their documentation produced by ethnomusicologists, oral historians, folklorists, and anthropologists. Other archival sources include diaries, correspondence, newspapers, advertising, broadsides, songsters, illustrations, local histories, popular literature, and photographs.

Access to resources

It is not always easy to gain access to the previously listed materials. There are, though, some standard reference tools which can assist researchers. These include library catalogues, bibliographies and discographies, indexing and abstracting sources, online databases, archival finding aids, government documents, organizations and specialists.

LIBRARY CATALOGUES Many libraries now have computer systems which provide online access to their materials, including books, journals and recordings. A new world of searching for information is open to users with this convenience. This is particularly true if the online system has keyword searching capability, where the user can search for words found anywhere in a bibliographic record. In addition to providing faster access to materials in both broad and narrow subject areas, it can provide easier access to collections of essays or to performers on a recording. Some institutions have begun to make indexes to archival and museum collections available online.

BIBLIOGRAPHIES AND DISCOGRAPHIES Searching systematically through bibliographies and discographies for information sources on a chosen topic is often considered essential in the early stages of research. Many sources for background information on a topic, as well as primary source materials of both historical and contemporary import, may not be consulted because they are hidden in obscure journals, monographic compilations of articles, or festschriften. There are, however, some excellent bibliographic and discographic guides and essays which may provide references to foundation materials. Individual entries may provide annotations or bibliographic guides may provide explanatory material to further guide in the research process. Many of these sources are included in the section below on geographical and topical bibliographies and discographies.

INDEXING AND ABSTRACTING SOURCES Indexing and abstracting sources generally provide bibliographic access to journal articles, and many also include bibliographic references to information on monographs, essays in collections, festschriften, and dissertations. Often cumulated yearly, less often in five-year intervals, they are sometimes cumbersome to use. Fortunately, many abstracting and indexing services are now available as CD–ROM products or as online databases, so that subject searches can take place over a wider span of years. The most useful major indexing and abstracting sources for ethnomusicological research have been *MLA International Bibliography of Books and Articles on the Modern Languages and Literature, RILM Abstracts (Répertoire International de Littérature Musicale)*, and *The Music Index*. Information on these sources and others is located below in the section on indexing and abstracting serial publications.

ONLINE DATABASES   While printed indexes and abstracts must be searched by finding one term at a time, such as an author or subject, online databases can be searched using a combination of terms such as: name, subject (or descriptor), date, journal name, or keyword. Bibliographic information, including abstracts and sometimes full texts, can be printed out or downloaded to disk for reformatting by the user. The advantages of these services include ease of use, speed, and currency (generally they are the most up-to-date sources for information). There are disadvantages too. They are generally expensive and some areas of inquiry do not lend themselves to computer research. Online coverage of 'early' journal literature (before 1970) is generally poor. For musicological and social science research *Arts and Humanities Citation Index*, *Social Science Citation Index*, *Humanities Index*, and *Social Sciences Index* are most helpful. Databases are available in two forms: (i) through a database vendor via dial-in access (WILSONLINE, DIALOG, BRS); or (ii) on compact disc (CD–ROM) accessed by microcomputer-based work stations which allow subscribers (usually libraries) to make this information available at no cost to the user. Subscribers typically are provided with updated discs on a monthly, bimonthly or quarterly basis.

ARCHIVAL FINDING AIDS   Finding aids for archival material are as varied as data formats found in a typical archive. As noted earlier, ethnomusicological research may draw on manuscripts, field recordings, field notes, visual data, and other supporting materials produced by ethnomusicologists, newspaper collections, early sheet music collections, and historical photographs. Full or partial access may be available through a card file, a printed index, a finding aid, or an online database. In some cases, when there is limited or no ready means to determine the contents of an archival collection, archivists or curators can provide the most direct assistance. Check resources such as the *International Directory of Archives* edited by Andre Vanrie (Munich, 1988) or *Directory of Archives and Manuscript Repositories in the United States* (Phoenix, 1988) for descriptive information about archival collections. For information about specific holdings of manuscript material there are guides for many countries available such as the *National Union Catalog of Manuscript Collections* (Washington, DC, 1962–), published annually, for material housed in the USA.

GOVERNMENT DOCUMENTS   Access to government documents, like other archival material, depends on local indexing and cataloguing practices. Some materials are indexed using CD–ROM sources, databases, or card files, while others are only available through handwritten ledgers. The scope of and access to government or public documents varies widely among repositories.

ORGANIZATIONS   Various professional, academic, public and private organizations can guide the researcher to museums, libraries, and private collections, as well as to individuals and groups who might provide information helpful in scholarly research. Look in directories of associations for information on organizations in specific locations. Two good sources include: *International Research Centers Directory* (Detroit, 1982–) and *Encyclopedia of Associations* (Detroit, 1956–).

SPECIALISTS Correspondence and personal discussion with scholars in the discipline can be an important source for information in any research.

A selective guide and directory

This directory provides lists of sources for information on ethnomusicological topics which can be found in a broad selection of research resources. The lists are not all inclusive. This is a selective guide to resources and organizations that are relatively accessible. The directory is divided into five sections: (i) Geographical and topical bibliographies and discographies; (ii) Indexing and abstracting serial publications; (iii) Journals; (iv) Archives and research centres; (v) Associations and organizations.

Bibliographic and Discographic Sources

The major goal of this brief bibliography of bibliographies and discographies is to provide information to researchers on general resources in the field. These, in turn, can include information on very specific topics. It should be especially useful to scholars beginning their research, leading them to both primary and secondary source materials.

The most up-to-date, comprehensive sources available are included in this listing of current bibliographic and discographic sources for ethnomusicology. Excluded are some older works which have been superseded, as well as bibliographies covering a smaller regional sphere or more specialized subject matter. The list is a convenience for researchers, but does not take the place, or deny the importance, of bibliographic and discographic information that can be found in articles and monographs on specific subjects. However, it is these bibliographic sources listed here that are seldom referred to in bibliographies of journal articles and monographs and therefore are sometimes difficult to identify.

This list cites geographical and topical source materials including encyclopedias, literature indexes, bibliographies and discographies organized by broad geographic regions. While the specific characteristics of each source vary, in general, these are guides to information on a specific geographic region and include references to journal articles, essays, books, as well as references to sound recordings and, sometimes, films. The title of the source does not always indicate whether or not aural and/or visual information is included in the citations.

Geographic and topical bibliographies and discographies

INTERNATIONAL

J. Kunst: *Musicologica: a Study of the Nature of Ethnomusicology, its Problems, Methods and Representative Personalities to which is Added a Bibliography* (Amsterdam, 1950, enl. 2/1955 as *Ethnomusicology*, 3/1959, The Hague: M. Nijhof), 303 pp.
'Current Bibliography, Discography and Filmography', in each issue of *EM*; compiled by J. C. Post, M. C. Russell and B. Dornfeld [other bibliographers in this series have included J. C. Hickerson, F. Gillis, L. Spear, N. Rosenberg, N. Yeh, and C. Rahkonen]
'Dissertations and Theses', in issues of *EM*, compiled by J. C. Post [orig. comp. F. Gillis]

V. H. Duckles and M. A. Keller: *Music Reference and Research Materials: an Annotated Bibliography* (New York: Schirmer Books, 1964, 4/1988)

F. Gillis and A. P. Merriam: *Ethnomusicology and Folk Music: an International Bibliography of Dissertations and Theses* (Middletown, CT: Wesleyan University Press, 1966), 148 pp.

P. Kennedy, ed.: *Films on Traditional Music and Dance: a First International Catalogue* (Paris: Unesco, 1970), 261 pp.

W. Laade: *Gegenwartsfragen der Musik in Afrika und Asien: eine grundlegende Bibliographie*, Sammlung musikwissenschaftlichen Abhandlunden, li (Baden-Baden: V. Koerner, 1971), 110 pp.

Archives of Traditional Music: *A Catalogue of Phonorecordings of Music and Oral Data Held by the Archives of Traditional Music: Archives of Traditional Music, Folklore Institute, Indiana University, Bloomington, Indiana* (Boston: G. K. Hall, 1975), 541 pp.

N. Dols, D. Niles, K. Culley and N. Yeh: *Music of the World: a Selective Discography* (Los Angeles: The Archive, 1977–85), 4 vols.

D. Kennington and D. L. Read: *The Literature of Jazz: a Critical Guide* (Chicago: American Library Association, 1980), 236 pp.

S. Sadie, ed.: *The New Grove Dictionary of Music and Musicians* (London: Macmillan; New York: Grove's Dictionaries of Music, 1980), 20 vols.

B. Hefele: *Jazz-Bibliography: International Literature on Jazz, Blues, Spirituals, Gospel and Ragtime Music with a Selected List of Works on the Social and Cultural Background from the Beginning to the Present* (New York: K. G. Saur, 1981), 368 pp.

E. S. Meadows: *Jazz Reference and Research Materials: a Bibliography*, Critical Studies on Black Life and Culture, xxii (New York: Garland, 1981), 300 pp.

D. Tudor: *Popular Music: an Annotated Guide to Recordings* (Littleton, CO: Libraries Unlimited, 1983), 647 pp.

D.-R. de Lerma: *Bibliography of Black Music* (Westport, CT: Greenwood, 1981–2, 1984), 4 vols.

I. Heskes, comp.: *The Resource Book of Jewish Music: a Bibliographical and Topical Guide to the Book and Journal Literature and Program Materials*, Music Reference Collection, iii (Westport, CT: Greenwood, 1985), 302 pp.

R. Iwaschkin: *Popular Music: a Reference Guide*, Music Research and Reference Guides, iv (New York: Garland, 1986), 658 pp.

E. Yassif: *Jewish Folklore: an Annotated Bibliography*, Garland Folklore Bibliographies, x; Garland Reference Library of the Humanities, no.450 (New York: Garland, 1986), 341 pp.

A. Seeger and L. S. Spear: *Early Field Recordings: a Catalogue of Cylinder Collections at the Indiana University Archives of Traditional Music* (Bloomington: Indiana University Press, 1987), 198 pp.

L. Jessup: *World Music: a Source Book for Teaching* (Danbury, CT: World Music Press, 1988), 63 pp.

B. Kernfeld, ed.: *The New Grove Dictionary of Jazz* (London: Macmillan; New York: Grove's Dictionaries of Music, 1988), 2 vols.

M. L. Hart, L. N. Howorth and B. M. Eagles: *The Blues: a Bibliographic Guide*, Music Research and Information Guides, vii; Garland Reference Library of the Humanities, no.565 (New York: Garland, 1989), 636 pp.

W. E. Richmond: *Ballad Scholarship: an Annotated Bibliography*, Garland Folklore Bibliographies, xiv; Garland Reference Library of the Humanities, no.499 (New York: Garland, 1989), 356 pp.

J. C. Hickerson: *An Inventory of the Bibliographies and Other Reference and Finding Aids Prepared by the Archive of Folk Culture* (Washington, DC: Library of Congress, Archive of Folk Culture, 1990)

A. B. Schuursma: *Ethnomusicology Research: a Selected Annotated Bibliography* (New York: Garland, in preparation)

A. P. Merriam: *African Music on LP: an Annotated Discography* (Evanston, IL: Northwestern University Press, 1970)

D. Varley: *African Native Music: an Annotated Bibliography* (Folkestone and London: Dawsons of Pall Mall, 1970), 116 pp.

International African Bibliography: Current Books, Articles and Papers in African Studies (London: Mansell Publishing House, 1971–)

R. M. Stone and F. J. Gillis: *African Music and Oral Data: a Catalog of Field Recordings, 1902–1975* (Bloomington: Indiana University Press, 1976), 412 pp.

R. M. Stone: 'Twenty-five Years of Selected Films in Ethnomusicology: Africa (1955–1980)', *EM*, xxvi (1982), 147

H. O. Emezi: 'A Bibliography of African Music and Dance: the Nigerian Experience, 1930–1980',

Ethnomusicology: an Introduction

Current Bibliography on African Affairs, xviii/2 (1985–6), 117–47.

Africa Bibliography (Manchester; Dover, NH: Manchester University Press, 1985–)

M. M. Rakotomalala: *Bibliographie critique d'intérêt ethnomusicologique sur la musique malagasy*, Travaux et documents, xxiii (Isoraka, Antananarivo: Museé d'art et d'archéologie, l'Université de Madagascar, 1986), 107 pp.

J. Gray: *African Music: a Bibliographic Guide to the Traditional, Popular, Art, and Liturgical Musics of Sub-Saharan Africa* (New York: Greenwood Press, 1991), 499pp.

EAST ASIA, SOUTHEAST ASIA, AND THE PACIFIC

Bibliography of Asian Studies (Ann Arbor, MI: Association for Asian Studies, 1965–)

A. M. Moyle: 'Source Materials: Aboriginal Music of Australia and New Guinea', *EM*, xv/1 (1971), 81

B.-S. Song: *An Annotated Bibliography of Korean Music*, Asian Music Publications, ser. A, no.2 (Providence, RI: Brown University, 1971), 250 pp.

K. Gourlay, comp.: *A Bibliography of Traditional Music in Papua New Guinea* (Port Moresby: Institute of Papua New Guinea Studies, 1974), 176 pp.

M. McClean: *An Annotated Bibliography of Oceanic Music and Dance*, Memoir of the Polynesian Society, no.41 (Wellington: Polynesian Society, 1977), 252 pp.; Suppl. (Auckland: Polynesian Society, 1981), 74 pp.

F. Lieberman: *Chinese Music: an Annotated Bibliography*, Garland Bibliographies in Ethnomusicology, i; Garland Reference Library of the Humanities, lxxv (New York: Garland, 2/1979) 257 pp.

Y. Minegishi: *Discography of Japanese Traditional Music* (Tokyo: The Japan Foundation, 1980), 56 pp.

D. Crisp, comp.: *Bibliography of Australian Music: an Index to Monographs, Journal Articles and Theses*, Australian Music Studies, i (Armidale: Australian Music Studies Project, 1982), 262 pp.

S. G. Nelson: *Documentary Sources of Japanese Music* (Tokyo: Research Archives for Japanese Music, 1986), 41 pp.

B. C. Stoneburner, comp.: *Hawaiian Music: an Annotated Bibliography*, The Music Reference Collection, no.10 (New York: Greenwood, 1986), 100 pp.

G. Tsuge: *Japanese Music: an Annotated Bibliography*, Garland Bibliographies in Ethnomusicology, ii; Garland Reference Library of the Humanities, no.472 (New York: Garland, 1986), 161 pp.

G. E. Koch, 'A Bibliography of Publications on Australian Aboriginal Music: 1975–1985', *Musicology Australia*, x (1987), 58

SOUTH AND WEST ASIA

E. Barnett, comp.: 'Special Bibliography: Art Music of India', *EM*, xiv/2 (1970), 278

P. F. Marks: *Bibliography of Literature Concerning Yemenite–Jewish Music*, Detroit Studies in Music Bibliography, xxvii (Detroit: Information Coordinators, 1973), 50 pp.

E. B. Barnett, comp.: *A Discography of the Art Music of India*, Society for Ethnomusicology, Special Series no.3 (Ann Arbor: Society for Ethnomusicology, 1975), 54 pp.

G. Kuppuswamy and M. Hariharan: *Indian Dance and Music Literature* (New Delhi: Biblia Impex Private Ltd, 1981), 156 pp.

W. J. Krüger-Wust: *Arabische Musik in Europäischen Sprachen: Eine Bibliographie* (Wiesbaden: Otto Harrassowitz, 1983), 124 pp.

M. S. Kinnear, comp.: *A Discography of Hindustani and Karnatic Music*, Discographies, no.17 (Westport, CT: Greenwood, 1985), 594 pp.

G. C. Kendadamath: *Indian Music and Dance: a Select Bibliography* (Varanasi: Indian Bibliographic Centre, 1986), 261 pp.

THE AMERICAS

HAPI: Hispanic American Periodicals Index (Los Angeles: UCLA Latin American Center Publications, 1970–)

B. Cavanaugh: 'Annotated Bibliography: Eskimo Music', *EM*, xvi/3 (1972), 479

M.-F. Guédon: 'Canadian Indian Ethnomusicology: Selected Bibliography and Discography', *EM*, xvi/3 (1972), 465

J. A. Huerta, ed.: *A Bibliography of Chicano and Mexican Dance, Drama, and Music* (Oxnard, CA: Colejo Quetzalcoatl, 1972), 59 pp.

410

M. E. Davis: *Music and Dance in Latin American Urban Contexts: a Selective Bibliography* (Brockport, NY, 1973), 20 pp.

P. K. Maultsby: 'Selective Bibliography: U.S. Black Music', *EM*, xix/3 (1975), 421

A. F. Thompson: *An Annotated Bibliography of Writings about Music in Puerto Rico*, MLA Index and Bibliography Series (Ann Arbor: Music Library Association, 1975), 34 pp.

C. Frisbie: *Music and Dance Research of Southwestern United States Indians: Past Trends, Present Activities, and Suggestions for Future Research* (Detroit: Information Coordinators, 1977), 109 pp.

D. S. Lee: *Native North American Music and Oral Data: a Catalogue of Sound Recordings 1893–1976* (Bloomington: Indiana University Press, 1979), 463 pp.

Handbook of Latin American Studies (Austin: University of Texas Press, 1979–)

R. Stevenson and others: *Caribbean Music History: a Selective Annotated Bibliography with Musical Supplement*, Inter-American Music Review Series, i/1 (Los Angeles: R. Stevenson, 1981), 112 pp.

R. A. Georges and S. Stern, comps.: *American and Canadian Immigrant and Ethnic Folklore: an Annotated Bibliography*, Garland Folklore Bibliographies, ii; Garland Reference Library of the Humanities, no.275 (New York: Garland, 1982), 484 pp.

S. A. Floyd and M. Reisser: *Black Music in the United States: an Annotated Bibliography of Selected Reference and Research Materials* (Milwood, NY: Krauss International, 1983), 234 pp.

W. M. Clements and F. M. Malpessi, comps.: *Native American Folklore, 1879–1979: an Annotated Bibliography* (Athens, OH: Swallow Press, 1984), 247 pp.

H. W. Hitchcock and S. Sadie, eds.: *The New Grove Dictionary of American Music* (London: Macmillan; New York: Grove's Dictionaries of Music, 1986), 4 vols.

T. E. Miller: *Folk Music in America: a Reference Guide*, Music Research and Reference Guides, v (New York: Garland, 1986), 424 pp.

I. L. Bradley: *A Selected Bibliography of Musical Canadiana* (Victoria, BC: University of Victoria, rev. 1987), 177 pp.

D. D. Krummel: *Bibliographical Handbook of American Music* (Urbana and Chicago: University of Illinois Press, 1987), 269 pp.

J. M. Spencer: *As the Black School Sings: Black Music Collections at Black Universities and Colleges with a Union List of Book Holdings* (New York: Greenwood Press, 1987), 185 pp.

D. Horn: *Literature of American Music in Books and Folk Music Collections: a Fully Annotated Bibliography* (Metuchen, NJ: Scarecrow, 1988), 556 pp.; Suppl. (1988), 570 pp.

EUROPE

Musikethnologische Jahresbibliographie Europas/Annual Bibliography of European Ethnomusicology (Bratislava: Slovenské národné múzeum, 1966–75), 10 vols.

D. Batser and B. Rabinovich: *Russkaia narodnaia muzyka: notograficheskii ukazatel', 1776–1973* (Moscow: Vses. izd-vo 'Sov. kompozitor', 1981–4), 2 vols.

M. P. Baumann: *Bibliographie zur ethnomusicologischen Literatur der Schweiz: mit einem Beitrag zu Geschichte, Gegenstand und Problemen der Volksliedforschung* (Winterthur: Amadeus, 1981), 312 pp.

M. E. A. Rehnberg: *Folkmusik i Sverige: bibliografisk hjälpreda* (Stockholm: Instituet för folklivsforskning, 1981), 133 pp.

P. Farwick and O. Holzapfel: *Deutsche Volksliedlandschaften: Landschaftliches Register der Aufzeichnungen im Deutschen Volksliedarchiv* (Freiburg: Das Archiv, 1983–)

A. Falassi: *Italian Folklore: an Annotated Bibliography* (New York: Garland, 1985), 438 pp.

J. E. Miller: *Modern Greek Folklore: an Annotated Bibliography*, Garland Folklore Bibliographies, ix; Garland Reference Library of the Humanities, no.451 (New York: Garland, 1985), 141 pp.

S. Biagiola: *Etnomusica: catalogo della musica di tradizione orale nelle registrazioni dell'Archivo etnico linguistico-musicale della Discoteca di Stato* (Rome: Discoteca di Stato, 1986), 887 pp.

J. B. Wolff and E. Kross: *Bibliographie der Literatur zum deutschen Volkslied: mit Stanortangaben an den wichtigsten Archiven und Bibliotheken der DDR*, Kleine Reihe Deutsche Volkslieder, vii–viii (Leipzig: Zentralhuas Publikation, 1987), 323 pp.

J. Porter: *The Traditional Music of Britain and Ireland: a Research and Information Guide*, Music Research and Information Guides, xi; Garland Reference Library of the Humanities, no.801 (New York: Garland, 1989), 408 pp.

D. L. Schaeffer, comp.: *Irish Folk Music: a Selected Discography*, Discographies, xxxi (New York: Greenwood, 1989), 180 pp.

W. Smialek: *Polish Music: a Research and Information Guide*, Music Research and Information Guides, xii (New York: Garland, 1989), 260 pp.

411

Indexing and abstracting serial publications in printed and online format

This part includes indexing and abstracting serial publications, in printed or online format, which consistently provide information to support ethnomusicological research. While every source listed is available in printed format, online access to many of the following indexing and abstracting publications is provided via specialized database vendors; major vendors noted for each entry include DIALOG, BRS and WILSONLINE. Many of the indexes are also available on CD–ROM. Each entry includes the following information:

Name of publication (place of publication, date) Database vendor, dates of coverage [if different from printed index] (Name used by vendor if different from printed index) [Brief abstract]; CD–ROM availability.

MLA International Bibliography of Books and Articles on the Modern Languages and Literature (New York: Modern Language Association, 1925–); DIALOG, WILSONLINE (*MLA International Bibliography*) [indexes book and journal articles in modern languages, literature and linguistics; also strong in folklore and music throughout the world]; available on CD–ROM

International volkskundliche Bibliographie/International Folklore [and Folklife] Bibliography/Bibliographie internationale des arts et traditions populaires (Bonn: Rudolf Habelt, 1939/41–)

The Music Index (Detroit: Information Coordinators, 1949–) [citations to articles and book reviews in over 200 journals; coverage is international]

Sociological Abstracts (San Diego: Sociological Abstracts, Inc., 1953–); BRS, DIALOG, 1963–; [abstracts and indexes literature in social and behavioural sciences; covers information from 1600 journals, conference papers and dissertations]

International Bibliography of Social and Cultural Anthropology (London: Tavistock; Chicago: Aldine; annual, 1955–) [classified index to articles, reviews and monographs with author index and subject index in French and English]

Current Contents: Arts & Humanities; Current Contents: Social & Behavioral Sciences (Philadelphia: Institute for Scientific Information, 1961–); BRS [includes tables of contents of journals and bibliographic records for each item; includes articles, reviews, letters, notes and editorials]

Dissertation Abstracts International (Ann Arbor: University Microfilms, 1961–); BRS, DIALOG (*Dissertation Abstracts International Online*) [indexes American and Canadian dissertations and theses at over 200 institutions; abstracts for dissertations are included after 1980; beginning in 1988 British and European dissertations and MA abstracts are included]; available on CD–ROM

America: History and Life (Santa Barbara: ABC–CLIO, 1964–); DIALOG [abstracts and indexes over 2000 journals in the sciences and humanities as well as monographs and dissertations; in addition to American and Canadian history, it is strong in American and Canadian social and cultural history including folklore, popular culture and ethnic studies]

RILM Abstracts, International Repertory of Music Literature/Répertoire International de Littérature Musicale (New York: RILM, 1967–); DIALOG (*Music Literature International*), 1971– [international database with abstracts from over 3000 journals; coverage is generally 4–6 years behind]

Social Science Citation Index (SSCI) (Philadelphia: Institute for Scientific Information, 1969–); BRS, DIALOG (*Social Scisearch*), 1972– [indexes significant articles from 4700 social and natural science journals and monographic series]; available on CD–ROM

Abstracts in Anthropology (Westport: Greenwood Press, 1970–) [abstracts and indexes journals in physical and cultural anthropology; an annual index is available for the more recent vols.]

Historical Abstracts (Santa Barbara: ABC–CLIO, 1973–); DIALOG [indexes and abstracts international historical literature from some 2000 journals and books; includes citations for dissertations beginning in 1980]

Humanities Index (New York: H. W. Wilson Co., 1974–); WILSONLINE, 1984– [citations to articles and book reviews in about 300 journals; international coverage]; available on CD–ROM

Social Sciences Index (New York: H. W. Wilson Co., 1974–); WILSONLINE, 1983– [citations to articles and book reviews in about 300 English language journals; international coverage]; available on CD–ROM

Religion Index One, Religion Index Two (New York: H. W. Wilson, 1975–); DIALOG, WILSONLINE (*Religion Index, ATLA Religion Database*), 1975– [indexes and abstracts articles from over 200 journals and about 300 multiple author works, including festschriften, collected essays, and proceedings; while the emphasis is on North American material and English language publications, other materials are also included]; available on CD–ROM

Arts and Humanities Citation Index (AHCI) (Philadelphia: Institute for Scientific Information, 1976–); BRS, DIALOG (*Arts and Humanities Search*), 1980– [international index which fully indexes 1300 arts and humanities journals and relevant articles from 5000 social and natural science journals]; available on CD–ROM

Anthropological Literature: an Index to Periodical Articles and Essays (Cambridge, MA: Tozzer Library, Harvard University, 1979–) [journals are selectively indexed; includes ethnic linguistics, cultural, geographical and author indexes]

Education Index (New York: H. W. Wilson Co., 1983–) [cites articles, editorials, reviews, in about 350 English-language periodicals, monographs, yearbooks; international coverage]; available on CD–ROM

Journals

The following is a list of current journals which consistently include information of interest to ethnomusicologists. This list is drawn largely from journals consulted over the years for 'Current Bibliography' in *EM*. Information provided for each entry includes: *Title*, organizational affiliation [if not reflected in title] (current place of publication, date of establishment); frequency; indexing sources.

The indexing sources are the indexing and abstracting serial publications available in either online or paper format described previously in this resource guide. Only the major indexing resources which are listed in this guide are included. The following abbreviations apply:

AH&L: America: History and Life
AHCI: Arts and Humanities Citation Index (Arts and Humanities Search)
Cc: Current Contents
EducInd: Education Index
HistAbst: Historical Abstracts
HumInd: Humanities Index
MLA: MLA International Bibliography
MusInd: Music Index
RILM: RILM Abstracts (Music Literature International)
SSCI: Social Science Citation Index (Social Scisearch)
SSI: Social Sciences Index

Acta Musicologica, International Musicological Society (Basel: Bärenreiter-Verlag, 1928–), half-yearly; *AHCI, Cc, MusInd, RILM*

African Music Journal, African Music Society (Grahamstown, South Africa: Rhodes University, 1954–); irregular; *AHCI, Cc, MusInd, RILM*

African Musicology (Nairobi: University of Nairobi, Institute of African Studies, 1983–); annual; *MLA*

American Music, Sonneck Society (Champaign, IL: University of Illinois, 1983–); quarterly; *AHCI, Cc, MusInd*

Anthropos: revue internationale d'ethnologie et de linguistique (Fribourg: Anthropos Institut, 1906–); half-yearly; *MLA, SSI*

413

Annual Review of Jazz Studies (New Brunswick, NJ: Institute of Jazz Studies, Rutgers University, 1973–); annual; *AHCI, MusInd, RILM*

Anuarul de folclor (Cluj Napoca: University of Cluj-Napoca, 1980–); annual

Arv: Journal of Scandinavian Folklore, Kungliga Gustav Adolfs Akademien – Royal Gustavus Adolphus Academy (Stockholm: Almqvist & Wiksell International, 1945–); annual; *AH&L, HistAbst, MLA*

Asian Folklore Studies (Nagoya: Nanzan University, Nanzan Anthropological Institute, 1942–); half-yearly; *AHCI, Cc, HumInd, MLA*

Asian Music, Society for Asian Music (Ithaca, NY: Society for Asian Music, 1968–); half-yearly; *AHCI, Cc, MLA, MusInd, RILM*

Balungan (Oakland, CA: American Gamelan Institute, 1984–); 2–3/year; *MusInd*

Bansuri (Calgary: Raga-Mala Performing Arts of Canada, 1985–); annual

Beiträge zur Musikwissenschaft (Berlin: Verlag Neue Musik, 1959–); quarterly; *Cc, MusInd, RILM*

Beiträge zur Jazzforschung/Studies in Jazz Research, International Society for Jazz Studies (Graz: International Society for Jazz Studies, 1969–); irregular; *RILM*

Black Music Research Journal, Center for Black Music Research (Chicago: Columbia College, 1980–); semiannual; *AHCI, MusInd, RILM*

Black Music Research Newsletter, Center for Black Music Research (Chicago: Columbia College, 1977–); semiannual; *AHCI, MusInd, RILM*

Black Perspective in Music (Cambria Heights, NY: Foundation for Research in the Afro-American Creative Arts, 1973–; annual; *Cc, MusInd, RILM*

Bluegrass Unlimited (Broad Run, VA: Bluegrass Unlimited, 1966–); monthly; *MusInd*

Blues Unlimited (London: Blues Unlimited Publications, 1963–); 4/year; *MLA*

Bulgarska musika (Sofia: Komiteta a Kultura, 1949–); 10/year; *MusInd*

Bulgarski folkor, Bulgarska Akademiia na Naukite (Sofia: Publishing House of the Bulgarian Academy of Sciences, 1975–); quarterly

Canadian Folk Music Bulletin/Bulletin de musique folklorique canadienne, Canadian Folk Music Society (Calgary: Canadian Folk Music Society, 1982–); quarterly; *MLA*

Canadian Folk Music Journal, Canadian Folk Music Society (Calgary: Canadian Folk Music Society, 1973–); annual; *MLA, MusInd*

Canu Gwerin/Folk Song, Welsh Folk Song Society (Gwynedd, Wales: Welsh Folk Song Society, 1909–); annual

Ceol: a Journal of Irish Music (Dublin, 1963–); irregular; *MLA, MusInd, RILM*

Česky lid/Czech People, Czechoslovak Academy of Sciences, Institute of Ethnography and Science of Folklore (Prague: Academia, 1892–); quarterly; *AH&L, MLA, HistAbst*

Chinese Music, Chinese Music Society of North America (Woodridge, IL: Chinese Music Society of North America, 1978–); quarterly; *MusInd, RILM*

College Music Symposium, College Music Society (Boulder: College Music Society, 1961–); annual; *AHCI, Cc, MusInd, RILM*

Country Dance and Song, Country Dance and Song Society of America (Northampton, MA: Country Dance and Song Society, 1968–); annual; *MusInd*

Cultural Anthropology, American Anthropological Association (Washington, DC: American Anthropological Association, 1986–); quarterly

Culture and Tradition (St John's, Nfld: Memorial University of Newfoundland, 1976–); annual; *MLA*

Culture musicali, Società Italiana di Etnomusicologica (Rome: Bulzoni Editore, 1982–); semiannual

Current Anthropology (Chicago: University of Chicago Press, 1960–); 5/year; *AH&L, Cc, HistAbst, MLA, SSCI, SSI*

Current Musicology (New York: Columbia University, 1965–); semiannual; *AHCI, Cc, HumInd, MusInd, RILM*

Dance Research Journal, Congress on Research in Dance (New York: Congress on Research in Dance, 1969–); semiannual; *AHCI, Cc, HumInd*

Demos: internationale ethnographische und folkloristische Informationen (Berlin: Akademie Verlag, 1960–); quarterly

Deutsches Jahrbuch für Volkskunde (Berlin, 1955–); annual; *AH&L, HistAbst.*

English Dance and Song, English Folk Dance and Song Society (London: English Folk Dance and Song Society, 1936–); 4/year; *MLA, MusInd, RILM*

Ethnologie française/French Ethnology (Paris: Editions Berger-Levrault, 1971–); quarterly

Ethnomusicology, Society for Ethnomusicology (Bloomington, IN: Society for Ethnomusicology,

1953–); quarterly; *AHCI, Cc, HumInd, MLA, MusInd, RILM, SSCI*

Etnografia Polska, Polska Akademia Nauk, Instytut Historli Kultury Materialnej (Wrocław: Ossolineum, 1958–); semiannual; *AH&L, HistAbst*

Finnish Music Quarterly (Helsinki: Performing Music Promotion Centre, Foundation for the Promotion of Finnish Music, 1985–); quarterly; *MusInd*

Folk Music Journal, English Folk Dance and Song Society (London: English Folk Dance and Song Society, 1965–); annual; *AHCI, Cc, MLA, MusInd*

Folklore, Folklore Society (London: Folklore Society, 1878–); semiannual; *AHCI, HumInd, MLA, RILM*

Folklore de France, Confédération Nationale des Groupes Folkloriques Français (Nîmes, 1950–); bimonthly

The Galpin Society Journal (Leicester: Galpin Society, 1948–); annual; *AHCI, Cc, MusInd, RILM*

Hogaku, Traditional Japanese Music Society (New York: City University of New York, 1983–); semiquarterly; *MusInd, RILM*

Indian Music Journal (Melkote: Tyaga Bharati Music Education Mission, 1964–); annual

Inter-American Music Review (Los Angeles: Robert Stevenson, 1978–); semiannual; *AHCI, MusInd, RILM*

International Folklore Review (London: New Abbey Publications, 1981–); annual; *MLA*

International Journal of Music Education, International Society of Music Education (Reading, 1967–); semiannual; *MusInd, RILM*

International Review of the Aesthetics and Sociology of Music (Zagreb: Muzicka Akademija u Zagrebu, 1970–); semiannual; *AHCI, Cc, MusInd, RILM*

In Theory Only, Michigan Music Theory Society (Ann Arbor, MI: University of Michigan School of Graduate Theory Association, 1975–); irregular; *MusInd, RILM*

Irish Folk Music Studies, Folk Music Society of Ireland (Dublin: Folk Music Society of Ireland, 1973–); annual; *RILM*

Israel Studies in Musicology (Ramat Aviv: Tel Aviv University, 1978–); annual; *RILM*

Jahrbuch des Österreichischen Volksliedwerkes (Vienna: Österreichischen Bundesverlag für Österreich, Wissenschaft und Kunst, 1952–); annual; *RILM*

Jahrbuch für musikalische Volks- und Völkerkunde, Freie Universität Berlin, Vergleichende Musikwissenschaft (Basel: Bärenreiter Verlag, 1968–); irregular; *RILM*

Jahrbuch für Volksliedforschung (Bielefeld: Deutsches Volksliedarchiv, 1928–); annual; *Cc, MLA*

Jazzforschung/Jazz Research, International Society for Jazz Research (Graz: International Society for Jazz Research, 1969–); annual; *MusInd, RILM*

JEMF Quarterly (Murfreesboro, TN: Center for Popular Music, 1968–); quarterly; *AHCI, Cc, MLA, MusInd, RILM*

Journal of American Folklore, American Folklore Society (Washington, DC: American Folklore Society, 1888–); quarterly; *AH&L, Cc, HistAbst, MusInd, SSCI*

Journal of Asian Studies, Association for Asian Studies (Ann Arbor, MI: University of Michigan, 1941–); 4/year; *AH&L, Cc, HistAbst, HumInd, MLA, SSCI*

Journal of Country Music (Nashville: Country Music Foundation, 1970–); quarterly; *AHCI, Cc, MLA, RILM*

Journal of Folklore Research (Bloomington, IN: Indiana University, Folklore Institute, 1964–); quarterly; *AH&L, Cc, HistAbst, MLA, MusInd*

The Journal of Musicological Research (London: Gordon and Breach Science Publishers, 1974–); 4/year; *AHCI, Cc, RILM*

Journal of Musicology (Berkeley: University of California Press, 1982–); quarterly; *AHCI, Cc, MusInd, RILM*

Journal of Popular Culture, Popular Culture Association (Bowling Green, OH: Bowling Green University Popular Press, 1967–); quarterly; *AH&L, AHCI, Cc, HistAbst, HumInd, MLA, MusInd, SSCI*

Journal of Research in Music Education, Society for Research in Music Education (Reston, VA: Music Educators National Conference, 1953–); quarterly; *AHCI, Cc, EducInd, MusInd, RILM, SSCI*

Journal of the American Musical Instrument Society (Vermillion, SD, 1975–); annual; *AHCI, Cc, MusInd, RILM*

Journal of the American Musicological Society (Richmond, VA: William Byrd Press, 1948–); quarterly; *AHCI, HumInd, MusInd, RILM, SSI*

Journal of the Indian Musicological Society (Baroda, India: Indian Musicological Society, 1970–); semiannual; *AHCI, Cc, MusInd, RILM*

Journal of the Music Academy, Madras (Madras: The Music Academy, 1930–); annual

415

Ethnomusicology: an Introduction

Kentucky Folklore Record, Kentucky Folklore Society (Bowling Green, OH: Western Kentucky University, 1955–); semiannual; *MLA, MusInd*

Laographia, Greek Folklore Society (Athens: Greek Folklore Society, 1909–); *AH&L, HistAbst, MLA*

Latin American Music Review/Revista de Musica Latino Americana (Austin: University of Texas Press, 1980–); semiannual; *AHCI, Cc, MLA, MusInd, RILM*

Living Blues: a Journal of the Black American Blues Tradition (University, MS: University of Mississippi, 1970–); 6/year; *MLA, MusInd, RILM*

Magyar Zene, Association of the Hungarian Musicians, Budapest (Budapest, 1960–); 6/year; *RILM*

Man (London: Royal Anthropological Institute of Great Britain and Ireland, 1966–); quarterly; *AH&L, Cc, HistAbstr, SSCI*

Miscellanea Musicologica: Adelaide Studies in Musicology (Adelaide: University of Adelaide, 1966–); annual; *MusInd, RILM*

Music Educators Journal, Music Educators National Conference (Reston, VA: Music Educators National Conference, 1914–); 9/year; *AHCI, Cc, EducInd, MusInd, RILM*

Musica Asiatica (New York: Oxford University Press, 1978–); irregular; *RILM*

Musica Judaica, American Society for Jewish Music (New York: American Society for Jewish Music, 1976–); annual; *MusInd, RILM*

Musicologica Slovaca (Bratislava, 1969–); irregular

Musicology Australia, Musicological Society of Australia (Canberra: Musicological Society of Australia, 1965–); annual; *MusInd, RILM*

Musikforum: Zeitschrift für musikalisches Volksschaften (Leipzig: Zentralhaus für Kulturarbeit, 1956–); 4/year; *MusInd, RILM*

Muzyka: Kwartalnick poswięcony historii i teorii muzyki oraz krytyce naukowej i artystycznej, Polska Akademiia Nauk, Instytut Sztuki (Warsaw: Polish Academy of Sciences, 1956–); quarterly; *MusInd, RILM*

Muzykal'naia fol'kloristika, Soyuz Kompozitorov Rossiiskoi SFSR, Fol'klornaya Komissiya (Moscow: Izdatel'stvo Sovetskii Kompozitor, 1973–); irregular; *MLA*

Muzyka narodov Azii i Afriki (Moscow: Sovetskii Kompozitor, 1969–); irregular

Národopisné aktuality (Strácnice: Ustav lidového umení ve Stráznici, 1963–); quarterly; *MLA*

Narodna tvorchist' ta etnografiia, Instytut mystetstvoznavstva, fol'kloru ta etnohrafii Akademii nauk Ukrains'koi SSR (Kiev: Ukraine, 1957–); quarterly

Neue Zeitschrift für Musik (Mainz: Schotts Söhne, 1834–); monthly; *Cc, MusInd, RILM*

New York Folklore, New York Folklore Society (Newfield, NY: New York Folklore Society, 1975–); quarterly; *AH&L, AHCI, Cc, HistAbst, MusInd*

Nord Nytt: Nordic Periodical for Folklife Studies (Lyngby: N E F A–Norden Institut for Europaeisk Folkelivsforskning, 1963–); irregular

North Carolina Folklore Journal, North Carolina Folklore Society (Boone, NC: North Carolina Folklore Society, 1948–); 2/year; *HistAbst, MLA, MusInd*

Orbis Musicae (Tel Aviv: Tel Aviv University, Department of Music, 1971–); biennial; *MusInd*

Österreichische Musikwissenschaft (Vienna: Musikverlag Elisabeth Hegelgasse, 1946–); monthly; *MusInd, RILM*

Pacific Review of Ethnomusicology (Los Angeles: Ethnomusicology Archive, 1984–); annual

Polish Music (Warsaw: Authors' Agency, 1966–); quarterly; *MusInd, RILM*

Popular Music (Cambridge: Cambridge University Press, 1982–); quarterly; *MusInd*

Popular Music and Society (Bowling Green, OH: Popular Press, 1971–); quarterly; *AHCI, Cc, MusInd, RILM*

Review of Popular Music, International Association for the Study of Popular Music (Berlin: IASPM, 1982–); 2/year

Revista de etnografie si folclor (Bucharest: Academia Romana, 1955–); 4/year; *MLA, RILM*

Revue de musicologie, Société Française de Musicologie (Paris: Société Française de Musicologie, 1917–); semiannual; *AHCI, Cc, MusInd, RILM*

Revue musicale de Suisse Romande (Yverdon-les-Bains, 1948–); quarterly; *MusInd, RILM*

Rivista Italiana di musicologia, Società Italiana di Musicologia (Florence: Casa Editrice Leo S. Olschki, 1966–); semiannual; *AHCI, Cc, MusInd, RILM*

Sangeet Natak, Sangeet Natak Akademi (New Delhi: Sangeet Natak Akademi, National Academy of Music, Dance and Drama, 1965–); quarterly

Selected Reports in Ethnomusicology (Los Angeles: University of California, 1966–); annual; *MLA, MusInd, RILM*

Sing Out! The Folk Song Magazine (Easton, PA: Sing Out Corporation, 1950–); quarterly; *AHCI, Cc, MLA, MusInd*

Slovensky Narodopis/Slovak Ethnography (Bratislava: Veda, 1956–); quarterly; *MLA*

416

South African Journal of Musicology/Suid-Afrikaanse tydskrif vir musiekwetenskap, Musicological Society of South Africa/Musiekwetenskapvereining van Suid-Afrika (Pretoria: Musicological Society of South Africa, 1981–); annual/semiannual

Sovetskaia etnografiia, Akademiia nauk SSSR i Narodnyi komissariat proszezhcheniia RSFSR (Moscow: Izdatel'stvo Akademii Nauk, 1931–); bimonthly; *AH&L, HistAbst, MLA*

Sovetskaia muzyka, Soyuz Kompozitorov SSSR (Moscow: Izdatel'stvo Sovetskii Kompozitor, 1933–); monthly; *MusInd, RILM*

Studia musicologica academia scientiarum hungaricae (Budapest: Akadèmiai Kiadó, 1961–); annual *MusInd, RILM*

Studia musicologica norvegica (Oslo: Universitetsforlaget, 1968–); annual; *MusInd, RILM*

Studies in Music (Nedlands: University of Western Australia, 1967–); annual; *MusInd, RILM*

Sumlen: Arsbok för vis- och folkmusikforskning, Samfundet för Visforskning (Stockholm, 1976–); annual; *MLA*

Suomen Antropologi/Antropologi i Finland (Helsinki: Suomen Antropologinen Seura, 1976–); quarterly; *MLA*

Svensk tidskrift för musikforskning (Uppsala: Svenska Samfundet för Musikforskning, 1919–); annual; *AHCI, MusInd, RILM*

Toyo ongaku kenkyu (Tokyo: Toyo Ongaku Gakkai, 1937–); *RILM*

Tradisjon: tidsskrift for folkeminnevitenskap (Oslo: Universitetsforlaget, 1971–); annual; *MLA*

Traditional Music (London: Alan Ward, 1975–); quarterly; *MusInd*

UCLA Journal of Dance Ethnology, Dance Ethnology Association (Los Angeles: Dance Ethnology Association, 1977–); annual

Umak nondan/Journal of the Science and Practice of Music (Seoul: Music Research Center, 1984–); annual; *RILM*

The World of Music/Le monde de la musique/Die Welt der Musik, International Institute for Comparative Music Studies and Documentation (Wilhelmshaven: Heinrichshofen, 1957–); quarterly; *AHCI, Cc, MusInd, RILM*

Yearbook for Traditional Music, International Council for Traditional Music (New York: International Council for Traditional Music, 1949–); annual; *MLA, MusInd, RILM*

Yuval, Jewish Music Research Centre (Jerusalem: Jewish Music Research Centre, Hebrew University of Jerusalem, 1966–); irregular; *RILM*

Zeitschrift für Volkskunde (Goettingen: Deutsche Gesellschaft für Volkskunde, 1905–); semiannual; *AHCI, Cc, MLA, MusInd*

Zvuk (Sarajevo: Savez Kompozitora Jugoslavije, 1955–); quarterly; *MusInd, RILM*

Archives and Research Centres with Archival Holdings

The following selective list of major archives and centres for ethnomusicological research with archival holdings is broadly divided by region of location. In many cases, archival and other research materials from a specific location may not be found in that country or region, but in a large international archive such as the Indiana University Archives of Traditional Music or the Archive of Folk Culture at the Library of Congress in Washington, DC. Included, when available, in each entry are the address of the centre and a date of establishment.

AFRICA
International Library of African Music. Rhodes University, Grahamstown, South Africa

ASIA AND THE PACIFIC
Archives and Research Center for Ethnomusicology (ARCE). American Institute of Indian Studies, B–29 Defence Colony, New Delhi 110024, India

Audio-Recording Collections (1889). Department of Anthropology, Bernice Pauahi Bishop Museum, Box 19000–A, Honolulu, HI 96819, USA

Australian Institute of Aboriginal Studies (AIAS) (1961). PO Box 553, Canberra, ACT 2601, Australia

Chinese Music Archives. Music Department, Chung Chi College, The Chinese University of
    Hong Kong
Institute of Papua New Guinea Studies Music Archive. PO Box 1432, Boroko, Papua New
    Guinea
Jerusalem Phono-Archives of Oriental and Jewish Music. 8 KKL–st., Entrance 5, 92428
    Jerusalem, Israel
Jewish Music Research Centre. Hebrew University of Jerusalem, Givat Ram Campus, PO Box
    503, Jerusalem 91004, Israel
National Film and Sound Archive. McCoy Circuit, Action ACT, GPO Box 2002, Canberra,
    ACT 2601, Australia
Oman Centre for Traditional Music (1985). Muscat, Oman
Phonothèque. Jewish National and University Library, Hebrew University, Jerusalem, Israel
Research Archives for Japanese Music. Ueno Gakuen College, 4–24–12 Higashi-ueno, Taito-ku,
    Tokyo, 110, Japan
Zhongquo Yinyue Yanjiu Sou [Chinese Music Research Institute] (1954). Beijing, PRC

THE AMERICAS
Archive of Folk Culture (1928). Library of Congress, American Folklife Center, Washington, DC
    20540, USA
Archive of Folk Song and Music (1960). Center for the Study of Comparative Folklore and
    Mythology, 1037 Graduate School of Management, University of California, Los Angeles,
    CA 90024, USA
Archive of Folklore and Folklife. University of Pennsylvania, 417 Logan Hall, Philadelphia,
    PA 19104, USA
Archive of Traditional Music. Catholic University of Peru, Institute Riva Agüera, Camará 459,
    Lima 1, Peru
Archives de folklore de l'Université Laval (1944). Bureau 5172, Pavillon Charles De Koninck,
    Cité Universitaire, Québec, Canada G1K 7P4
Canadian Centre for Folk Culture Studies (1841). Canadian Museum of Civilization, 100
    Laurier Street, PO Box 3100, Station B, Hull, Québec, Canada J8X 4H2 [Formerly National
    Museum of Man]
Center for Black Music Research (1983). Columbia College, Chicago, IL, USA
Center for Ethnomusicology (1964–5). Columbia University, 417 Dodge Hall, New York,
    NY 10027, USA
Center for Intercultural Studies in Folklore and Ethnomusicology (1967). SSB 3.106, Austin,
    TX 78712, USA
Center for Research and Development of Cuban Music. Havana, Cuba
Center for Southern Folklore Archives (1972). Box 40105, Memphis, TN 38174, USA
Center for the Study of Comparative Folklore and Mythology (1962). University of California,
    Los Angeles, CA 90024, USA
Center for the Study of Popular Culture. Bowling Green State University, Bowling Green,
    OH 43403, USA
Centre d'études sur la langue, les arts et les traditions populaires des francophones en Amérique
    du Nord (CELAT)/Center for the Study of the Language, Art, and Culture of Francophones
    in North America (1976). Laval University, Pavillon Charles De Koninck, Cité Uni-
    versitaire, Québec, Canada G1K 7P4
Ethnic Folk Arts Center (1966). 325 Spring Street, Room 314, New York, NY 10013, USA
Ethnographic Audio Archive. Lowie Museum of Anthropology, 103 Kroeber Hall, University of
    California, Berkeley, CA 94720, USA
Ethnomusicology Archive (1961). Department of Music, University of California, Los Angeles,
    CA 90024, USA
Ethnomusicology Archive (1974). School of Music, The Florida State University, Tallahassee,
    FL 32306, USA
Indiana University Archives of Traditional Music (1936). Morrison Hall, Indiana University,
    Bloomington, IN 47405, USA
Indiana University Folklore Archives. Morrison Hall, Indiana University, Bloomington,
    IN 47405, USA
Institute of Jazz Studies (1952). Rutgers University, 135 Bradley Hall, Newark, NJ 07102, USA
John Donald Robb Archive of Southwestern Music (1964). Fine Arts Library, Fine Arts Center,
    University of New Mexico, Albuquerque, NM 87131, USA

Memorial University of Newfoundland Folklore and Language Archive (MUNFLA) (1968). Department of Folklore, Memorial University of Newfoundland, St John's, Newfoundland, Canada A1C 5S7

National Anthropological Archives. Natural History Building, MRC 152, Smithsonian Institution, Washington, DC 20560, USA

Northeast Archives of Folklore and Oral History. Department of Anthropology, South Stevens Hall, Room B, University of Maine at Orono, Orono, ME 04469, USA

Provincial Archives of British Columbia. Sound and Moving Image Division, 655 Belleville Street, Victoria, British Columbia, Canada V8V 1X4

Research Center for Musical Iconography (RCMI) (1971). The City University of New York, 33 West 42nd Street, New York, NY 10036, USA

Smithsonian Folklife Program Archives. Office of Folklife Programs, Smithsonian Institution, 955 l'Enfant Plaza, Suite 2600, Washington, DC 20560, USA

Southern Folklife Collection. University of North Carolina at Chapel Hill, Chapel Hill, NC 27514, USA [includes John Edwards Memorial Collection]

UCLA Folklore Archives (1960). Center for the Study of Comparative Folklore and Mythology. 1037 Graduate School of Management, University of California, Los Angeles, CA 90024, USA

University of California Folklore Archives (1963). 110 Kroeber Hall, University of California, Berkeley, CA 94720, USA

University of Illinois Archive of Ethnomusicology (1971). School of Music, 2136 Music Building, 1114 West Nevada Street, Urbana, IL 61801, USA

University of Mississippi Blues Archive (1984). Farley Hall, University of Mississippi, University, MS 38677, USA

University of Pennsylvania Folklore Archives (1963). Folklore and Folklife Department, 417 Logan Hall CN, University of Pennsylvania, PA 19101, USA

University of Washington Ethnomusicology Archives (1962). School of Music, DN–10, University of Washington, Seattle, WA 98195, USA

William Ranson Hogan Jazz Archive (1958). Howard–Tilton Memorial Library, Tulane University, New Orleans, LA 70118, USA

World Music Archives (1965). Olin Library, Wesleyan University, Middletown, CT 06457, USA

EUROPE

Archives Internationales de Musique Populaires (AIMP). Genf, Switzerland

Bibliothèque National. Départment de la Phonothèque Nationale et de l'Audiovisuel, 2 rue de Louvois, 75002 Paris, France

British Library National Sound Archive. 29 Exhibition Rd., London SW7 2AS, UK

Centre for English Cultural Traditions and Language. Sheffield, UK

Centre d'études d'Asie Mineure. 14, rue Navarinou, Athens, Greece

Centre du recherches du folklore Hellénique. Académie d'Athènes, Leophoros Sygrou 129, Athens 405, Greece

Dansk Folkemindesamling/Danish Folklore Archives (DFS). Birketinget 6, 2300 Copenhagen S, Denmark

Deutsches Volksliedarchiv. Silberbackstrasse 13, D–7800 Freiburg am Breisgau, Germany

Etnomusicologisch Centrum 'Jaap Kunst'. Universiteit Van Amsterdam, Keizersgracht 73, NL–1002 Amsterdam, Netherlands

Etno-Folkloristisk Institutt. Universitetet i Bergen, N–5000 Bergen, Norway

Fonogrammarkhiv. Institut russkoi literatury Akademii nauk SSSR. St Petersburg, Russia

Institute of Folklore Research/Zavod za Istrazivanje Folklore. Institute for Philology, Socijalisticke Revolucije 17/IV, YU–41000 Zagreb, Yugoslavia

Institut za Folklor pri Bulgarskata Akademiia na Naukite (1988). Sektor za Musika, ulitza Moskovska 6–a, 1000 Sofia–C, Bulgaria

Institut po problemi na izkustvoznanieto pri Bulgarskata Akademiia na Naukite (1988). Sektor za Etnomusikologiia, Evlogi Georgiev No. 11, 1504 Sofia, Bulgaria

International Archives of Folk Music (IAFM)/Archives internationales de musique populaire (AIMP) (1944). Laurent Aubert, Musée d'ethnographie, de la Ville de Genève, 65–67 Cark–Vogt, CH–1205 Geneva, Switzerland

Kabinet narodnoi muzyki. Moskovskaia gos. konservatoriia. Moscow, Russia

M.Merlier Folk Music Archives (MFA). 11 Kydathenaion Str, 105.59, Athens, Greece

Musée de l'Homme. Départment d'Ethnomusicologie, Palais de Chaillot, Place du Trocadéro, 75116 Paris, France

Musikkvitenskapelig Institutt. Universitetet i Trondheim, N–7055 Dragvoll, Norway

Národopisny institut, Slovenskej akadémie vied [Ethnographic Institute of the Slovak Academy of Sciences], Klemensova 19, 88416 Bratislava, Czechoslovakia

Phonogrammarchiv, Österreichischen Akademie der Wissenschaften. Licbiggasse 5, A 1010 Vienna, Austria

Peloponnesian Folklore Foundation. Vas. Alexandrou 1, Nafplion, Greece

School of Scottish Studies, Sound Archive. University of Edinburgh, 27 George Square, Edinburgh EH8 9LD, Scotland

Schweizerisches Volksliedarchiv. Basel, Switzerland

Sekcia hudobnej vedy, Umenovedny ustav Slovenskej akademie vied. Fajnorovo nabrezie, 1, Bratislava, Czechoslovakia

Svenska litteratursallskapet archiv i Finland. Fabianskatan 7 B, SF–00180 Helsinki, Finland

Svenskt Musikhistoriskt Arkiv (SMA) (1965). Box 16326, S–10326 Stockholm, Sweden

Svenskt Visarchiv (SVA) (1950). Hagagatan 23 A, S–11347 Stockholm, Sweden

Ustav pro etnografii a folkloristiku Ceskoslovenske akademie ved [Institute for Ethnography and Folklore Research of the Czech Academy], Lazarská 8, 120 00 2, Prague, Czechoslovakia

Vaughan Williams Memorial Library. English Folk Dance and Song Society, Cecil Sharp House, 2 Regents Park Road, London NW1 7AY, UK

Zavod za Instrazivanje Folklora [Institute for Philology and Folklorsitics-Institute for Folklore Research], Library, Socijalisticke Revolucije 17/IV, YU–41000 Zagreb, Yugoslavia

Associations and Organizations

Listed below are associations and organizations which people engaged in ethnomusicological research may want to contact during a stage of their research. This, too, is a selective list. Organized by broad region of location, it is important to note that many of the organizations are international in scope, and that some, though located in the USA or Europe, exist primarily to support musicological study of another region. Included in the listing are:

Organization name (date of establishment [when known]); address; *Official publication*

AFRICA

African Music Association (AMA)/Société Africaine de musique (SAM), University of Zambia, Lusaka, Zambia

African Music Society (1947), Rhodes University, Grahamstown 6140, South Africa; *African Music*

Musicological Society of South Africa/Musikwetens kapvereiniging van Suid Afrika, PO Box 29950, Sunnyside 0132, Pretoria, South Africa

ASIA AND PACIFIC

Asia Dance Association, Dept 623 Tongsan APT, 669 It'aewon–dong, Tongsan-su, Seoul 140, Korea

Indian Musicological Society (1970), Jambu Bet, Dandia Bazar, Baroda 390 001, India; *Journal of the Indian Musicological Society*

Musicological Society of Australia (1963), GPO Box 2404, Canberra, ACT 2601, Australia; *Musicology Australia*

Nippon Ongaku Gakkai/Musicological Society of Japan (1949), Tokyo National University of Fine Arts and Music, Ueno Park, Taito-ku, Tokyo 110, Japan

Society for Ethnomusicological Research in Hong Kong (SERHK) (1988), Chinese University of Hong Kong, Hong Kong

Tôyô Ongaku Gakkai/Society for Research in Asiatic Music (1936), Seiha Hogaku Kaikan, Ichigaya Sanai-cho 3, Shinjuku, Tokyo 162, Japan

420

American Anthropological Association (1902), 1703 New Hampshire Ave. NW, Washington, DC 20009, USA; *American Anthropologist*

American Folklore Society (1888), 1703 New Hampshire Avenue NW, Washington, DC 20009, USA; *Journal of American Folklore*

American Musical Instrument Society (AMIS (1971), c/o The Shrine to Music Museum, 414 East Clark St, Vermillion, SD 57069, USA; *Journal of the American Musical Instrument Society*

American Musicological Society (AMS) (1934), 201 South 34th St, Philadelphia, PA 19104, USA; *Journal of the American Musicological Society*

American Society for Jewish Music (ASJM) (1974), 155 Fifth Ave., New York, NY 10010, USA; *Musica Judaica*

Association for Asian Studies (AAS) (1941), One Lane Hall, University of Michigan, Ann Arbor, MI 48109, USA; *Journal of Asian Studies*

Association for Recorded Sound Collections (ARSC), PO Box 75082, Washington, DC 20013, USA

Canadian Folk Music Society (CFMS)/Société Canadienne de Musique Folklorique (1956), Box 4232, Station C, Calgary, Alberta, Canada T2T 5N1; *Canadian Folk Music Bulletin/Canadian Folk Music Journal*

Chinese Music Society of North America (1976), One Heritage Plaza, Woodridge, IL 60517, USA; *Chinese Music*

Congress on Research in Dance (1965), 35 West 4th St, Rm 675–D, University of New York, New York, NY 10003, USA; *Dance Research Journal*

Council for Research in Music Education (CRME) (1963), c/o School of Music, University of Illinois, Urbana, IL 61801, USA; *Bulletin of the Council for Research in Music Education*

Country Dance and Song Society of America (1915), 505 Eighth Ave., Room 2500, New York, NY 10018, USA; *Country Dance and Song*

Country Music Foundation (1964), 4 Music Square East, Nashville, TN 37203, USA; *Journal of Country Music*

Folklore Studies Association of Canada, Canadian Folklore, PO Box 11217, Station H, Nepean K2H 7T9 Ontario, Canada

Foundation for Research in the Afro-American Creative Arts, P.O. Drawer I, Cambria Heights, NY 11411, USA; *The Black Perspective in Music*

Inter-American Music Council/Conseil interaméricain de musique/Consejo Interamericano de Música (CIDEM) (1956), c/o Efraín Paesky, 1889 F Street, NW, 510–B, Washington, DC 20006, USA

International Council for Traditional Music (ICTM)/Conseil international de la musique traditionelle (CIMT)/Consejo Internacional de Música Tradicional (1947), c/o Center for Ethnomusicology, Dept. of Music, Columbia University, New York, NY 10027, USA; *Yearbook for Traditional Music*

Music Educators National Conference (1907), 1902 Association Dr., Reston, VA 22091, USA; *Journal of Research in Music Education*; *Music Educators Journal*

Popular Culture Association (PCA) (1969), Popular Culture Center, Bowling Green State University, Bowling Green, OH 43403, USA; *Popular Music and Society*; *Journal of Popular Culture*; *Journal of American Culture*

Society for Asian Music (1959), Department of Asian Studies, 388 Rockefeller Hall, Cornell University, Ithaca, NY 14853, USA; *Asian Music*

Society for Ethnomusicology (1955), Morrison Hall, Indiana University, Bloomington, IN 47405, USA; *Journal of Ethnomusicology*

Sonneck Society (1974), c/o Kate Keller, 13125 Scarlet Oak Dr., Darnestown, MD 20878, USA; *American Music*

Traditional Japanese Music Society, City University of New York, Graduate Center, 33 West 42nd Street, 10th Floor, New York, NY 10036, USA

English Folk Dance and Song Society, Cecil Sharp House, 2 Regents Park Road, London NW1 7AY, UK; *English Dance and Song*

Folk Music Society of Ireland (FMSI)/Cumann Cheol Tire Eireann (CCTE) (1971), 15 Henrietta Street, Dublin 1, Rep. of Ireland; *Irish Folk Music Studies*

The Folklore Society (1878), University College, Gower Street, London WC1E 6BT, UK; *Folklore*

The Galpin Society (1946), c/o Pauline Holden, 38 Eastfield Rd., Western Park, Leicester LE3 6FE, UK; *Galpin Society Journal*

Institut für Jazzforschung/International Society for Jazz Research, Hochschule für Musik und darstellende Kunst, Leonhardt 15, A–8010 Graz, Austria; *Jazzforschung*

International Archives of Folk Music (IAFM)/Archives internationales de musique populaire (AIMP) (1944), Laurent Aubert, Musée d'ethnographie, de la Ville de Genève, 65–67 Cark-Vogt, CH–1205 Geneva, Switzerland

International Association for the Study of Popular Music (IASPM)/Association internationale pour l'étude de la musique populaire (1981), c/o Peter Wicke, Forschungszentrum Populäre Musik, Berich Musikwissenschaft, Humboldt–Universitat–Berlin, Am Kupfergraben 5, DDR–1080, Berlin, Germany; *Review of Popular Music*

International Dance Council (IDc)/Conseil international de la danse (CIDD), Nicole Luc-Maréchal, c/o Unesco, Lureau S2 60, 1 rue Miollis, F–75732 Paris CEDEX 15, France

International Institute for Comparative Music Studies and Documentation (IICMSD)/Institut international d'études comparatives de la musique et de documentation musicale/Internationales Institut für vergleichende Musikstudien und Dokumentation (1963), Winklerstrasse 20, D–1000 Berlin 33, Germany; *The World of Music*

International Music Council (IMC)/Conseil international de la musique (CIM) (1949), 1 rue Miollis, F–75732 Paris CEDEX 15, France

International Musicological Society (IMS)/Société internationale de musicologie (SIM)/ Sociedad Internacional de Musicología (SIM)/Internationale Gesellschaft für Musikwissenschaft (IGMW) (1927), Postfach 1561, CH–4001 Basel, Switzerland; *Acta Musicologica*

International Society for Music Education (ISME)/Société internationale pour l'éducation musicale/Sociedad Internacional de Educación Musical/Internationale Gesellschaft für Musik-Erziehung (1967), University of Reading, Music Education Centre, Reading RG6 1HY England; *International Journal of Music Education*

Nordic Association for Folk Dance Research/Association nordique d'étude des danses populaires/ Nordisk Förening för Folkdansforskning (1977), Egil Bakka, Rädet for Folkemusikk og Folkedans, Universitetssentret, N–7055 Dragvoll, Norway

Società Italiana di Etnomusicologia (1966), Bulzoni Editore, Via di Liburni 14 00185, Rome, Italy; *Rivista Italiana di musicologia*

Société française d'Ethnomusicologie (1917), Paris, France; *Revue de musicologie*

Major Instrument Collections

Laurence Libin

Musical instruments of all types are collected for many reasons – for use in performance, as objects of veneration or visual art, to furnish ethnological and historical evidence, to illustrate technological developments and serve as models for new construction, for financial investment and sale, and merely to satisfy curiosity. Amateur and professional musicians, wealthy aristocrats, religious and municipal bodies, schools and museums are among those who amass instruments for one reason or another. Criteria distinguishing successful modern collections include not merely size, but also quality and accessibility of holdings, condition and documentation of individual objects, and integrity or coherence of the whole. This article outlines the history of instrument collecting with attention to the motives and conditions that influence collectors, and deals with assemblages of musical instruments gathered intentionally and more or less permanently. Instruments awaiting dispersal (e.g. in a dealer's or maker's shop) or accumulated apparently by chance are considered only in passing.

Pre-Christian and non-European

Assemblage and deliberate preservation of groups of instruments is an ancient but not a universal practice. Little evidence exists of large-scale collecting outside urban centres; nomads, subsistence-level tribes and those occupying hostile environments may not save instruments at all. Though native Americans seldom preserved collections of instruments, descendants of the Aztecs still occasionally hoarded specimens of the *teponaztli* and *huehuetl* in the 1950s. Elsewhere, particularly in settled societies where ensemble performance predominates, collections associated with worship or venerated in their own right are not uncommon; notable examples include New Guinean slit-drums, East African royal drums, and ceremonial instruments in Himalayan monasteries. Such groups may be of substantial size: the Tibetan monastery at Tin-ge owned at least 12 bone trumpets, four long trumpets, and hundreds of cymbals, drums, small bells, and other ritual noisemakers. Special ceremonies, taboos and skills connected with their manufacture and use reinforce the instruments' extra-musical connotations among non-literate societies; revered collections may thus be said to express a people's history and beliefs. But largely because of political factors and the greed of Western collectors many native assemblages have been dispersed, injuring continuity of traditional practices in affected areas such as central Java, where late 18th- and early 19th-century rulers of some principalities maintained three complete gamelans. Although national pride and affluence have led to re-establishment of collections in some former colonies, the most extensive repositories occur today in urbanized, literate societies with long histories of instrumental art music.

The oldest extant groups of instruments, dating back some 6000 years, do not represent intentionally preserved collections. Late Roman and early medieval instrument groups, usually fragmentary and found in northern European mounds, may similarly be coincidental. Since relatively few ancient instruments survive, however, such small archaeological assemblages demand attention. Archaeological departments of art and history museums often include instruments that are not catalogued with the institutions' main instrument collections, but are accompanied by excavation data without which the objects might be valueless to scholars. A major responsibility of modern collectors is to obtain accurate documentation of their instruments and to transmit this information with the instruments should they change ownership; in this respect archaeological and ethnographic collectors generally have been conscientious.

Quite apart from accidental accumulation, the thoughtful collection of instruments predates the Christian era. History records the jealous guarding of many individual instruments, including even a fake 'lyre of Paris' that Plutarch mentioned as being kept in Troy in 334 BC; references to collections are less common, but although well-known passages in *2 Chronicles* and *Daniel* may be late and unreliable there is no reason to doubt that collections of instruments formed part of the sacred property both of Solomon's temple and of Nebuchadnezzar's band. The Second Temple seems to have owned a small orchestra of lyres, harps, horns, trumpets, oboes and cymbals, and there is much evidence of earlier collections used in ritual and entertainment.

Besides collecting instruments for ensemble performance, many pre-Christian peoples hoarded apotropaic (evil-averting) and votive instruments for inclusion at burials. Cult instruments brought together to be entombed constitute the oldest extant true collections. Tutankhamun's tomb (*c*1352 BC) yielded pairs of trumpets and sistra, but most Egyptian burial collections consist only of jingles or votive clappers. Of greater interest to musicians is an assemblage excavated in 1972 from the 2100-year-old tomb of a Chinese noblewoman near Changsha, Hunan province. This includes models of performers playing miniature instruments, as well as real instruments in a state of fine preservation. The Elgin auloi and fragmentary lyre now in the British Museum, from a 5th-century BC Athenian tomb, were likewise once playable. Despite topical inscriptions such as occur on bronze ceremonial instruments excavated in 1955 from the 5th-century BC tomb of the Marquis of Zai, Shouxian county, Anhui province, such interred collections were probably never intended to be seen again in this world.

After the destruction of instruments ordered by Emperor Shihuangdi (221–206 BC) China again became the home of remarkable collections intended for use in performance. Unlike Indian courts, where small ensembles predominated despite the wealth of instruments available, Tang court ministries and conservatories of music involved hundreds of musicians playing about 50 kinds of instrument, often in large orchestras. The cosmopolitan Tang court conservatory (established AD 714) collected not only the finest Chinese instruments but also foreign ones brought from trade centres as far west as Bukhara, gifts to the music-loving Emperor Xuanzong (712–56). In quality and quantity, as well as in geographical scope, his repositories dwarfed any known in Europe for nearly the next 1000 years. Some idea of those holdings may be gained from the dozens of superbly decorated instruments still preserved at the Japanese Imperial Treasury of Shōsōin at Nara; many of these were played by foreign musicians at the unveiling of a Buddha at Tōdaiji temple in 752.

Under the Song dynasty (960–1280) some Chinese shrines employed as many as 120 *qin*, 120 *se*, 200 *sheng*, 20 oboes and percussion. In 1114 the emperor continued the practice of instrument exchange on a grand scale by sending to Korea a collection that included ten sets each of stone chimes and bells.

Medieval

Despite ample iconographic evidence of the many types of instrument assembled at medieval European music centres and despite extant descriptions of occasional large ensembles, we know of no permanent instrument collections of the Middle Ages that approached in size those of contemporary East Asia. Those European instruments which were held in highest regard were complex, rare and probably outside the mainstream of musical activity. There seem to have been no significant collections as such during the earlier Middle Ages. Instrumental music had been discouraged for religious reasons, but even in Islamic Spain, where by 755 Córdoba under the caliphate had become an important music centre, instruments appeared only in small groups except on extraordinary occasions. Since solo and small ensemble music predominated there was no reason to assemble large numbers of instruments for use in performance as in China, and few medieval nobles could afford to employ more than a handful of musicians. While the Church Fathers' censure of secular musical pleasures might not have been taken too seriously, little energy was spent in preserving what could be considered mere tools. Apart from such things as church bells, only those few instruments that found their way to treasuries among other objects valued for appearance, precious materials, or historical associations were saved intentionally. It is likely that the musicians' plain, perishable tools, of which itinerant players seldom owned more than they could carry, simply wore out.

Gradually the rise of polyphony created a demand for more and better-blending instruments. Ceremonial performance called for loud wind instruments like those owned by London's Goldsmiths' Company band, enriched in 1391 by purchase of new trumpets, clarions, shawms, a bombard and a bagpipe – perhaps, with some drums, a guild's typical collection. Domestic music required softer instruments; in 1425 the Parisian Jacques Duchié owned 'harps, organs, vielles, gitterns, psalteries and others, all of which he knew how to play'. Contemporary writers frequently mentioned amateur virtuosos; Sollazo in Simone Prodenzani's *Il Saporetto* (*c*1400), who could play any instrument, may have had authentic counterparts who owned a variety of instruments. The court musician's status had much to do with the formation of collections, for example at the Burgundian courts where noble children took lessons on richly decorated instruments from Philip the Bold's 28 musicians (1367). Yet there is no evidence that groups of the loveliest instruments were set apart from ordinary use to be appreciated as art objects.

Renaissance to 1800

The flourishing of instrument collections during the Renaissance, especially in Italy, is best understood in the context of collecting in general. With increasing wealth and ease of travel, collectors gathered great numbers of exotic objects for both amusement and instruction. Competition led to ostentation, since according to Matarazzo 'it belongs to the position of the great to keep horses, dogs, . . . court jesters, singers and foreign animals', and the largest number of different specimens was most impressive. The contemporaneous development of idiomatic instrumental music elevated the status of instrument makers, who in some towns were protected by professional guilds. Growth of instrument families in all pitch ranges made it desirable to obtain complete consorts, adding new varieties as they became fashionable. Fulfilling aristocratic demands for instruments of utmost magnificence, makers produced art objects worthy of display in private *musei* and *Wunderkammern*; an impression of these studios survives in the intarsias that lined Federigo da Montefeltro's studios at Urbino and Gubbio. By commissioning elegant instruments towns and churches joined the nobility and rich merchants in demonstrating prosperity and good taste. All these factors encouraged instrument collecting.

With important exceptions noted below, most of the Renaissance and Baroque collections have become dispersed. Some idea of their contents can be gained from various published inventories and descriptions. A 1503 inventory of Isabella of Castile's royal alcázar reveals about 20 instruments, some old and broken, a modest assemblage used mainly in performance. A century later Philip II's royal palace in Madrid boasted not only 136 wind, 44 string and 11 keyboard instruments, but also ten Chinese instruments (1602 inventory; the collection, part of which Philip inherited from his aunt, Queen Mary of Hungary, was dispersed through sale a few years later). Wind instruments likewise far outnumbered strings at Henry VIII's Westminster (1547 inventory), where Philip van Wilder had in his charge about 320 instruments (not counting gilt horns, drums and the like), including 40 keyboards. Raymond Fugger's music chamber in Augsburg held (in 1566) nearly 400 instruments, including over 100 flutes and recorders, about 140 lutes and many violins and harpsichords by famous makers, gathered from all over Europe. The Berlin court orchestra owned (in 1582) 72 instruments, 60 of them wind, while Archduke Ferdinand II of the Tyrol's collections (1596) comprised over 230 costly instruments, nearly 80% wind. Ferdinand's personal collection, now at the Vienna Kunsthistorisches Museum, was kept at his Ambras residence; his musicians drew on another repository at Innsbruck. French 16th-century collections were far less impressive, but Jean de Badonvilliers, councillor to François I, left a number of string and keyboard instruments at his death in 1544. Charles IX of France reputedly added Amati violins to the royal collection about 1564. A 1603 inventory of the Hengrave Hall collection survives; in that year the royal collection provided violins for Queen Elizabeth's funeral.

Woodwind instruments usually outnumbered strings in Renaissance repositories, but have not survived in such profusion. Wooden flutes and reed instruments, being cheaper and offering less opportunity for decoration than strings, were considered less worth preserving when they became obsolete; they were also harder to modernize (ivory ones were more precious and often elaborately carved, but less useful in performance; hence they survive in relatively high numbers). Wind instruments in sets often belonged to repositories heavily drawn on by professional performers. The Kassel Hofkapelle inventories of 1573, 1613 and 1638 record loans to the count's musicians; there and elsewhere it appears that valuable, decorated keyboard instruments seldom left their usual chambers (hence more harpsichords and organs occur in inventories than one might expect since one or more might have had to be kept wherever music was often performed). These stationary, seldom lent instruments are more likely than most to have become 'collectors' items'.

Only gradually did connoisseurs evolve the concept of a collection as a work of art, capable of displaying internal harmony and of expressing its owner's taste. Private collectors rather than institutional buyers were mainly responsible for developing this attitude, and Italy in particular was full of collectors. Venice boasted Agostino Amadi, Luigi Balbi, Marco Contarini (whose collection passed to the Correr family and parts of which came to the Paris and Brussels conservatory collections), Leonardo Sanudo and Catarino Zeno; in Bologna lived Ferdinando Cospi; in Ferrara, Antonio Goretti; in Florence, Ridolfo Sirigatti; in Padua, Enea degli Obizzi (whose collection is now in the Vienna Kunsthistorisches Museum); in Rome, Michele Todini and Athanasius Kircher; and in Milan, Manfredo Settala. Finally, there were the more renowned d'Este, Sforza and Medici families. According to Bottrigari, Isabella d'Este's nephew Alfonso II kept his collection in two great chambers where his musicians played; the instruments were arranged by category, and separated according to whether they were played or 'different from those . . . usually made today', and included Vicentino's *arcicembalo* and a set of crumhorns now in the Brussels Conservatory collection.

In Spain and Portugal, noteworthy collections belonged to the Duke of Calabria at Valencia and to Queen Mary of Hungary. Northwards were the private holdings of Jean Baptiste Dandeleu, Caspar Duitz, Hendrick van Brederode, and Constantijn Huygens. Hans Burgkmair's *Triumphzug* illustrates instruments from Maximilian I's Hofkapelle. A certain Felix Platter owned instruments in Basle.

In 1659 Elias Ashmole received a Guinea Coast drum from Johan Tradescant the younger, whose 1656 Musaeum Tradescantianum catalogue records several African and Indian drums under the heading 'Warlike Instruments' (a Guinea drum and a fragment of a side-blown horn remain in the Ashmolean collection, Oxford); similar instruments had been illustrated by Praetorius (*Theatrum instrumentorum*, 1620). Athanasius Kircher's museum at Rome contained instruments discussed in his *Musurgia universalis* (1650); and Filippo Bonanni, curator of Kircher's collection from 1698, drew on

Kircher's text as well as Marin Mersenne's *Harmonie universelle* (1636–7) for his own *Gabinetto armonico* (1722). Michele Todini's *Dichiaratione della galleria armonica* (1676) describes his own idiosyncratic collection, which included curious instruments of his own design; his extraordinary harpsichord flanked by figures of Polyphemus and Galatea survives in the Metropolitan Museum of Art, New York. Todini exhibited his collection publicly, and Winternitz (1966) believed that it might have constituted 'the first museum exclusively devoted to musical intruments'.

Of particular interest later in the Baroque era were the keyboard instruments in collections of Cosimo III and Ferdinand de' Medici (supervised by Bartolomeo Cristofori after 1716), Cardinal Ottoboni and Queen Maria Barbara de Braganza. A distinguished private collection belonged to the Englishman Samuel Hellier in the mid-18th century, including the Stradivari violin now known by his name. By that time it was common for collectors to obtain antique instruments at public sales.

Some outstanding 18th-century musicians were collectors. The celebrated castrato Farinelli owned several precious keyboard instruments (nicknamed 'Coreggio', 'Rafael', 'Titian' and so on), some inherited from Queen Maria Barbara; his testament (1782) specifies that his collection, formed for playing domestic music, should be perpetually preserved in good order along with his music library for the exclusive enjoyment of devoted musicians. Bach at his death owned 19 instruments estimated at nearly a third of the entire value of his estate. Curatorial responsibilities may have stimulated other notable composers of instrumental music. In 1673 Henry Purcell was apprenticed to John Hingeston, Charles II's instrument keeper, as an unpaid 'keeper, maker, mender, repayrer and tuner of the regalls, organs, virginalls, flutes and recorders and all other kind of wind instruments whatsoever'; ten years later Purcell succeeded Hingeston. One of Haydn's contractual responsibilities as Esterházy's vice-Kapellmeister was to look after the instruments and order new ones for the prince's orchestra. Vivaldi's duties at the asylum of the Pietà included the purchase of instruments.

19th and 20th centuries

The French Revolution sounded the death-knell of aristocratic hoarding. From then on middle-class utilitarian ideals underlay the evolution of public collections, first shown by the ambitious 'collection of antique or foreign instruments and also for those in present use which by virtue of their perfection may serve as models' proposed for the new Paris Conservatoire by the 1795 National Convention. Sadly, most of the treasures inventoried for the *Commission temporaire des arts* perished as firewood during the winter of 1816, and it was not until 1864 that the Conservatoire's museum began with the acquisition of 230 instruments from Louis Clapisson. This was followed in the 1870s by the creation of the Brussels Conservatory's museum from the private collections of F.-J. Fétis, Victor-Charles Mahillon and others; then in 1888 came the acquisition of Paul de Wit's first collection by the Berlin Königliche Hochschule für Musik. Perhaps the oldest institutional collection still thriving is that of the Gesellschaft der Musikfreunde in Vienna, begun in 1824 with the acquisition of F. X. Glöggl's instruments and administered in trust since 1938 by the Kunsthistorisches Museum; this repository holds both the Ambras and Obizzi collections, combined by Julius Schlosser in 1916 to form the Sammlung alter Musikinstrumente.

By the 18th century the notion of musical progress had become tied to technical improvement in instrumental manufacture. Growing concern with design standards for mass-produced goods led in the 19th century to the founding of museums of decorative arts in which old instruments occupied an honoured place; London's Victoria and Albert Museum is an example. Loan exhibitions encouraged competition among makers and confirmed the importance of exposing foreign models; one instance is the gamelan that so impressed Debussy at the 1889 Paris Exhibition. Temporary loan exhibitions enjoyed much popularity in England, where an important pioneering display took place in 1872 at the South Kensington (now the Victoria and Albert) Museum. Others followed, some producing useful catalogues: Milan (1881), Bologna and Brussels (1888), Vienna (1892), Chicago (1893), London (Crystal Palace, 1900), Boston (Horticultural Hall, 1902), and again London (Fishmongers' Hall, 1904). The Fishmongers' Hall catalogue explained the motive for such exhibitions: 'to enable all interested in music under its various aspects to contrast, as a fruitful means of instruction, its past with its present condition – to estimate its growth and development, and to observe what progress has been made in the work of the instrument maker'.

Darwinian theories of evolution, scientific interest in acoustics, easy contact with colonial areas and abundant funds encouraged 19th-century collectors whose holdings became the nuclei of many museum collections. Some museums emphasized educational objectives while catering to middle-class tourists with a taste for the exotic; others became archival, veritable Noah's arks of primary source material for research. Many institutions inherited problems as well as benefits from the acquisition of instrument hoards offered by amateurs whose wealth and enthusiasm usually offset their understandable lack of discernment. Most private collectors were rich dilettantes with little musical knowledge; others were professional performers or instrument manufacturers; only a few were music scholars of the first rank. Yet so readily available were fine antiques during the 'golden age' of collecting (up to World War I) that, whether through careful search or mere luck, collectors of every level of sophistication accumulated and eventually gave to museums many significant instruments (as well as many fakes). Abundant donations created the chief task facing 20th-century museums: not acquisition, but the refinement of often haphazard assemblages.

By mid-century the pace of acquisition had slowed: irrelevant, damaged and duplicate material cluttered valuable storage space; legal restrictions on export of national treasures and rocketing prices further inhibited growth. Museums turned to selecting instruments for their rarity or to fill significant gaps in coverage rather than trying to obtain several samples of every type. Emphasis fell on the publication of accurate catalogues, production of recordings and technical drawings, and scientific conservation and restoration. The Comité International des Musées et Collections d'Instruments de Musique was formed within the International Council of Museums, and soon gave birth to the International Association of Musical Instrument Collectors (reabsorbed by CIMCIM in 1975). Discussions within these organizations raised hope that universally acceptable cataloguing procedures might be established.

From the 1980s, wealthy Japanese collectors evinced strong interest in Western as well as Asian instruments and acquired important European and American holdings including major private collections of Robert Rosenbaum and Hans Schambach from New York, both to be housed in new facilities in Japan. At the same time, agreements restricting international transport and sale of ivory and tortoiseshell created obstacles for museums as well as for private collectors, for example greatly complicating loans of instruments for exhibitions. Development of techniques such as dendrochronology for dating and authenticating wooden objects led to realization that many bowed instruments in public collections may be of more recent manufacture or more drastically altered than had been previously suspected; consequently, many long-held attributions were challenged and a more realistic view of the development of viols and violins, especially in Italy, began to emerge.

The relative claims of conservation and restoration became another topic of widespread controversy. Conservation, a fundamental responsibility underlying the permanence of collections and survival of objects, involves a policy of minimum handling, 'climate' and air quality control, proper lighting, disaster and burglar alarms and, on occasion, chemical treatment. In these circumstances, and barring catastrophes like the Florence floods of 1966, instruments may remain in stable condition indefinitely, and collections that receive thoughtful attention in this respect can increase greatly in value and usefulness quite apart from the acquisition of new items. The potential benefits of restoration to playing condition must always be weighed against possible destruction of original evidence. Leading centres of conservation and restoration include the Germanisches Nationalmuseum, Nuremberg, and the Smithsonian Institution's National Museum of American History, Washington, DC.

List of collections

This list includes the most important and largest modern permanent collections (numbers of instruments are approximate); many others contain noteworthy instruments. Detailed information about collections is available from organizations such as the American Musical Instrument Society (USA), the Galpin Society (Great Britain), the Gesellschaft der Freunde alter Musikinstrumente (Switzerland), the Kommission für Instrumentenkunde der Gesellschaft für Musikforschung (Germany) and the Comité International des Musées et Collections d'Instruments de Musique (of the International Council of Museums), and from the publications listed in the bibliography below.

ANGOLA
DUNDO. Museu do Dundo, Missão de Recolha do Folcloro Musical. 100 central African, mainly from the Luanda district

ARGENTINA
BUENOS AIRES. Museo de Instrumentos Indigenas y Folklóricos del Instituto Nacional de Musicologia. 210 from Argentina and neighbouring countries
LA PLATA. Private collection of Emilio Azzarini. 700, especially native South American and musical boxes
——. Facultad de Ciencias Naturales y Museo. 150 ethnic

AUSTRALIA
NEDLANDS. Department of Music, University of Western Australia. A new and growing general collection, including the J. Payton collection of European instruments
D. Casson: *Collection of Musical Instruments* (1974) [check-list]

SYDNEY. Museum of Applied Arts and Sciences. Mainly European with some Chinese and Japanese, including a collection of Australian violins

AUSTRIA

GÖTTWEIG. Musikarchiv Stift Göttweig. 50 European, on loan from Benedictine Abbey

GRAZ. Landesmuseum Joanneum. 150 general

H. Sowinski: 'Steirische Volksmusikinstrumente', *Das Joanneum*, iii (1940)

INNSBRUCK. Kunsthistorische Sammlungen Schloss Ambras. 11 European art and folk instruments from the 16th and 17th centuries and 4 non-European

L. Luchner: *Kunsthistorische Sammlungen Schloss Ambras* (1959)

——. Tiroler Landesmuseum Ferdinandeum. 275 European

F. Waldner: 'Verzeichnis der Musikinstrumente in der Sammlung des Museum Ferdinandeum', *Zeitschrift des Ferdinandeums für Tirol und Vorarlberg*, lix (1915); 'Die Musiksammlung', *Tiroler Landes-museum im Zeighaus* (1973)

LINZ. Oberösterreiches Landesmuseum. 238, mainly European

O. Wessely: *Die Musikinstrumentensammlung des Oberösterreichen Landesmuseums*, Katalog des Ober-österreichen Landesmuseums, ix (1952)

SALZBURG. Museum Carolino Augusteum. 300, mainly European

K. Geiringer: *Alte Musikinstrumente im Museum Carolino-Augusteum Salzburg: Führer und beschreibendes Verzeichnis* (Leipzig, 1932); K. Birsak: 'Die Holzblasinstrumente im Salzburger Museum Carolino-Augusteum: Verzeichnis und entwicklungs-geschichtliche Untersuchungen', *Salzburger Museum Carolino-Augusteum Jahresschrift*, xviii (1973); K. Birsak: 'Die Blechblas-instrumente im Museum Carolino-Augusteum', ibid, xx (1976)

VIENNA. Gesellschaft der Musikfreunde in Wien. General, mostly on loan to the Kunsthistorisches Museum

E. Mandyczewski: *Zusatzband zur Geschichte der k. k. Gesellschaft der Musikfreunde in Wien* (1912)

——. Kunsthistorisches Museum, Sammlung alter Musikinstrumente. 1000, mainly 16th- to 19th-century European, including the collections of Archduke Ferdinand in Schloss Ambras, the Este-Obizzi and the Gesellschaft der Musikfreunde (on loan)

J. von Schlosser: *Die Sammlung alter Musikinstrumente beschreibendes Verzeichnis* (1920/R1970); V. Luithlen: *Saiteninstrumente (Klaviere, Streichinstrumente, Zupfinstrumente) Verzeichnis* (1941); V. Luithlen: *Katalog der Sammlung alter Musikinstrumente*, i: *Saitenklaviere* (1966)

——. Museum für Völkerkunde. 7000 non-European

A. Janata: *Aussereuropäische Musikinstrumente* (1961)

——.Österreiches Museum für Volkskunde. 200, mainly from Austria and the Alps

K. Klier: *Volkstümliche Musikinstrumente in den Alpen* (1956)

BELGIUM

ANTWERP. Etnografisch Museum. 200, African, Asian, Australian, Oceanian

——. Museum Vleeshuis. 500, mainly European; contains collections formerly in the Steen Museum and the Koninklijk Vlaams Muziekconservatorium, Antwerp

P. Génard: *Catalog du Musée d'antiquités d'Anvers* (1894); *Stad Antwerpen, oudheidkundige musea, Vleeshuis: catalogus V. muziek-instrumenten* (1956), *catalogus V-bis* (1967); J. Lambrechts-Douillez: *Antwerpse klavecimbels in het Museum Vleeshuis* (1970)

——. Volkskundemuseum. 360 folk instruments

——. Private collection of J. A. Stelfeld

BRUGES. Musée Gruuthuse. List in *Glareana*, xxiii/2 (1974)

BRUSSELS. Musée Instrumental du Conservatoire Royal de Musique. 5000 of all types and provenances, including the Tagore (Indian), Fétis, Contarini-Correr (17th-century Italian) and Snoeck (Low Countries) collections

V. Mahillon: *Catalogue descriptif et analytique du Musée instrumental du Conservatoire royal de musique de Bruxelles*, i-v (1880–1922); C. C. Snoeck: *Catalogue de la collection d'instruments de musique flamands et néerlandais de C. C. Snoeck* (1903); *Instruments de musique: XVIème et XVIIème siècles* (1969) [exhibition catalogue]; *Instruments de musique: XVIème et XVIIème siècles* (1972) [exhibition catalogue]; N. Meeùs: *Musical Instruments* (1974) [exhibition catalogue]; *The Brussels Museum of Musical Instruments Bulletin* [annual journal of work done in the Brussels Museum]

——. Musées Royaux d'Art et d'Histoire. 400 general

TERVUREN. Musée Royal de l'Afrique Centrale. 10,000, mainly from the former Belgian Congo

F. J. de Hen: *Beitrag zur Kenntnis der Musikinstrumente aus Belgisch Kongo und Ruanda-Urundi* (1960); G. Knosp: *Enquête sur la vie musicale au Congo belge 1934–1935* (1968)

BENIN

PORTO-NOVO. Institut de Recherches Appliquées. 150 Beninese

BRAZIL

BELÉM. Museu Paraense Emílio Goeldi. 400 Brazilian
RIO DE JANEIRO. Museu Nacional da Universidade Federal do Rio de Janeiro. 1300 Brazilian
SÃO PAULO. Museu Paulista da Universidade de São Paulo. 200 Brazilian wind and percussion
Revista do Museu Paulista

BURUNDI

GITEGA. Musée National. Instruments of central Africa

CANADA

OTTAWA. National Museum of Man, Canadian Centre for Folk Culture Studies, and Ethnology
Division. Over 1600, mainly ethnic, especially Indian and Eskimo
R. Carlisle: *Folk Music in Canada – 1974* (1974)
TORONTO. Royal Ontario Museum. European art instruments, including the R. S. Williams
Collection
L. Cselenyi: *Musical Instruments in the Royal Ontario Museum* (1971)
VANCOUVER. Ethnography Museum, University of British Columbia. 300, North American tribal
cultures
——. Private collection of Baron and Baroness Giulio Gatti-Kraus. European art instruments
formerly in the collection of Alessandro Kraus

CHINA

T'AIPEI (TAIWAN). Exhibition Rooms, Institute of History and Philology, Academia Sinica. 100
Asian, especially excavated ancient Chinese instruments

COLOMBIA

BOGOTÁ. Museo Organilogico Folklorico Colombiano. 110 Colombian; museum guide in
preparation
MEDELLÍN. Museo Universitario. 140 Colombian

COMMONWEALTH OF INDEPENDENT STATES (formerly USSR)

DUSANBE. Muzei Muttachidai Respublikawii Ta'richi Kisch-wazschinosi wa San'ati Taswiri.
100 from Tajikistan
ST PETERSBURG (formerly LENINGRAD). Muzey Antropologii i Etnografii imeni Petra I. 1500
ethnographic, mainly Asian, including Peter the Great's collection (founded 1714)
G. I. Blagodatov: *Katalog sobraniya muzïkal'nïkh instrumentov* (1972)
——. Gosudarstvennïy Muzey Etnografii Narodov SSSR. 1500 ethnographic
——. Institut Teatra, Muzïki i Kinematografii [State Institute for Theatre, Music and
Cinematography]. 3000, mainly European art instruments
G. I. Blagodatov: *Katalog sobraniya muzïkal' nïkh instrumentov* (1972)
MOSCOW. State Central Museum of Musical Culture. 1900, mainly European art and folk
instruments, especially from the former USSR
——. State Collection of Antique Bowed Instruments. 240 European art instruments
——. State Historical Museum. 200, mainly European and Asian art and folk instruments
TBILISI. State Museum of Georgia. 130 ethnic, especially string
D. Arakishvili: *Opisaniye i obmer narodnïkh muzïkal'nïkh instrumentov* (1940)

CZECHOSLOVAKIA

BRATISLAVA. Hudobné Oddělenie, Slovenské Národné Muzeum [Music Division, Slovak
National Museum]. 1000, mainly European art and folk
Hudobné zbirky Slovenského národného muzea/Musiksammlungen des Slowakischen Nationalmuseums (1975)
MARTIN. Slovenské Národné Muzeum, Etnograficky Ústav. [Slovak National Museum,
Ethnographical Institute]. 270, mainly Slovak
PRAGUE. Národni Muzeum [National Museum]. 2180, especially European art instruments,
Czech string and other orchestral, and keyboard
Museum of Musical Instruments (1973) [exhibition catalogue]

DENMARK

COPENHAGEN. Musikhistorisk Museum. 1370 general
A. Hammerich: *Musikhistorisk Museum* (1909, 2/1911); suppl. by M. Andersen (1960)
——. Nationalmuseet. 1000 ethnic, especially Asian
——. Carl Claudius' Musikhistoriske Samling. 715, mainly European art instruments
(transferred to Musikhistorisk Museum)
G. Skjerne: *Carl Claudius' samling af gamle musikinstrumenter* (1931)
LYNGBY. Danish Agricultural Museum. 250 cowbells, mainly European and Asian

ECUADOR

QUITO. Casa de la Cultura Ecuatoriana, Pedro Pablo Traversari Collection. 400 European and South American
R. Rephann: *A Catalogue of the Pedro Traversari Collection* (1978)

EGYPT

CAIRO. Mathaf al-Misri [Egyptian Museum]. Ancient Egyptian instruments
H. Hickmann: *Catalogue général des antiquités égyptiennes du Musée du Caire: instruments de musique* (1949)

FIJI ISLANDS

SUVA. Fiji Museum. Instruments of the Fiji Islands

FINLAND

HELSINKI. Suomen Kansallismuseo. 900, in departments of Finnish, Finno-Ugric and Foreign Ethnography
TURKU. Sibeliusmuseum (Åbo Akademi). 500 general

FRANCE

BOURG-LA-REINE. Private collection of Aristide Wirsta. 100 French bows
LA COUTURE-BOUSSEY. Musée Communal d'Instruments de Musique à Vent. 300 wind
PARIS. Private collection of Max Millant. 100 18th- and 19th-century bows
——. Musée des Arts et Traditions Populaires. 3000 European folk instruments, mainly French
——. Musée de l'Homme. 7000 folk and non-European instruments
G. Dournon-Tourelle and J. Wright: *Les guimbardes du Musée de l'homme* (1978)
——. Musée de la Musique. 2700, mainly European instruments incorporating former collections of A. L. Clapisson, Geneviève Thibault and the Conservatoire National Supérieur de Musique
G. Chouquet: *Le Musée du Conservatoire national de musique: catalogue raisonné des instruments* (1875, 2/1884); suppls. (1894, 1899, 1903)
——. Musée du Louvre, Département des Antiquités Egyptiennes. 130 ancient Egyptian
C. Ziegler: *Les instruments de musique égyptiens au Musée du Louvre* (1979)
——. Private collection of S. Péria. 1200, mainly bells and percussion (including the Horn collection)

GERMANY

BERLIN. Museum für Völkerkunde. 2480 general, mainly non-European
C. Sachs: *Die Musikinstrumente Indiens und Indonesiens* (1915, 2/1923); K. Reinhard: *Klingende Saiten: Musikinstrumente aus drei Kontinenten* (1965) [exhibition catalogue]; K. Reinhard: *Trommeln und Trompeten* (1967) [exhibition catalogue]; U. Wegner, *Afrikanische Saiteninstrumente* (1984)
——. Musikinstrumenten-Museum des Staatlichen Instituts für Musikforschung. 1700 general, mainly European art instruments, including the de Wit and Snoeck collections
O. Fleischer: *Führer durch die Sammlung alter Musikinstrumente* (1892); C. C. Snoeck: *Catalogue de la collection d'instruments de musique anciens ou curieux* (1894); C. Sachs: *Sammlung alter Musikinstrumente bei der Staatlichen Hochschule für Musik zu Berlin* (1922); A. Berner: *Die Berliner Musikinstrumenten-Sammlung* (1952); I. Otto: *Musikinstrumenten-Museum Berlin* (1965); I. Otto, ed.: *Das Musikinstrumenten-Museum Berlin* (1968)
——. Ägyptisches Museum der Staatlichen Museen zu Berlin. From the collection once in the Ägyptisches Museum, West Berlin
C. Sachs: *Die Musikinstrumente des alten Ägyptens* (Berlin, 1921)
BIEBRICH. Musikhistorisches Museum Heckel-Biebrich (private). 150 wind, mainly bassoons
F. Groffy: *Musikhistorisches Museum Heckel-Biebrich: Fagotte* (1968)
BOCHUM. Städtische Musikinstrumentensammlung Grumbt bei der Stadtbücherei Bochum. 230 instruments
F. Ernst: catalogue in *Glareana*, xiv/1 (1965)
BREMEN. Übersee-Museum. 820 non-European, mainly African and Oceanian
BRUNSWICK. Städtisches Museum. 285 general, including Grotrian-Steinweg collection
H. Schröder: *Verzeichnis der Sammlung alter Musikinstrumente im Städtischen Museum Braunschweig* (1928); D. Hecht: *Katalog der afrikanischen Sammlung im Städtischen Museum Braunschweig* (1968)
DARMSTADT. Hessisches Landesmuseum. 120 general, mainly European from the Hüpsch collection
Grossherzogliches Hessisches Landesmuseum: Führer durch die Kunst- und Historischen Sammlungen (1908)
DÜREN. Private collection of Josef Zimmerman. 150 European woodwind

J. Zimmerman: *Von Zinken, Flöten und Schalmeien: Katalog einer Sammlung historischer Holzblasinstrumente* (1967)

EISENACH. Bachhaus. 450, including the Obrist collection

E. Buhle: *Verzeichnis der Sammlung alter Musikinstrumente im Bachhaus zu Eisenach* (1913, 3/1939); H. Heyde: *Historische Musikinstrumente im Bachhaus Eisenach* (1976)

FRANKFURT AM MAIN. Städtisches Museum für Völkerkunde. 300, mainly non-European

FRANKFURT AN DER ODER. Museum Viadrina, Reka collection. 370 European, mainly 18th and 19th centuries

H. Heyde: *Historische Musikinstrumente der Staatlichen Reka-Sammlung* (1989)

GÖTTINGEN. Ethnographische Sammlung des Instituts für Völkerkunde der Universität Göttingen. 290 non-European, mainly African

——. Musikinstrumentensammlung des Musikwissenschaftlichen Instituts der Universität Göttingen. 1020 general, including the Moeck collection

HALLE. Händel-Haus. 550, mainly European art instruments, including parts of the Neupert and Rück collections

K. Sasse: *Katalog zu den Sammlungen des Händel-Hauses*, v (1966) [keyboard]; vi (1972) [string]

HAMBURG. Museum für Hamburgische Geschichte. 300 European art and folk instruments

H. Schröder: *Verzeichnis der Sammlung alter Musikinstrumente* (1930)

LEIPZIG. Musikinstrumenten-Museum der Universität. 3000 general, especially 16th- to 20th-century European, including the Heyer, de Wit, Ibach and Kraus collections

P. de Wit: *Kurz-gefaszter Katalog aller im Musikhistorischen Museum von Paul de Wit vorhandenen Musik-Instrumente* (1893); A. Kraus: *Catalogo della collezione etnografico-musicale Kraus in Firenze* (1901); P. de Wit: *Katalog des Musikhistorischen Museums von Paul de Wit* (1903); G. Kinsky: *Musikhistorisches Museum von Wilhelm Heyer in Köln*, i (1910); ii (1912); G. Kinsky: *Kleiner Katalog der Sammlung alter Musikinstrumente* (1913); H. Schultz: *Führer durch das musikwissenschaftliche Instrumenten-Museum der Universität Leipzig* (1929); P. Rubart: *Führer durch das Musikinstrumenten-Museum der Karl-Marx-Universität Leipzig* (1955, 2/1964); *Katalog* i, H. Heyde: *Flöten* (1978); ii, H. Heyde: *Trompeten, Posaunen, Tuben* (1980); iv, H. Henkel: *Clavichorde* (1981); v, H. Heyde: *Hörner und Zinken* (1982); vi, K. Gernhardt, H. Henkel and W. Schrammek: *Orgel-Instrumente, Harmoniums* (1983)

LÜBECK. Museum für Kunst und Kulturgeschichte der Hansestadt Lübeck, St Annen-Museum. 120, mostly string and brass of local origin

G. Karstädt: 'Die Sammlung alter Musikinstrumente im St. Annen-Museum', *Lübecker Museumshefte*, ii (1958)

MARKNEUKIRCHEN. Musikinstrumenten-Museum. 1500 general, mainly European

Katalog des Gewerbemuseums Markneukirchen (1908); E. Wild: *Führer durch das Musikinstrumenten-Museum der Stadt Markneukirchen* (1967)

MUNICH. Bayerisches Nationalmuseum. 340 European art and folk instruments

K. A. Bierdimpfl: *Die Sammlung der Musikinstrumente des Baierischen Nationalmuseums* (1883); A. Ott: *Ausstellung Alte Musik, Instrumente, Noten und Dokumente aus drei Jahrhunderten* (1951)

——. Deutsches Museum von Meisterwerken der Naturwissenschaft und Technik. 1400 European

F. Fuchs: *Der Aufbau der technischen Akustik im Deutschen Museum* (1963); H. Seifers: *Die Blasinstrumente im Deutschen Museum* (1976)

——. Städtische Musikinstrumentensammlung. 3000 general, mainly non-European, including the Georg Neuner collection

A. Ott: *Ausstellung Alte Musik, Instrumente, Noten und Dokumente aus drei Jahrhunderten* (1951)

NUREMBERG. Germanisches Nationalmuseum. 2200 general, including the Rück (Western art instruments) and Neupert collections (keyboard)

H. Neupert: *Das Musikhistorische Museum Neupert in Nürnberg* (1938); J. H. van der Meer: 'Die Klavierhistorische Sammlung Neupert', *Anzeiger des Germanischen Nationalmuseums* (1969); J. H. van der Meer: *Wegweiser durch die Sammlung historischer Musikinstrumente* (1971)

STUTTGART. Württembergisches Landesmuseum. 150 European, particularly 16th- to 20th-century keyboard

H. H. Josten: *Württembergisches Landesgewerbemuseum: die Sammlung der Musikinstrumente* (1928)

GHANA

ACCRA. Ghana National Museum. 275 African

GREAT BRITAIN

BIRMINGHAM. Historic Instrument Collection of the School of Music. Includes the Key Collection and many bows by John Dodd

W. H. Morris: *Catalogue of Musical Instruments in the Possession of the School* (1953); J. J. Morris and S. Daw: *Catalogue of the Historic Instruments of the Birmingham School of Music Collection* (1975)

BRIGHTON. Brighton Museum and Art Gallery. General, including the Potter and Albert Spencer collections

CAMBRIDGE. University Museum of Archaeology and Ethnology. Large general collection

——. Private collection of Laurence Picken. Mainly ethnic instruments

CARDIFF. Amgueddfa Werin Cymru [Welsh Folk Museum]. 120, mainly Welsh, especially harps

DUNDEE. Albert Institute. Includes the Alexander Simpson keyboard collection

EDINBURGH. Edinburgh University Collection of Historic Musical Instruments. Western art instruments, including the Russell Collection of harpsichords and clavichords

G. Melville-Mason: *European Musical Instruments* (1968); S. Newman and P. Williams: *The Russell Collection and Other Early Keyboard Instruments* (1968); A. Myers, *Historic Musical Instruments in the Edinburgh University Collection*, i (1990)

GLASGOW. Art Gallery and Museum. 370, including the R. Glen (European) and the H. G. Farmer (general) collections

GOUDHURST, KENT. Finchcocks Living Museum of Music. 60 keyboard, mainly 18th and early 19th century

HASLEMERE. Dolmetsch Collection. Acquired by Horniman Museum

ILFORD, ESSEX. Private collection of Eric Halfpenny

JERSEY, CHANNEL ISLANDS. Société Jersiaise

R. Falle: 'A List of the Musical Wind Instruments in the Museum of the Société Jersiaise', *Société Jersiaise Bulletin*, xvi (1954)

KILMARNOCK. Private collection of Lord Howard de Walden. Includes part of the Van Raalte Collection

LEWES, SUSSEX. Sussex Archaeological Institute. 250 ethnic, including the Mummery Collection

LIVERPOOL. Merseyside County Museums. Includes the Rushworth and Dreaper collection

The Rushworth and Dreaper Collection of Antique Musical Instruments and Historical Manuscripts (1927)

LONDON. British Museum. Ethnic and archaeological material

R. D. Anderson: *Catalogue of Egyptian Antiquities in the British Museum*, iii (1976)

——. Fenton House. Keyboard instruments, including the G. H. Benton Fletcher Collection

R. Russell: *The Musical Instruments in Fenton House, Hampstead* (1953); R. Russell: *The Benton Fletcher Collection of Early English Musical Instruments at Fenton House* (1955); R. Russell: *Catalogue of Early Keyboard Instruments at Fenton House* (1975)

——. Horniman Museum. 5000, general, including the collections of Percy Bull, Adam Carse and the Dolmetsch Collection

A. Carse: *The Horniman Museum: List of the Instruments included in the Adam Carse Collection of Musical Wind Instruments* (1947); A. Carse: 'The Adam Carse Collection of Musical Wind Instruments', *GSJ*, ii (1949); J. Jenkins: *Musical Instruments* (1958, 2/1970); E. A. K. Ridley: *Wind Instruments of European Art Music in the Horniman Museum* (1974); *The Dolmetsch Collection of Musical Instruments* (1981)

——. Royal College of Music. 450, mainly European art instruments, including the Day, Tagore, Donaldson, Hipkins and Ridley collections

G. Dyson: *The Royal College of Music Catalogue of Historical Instruments, Paintings, Sculpture, and Drawings* (1952); *The Ridley Collection of Musical Wind Instruments in Luton Museum* (1957)

——. Victoria and Albert Museum. European art instruments, collected mainly by Carl Engel, and the C. R. Day collection of Indian instruments

C. Engel: *A Descriptive Catalogue of Musical Instruments in the South Kensington Museum* (1870); R. Russell: *Catalogue of Musical Instruments*, i: *Keyboard Instruments* (1968; rev. edn. by H. Schott in preparation); A. Baines: *Catalogue of Musical Instruments*, ii: *Non-keyboard Instruments* (1968); *Musical Instruments as Works of Art* (1968)

MANCHESTER. Royal Northern College of Music. General, including the Henry Watson collection

H. Watson: *The Royal Manchester College of Music: Catalogue of the Henry Watson Collection of Musical Instruments* (1906)

NEWCASTLE UPON TYNE. Museum of the Society of Antiquaries. Includes the collection of W. A. Cocks

OXFORD. Ashmolean Museum. String and keyboard, including the Hill Collection, and 17th-century non-European

T. Dart: 'The Instruments in the Ashmolean Museum', *GSJ*, vii (1954); D. D. Boyden: *Catalogue of the Hill Collection of Musical Instruments in the Ashmolean Museum* (1969)

——. Philip Bate Collection of Historical Wind Instruments, University of Oxford, Faculty of Music. 500 European woodwind and brass, including part of the Reginald Morley-Pegge collection,

the loan collection of Anthony Baines and the Edgar Hunt collection
A. Baines: *The Bate Collection of Historical Wind Instruments: Catalogue* (1976)
——. Pitt Rivers Museum, University of Oxford. 5000, mainly non-European
A. Baines: 'Bagpipes', *Occasional Papers on Technology*, ix (1960)
WIGAN. Central Library. Includes the William Rimmer Collection
YORK. Castle Museum
G. B. Wood: *Musical Instruments in the York Castle Museum* (1938)

GREECE
ATHENS. Private collection of Fivos Anoyanakis. 300 Greek folk instruments
Greek Folk Musical Instruments (1965) [exhibition catalogue]; F. Anoyanakis: *Greek Popular Musical Instruments* (1979)
——. Private collection of Despina Mazaraki. 150 pipes

HONG KONG
HONG KONG. Archives of Chinese Music, Chung Chi College. New, growing collection of Chinese instruments, many modern

HUNGARY
BUDAPEST. Magyar Nemzeti Múzeum, Zenetörténeti Gyüjteménye [Hungarian National Museum, Music History Collection]. 380 European, including the Delhaes (string and keyboard) and Schunda (mainly wind) collections, and 18th-century wind instruments from the Cathedral of Györ
G. Gábry: *Old Musical Instruments* (1969)
——. Néprajzi Múzeum [Ethnographic Museum]. 385 ethnic

INDIA
CALCUTTA. Indian Museum. 240 Indian, Burmese, Tibetan, including collections of the Asiatic Society of Bengal, S. M. Tagore and Verrier Elwin
A. M. Meerwarth: *A Guide to the Collection of Musical Instruments in the Ethnographic Gallery of the Indian Museum* (1917)
JAIPUR. Maharaja of Jaipur Museum. 200 Indian classical
MADRAS. Sangita Vadyalaya. 250, mainly Indian, used for educational purposes
NEW DELHI. Sangeet Natak Akademi. 250 Indian folk and classical

INDONESIA
JAKARTA. National Museum. Gamelan instruments

IRELAND
DUBLIN. National Museum of Ireland. 350 general, mainly European art instruments

ISRAEL
HAIFA. Muzéon Vesifaiyya LeMusiga [Haifa Music Museum and Library]. 500, mainly ethnic and Jewish
JERUSALEM. Private collection of Edith Gerson-Kiwi. 300, mainly Arabic and Persian; exhibition catalogue (1963)
——. Rubin Academy of Music. European and ethnic, including the Koussevitzky and Bellison collections
Musical Instruments bequeathed by the Late Conductor Dr. Serge Koussevitsky to the State of Israel (1953)

ITALY
BOLOGNA. Civico Museo. 190 general, especially Bolognese wind instruments and early lutes
Raccolta di antichi strumenti armonici (1880); P. Ducati: *Catalogo-guida* (1923)
——. Private collection of L. F. Tagliavini. Historic keyboard instruments
J. H. van der Meer et al.: *Clavicembali e spinette del XVI al XIX secolo* (1986)
CREMONA. Museo Stradivariano, Materials from the workshop of Antonio Stradivari.
A. Mosconi: *Il Museo Stradivariano di Cremona* (1987)
FLORENCE. Museo degli Strumenti Musicali del Conservatorio di Musica 'L. Cherubini'. 220, mainly 16th- to 19th-century European, including Medici instruments
L. Bargagna: *Gli strumenti musicali raccolti nel Museo del R. Istituto L. Cherubini a Firenze* (1911); V. Gai: *Gli strumenti musicali della corte Medicea e il Museo del Conservatorio 'Luigi Cherubini' di Firenze* (1969); *Antichi strumenti dalla raccolta dei Medici e dei Lorena alla formazione del Museo del Conservatorio di Firenze* (1980)
——. Private collection of Alessandro Kraus. See Leipzig and Vancouver
MILAN. Civico Museo degli Strumenti Musicali, Castello Sforzesco. 640 general, mainly European art instruments
N. and F. Gallini: *Museo degli strumenti musicali* (1963)

ROME. Museo Strumentale Antico e Moderno dell'Accademia Nazionale di Santa Cecilia. 200, mainly European, including string instruments and the Gorga collection
Museo strumentale (1963) [exhibition catalogue]
——. Museo 'Luigi Pigorini'. 500 ethnic, mainly African, Oceanian and American
VATICAN CITY. Pontifico Museo Missionario Etnologico. 300 non-European donated by missionary orders since 1926
VERONA. Accademia Filarmonica. European 16th- to 19th-century art instruments, including instruments formerly in the Museo Civico, Verona

JAPAN

HAMAMATSU. [?; information]. Former private collection of Robert Rosenbaum.
NARA. Imperial Treasury, Shōsōin. 200 ancient instruments
K. Hayashi and others: *Shōsōin no gakki* [Musical Instruments in the Shōsōin treasury] (Tokyo, 1967) [with Eng. summary]
TOKYO. Musashino Ongaku Daigaku [Musashino Music Academy]. General, including East Asian instruments and European string instruments and bows
S. Kikuchi and O. Yamaguchi: *Catalogue, Museum of Musical Instruments, Musashino Academiae Musicae* (1969)
——. Institute for the Study of Musical Instruments, Ueno Gakuen College. Several hundred, mainly European, 17th–19th centuries.
S. Takeuchi et al.: *Catalogue of the European Musical Instruments . . .* (1980)
——. Gakkigaku Shiryokan, Kunitachi College of Music. Several thousand from all cultures.
S. Gunji et al.: *The Collection of Musical Instruments* (1986)
——. Koizumi Fumio Memorial Archives, Tokyo Geijutsu Daigaku. 650, mainly Asian.
T. Gen'ichi: *Catalogue of the Musical Instrument Collection* (1987)
——. Private collection of Dr. H. Iino. 300 flutes and recorders
——. Private collection of Akira Tsumura. Several hundred banjos, guitars and ukuleles, mainly American.
A. Tsumura, *Banjos: The Tsumura Collection* (1984); *Guitars: The Tsumura Collection* (1987)

KENYA

NAIROBI. National Museum. 150–200, of Kenyan tribes

KOREA

SEOUL. National Classical Music Institute. 70 traditional Korean instruments used in perf.

MALAYSIA

KUCHING. Sarawak Museum. 130 South-east Asian, especially Borneo

MEXICO

MEXICO CITY. Instituto Nacional de Bellas Artes, Investigaciones Musicales. 190 pre-Columbian and ethnic
——. Museo Nacional de Antropología. Mexican archaeological and ethnographical instruments
——. Laboratorio Museográfico, Universidad Ibero-Americana. Pre-Columbian and colonial Mexican instruments
R. Hellmer: *Panorama del instrumento musical en Mexico* (1968) [exhibition guide]

NETHERLANDS

AMSTERDAM. Tropen Museum. 2700, mainly Indonesian
P. Wirtz: *A Description of Musical Instruments from Central North Eastern New Guinea* (1952)
GRONINGEN. Groninger Museum voor Stad en Lande. Instruments from medieval artificial mounds
F. Crane: *Extant Medieval Musical Instruments* (1972)
THE HAGUE. Gemeentemuseum, Music Department. 2600 general, including the D. F. Scheurleer, G. Alsbach, Rijksmuseum and Carel van Leeuwen Boomkamp collections
L. J. Plenckers: *Hoorn-en trompetachtige blaasinstrumenten.* Catalogues of the Music Library and Musical Instruments Collection, ed. C. C. J. von Gleich, i (1970); C. van Leeuwen Boomkamp and J. H. van der Meer: *The Carel van Leeuwen Boomkamp Collection of Musical Instruments* (1971); C. von Gleich: *Toetsinstrumenten uit de Lage Landen* (1978)
LEEUWARDEN. Fries Museum. Instruments from medieval mounds
F. Crane: *Extant Medieval Musical Instruments* (1972)
LEIDEN. Rijksmuseum voor Volkenkunde. 540 ethnic
ROTTERDAM. Museum voor Land- en Volkenkunde. 1300, mainly African, Asian, Australian and Oceanian
UTRECHT. Instituut voor Muziekwetenschap der Rijksuniversiteit. 300 general

437

H. J. van Royen: *Beschrijving van een muziekinstrument in het Instituut voor muziekwetenschap der Rijksuniversiteit te Utrecht* (1965)
——. National Museum van Speelklok tot Pierement. 600 mechanical instruments, 18th- to 20th-century

NEW ZEALAND
AUCKLAND. Auckland Institute and Museum. 100 Polynesian and Melanesian, especially Maori wind
WELLINGTON. Dominion Museum. 190 New Zealand and Oceanian
——. Private collection of Zillah and Ronald Castle. 400 general, especially instruments of colonial New Zealand
R. and Z. Castle: *Old Instruments in New Zealand* (n.d.)

NIGERIA
JOS. Jos Museum. 325 African
LAGOS. Nigerian Museum. 465 African

NORWAY
OSLO. Etnografisk Museum, University of Oslo. 300 non-European, including Chinese instruments from King Oscar II
——. Norsk Folkemuseum. 270, mainly Norwegian folk and European art instruments
H. Fett: *Musik-Instrumenter Katalog* (1904)
——. Norwegian State Academy of Music. 500 general, mainly European, including many Hardanger fiddles, and the Lindeman and Gurvin collections
TRONDHEIM. Ringve Musikhistorisk Museum. 1200 general, including Bachke collection
K. Michelsen: *Katalog over musikalieutstillingen* (1975) [exhibition catalogue]; P. A. Kjeldsberg: *Musikinstrumenter ved Ringve Museum* (1976)

PHILIPPINES
QUEZON CITY. College of Music, University of the Philippines. 300 Philippine and Asian

POLAND
KRAKÓW. Muzeum Etnograficzne [Ethnographic Museum]. 125 European, 50 non-European
POZNAŃ. Muzeum Narodowe [National Museum]. 755 general, especially Polish
Z. Szulc: *Muzeum wielkopolskie: katalog instrumentón muzycznych* (1949); 'Muzeum instrumentów muzycznych w Poznaniu, historia zbiorow', *Kronika miasta Poznania* (1959)
WARSAW. Państwowe Muzeum Etnograficzne [National Museum of Ethnology]. 500 ethnic, mainly African and Polish
WROCLAW. Schlesisches Museum für Kunstgewerbe und Altertümer.
P. Epstein and E. Scheyer: *Führer und Katalog zur Sammlung alter Musikinstrumente* (1932)

PORTUGAL
LISBON. Museu Etnografico do Ultramar [Museum of the Lisbon Geographical Society]. 100 from former Portuguese colonies
——. Museu Instrumental do Cónservatório Nacional. 524 European string, wind, percussion and keyboard, including the Alfredo Keil, Lambertini and Lamas collections; many instruments from Portugal
Breve noticia dos instrumentos de musica antigos e modernos da collecção Keil (1904); M. A. Lambertini: *Primeiro nucleo de um museo instrumental em Lisboa; catálogo summario* (1914); *Boletim do Cónservatório nacional e revista panorama*, 4th ser., xiii (1965); G. Doderer: *Clavicordios portugueses do século dezoito* (1971)

SENEGAL
DAKAR. Musée d'Art Africain, University of Dakar. 1300 Senegalese

SINGAPORE
SINGAPORE. National Museum. 400 Malaysian and Indonesian

SOUTH AFRICA
CAPE TOWN. South African Cultural History Museum. 320, mainly African (Zambia, Congo, South Africa)
——. South African College of Music, University of Cape Town. 523, comprising the Percival R. Kirby Collection (formerly in Africana Museum, Johannesburg)
P. R. Kirby: *The Musical Instruments of the Native Races of South Africa* (1934, 2/1953); M. M. de Lange: *Catalogue of the Musical Instruments in the Collection of Professor Percival R. Kirby* (1967)
JOHANNESBURG. Africana Museum. 326, mainly indigenous South African

438

SPAIN

BARCELONA. Museo Municipal de Musica. 1030, mainly European folk instruments
GIJÓN ASTURIAS. Museo Internacional de la Gaita. Bagpipes and related materials
R. Meré: *Catálogo* (1970)

SWEDEN

GÖTEBORG. Etnografiska Museet, 2000 folk instruments, mainly African, and some 18th-century Chinese instruments
——. Historiska Museet. 280 European, especially woodwind and instruments of w. Sweden
O. Thulin: *Historiska avdelningen Göteborgs museum; musikinstrument* (1931)
HÄLSINGBORG. Hälsingborgs Museum. 155, mainly European art and folk instruments
D. Fryklund: 'Samlingen av musikinstrument i Hälsingborgs museum', *Kring Kärnan: Hälsingborgs museums årsskrift* (1939)
LUND. Kulturhistoriska Museet. 360 European
F. Crane: *Extant Medieval Musical Instruments* (1972)
SKARA. Västergötlands Fornmuseum. 240 European
S. Welin: *Musikhistoriska avdelningen vid Västergötlands fornmuseum i Skara* (1924)
STOCKHOLM. Etnografiska Museet. 2200 ethnic, mainly African and American
——. Musikmuseet. 5000, including the collection of Swedish folk instruments from the Nordiska Museet and the Neydall collection
J. Svanberg: *Musikhistoriska museet i Stockholm instrumentsamling* (1902); H. Boivie: *Nordiska museet, musikavdelningen* (1911); T. Norlind: 'Musikhistoriska museet i Stockholm', *STMf*, ii (1920)
——. Statens Historiska Museum. Medieval instruments
F. Crane: *Extant Medieval Musical Instruments* (1972)
——. Stiftelsen Musikkulturens Främjande och Memoria Musica. 500 general, including the Nydahl collection

SWITZERLAND

BASLE. Historisches Museum. 1500, mainly European, including the Lobeck and Bernouilli collections
K. Nef: *Historisches Museum Basel: Katalog IV: Musikinstrumente* (1906); W. Nef and P. Heman: *Alte Musikinstrumente in Basel* (1974)
——. Museum für Völkerkunde and Schweizerisches Museum für Volkskunde. 2000, mainly non-European
BERNE. Bernisches Historisches Museum, Historical and Ethnographical departments. 120 European folk instruments, mainly from Berne, and 300 non-European, mainly Asian, African and South American
GENEVA. Musée d'Instruments Anciens de Musique de Genève. 300, mainly European art instruments, including the Fritz Ernst collection
——. Musée d'Ethnographie. 250 general, especially African and South American
G. Montadon: *La généalogie des instruments de musique et les cycles de civilisation: étude suivie du catalogue raisonné des instruments de musique* (1919); M. Lobsiger-Dellenbach: *Népal: catalogue de la collection d'ethnographie* (1954)
LUCERNE. Richard-Wagner-Museum. 170, general, including the Schumacher collection
H. Schumacher: *Katalog zu der Ausstellung von Musikinstrumente früherer Zeiten* (1888); R. Vannes: *Katalog der städtlichen Sammlung alter Musikinstrumente im Richard-Wagner-Museum, Tribschen* (1956)
NEUCHÂTEL. Musée d'Ethnographie de Neuchâtel. 1200 ethnic, especially African, including the Bardout collection
F. Borel: *Les Sanza* (1986)
ZURICH. Kunstgewerbemuseum. 350 general, mainly European art instruments, including the Hug collection
Musikinstrumente: Wegleitung 247 des Kunstgewerbemuseums der Stadt Zürich (n.d.)
——. Schweizerisches Landesmuseum. 120 European, especially Swiss folk instruments
Die Zithern der Schweiz (1974) [exhibition catalogue]

TANZANIA

DAR ES SALAAM. National Museum of Tanzania. 120, mainly Tanzanian

UGANDA

KAMPALA. Uganda Museum. 500, mainly traditional African
K. Wachsmann: *The Uganda Museum: Report for the Years 1950–1* (1952)

439

UNITED STATES OF AMERICA

ALBUQUERQUE (NM). Maxwell Museum of Anthropology, University of New Mexico. 600, mostly native American and east African, including the Kidd collection

ANN ARBOR (MI). Stearns Collection, University of Michigan. 2000 general, especially European and East Asian

B. Smith: *Two-hundred forty-one European Chordophones in the Stearns Collection. . .* (1977)

A. A. Stanley: *Catalogue of the Stearns Collection of Musical Instruments* (1918, rev. 2/1921); R. A. Warner: 'The Stearns Collection of Musical Instruments', *Journal of the Viola da Gamba Society of America*, ii (1965)

BERKELEY (CA). Robert H. Lowie Museum of Anthropology, University of California. 1050 ethnic

——. Department of Music, University of California. 160 Western, including the Ansley K. Salz collection of string instruments

D. D. Boyden: *Catalogue of the Collection of Musical Instruments in the Department of Music* (1972)

BLOOMINGTON (IN). Indiana University Museum. 700, including the Frances Cossard (mostly Japanese), Ellison (Plains Indian), Carl Anton Worth (Sundanese and Javanese) and Herzog-Hornbostel collections

P. Gold: *Traditional Music of the World* (1968) [exhibition guide]

BOSTON (MA). Museum of Fine Arts. 800, including the Leslie Lindsey Mason collection (formerly Francis Galpin's) and 300 ethnic instruments, mainly Chinese and Northwest Coast Indian

N. Bessaraboff: *Ancient European Musical Instruments in the Leslie Lindsey Mason Collection* (1941); B. Lambert: *Checklist of Instruments on Exhibition* (1983)

CAMBRIDGE (MA). Peabody Museum of Archaeology and Ethnology, Harvard University. 2000 ethnic

CINCINNATI (OH). Cincinnati Art Museum. 800 general, including the William Howard Doane collection

Musical Instruments (1949) [exhibition guide]

CHICAGO (IL). Field Museum of Natural History. Thousands, all except European cultural areas

DETROIT (MI). Detroit Institute of Arts, Edith J. Freeman collection. 300 general

Music and Art (1958) [U. of Minnesota exhibition guide]; *Musical Instruments Through the Ages* (1952) [Toledo Museum of Art exhibition guide]

HONOLULU (HI). Bernice P. Bishop Museum. 450, mainly Hawaiian and Oceanian

——. Music Department, University of Hawaii. Large ethnic collection

LOS ANGELES (CA). Institute of Ethnomusicology, University of California. 1000 non-Western art instruments, especially south-east Asian, most in playing condition

——. Museum of Cultural History, University of California. 300 ethnic, especially New Guinean and African

MIDDETOWN (CT). World Music Collection, Wesleyan University Music Department. 500, mainly ethnic, especially Asian, most in playing condition

NASHVILLE (TN). Roy Acuff Museum, Opryland. Folk and popular instruments, mainly American fretted types.

D. Green and G. Gruhn: *Roy Acuff's Musical Collection at Opryland* (1982)

NEWARK (NJ). Newark Museum. 300, mainly ethnic, especially African and Tibetan, but including the Russell Barkley Kingman collection of European art instruments

The Museum, xiv/1 (1962); *Catalogue of the Tibetan Collection*, ii (1950)

NEW HAVEN (CT). Peabody Museum of Natural History, Department of Anthropology, Yale University. 1000 ethnic

——. Yale University Collection of Musical Instruments. 450, mainly European art instruments, including the Belle Skinner, Emil Herrmann (string), Albert Steinert (formerly at Rhode Island School of Design), Morris Steinert and Robyna Neilson Ketchum (bells) collections

M. Steinert: *Catalogue of the Morris Steinert Collection* (1893); W. Skinner: *The Belle Skinner Collection of Musical Instruments* (1933); S. Marcuse: *Checklist of Western Instruments*, i: *Keyboard Instruments* (1958); S. Marcuse: *Musical Instruments at Yale* (1960); R. Rephann: *Checklist: Yale Collection of Musical Instruments* (1968)

NEW YORK (NY). American Museum of Natural History. 4000 ethnic, especially African, American and Oceanian

——. Private collection of Janos Scholz. 200 viola da gamba and cello bows

——. Metropolitan Museum of Art. 5000 general, in several departments but especially the Department of Musical Instruments, including the Drexel and Crosby Brown collections

M. E. Brown and W. A. Brown: *Musical Instruments and Their Homes* (1888); F. Morris and others: *Catalogue of the Crosby Brown Collection of Musical Instruments of All Nations* (1901–14); E. Winternitz: *Keyboard Instruments in the Metropolitan Museum of Art* (1961); E. Winternitz: 'The Crosby Brown Collection . . . its Origin and Development', *Metropolitan Museum Journal*, iii (1970); L. Libin: *American Musical Instruments in The Metropolitan Museum of Art* (1985); L. Libin: *Keyboard Instruments* (1989)

——. Private collection of Murtogh Guinness. Musical automata
——. Museum of the American Indian: Heye Foundation. 4000 native American
——. Private collection of Jacques Français. Bowed and plucked strings
——. Private collection of Henryk Kaston and Hans Schambach. Bows, pochettes, violins
——. Private collection of Frederick R. Selch. American instruments
——. Private collection of Nathaniel Spear Jr. Bells.

N. Spear Jr: *A Treasury of Archaeological Bells* (1978)

OKLAHOMA CITY (OK). Private collection of Richard W. Payne. 500 flutes, especially native American

PHILADELPHIA (PA). University of Pennsylvania Museum. 600, mainly ethnic, especially African and West Asian

ST PAUL (MN). Schubert Club Museum. 1000 general, including 100 keyboards and the former William and Ida Kugler collection

SALEM (MA). Peabody Museum. 400 ethnic, especially Chinese and Japanese

TEMPE (AZ). Laura Boulton collection, University of Arizona. 300 ethnic

L. Boulton: *Musical Instruments of World Cultures* (1972, rev. 2/1975)

URBANA (IL). University of Illinois (especially the Department of Anthropology, Archives of Ethnomusicology and World Heritage Museum). 220, mainly archaeological and ethnographical

J. R. Haefer: *A Checklist of Folk and Non-European Musical Instruments in University of Illinois Collections* (1974)

VERMILLION (SD). Shrine to Music Museum. 5000 general, including the Arne B. Larson and Witten collections

A. B. Larson: *Catalog of the nineteenth-century British brass instruments . . .* (1974); G. M. Stewart: *Keyed Brass Instruments . . .* (1980); T. E. Cross: *Instruments of Burma, India, Nepal, Thailand and Tibet* (1982) G. Stewart: *Keyed Brass Instruments* (1980); T. Cross: *Instruments of Burma, India, Nepal, Thailand, and Tibet* (1982)

WASHINGTON (DC). United States National Museum (Smithsonian Institution), National Museum of American History. 2000 European and American, especially brass, keyboard and folk instruments

F. Densmore: *Handbook of the Collection of Musical Instruments in the United States National Museum* (1927); C. Hoover and S. Odell: *A Checklist of Keyboard Instruments at the Smithsonian Institution* (1967, rev. 2/1975); J. Fesperman: 'Music and Instruments at the Smithsonian Institution', *CMc* (1968), no.6; H. Hollis: *Pianos at the Smithsonian Institution* (1971); C. Hoover: *Harpsichords and Clavichords* (1971); C. Hoover: *Music Machines American Style* (1971)

——. United States National Museum (Smithsonian Institution), Museum of Natural History, Office of Anthropology. 3300 ethnic, especially African and Oceanian

F. Densmore: *Handbook of the Collection of Musical Instruments in the United States National Museum* (1927); D. L. Thieme: *A Descriptive Catalogue of Yoruba Musical Instruments* (diss., Catholic U. of America, 1969)

——. Library of Congress, Music Division. The Gertrude Clarke Whittall Foundation (5 Stradivari), H. Blakiston Wilkins (5 strings), Thai Ceremonial (10 Thai) and Dayton C. Miller (1500 flutes) collections

W. D. Orcutt: *The Stradivari Memorial at Washington, the National Capitol* (1938); L. E. Gilliam and W. Lichtenwanger: *The Dayton C. Miller Flute Collection: a Checklist of the Instruments* (1961); M. Seyfrit: *Musical Instruments in the Dayton C. Miller Flute Collection*, i (1982)

WILLIAMSBURG (VA). Colonial Williamsburg. 200, mainly English and American, in several departments

VENEZUELA

CARACAS. Museo Organologico, Instituto Interamericano de Etnomusicologia. 700, mainly ethnic, including Aretz and Ramón y Rivera collections

YUGOSLAVIA

BELGRADE. Etnografski Muzej. 340 Yugoslav folk instruments; catalogue (1957)

ZAGREB. Etnografski Muzej. 410, mainly European folk instruments

——. Muzej za Umjetnost i Obrt [Museum of Decorative Art]. 160, mostly European art instruments

ZAMBIA
ISOKA. Jean-Jacques Corbeil collection, Catholic Church. 120 Bemba instruments

Bibliography

GENERAL

M. Todini: *Dichiaratione della galleria armonica* (Rome, 1676)
A. Bruni: *Un inventaire sous la Terreur* (Paris, 1890)
E. de Bricqueville: 'Les collections d'instruments de musique aux XVIe, XVIIe et XVIIIe siècles', *Un coin de la curiosité: les anciens instruments de musique* (Paris, 1895), 15
G. Kinsky: 'Musikinstrumenten-Sammlung in Vergangenheit und Gegenwart', *JbMP 1920*, 47
C. Sachs: 'La signification, la tâche et la technique muséographique des collections d'instruments de musique', *Mouseion*, xxvii-xxviii (1934), 153–84
T. Norlind: *Systematik der Saiteninstrumente (Musikhistorisches Museum, Stockholm)*, i: *Geschichte der Zither* (Hanover, 1936); ii: *Geschichte des Klaviers* (Hanover, 1939)
D. H. Boalch: *Makers of the Harpsichord and Clavichord 1440–1840* (London, 1956, 2/1974)
A. Berner: 'Instrumentensammlungen', *MGG*
G. Thibault: 'Les collections privées de livres et d'instruments de musique d'autrefois et d'aujourd'hui', *HMYB*, xi (1961), 131
F. Hubbard: *Three Centuries of Harpsichord Making* (Cambridge, MA, 1965, 2/1967)
A. C. Baines: *European and American Musical Instruments* (New York, 1966)
E. Winternitz: *Die schönsten Musikinstrumente des Abendlandes* (Munich, 1966; Eng. trans. 1967)
F. J. Hirt: *Stringed Keyboard Instruments 1440–1880* (Boston, 1968)
H. K. Goodkind: *Violin Iconography of Antonio Stradivari* (Larchmont, NY, 1972)
W. Stauder: *Alte Musikinstrumente* (Brunswick, 1973)
W. Lichtenwanger and others: *A Survey of Musical Instrument Collections in the United States and Canada* (Ann Arbor, 1974)
E. M. Ripin: *The Instrument Catalogs of Leopoldo Franciolini* (Hackensack, NJ, 1974)
J. Jenkins, ed.: *International Directory of Musical Instrument Collections* (Buren, 1977)
J. H. van der Meer: 'Ältere und neuere Literatur zur Musikinstrumentenkunde', *AcM*, li (1979), 1–50

INVENTORIES

In addition to the inventories cited by Berner, the following are of special interest:
L. Puliti: 'Cenni storici della vita del . . . Ferdinando dei Medici . . . e della origine del pianoforte', *Atti dell'Accademia del Real istituto musicale di Firenze* (Florence, 1874)
F. Waldner: 'Zwei Inventarien aus dem 16. and 17. Jahrhundert', *SMw*, iv (1916)
F. A. Drechsel: 'Alte Dresdener Instrumenten Inventare', *ZMw*, x (1927–8), 495
A. C. Baines: 'Two Cassel Inventories', *GSJ*, iii (1950), 30
S. Marcuse: 'The Instruments of the King's Library at Versailles', *GSJ*, xiv (1961), 34
S. Hellier: 'A Catalogue of Musical Instruments', *GSJ*, xviii (1965), 5
M. McLeish: 'An Inventory of Musical Instruments at the Royal Palace, Madrid, in 1602', *GSJ*, xxi (1968), 108

CATALOGUES OF MAJOR 20TH-CENTURY LOAN EXHIBITIONS

Musée rétrospectif de la classe 17, instruments de musique (Paris, 1900) [Paris Exhibition]
Catalogue of the Exhibition (Boston, 1902) [Chickering & Sons, Horticultural Hall]
An Illustrated Catalogue of the Music Loan Exhibition (London, 1909) [Worshipful Company of Musicians, Fishmongers' Hall, 1904]
K. Meyer: *Katalog der internationalen Ausstellung: Musik im Leben der Volker* (Frankfurt am Main, 1927)
A. Ott: *Ausstellung Alte Musik: Katalog* (Munich, 1951) [Bayerisches Nationalmuseum]
V festival Gulbenkian de musica: exposição internacional de instrumentos antigos (Lisbon, 1961) [Palácio Foz]
P. Sambamoorthy: *Catalogue of the Musical Instruments Exhibited in the Government Museum, Madras* (Madras, 3/1962)
Mostra di antichi strumenti musicali (Modena, 1963) [Teatro Comunale]

R. Bhavan: *Indian Folk Musical Instruments* (New Delhi, 1968) [Sangeet Natak Akademi]

The Galpin Society, 21st Anniversary Exhibition: an Exhibition of European Musical Instruments (Edinburgh, 1968) [Reid School of Music, U. of Edinburgh]

Exposition des instruments de musique des XVIème et XVIIème siècles, organisée par le Musée instrumental de Bruxelles en l'Hôtel de Sully à Paris, juin, 1969 (Brussels, 1969)

K. Laarne: *Catalogus van de tentoonstelling gewijd aan muziekinstrumenten uit de XVIe en XVIIe eeuw behorend tot het Instrumentenmuseum van Brussel* (Brussels, 1972)

Eighteenth Century Musical Instruments: France and Britain (London, 1973) [Victoria and Albert Museum]

R. J. M. van Acht and others: *De ontwikkeling van de blaasinstrumenten vanaf 1600* (Kerkrade, 1974) [Kasteel Ehrenstein]

J. Jenkins and P. Rovsing Olsen: *Music and Musical Instruments in the World of Islam* (London, 1976) [Horniman Museum]

S. Pollens: *Forgotten Instruments* (Katonah, NY, 1980) [Katonah Gallery]

P. T. Young: *The Look of Music; rare musical instruments 1500–1900* (Vancouver, 1980) [Vancouver Museums & Planetarium Association]

L'instrument de musique populaire (Paris, 1980) [Musée national des arts et traditions populaires]

Instruments de musique espagnols du XVIe au XIXe siècle (Brussels, 1985)

Made for Music; an exhibition to mark the 40th anniversary of the Galpin Society . . . (London, 1986) [Sotheby's]

Clavicembali e spinette dal XVI al XIX secolo (Bologna, 1986) [Chiesa di San Giorgio in Poggiale]

M. C. Poma, ed.: *Capolavori di Antonio Stradivari* (Cremona, 1987) [Palazzo Comunale]

Die Klangwelt Mozarts (Vienna, 1991) [Kunsthistorisches Museum]

The Spanish Guitar (New York, 1991) [Metropolitan Musem of Art]

Classification of Musical Instruments

ERICH M. VON HORNBOSTEL, CURT SACHS

Treatises on systems of classification are by and large of uncertain value. The material to be classified, whatever it may be, came into existence without any such system, and grows and changes without reference to any conceptual scheme. The objects to be classified are alive and dynamic, indifferent to sharp demarcation and set form, while systems are static and depend upon sharply drawn demarcations and categories.

These considerations bring special difficulties to the classifier, though also an attractive challenge: his aim must be to develop and refine his concepts so that they better and better fit the reality of his material, sharpen his perception, and enable him to place a specific case in the scheme quickly and securely.

A systematic arrangement for musical instruments concerns first of all musicologists, ethnologists, and curators of ethnological collections and those of cultural history. Systematic arrangement and terminology are urgently needed, however, not only for collections of material, but also for their study and in its interpretation. He who refers to a musical instrument by any name or description he pleases, being unaware of the points which matter, will cause more confusion than if he had left it altogether unnoticed. In common speech technical terms are greatly muddled, as when the same instrument may be indiscriminately called a lute, guitar, mandoline or banjo. Nicknames and popular etymology also mislead the uninitiated: the German *Maultrommel* is not a drum, nor the English jew's (properly 'jaw's') harp a harp, nor the Swedish *mungiga* a geige ('fiddle'), nor the Flemish *tromp* a trumpet; only the Russians are correct when they call this same instrument, a plucked lamella, by the uncommitted term *vargan* (from Greek *organon*, 'instrument'). Homonyms are no less dangerous than synonyms: the word 'marimba', for instance, denotes in the Congo the set of lamellae usually called 'sansa', but elsewhere it denotes a xylophone. Ethnological literature teems with ambiguous or misleading terms for instruments, and in museums, where the field-collector's report has the last say, the most senseless terms may be perpetuated on the labels. Correct description and nomenclature depend upon knowledge of the most essential criteria for the various types – a condition which, as a visit to a museum will show, is hardly ever met. One will find, for instance, that oboes, even when still in the possession of the double reed which unmistakably proclaims them for what they are, are noted as flutes, or at best as clarinets; and should the oboe have a brass bell one may be certain of the label 'trumpet'.

A system of classification has theoretical advantages as well as practical uses. Objects which otherwise appear to be quite unrelated to each other may now become associated, revealing new genetic and cultural links. Herein will always be found the leading test of the validity of the criteria upon which the system is based.

The difficulties which an acceptable system of classification must surmount are very great, since that which suits one era or nation may be unsuitable as a foundation for the instrumental armoury of all nations and all times. Thus the ancient Chinese based their classification on material, distinguishing between instruments made of stone, metal, wood, gourd, bamboo, hide and silk; consequently, to them, trumpets and gongs, stone harmonicas and marble flutes, shawms and clappers, each belonged together.

Our own present-day practice does not amount to much more. Sound-instruments are divided into three major categories: stringed instruments, wind instruments and percussion instruments. This cannot be defended even on the grounds that it satisfies day-to-day requirements. A large number of instruments cannot be fitted into any of the three groups without placing them in an unnatural position, like the celesta, which, as a percussion instrument, is brought into close proximity to drums and so on. As a remedy one introduces a fourth group under the disconcerting heading 'miscellaneous' – in any systematic grouping an admission of defeat. Moreover, the current classification is not only inadequate, but also illogical. The first requirement of a classificatory system is surely that the principle of demarcation remains the same throughout for the main categories. Our customary divisions, however, follow two different principles, stringed instruments being distinguished by the nature of the vibrating substance but wind and percussion by the mode of sound-excitation – ignoring the fact that there are stringed instruments which are blown, like the Aeolian harp, or struck, like the pianoforte. The customary subdivisions are no better. Wind instruments are divided into woodwind and brass, thus giving a subordinate criterion of differentiation, namely, material, an unjustifiable predominance and flagrantly disregarding the fact that many 'brass' instruments are or were once made of wood, like cornetts, serpents and bass horns, and that in any case many 'woodwind instruments' are optionally or invariably made of metal, as flutes, clarinets, saxophones, sarrusophones, tritonicons etc.

The objections which can be raised against the crudity of the customary divisions are now familiar to organology (*Instrumentenkunde*), and in recent decades scholars have made more than one attempt to attain something more satisfactory. Leaving aside classifications which have owed their structure to the peculiarities of this or that collection, catalogues have latterly in general adopted a system which Victor Mahillon has used since 1888 for his comprehensive catalogue of the Museum of the Brussels Conservatoire.

Mahillon takes the nature of the vibrating body as his first principle of division, and thus distinguishes between instruments (i) whose material is sufficiently rigid and at the same time sufficiently elastic to undergo periodic vibration, and named by him 'self-sounding instruments' (*instruments auto-phones*; for reasons which Sachs has explained in his *Reallexikon der Musik-*

instrumente, Berlin, 1913, p. 195*a*, we prefer the term idiophones); (ii) on which sound waves are excited through the agency of tightly stretched membranes; (iii) in which strings vibrate; and lastly (iv) in which a column of air vibrates. Thus he distinguishes four categories: self-sounders, membrane instruments, stringed and wind instruments. Besides the uniformity of its principle of division, the system has the great advantage in that it is capable of absorbing almost the whole range of ancient and modern, European and extra-European instruments.

Mahillon's system of four classes deserves the highest praise; not only does it meet the demands of logic, but also it provides those who use it with a tool which is simple and proof against subjective preferences. Moreover, it is not so far removed from previously used divisions as to offend well-established custom.

It has seemed to us, however, that the four-class system stands in pressing need of development in fresh directions. Mahillon started on the basis of the instruments of the modern orchestra, with which, as an instrument manufacturer and musician, he was in closest contact, and it was these which gave him the initial challenge to work out his system. Then, as the collections of the Brussels museum grew under his direction, he explored over years of relentless effort the limitless field of European and exotic organology. Inevitably a newly acquired specimen would now and then fail to fit into the system, while certain subdivisions which figure importantly among European instruments – e.g. those of keyboard and mechanical instruments – assumed an unwarrantably prominent place. Mahillon had indeed been led, for the sake of the European instruments, to juxtapose categories which did not logically build a uniform concept. Thus he divided the wind instruments into four branches, (i) reed instruments (*instruments à anche*); (ii) mouth-hole (*instruments à bouche*); (iii) polyphone instruments with air reservoir and (iv) cup-mouthpiece instruments (*instruments à embouchure*). Consider too the drums, which he grouped as frame drums, vessel drums and double-skin drums; he consequently divided the skin drums corresponding to our side- and kettle-drums – and likewise the autophones – into instruments of untuned pitch (*instruments bruyants*) and those of tuned pitch (*à intonation déterminée*). This is an awkward distinction, since a wide range of transitional sounds occurs between pure noises and noise-free tones; indeed, save for a few laboratory instruments, there are no sound-producers that can truly be said to yield either pure noise or pure tones, the sounds of all the usual musical instruments being more or less wrapped in noise. Mahillon later seems to have sensed this when he contrasted noise-instruments with those *à intonation nettement* or *intentionellement déterminée*; but the criterion is subjective and as a rule incapable of proof.

In general, Mahillon was right to subdivide the four main classes into 'branches' differentiated by playing action. Yet for stringed instruments it was a dubious procedure; a violin remains a violin whether one bows it with a bow, plays it pizzicato with the fingers, or strikes it *col legno*. Perhaps this seems a lopsided argument, since the violin is, after all, designed to be bowed. But there are other instances. One could cite instruments whose playing action has changed in the course of time but whose form has remained unaltered. This was the case, for example, with the ancient Celtic *crowd*, which can be proved to have been plucked in the earliest times, but which came to be bowed in the

High Middle Ages: should the history of instruments therefore deal with it half in a chapter on plucked stringed instruments and half in one on bowed, although the instrument itself remains just the same? Then there is the psaltery, which is turned into a dulcimer (*Hackbrett*) when the player uses beaters; should one, in a collection, separate the psalteries, otherwise indistinguishable from each other, into two groups on the grounds that in one country of origin it was customary to pluck it but in another to beat it? Should I place the clavichord and the pianoforte side by side but house the harpsichord with the guitars because its strings are plucked?

All these considerations have persuaded us to undertake afresh the attempt to classify musical instruments. We were fortunate in having at our disposal as a ready-made base the large and extensively described collections of the Brussels museum out of which Mahillon's system had grown. At the same time we are aware that with increasing knowledge, especially of extra-European forms, new difficulties in the way of a consistent classification will constantly arise. It would thus seem impossible to plan a system today which would not require future development and amendment.

Like Mahillon, we accept the physical characteristics of sound-production as the most important principle of division; but even at this point considerable difficulties are met since acoustic physics has so far covered but the smallest fraction of the preliminary investigations. Thus inadequate research has yet been undertaken on the sound-production of the bull-roarer, the vibratory manner in north-west American 'ribbon-reeds', the vibration events in bells, gongs, kettledrums, plucked drums, and wind instruments with free reeds and finger-holes. To such difficulties must be added others arising from the morphology of instruments. The problem of defining the term 'frame drum' (*tamburin*), for example, is scarcely capable of satisfactory solution; undoubtedly the typical frame drum represents a concise concept not to be disregarded in any classificatory system, but the transition between this and the pronouncedly tubular drum occurs without a break, often making it impossible to decide on the basis of shape whether a specimen belongs to the one kind or to the other.

Other obstacles in the path of the classifier are instruments showing adulterations between types (*Kontaminationen*). The fact of adulteration should be accounted for by placing such instruments in two (or more) groups. In museums and catalogues these cases will be arranged according to the dominant characteristic, but cross-references to other characteristics should not be omitted. Thus, among instruments of every class one may find rattling devices which belong to the inventory of idiophones – a feature which cannot be taken into account when placing the instrument in the classification. But where the adulteration has led to an enduring morphological entity – as when kettledrum and musical bow combine in the spike lute – it must have a place of its own within the system.

We must refrain from arguing our subdivisions in detail. Whosoever will check these critically, or test them in practice, will doubtless repeat the lines of thought which are not set out here, with minor variations of his own.

In classifications it is often customary to indicate the ranking of divisions within the system by means of specific headings, as especially in zoology and botany with expressions like class, order, family, genus, species, variant. In the

447

study of instruments, Mahillon himself felt this need and met it by introducing the terms *classe, branche, section, sous-section*; on Gevaert's advice he refrained from using the term 'family' on account of its widely known use for instruments of like design but of different sizes and pitches.

We consider it inadvisable to maintain consistent headings throughout all rubrics for the following reasons. The number of subdivisions is too big to manage without bringing in a petty superfluity of headings. Moreover, in any system one must leave room for further division to meet special cases, with the result that the number of subdivisions could for ever increase. We have purposely not divided the different main groups according to one uniform principle, but have let the principle of division be dictated by the nature of the group concerned, so that ranks of a given position within a group may not always correspond between one group and another. Thus terms like 'species' may refer in one case to a very general concept but in another to a highly specialized one. We therefore propose that the general typological headings be restricted to the topmost main groups, though one could, like Mahillon, speak of the four main groups as classes, of the next divisions (with a two-unit symbol [*zweiziffrig*]) as sub-classes, the next (three-unit) as orders, and the next (four-unit) as sub-orders.

We have refrained from providing a subdivision containing no known existing representative, save in cases where a composite type may be assumed to have had a precursor in a simpler type now extinct. Thus it can be assumed from analogy with numerous types that Man rubbed a solid, smooth block of wood with the moist hand before he ever carved a series of differently pitched tongues by cutting notches into the block, as in the friction block of New Ireland. Again, where the wealth of forms is exceptionally vast, as with rattles, only the more general aspects of their classification can be outlined in the scheme, and these will certainly require further elaboration.

In general we have tried to base our subdivisions only on those features which can be identified from the visible form of the instruments, avoiding subjective preferences and leaving the instrument itself unmeddled with. Here one has had to consider the needs not only of museum curators but also of field workers and ethnologists. We have carried the subdivisions as far as seemed important for the observation of cultural history and detail, though the plan of the whole classification makes possible its application to the material either summarily or in great detail as desired; general treatises and smaller collections may not require to follow our classification to its last terms, while specialist monographs and catalogues of large museums may well wish to extend it in further detail.

The application of our findings in describing and cataloguing is substantially facilitated by use of the Dewey numerical system (since the numerical arrangement for the Bibliographie Internationale of musical instruments applies only to European instruments, and is anyhow as inadequate as can be, we have planned our own numerical order independently). If those in charge of large collections who issue catalogues in the future decide to accept our numerical arrangement, it will become possible to find out at first glance whether a given type of instrument is represented in the collection.

The ingenuity of Dewey's idea lies in the exclusive use of figures, replacing the more usual conglomeration of numbers, letters and double letters by decimal fractions. These are so used that every further subdivision is indicated by adding a new figure to the right-hand end of the row; a zero before the decimal point being always omitted. Thus it becomes possible not only to pursue specification to whatever limits one desires and with never any trouble in the manipulation of the numbers, but also directly to recognize from the position of its last figure the ranking of a given term within the system.

It is also feasible in a row of numbers to divide off any set of figures by points. Say, for example, that it is a bell chime (*Glockenspiel*) which is to be coded and placed in the system. In the context of the system we are dealing with an idiophone, the class to which the initial code-figure 1 is allotted. Since the instrument is struck it belongs to the first sub-class, and so another 1 is added (struck idiophones = 11). Further addition of relevant code-figures produces the ranking 111 since it is struck directly; and then, as a struck-upon (i.e. percussion) idiophone, it earns a fourth figure, in this case 2 (1112 = percussion idiophones). Further specification leads to 11124 (percussion vessels), 111242 (bells), 1112422 (sets of bells), 11124222 (sets of hanging bells) and 111242222 (ditto with internal strikers) – obviously, everyone must decide for himself how far to go in a given case. Instead of the unmanageable number now arrived at, we write 111.242.222. The first cluster shows that we are dealing with an idiophone that is struck directly, while the second and third together imply that we are dealing with bells.

Common considerations among all instruments of a class – e.g. with membranophones the method of fixing the skin, and with chordophones the playing method – may be noted with the aid of figures appended to the essential code-number by a dash: the pianoforte would be entered as 314.122–4–8 and the harpsichord 314.122–6–8, because 8 represents the keyboard, 4 the hammer playing-action and 6 the plectrum playing-action, both instruments having the same main number indicating board zithers with resonator box.

Any of the subordinate criteria of division may, if desired, easily be elevated and treated as a higher rank in the classification, by switching the positions of figures. Thus, for a bagpipe in which chanter and drone are both of the clarinet type, the code-number would read 422.22–62, i.e. a set of clarinets with flexible air reservoir. But if, for instance, in a monograph on bagpipes, one wished to especially distinguish these (i.e. chanter and drone) features, one could write 422–62:22, i.e. reed instrument with flexible air reservoir whose pipes are exclusively clarinets.

Conversely, in order to bring closer together groups which are separated in the system, it is possible to turn a main criterion of division into a subordinate one without destroying the system: one simply replaces the first relevant figure by a point (.) and then adds it after a square bracket (]) at the end of the number. Thus in the example of bagpipes, it might be important to specify these instruments as always polyorganic (i.e. composed of several single instrumental units) but with components which are sometimes clarinets and sometimes oboes; instead of 422–62:22 = reed instrument (*Schalmeieninstrument*), with flexible air reservoir, polyorganic, composed of clarinets, it might be preferable to write 422–62:.2 = set of reedpipes (*Schalmeienspiel*) with flexible air reservoir = bagpipe, and then to differentiate further by writing 422–62:.2]1 = bagpipe of oboes, or 422–62:.2]2 = bagpipe of clarinets. (This use of the symbols –:] is slightly different from that of the Classification

Bibliographique Décimale, but is nevertheless within its spirit. The rules are: the dash is employed only in connection with the appended figures listed in the tables at the end of each of the four main sections; subdivisions beyond these are preceded by a colon [thus 422–62 = reed instrument with flexible air reservoir, but 422–6:2 = 422.2–6 = oboe with air reservoir]: subdivision answering to the omission of a figure is preceded by a square bracket.)

Other specifications applying to a subordinate group are suffixed to the code-figures of the latter, e.g. 422–62:.2]212 = a bagpipe of clarinets with cylindrical bore and finger-holes.

These innumerable cases in which an instrument is composed of parts which in themselves belong to different groups of the system could be indicated by linking appropriate figures by a plus sign. One then avoids repetition of a number common to both such parts, writing this number once and following it with a point: a modern trombone with slide and valve would then appear not as 423.22 + 423.23, but as 4232.2 + 3, and similarly bagpipes composed partly of clarinets and partly of oboes, as cited above, would become 422.62:.2]1 + 2.

In certain circumstances it may be necessary not only to rearrange the rankings to the concepts and create new subdivisions, but also to incorporate into the higher ranks of the classification some criterion which has purposely not so far been used. There is nothing to prevent this being done, and we should like to illustrate it by a final example, at the same time showing how we envisage the development of our system for special purposes. Let us imagine the case of a monograph on the xylophone. The system divides struck idiophones (111.2) by the shape of the struck bodies, thus: struck sticks (111.21), struck plaques (111.22), struck tubes (111.23) and struck vessels (111.24). Xylophones could fall into any of the first three, but the shape of the sounding bodies is here of little relevance – the transition from sticks to plaques being quite fluid – and so the fifth figure may be removed, and, if desired, added as]2 at the end. For the sixth figure we insert 2, if the description is to concern only multi-tone instruments, giving 1112. .2 = sets of struck idiophones (*Aufschlagspiele*). We must, however, exclude sounding bodies of metal, stone, glass etc, and must therefore create a subdivision according to material which the system does not already provide, thus:

1112.21 = xylophone	sounding bodies of wood
1112.22 = metallophone	sounding bodies of metal
1112.23 = lithophone	sounding bodies of stone
1112.24 = crystallophone	sounding bodies of glass

Further stages in this classification of the xylophone would make use of morphological criteria significant from an ethnological point of view:

Classification

1112. .21.1	*Bedded xylophone*: the sounding bodies rest on an elastic foundation
1112. .21.11	*Log xylophone*: the foundation consists of separate logs, there is generally a shallow pit in the ground beneath the sounding bodies (found in Oceania, Indonesia, East and West Africa)
1112. .21.12	*Frame xylophone*: the bearers are joined by cross rods or bars
1112. .21.121	*Rail xylophone*: the frame hangs from the player's neck on a sling and is kept clear of his body by a curved rail (South-east, East and West Africa)
1112. .21.122	*Table xylophone*: the frame is borne on a trestle (Senegambia)
1112. .21.13	*Sledge xylophone*: the sounding bodies lie across the edges of two boards (Central Africa)

1112. .21.14	*(Bedded) trough xylophone*: the sounding bodies lie across the edges of a trough- or box-shaped vessel (Japan)
1112. .21.2	*Suspension xylophone*: the sounding bodies lie on two cords without any other foundation
1112. .21.21	*(Free) suspension xylophone*: without case (Cochin China)
1112. .21.22	*(Suspension) trough xylophone*: with trough-shaped box (Burma, Java)

Rail xylophones and table xylophones are to be further subdivided thus: 1 without resonators; 2 with resonators; 21 with resonators suspended singly; 22 with resonators struck into a common platform. The resonators, in most cases gourds, often have holes sealed by a membrane, showing adulteration with 242 (vessel kazoos). Possibly the method of mounting the membranes (directly, or over a cone-shaped frame) will demand another subdivision. One can, however, dispense with adding another number since frame xylophones without resonators are unknown.

The systematic survey of musical instruments which now follows in tabular form is meant equally to serve the purposes of identification. Hence the descriptions of characteristics are here and there expanded to include warnings against likely misunderstandings and confusion.

Explanations and examples are kept to a minimum; the former are not intended as descriptions, nor the latter as notes on the history of cultures. Also, visual study of specimens far outvalues pages of written description. The expert will know what we are driving at, while the layman will be able to find his bearings with the aid of a visit to a museum.

Classification

1	**Idiophones** the substance of the instrument itself, owing to its solidity and elasticity, yields the sounds, without requiring stretched membranes or strings
11	STRUCK IDIOPHONES the instrument is made to vibrate by being struck upon
111	*Idiophones struck directly*: the player himself executes the movement of striking; whether by mechanical intermediate devices, beaters, keyboards, or by pulling ropes etc. is immaterial; it is definitive that the player can apply clearly defined individual strokes and that the instrument itself is equipped for this kind of percussion
111.1	*Concussion idiophones or clappers*: two or more complementary sonorous parts are struck against each other
111.11	*Concussion sticks or stick clappers* – found in Vietnam, India and the Marshall Islands
111.12	*Concussion plaques or plaque clappers* – found in China and India
111.13	*Concussion troughs or trough clappers* – found in Burma
111.14	*Concussion vessels or vessel clappers*: even a slight hollow in the surface of a board counts as a vessel
111.141	*Castanets*: vessel clappers, either natural, or artificially hollowed out
111.142	*Cymbals*: vessel clappers with everted rim
111.2	*Percussion idiophones*: the instrument is struck either with a non-sonorous object (hand, stick, striker) or against a non-sonorous object (human body, the ground)
111.21	*Percussion sticks*
111.211	*(Individual) percussion sticks* – found in Japan, Vietnam and the Balkans (also the triangle)
111.212	*Sets of percussion sticks*: several percussion sticks of different pitch are

451

	combined to form a single instrument (all xylophones, as long as their sounding components are not in two different planes)
111.22	*Percussion plaques*
111.221	*(Individual) percussion plaques* – found in the oriental Christian Church
111.222	*Sets of percussion plaques* (lithophone [China], and most metallophones)
111.23	*Percussion tubes*
111.231	*(Individual) percussion tubes* (slit drum, tubular bell)
111.232	*Sets of percussion tubes* (tubaphone, tubular xylophone)
111.24	*Percussion vessels*
111.241	*Gongs*: the vibration is strongest near the vertex
111.241.1	*(Individual) gongs* – found in South and East Asia (including the so-called metal drums, or rather kettle-gongs)
111.241.2	*Sets of gongs* (gong-chimes) – found in South-east Asia
111.242	*Bells*: the vibration is weakest near the vertex
111.242.1	*(Individual) bells*
111.242.11	*Resting bells*: the cup is placed on the palm of the hand or on a cushion; its mouth faces upwards – found in China, Indochina [now Vietnam] and Japan
111.242.12	*Suspended bells*: the bell is suspended from the apex
111.242.121	*Suspended bells struck from the outside*: no striker is attached inside the bell, there being a separate beater
111.242.122	*Clapper bells*: a striker (clapper) is attached inside the bell
111.242.2	*Sets of bells* [chimes] (subdivided as 111.242.1)
112	*Indirectly struck idiophones*: the player himself does not go through the movement of striking; percussion results indirectly through some other movement by the player. The intention of the instrument is to yield clusters of sounds or noises, and not to let individual strokes be perceived
112.1	*Shaken idiophones or rattles*: the player executes a shaking motion
112.11	*Suspension rattles*: perforated idiophones are mounted together, and shaken to strike against each other
112.111	*Strung rattles*: rattling objects are strung in rows on a cord (necklaces with rows of shells)
112.112	*Stick rattles*: rattling objects are strung on a bar (or ring) (sistrum with rings)
112.12	*Frame rattles*: rattling objects are attached to a carrier against which they strike
112.121	*Pendant rattles*: rattling objects are hung from a frame (dancing shield with rattling rings)
112.122	*Sliding rattles*: non-sonorous objects slide to and fro in the slots of the sonorous object so that the latter is made to vibrate; or sonorous objects slide to and fro in the slots of a non-sonorous object, to be set in vibration by the impacts (*angklung*, sistrum with rods [recent])
112.13	*Vessel rattles*: rattling objects enclosed in a vessel strike against each other or against the walls of the vessel, or usually against both. NB The Benue gourd rattles with handle, in which the rattling objects, instead of being enclosed, are knotted into a net slipped over the outer surface, count as a variety of vessel rattle (fruit shells with seeds, 'pellet bells' enclosing loose percussion pellets)
112.2	*Scraped idiophones*: the player causes a scraping movement directly or indirectly: a non-sonorous object moves along the notched surface of a sonorous object, to be alternately lifted off the teeth and flicked against them; or an elastic sonorous object moves along the surface of a notched non-sonorous object to cause a series of impacts. This group must not be confused with that of friction idiophones
112.21	*Scraped sticks*: a notched stick is scraped with a little stick
112.211	*Scraped sticks without resonator* – found in South America, India (notched musical bow) and Congo
112.212	*Scraped sticks with resonator* – found in East Asia (ŏ)
112.22	*Scraped tubes* – found in south India
112.23	*Scraped vessels*: the corrugated surface of a vessel is scraped – found in South America and the Congo region

112.24	*Scraped wheels or cog rattles*: a cog wheel, whose axle serves as the handle, and a tongue fixed in a frame which is free to turn on the handle; when whirled, the tongue strikes the teeth of the wheel one after another – found in Europe and India
112.3	*Split idiophones*: instruments in the shape of two springy arms connected at one end and touching at the other: the arms are forced apart by a little stick, to jingle or vibrate on recoil – found in China, Malacca [now West Malaysia], Iran and the Balkans
12	PLUCKED IDIOPHONES lamellae (i.e. elastic plaques), fixed at one end, are flexed and then released to return to their position of rest
121	*In the form of a frame*: the lamella vibrates within a frame or hoop
121.1	*Clack idiophones* (cricri): the lamella is carved in the surface of a fruit shell, which serves as a resonator – found in Melanesia
121.2	*Guimbardes* (jew's harps): the lamella is mounted in a rod or plaque-shaped frame and depends on the player's mouth cavity for resonance
121.21	*Idioglot guimbardes*: the lamella is carved in the frame itself, its base remaining joined to the frame – found in India, Indonesia and Melanesia
121.22	*Heteroglot guimbardes*: a lamella is attached to a frame
121.221	*(Single) heteroglot guimbardes* – found in Europe, India and China
121.222	*Sets of heteroglot guimbardes*: several heteroglot guimbardes of different pitches are combined to form a single instrument – found in Aura
122	*In board or comb-form*: the lamellae are tied to a board or cut out from a board like the teeth of a comb
122.1	*With laced-on lamellae*
122.11	*Without resonator* (all lamellaphones on a plain board)
122.12	*With resonator* (all lamellaphones with a box or bowl below the board)
122.2	*With cut-out lamellae* (musical boxes): pins on a cylinder pluck the lamellae – found in Europe
13	FRICTION IDIOPHONES the instrument is made to vibrate by friction
131	*Friction sticks*
131.1	*(Individual) friction sticks* (unknown)
131.2	*Sets of friction sticks*
131.21	*With direct friction*: the sticks themselves are rubbed (nail violin, nail piano, Stockspiele)
131.22	*With indirect friction*: the sticks are connected with others which are rubbed and, by transmitting their longitudinal vibrations, stimulate transverse vibration in the former (Chladni's euphon)
132	*Friction plaques*
132.1	*(Individual) friction plaques* (unknown)
132.2	*Sets of friction plaques* [*livika*] – found in New Ireland
133	*Friction vessels*
133.1	*(Individual) friction vessels* – found in Brazil (tortoise shell)
133.2	*Sets of friction vessels* (verillon [glass harmonica])
14	BLOWN IDIOPHONES the instrument is made to vibrate by being blown upon
141	*Blown sticks*
141.1	*(Individual) blown sticks* (unknown)
141.2	*Sets of blown sticks* (Äolsklavier)
142	*Blown plaques*
142.1	*(Individual) blown plaques* (unknown)
142.2	*Sets of blown plaques* (piano chanteur)

Suffixes for use with any division of this class:

8	*With keyboard*
9	*Mechanically driven*
2	**Membranophones** the sound is excited by tightly stretched membranes
21	STRUCK DRUMS the membranes are struck
211	*Drums struck directly*: the player himself executes the movement of striking; this includes striking by any intermediate devices, such as beaters, keyboards etc; drums that are shaken are excluded

211.1	*Kettledrums* (timpani): the body is bowl- or dish-shaped
211.11	*(Separate) kettledrums* (European timpani)
211.12	*Sets of kettledrums* (West Asian permanently joined pairs of kettledrums)
211.2	*Tubular drums*: the body is tubular
211.21	*Cylindrical drums*: the diameter is the same at the middle and the ends; whether or not the ends taper or have projecting discs is immaterial
211.211	*Single-skin cylindrical drums*: the drum has only one usable membrane. In some African drums a second skin forms part of the lacing device and is not used for beating, and hence does not count as a membrane in the present sense
211.211.1	*Open cylindrical drums*: the end opposite from the membrane is open – found in Malacca [now West Malaysia]
211.211.2	*Closed cylindrical drums*: the end opposite from the membrane is closed – found in the West Indies
211.212	*Double-skin cylindrical drums*: the drum has two usable membranes
211.212.1	*(Individual) cylindrical drums* – found in Europe (side drum)
211.212.2	*Sets of cylindrical drums*
211.22*	*Barrel-shaped drums*: the diameter is larger at the middle than at the ends; the body is curvilinear – found in Asia, Africa and ancient Mexico
211.23	*Double-conical drums*: the diameter is larger at the middle than at the ends; the body is rectilinear with angular profile – found in India (*mṛdaṅga*)
211.24*	*Hourglass-shaped drums*: the diameter is smaller at the middle than at the ends – found in Asia, Melanesia and East Africa
211.25*	*Conical drums*: the diameters at the ends differ considerably (minor departures from conicity, inevitably met, are disregarded here) – found in India
211.26*	*Goblet-shaped drums*: the body consists of a main section which is either cup-shaped or cylindrical, and a slender stem; borderline cases of this basic design, like those occurring notably in Indonesia, do not affect the identification, so long as a cylindrical form is not in fact reached (*darabukka*)
211.3	*Frame drums*: the depth of the body does not exceed the radius of the membrane; NB the European side drum, even in its most shallow form, is a development from the long cylindrical drum and hence is not included among frame drums
211.31	*Frame drums (without handle)*
211.311	*Single-skin frame drums* (tambourine)
211.312	*Double-skin frame drums* – found in North Africa
211.32	*Frame drum with handle*: a stick is attached to the frame in line with its diameter
211.321	*Single-skin frame drums with handle* (Inuit)
211.322	*Double-skin frame drums with handle* – found in Tibet
212	*Rattle drums* (sub-divisions as for drums struck directly, 211): the drum is shaken; percussion is by impact of pendent or enclosed pellets, or similar objects – found in India and Tibet
22	PLUCKED DRUMS a string is knotted below the centre of the membrane; when the string is plucked, its vibrations are transmitted to the membrane – found in India (*gopīyantra, ānandalaharī*)
23	FRICTION DRUMS the membrane is made to vibrate by friction
231	*Friction drums with stick*: a stick in contact with the membrane is either itself rubbed, or is employed to rub the membrane
231.1	*With inserted stick*: the stick passes through a hole in the membrane
231.11	*Friction drums with fixed stick*: the stick cannot be moved; the stick alone is subjected to friction by rubbing – found in Africa
231.12	*Friction drums with semi-fixed stick*: the stick is movable to a sufficient extent to rub the membrane when it is itself rubbed by the hand – found in Africa
231.13	*Friction drums with free stick*: the stick can be moved freely; it is not itself rubbed, but is employed to rub the membrane – found in Venezuela

231.2	*With tied stick*: the stick is tied to the membrane in an upright position – found in Europe
232	*Friction drum with cord*: a cord, attached to the membrane, is rubbed
232.1	*Stationary friction drum with cord*: the drum is held stationary – found in Europe and Africa
232.11	*Single-skin stationary drums with friction cord*
232.12	*Double-skin stationary drums with friction cord*
232.2	*Friction drum with whirling stick*: the drum is whirled on a cord which rubs on a [resined] notch in the holding stick (*Waldteufel* [cardboard buzzer]) – found in Europe, India and East Africa
233	*Hand friction drums*: the membrane is rubbed by the hand
24	SINGING MEMBRANES (KAZOOS) the membrane is made to vibrate by speaking or singing into it; the membrane does not yield a note of its own but merely modifies the voice – found in Europe and West Africa
241	*Free kazoos*: the membrane is incited directly, without the wind first passing through a chamber (comb-and-paper)
242	*Tube or vessel-kazoos*: the membrane is placed inside a tube or box – found in Africa (while also East Asian flutes with a lateral hole sealed by a membrane exhibit an adulteration with the principle of the tube kazoo)

Suffixes for use with any division of this class:

6	*With membrane glued to drum*
7	*With membrane nailed to drum*
8	*With membrane laced to drum*
81	*Cord- (ribbon-)bracing*: the cords are stretched from membrane to membrane or arranged in the form of a net, without employing any of the devices described below
811	*Without special devices for stretching* – found everywhere
812	*With tension ligature*: cross ribbons or cords are tied round the middle of the lacing to increase its tension – found in Sri Lanka
813	*With tension loops*: the cords are laced in a zig-zag; every pair of strings is caught together with a small ring or loop – found in India
814	*With wedge bracing*: wedges are inserted between the wall of the drum and the cords of the lacing; by adjusting the position of the wedges it is possible to control the tension – found in India, Indonesia and Africa
82	*Cord-and-hide bracing*: the cords are laced at the lower end to a non-sonorous piece of hide – found in Africa
83	*Cord-and-board bracing*: the cords are laced to an auxiliary board at the lower end – found in Sumatra
84	*Cord-and-flange bracing*: the cords are laced at the lower end to a flange carved from the solid – found in Africa
85	*Cord-and-belt bracing*: the cords are laced at the lower end to a belt of different material – found in India
86	*Cord-and-peg bracing*: the cords are laced at the lower end to pegs stuck into the wall of the drum – found in Africa

NB 82 to 86 are sub-divided as 81 above

9	*With membrane lapped on*: a ring is slipped over the edge of the membrane
91	*With membrane lapped on by ring of cord* – found in Africa
92	*With membrane lapped on by a hoop*
921	*Without mechanism*: European drum
922	*With mechanism*
9221	*Without pedal*: machine timpani
9222	*With pedals*: pedal timpani

*To be sub-divided like 211.21

3	**Chordophones** one or more strings are stretched between fixed points
31	SIMPLE CHORDOPHONES OR ZITHERS the instrument consists solely of a string bearer, or of a string bearer with a resonator which is not integral and can be detached without destroying the sound-producing apparatus

311	*Bar zithers*: the string bearer is bar-shaped; it may be a board placed edgewise
311.1	*Musical bows*: the string bearer is flexible (and curved)
311.11	*Idiochord musical bows*: the string is cut from the bark of the cane, remaining attached at each end
311.111	*Mono-idiochord musical bows*: the bow has one idiochord string only – found in New Guinea (Sepik River), Togo
311.112	*Poly-idiochord musical bows or harp-bows*: the bow has several idiochord strings which pass over a toothed stick or bridge – found in West Africa, among the Fang
311.12	*Heterochord musical bows*: the string is of separate material from the bearer
311.121	*Mono-heterochord musical bows*: the bow has one heterochord string only
311.121.1	*Without resonator* (NB if a separate, unattached resonator is used, the specimen belongs to 311.121.21; the human mouth is not to be taken into account as a resonator)
311.121.11	*Without tuning noose* – found in Africa (*ganza*)
311.121.12	*With tuning noose*: a fibre noose is passed round the string, dividing it into two sections – found in south equatorial Africa
311.121.2	*With resonator*
311.121.21	*With independent resonator* – found in Borneo
311.121.22	*With resonator attached*
311.121.221	*Without tuning noose* – found in South Africa (*hade, thomo*)
311.121.222	*With tuning noose* – found in South Africa, Madagascar (*hungo*)
311.122	*Poly-heterochord musical bows*: the bow has several heterochord strings
311.122.1	*Without tuning noose* – found in Oceania (*kalove*)
311.122.2	*With tuning noose* – found in Oceania (*pagolo*)
311.2	*Stick zithers*: the string carrier is rigid
311.21	*Musical bow cum stick*: the string bearer has one flexible, curved end (NB stick zithers with both ends flexible and curved, like the Basuto bow, are counted as musical bows) – found in India
311.22	*(True) stick zithers*: NB round sticks which happen to be hollow by chance do not belong on this account to the tube zithers but are round-bar zithers; however, instruments in which a tubular cavity is employed as a true resonator are tube zithers
311.221	*With one resonator gourd* – found in India (*ṭuila*), Celebes [now Sulawesi]
311.222	*With several resonator gourds* – found in India (*vīṇā*)
312	*Tube zithers*: the string bearer is a vaulted surface
312.1	*Whole-tube zithers*: the string carrier is a complete tube
312.11	*Idiochord (true) tube zithers* – found in Africa and Indonesia (*valiha*)
312.12	*Heterochord (true) tube zithers*
312.121	*Without extra resonator* – found in South-east Asia (*čhakhē*)
312.122	*With extra resonator*: an internode length of bamboo is placed inside a palm leaf tied in the shape of a bowl – found in Timor
312.2	*Half-tube zithers*: the strings are stretched along the convex surface of a gutter
312.21	*Idiochord half-tube zithers* – found in Flores
312.22	*Heterochord half-tube zithers* – found in East Asia (*qin*, koto)
313	*Raft zithers*: the string bearer is composed of canes tied together in the manner of a raft
313.1	*Idiochord raft zithers* – found in India, Upper Guinea, central Congo
313.2	*Heterochord raft zithers* – found in the north Nyasa region
314	*Board zithers*: the string bearer is a board; the ground too is to be counted as such
314.1	*True board zithers*: the plane of the strings is parallel with that of the string bearer
314.11	*Without resonator* – found in Borneo
314.12	*With resonator*
314.121	*With resonator bowl*: the resonator is a fruit shell or similar object, or an artificially carved equivalent – found in the Nyasa region
314.122	*With resonator box (box zither)*: the resonator is made from slats (zither, dulcimer, piano)

456

314.2	*Board zither variations*: the plane of the strings is at right angles to the string bearer
314.21	*Ground zithers*: the ground is the string bearer; there is only one string – found in Malacca [now West Malaysia], Madagascar
314.22	*Harp zithers*: a board serves as string bearer; there are several strings and a notched bridge – found in Borneo
315	*Trough zithers*: the strings are stretched across the mouth of a trough – found in Tanganyika [now part of Tanzania]
315.1	*Without resonator*
315.2	*With resonator*: the trough has a gourd or a similar object attached to it
316	*Frame zithers*: the strings are stretched across an open frame
316.1	*Without resonator* (perhaps among medieval psalteries)
316.2	*With resonator* – found in West Africa (*kani*)
32	COMPOSITE CHORDOPHONES a string bearer and a resonator are organically united and cannot be separated without destroying the instrument
321	*Lutes*: the plane of the string runs parallel with the soundtable
321.1	*Bow lutes or pluriarcs*: each string has its own flexible carrier – found in Africa (*nsambi*)
321.2	*Yoke lutes or lyres*: the strings are attached to a yoke which lies in the same plane as the soundtable and consists of two arms and a cross-bar
321.21	*Bowl lyres*: a natural or carved-out bowl serves as the resonator (East African lyre)
321.22	*Box lyres*: a built-up wooden box serves as the resonator (kithara, crwth)
321.3	*Handle lutes*: the string bearer is a plain handle; subsidiary necks are disregarded, as are also lutes with strings distributed over several necks, like the harpo-lyre, and those like the lyre-guitars, in which the yoke is merely ornamental
321.31	*Spike lutes*: the handle passes diametrically through the resonator
321.311	*Spike bowl lutes*: the resonator consists of a natural or carved-out bowl – found in Persia [now Iran], India, Indonesia
321.312	*Spike box lutes or spike guitars*: the resonator is built up from wood – found in Egypt (*rabāb*)
321.313	*Spike tube lutes*: the handle passes diametrically through the walls of a tube – found in China, Indochina [now Vietnam]
321.32	*Necked lutes*: the handle is attached to or carved from the resonator, like a neck
321.321	*Necked bowl lutes* (mandolin, theorbo, balalaika)
321.322	*Necked box lutes or necked guitars* (violin, viol, guitar); NB a lute whose body is built up in the shape of a bowl is classified as a bowl lute
321.33	*Tanged lutes*: the handle ends within the body resonator
322	*Harps*: the plane of the strings lies at right angles to the sound table; a line joining the lower ends of the strings would point towards the neck
322.1	*Open harps*: the harp has no pillar
322.11	*Arched harps*: the neck curves away from the resonator – found in Burma and Africa
322.12	*Angular harps*: the neck makes a sharp angle with the resonator – found in Assyria, ancient Egypt, ancient Korea
322.2	*Frame harps*: the harp has a pillar
322.21	*Without tuning action* (all medieval harps)
322.211	*Diatonic frame harps*
322.212	*Chromatic frame harps*
322.212.1	*With the strings in one plane* (most early chromatic harps)
322.212.2	*With the strings in two planes crossing one another* (the Lyons chromatic harp)
322.22	*With tuning action*: the strings can be shortened by mechanical action
322.221	*With manual action*: the tuning can be altered by hand levers (hook harp, dital harp, harpinella)
322.222	*With pedal action*: the tuning can be altered by pedals
323	*Harp-lutes*: the plane of the strings lies at right angles to the soundtable; a line joining the lower ends of the strings would be perpendicular to the neck; notched bridge – found in West Africa (*kasso*)

457

Suffixes for use with any division of this class:

4	*Sounded by hammers or beaters*
5	*Sounded with bare fingers*
6	*Sounded by plectrum*
7	*Sounded by bowing*
71	*With a bow*
72	*By a wheel*
73	*By a ribbon (Band)*
8	*With keyboard*
9	*With mechanical drive*

4 **Aerophones** the air itself is the vibrator in the primary sense

41   FREE AEROPHONES the vibrating air is not confined by the instrument

411   *Displacement free aerophones*: the airstream meets a sharp edge, or a sharp edge is moved through the air. In either case, according to more recent views, a periodic displacement of air occurs to alternate flanks of the edge (whip, sword-blade)

412   *Interruptive free aerophones*: the airstream is interrupted periodically

412.1   *Idiophonic interruptive aerophones or reeds*: the airstream is directed against a lamella, setting it in periodic vibration to interrupt the stream intermittently. In this group also belong reeds with a 'cover', i.e. a tube in which the air vibrates only in a secondary sense, not producing the sound but simply adding roundness and timbre to the sound made by the reed's vibration; generally recognizable by the absence of finger-holes (organ reed stops)

412.11   *Concussion reeds*: two lamellae make a gap which closes periodically during their vibration (a split grass-blade)

412.12   *Percussion reeds*: a single lamella strikes against a frame

412.121   *Individual percussion reeds* – found in British Columbia

412.122   *Sets of percussion reeds* (the earlier reed stops of organs)

412.13   *Free reeds*: the lamella vibrates through a closely fitting slot

412.131   *(Individual) free reeds* (single-note motor horn)

412.132   *Sets of free reeds*: NB in instruments like the Chinese *sheng* the finger-holes do not serve to modify the pitch and are therefore not equivalent to the finger-holes of other pipes (reed organ, mouth organ, accordion)

412.14   *Ribbon reeds*: the airstream is directed against the edge of a stretched band or ribbon. The acoustics of this process has not yet been studied – found in British Columbia

412.2   *Non-idiophonic interruptive instruments*: the interruptive agent is not a reed

412.21   *Rotating aerophones*: the interruptive agent rotates in its own plane (sirens)

412.22   *Whirling aerophones*: the interruptive agent turns on its axis (bullroarer, whirring disc, ventilating fan)

413   *Plosive aerophones*: the air is made to vibrate by a single density stimulus condensation shock (pop guns)

42   WIND INSTRUMENTS PROPER the vibrating air is confined within the instrument itself

421   *Edge instruments or flutes*: a narrow stream of air is directed against an edge

421.1   *Flutes without duct*: the player creates a ribbon-shaped stream of air with his lips

421.11   *End-blown flutes*: the player blows against the sharp rim at the upper open end of a tube

421.111   *(Single) end-blown flutes*

421.111.1   *Open single end-blown flutes*: the lower end of the flute is open

421.111.11   *Without finger-holes* – found in Bengal

421.111.12   *With finger-holes* – found almost worldwide

421.111.2   *Stopped single end-blown flutes*: the lower end of the flute is closed

421.111.21   *Without finger-holes* (the bore of a key)

421.111.22   *With finger-holes* – found especially in New Guinea

421.112   *Sets of end-blown flutes or panpipes*: several end-blown flutes of different pitch are combined to form a single instrument

458

421.112.1	*Open panpipes*
421.112.11	*Open (raft) panpipes*: the pipes are tied together in the form of a board, or made by drilling tubes in a board – found in China
421.112.2	*Open bundle (pan)pipes*: the pipes are tied together in a round bundle – found in the Solomon Islands, New Britain, New Ireland and the Admiralty Islands
421.112.21	*Stopped panpipes* – found in Europe and South America
421.112.3	*Mixed open and stopped panpipes* – found in the Solomon Islands and South America
421.12	*Side-blown flutes*: the player blows against the sharp rim of a hole in the side of the tube
421.121	*(Single) side-blown flutes*
421.121.1	*Open side-blown flutes*
421.121.11	*Without finger-holes* – found in south-west Timor
421.121.12	*With finger-holes* (European flute)
421.121.2	*Partly stopped side-blown flutes*: the lower end of the tube is a natural node of the pipe pierced by a small hole – found in north-west Borneo
421.121.3	*Stopped side-blown flutes*
421.121.31	*Without finger-holes*
421.121.311	*With fixed stopped lower end* (apparently non-existent)
421.121.312	*With adjustable stopped lower end* (piston flutes) – found in Malacca [now West Malaysia] and New Guinea
421.121.32	*With finger-holes* – found in east Bengal and Malacca [now West Malaysia]
421.122	*Sets of side-blown flutes*
421.122.1	*Sets of open-blown flutes* (chamber flute orum)
421.122.2	*Sets of stopped side-blown flutes* – found in north-west Brazil, among the Siusi
421.13	*Vessel flutes (without distinct beak)*: the body of the pipe is not tubular but vessel-shaped – found in Brazil (Karaja) and the Lower Congo (Bafiote)
421.2	*Flutes with duct, or duct [fipple] flutes*: a narrow duct directs the airstream against the sharp edge of a lateral orifice
421.21	*Flutes with external duct*: the duct is outside the wall of the flute; this group includes flutes with the duct chamfered in the wall under a ring-like sleeve and other similar arrangements
421.211	*(Single) flutes with external duct*
421.211.1	*Open flutes with external duct*
421.211.11	*Without finger-holes* – found in China and Borneo
421.211.12	*With finger-holes* – found in Indonesia
421.211.2	*Partly stopped flutes with external duct* – found in Malacca [now West Malaysia]
421.211.3	*Stopped flutes with external duct*
421.212	*Sets of flutes with external duct* – found in Tibet
421.22	*Flutes with internal duct*: the duct is inside the tube. This group includes flutes with the duct formed by an internal baffle (natural node, block of resin) and an exterior tied-on cover (cane, wood or hide)
421.221.1	*Open flutes with internal duct*
421.221.11	*Without finger-holes* (European signalling whistle)
421.221.12	*With finger-holes* (recorder)
421.221.2	*Partly stopped flute with internal duct* – found in India and Indonesia
421.221.3	*Stopped flutes with internal duct*
421.221.31	*Without finger-holes*
421.221.311	*With fixed stopped lower end* (European signalling whistle)
421.221.312	*With adjustable stopped lower end* (piston pipes [swannee whistle])
421.221.4	*Vessel flutes with duct*
421.221.41	*Without finger-holes* (zoomorphic pottery whistles) – found in Europe and Asia
421.221.42	*With finger-holes* (ocarina)
421.222	*Sets of flutes with internal duct*
421.222.1	*Sets of open flutes with internal duct*
421.222.11	*Without finger-holes* (open flue stops of the organ)
421.222.12	*With finger-holes* (double flageolet)
421.222.2	*Sets of partly stopped flutes with internal duct* (*Rohrflöte* stops of the organ)
421.222.3	*Sets of stopped flutes with internal duct* (stopped flue stops of the organ)

459

422	*Reedpipes*: the airstream has, through means of two lamellae placed at the head of the instrument, intermittent access to the column of air which is to be made to vibrate
422.1	*Oboes*: the pipe has a [double] reed of concussion lamellae (usually a flattened stem)
422.11	*(Single) oboes*
422.111	*With cylindrical bore*
422.111.1	*Without finger-holes* – found in British Columbia
422.111.2	*With finger-holes* (aulos, crumhorn)
422.112	*With conical bore* (European oboe)
422.12	*Sets of oboes*
422.121	*With cylindrical bore* (double aulos)
422.122	*With conical bore* – found in India
422.2	*Clarinets*: the pipe has a [single] 'reed' consisting of a percussion lamella
422.21	*(Single) clarinets*
422.211	*With cylindrical bore*
422.211.1	*Without finger-holes* – found in British Columbia
422.211.2	*With finger-holes* (European clarinet)
422.212	*With conical bore* (saxophone)
422.22	*Sets of clarinets* – found in Egypt (*zummara*)
422.3	*Reedpipes with free reeds*: the reed vibrates through [at] a closely fitted frame. There must be finger-holes, otherwise the instrument belongs to the free reeds 412.13 – found in South-east Asia
422.31	*Single pipes with free reeds*
422.32	*Double pipes with free reeds*
423	*Trumpets*: the airstream passes through the player's vibrating lips, so gaining intermittent access to the air column which is to be made to vibrate
423.1	*Natural trumpets*: without extra devices to alter pitch
423.11	*Conches*: a conch shell serves as trumpet
423.111	*End-blown*
423.111.1	*Without mouthpiece* – found in India
423.111.2	*With mouthpiece* – found in Japan
423.112	*Side-blown* – found in Oceania
423.12	*Tubular trumpets*
423.121	*End-blown trumpets*: the mouth-hole faces the axis of the trumpet
423.121.1	*End-blown straight trumpets*: the tube is neither curved nor folded
423.121.11	*Without mouthpiece* (some alphorns)
423.121.12	*With mouthpiece* – found almost worldwide
423.121.2	*End-blown horns*: the tube is curved or folded
423.121.21	*Without mouthpiece* – found in Asia
423.121.22	*With mouthpiece* (lurs)
423.122	*Side-blown trumpet*: the mouthpiece is in the side of the tube
423.122.1	*Side-blown straight trumpets* – found in South America
423.122.2	*Side-blown horns* – found in Africa
423.2	*Chromatic trumpets*: with extra devices to modify the pitch
423.21	*Trumpets with finger-holes* (cornetti, key bugles)
423.22	*Slide trumpets*: the tube can be lengthened by extending a telescopic section of the instrument (European trombone)
423.23	*Trumpets with valves*: the tube is lengthened or shortened by connecting or disconnecting auxiliary lengths of tube – found in Europe
423.231	*Valve bugles*: the tube is conical throughout
423.232	*Valve horns*: the tube is predominantly conical
423.233	*Valve trumpets*: the tube is predominantly cylindrical

Suffixes for use with any division of this class:

6	*With air reservoir*
61	*With rigid air reservoir*
62	*With flexible air reservoir*
7	*With finger-hole stopping*
71	*With keys*

460

72	*With Bandmechanik* (presumably a perforated roll or ribbon)
8	*With keyboard*
9	*With mechanical drive*

This entire article is reproduced from E. M. von Hornbostel and Curt Sachs: 'Systematik der Musikinstrumente', *Zeitschrift für Ethnologie*, xlvi (1914), 553–90; Eng. trans. by A. Baines and K. P. Wachsman as 'Classification of Musical Instruments', *GSJ*, xiv (1961), 3; reproduced by permission of Limbach Verlag, Berlin

Pitch Measurement

KATHRYN VAUGHN

The purpose of measurement is to gain relevant information about events or objects which may contribute to the deeper understanding of the relations between these objects or events. Measurement is not an end in itself and by definition necessarily breaks natural things into unnaturally reduced bits of information. The apparent continuity which permeates the 'real' world is disregarded temporarily in favour of a more discrete and particularized world view. It does not follow, however, that the process of measuring something is consequently 'unreal' or invalid.

Of all the arts, music most lends itself to scientific investigation and to mathematical analysis. For this reason much attention has been paid to the measurement of various parameters of musical sound as well as to the physiological processes involved in producing and perceiving music. In the developing field of ethnomusicology pitch measurement has been important for the study of various tuning systems and to some extent as an aid to transcription. In light of the remarkable progress in technology and in the study of music perception since the 1980s, certain assumptions regarding the concept of pitch recognition as well as the methodology of measurement need to be re-examined. The purpose here is to give a brief overview of the major new discoveries in pitch perception and to present a quick and easy method of calculating scales and intervals.

The question of pitch

Before attempting to document pitch or tuning information from a particular music culture, it is helpful to have some understanding of the nature of the physical and cognitive processes involved in the production of and perception of musical sound. Misunderstandings about the physical aspects of musical sound and the limitations of measuring devices can lead to misrepresentation of the music and the musical context. For the most part, looking at the detail of tuning and pitch patterns is one analytical strategy for studying music as a process of pattern-making. The goal of this type of analysis is to identify invariant properties of scale systems and melodic shapes which can then help to identify musical traits. It is important, therefore, to be aware of the range of significant variation for a given musical parameter, both for the listeners and the performers.

Several excellent sources address these questions. *Music Cognition* (Dowling and Harwood, 1986) contains a comprehensive overview of current theory concerning pitch perception and melodic pattern recognition. C. L. Krumhansl's *Cognitive Foundations of Musical Pitch* (1990) is the most recent and in-depth work on the subject. Other useful references are included in the bibliography.

To answer the question most briefly, pitch is a cognitive construct. The perception of pitch is a function of 'the ear' in the sense that musicians have always used the term. Our 'ear' is a complex interaction of the peripheral auditory system and the activities of the brain and mind (considerable debate over the relation between mind and brain still exists). Hearing a given pitch involves the awareness of a particular type of periodic sound vibration and further processing by the central nervous system. Although there is a connection between the frequency of the external vibration and the perception of pitch, the exact reason for this is still unknown. Although a reasonably reliable relationship exists between the external signal (the sound wave) and the perception of pitch, the information from frequency counters such as a stroboconn must be tempered with a realistic view of the musical context.

Pitch tracking devices now exist that are designed to work more like the human ear (*see* Chapter V, 'Transcription', for information on mechanical transcription). These devices are really frequency measuring devices which may or may not use a perceptual basis to interpret the frequency information before sending it out to the user. Acquiring frequency information over a period of time, at least a second or two, is preferable to using a frequency counter. Computer programs which digitally sample sound can be used to extract pitch information as well. Methods which give some picture of the minute frequency fluctuations over time help to determine which frequencies are significant enough to be called 'pitch areas' of the musical system.

Experimental studies in pitch perception have raised two important points to bear in mind when formulating any claim about significant pitch relations within a musical system. (i) The perception of a pitch in an isolated context (i.e. the careful tuning of an instrument) is quite distinct from the perception of pitch categories in a sequential (melodic) or harmonic context, such as occurs in the performance of music. (ii) The effect of timbre on pitch identification is not known. We do not fully understand exactly how much the spectral components of a sound contribute to the perception of a pitch from a wave form of a given fundamental frequency. The first point explains why it is sometimes difficult to tune an instrument during a performance while surrounded by ongoing music. The second point is related to the forgiving context we find while singing in a resonant environment.

Pitch perception is much less precise in a musical context than when identifying isolated tones. Although this idea is nothing new for ethnomusicologists, it is surprising to find claims for scale systems being made on the basis of data analysis built on mixed measurements (i.e. measurements consolidated both from performance data and from recordings of instruments being carefully tuned). It has been shown that pitch discrimination in the context of a scale is very coarse, falling within a window of at least 50 cents (one quarter-tone) on either side of the actual frequency. This research should be taken into account when presenting measurements on variations in scale types either cross-culturally or intra-culturally. Much misinterpretation of scale variation within a musical culture has been due to this problem. Measuring pitch and inter-pitch distance is accomplished by analysing an analog or digital representation of the performance or production of musical sound. The nature of the machines which help us do this is to transform air pressure fluctuation into a measure of voltage amplitude. Formulating theories about significant differences in tuning systems or structural aspects of melody comes into the realm of perception and involves the listener. For this reason, allowances should be made for the limitations of perception which machines do not have.

The recorded material contained in ethnomusicology archives and elsewhere is an enormously valuable storehouse of information about the way people make music and create culture. So much has yet to be learned about the pattern-making processes of all human beings that thorough study of such a wide variety of musical material can only prove to be an asset.

What are cents?

The cents system was originally designed by Alexander J. Ellis to help relate the physical frequencies of musical sounds to the 'sensation of tone' as H. L. F. Helmholtz (1863) so aptly put it. In his pioneering work on the physics of musical sound Helmholtz discovered that there was some relation between the frequency of a vibrating medium and the pitch percept. He deduced that the ear was a frequency analyser and in some way processed sound in an additive, logarithmic fashion that was based on the physiology of the ear.

For example, take the perception of the octave. Although the term is derived from a Western idea of eight tones surrounding a sequence of the seven sequential tones of a diatonic scale, the recognition of octave equivalence is a universal human trait. The ratio of frequencies from one pitch to its octave equivalent is 2/1. This means one periodic vibration is fluctuating twice as fast as the other. If one were to strike the air as fast as 220 times per second, then everyone in the room would hear a tone. That tone would sound identical to A3, the A below middle C on the piano. Striking the air faster and faster would cause the apparent pitch to continue to change. At the point where the air pressure fluctuates at a rate of 440 cycles per second (or 440 Hz) the tone is recognized as the octave above A3. Double that frequency and one will hear the tone A5 (880 Hz).

Tone 1	220 Hz	2^0	(2×1)
Tone 2	440 Hz	2^2	(2×2)
Tone 3	880 Hz	2^3	$(2 \times 2 \times 2)$

Through this progression we hear three tones which belong to the same pitch category. Tone 3 is perceived as two octaves above Tone 1, even though the frequency has been increased exponentially. The logarithm is the inverse of the exponential function. Helmholtz reasoned we are not hearing frequencies directly, but in some way process them additively. Otherwise, we would hear an octave at 660 Hz.

$$220 \times 1 = 220 \qquad (220 + 0) \qquad\qquad = 220$$
$$220 \times 2 = 440 \qquad (220 + 220) \qquad\quad = 440$$
$$220 \times 3 = 660 \qquad (220 + 220 + 220) \quad = 660$$

Calculating cents

Sounds are heard additively rather than multiplicatively because of the physiology of the ear. Ellis's paper formulating a linear measure of pitch he called 'cents' can be found in Helmholtz (1863). Although the theory is grounded in the Western notion of equal temperament with 12 tones embedded in the octave, the concept is an elegant transformation of frequency distance into pitch distance.

The definition of one cent is 1/100 of a semitone. Ellis considered that there are 12 semitones per octave, therefore there are 1200 cents per octave. That the number of cents per octave is 1200 is incidental to the theoretical basis. One can just as easily calculate a cent based on an octave of 1000 divisions or even 5. By convention, the 1200-cent octave is most accepted and for the sake of clarity ethnomusicologists have held with 1200 cents per octave as the standard.

The logarithmic function is additive. See the Appendix for proof of this.

If C is allowed to represent 1 cent, then C will be the number of 1200ths in the interval (I)

and

$$I = \left[2^{\frac{1}{1200}} \right]^{C}$$

Therefore the formula to calculate the number of cents in a given interval is:

$$C = \log I \times \left[\frac{1200}{\log 2} \right]$$

where
      I = the ratio of the two frequencies f_2 and f_1
      C = the number of cents in the interval
      log = logarithm in any base

Historically, tables of cents have been constructed for hands-on calculation of intervallic distance in cents. The simplest of these, such as those of Erich M. von Hornbostel (1921) and Heinrich Husmann (1952), involve linear interpolation, a method no longer in use for such elementary problems. For an excellent survey of various methods of cents approximation and the cents tables see Frederic Lieberman (1971).

Tables are no longer necessary, as it is a simple matter to find exact cents measurement using the most inexpensive hand-held calculator. Following is a step-by-step guide to entering the formula into the most basic calculator. More sophisticated calculators have features that make entering formulas a bit more direct.

465

SUMMARY OF OPERATIONS
 1. Divide 1200 by the log of 2; store the result in memory or write it down
 2. Divide the larger frequency by the smaller, call this result the interval I
 3. Recall the result of step 1 and multiply that times the log of interval I

STEP-BY-STEP EXAMPLE FOR THE OCTAVE A220 TO A440;
 Keys pressed
  › Clear
  › 1200
  › Division symbol
  › log button
  › 2
  › =   (ans: 3986.31 if you use Ln)
  › press store symbol or write down 3986
  › 440
  › division symbol
  › 220
  › =   (ans: 2 – the ratio of I)
  › save the result (2)
  › Clear
  › Recall button or enter 3986
  › ×
  › log button
  › 2   (the ratio I)
  › =   (ans: 1.1999..)

The result should be extremely close to 1200, depending on how many significant digits of (1200/log2) you decide to keep. The more you retain the closer the result will be to 1200. It does not matter which logarithmic base you choose as long as you are consistently pressing the same one throughout the calculation. The Ln button is the natural log with a base of the irrational number e; the log symbol is gives the result in base 10. This does not affect the result as they are all proportional to each other by a constant.

Appendix

DERIVATION OF THE CENTS FORMULA

$$I = \left[2^{\frac{1}{1200}} \right]^{(C)}$$

$$I = 2^{\frac{C}{1200}}$$

$$\log (I) = \frac{C}{1200} \ (\log 2)$$

$$\log(I) \times 1200 = C \times (\log 2)$$

$$\log(I) \times \left[\frac{1200}{\log(2)}\right] = C$$

Therefore the formula to calculate the number of cents in a given interval is:

$$C = \log(I) \times \left[\frac{1200}{\log(2)}\right]$$

WHY ELLIS'S SYSTEM WORKS

Approximation of the logarithm is an additive function.

$$\sum_{k-1}^{n}\left(\frac{1}{k}\right) = 1 + \tfrac{1}{2} + \tfrac{1}{3} + \tfrac{1}{4} + \ldots \frac{1}{n} \approx \log(n)$$

We hear sounds additively rather than multiplicatively.

$$\log_x x = 1$$
$$2^2 = 4$$
$$\log_2 2^2 =$$
$$2 \times (\log_2 2) = 2$$

$$\left\{\begin{array}{l} 2^2 = 4 \\ \log_2 2^2 = 2 \\ 2 \times (\log_2 2) = 2 \end{array}\right\}$$

4 is not the same as 2
(we hear 2)

EXAMPLE

Definition: semitone (½ step) is $\frac{1}{12}$ of octave

$$\left[\frac{a}{b}\right]^{(12)} = \frac{2}{1}$$

$$\frac{a}{b} = 2^{\frac{1}{12}}$$

Then: the interval of one whole step, I, is

$$I = \left[2^{\frac{1}{12}}\right]^{(2)} = 2^{\frac{1}{6}} \quad \text{Recall } 2^{\frac{1}{12}} \times 2^{\frac{1}{12}} = 2^{\frac{1}{12} + \frac{1}{12}} = 2^{\frac{2}{12}}$$

Then: the frequency ratio for C ½ steps is

$$\left[2^{\frac{1}{12}}\right]^{(C)} = 2^{\frac{C}{12}}$$

If C is allowed to represent one cent, then C will be the number of 1200[ths] in the interval.

Bibliography

The references here include sources for information on acoustics and pitch perception that relate to the problems of measurement. In addition to those mentioned previously, the following are especially salient. Deutch (1982) includes many thorough articles on all major aspects of music psychology. Pierce (1983) presents a beautiful and detailed overview of musical acoustics, and Sundberg's study of the human voice is a landmark work. Chamberlain (1986) is one of the best and most accessible sources on the newest signal processing technology.

Ethnomusicology: an Introduction

H. L. F. Helmholtz: *Die Lehre von den Tonempfindung als physiologische Grundläge fur die Theorie der Musik* (Brunswick, 1863; Eng. trans. by A. J. Ellis, 1875/R1954 as *On the Sensations of Tone*)

A. J. Ellis: 'On the calculation of cents from interval ratios', in Helmholtz (1863, Eng. trans. 1875/R1954)

E. M. von Hornbostel: 'Eine Tafel zur Logarithmischen Darstellung von Zahlenverhaltnissen', *Zeitschrift fur Physik*, vi (1921), 29

H. Fletcher: 'The Physical Criterion for Determining the Pitch of a Musical Tone', *Phys. Rev.*, xxiii (1924), 427

J. F. Schouten: 'The Perception of Subjective Tones', *Proc. Kon. Ned. Akad. Wetensch.*, xli (1938), 1086

——: 'The Residue: a New Component in Subjective Sound Analysis', *Proc. Kon. Ned. Akad. Wetensch.*, xliii (1939), 356

H. Husmann, 'Cents', *MGG*

C. A. Taylor: *The Physics of Musical Sound* (New York, 1965)

R. J. Ritsma: 'Frequencies Dominant in the Perception of the Pitch of Complex Sounds', *Journal of the Acoustical Society of America*, xlii (1967), 191

A. W. Slawson: 'Vowel Quality and Musical Timbre as Functions of Spectrum Envelope and Fundamental Frequency', *Journal of the Acoustical Society of America*, xliii (1968), 101

H.-P. Reinecke: *Cents Frequency Period: Calculations Tables for Musical Acoustics and Ethnomusicology* (Berlin, 1970)

F. Lieberman: 'Working with Cents: a Survey', *EM*, xv/1 (1971), 236

D. A. Ronkin: 'Changes in Frequency Discrimination Caused by Leading and Trailing Tones', *Journal of the Acoustical Society of America*, li (1972), 1937

J. G. Roederer: *Introduction to the Physics and Psychophysics of Music* (Berlin and New York, 1975)

R. Plomp: *Aspects of Tone Sensation* (New York, 1976)

E. C. Carterette and M. P. Friedman: *Handbook of Perception* (New York, 1978)

W. J. Dowling and J. C. Bartlett: 'The Importance of Interval Information in Long-term Memory for Melodies', *Psychomusicology*, i (1981), 30

D. J. Getty and J. Howard, eds.: *Auditory and Visual Pattern Recognition* (Hillsdale, NJ, 1981)

G. J. Balzano: 'The Pitch Set as a Level of Description for Studying Musical Pitch Perception', *Music, Mind and Brain*, ed. M. Clynes (New York, 1986)

D. Deutsch, ed.: *The Psychology of Music* (New York, 1982)

R. Plomp: 'The Perception of Musical Tones', *The Psychology of Music*, ed. D. Deutsch (New York, 1982)

J. R. Pierce: *The Science of Musical Sound* (New York, 1983)

J. A. Sloboda: *The Musical Mind: the Cognitive Psychology of Music* (Oxford, 1985)

H. Chamberlain: *Music and Microprocessors* (New York, 1986)

W. J. Dowling and D. L. Harwood: *Music Cognition* (Orlando, FL, 1986)

C. K. Monahan and E. C. Carterette: 'The Effect of Melodic and Temporal Contour on Recognition Memory for Pitch Change', *Perception and Psychophysics*, xli (1987), 576

J. Sundberg: *The Science of the Singing Voice* (Dekalb, IL, 1987)

C. L. Krumhansl: *The Cognitive Foundations of Musical Pitch* (Oxford, 1990)

468

REFERENCE AID 5

National Mains Frequencies and Voltages; Television Standards

The ethnomusicologist, when working away from his or her home country, must be aware of the wide variety of mains electrical supplies and incompatible television systems that will be encountered.

Provided that AC (alternating current) mains is available the local supply can be transformed as necessary to run equipment or charge batteries. If only DC (direct current) is available, the researcher will require enough batteries to power equipment, or will need custom-made chargers especially designed for use with DC mains supplies.

The major colour television standards are: NTSC, 525 line, 60Hz (American); PAL, 625 line, 50Hz (France, former French colonies, parts of Eastern Europe). The researcher would normally record video films using his home country's TV system. This may necessitate transporting TV monitors across the world to permit replay of material to local audiences. Video tapes originating on one system may be converted to another by use of a TV standards converter with virtually no loss of quality, so permitting international exchange of information.

Country	Frequency; voltage	TV standard	Sets per person
Abu Dhabi (UAE)	50Hz; 240V	PAL	n.a.
Afghanistan	50Hz; 220V	PAL, SECAM	1/709
Ajman (UAE)	50Hz; 230V	PAL	
Alaska (USA)	60Hz; 120/240V	NTSC	
Albania	n.a.	PAL	1/10
Algeria	50Hz±1.5%; 220V, 127/220V±10%	PAL	1/15
Andorra	50Hz; 220V	PAL	1/12
Angola	50Hz; 220V	PAL	1/228
Antigua and Barbuda	60Hz; 230V	NTSC	n.a.
Antilles, Netherlands		NTSC	n.a.
– Bonair, Curaçao	50Hz; 127, 220V		
– St Martin	60Hz; 115, 120, 127V		
Argentina	50Hz±1%; 220, 225V±10% DC 220, 440V	PAL	1/4
Aruba	60Hz; 115, 120, 127V	NTSC	n.a.
Australia	50Hz±0.1%; 240V±6%	PAL	1/2
Austria	50Hz±0.1%; 220V±5%	PAL	1/2.8
Azores	50Hz; 110, 220V	PAL – USAF base NTSC	n.a.
Bahamas	60Hz; 120V, 120/240V	NTSC	1/4.6
Bahrain	50Hz±2%; 230V 6%, 60Hz±2%; 110V±6%	PAL	1/2.3

469

Country	Frequency; voltage	TV standard	Sets per person
Bangladesh	50Hz±0.5%; 220, 230V±5%	PAL	1/244
Barbados	50Hz±0.4%; 110/190V, 115/200V, 120/208V±6%	NTSC	1/3.9
Belgium	50Hz±3%; 220V, 127/ 220V±10%	PAL – AFN NTSC	1/3.2
Belize	60Hz±0.1%; 110/220V	NTSC	n.a.
Benin	50Hz±1%; 220V±10%	SECAM	1/272
Bermuda	60Hz±1%; 120/208V, 120/ 240V±5%	NTSC	n.a.
Bhutan	n.a.	no TV service	—
Bolivia	50Hz±1%; 115/230V±5%	NTSC	1/16
Botswana	50Hz; 220V	PAL	n.a.
Brazil	60Hz; 110, 127, 220V; 50Hz, 110, 127, 220V	PAL–M*	1/4
Brunei Darussalam	50Hz; 230V±15%	PAL	1/4.7
Bulgaria	50Hz±0.1%; 220V±5%	SECAM	1/5.3
Burkina Faso	50Hz; 220V	SECAM	1/205
Burma (Myanmar)	50Hz; 230V	NTSC	1/592
Burundi	50Hz; 220V+0/−25%	SECAM	n.a.
Cameroon	50Hz±2%; 127, 220, 127/220V±5%	PAL	n.a.
Canada	60Hz±0.02%; 120/240V +4/−8%	NTSC	1/1.7
Canary Islands	50Hz; 127, 220V	PAL	n.a.
Cape Verde Islands	n.a.	no TV service	—
Cayman Islands	60Hz±1%; 120/240V±5%	NTSC (taped)	n.a.
Central African Republic	50Hz; 220V	no TV service	—
Chad	50Hz; 220V	no TV service	—
Channel Islands (UK)	50Hz; 230V, 240V	PAL	n.a.
Chile	50Hz; 220V	NTSC	1/5.5
China (People's Republic)	50Hz; 220V±7%	PAL	1/12
China (Republic of Taiwan)	60Hz±4%; 110, 220, 110/220V±10%	NTSC	1/3.2
Colombia	60Hz±1%; 110/220V, 120/240V, 150V±10%	NTSC	1/5.6
Commonwealth of Independent States	50Hz±1%; 127, 127/220V, 220V	SECAM	1/3
Congo	50Hz; 220V	SECAM	1/375
Costa Rica	60Hz; 120V	NTSC	1/6.1
Cuba	60Hz; 115, 120V	NTSC	n.a.
Cyprus	50Hz±1%; 230V±2.5%	Turkish PAL Greek PAL transcoded SECAM	1/3.4
Czechoslovakia	50Hz±0.1%; 220V±10%	SECAM	1/3.7
Denmark	50Hz±0.4%; 220V±10%	PAL	1/2.7
Diego Garcia	60Hz; n.a.	US Forces TV NTSC	n.a.
Djibouti	50Hz±4%; 220V±7%	SECAM	1/35
Dominica	50Hz; 230V	no TV service	—
Dominican Republic	60Hz; 110V	NTSC	1/12
Dubai (UAE)	50Hz±0.5%; 220V±3%	PAL	n.a.
Easter Island	n.a.	n.a.	n.a.

Country	Frequency; voltage	TV standard	Sets per person
Ecuador	60Hz; 110, 120, 127V	NTSC	1/17
Egypt	50Hz±1%; 220V±10%	SECAM	1/13
El Salvador	60Hz±1%; 115, 230V±5%	NTSC	1/12
Equatorial Guinea	50Hz; 220V	n.a.	n.a.
Ethiopia	50Hz; 220V	PAL	1/679
Falkland Islands	50Hz±3%; 230V±2.5%	PAL (taped)	n.a.
Fiji	50Hz±1%; 240V	n.a.	n.a.
Finland	50Hz±0.5%; 230V±10%	PAL	1/2.7
France	50Hz±1%; 127,220V, 127/220V±10%	SECAM	1/2.5
Fujairah (UAE)	50Hz±0.5%; 230V±3%	PAL	
Gabon	50Hz; 220V	SECAM	1/33
Galapagos Islands	n.a	NTSC	n.a.
Gambia	50Hz; 230V±5%	n.a.	n.a.
Germany – eastern	50Hz±0.3%; 220, 127, 127/220V±5%	SECAM	1/2.7
western	50Hz±0.3%; 220V±10%	PAL Forces Broadcasting NTSC, PAL	1/2.6 n.a.
Ghana	50Hz±5%; 230, 250V±10%	PAL	1/77
Gibraltar	50Hz±1%; 240V±6%	PAL	n.a.
Greece	50Hz±1%; 220V±5%	SECAM	1/5.7
Greenland (Kalaallit Nunaat)	50Hz; 220V USAF	PAL NTSC	n.a.
Grenada	50Hz; 230V	n.a.	n.a.
Guadeloupe	50Hz; 220V; 60Hz; 220V	SECAM	n.a.
Guam	60Hz±1%; 120, 120/208V, 120/240V, 240V +8/−10%	NTSC	n.a.
Guatemala	60Hz±1.7%; 120/240V ±10%	NTSC	1/18
Guiana, French	50Hz; 127, 220V	SECAM	n.a.
Guinea (Republic of)	50Hz; 220V	PAL	n.a.
Guinea-Bissau	50Hz; n.a.	n.a.	n.a.
Guyana (Republic of)	50Hz; 60Hz; 110V, 220V	NTSC	n.a.
Haiti	60Hz; 110, 115, 220, 230V	NTSC	1/218
Hawaii (USA)	60Hz; 120, 120/240V±10%	NTSC	n.a.
Honduras	60Hz; 110V	NTSC	1/31
Hong Kong	50Hz±5%; 200V±10%	PAL	n.a.
Hungary	50Hz±2%; 220V+5/−10%	SECAM	1/2.5
Iceland	50Hz±0.1%; 220V	PAL	1/3.3
India	50Hz±3%; 230, 250V±6% DC 220, 225, 230, 300V±6%	PAL	1/62
Indonesia	50Hz±2%; 127, 127/220V ±5%	PAL	1/24
Iran	50Hz±5%; 220V±15%	SECAM	1/23
Iraq	50Hz; 220V±5%	SECAM	1/18
Ireland	50Hz; 230V	PAL	1/3.8
Israel	50Hz±0.2%; 230V±6%	PAL	1/6.9
Italy	50Hz±0.4%; 127/220V, 220V±10%	PAL	1/3.9
Ivory Coast	50Hz; 220V	SECAM	1/19
Jamaica	50Hz±1%; 110/220V±6%	NTSC	1/6.1
Japan – east	50Hz±0.2%; 100V, 100/200V	NTSC	1/4.1

Country	Frequency; voltage	TV standard	Sets per person
Japan – west	60Hz±0.1%; 100V, 100/200V, 105/210V		
Johnston Atoll	60Hz; 110V	USAF, NTSC	n.a.
Jordan	50Hz; 220V	PAL	1/12
Kampuchea	50Hz; 120, 120/208V, 220V	SECAM	n.a.
Kenya	50Hz; 240V±6%	PAL	1/118
Korea – North	50Hz+0/−5%; 220V+7/−14%	PAL	n.a.
South	60Hz; 100V	NTSC	1/4.9
Kuwait	50Hz; 240V	PAL	1/2.4
Laos	50Hz±8%; 220V±6%	PAL	n.a.
Lebanon	50Hz; 110, 220V	SECAM	1/3.4
Leeward Islands	60Hz; 230V	NTSC	n.a.
Lesotho	50Hz; 220V	PAL	n.a.
Liberia	60Hz±3.3%; 120, 120/240V±1.7%	PAL	1/55
Libya	50Hz; 127, 230V	SECAM	1/13
Liechtenstein	50Hz±0.5%; 220V±10%	PAL	n.a.
Luxembourg	50Hz±0.5%; 220, 127/ 220V±10%	PAL, SECAM	1/4
Macau	50Hz; 110, 220V	PAL	n.a.
Madagascar	50Hz±2%; 127, 220V ±20%	SECAM	n.a.
Madeira	50Hz±1%; 220V±5%	PAL	n.a.
Malawi	50Hz; 230V	n.a.	n.a.
Malaysia	50Hz±1%; 230V, 240V +5/−10%	PAL	1/10
Maldives	50Hz; n.a.	PAL	n.a.
Mali	50Hz; 220V	SECAM	n.a.
Malta	50Hz±1%; 240V±5%	PAL	n.a.
Mariana Islands	60Hz±1%; 120/240V ±10%	NTSC	n.a.
Martinique	50Hz; 127, 220V	SECAM	n.a.
Mauritius	50Hz±1%; 230V±6%	SECAM	1/8.2
Mexico	60Hz±0.2%; 127, 220V ±6%	NTSC	1/8.7
Micronesia (including Marshall Islands and YAP)	60Hz; n.a.	NTSC	n.a.
Midway Island	60Hz; 120V	NTSC	n.a.
Monaco	50Hz; 127, 220, 127/ 220V	Italian PAL French SECAM	n.a.
Mongolia	n.a.	SECAM	1/18
Montserrat	60Hz; 230V	SECAM	n.a.
Morocco	50Hz; 110, 115, 127, 190, 200, 220V	SECAM	1/19.2
Mozambique	50Hz; 220V	PAL	1/425
Namibia	50Hz; 220V	PAL	1/42
Nauru	50Hz; 240V	no TV service	—
Nepal	50Hz±1%; 230V±10%	PAL	n.a.
Netherlands	50Hz±0.4%; 220V±6%	PAL	1/3.2
New Caledonia	50Hz±1%; 220V±10%	SECAM	n.a.
New Zealand	50Hz±1.5%; 230V±5%	PAL	1/3.5
Nicaragua	60Hz; 120, 120/240V	NTSC	1/17

472

Country	Frequency; voltage	TV standard	Sets per person
Niger	50Hz±1%; 220V±2.5%	SECAM	1/277
Nigeria	50Hz±2%; 220, 230V ±10%	PAL	1/20
Norway	50Hz±0.2%; 230V±10%	PAL	1/2.9
Oman	50Hz; 240V	PAL	1/1.4
Pakistan	50Hz; 230V	PAL	1/73
Palau	50Hz; 115V	NTSC	n.a.
Panama	60Hz±0.2%; 110, 110/220V, 120, 120/240V±5%	NTSC	1/4.9
Papua New Guinea	50Hz±2%; 240V±5%	PAL	1/14
Paraguay	50Hz±1%; 220V±5%	PAL	1/12
Peru	60Hz; 220, 225V	NTSC	1/13
Philippines	60Hz±5%; 110, 110/220V, 120, 120/240V, 220, 240V±5%	NTSC	1/8
Poland	50Hz±1%; 220V±5%	SECAM	1/3
Polynesia	60Hz±2.5%; 220V±10%	SECAM	n.a.
Portugal	50Hz±1%; 220V±5%	PAL	1/6.4
Puerto Rico	60Hz±10%; 120/240V±10%	NTSC	n.a.
Ras Al-Khaimah (UAE)	50Hz±0.5%; 230V±3%	PAL	n.a.
Réunion	50Hz; 220V	SECAM	n.a.
Romania	50Hz±1%; 220V±5%	PAL	1/6
Rwanda	50Hz±1%; n.a.	no TV service	—
Sabah and Sarawak	50Hz±0.5%; 240V±6%	PAL	n.a.
St Kitts and Nevis	60Hz; 230V	NTSC	n.a.
St Lucia	50Hz; 240V	NTSC	1/28
St Pierre et Miquelon	50Hz; 115V	SECAM	
St Vincent	50Hz; 230V	NTSC	n.a.
Samoa – American	50Hz; 230V	NTSC	n.a.
Western	50Hz; 230V	no TV service	—
San Andres Island	60Hz±1%; 110/220V, 120/240V±10%	NTSC	n.a.
San Marino	50Hz±0.4%; 127/220V, 220V±10%	PAL	1/3.4
Sao Tomé et Principe	50Hz; 220V	no TV service	—
Saudi Arabia	60Hz±0.5%; 50Hz; 127/220V±5%	SECAM, PAL	1/3
Senegal	50Hz; 127V	SECAM	1/31
Seychelles	50Hz; 230V	PAL	1/3
Sharjah (UAE)	50Hz±0.5%; 230V±3%	PAL	n.a.
Sierra Leone	50Hz; 230V	PAL	1/114
Singapore	50Hz±1%; 230V±6%	PAL	1/4.9
Solomon Islands	50Hz; 240V	n.a.	n.a.
Somalia	50Hz; 110, 220, 230V	PAL	n.a.
South Africa	50Hz±2.5%; 220, 230, 250V±5% DC 230V, 25Hz; 220V	PAL	1/13
Spain	50Hz±3%; 127, 127/220V, 220V±7%	PAL	1/2.6
Sri Lanka	50Hz±2%; 230V±6%	PAL	
Sudan	50Hz; 240V	PAL	1/23
Surinam	60Hz; 115, 127V	NTSC	1/10
Swaziland	50Hz±2.5%; 230V±6%	PAL	n.a.
Sweden	50Hz±0.2%; 220V±10%	PAL	1/2.4
Switzerland	50Hz±0.5%; 220V±10%	PAL	1/2.9
Syrian Arab Republic	50Hz; 115, 220V	SECAM, PAL	1/26.5

473

Country	Frequency; voltage	TV standard	Sets per person
Tanzania	50Hz; 230V	PAL	n.a.
Thailand	50Hz±1%; 220V±5%	PAL	1/11
Tibet (China)	50Hz; 220V	PAL	n.a.
Togo	50Hz; 220, 127V	SECAM	1/152
Tonga	50Hz; 240V	no TV service	—
Trinidad and Tobago	60Hz±5%; 115, 230V, 115/230V±6%	NTSC	1/3.6
Tunisia	50Hz±1%; 110, 127, 220V±5%	SECAM	1/15
Turkey	50Hz±1%; 230V±10%	PAL	1/6.8
Tuvalu	n.a.	n.a.	n.a.
Uganda	50Hz±0.1%; 240V±5%	PAL	1/178
United Arab Emirates	50Hz±0.5%; 220, 230, 240V±3%	PAL	1/12
UK	50Hz±1%; 220, 230, 240V±6%	PAL	1/3
Uruguay	50Hz±1%; 220V±6%	PAL	1/5
USA	60Hz±0.3%; 120, 120/208V, 120/240V±10%	NTSC	n.a.
USSR *see* Commonwealth of Independent States			
Vanuatu	n.a.	n.a.	n.a.
Venezuela	60Hz; 120V	NTSC	1/6.6
Vietnam	50Hz±0.1%; 120, 127, 220V±10%	NTSC/SECAM	1/30
Virgin Islands – American	60Hz; 110, 120V	NTSC	n.a.
British	60Hz; 110, 120V	NTSC	n.a.
Wallis Island	n.a.	SECAM	n.a.
Yemen Arab Republic	50Hz; 220V	PAL	1/56
Yemen (People's Democratic Republic of)	50Hz±1%; 230V, 250V±4%	NTSC	n.a.
Yugoslavia	50Hz; 220V	PAL	1/5.7
Zaire	50Hz; 220V	SECAM	1/2,035
Zambia	50Hz±2.5%; 220V±4%	PAL	1/94
Zanzibar	50Hz; 230V	PAL	n.a.
Zimbabwe	50Hz±2.5%; 225V, 240V±5%	PAL	1/71

Note: PAL–M is 525 line, 60Hz; PAL, SECAM are 625 line, 50Hz; NTSC is 525 line, 60Hz

Index

212-354-5500

1800 233-4830